JOHN KEATS

VOLUME I

Books by Amy Lowell

PUBLISHED BY

HOUGHTON MIFFLIN COMPANY

Poetry

LEGENDS

PICTURES OF THE FLOATING WORLD

CAN GRANDE'S CASTLE

MEN, WOMEN AND GHOSTS

SWORD BLADES AND POPPY SEED

A DOME OF MANY-COLOURED GLASS

A CRITICAL FABLE

(IN COLLABORATION WITH FLORENCE AYSCOUGH)

FIR-FLOWER TABLETS: POEMS TRANSLATED FROM THE CHINESE

Prose

TENDENCIES IN MODERN AMERICAN POETRY

SIX FRENCH POETS: STUDIES IN CONTEMPORARY LITERATURE

JOHN KEATS

LIFE MASK OF KEATS

From a copy of the original mask in the possession of the author

JOHN KEATS

BY
AMY LOWELL

WITH ILLUSTRATIONS

VOLUME I

BOSTON AND NEW YORK
HOUGHTON MIFFLIN COMPANY
The Riverside Press Cambridge

PUBLISHED FEBRUARY, 1925
REPRINTED FEBRUARY, 1925
REPRINTED MARCH, 1925

The Riverside Press
CAMBRIDGE · MASSACHUSETTS
PRINTED IN THE U.S.A.

TO

A. D. R.

THIS, AND ALL MY BOOKS

A. L.

PREFACE

To add another to the long list of books on Keats seems to demand, if not an excuse, at least an explanation. My reasons for undertaking what at first sight appears an act of supererogation have a certain cogency, however, and this cogency lies in the unexpected wealth of new material existing uncharted and almost unexplored in the libraries of American collectors. America has always been greatly interested in Keats, and from the very beginning American enthusiasts have been indefatigable in their efforts to obtain manuscripts, letters, books owned by Keats, anything, in short, which touched even remotely on the brief life history of the poet. For years I had been one of this band of collectors, but I scarcely knew how successful my quest had been until, in 1921, I was asked to deliver a commemorative address on the one hundredth anniversary of Keats's death at Yale University, as one of the lectures of the Francis Bergen Foundation. In preparing that address, I discovered so much that was fresh and unknown, so many little collateral facts of importance, that only a tithe of the information so gained could find place in the limits of an hour's talk. Realizing that, if my own collection could yield so much, the collections of others must also contain a great deal of which biographers and commentators were unaware, I decided that there was room for a new biography which should incorporate all the available material and make it accessible to students of Keats.

My intention in writing this book has been by no means to supplant existing biographies, but to add to them, and this I hope will be clearly understood. I should not have attempted a complete biography had it been possible to present all that I have discovered in any other way, but the knowledge gained, spread as it is over the whole of Keats's life, could be properly understood only by placing it in a chronological pattern.

This was my chief reason for writing the book; there was, however, another. It lay simply in the passage of time. Many as are the books on Keats, their authors have belonged, I think without exception, to the nineteenth century, in attitude if not in fact. But a new generation of poets and critics now holds the stage, and the twentieth century has been silent in regard to Keats. Yet a great poet has something to give to every generation, and it has seemed to me time that mine should set down its impressions and put its particular view on record. I do not pretend to speak as the universal voice of an era, merely as one voice existing in that era; but this opinion has led me to add a certain amount of criticism to the biography proper, which criticism will be considered sympathetic or the reverse principally, I believe, according to whether the individual reader derive his impressions from the mental impulses of the last century or of this.

Before going any farther, I wish to make an apology. In July, 1914, I met Sir Sidney Colvin, then preparing his great book on Keats, in London. I told him that I possessed a good deal of Keats material, and promised, at his desire, to send him a list of it. But before my return to America, the war broke out, and shortly after, I fell seriously ill. These two facts made it impossible for me to keep my promise immediately, and before I was able to do so, his biography appeared. At the time, I had no intention of writing on Keats myself, and was deeply chagrined to discover that it was too late to send the list. I can only say that Sir Sidney Colvin has most graciously forgiven me, and granted me his permission to quote freely from his book. My indebtedness to him will be found recorded again and again throughout these two volumes.

Keats and his poetry are so much of a piece, that I have

followed a rather unusual method in dealing with the two aspects of his character, the personal and the poetic. I have given his life as a whole, bringing in the poems at intervals as they occurred to him. My object has been to make the reader feel as though he were living with Keats, subject to the same influences that surrounded him, moving in his circle, watching the advent of poems as from day to day they sprang into being. I have tried to bring back into existence the place, the time, and the society in which Keats moved. A host of commentators have dealt with him solely in his quality of poet functioning in the timeless area of universal literature; my endeavour has been to show him as a particular poet, hindered and assisted by his temperamental bias as a man, writing in a certain *milieu*. For this reason, I have considered that no detail which could add vividness to the picture is unimportant, nothing which could clarify his psychological processes too slight to be mentioned. Keats's life was so short that it is possible to follow it with a minuteness which could not be accorded to a poet who had lived the usual span of man's existence.

I have quoted freely, both from published and hitherto unpublished sources, convinced that first-hand evidence is always preferable to a hundred-year-after paraphrase. And I have spared no space to make clear my reasons for any altered date or departure from an accepted point of view. The sources for the quotations will be found at the bottom of the pages, and being there, I have not thought it necessary to give any farther catalogue of the books consulted. In the quotations, words in parentheses were in the original manuscripts, words in brackets have been added by me or by previous commentators. In quoting poems published in Keats's lifetime, I have followed the texts of the first editions. For those poems published after his death, I have followed the manuscripts wherever such were obtainable; where manuscripts were non-existent or inaccessible, I have taken Mr. Buxton Forman's readings in his Complete Edition. In the case of poems recently discovered, I have adopted Professor de Sélincourt's text. All letters and manuscripts are quoted exactly as they were written. I have altered neither spelling nor punctuation, and have let even abbreviations stand. In three Appendices I have given a chronological list of Keats's poems compiled with reference to the most recent discoveries; an unknown fragment of a poetical play in the Morgan Library; and various underscored passages and annotations found in books owned by Keats and never before published.[1]

As I have already said, my work has been principally among American collections, as I believed that the material in England had been exhaustively gone over by previous students, but I have examined both the Dilke Collection at Hampstead and that in the British Museum. Lord Crewe's collection I have not seen nor made any attempt to see, knowing it to have been thoroughly tabulated and made use of by the late H. Buxton Forman and Sir Sidney Colvin. The debt owed to these two gentlemen by all students of Keats is incalculable. Nothing can be done to-day without constant reference to their works. In the case of Mr. Buxton Forman, I have used chiefly his Complete Edition, in five small volumes, published in 1900–1, augmenting it with his earlier Library Edition, which though fuller in detail lacks the later information of the small edition. Whenever possible I have gone to the original sources quoted by him or Sir Sidney Colvin.

Professor de Sélincourt's editions of Keats's poems, particularly the Fourth Edition, have been invaluable, and to his courtesy I owe the permission to quote from them. It is a pleasure to record my thanks for his kindness and encouragement.

It has been my good fortune to run across a number of letters of Fanny Brawne's, quite unknown to students. I

[1] A fourth Appendix contains material which arrived too late to be mentioned above.

have been allowed to quote these in excerpts only, but indeed to give them in full would require an entire volume. To me, they make Fanny Brawne for the first time plausible; we see her at last as she was, not as egregious and erroneous legend has hitherto depicted her. To have been able, through these letters, to raise the cloud of malign misconstructions which has long obscured her, has been one of the chief satisfactions of my researches.

The list of my indebtedness to my brother collectors, and to many other people who have helped me by information or otherwise, is long, for I have met with the utmost cordiality on every side. First and foremost come the owners or custodians of the great collections. To Mr. J. P. Morgan of New York, owner of the Morgan Library, which he has just formally put at the service of students, but which has in fact always been at their service, assisted by the expert advice of its remarkable librarian, Miss Belle da Costa Greene, I am deeply obliged. Through Miss Greene's kindness I have had free access to the Library for the past four years, and have been permitted to make such transcripts of manuscripts as I needed. Mr. F. Holland Day of Norwood, Mass., has given me copies of three unpublished letters of Keats and various letters of his friends, as well as many photographs and pictures, among them a most interesting pencil drawing of Keats from a note-book of his brother Tom's. Mr. Day has also greatly aided me with his advice and detailed knowledge of Keats's life, and supplied me with newspaper clippings and magazine articles difficult to find. His unique collection of Keats presentation copies has added some valuable bits to my biographical data. Mr. Louis A. Holman of Boston, an indefatigable collector of Keatsiana, and the owner of the largest collection of prints and illustrations relating to Keats in the world, has opened his entire store to me. His note-books, the result of infinite labour, have been of the greatest service. Mr. Frank B. Bemis of Boston has also offered me every facility in his power, to him I owe a most important letter from Tom Keats, and the inscriptions in some of his presentation copies of Keats's books have been particularly significant. Mr. William A. White of Brooklyn has been most kind. Through him I have had access to a manuscript of *Lamia*[1] as well as the proof-sheets of that poem, and his courtesy has enabled me to find and recognize one of the only two first editions of Drayton's *Endimion and Phœbe* known to exist, which is now in his possession. The Keats Memorial Association of Hampstead, England, through its most courteous secretary, Mr. William E. Doubleday, placed the Dilke Collection at my unreserved disposal, and Mr. Doubleday personally undertook to obtain for me various permissions from people in England for which I am profoundly grateful. In the notes, these large collections are referred to as Morgan Collection, Day Collection, Dilke Collection, etc.

For the owners of one or more items, my thanks are due to Mr. Lucius Wilmerding of New York, for permission to quote the annotations in a copy of *Palmerin of England*; to Mr. William M. Elkins of Philadelphia, for allowing me to examine a copy of Keats's *Poems* formerly owned by Thomas Richards; to Mr. James Freeman Clarke of Boston, for permission to transcribe one of Keats's Scotch letters given by George Keats to his grandfather; to Mr. W. van R. Whitall of Pelham Manor, New York, for sending me Woodhouse's copy of *Endymion* for examination and transcription and for a photograph of an oil portrait of Woodhouse belonging to him; to Professor Edward S. Burgess of New York University, for an unpublished letter of George Keats, and for his transcription of Keats's notes written by Marianne Reynolds into a copy of *Paradise Lost* from the copy given by Keats to Mrs. Dilke now in the Dilke Collection; to Mr. A. Edward Newton of Philadelphia, for permission to reproduce a silhouette of Keats as a boy; to the National Portrait Gallery, London, for permission to reproduce a pencil drawing of Keats by Brown; to Mrs.

[1] Now in the Bemis Collection.

Herbert L. Wild, grand-daughter of Joseph Severn, for the reproduction of a silhouette of Keats; to Miss Fanny Speed MacDonald, great grand-daughter of George Keats, for a photograph of an engraving of a water colour sketch of Tom Keats by Joseph Severn; to Mr. Oliver R. Barrett of Chicago, for photographs of Keats's passport in his possession; to Dr. Roderick Terry of Newport, Rhode Island, for allowing me to quote the poem *Hither, hither, love*, the manuscript of which is owned by him; to Mrs. Roland Gage Hopkins of Brookline, Mass., for two unpublished letters of Keats; to Mr. Rosewell Page of Richmond, for transcribing the title-page and inscription of a Greek Testament which belonged to Keats now in his possession; to the Authors' Club of New York, for allowing me to transcribe Keats's annotations in a copy of *Guzman d'Alfarache*.

Other people who have helped me in various ways are: Mrs. Samuel A. Hartwell, a grand-daughter of George Keats, by giving me much information about the Keats family in America, and compiling for me a genealogy of George Keats's descendants; Mrs. Thomas Hardy, by sending me information about the Keats family in Dorsetshire; Dr. John B. Hawes 2nd, by examining a health history of Keats which I made out for him and permitting me to quote his opinion upon it; Dr. Abner Post, by also examining the health history and allowing me to quote the result of his investigations; the Rev. Dr. Leigh H. Nixon, Librarian of the Westminster Cathedral Library, by sending me information in regard to a copy of Drayton's *Endimion and Phœbe* in that Library; Mr. Gardner Teall, by telling me of the whereabouts of Keats's copy of *Guzman d'Alfarache*; Mr. Claude L. Finney of the University of Michigan, by according me permission to quote from his unpublished thesis, *Shakespeare and Keats*, in the Widener Library, Harvard University; Professor Ralph Leslie Rusk of the University of Indiana, by giving me leave to quote one of Keats's Scotch letters discovered by him in an old copy of the *Western Messenger* which he reprinted in the *North American Review*, and Miss Elisabeth Cutting, the editor of that magazine, by adding her necessary permission to his; Mr. S. Foster Damon, by making for me a list of the derivations of the alchemical and astrological allusions in Keats's *Cap and Bells*; and Miss Margaret Shepard, by allowing me to reproduce a photograph taken by her of the Piazza di Spagna, Rome.

To my friend, Professor John Livingston Lowes of Harvard, I owe so much that it is impossible to tabulate the sum of my indebtedness. His enthusiasm, encouragement, and sympathy during the entire time that I have been at work on the book have been unfailing. To his knowledge and imaginative insight I owe many suggestions as to the possible sources of some of the poems, which suggestions I have followed up with most fruitful results.

To Professor William Lyon Phelps of Yale is due the initial impulse which led me to undertake the book, for it was he who invited me to deliver the anniversary address at New Haven. I hereby express my thanks.

Others whose assistance I cannot leave unrecorded are Dr. Theodore J. Eastman, who has given me much advice on the medical aspects of Keats's life; Dr. George Watson Cole, librarian of the Henry E. Huntington library at Pasadena, who, together with his assistant, Mr. Cecil K. Edmonds, set me on the track which led to the discovery of a copy of Drayton's *Endimion and Phœbe* in a place where Keats might have seen it; Professor John R. Slater of the University of Rochester, who examined for me a presentation copy of Keats's *Endymion* formerly in the possession of Mrs. Bertha L. Bolton of that city; my niece, Mrs. Orme B. Clarke of London, who obtained for me a copy of the entry of the marriage of Keats's parents in the Register Book of Marriages of Saint George's Church, Hanover Square, and the Rev. Prebendary Thicknesse who made the copy.

For transcriptions of letters and poems which I have been unable to use, I wish to thank the well-known booksellers, Mr. Gabriel Wells, and Mr. Edgar H. Wells, both of New York, Mr. Charles Sessler of Philadelphia, and Mr. John Howell of San Francisco; also Mr. Jerome Kern of New York.

Mr. Charles K. Bolton, librarian of the Boston Athenæum, Mr. William C. Lane, librarian of the Widener Library, and Mr. Walter B. Briggs, assistant librarian of the Widener Library, have afforded me very material assistance in many ways for which I am most grateful.

I cannot close this list without mentioning my secretaries, Mrs. Charles W. Alexander and Mrs. Willis C. Carling, whose unwearying labours have so materially lightened mine. By their devotion, complete indifference to the passage of time, and enthusiastic eagerness, a long and difficult task has been made almost easy and brought to a conclusion in a surprisingly short time.

If I have forgotten any one I should have remembered, I shall be very sorry; but I beg all such persons, if any there be, to pardon the oversight as one of the head not of the heart.

Amy Lowell.

Brookline, Mass.
October 10, 1924.

CONTENTS

VOLUME I

LIST OF ILLUSTRATIONS

VOLUME I

JOHN KEATS

VOLUME I

JOHN KEATS

CHAPTER I

FROM BOY TO MAN

THE leaves were turning brown, and fluttering down in companies to be scuffled carelessly underfoot by passers-by in the squares, and parks, and graveyards — any-where, in fact, where there were leaves to turn brown and fall. In the West End of London, shuttered houses gazed blankly at empty streets, except when caretakers flung open their wide doors and revealed glimpses of darkened halls echoing with emptiness. Drawing-rooms slumbered, swathed in cambric coverings. Rats scuttled unmolested across the floors of deserted stables. Footman's knock and postman's bell were events of rare occurrence. The West End, or rather that important part of it composed of strictly human elements, was scattered all over Great Britain: it cultivated its magnificent gardens in every shire in England; it killed exuberantly, bagging birds and beasts with unabatable ardour from Scotland to Land's End; it sipped and bathed and attended routs and con-certs at Bath; or, if it happened to be in the Prince of Wales's set, briefly sojourned in the wake of that fantastic gentleman whither fancy led him, which on this particular Autumn, having just broken with Mrs. Fitzherbert, was not Brighton. But, whatever its temper, as it bumped and rolled in its own carriages toward its chosen destinations, the sight of broad fields and finely timbered parks caused it to thank its stars with fervour that the English channel separated it from France, still in the clutches of the Reign of Terror. Wherever the world of fashion might have betaken itself, it had betaken itself somewhere. The West End was deserted, and nowhere was its desertion more noticeable than it was of a Sunday in its favourite church, Saint George's, Hanover Square.

But although the meagre congregation which gathered for its Sunday services could not boast a single denizen of the quarter, it was still, in the eyes of the parishioners of less favoured edifices, the most desirable church in all London to be married in. It was not uncommon for aspirants to matrimony from other parishes to hire rooms within the area of its jurisdiction and deposit bags or wearing apparel in them in order that its hallowed influence might shed its blessing on their marriage vows. This was snobbish, no doubt, but it also showed a praiseworthy desire to rise in the world, and was probably the reason, and very likely the method of procedure, which induced two young persons who lived in Finsbury to be married there. These persons were Frances Jennings, daughter of John Jennings, a livery-stable keeper at the sign of the Swan and Hoop, Finsbury Pavement, Moorfields, and her father's trusted head ostler, Thomas Keats. So they appeared to themselves; to us, they appear uniquely as the future father and mother of John Keats.

If the choice of Saint George's as the scene of the wedding ceremony was for any other reason than that I have stated, I do not know what it was; unless, indeed, the marriage were in the nature of a runaway match owing to some objection on the part of the bride's parents, whose own notions of rising in the world may have taken another direction, but their evident sense of the probity of Thomas Keats, which as events prove was great, does not seem to point in this direction. However that may be, the marriage took place at Saint George's on Thursday, October ninth, 1794.

SAINT GEORGE'S, HANOVER SQUARE

From a print in Ackerman's "Repository of the Arts," 1812

Author's Collection

The register of the church reads as follows:

Thomas Keats and Frances Jennings

Both of this Parish, were married in this Church by *Banns* this *Ninth* day of *October* in the year *1794*.

By me, *J. Downes, Curate.*

This marriage was solemnized between us { *Thomas Keats.* *Frances Jennings.*

In the presence of { *John Brough* *Mary Sut*

Who John Brough and Mary Sut were, no one knows. They appear and disappear with their signatures. Their presence, and the absence of Mr. and Mrs. Jennings, gives some colour to the disapproval theory, but subsequent occurrences do not seem to bear it out. At any rate, the young couple returned to the Swan and Hoop, and there, one year later, their first son, John Keats, was born.

There is some doubt as to whether October twenty-ninth or October thirty-first was his birthday. Everyone connected with Keats seems to have believed that he was born on October twenty-ninth, but in the baptismal register at St. Botolph's Church, Bishopsgate, where he was christened on December eighteenth, 1795, is a marginal note, said to be in the handwriting of the rector, Dr. Conybeare, stating that he was born on October thirty-first. This appears to me the flimsiest evidence, as the rector could know nothing of the matter except what he was told and may very possibly have mistaken what was said.

Keats is supposed to have been a seven months child, but he seems to have suffered from none of the disabilities which usually hamper such children. For sixteen months, John remained the only child; but on February twenty-eighth, 1797, another son, George, was born; and on November eighteenth, 1799, still another, who was named Thomas after his father. Since these two brothers play a very large part in Keats's life, it is important to remember their relative ages. A fourth son, Edward, born in 1801, died in infancy, and the only girl, Frances Mary, did not arrive upon the scene until June, 1803.

Of Keats's ancestry, we know next to nothing. The name is a fairly common one in England under various spellings, but all attempts hitherto made through baptismal registers, etc., to trace the origin of Thomas Keats, John's father, have failed. Sir Sidney Colvin says that, according to his information, Thomas Keats was born in 1768, but as he does not reveal the source from which he obtains this fact, we are almost as much in the dark as ever. The most plausible suggestion is that communicated by Mr. Thomas Hardy to Sir Sidney Colvin, and again mentioned in a letter to me from Mrs. Hardy. Mrs. Hardy's letter is a little fuller in detail than Sir Sidney's account, and the detail gives the matter a more likely possibility. Mrs. Hardy says that in her husband's youth "there was a family named Keats living two or three miles from here [Dorchester], who, Mr. Hardy was told by his father, was a branch of the family of the name living in the direction of Lulworth, where John Keats is assumed to have landed on his way to Rome (it being the only spot on this coast answering to the description). They kept horses, being what is called 'hauliers,' and did also a little farming. They were in feature singularly like the poet, and were quick-tempered as he is said to have been, one of them being nicknamed 'light-a-fire' on that account. All this is very vague, and may mean nothing, the only arresting point in it considering that they were of the same name, being the facial likeness, which my husband says was very strong. He knew two or three of these Keatses." An additional weight given to this suggestion is Severn's remark that, when he and Keats visited the spot identified as Lulworth in one of the many irritating delays to which wind-driven vessels were so often subjected and which tormented the passengers on the "Maria Crowther" for two weeks after sailing from Gravesend, Keats "was in a part that he already knew." We are not aware that Keats was ever in the neighbourhood, for Sir Sidney's idea that he may have broken the homeward journey from Teignmouth at Dorchester, and visited Lulworth Cove then, breaks down in face of an unpublished letter from Tom Keats that I shall quote in due course, in which he says that after leaving Bridport "we travelled a hundred miles in the last two days." This certainly leaves no time for sight-seeing, so that, if Severn be correct in thinking that Keats was familiar with the Lulworth "caves and grottoes," his familiarity must date from a boyhood visit of which we have no record, made perhaps while staying with relations. This is all mere guess-work, of course, but it is the nearest we can approach to a genealogy of the Keats family. Against this, is the statement of Señora Llanos (Fanny Keats) that she remembered hearing as a child that her father came from Cornwall, near Land's End. Again Sir Sidney is my authority, but again he neglects to mention his; so whether Señora Llanos's recollection is down in black and white somewhere, or is merely the product of hearsay remembrance on some one's part, we cannot tell.

The origin of Keats's maternal grandfather is equally to seek. There is an entry of a marriage between a John Jennings and a Catherine Keate at Penryn, Cornwall, in 1770, and Sir Sidney Colvin conjectures that this entry may point to the fact of Jennings and his head man, Thomas Keats, being relatives; but Jennings is a usual patronymic enough in that part of Great Britain, and John is a name of no use at all for purposes of identification wherever English is spoken. What explodes Sir Sidney's conjecture into thin air, however, is the recently discovered knowledge that Mrs. Jennings was a Yorkshire woman.[1] The present Keats family believe that Mr. Jennings was more than an ordinary livery-stable keeper. One of the granddaughters

[1] Abbey Memoir in Author's Collection.

of George Keats remembers her grandmother to have said that he ran a line of coaches. I cannot pretend to have examined all the coach registers of the period, but he certainly was not one of the larger coach proprietors, as I can find no mention of him among these in the dozen or two volumes on the subject which I have consulted, therefore I think it more likely that he was one of the many jobbers who "horsed" someone else's coaches for a certain number of miles on their journey. That he was successful in his business is shown by his having retired with a competence. From an unpublished Memoir [1] compiled by Keats's publisher, Taylor, after a conversation with Keats's quondam guardian, Richard Abbey, in 1827, and sent by Taylor to Woodhouse, we learn of Mr. Jennings that "he was excessively fond of the pleasures of the Table and 4 days in the week his wife and family were occupied in preparing for the Sunday's Dinner. He was a complete Gourmand." There is no doubt, however, as to the maliciousness of tone of Abbey's communications, and I think they must be taken with a grain of salt; but since they are the only ones we have concerning Keats's grandfather and grandmother, and are very open in dealing with the character of Keats's mother, they are of the utmost importance.

Through this Memoir, we learn that Mrs. Jennings was a native of the village of Colne, at the foot of Pendlekill, in Yorkshire. Abbey came from the same village, and probably knew Mrs. Jennings from childhood. He seems to have been strongly prepossessed in her favour and gives an instance of her charitable disposition in befriending an unfortunate woman, also from Colne, and after the woman's death bestirring herself to succour her children. He does not seem to have liked her husband and appears to have almost hated her daughter, but whether his dislike — in the former case, at least — was well grounded or not, who can say.

[1] Author's Collection.

There seems to be no doubt that Mrs. Jennings was a good and worthy woman. George Keats, writing to Dilke in April, 1828,[1] speaks of his grandfather Jennings as "extremely generous and gullible," but adds "I have heard my Grandmother speak with enthusiasm of his excellencies." He goes on to tell his correspondent that "Mr. Abbey used to say that he never saw a woman of the talents and sense of my grandmother, except my mother." Naturally George had never seen the Memoir written by Taylor after his talk with Abbey. But considering what Abbey permitted himself to say to Taylor about George Keats's mother on that occasion, George's letter to Dilke leaves us wondering who is lying. Is George attributing sentiments to Abbey which the latter never held in order to throw dust in Dilke's eyes, or had Abbey hypocritically said this to George, or was Abbey letting malice get the better of truth when he spoke to Taylor? The wisest course is to believe neither George nor Abbey implicitly, but to take a middle view between the two and suppose Keats's mother to have been a woman of strong passions and appetites, with no particular desire to curb either, but with something redeeming and attractive about her just the same.

I have debated with some care the advisability of quoting what Abbey says of Mrs. Keats in this Memoir. But believing, as I do, that where so much has been told all should be recorded, realizing also that half truths never lead to fair conclusions, and that a great man can stand complete revelation; considering again that no adequate psychological study of a man's life and character can be made if we fail to take his inheritance into account, I have decided to quote the important parts of the Memoir in full, always cautioning my readers to notice that Abbey was undoubtedly exaggerating to a greater or lesser extent, and that he evidently gloated on blackening the character of

[1] Original letter in Author's Collection.

Mrs. Keats whom he seems to have quite cordially detested.

Here, then, is Taylor's paraphrase of Abbey's communications, continuing directly from the description of Mr. Jennings's love of eating:

> "His Daughter in this respect somewhat resembled him, but she was more absolutely the Slave of her appetites, attributable probably to this for their exciting cause. At an early Age she told my informant, Mr. Abby, that she must and would have a Husband; and her passions were so ardent, he said, that it was dangerous to be with her. She was a handsome, little woman. Her features were good and regular, with the exception of her mouth which was unusually wide. A little circumstance was mentioned to me as indication of her Character — She used to go to a Grocer's in Bishopsgate Street, opposite the Church, probably out of some liking for the owner of the Shop, — but the man remarked to Mr. Abby that Miss Jennings always came in dirty weather, and when she went away, she held her clothes very high on crossing the street, and to be sure, says the Grocer, she has uncommonly handsome Legs. He was not, however, fatally wounded by Cupid the Parthian.
>
> But it was not long before she found a Husband, nor did she go far for him — a Helper in her Father's Stable appeared sufficiently desirable in her Eyes to make her forget the Disparity of their Circumstances, and it was not long before John Keats had the Honour to be united to his Master's Daughter."

After spattering Mr. Keats's character to the best of his ability — a spattering to which I shall have occasion to refer in a moment, but with its antidotes in the shape of less prejudiced accounts — Abbey describes his death with infinite malice and unveracity. The Memoir continues, in Taylor's words:

> "I think it was not more than 8 Months after this Event that Mrs. Keats again being determined to have a Hus-

band, married Mr. Rawlins, a Clerk in Smith Payson and Co.'s — I know very little of him further than that he would have had a Salary of 700£ a year eventually had he continued in his Situation. I suppose therefore that he quitted it on becoming the Proprietor of the Livery Stable by his Marriage with Mrs. Keats, but how long the concern was carried on, or at what period Mr. Jennings died, or relinquished it, I didn't learn. It is perhaps sufficient to know that Rawlins also died after some little Time, and that his Widow was afterwards living *as* the wife of a Jew at Enfield, named Abraham."

Here follows the account of Mrs. Jennings from which I have already quoted, and Taylor again returns to Mrs. Rawlings (for it was not Rawlins, as Taylor supposed) as painted by Abbey:

> "Her unhappy Daughter after the Death of her first Husband, became addicted to drinking and in the love of the Brandy Bottle found a temporary gratification to those inordinate appetites which seem to have been in one Stage or other constantly soliciting her. The Growth of this degrading Propensity to liquor may account for the strange Irregularities — or rather Immorality of her after-Life. I should imagine that her Children never saw her, and would hope that they knew not all her Conduct."

We should hope not indeed, if this account of her were strictly true. That it is not, we can guess by the tone of it. Abbey had a good listener in Taylor, and he gave himself the luxury of speaking as he felt. Taylor, in spite of a certain shrewdness, seems to have been considerably gulled by Abbey's speciousness. Both the gulling and the shrewdness appear in this paragraph:

> "Abby is a large stout good-natured looking man with a great Piece of Benevolence standing out of the Top of his Forehead." [It was the age of phrenology.] "As he spoke of the Danger of being alone with Miss Jennings I looked to see if I discern any of the Lineaments of the

young Poet in his Features, but if I had heard the whole of his Story I should have banished the Thought more speedily than it was conceived — never were there two people more opposite than the Poet and this good Man."

We may banish the thought, too, not because Abbey had a "Piece of Benevolence" sticking out of the "Top of his Forehead," but because the idea is completely absurd. But we may thank Taylor for the suggestion since it carries a wide train of possibilities in its wake. Granted that where there is smoke there is fire, Mrs. Keats probably did have qualities leading her to indiscretions, it is not unlikely that she was at once over-sexed and under-educated; that she was weak in self-control seems evident, but what the Memoir goes far to show is that Abbey had received, or thought he had received, some injury from her, an injury which looks very much as though it were a snub. Was Abbey, a married man, unduly attracted by the exuberant young lady, and did he dare something which she resented? His false witness against her husband points to something of the sort. What is a respectable, middle-aged man doing gossiping with a near-by grocer on the subject of a young lady's legs? Something on the part of his caller must have led the grocer on to these revelations. Abbey was, I fear, spying upon Miss Jennings, trying to find out whom she did look upon since she would not look at him. It is not a pretty story, and the gusto with which Abbey related it to Taylor is greatly against him. When Abbey began to speak of things which Taylor knew about, Taylor found him inaccurate, as we can see by this sentence at the end of the Memoir:

"There is the whole of what he told me respecting John Keats, excepting such particulars as I was better acquainted with perhaps than he himself."

I shall have occasion to come back to the Memoir again, but not in this connection.

Before judging Mrs. Keats, we should look at her through other eyes. George Keats, writing to Dilke in 1825,[1] has this to say of his mother:

> "My mother I distinctly remember, she resembled John very much in the Face was extremely fond of him and humoured him in every whim, of which he had not a few, she was a most excellent and affectionate parent and as I thought a woman of uncommon talents, she was confined to her bed many years before her death by a rheumatism and at last died of a Consumption, she would have sent us to harrow school as I often heard say, if she could have afforded."

Making all allowances for a son's enthusiasm, still this is clearly not the debauched woman depicted by Abbey. In a later letter, the one already referred to, of April, 1828, George contradicts this earlier statement in one particular, for he says: "I do not remember much of my mother," yet he strengthens his impression of her character by adding "but her prodigality, and doting fondness for her children, particularly John, who resembled her in the face."

Cowden Clarke says [2] that Mrs. Keats was "tall, of good figure, with large, oval face, and sensible deportment." She must have been about twenty-eight when Clarke first met her, having been born in 1775. From such very conflicting accounts as these, it seems not too difficult to reconstruct the character of Mrs. Keats. She was certainly a vivacious woman, fond of everything gay and lively, sensuous, ardent in pursuit of any aim, and clever beyond the majority of her sex and station; the sort of person, in short, only too likely to be misunderstood in the narrow circle of her acquaintance. That Keats got his sensuous vigour from his mother seems self-evident; that he sublimated her somewhat raw instincts through the medium of poetry into an ardour for sheer beauty, is a fact

[1] Original letter in Author's Collection.
[2] *Recollections of Writers*, by Charles Cowden Clarke.

which should be easily understood by students of modern psychology. John loved his mother passionately, as is no wonder. He was her first born, and from George's account we can see that she lavished a very special love on him. Buxton Forman records that, during her last illness, John (presumably in some vacation from school) often sat up with her all night, seeing that she got her medicine at the proper times, preparing the nourishment prescribed for her, and reading novels aloud to her, and Clarke says that at her death, which occurred when John was fourteen, his grief was deep and bitter, so much so that in his desolation he hid himself under the master's desk. Poor little shaver, so pitiably unable to cope with his first great sorrow!

Of Thomas Keats, John's father, we know somewhat more; although George, in the letter to Dilke already quoted, says he remembers nothing of his father except that he had dark hair. As Thomas Keats did not die until George was seven, this lack of all recollection is strange. It can only be accounted for by supposing Thomas Keats to have been very much engaged by his business. Cowden Clarke has left us a very careful portrait of him, however. Clarke speaks of him as "a man of so remarkably fine a commonsense, and native respectability, that I perfectly remember the warm terms in which his demeanor used to be canvassed by my parents after he had been to visit his boys. John was the only one resembling him in person and feature." And elsewhere Clarke says: "I have a clear recollection of his lively and energetic countenance, and particularly when seated on his gig and preparing to drive his wife home after visiting his sons at school."

Clarke was apparently wrong as to feature, for George may be trusted to know whether or not John took after his mother in that respect, unless his remembering only that his father had dark hair indicates that he had quite forgotten what he looked like. But the rest of Clarke's description is undoubtedly correct. Thomas Keats was a short, powerfully built man, like his eldest son, with an ambition and perseverance above the average and with a good mind.

Now that we know how Thomas Keats impressed people of the type of Clarke's father and mother, we may return to the Memoir and see Abbey's malice in full swing, and also deduce, through his prejudice, a little more of the character of Keats's father.

To Abbey's jaundiced eyes, Thomas Keats

> "did not profess or display any just Accomplishments. Elevated perhaps in his notions by the Sudden Rise in his Fortunes he thought it became him to act somewhat more the Man of Consequence than he had been accustomed to do — but it was still in the way of his Profession — He kept a remarkably fine Horse for his own Riding, and on Sundays would go out with others who prided themselves on the like Distinction, to Highgate, Highbury, or to some other place of public Entertainment for Man and Horse. — At length one Sunday night, he was returning with some of his jolly Companions from a Carouse at one of these Places, riding very fast, and most probably very much in Liquor, when his Horse leaped upon the Pavement opposite the Methodist Chapel in the City Road and falling with him against the Iron Railings so dreadfully crushed him that he died as they were carrying him Home."

Abbey distorts facts with a diabolical cleverness. Thomas Keats did die from his horse falling with him, but he lived for seven hours at least after the event. He had been dining out, at Southgate, but where was the harm of that? There is no reason at all to suppose that he was drunk, that is a pure invention of Abbey's, for even he ushers in the statement with a "most probably." Why should not a stable-keeper ride a good horse? In those days, everyone who could kept a good riding horse, many men still preferring to make journeys on horseback rather than in a vehicle. Thomas Keats dealt in horses; they were not a luxury, but part of his business stock. That he displayed many "just Accomplishments," is proved by Clarke's remembrance of him. Yet, with all the falsity of accent in Abbey's account, one trait in Thomas Keats's character stands out clearly: his ambition to better his condition, to rise in the world. He was no "helper" in the stable, as Abbey insinuates, but the foreman of the establishment, at the time of his marriage; and when he kept the fine horse which so annoyed Abbey, he had become, by the retirement of his father-in-law, its ostensible proprietor. Bettering his condition was apparently one of the dearest wishes of his heart, and there is no reason to suppose that he wished only the froth of such betterment. The frill of being married at Saint George's need not blind us to the realization that beneath it lay both a refined taste and a solid appreciation of the value of education and good manners. Thomas Keats was civilized beyond his class, or endeavoring to become so — and what is strange in that, seeing he was the father of John Keats?

How Keats came by his poetry has been a wonder to all his biographers. But we know more of the workings of the subconscious brain and the whys of genius than the then state of science permitted most of them to do. Mrs. Keats was passionate and weak; Thomas Keats was, or appears to have been, strong; the grandmother Jennings was certainly a woman of good sense. That there was intellect somewhere, must have been the case; at any rate, there was admiration of intellect, or Mr. and Mrs. Keats would not have considered sending the boys to Harrow, as George Keats says they did. Harrow meant not only a classical education, it meant association with boys of a better class than their own. But this is only snobbishness to a half-vision, there is plenty of evidence that Thomas Keats's snobbishness was the shell of an ideal. Here, in father, mother, and grandmother, are a series of inheritances which may well have produced a poet. Even imagination plays a part, for what was the ideal but an imagined one? Such a high reach for their sons shows an almost fantastic fancy on the part of both father and mother, and a fancy they were willing to abide by. Keats refined upon the imagination as he refined upon the passion, and his intellectual strength forged for both a medium of expression. In other words, character in his case made for creation. This is no new thing; everyone knows that the artist's temperament without the artist's power to create fills our sanitariums with neurotics. Reading between the lines of Abbey's Memoir, it seems likely that Mrs. Keats verged toward this state in her later years; but, poor creature, difficult as she may have been to her family, she did her son an infinite service. Her sympathy with John proves potentialities that she fatally lacked the power of turning into facts. What she had not, strength of character, her husband had, and between them they made their son, transmitting to him much that was unfortunate, it is true, but dowering him with the uncomfortable treasure of genius. Yet there is one question which no probing will satisfactorily answer: Why is there no mention of his parents in any of Keats's letters, even in those to his brothers and sister? There is but one exception to this throughout the correspondence, but the connection in which it occurs is most significant. Writing his third letter to Fanny Brawne from Shanklin, Keats seals it with an old seal of his father's, which he comments upon in this way: "My seal is mark'd like a family table cloth with my Mother's initial F for Fanny: put between my Father's initials." We have no other evidence of Keats's having used this seal, although, of course, he may have done so, but the reason for his using it here is obvious. Keats attached a good deal of weight to seals, as we shall see later. He could speak to Fanny Brawne as he could to no one else, naturally; the jest about the table-cloth is to ease an overflow of tenderness, and in his situation a "family table cloth" was not without meaning. Leigh Hunt says [1] that Keats never spoke of the livery-stable, and thinks it was "out of a personal soreness which the world had exasperated." If this suspicion of Hunt's be correct, the less man Keats. Let us not seek our answer too far, with Abbey's ugly communication staring us in the face, but even supposing that it contains some grains of truth, Keats's reticence is more likely to have been caused by a feeling of sacredness toward his dead parents than to any sudden revelation of regrettable traits in his mother's character. Knowing how much he loved her, we may suspect a grief with which harness buckles have nothing to do, and a bereavement too deep to be chattered about.

Stepping out of the bounds of immediate descent, Keats's relations appear to have been few and to have played no part at all in his life. On the authority of Clarke, we learn that he had two uncles, brothers of his mother. Our information concerning one of them stops at the mere facts of his existence and early death; the other was a Lieutenant of Marines, Midgley John Jennings, who is supposed to have served in Admiral Duncan's flagship in the action off Camperdown. A family legend has it that this gentleman, being very tall, was a special target for the enemy, who, in spite of his height, failed to hit him. Tales of his valour during the engagement seem to have been current in his old school. I am told by Mr. Holman that naval records [2] show no such person in the roster of the ship's company of the "Venerable," Duncan's flagship. At that time, Jennings was a Second Lieutenant, his promotion to First Lieutenant came in 1799, and he was made Captain in 1808. He survived his promotion to a captaincy by a few months only, as he died on October eighth, 1808. By what inaccuracy his name fails to appear among those serving in the "Venerable," we do not know. His whereabouts dur-

[1] *Lord Byron and his Contemporaries*, by Leigh Hunt.

[2] Memorandum from Public Records Office. June 24, 1913.

ing the engagement has not been traced in the Marine Office Commission Books, but there is a gap in them from 1796 to 1800. That Second Lieutenant Midgley John Jennings, Royal Marine officer, was present at the battle off Camperdown, if not in the "Venerable," then in some other vessel of the fleet, there is no reason whatever to doubt. Edward Holmes, a school-fellow, remembers that [1] "Jennings their sailor relation was always in the thoughts of the brothers, and they determined to keep up the family reputation for courage." Years seem to have dimmed the brightness of the gallant lieutenant's appeal, for he is never once alluded to in the letters, not even when his widow threatens to bring a lawsuit against Abbey, which threat had the effect of seriously incommoding his niece and nephews for some time.

Not long after his daughter's marriage, Mr. Jennings retired from active business, and, leaving his stable in the competent hands of his son-in-law, went to live at Ponders End. For some time after this, Thomas Keats and his wife continued to live at the Swan and Hoop, but before long, probably owing to an increasing prosperity, they moved to Craven Street, City Road. As this new house was only half a mile North of the stable, it was both convenient for business and one of those evident rises in the world so dear to Thomas Keats's heart. From living over a stable to living in a separate house at some distance was no mean gain in those days, and we can imagine the rejoicing which the move occasioned. Some of the younger children, I do not know how many, were born in the Craven Street house.

Of Keats's childhood, we know practically nothing; for I cannot take much stock in the only anecdotes which have come down to us. One derives from Haydon, who dresses it up in his melodramatic style until it loses all semblance of reality. Boiled down to probable fact, the story is that

[1] *Life of John Keats*, by Sir Sidney Colvin.

once, when Mrs. Keats was ill and had been ordered perfect quiet, John, having got hold of an old sword somewhere, mounted guard in front of her door and would allow no one to go into her room. The other tale, also recorded by Haydon, but with less flourish and furor, he says he got from George Keats. An old lady, whom Haydon[1] identifies as a Mrs. Grafty of Craven Street, Finsbury, who had known the boys when they were children, encountering George on some occasion asked him the natural question: "What is John doing?" On George's telling her that John had determined to be a poet, the old lady remarked that such a decision was very odd, because, when he could only just speak, he had a habit of ignoring questions asked him and instead would make a rhyme to the last word spoken by the questioner, after which astonishing behaviour he would laugh as though mightily pleased with himself. In a child of two or three this would surely be remarkable, if it were true. I, for one, do not believe a word of it. It is just the kind of thing that old ladies always recollect of children in after years, but affection and the usual desire of the old to link themselves to the young are the sources of memory.

I have already mentioned that Thomas Keats aspired to Harrow as the school for his sons, but here his imagination outran his pocket. Try as he would, his income would not stretch to such a flight. We can understand with what disappointed reluctance he abandoned the ambitious scheme and decided to follow his father-in-law's example and send his sons to the excellent school kept by Mr. John Clarke at Enfield, ten miles from London. So to Enfield John went in 1803, and either with him, or immediately after, went George.

It was a charming place, architecturally, this Enfield school. Cowden Clarke begins his paper on Keats with a description of it:

[1] *Autobiography and Journals of Benjamin Robert Haydon*, edited by Tom Taylor.

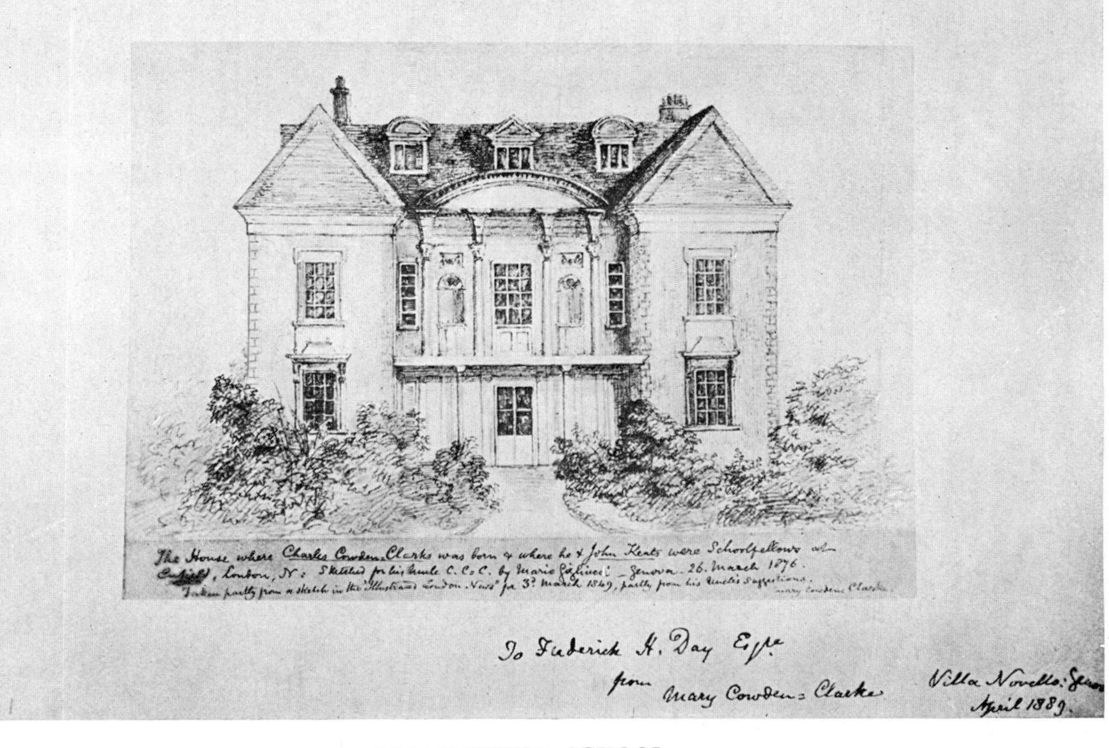

THE ENFIELD SCHOOL

From a sketch by Mario Cigliucci in the possession of F. Holland Day, Esq.

"The house had been built by a West India merchant in the latter end of the seventeenth or beginning of the eighteenth century. It was of the better character of the domestic architecture of that period, the whole front being of the purest red brick, wrought by means of moulds into rich designs of flowers and pomegranates, with heads of cherubim over niches in the centre of the building."

So perfect an example was it of a certain type of decoration, that, when it was finally pulled down, the middle of the façade was placed in the Victoria and Albert Museum, South Kensington, where it now is. Attached to the house was a large garden with an arbour, adding just the touch needed to temper the arabesqued brickwork with glimpses of variously tinted green.

This stimulatingly fruity façade, stuffed away from human intercourse in the South Kensington Museum, was once witness to some such scene as this: Two little fellows, six and seven years old respectively, driven out from town in their father's gig, a little awe-stricken probably, a little tearful undoubtedly, at least when their father drove away and left them to face that most terrible of experiences, the first day at a new school.

George was the younger by sixteen months, but so much taller was he than John that Clarke thought he was the older of the two and apparently never found out his mistake. He speaks of John as "the youngest individual in a corporation of between seventy and eighty youngsters," he was "one of the little fellows who had not wholly emerged from the child's costume." We know the dress well from innumerable prints — frilled collar, short jacket, pearl buttons as large as half-crowns, tasselled cap. Two little boys, with home and mother ten miles away, gaped at by "seventy or eighty youngsters," jeered at and teased in the merry fashion of English youth a century ago. Brutal, we should call it; no school of to-day would permit the type of "hazing" which pertained in English schools to a very recent date. We cannot suppose that the Keats boys escaped until they had made good their title to be let alone. But John was a pugnacious little chap, as all accounts show. Cowden Clarke speaks of his

> "highly pugnacious spirit, which, when roused, was one of the most picturesque exhibitions — off the stage — I ever saw. One of the transports of that marvelous actor, Edmund Kean . . . was its nearest resemblance; and the two were not very dissimilar in face and figure. Upon one occasion, when an usher, on account of some impertinent behaviour, had boxed his brother Tom's ears, John rushed up, put himself in the received posture of offense, and, it was said, struck the usher — who could, so to say, have put him into his pocket. His passion at times was almost ungovernable; and his brother George, being considerably the taller and stronger, used frequently to hold him down by main force, laughing when John was in 'one of his moods' and was endeavouring to beat him. It was all, however, a wisp-of-straw conflagration; for he had an intensely tender affection for his brothers, and proved it upon the most trying occasions. He was not merely the 'favourite of all' like a pet prize-fighter, for his terrier courage; but his high-mindedness, his utter unconsciousness of a mean motive, his placability, his generosity, wrought so general a feeling in his behalf, that I never heard a word of disapproval from any one, superior or equal, who had known him."

Clarke also mentions his "brisk, winning face," a detail which must not be omitted.

Edward Holmes, a school-fellow, and later the author of a *Life of Mozart*, tells the same story: [1]

> "He would fight any one — morning, noon, and night, his brother among the rest. It was meat and drink to him."

George Keats, who knew his brother intimately, also bears witness to this trait in John's character, but with an even stronger qualification, based on a more under-

[1] Houghton MSS. Crewe Collection. Quoted by Sir Sidney Colvin.

standing knowledge, than Clarke. He speaks of John's "nervous, morbid temperament":

> "From the time we were Boys at school where we loved, jangled, and fought alternately until we separated in 1818 I in a great measure relieved him by continual sympathy, explanation, and inexhaustible spirits, and good humour, from many a bitter fit of hypochondriasm."

This is from the letter written to Dilke in 1825. In another letter, also to Dilke, in 1830,[1] he enlarges upon the subject:

> "I loved him from boyhood even when he wronged me, for the goodness of his heart and the nobleness of his spirit, before we left school we quarrelled often and fought fiercely, and I can safely say and my schoolfellows will bear witness that John's temper was the cause of all, still we were more attached than Brothers ever are — After we left school we never passed an opposing word."

And earlier in the same letter:

> "John was open, prodigal, and had no power of calculation whatever. John's eyes moistened, and his lip quivered at the relation of any tale of generosity of benevolence or noble daring, or at sights of loveliness or distress — he had no fears of self thro interference in the quarrels of others, he would at all hazards, without calculating his power to defend, or his reward for the deed, defend the oppressed or distressed with heart and soul with hand and purse."

Since the man exists in embryo in the child, with these evidences of an older Keats we can construct the little fellow, eight years old, who found himself gazed upon by such a host of alien eyes in the strange school-yard, and we can see him showing the others that here was something to beware. But the extreme sensitiveness which George calls "nervous," "morbid," "hypochondriasm," was even then a part of his make-up, that hyper-delicacy

[1] Author's Collection.

of the nerves of both physical and mental sensation which none of his biographers have sufficiently understood and made allowance for, which was the cause of his poetry on the one hand, and, on the other, of the pitiful letters to Fanny Brawne.

Whatever happened in the school-yard that afternoon, however much like a bantam cockerel bristling for a fight he may have appeared to the other boys, one knows for a certainty what bedtime meant when it came, with his heart bursting with homesickness; and we do not need to be told that he stuffed his bed-clothes into his mouth so that no one should hear the sobs he could not control. For he was his mother's son, and poetry had not yet come to relieve him of overcharged emotion.

The seven and a half, or eight, years (we do not know at what period of the year the boys entered school for the first time, but John left at the end of the Summer term in 1811) of Keats's school life should be taken all of a piece. In order to consider them so, I shall give here a brief outline of the most material events of family history during the years immediately following his entrance.

Hardly more than a year after sending John and George to school, Thomas Keats was killed in the accident of which I have already spoken. I think it very unlikely that this accident was due to liquor or other inadvertence on Mr. Keats's part. Horses are always liable to slip on pavement or cobble-stones, and death seems to have been due to the hitting of Thomas Keats's head on an iron railing rather than to the fall itself. Here is a sober account of the accident printed in the *Times* for Tuesday, April seventeenth, 1804:

> "On Sunday Mr. Keats, livery-stable keeper in Moorfields, went to dine at Southgate; he returned at a late hour, and on passing down the City-road, his horse fell with him, when he had the misfortune to fracture his skull. It was about one o'clock in the morning when the watch-

> man found him, he was at that time alive, but speechless; the watchman got assistance, and took him to a house in the neighbourhood, where he died about 8 o'clock."

Their father's death was a more bitter blow to the Keats family than any one could have foreseen. At one stroke, the home was broken up, and with it all those fanciful and affectionate schemes for the future went by the board. The boys did advance in the world, but by their own efforts alone. No careful, wise, and enthusiastic guidance was ever theirs for the asking again. They were pitchforked and tumbled into work they hated without having their wishes consulted in any particular. Their father's direction for them as boys was followed until they had outgrown it; but, after that, they were the constant victims of a narrow-minded opposition which took no account of temperament or aptitude.

To Mrs. Keats, the blow was as devastating as it was destined to be later for her children. Her marriage seems to have been extremely happy. She and her husband were evidently congenial in tastes and outlook; they were young people, stepping boldly on in the world, prospering and deserving to do so. Now all was changed. Frances Keats was clearly not a woman who could live alone; nor does she seem to have been a woman of capacity in affairs. There appears to have been no question of her father's returning to the stable, and we can imagine that Mrs. Keats made a poor job of it as proprietor in her own right. Had she been like other women of her time, place, and profession, notably the famous Mrs. Mountain of the Saracen's Head, Snow Hill, or Mrs. Nelson, of the Bull Inn, Aldgate, who not only "horsed" coaches, but owned them, and ruled their coachmen, guards, and stablemen with firm hands and single-minded shrewdness, all would probably have gone well with her and her children. It was not in her to do any such thing. She was clinging, loving, ardent, but she was not self-sustaining. It was therefore natural that within a year she should have taken another husband in the person of the Rawlings of Abbey's story. But Rawlings was far from being another Thomas Keats. It may be questioned whether Mrs. Keats was ever so attractive in his eyes as the stable. It is no wonder, then, that the marriage turned out badly. Mrs. Rawlings left her husband after a short experience of life with him, and seems to have left the stable to him on her departure.

The relations of Jennings, Thomas Keats, Mrs. Keats, and Rawlings with the stable are very obscure. Since Mr. Jennings died with money enough to leave his wife comfortably off and bequeath legacies to his children and grandchildren, and the loss of the stable to Rawlings does not seem to have affected his income, it is possible that Thomas Keats had already bought him out. By leaving Rawlings, Mrs. Keats lost all claim to whatever property she had brought to the marriage, and Rawlings seems to have accepted the situation and the stable with perfect calm. She must have lost her whole share in it by running away, for she left her children nothing when she died, and Rawlings evidently felt under no obligation to provide for them. If the Jew named Abraham were not a fiction of Abbey's brain, she probably went to him on leaving Rawlings. But that connection also went wrong, and it was a broken woman, sick, lonely, and hopeless, who returned to her mother's house, never to move again.

There is no means of finding out how long it took all these things to happen. Mr. Jennings died at Ponder's End on May eighth, 1805, leaving something over £13,000. His will,[1] which was drawn on February first, 1805, bequeathed a capital yielding an income of £200 a year to his widow outright, together with all the household furniture, etc., and another carrying a yearly income of £50 to his daughter, with reversion to her Keats children after her

[1] *Reports of Chancery*, Vol. XIII, by Francis Vesey, Jr.

death; he also bequeathed £1000 to each of the children to be held in separate trusts and not divided until the youngest should come of age.[1] To his son, Midgley John Jennings, he left £2000 in East India stock and £1900 in "Bank Security called the New Fives"; apparently this money was merely a life estate to be returned to the main trust in the event of his son's death, but, if Mrs. Midgley John Jennings should survive her husband, she was to receive the sum of £500. Charles Danvers, Midgley John Jennings, and Alice Jennings were named as executors and executrix, but the will was proved by Mrs. Jennings and Lieutenant Jennings only, Danvers probably refusing to serve.

Mr. Jennings may have supposed that these bequests would account for his entire capital, but, as a matter of fact, there was a certain sum still remaining after the provisions of the will had been fulfilled. It was thought best that the disposal of this money should be determined by the Court of Chancery. For this reason, a friendly suit was brought by Mrs. Rawlings against her mother and brother as executors under her father's will. The suit dragged on for nearly twenty years, until all the principals were dead. It was finally disposed of in 1823–24, when John Keats had been dead for three years and Tom for five. Most of the financial difficulties suffered by the family were due to this Chancery suit.

I have assumed that Mr. and Mrs. Jennings, on leaving the Swan and Hoop, went to live at Ponder's End, because it was there that Mr. Jennings died. It must have been almost immediately after his death, therefore, that Mrs. Jennings moved to Church Street, Edmonton; her name appears in the Rate Books of Lower Edmonton first in 1806. If Sir Sidney Colvin's surmise that Mrs. Rawlings's return to her mother's house and her father's death were practically synchronous, it was to the Edmonton house

[1] Colvin.

that Mrs. Rawlings returned. For five years she lived there, until her death in 1810. So the scene is set for Keats's school life. London passes out of his orbit; his life revolves between the Clarke school at Enfield and his grandmother's house at Edmonton.

Exactly when Tom joined his brothers at school is not known, but probably as soon as he was considered old enough. At whatever age he went, we may be sure it was too soon for his health. He was a very delicate boy, and schools in those days were for the strong. I know no more pathetic record than the tablets put up to the memory of poor little boys who died at school in the cloister of Winchester College, for example, realizing as we must that most of these deaths were due to insufficient care and unwise medical treatment. Tom Keats never outgrew his delicacy. On the contrary, his life was one steady march toward the consumption which finally killed him at the age of nineteen.

Beyond Enfield and Edmonton was the world, and the world in 1805 deserves some notice. On December second, 1804, Napoleon had been consecrated and crowned as "Emperor of the French." This magnificent ceremony had been performed by no less a person than the Pope, Pius VII, especially imported for the occasion, and thereafter "induced" to remain for four months in Paris to obviate any consequences that might accrue on his immediate return to Rome. His benediction thus summarily extorted, Napoleon preferred to be alone responsible for the more important part of the affair; he arranged that the actual crowning should be done by the greatest man in the world at that time — he crowned himself. Anxious to establish the new imperial household with all possible speed, Napoleon was summoning home all those *émigrés* who were willing to become a part of the new order; but, considering that France was at war with England, Russia, Austria, and Sweden, they could return but slowly.

For two years, Napoleon had been threatening to invade England. His great camp on the sands at Boulogne had been matched by camps up and down the English coast on the opposite side of the channel. Not one comfortable night had the dwellers in the coast villages of Sussex, Kent, Hampshire, and Dorsetshire known in all that time. Now, with the new coalition against France entered into by the four countries I have named, conditions on the Rhine frontier required attention, and Napoleon was obliged to withdraw his troops from Boulogne to send them hot-foot to meet the advancing Austrians, whom he defeated at Ulm on October seventeenth, 1805. England's part in the war at this time was purely naval; but, restricted as it was, it was thorough, for four days after Ulm, on October twenty-first, the British fleet under Nelson wiped the combined French and Spanish fleets practically out of existence at the the Battle of Trafalgar, and the menace of invasion became an old wives' tale for a hundred and ten years, when it once more raised its grim head in another connection during the Great World War we have just past through. Beaten at sea, Napoleon was at the height of his glory on land, and at the Battle of Austerlitz, fought in the December following, the combined Russians and Austrians were defeated.

One can imagine the excitement that these stirring events must have brought to a boys' school. For, although both army and navy were made up of professional fighters, many of the boys must have had relations in one or other service; and, while conscription was not resorted to, a robust and unsentimental government winked its eye at lies, cajolements, much treating with brandy, whiskey, etc. on the part of recruiting sergeants, and the even more abominable kidnapping methods resorted to by the navy press-gangs.

George the third was king, during his last lucid interval before going hopelessly insane in 1811. William Pitt was prime minister, until his death in January, 1806. When anything went wrong, the *habeas corpus* act was suppressed until it went right again, as in Robert Emmet's easily quashed insurrection in Ireland in 1803. Persons so misguided as to steal sheep or pick pockets, if not hanged at once, were transported to Botany Bay in Australia. Slaves, although not permitted in England, were freely brought to the British holdings in the West Indies. India was falling, piece by piece, under British rule in the shape of the East India Company.

A series of petty indignities connected with the "right of search," an extension of the press-gang policy, offered by British ships to American ships at sea, was leading up to the war of 1812. Fleets of merchant ships convoyed by men-of-war as a safeguard, not only against enemies, but against African and Asian pirates or random buccaneers, crossed the seas constantly to India, China, and the West Indies. Japan alone remained impenetrable and unknown.

It is strange to look back and think of these things and realize how little they seem to have affected the life of the ordinary English citizen of that time. A few travelled people, chiefly of the nobility, who had rejoiced in the efficient succour rendered by Nelson and Lady Hamilton to the Neapolitan Bourbons in 1799, must have grieved to know that Napoleon had proclaimed himself King of Italy, with Eugene Beauharnais as Viceroy of Naples.

Life, as the ordinary citizen knew it, was a much quieter affair than such events might lead one to suppose. Considering that there were no railroads, people got about the country with a remarkable persistence and dispatch. The nobility travelled in its own carriages; the gentry made use of the innumerable post-chaises with relays of horses; for those of more moderate incomes, there were excellent coach lines running in every direction for which bookings were obtained at inns with picturesque names like "The Swan with Two Necks" or "The Bull and

Mouth"; and, if pressed for time, the extraordinarily swift mail-coaches left the London Post Office every evening at sundown. Letters, rarely prepaid, were folded, with the flap fastened down by sealing-wax, and sent to be paid at what we should consider an inordinately high rate by the recipient, unless the sender were lucky enough to obtain a frank from some great personage; they crossed the seas in sailing packets, usually confided in bundles to someone's acquaintance who was making the voyage, in order to save the really great expense of over-seas postage. And yet all the world, the English world, wrote and wrote prodigiously. By means of innumerable letters, we may know the period as though it were our own. Apologies to correspondents for the amount they will have to pay are frequent, but no instance in which a correspondent has been urged to write more briefly has ever come to my attention. Keats prepaid only his letters to Fanny Brawne, a fact worth noticing, I think.

Police, there were none. In London, their place was taken by a rather inefficient body of men known as "the watch," who paraded their various beats in ones or twos, armed with staves and lanterns, shouting out the hours of the night and the type of weather prevailing, and when not so engaged huddled in sentry-boxes placed up and down the town for their accommodation. The streets were lit at night by means of oil lamps; small whale-oil lamps were sometimes used in houses, but candles, tallow or wax, were the common form of domestic lighting. Huge cut-glass chandeliers, the smooth facets of which were purposely designed to increase the light of the candles, illuminated public halls, ball-rooms, and theatres. The stage was in one of its most flourishing periods, with Mrs. Siddons and her brother, John Kemble, as its chief stars; Italian opera was in high vogue, varied by occasional excursions into Mozart, etc. The two great theatres, Drury Lane and Covent Garden, alternated seasons of opera and plays. Shakespeare was acted constantly, while a light English opera, built more or less upon the favoured Italian model, had a large following. Smaller theatres, considered of no standing, gave entertainments consisting of clownings, squibs, and comic songs; they were the forerunners of our vaudeville houses, but had no such patronage as these enjoy.

The great school of portrait painters was slowly giving place to a school of landscape painters, among them Turner and Constable. An immense hope and ferment were in the air. Even those who had believed that the French Revolution was to mark the beginning of Paradise on earth, and who owned to a bitter and disillusioning disappointment, had been, nevertheless, so wrought upon and ploughed into, that they were, however unwittingly, seed-ground for new ideas. Even when, ten years later, the Battle of Waterloo proclaimed the permanence of existing order, the ferment of thought could not altogether be stayed. In literature, it made Coleridge, Wordsworth, Shelley — it made Keats. Already, in 1805, literature was undergoing a rejuvenation. That the world scarcely realized it, is nothing. We can see that it was there. In 1796, a modest little volume had been printed by one Cottle of Bristol; it was entitled *Poems on Various Subjects* and was by Samuel Taylor Coleridge. Two years later appeared the epoch-making *Lyrical Ballads* by Coleridge and Wordsworth, which contained *The Ancient Mariner*; and, in 1807, Wordsworth's *Poems* was published. But before this (bombshells, had they been but better known), were the books of William Blake: *The Songs of Innocence* and *The Book of Thel*, both ready for distribution in 1787, *The Marriage of Heaven and Hell*, 1790, and in 1793 *The Gates of Paradise* and *The Visions of the Daughters of Albion*. The world took no notice of Blake, and but little of Wordsworth; it was still concerned with Cowper, Burns, Crabbe, etc., and the light it saw and hailed as the coming star was the very dubious one of Sir Walter Scott's ballads. But the real light was there, all the same, the light kindled by the bonfire dreams of a world rejuvenation. Keats was not one of its earliest rays, but he came at the time of its day-spring and did his share to increase its brilliance.

I have taken so much space to recapitulate what everybody knows, because the world I have briefly sketched is not only the setting for the years of Keats's school-days, but for practically his whole life. So modern in many ways is this world of a hundred years ago, that we are surprised at its occasional differences from the one we live in. I think we, to-day, can understand Keats better than the men of previous generations could. They were nearer to him in time, but not in temper; for — strange paradox! — Keats was an almost completely modern man. Once grasp that idea, and a good many of his difficulties with life and with poetry become comprehensible.

I do not mean for a moment that he *wrote* as the modern poets do, but that he *thought* as they do, and as his contemporaries most emphatically did not. Take the letters of the time — Shelley's, Byron's, Hunt's, Miss Edgeworth's, almost any you like — and you are conscious of a different strain of thought, feeling, and expression from ours. In Keats's letters, you are conscious of nothing of the kind. Occasional references to the world we have been considering appear in them, of course, but they are mere incidents, and do not, for one moment, make the letters "quaint" to us, as old letters usually are.

We know the time very well from innumerable sources, and perhaps from none better than the novels of Jane Austen. No one can deny that Jane Austen's books are very much alive, but they date, the period is always present to us as we read. Where is the period in Keats's letters? Right here, now, in our own minds. George Keats's epistolary style is old-fashioned and stiff; Severn's is old-fashioned and sentimental; Bailey's is old-fashioned and cumbersome; but Keats himself, even with the difference of a turn of phrase here and there, is all of to-day. Any real consideration of Keats's life must keep constantly in view the world he lived in, and the type of man he was living in this world. His life was one long, blind struggle to outdistance his mental environment. Insufficiently equipped, uncertain of his way, not even thoroughly aware of his own goal, unwisely guided by his friends, ignorantly and cruelly criticized by his enemies, buffeted by the hurricanes of his own changing ideas, Keats died at the age of twenty-five still unformed in many ways, profoundly discouraged and dissatisfied, but leaving behind him a body of work in his poems which does not die because of qualities in it even more important to mankind than those which appear on the surface, and in his letters a possibly no less valuable legacy to the student of psychology and a volume of perennial charm to the ordinary reader.

John Clarke's school was one of the many academies dotted over England, designed to impart a moderate degree of education to the sons of professional men of meagre incomes and tradesmen of the better class. It did not aspire to turn out thoroughly well-grounded classical scholars nor embryonic mathematicians. It taught the three "Rs" and taught them well. Latin, of course, bulked large in the curriculum, but if Greek were taught at all, Keats did not take it. There were rudiments of science — astronomy, geology, botany probably, possibly a little physics — and there was French, this last made easy by the hosts of needy Frenchmen escaped from revolutionary France. Probably French has never been so well taught in England as it was at just that time, and Keats learnt to read it with perfect ease. The Latin he acquired, if not a great deal, was serviceable, and gave him considerably more than itself. But the important thing about the school for Keats was that the headmaster's son acted as one of the ushers, and this son was Charles Cowden Clarke.

During the first part of his school life, Keats gave no indication of extraordinary intellectual power. He was the ordinary happy, rough-and-tumble school-boy. He was fond of games; Holmes[1] says: "In all active exercises he excelled." On half-holidays and during vacations, he loved to roam about the fields and paddle in brooks and ponds, and he was fond of making pets of wild and irreconcilable animals. Writing to Fanny Keats, many years later, he asks her to tell him what she would like him to give her, adding: "Anything but live stock. Though I will not now be very severe on it, remembering how fond I used to be of Goldfinches, Tomtits, Minnows, Mice, Ticklebacks, Dace, Cock Salmons and the whole tribe of the Bushes and Brooks: but verily they are better in the Trees and water."

We can easily see how indulgent, not only his mother, but his grandmother also, must have been, to allow him to bring his incongruous pets home in such casual profusion. Love was not lacking in the Edmonton home, that is certain. He tells the whole story in a doggerel rhyme of reminiscence sent in another letter to his sister:

"There was a naughty Boy
A naughty boy was he
He kept little fishes
In washing tubs three
In spite
Of the might
Of the Maid
Nor afraid
Of his Granny-good —
He often would
Hurly burly
Get up early
And go
By hook or crook
To the brook
And bring home
Miller's thumb

[1] Colvin.

Tittlebat
Not over fat
Minnows small
As the stall
Of a glove

. . .

O he made
'Twas his trade
Of Fish a pretty Kettle
A Kettle — A Kettle
Of Fish a pretty Kettle
A Kettle!"

The kettle is evidently a quotation from the expressed view of the mighty maid, with difficulty subdued by the good grandmother. Sir Sidney Colvin has given us so pleasant a picture of this brook that I cannot do better than quote it here:

[1] "Despite the changes which have overbuilt and squalidly or sprucely suburbanized all those parts of Middlesex, the Pymmes brook still holds its course across half the county, is still bridged by the main street of Edmonton, and runs countrywise, clear and open, for some distance along a side street on its way to join the Lea."

Again, Sir Sidney describes the countryside, which was the scene of Keats's half-holiday excursions:

[2] "Across the levels of the Lea valley . . . rose the softly shagged undulations of Epping forest, a region which no amount of Cockney frequentation or prosaic vicinity can ever quite strip of its primitive romance. Westward over Hornsey to the Highgate and Hampshire heights, north-westward through Southgate towards the Barnets, and thence in a sweep by the remains of Enfield Chace, was a rich tract of typically English country, a country of winding elm-shadowed lanes, of bosky hedge and thicket and undulating pasture and corn-land charmingly diversified with parks and pleasances."

[1] Colvin. [2] *Ibid.*

KEATS AS A CHILD

From a silhouette in the possession of A. Edward Newton, Esq.

Keats learnt the country, and its fauna and flora, practically by heart. Touches of his boyhood sports in it crop up here and there in his poems. In *Sleep and Poetry*, we have a school-boy "riding the springy branches of an elm" and "a pigeon tumbling in clear summer air," and the brook and his games with it are in *Endymion*, when he remembers that he used to "bubble up the water through a reed" and

> ". . . make me ships
> Of moulted feathers, touchwood, alder chips,
> With leaves stuck in them,"

and also, in the same poem, we have a recollection of looking

> "Athwart the sallows of a river nook
> To catch a glance at silver throated eels."

These were the high lights of his inconsequential early years at the Clarke school. But we must not forget the low lights, recorded by his brother George. The moments of misery over some trifle of huge import to him at the time, the fits of the "blues" which came so suddenly and wrought such havoc. He kept these things for his brothers, although Holmes seems to have been an occasional witness of their results. Clarke, naturally, knew nothing of them, but George's testimony is enough.

Games, fights, and rambles, with an overbalanced proportion of "blue devils" to temper their delights, and about as much study as could be got along on, seem to have made up Keats's life in his first school years. Holmes[1] refers to "his extraordinary vivacity and personal beauty," which with the farther remark that "his sensibility was as remarkable as his indifference to be thought well of by the master as 'a good boy' and to his tasks in general," rounds out his portrait for us. But, Holmes adds, and we must

[1] Colvin.

ponder his expression: "He was in every way the creature of passion." Once more in this we see his mother's son, more exactly like her than he will ever be again. For his mind has not waked up, and he has not yet been taken possession of by his intellectual faculties.

All at once it came — the love of literature — and with passion, naturally, what else could one expect. Keats's was not a character of half measures. He may not have cared a rap for the master's opinion, but he seems to have done well enough in his classes, for Clarke says that "he was a most orderly scholar." But when it came — it came! Order gave place to profusion. Holmes is firm on the point "that he was not literary," but that "this taste came out rather suddenly and unexpectedly." He dates it "about the year before he left school." Clarke speaks of it as occurring in "the last two or three successive half years before he left school." Suddenly books started into life for him. He probably cared as little for the encomiums of his masters as ever, but he began to care a lot for the studies themselves. Clarke's account shows his manner of work, quite passionately unbalanced, of course:

> "He was at work before the first school-hour began and that was at seven o'clock; almost all the intervening times of recreation were so devoted; and during the afternoon holidays, when all were at play, he would be in the school — almost the only one — at his Latin or French translation; and so unconscious and regardless was he of the consequences of so close and persevering an application, that he never would have taken the necessary exercise had he not been sometimes driven out for the purpose by one of the masters."

The bad habit of recording events in different groupings, so dear to the hearts of biographers, has obscured a governing cause for this change of direction in Keats's life. His mother died of consumption in February, 1810. We have already seen how close was the tie between Keats and his mother, we know how deeply her death affected him. It shook his world to its foundation; it broke his life to bits. But grief is a great maturer. I believe that this intimate experience with sorrow started Keats's intellectual faculties functioning as they never had before. He must have speculated on, and fiercely combatted with, death; and, seeking the reason for bereavement, cudgelling his mind for some explanation of the cruel paradox of life always reaching an end, of love snapped off and bleeding, suddenly stumbled upon a dormant part of himself.

With his life changed and shattered, we can conceive that home holidays were more sad than merry. Many men, in his then state of mind, have flung over their responsibilities and sought to flee sorrow by change of scene and activity. Keats was not his own master; he could not change his scene, but he could alter his mode of life. Books came to him like a soporific saturated with dreams. With his vivid imagination, he could literally live in them. Even the dull work of prescribed translation could be made to deaden the ache of his loss if he set at it hard enough. If he played, or rambled, or fought, he could still think, and thinking meant to open himself to the intolerable agony of missing; but if his thinking faculties were engrossed in hard work, the nerves of sensation were for the moment numb. Considering that Keats was, innately, one of the most literary of men, what was begun as a relief from pain ended by becoming a conscious delight. Not the lessons, we can hardly suppose that Keats revelled in them for their own sakes, but the books he read for pleasure, and Latin and French exercises quickly took on the aspect of means by which he would be enabled to read more books.

He read everything he could lay his hands on, and he read with an extremely eager and brilliantly active imagination. Clarke thinks that "he must, in those last months, have exhausted the school library, which consisted principally of abridgements of all the voyages and travels of any note; Mavor's collection, also his *Memorial History*, Robertson's histories of Scotland, America, and Charles the Fifth; all Miss Edgeworth's productions, together with many other works well calculated for youth. The books, however, that were his constantly recurring sources of attraction were Tooke's *Pantheon*, Lemprière's *Classical Dictionary*, which he appeared to *learn*, and Spence's *Polymetis*." Holmes[1] adds to this formidable list, *Robinson Crusoe* and "something about Montezuma and the Incas of Peru," these last probably out of Robertson or Marmontel. Holmes continues:

> "He must have read Shakespeare as he thought that 'no one would dare to read *Macbeth* alone in a house at two o'clock in the morning.'"

This remark is refreshing as showing that even in the first flush of literary interest Keats was no pedant, but a perfectly healthy, sensible, imaginative boy of fifteen. Except for Miss Edgeworth, nothing is said in these lists of current popular authors, but Keats admitted later to an adolescent admiration for Beattie's *Minstrel* and Mrs. Tighe's sentimental effusion *Psyche*, and we must not overlook the novels he had been in the habit of reading to his mother.

"Always in extremes," is Holmes's summary of him, "in passions of tears or outrageous fits of laughter"; now to these were added positive debauches of reading. The Clarke school must have been an easy-going place, for Clarke writes:

> "In my 'mind's eye' I now see him at supper (we had our meals in the schoolroom) sitting back on the form, from the table, holding the folio volume of Burnet's *History of his Own Time* between himself and the table, eating his meal from beyond it."

Under these circumstances, we are not surprised to learn

[1] Colvin.

from Clarke that "for the last two or three successive half years of his remaining at school . . . he took the first prize by a considerable distance."

These prizes seem to have consisted of books or silver medals, but which meant the most we can only conjecture, although Clarke does say that books were given for voluntary work done in recreation hours. The first prize which we know of Keats's receiving [1] was a book so odd in character that we can only account for it by remembering that most of the boys in the Clarke school were undoubtedly destined for trade; it was Kaufmann's *Dictionary of Merchandise*. It is inscribed: "Mr. Clarke's School at Enfield. Awarded to Master John Keats as a Reward of Merit. 1809." Did Keats, the vivacity of whose reading appetite was only just beginning, attempt to read his prize, we wonder? The second prize he received was a silver medal.[2] It bears on one side the inscription: "Prize medal. Rev. Wm. Thomas's Academy, Enfield. 1810. Awarded to Master J. Keats"; on the other side is a Latin inscription: "*Stadium doctrinæ arduum & difficile sit nihilominus Finis gloriosus erit*," and the words "*Audivit Clarkenem*" running round the edge. The school, on Cowden Clarke's authority, is usually spoken of as Mr. John Clarke's school, and John Clarke was certainly the head-master in Keats's time. But evidently he either acted as manager of an academy of which Mr. Thomas was the—presumably retired—proprietor, or, more likely, he had succeeded to a school once run by Mr. Thomas. The name of Mr. Thomas might tend to throw some doubt on the authenticity of the medal, but one of George Keats's granddaughters distinctly remembers seeing it often at her grandmother's when she was a child. The third prize won by Keats was again a book, Bonnycastle's *Introduction to Astronomy*, and this time the inscription reads:

[1] *Letters and Poems of John Keats*, by John Gilman Speed.
[2] Author's Collection.

"Assigned as a Reward of Merit to Ma[r] *John Keats* at Mr. Clarke's Enfield *Mids.* 1811." Since in both these books the school is spoken of as "Mr. Clarke's," I think it probable that the die for the silver medal was made when the school was in the Rev. William Thomas's hands, and that, to save the expense of a new die, the old one was still used, with the words "*Audivit Clarkenem*" added. If this speculation be true, it argues a very special thriftiness on the part of Mr. Clarke, who had had the school for over twenty years by this time; yet it seems more probable than that the medal should be struck for a master who did not take possession until at least two years later. Keats left school at the end of the midsummer term, but for some reason he was given a fourth book the next year, Ovid's *Metamorphoses*, not, probably, as a prize, but as a mark of friendship and approbation, since in it is written in a flourishing hand with much ornamental underlining: "John Keats emer: 1812." John Keats, *emeritus*, for he was no longer a scholar. That Keats received several books and only one medal, and that in 1810, goes far to substantiate my theory that it was precisely in 1810, the year of his mother's death, that Keats did his hardest studying apart from his reading for pleasure.

At this point, we must go back a little and take up the family fortunes once more. Her daughter's death seems to have startled Mrs. Jennings into the realization that she alone was left to care for her four young grandchildren. She was no longer even middle-aged, and the death of her husband, son, son-in-law, and daughter, all occurring within six years, must have shaken her considerably. She was the sole stay of her daughter's little family, and that family consisted of three boys, the oldest on the eve of growing up, and one little girl of seven years old. The thought of bringing up three obstreperous boys all alone probably appalled her, and the little girl would need care for many years to come. Taking heed of her advanced age — she was seventy-

SILVER MEDAL WON BY KEATS AT SCHOOL (BOTH SIDES)

Photographed from the original medal in the possession of the author

four — she wisely decided to protect the children from all eventualities. I say "wisely," because the idea was a wise one, but the persons selected to carry it out were not a good choice. Mrs. Jennings did not, probably, have a very large acquaintance to choose from, and it cannot have been easy to find any one willing to assume the guardianship of four children. Her old friend and fellow townsman, Richard Abbey, now a prosperous wholesale coffee and tea merchant with a warehouse and counting-room at 4 Pancras Lane, London, seemed the natural person to whom she could turn. She could not have guessed his hostility to her daughter and Thomas Keats, or she would not have designated him as guardian for their children. Blind to this side of Abbey, she did choose him, but associated with him another merchant, Rowland Sandell. The deed putting the children under the guardianship of these two men was executed in the July following her daughter's death. At the same time, she appointed them trustees of a trust to become active from that date, consisting of the best part of the property she had received from her husband. This trust was to be administered solely for the benefit of the children. Mrs. Jennings lived four years after this arrangement was made, but as it was to take effect at once, that meant that she virtually resigned control over the children from that moment. She must have felt herself very weary and old to do such a thing, and her doing so proved her complete confidence in the guardians she had appointed.

Rowland Sandell resigned his position very soon, probably long before Mrs. Jennings's death, for there is no farther question of him after the drawing of the deed. But Mr. Abbey took up his new responsibility at once, and thoroughly, with, as far as we know, perfect concurrence on the part of Mrs. Jennings. The boys remained at school, Fanny with her grandmother, and so things continued for a year.

What Abbey was, or was not, it is a little difficult to say.

George Keats, who seems to have got on well with him, speaks of him as sensible and worthy; John, on the other hand, clearly regarded him as incompetent, fussy, and disagreeable. Fanny Keats, who lived with him and his wife after her grandmother's death, gives the impression of having been thoroughly unhappy in the connection, and to have felt no love for either his wife or him. Dilke, who took over Fanny's property when she came of age, considered that Abbey had muddled things badly. Taylor, in the letter[1] I have so often quoted, speaks of his kindness and generosity; but Taylor apparently received much of this impression from Abbey's own mouth, which may not be an entirely trustworthy source. What Taylor does say of him clearly proves him to have been set in his ways, with little or no elasticity of mind or temperament. Taylor records, in this letter, an anecdote told him by a Mr. Macauley who, meeting Abbey at the Girdler's[2] Dinner, scarcely knew him: "The reason," in Taylor's words, "was this, he had that Day put on Trousers for the first Time having worn till then white Cotton Stockings and Breeches and half-Boots. When for a long Time there had been no other Man on the Exchange in that Dress — and he was become so conspicuous for it as to be an Object of attention in the Streets, he had at last resolved to come into the Fashion."

Unimaginative, conservative, opinionated, and utterly without capacity, such seems to have been Abbey's character from whatever angle we view him. Probably the cruelty of which he often seems guilty arose from sheer stupidity. He may have tried to do well by his charges, but always in his own way without regard to their feelings. He liked George, tolerated Fanny, and entirely disapproved of John and Tom, which disapproval led him to

[1] Abbey Memoir. Author's Collection.

[2] One of the City Companies. Girdlers — makers of girdles — as a separate trade now extinct.

misconstrue their actions at every turn. He seems to have gritted his teeth over his trust and grimly done his best, with all the well-meaning severity of a blundering, narrow-minded, bustling fool.

As I have said, during the first year of Abbey's guardianship, he permitted things to remain in *statu quo*. Then the sight of a boy going on for sixteen, wasting the formative years over studies which, so far as Abbey could see, led to no profitable end, was more than he could bear. To be sure, John was not penniless. In the first place, there was his share of the small trust placed in Abbey's hands by Mrs. Jennings. Farthermore, there was his reversionary right to a fourth of his mother's legacy, and the one thousand pounds directly bequeathed to him by his grandfather, to say nothing of the money tied up in Chancery. But Abbey was shrewd enough to realize that all this amounted in immediate fact to very little. Mrs. Jennings's total capital, before making the trust, produced only two hundred pounds a year, and the capital itself was liable to the vicissitudes of all invested moneys, while the sum which constituted the trust was necessarily less; Mrs. Rawlings's reverted legacy would yield her children only about twelve pounds a year each. As to the direct bequest, that could not be touched until Fanny Keats came of age, which would not happen for fourteen years; and the money tied up in Chancery was not worth considering at all to any one who knew the habit of suits in Chancery. The money to be counted upon, present and due, would make a nice little nest-egg for each of the children to start out in the world, which was what it was intended for. But the boys must start, as soon as they reached an age to do so. That was Abbey's very sensible opinion, and probably every one else's also, and when I say "every one," I include the boys themselves. This granted, Abbey submitted that John's time for starting had come, possibly George's also. In George's case, the matter was simple.

Abbey was willing to take him into his counting-house, George was willing to go. So that was settled.

It was considerably more difficult to know what to do with John. A fellow who had taken three first prizes at school, and who showed not the slightest interest in business, was obviously destined by nature for a profession. So thought Abbey. If Thomas Keats had been alive, he would probably have seen "Oxford" or "Cambridge" written in letters of flame upon the sky, and strained his every nerve to fulfil such an obvious prophecy. But Thomas Keats was dead, and the Clarke school did not prepare for the universities. John himself had no desire except to read all and every day, which, as even he doubtless admitted, was not exactly in line with adopting a profession.

We can imagine the family conclaves, with Abbey, Mrs. Jennings, and John, all discussing the important question of what John was to do. The church meant a university career — out of the question; the army may have been canvassed, and the navy, but Lieutenant Jennings was dead, and Abbey's aspirations were of a more modest order. What, except reading, had John shown an aptitude for? Mrs. Jennings recollected his careful and efficient tending of his mother. Here was something to cling to. John could be a surgeon. Surgery, in those days, occupied a position mid-way between a trade and a profession. It was not so long since surgeons had been barbers as well, even now they were apothecaries. The physicians were a higher grade, in public opinion. To be a physician, one had to undergo an arduous course of study, preferably at Edinburgh, and spend long years in training; it was beyond bounds in Abbey's philosophy to think of John becoming a physician, but a surgeon might be considered. Physicians were gentlemen and were addressed as "Dr."; surgeons were ordinary men like one's self and were called simply "Mr." like everybody else. How great surgeons like Astley

Cooper became such, no one could guess; they happened, remarkably happened, occasionally, but Abbey harboured no such glorious desire for John Keats. A good, honest country doctor, riding round in a gig, pulling teeth, compounding pills and potions, setting bones indifferent well, and earning enough to keep a decent house over his head, that was enough. And this could be accomplished. "Well, John, how does it strike you?" we can suppose Abbey asking, and John seems to have made no objection.

A Mr. Thomas Hammond, surgeon, living in Church Street, Edmonton, probably well known to Mrs. Jennings, and certainly not unknown to Keats, as he was often called to the Clarke school, was in need of an apprentice. Here was opportunity. Abbey, with characteristic promptness, took it. Keats was withdrawn from school at the end of the Midsummer term of 1811 and bound apprentice to Mr. Hammond.

George Keats, writing to Dilke in 1824,[1] says that Keats paid "two hundred Guineas and expenses" to Mr. Hammond. This appears to have been an error on George's part, as the sum paid by a surgeon's apprentice in those days was forty pounds. I am inclined to doubt the accuracy of George's financial statements to Dilke, as they do not seem, in certain instances, to tally with others made by him in letters contemporary to the events. Later in the same letter he speaks of a "premium" of two hundred pounds having been paid to Mr. Hammond, and apprenticeship fees of thirty pounds. For a surgeon to exact a premium over and above the usual fees, does not seem to have been the general custom, and I cannot but think that George's memory played him false on the subject.

Sir William Osler,[2] speaking of an indenture of a sur-

[1] Author's Collection.

[2] In an address on Keats delivered before the Johns Hopkins Historical Club in October, 1895. Published in the *Johns Hopkins Hospital Bulletin*, 1896.

geon's apprentice which was made out for his uncle in 1811, says:

> "The surgeon, for a consideration of £40, without board, undertook the care and education of the apprentices, of whom there were often three or four . . . The young apprentice promised not 'to haunt taverns or playhouses, not to play at dice or cards, nor absent himself from his said master's service day or night unlawfully, but in all things as a faithful apprentice he shall behave himself towards his said master and all his during the said time.'"

Keats was bound for five years, the usual term, and the "expenses," mentioned by George Keats probably refer to his board which the fee itself did not cover. The fee and expenses were paid by Abbey out of John's share of the money in his (Abbey's) hands.

A surgeon's apprentice in those days was a sort of handy general house and stable boy. He made up medicines, tended the shop, ran errands, went with his master on his rounds and held the horse, did, in fact, whatever there was to do in connection with the odds and ends of practice, and, as he became more proficient, acted as his master's assistant by doing all those things which we are accustomed to see done by an office nurse. His education depended entirely on the type of man he was apprenticed to. If his master lived up to his part of the bargain, he might learn a great deal; if his master were lazy or incompetent, the time of his apprenticeship was wasted. But, whatever the master, the circumstances were such that a bright boy could pick up much more than he was actually taught. Keats was a very bright boy. Leaving his genius entirely out of the question, his was a mind of very exceptional capacity. The fact is that, willy nilly, he became a good doctor. In the case of his own fatal illness, it is always his diagnoses which are right and those of his attending physicians which are wrong. Whatever was interesting, interested him, even

DR. HAMMOND'S HOUSE, EDMONTON

From a photograph taken by F. Holland Day, Esq.

if other things interested him more. He simply could not help learning, he had that sort of mind.

Clarke says that he liked his new job, for "with the exception of the duty he had to perform in the surgery — by no means an onerous one — his whole leisure hours were employed in indulging his passion for reading and translating." Clarke makes no mention of book tasks, but there must have been some. He must have studied anatomy and physiology, and got a considerable amount of his *materia medica* by heart. But evidently these things came to him easily and quickly. His habit of concentrated study helped him there. Mr. Hammond kept two apprentices, which presupposes a fairly large practice; but, however that may have been, Keats seems to have had plenty of spare time, and on the whole he does not appear to have objected to the place — at first, at any rate. Clarke thinks his apprenticeship was "the most placid period of his painful life."

Here let me point out a common mistake made by many people, and in this sentence by Clarke in his words "painful life." Taken as a whole, Keats's life was painful. The bereavements of his earlier, and the griefs of his later, life must have made it so. But we should never forget that in these few years of his growing poetic talent he was supremely happy, as happy as his passionate temperament allowed him to be. He had a genius for friendship, a saving and joyous sense of humour, and a fund of animal spirits, while, together with all this, he realized an ever increasing power of creative force within him than which nothing is more satisfying to the possessor. Nothing in life equals the pain and the joy of successful artistic creation except the fulfilment of reciprocated love, and in these early years Keats had not arrived at love, creation contented him. If he had deep and devastating sorrows, he had also moments of extreme happiness. The cheerful years, from 1811 to his brother Tom's increasing illness in the early Spring of

1818, must not be counted out when we consider the sum total of his life.

One of the voluntary tasks which Keats had undertaken before leaving school was a written translation of Virgil's *Æneid*. This he finished at Edmonton. Probably the work took him some years to get through, for when he was, Clarke thinks, "mayhap under fourteen," he had hazarded to his friend the opinion that beneath all the incidental attractiveness of the *Æneid*, there was a feebleness in its structure. "The expression," says Clarke, "riveted my surprise," as well it might, coming from a boy. This is the first evidence of Keats's critical faculty on record. In after years, his critical judgment proved that, had he lived, he would probably have been one of the foremost critics in English literature. But, as is usually the case, his critical faculty developed more slowly than his poetical; and even when, later, his criticisms on work not his own were shrewd and sure, he was apt to go astray where he himself was concerned. Only toward the very end was he able to apply to his own work the seeing eye with which he regarded that of others.

Long before he left school, Keats had exhausted the resources of the school library and formed the habit of borrowing from the private stock of the good-natured Clarke. The influence of Clarke was invaluable to Keats. Eight years his senior, Clarke was ahead of him in knowledge of books and literary appreciation. Clarke was a very generous and enthusiastic fellow, full of sympathy for Keats's pursuits, and indefatigable in following his own. He tells us himself that he would often walk the twelve miles to Covent Garden Theatre to see Mrs. Siddons as Lady Macbeth or Queen Constance, or her brother, John Kemble, as Coriolanus or Brutus, and, walking home again in the middle of the night, consider his evening well worth the twenty-four mile tramp. When Edmund Kean burst upon the London stage, his excitement knew no bounds;

it was he who impregnated Keats with his immense enthusiasm for that remarkable actor.

Among other things which Clarke lent to Keats were successive numbers of Leigh Hunt's *Examiner*, to which his father, John Clarke, was a regular subscriber. The *Examiner* was liberal in its politics, and literary in its interests. Whatever Hunt's faults, his writing was of the kind which reads itself. The paper must have been singularly attractive to Keats, who doubtless swallowed its opinions whole; Clarke says that it, and Burnet's *History of His Own Time*, "no doubt laid the foundation of his love of civil and religious liberty." Clarke tells an amusing tale in this connection. It seems that Keats once told him, smiling, that Abbey, on asking what books Clarke was lending to him, declared that "if he had fifty children he would not send one of them to that school." But it speaks not badly for Abbey that, although his patriotic sensibilities were outraged, he made no attempt to discourage Keats's intimacy with Clarke; nevertheless, this knowledge may have hastened his removal of George and Tom from the dangerous atmosphere.

That Keats missed the school and Clarke, goes without saying. Luckily Edmonton was only a little over two miles from Enfield, a distance easily accomplished on an off afternoon, with plenty of time left for a visit before he had to start back. Clarke states that he used to walk over five or six times a month, and he always came either with a book to read, or one he had finished and wanted to exchange for another. Here, in the arbour at the end of the garden, the two young fellows would sit, and talk, and read. They read Shakespeare. Clarke recollects that once when reading *Cymbeline* aloud Keats's eyes filled with tears and his voice shook in the passage where Imogen, after the departure of Posthumous, says that she would have watched him

"... 'till the diminution
Of space had pointed him sharp as my needle,
Nay, follow'd him, till he had *melted from*
The smallness of a gnat to air, and then
Have turn'd mine eye and wept."

The italics are Clarke's, and show that Keats must have been especially struck by this particular expression, proving a literary instinct already on the alert even through the emotion which the purely human side of the passage evoked in him.

On one occasion, when, Clarke thinks, Keats "may have been sixteen years old" — they were, he remembers perfectly, in the old arbour — Clarke read aloud Spenser's *Epithalamium*. Keats's "features and exclamations were ecstatic," declares Clarke. "How often, in after-times, have I heard him quote these lines:

'Behold, while she before the altar stands,
Hearing the holy priest that to her speaks,
And blesses her with his two happy hands,
How the red roses flush up to her cheeks!
And the pure snow, with goodly vermeil stain,
Like crimson dyed in grain,
That even the angels, which continually
About the sacred altar do remain,
Forget their service and about her fly,
Oft peeping in her face, that seems more fair,
The more they on it stare;
But her sad eyes, still fasten'd on the ground,
Are governèd with goodly modesty,
That suffers not one look to glance awry,
Which may let in a little thought unsound.'"

That night Keats took back with him to Edmonton the first volume of the *Faerie Queene*, and he went through it, Clarke told Lord Houghton, "as a young horse would through a spring meadow — ramping."

What, in any individual case, starts a poet writing?

That would be an interesting inquiry, if there were means to answer it in a sufficient number of cases to make the question worth while. Granted the faculty to be lying in wait, what, in the majority of poets, is the one touch needed to set it going in words? Clearly, in Keats's case, the answer is — the reading of Spenser. The result was the lines, *Imitation of Spenser.* Brown told Lord Houghton that the poem was the earliest one Keats was known to have written. Brown probably got this from Keats himself. Keats may, of course, have tried his hand at something before, but the fact that he included the *Imitation* in his first volume, and left out so many poems that succeeded it, proves that he had conceived a special affection for it and that this affection was shared by his brothers also. A first poem is simply a wonder, a miracle, to a young poet, and the young poet's friends and family. Apart, therefore, from Brown's statement, we can believe that it was his first attempt by the evidence of its preservation, for its fate was greater than it deserved. It is, in truth, a pretty feeble thing; a fragment of poetical copy, marvelous to Keats and his brothers because neither he nor they knew that he had it in him to do even that, but with little other interest. Of course he viewed it with partial eyes, but not so partial as to show it to the eight-years-older Clarke. To us, who are not partial, it contains one good passage, that in which Keats describes the island:

> "It seem'd an emerald in the silver sheen
> Of the bright waters."

As a poem, it is characteristic only in a certain sensuous delight in picture.

The truth is that Keats learnt to write poetry very slowly and unsteadily. His was no precocious talent. It took him a long time to learn what not to do, for he shows his genius in being over luxuriant from the start, with almost every worst fault which a poet can be heir to. Even when he began to get his bearings and write the poetry which has made his fame, he was often guilty, at one and the same moment, of pieces of so weak and sentimental a kind that one wonders how, with the power to write the first, he could possibly have been able to write the others. Truly, to study Keats is to be baffled again and again. But we must not forget that the strange interest which the man inspires has caused all his failures to be brought into notice; a cruelty which no other poet has suffered to a like extent.

We can imagine with what speed Keats rushed up to London to show his *Imitation* to his brothers. Brown dates the poem two years later than Clarke, when Keats was eighteen, not sixteen; but it does not make a pennyworth of difference at which age he wrote it, for it seems to have been the first of his poems of which we are cognizant, at any rate.

We know very little about these apprentice years, except what Clarke can tell us. One of the boys at the Clarke school, Richard Hengist Horne — the subsequent author of *Orion*, but known chiefly as the friend and correspondent of Mrs. Browning and the editor of two volumes of her letters — remembers an amusing little incident.[1] It seems that one day, when Mr. Hammond was called professionally to the school, Keats was left outside to look after the horse and gig. Horne had come to the school after Keats's departure, but tales of Keats's prowess as a fighter still lingered there, and Horne, peeking at him as he sat in the gig, was dared by the other fellows to snowball the "old boy." No decent youngster will take a dare, but Horne seems to have let fly from behind, which was not too bold of him. He hit Keats squarely in the back and then took to his heels before Keats could jump out of the gig and catch him.

We cannot suppose that the apprenticeship was all plain sailing. In a letter, written in 1819, speaking of the renewal of the tissues every seven years, Keats remarks:

[1] Buxton Forman.

"This is not the same hand which seven years ago clenched itself at Hammond." It was within a year of his beginning his work at the surgery that he was moved to shake his fist at his master, according to that, but nothing seems to have come of the episode. Perhaps the gesture was made behind the doctor's back; perhaps it was a gunpowder flash of temper which the wise doctor thought best to ignore. Keats, with his mind on poetry, cannot have been a perfectly satisfactory assistant, but neither can a young man of his brains and sense of justice have been an altogether unsatisfactory one. We may conjecture that the jealousy of a less intelligent co-worker, about whose early years no one was making inquiry, prompted the remarks of his brother apprentice to the effect that "he was an idle loafing fellow, always writing poetry."

The Enfield school was not the only place to which Keats resorted on his days out. He got into the very natural habit of running up to London to see his brothers. I say "brothers," because Tom had joined George in Mr. Abbey's employ before Keats left Edmonton, although just when, we do not know. George, sociable fellow that he was, had made friends in London; among them, the family of a deceased naval officer named Wylie. There was Mrs. Wylie, a daughter Georgiana, and two sons. Georgiana Wylie was a very remarkable woman. She was only a child of eleven at this time, however, but George Keats seems to have fallen in love with her at a very early date. The steadiness of George's career cannot be entirely imputed to his character. Unlike his brothers, he had an anchor in his love for Miss Wylie. To her, then, we can ascribe most of the happiness and good fortune which the family was to know. Her effect upon George, and the consequent effect upon John, cannot be over-estimated. George had also become intimate with another family of well-to-do tradespeople named Matthew. In this family were two daughters, Caroline and Anne, who brought in their train a cousin, George Felton Matthew. Keats naturally inherited these friends from George, and saw a great deal of them whenever he was in town. George Felton Matthew quickly became his most intimate friend after Cowden Clarke.

The outings in London probably included various jaunts to public resorts. Sir Sidney Colvin states that Keats's second known poem, written in August, 1814, *Fill for me a Brimming Bowl*, was written to a lady seen at Vauxhall. This fact he gets from the Woodhouse transcript in Lord Crewe's collection, although he does not explicitly say so; but in the Woodhouse Book in the Morgan collection, where the poem is copied twice, there is no mention of it.

Fill for me a Brimming Bowl is a singularly poor poem, far poorer than the *Imitation of Spenser*. It is only interesting as being in the octosyllabic metre afterwards employed in *Fancy*, *Bards of Passion*, and the *Eve of St. Mark*.

The reading continued with unabated ardour, but exactly what it consisted of besides Shakespeare and Spenser, we can only guess. Probably the Elizabethans and Milton played the greatest part in it. But there were modern poets who must have claimed his attention. Wordsworth's *Poems*, as we have seen, came out when he was only twelve, but we know that he was familiar with them; the first two cantos of Byron's *Childe Harold* appeared in 1812, and his *Giaour* and *Bride of Abydos* in 1813. Keats was too much of a poet to be impressed by Walter Scott's ballads, but Wordsworth's *Excursion* interested him profoundly.

All this time, Keats had been living with Mr. Hammond, but his grandmother's house was in the same street, the house he had known as home for so many years. Mrs. Jennings was getting very old, but her kindness and affection must have always made a ready welcome for John, and his little sister Fanny was there too, whenever he felt inclined to run over and play with her. Keats never seems to have had much interest in children, the few he encountered are referred to chiefly as bothering him by their noisy playing; but then, he was never intimate with them. Fanny Keats he evidently loved devotedly. George Keats, writing to his sister in 1825, refers to "times which I expect you have almost forgotten, when we lived with our grandmother at Edmonton, and John, Tom and myself were always devising plans to amuse you, jealous lest you should prefer either of us to the others." The Keats children were extraordinarily fond of one another. Although his grandmother was very old and his sister very young, the Church Street house was a home, and the last Keats was ever to know. Now, in December, 1814, Mrs. Jennings died, and was buried at St. Stephen's, Colman Street, on December nineteenth. This changed everything. Fanny Keats went to live with the Abbeys at their house in Marsh Street, Walthamstow, and Keats found himself alone in a town full of memories for him which must have made his virtual solitude at Mr. Hammond's even more lonely.

The immediate effect of his grandmother's death was a poem, consisting of two quatrains, entitled simply *On Death*. It is a pathetic little piece, of no merit poetically, but it shows real feeling as distinguished from the mere effort to "write poetry" evident in the *Imitation* and the *Brimming Bowl*. For the first time, Keats gets himself into a poem. There is no artificiality here; this is plain, untaught emotion. As the poem is very little known, I will quote it, for it gives the first expression to a side of Keats that we should never forget, the side which suffered, and questioned, and found no answer.

"ON DEATH

I.

Can death be sleep, when life is but a dream,
  And scenes of bliss pass as a phantom by?
The transient pleasures as a vision seem,
  And yet we think the greatest pain's to die.

2.

How strange it is that man on earth should roam,
And lead a life of woe, but not forsake
His rugged path; nor dare he view alone
His future doom which is but to awake."

The boy in Keats is fading, giving place to the man. A certain boyish tenderness is sinking down in him, down where he can rarely come at it. Tender he will always be, but as a man is tender. The boy's clinging tenderness goes, with the realization that the older generation who loved and cherished him is gone. His grandmother may have meant little to him in the last years, but she was a symbol, something that was his, a chain to hold and sustain him, something that gave him roots and reasons beyond his understanding. Now he sees himself the oldest of the family, with only younger brothers to support him. It is as if his whole past had suddenly been chopped away, leaving him swinging in the air with no natural connection with anything. Abbey is nothing, worse than nothing. He is that odious thing, a governor without affection, a ruler without sympathy, an absolute master with no tie of blood to make obedience appear just. Keats would be less lonely if he were all alone, with merely his brothers. Abbey's is a mock paternity, and Keats hates the relation with his whole soul. We can suppose that Mrs. Jennings made a sort of buffer between the two; without her, they must inevitably grind upon each other until the end. Abbey's indifference to everything Keats cares for is to the younger man an intolerable burden. Edmonton, the surgery, Hammond — all become suddenly unbearable. He simply must be near his brothers and feel them near him as a kind of poultice to his jangling nerves. For the second time in his life he craves a change of scene and activity. But how can he persuade Abbey to let him break his indentures? So he sets to work at his poetry harder than he has ever done before.

Keats was always a student of his art, so it is quite natural to find that the poem immediately following on the simple quatrains he used to express his very real sorrow in the lines, *On Death*, should be couched in sonnet form. It is addressed *To Byron*. Lord Houghton dates the sonnet simply "December, 1814," but one line in it proves it to have been written after Mrs. Jennings's death:

> "O'ershadowing sorrow doth not make thee less
> Delightful."

The lonely boy of nineteen found a solace in Byron which the greater poets of his real admiration could not, at the moment, give him. To us, Byron is the supreme poet of irony; to his contemporaries, particularly his youthful contemporaries, he was the very rapture of divining sympathy. His touch was both wound and healing, an intimate connection joining soul with brother soul. Keats grew to rate Byron at a true valuation, but we need not expect to find him at nineteen so very different from other young men of his time. The sonnet shows that he fairly soaked in Byron at this period. He was having a hard time, and Byron helped him over it, so the better for Byron. We, knowing Keats's later opinion, may smile a little as we read, but, understanding the circumstances, the smile, I think, will not be very broad; and, although Keats was quite serious in his attitude, and was surprisingly unconscious of any ironic intent, there is good criticism in the last two lines of the sonnet, a criticism which he would have hotly denied at the time, but which stands, nevertheless, in the backhanded fashion which Keats never meant. The lines are:

> "Still warble, dying swan! still tell the tale
> The enchanting tale, the tale of pleasing woe."

We should note in passing the lines:

"As when a cloud the golden moon doth veil,
Its sides are ting'd with a resplendent glow,
Through the dark robe oft amber rays prevail,
And like fair veins in sable marble show."

So early did the moon take possession of Keats's poetry. This passage proves that already Keats had learnt how to see. Cloudy moonlight is a difficult thing to get into verse, and Keats does not quite succeed with it here. But he knows the effect he is trying for, his attempted picture is the product of keen observation. In the expression, "shining beamily," we see Keats already employing what is to become one of the chief elements of his own peculiar idiom.

As a first attempt at a sonnet, *To Byron* is not bad. To be sure, the octave runs directly into the sestet, and the poem is all of a piece without the oblique changes of direction between the two sections which make the charm of a sonnet. But it is a fairly successful performance technically, on the whole. It will be observed that the sonnet follows the Petrarchan form.

Still another poem, a sonnet entitled *On Peace*, may possibly belong to 1814, although it is quite likely to have been written as late as the Summer of 1815. As there is a doubt as to its exact date, I have put it as the last of the 1814 sonnets, although I am certain it was not written then. It must, I think, belong either to the Summer of 1814, or the Summer of 1815, for it is clearly written either after Napoleon's banishment to Elba, or after Waterloo. It would be interesting to know which, for, in the former case, it would precede *To Byron*, and be the first sonnet by Keats of which we have cognizance. It is evidently a set piece, and from the type of expression in it I am inclined to place it after Waterloo, in the early Summer of 1815. It is quite unimportant, except for the fact that it stands as an essay, and the sole essay, in the Shakespearian sonnet form attempted by Keats, at least so far as we know, before 1818;

but still it is here to prove that he had tried his hand at the form very early in his writing life. The octave of the sonnet is perfectly Shakespearian; the sestet is bastard. The first line of it rhymes with the last line of the octave. The sestet rhymes A.A.B.A.B.B. One might almost suppose the poem to be an experiment, but at this period Keats was not experimenting beyond already existing forms, writing within them was still too much of an experiment as it was.

I shall make some study of Keats's employment of the sonnet a little later on. But now, when he had written only two (supposing the poem to have been written in 1814), such a study seems out of place. It will easily be seen that, whenever it was written, it was not written in December, 1814, for it is quite out of key with his mood at that time.

Since, from this point on, the story of Keats's life and the story of his poems run parallel, I must explain here one of the chief sources of much in both narrative and criticism which will be new to my readers. There is in the possession of Mr. J. P. Morgan, of New York, a large bound volume of manuscripts. The greater part of the volume consists of letters, written to either Woodhouse or Taylor. These letters are not transcripts, but original holographs, and none of them is from Keats. The latter half of the book is given up to transcripts of poems by Keats and others, copied by Woodhouse. This last section is headed, in Woodhouse's handwriting: "Poems, &c. by, or relating to, John Keats. All that are not by Keats, have the names of the authors added. R. Woodhouse, Nov. 1818. Temple." The volume had an ambitious purpose, for later in it Woodhouse says:

> "There is a great degree of reality about all that Keats writes: and there must be allusions to particular circumstances, in his poems: which would add to their beauty and interest, if properly understood. — To arrest some few of these circumstances, and bring them to view in connection with the poetic notice of them, is one of the objects of this

> collection — and of the observations — as it is of the notes in the interleaved copies of his published works. R. D. W."

Woodhouse's high opinion of Keats is shown by his adding the following note:

> "How valuable would such notes be to Shakespeare's sonnets, which teem with allusions to his life, & its circumstances, his age, his loves, his patrons, etc.'

Unfortunately Woodhouse makes not a few mistakes. In one place, after copying a poem, he is obliged to add "Keats said this day that he did not write this poem." In other places he has evidently confused his poems and the information relating to them, as in a sonnet, *The Poet*, where he states, as he does to several of the poems, "This song was written at the request of some young ladies who were tired of singing the words printed with the air and desired fresh words to the same tune." As the sonnet form could not possibly have been sung to the sort of "air" current at the time, or, I believe, at any time, Woodhouse has evidently connected a note belonging to one poem with another. In other instances, more authentic information shows us that the dates appended to the poems are wrong. In the valentine and sonnet which we know to have been addressed to Georgiana Wylie, he states that the young lady's name was "Miss Mary F." although, under the date of February, 1819, he says, "He this day said they both related to the same person." We can only suppose that Keats, while telling him that the first was written as a valentine for George to send, purposely misled him as to the name out of delicacy. It will be seen, then, that Woodhouse's information must be weighed carefully before it is accepted as gospel. There are quite a number of poems in the book to which Woodhouse appends the author's names, but which, for one reason or another, he has thought fit to copy. For this reason, I am quite sure that Professor de Sélincourt is wrong in thinking that *Stay, Ruby-Breasted Warbler, Stay* must be by John Keats and not George simply because it appears in one of Woodhouse's volumes of transcripts. A commentator must walk charily in the midst of such confusion, and temper faith with criticism. I have unhesitatingly adopted two hitherto unpublished poems as being without doubt by Keats; another, of which I am doubtful, I have relegated to an appendix; a fifth I have rejected as impossible for Keats to have written, although it may very well be by Reynolds. We must not, however, under-rate Woodhouse's very valuable information because of occasional inaccuracies. I only wish to point out that he is not, in all things, infallible. A few selections from this volume, notably the list of Keats's books, were copied and sent to Sir Sidney Colvin, but the bulk of the volume has never before been read. Through the courtesy of Mr. Morgan, and the kindness of his very able librarian, Miss Belle da Costa Greene, I have been permitted not only to examine the book, but to transcribe it in full. It has been most interesting to find the answers to certain letters in this book in my own collection. The result of the two records is a fuller story of various events in Keats's life than it has been possible to give hitherto.

Woodhouse puts 1815 as the date for the sonnet *To Chatterton*, and I think we shall not be wrong in attributing it to early in the year. The state of mind in which Keats then was, must have made Chatterton, after Byron and for a different reason, very sympathetic reading. In the first place, Chatterton was young and unfortunate, and he was much more unfortunate than Keats could imagine himself to be, which was comforting. The Bristol merchants thought little of him; Abbey had no opinion of Keats, at least of that side of Keats which mattered in his own eyes. Chatterton ached for London just as Keats was doing. Then, too, Keats had an innate love for the age of chivalry. Tales of knights and ladies never lost their charm for him, from the moment when he encountered them in Spenser to the last year before he left England, when he was reading the old Spanish romance, *Palmerin of England*. But, after all, I think it was more Chatterton himself and his unhappy fate which produced the sonnet than the Rowley poems, although these had a considerable effect on Keats, a greater effect than they deserve probably.

Boys of nineteen do not mourn forever, and it need not surprise us that in February Keats was moved to write a poem *To Hope*. A very youthful poem is this, but a pleasant one. Keats does so enjoy writing it, and is so pleased with the varying refrain which ends each of his stanzas. In the second stanza his beloved moon is brought in as comforter:

> "Whene'er I wander, at the fall of night,
> Where woven boughs shut out the moon's bright ray,
> Should sad Despondency my musings fright,
> And frown, to drive fair Cheerfulness away,
> Peep with the moon-beams through the leafy roof,
> And keep that fiend Despondence far aloof."

Beginning with himself, the poem ends with a bombastic invocation to liberty, in the good, old, stilted, eighteenth century manner. Keats is trying all the styles with a positively childish ardour. On account of the beginning of the poem, when Keats's quondam gloom still overshadows him, I am inclined to put *To Hope* before the sonnet *Written on the Day that Mr. Leigh Hunt left Prison*, although that event occurred on the second of February , 1815. *To Hope* was printed in the *Poems*, 1817, and there dated, "February, 1815." There is really no reason why the two poems should not have been written on the same day, or *To Hope* may have been written on the first. Keats clearly works himself into complete writing cue before the end of the poem, finishing in a mood quite other from that in which he began, and, after the sonnet to Hunt, is in such fine fettle that he decides the latter poem good enough to show to Clarke.

Keats had been feeding upon Hunt in the pages of Hunt's paper, the *Examiner*, for some years, as we have seen. In March, 1812, the Hunt brothers, Leigh and John, had published a violent diatribe against the Prince Regent, for which "libel" they were tried, and sentenced to two years' imprisonment, Leigh Hunt in Horsemonger Lane Prison, John Hunt in Pentonville, and fined a thousand pounds. This treatment, of course, made martyrs of them in the eyes of their followers, and of these, in his own estimation, was John Keats. Keats did not dig very far into the causes and effects of the case, doubtless. He simply glowed with indignation at this infringement of the rights of free speech in the case of a citizen who wrote so pleasantly as Hunt. The two years over and Hunt once more a free man, Keats wrote a sonnet and dashed off with it to find Clarke. Clarke was also a follower of Leigh Hunt and a friend as well, and on this particular occasion, which Professor de Sélincourt dates as February third, he was walking up to London to congratulate the beloved martyr on his liberation. Keats met him on the way, and turned back with him. "At the last field-gate, when taking leave," says Clarke, "he gave me the sonnet. . . How clearly do I recall the conscious look and hesitation with which he offered it!" Clarke feels quite certain that this was the first evidence he had that Keats was writing poetry. He only says "feels," but as the knowledge made such an impression upon him, his assumption is probably quite correct.

And what of the sonnet? Nothing, I fear. It is a feeble sonnet. The putting of Spenser and Milton into the poem is interesting, and particularly the adding of Hunt to the party in the lines:

> "To regions of his own his genius true
> Took happy flights."

Spenser, Milton, and Hunt on an equality opens a wide door to Keats's point of view at the time.

The next poem which Keats wrote, also in February, was the somewhat pretentious *Ode to Apollo*. It is a long and very dull poem, as he evidently knew, for he did not print it in his *Poems*. He must have scrapped it in his mind, for, as Woodhouse points out, the expression "laurel'd peers," in stanza four, is used again in the sonnet: *To my Brother George*.

In the Woodhouse Book in the Morgan Library is an unpublished poem, which, as it is only partially dated, I have been obliged to place. From all the evidence procurable, it seems likely that the poem was written in May, 1815. Hunt's liberation had aroused Keats to a fine fervour of patriotism, the new patriotism which denounced "Minions of Grandeur," in the words of the Leigh Hunt sonnet. The bells ringing the anniversary of Charles II's restoration went against Keats's grain, and out came this little burst of indignation:

[1] "LINES WRITTEN ON 29 MAY — THE ANNIVERSARY OF CHARLES'S RESTORATION — ON HEARING THE BELLS RINGING.

Infatuate Britons, while you still proclaim
His memory, your direst, foulest shame?
Nor patriots revere?
Oh! while I hear each traitorous lying bell,
'Tis gallant Sydney's, Russel's, Vane's sad knell,
That pains my wounded ear."

The question marks seem oddly out of place, but I copy the transcript. The poem needs no comment. It is a boyish effusion, but all in line with Keats's attitude in these early years.

It is largely these *Lines on Charles II's Restoration* which incline me to believe that the sonnet *On Peace* was written in June, 1815, immediately after the Battle of

[1] Woodhouse Book. Morgan Collection.

Waterloo. During the whole Spring, Keats seems to have been much agitated politically, and the Battle of Waterloo was a subject not easy to let pass unsignalized by a budding poet. *On Peace* is more advised in treatment than the *Imitation of Spenser*, or *Fill for me a Brimming Bowl*, which, if *On Peace* were written in the Summer of 1814, were the only poems which had preceded it. The chief reason for supposing it to belong to 1814 is the clumsy mismanagement of the sonnet form, but against that is the plausible conjecture that Keats, having by the Summer of 1815 tried his hand at two Petrarchan sonnets, was impelled to attempt the Shakespearian. I think, however, that this is flimsy evidence balanced against the known preoccupation of Keats's mind with politics in the latter year.

What is worth remarking in these poems is Keats's growing tendency to write. He delights in using his pen. Young poets usually begin with expressions of personal emotion, but with Keats the mere act of composing seems to have been all the emotion he needed. So far, the only lines he has written not prompted by anything save the giving vent to feeling are those *On Death*. Everything is grist to his mill, and everything is literary. He loved poetry as an art, and forgot himself in its creation. Teeming with emotion of one kind or another as he always was, when he sat down to give it expression the artist took charge of his pen, which, in the final count, is why he is so great a poet. The mark of the minor poet is that he can never forget himself; the proof of greatness lies just in the fact that the artist transcends the man.

When Keats published his *Poems*, 1817, immediately after the dedication appeared this notice:

> "The Short Pieces in the middle of the Book, as well as some of the Sonnets, were written at an earlier period than the rest of the Poems."

Months appeared ages in those days, as, with the exception of the *Imitation of Spenser*, the earliest of the "short pieces," *To Hope*, was written only twenty-two months before the latest poems, *Sleep and Poetry* and the sonnet *To Kosciusko*. But when one is growing up hand over fist, and changing almost over night, two years is a veritable age.

Four of these short poems evidently belong to the Summer or early Autumn of 1815. One is a sequence of three sonnets, without a title, addressed to "Woman!" carefully generalized. It is a juvenile production which needs no farther characterization. Two others, in the tripping metre of Thomas Moore, whose *Irish Melodies*, published in 1807, were very much the fashion, are mere jingles snapped off to a catchy tune. In them we see a boy having a good time making rhymes for a couple of silly girls. These girls were the Misses Matthew already referred to. How silly they were, can be seen by the following account given by Sir Sidney Colvin:

> [1] "One of the sisters, asked in later life for her recollections of the time, replied in a weariful strain of evangelical penitence for the frivolities of those days, and found nothing more to the purpose to say of Keats than this:—'I cannot go further than say that I always thought he had a very beautiful countenance and was very warm and enthusiastic in his character. He wrote a great deal of poetry at our house but I do not recollect whether I ever had any of it, I certainly have none now; Anne had many pieces of his.'"

By which we observe that Anne was more attractive than Caroline. The poems are entitled respectively *To Some Ladies*, and *On Receiving a Curious Shell and a Copy of Verses*. The Matthew family, including the cousin, George Felton, were at Hastings, and from thence sent Keats "a copy of Tom Moore's 'Golden Chain,' and a most beau-

[1] Colvin.

tiful Dome shaped shell," to quote from a transcript of the poem by George Keats. Why Keats reprinted these poems in his book, as he did, can only be answered by remembering how very immature he was, and that Moore's poems were liked by Hunt. Yet even Hunt could not stomach these nerveless copies of a type of verse which, in Moore's hands, was not without charm. In his review of the 1817 volume in the *Examiner*, he admits that these earlier poems "might have been omitted, especially the string of magistrate-interrogations about a shell and a copy of verses."

Shells and poetry books were not the only presents which Keats received from young ladies. Whether it was the Misses Matthew or some other friend whose name we have never heard who sent him a laurel crown for fun, there is no means of finding out, but a poem, entitled *To a young Lady who sent me a Laurel Crown* seems to belong to this year. It certainly does not refer to the laurel crowning at Leigh Hunt's, which took place about a year later. The *Hymn to Apollo* usually printed immediately after it, Woodhouse definitely states[1] to have been written after the laurel crowning at Hunt's. Woodhouse calls it *Ode to Apollo*, which puzzled me until I discovered that, in the first Woodhouse Commonplace Book,[2] it was copied under the title *Fragment of an Ode to Apollo*. So, gradually, as the years go on and new manuscripts and transcripts are recovered, we are enabled to place more and more poems where they rightfully belong.

To return to the *Laurel Crown* sonnet. Evidently Keats had been in one of his gloomy fits the night before it was written, and had poured out his disgust, or distrust, or forebodings, to the lady to whom it was addressed. This attitude of the night before is the chief reason which leads me to place the poem before his going to London, although I admit it possible that it may have been written in

[1] Woodhouse Book. Morgan Collection.
[2] Owned by Sir Sidney Colvin.

November when he was in the mood which brought out the *Epistle to George Felton Matthew.* The earlier date seems more likely, however, for to sally forth hunting laurel on a chill November day does not commend itself to reason, and do florists keep laurel handily by for the emergency of genius? That the sonnet was not written during his first weeks in London, the whole tone of it declares. Whoever wove the wreath, it was a pretty gesture to rally Keats's spirits and stir his sick ambition with it. And the ruse succeeded, as the sonnet shows. It is much more virile than any other of these very early poems, and written with his delightful mocking humour, the first evidence of it in verse. There is a nice bravado about it, and none of the saccharine sentimentality which marks his serious poems of the period. We can imagine it to have been written after some bout with Abbey, in which the misguided and much tried guardian had undertaken to give a little "advice" about not wasting one's time scribbling. The lady's pin-prick worked, Keats gets himself together with a jerk and exclaims:

> "Lo! who dares say, 'Do this?' Who dares call down
> My will from its high purpose? Who say, 'Stand,'
> Or 'Go?' This mighty moment I would frown
> On abject Cæsars — not the stoutest band
> Of mailed heroes should tear off my crown;
> Yet would I kneel and kiss thy gentle hand."

This is not the way Keats writes to Caroline and Anne Matthew. We like this girl, but who was she? Her action is quite in character with Georgiana Wylie, but that young lady was only thirteen. We, who love John Keats, salute you, wise and witty incognita, you gave him courage to do farther battle with Mr. Cæsar Abbey.

Success is to the strong, and Keats, thus nerved, persevered and won. Somehow, by specious arguments or obstinate resistance, he at last persuaded Abbey that he should do better by studying in London than by remaining with Mr. Hammond for the final year of his apprenticeship. Hammond does not seem to have made any objection to the indentures being broken, and it was by common agreement between Abbey, Hammond, and Keats, that, some time in September probably, the latter packed up his clothes, his prize books and what others he had been able to acquire, and his slim bundle of manuscripts, and set off for London to walk the hospitals.

with Mr. Hammond for the final year of his apprenticeship. Hammond does not seem to have made any objection to the indentures being broken, and it was by common agreement between Abbey, Hammond, and Keats, that, some time in September probably, the latter packed up his clothes, his spare books and what others he had been able to acquire, and his slim bundle of manuscripts, and set off for London to walk the hospitals.

CHAPTER II

LONDON AND POETRY

IT needs no stretch of the imagination to picture the state of Keats's mind during the eight miles to London on that September day. Did he walk, and leave his precious portmanteau to be sent on by wagon, or did he ride up to town on the top of the coach with the portmanteau safely stowed away in the boot? Historically speaking, the journey is a blank. But whether he walked, or spanked along behind four lively horses to the tune of jingling harness and the guard's busy horn, even supposing that it rained cats and dogs and the drops trickled down his neck, we know very well that his spirits were bubbling over with excitement, that he felt exactly like a knight of romance starting forth in quest of high adventure in the green forest. He was free of Hammond, thank God! He was nobody's apprentice, but a free man, and in another year he would be his own man, come of age and out of Abbey's jurisdiction. But, in all this, not a thought of abandoning his profession seems to have occurred to him. Poetry was his avocation, but his vocation was surgery, and he had every intention of sticking to it. A man can have a religion by which he lives and yet go about his daily work. Keats's attitude toward poetry was a good deal like this. He fed on it in his heart, he intended to devote all his leisure time to it, but his job was to become an apothecary and surgeon, and so ingrained was the idea that he does not, at this period, seem to have questioned it.

His first business on reaching London must have been to find a lodging. George and Tom were living at Mr. Abbey's at 4 Pancras Lane. Abbey seems to have lodged some of his employees at his business quarters, and to have had rooms there for himself and his family also which they occupied from time to time; usually, however, he lived at Walthamstow, coming in to town every day in true suburban fashion. There appears to have been no thought of Keats's joining his brothers in Pancras Lane. The hospitals at which he proposed to study, Guy's and St. Thomas's, which in those days were united, were on the other side of the river, in Southwark. Keats found a lodging near them, at 8 Dean Street, Borough. He was not in love with the Borough. In a letter, written somewhat later to Clarke, he describes it as "a beastly place in dirt, turnings, and windings." Dean Street was the first turning to the right after crossing London Bridge, and the house was "nearly opposite a meeting." So there we have it as it showed itself to Keats, and we must agree with him that the spot was not alluring.

There is every reason to suppose that Keats took a week or so to look about and settle down before presenting himself at the hospital. We can imagine him knocking up all his acquaintance, and more especially frequenting the Matthew family, who seem to have attracted him greatly just at this time, an attraction which quickly died down, for after the first year or so we hear nothing more of them. The first of October, however, saw him entered as a student at Guy's.

The various registers of Guy's hospital contain these records: First: "Oct. 1, 1815. John Keats (no 57) 6 Mo[nths]. Place of education, Mr. T. Hammond, Edmonton. Office fee £1.2s." Under the entry: "Dressers of the Surgeons, Guy's Hospital," beside the heading, "Pupil," appears: "Oct. 2. 1815. John Keats. (Mr. L.) $\frac{6}{12}$ Mo[nths]." On this occasion, he paid a fee of £25.4s. On October 29, 1815, is entered: "Mr. Jno. Keats had returned to him £6.6s, he becoming a dresser." A final entry reads as follows: "Entered, March 3, 1816, John Keats. Under whom: Mr. L. Time: 12 mo[nths]. Whence they come: From Edmonton. S. Office. £1.1s.0d." October first, 1815, was a Sunday, which accounts for the fact that Keats was merely entered on the books on that day, and his assignment to a particular surgeon not made until the next day, Monday.

The death blow to the surgical career of John Keats is contained in the modest little parenthetical legend "(Mr. L.)." For Mr. Lucas was clearly not the man to inspire a rather half-hearted assistant with enthusiasm. John Flint South, a well-known surgeon, who was a contemporary of Keats's and a pupil at Guy's at the same period, has described Lucas very vividly:

> [1] "A tall ungainly awkward man, with stooping shoulders and a shuffling walk, as deaf as a post, not overburdened with brains, but very good-natured and easy, and liked by every one. His surgical acquirements were very small, his operations generally badly performed, and accompanied with much bungling, if not worse."

Had Keats the good fortune to have been appointed dresser to the very magnetic, lightning-minded, and enthusiastic Astley Cooper, not yet a baronet, his interest in his work would have been augmented tenfold. He worked hard, as is shown by a note-book [2] on his courses of anatomy and surgery. The notes are full and explicit. Little drawings appear occasionally among them, a flower or two absent-mindedly jotted down, probably when the lecturer grew dull or diffuse, but there is nothing odd in that.

The life of a medical student, particularly when he is also something very nearly corresponding to an "intern" in our modern hospitals, is an arduous and fatiguing one. Keats had longed to come to London, but he had had no idea what he was coming to, or how the city would affect him. He had not realized how much harder he would have to work, attending lectures, dissecting specimens, and assisting at operations, than he had ever been obliged to do at Mr. Hammond's. His courses consisted of two on anat-

[1] Feltoe's *Memories of J. F. South.* [2] Dilke Collection.

omy and physiology, two on the theory and practice of medicine, two on chemistry, and one on *materia medica.*

At first, we can believe that the excitement of being a grown man living in lodgings was extremely agreeable. Nothing is more assuring to youth than the possession of a latch-key, but the delight soon wears off. London in Autumn is not a cheery place, and Keats was in a very dingy quarter. A man who has tramped up and down stairs from ward to lecture-room and back again, hour after hour; who has patiently followed his surgeon on his rounds, and made others alone, shuddering with a new responsibility; who comes home, dog-tired, to a cold grate and hideous, shabby furniture, with pages of notes to digest and more walking to a chop-house to get his dinner; such a man, if he wants all his energy to write poetry and has never lived away from trees and fields before, cannot be expected to keep his spirits always at concert pitch. Keats, in fact, became a little homesick, and more than a little lonely. Add to this the discouraging realization that there was no home to be homesick for. He must have thought often of the days when his mother was always ready to comfort and sympathize with him. A mother is a woman, and a motherless boy mixes up his longings for his mother with his general need of a woman's tenderness. He may not put it so to himself, but that is the fact. Keats never got over his need for a mother; and we must never forget this salient trait in his character. He was always seeking to fill up a void in his life of which he was only half aware. He tried to fill this emptiness with friendship, with love for his brothers, but man cannot take the place of woman to another man. One of the many reasons for Keats's failure in his relations with Fanny Brawne was that he sought in her a mother as well as a lover, and she had not yet grown up enough to stand to him in both capacities. But I anticipate. All I wish to point out here is that his very loneliness, the empty room where he found things just as he had left them, the door opening to chilly silence, all this, operating on his adolescence without its usual corrective, the composing of poetry, caused him to speculate a little, ever so little, on the idea of woman and her possibilities to man. It was only a sort of moon-calf attitude, and not entirely unexperienced before — witness the sonnet sequence I have mentioned as probably written during this Summer. The idea was a bit twinging at times, that was all, but we find it creeping into his poetry. A boy of twenty who never speculates about love would be a monster unknown to Nature. Indeed, Keats's early poems are rather remarkable for the absence of love in them. That side of him took a long while to mature. It is loneliness which brings it out now, and its expression is wistfully cool, if I may so express it.

In the short, dreary November days, Keats wrote a sonnet. All that I have been saying is to be found in it, and as it is one of the least known of his poems, I will give it here:

"O Solitude! if I must with thee dwell,
Let it not be among the jumbled heap
Of murky buildings; climb with me the steep, —
Nature's observatory — whence the dell,
Its flowery slopes, its river's crystal swell,
May seem a span; let me thy vigils keep
'Mongst boughs pavillion'd, where the deer's swift leap
Startles the wild bee from the fox-glove bell.
But though I'll gladly trace these scenes with thee,
Yet the sweet converse of an innocent mind,
Whose words are images of thoughts refin'd,
Is my soul's pleasure; and it sure must be
Almost the highest bliss of human-kind,
When to thy haunts two kindred spirits flee."

"The highest bliss of human-kind" — but he had never experienced it, poor boy! The kindred spirit had no existence in reality.

In spite of the anatomy, and chemistry, and *materia medica*, Keats had found time to solace his longing for fields and trees and brooks by reading Wordsworth, for

Keats's wild bee in a foxglove bell comes straight out of Wordsworth's sonnet on the sonnet, in his *Poems*, 1807:

> "... bees that soar for bloom,
> High as the highest Peak of Furness Fells,
> Will murmur by the hour in Foxglove bells."

In the *Solitude* sonnet, Keats is lonely, but he is not absolutely discouraged. By the time the next poem was written, he was beginning to find how very badly his vocation and his avocation jibed. It took the form of an *Epistle to George Felton Matthew*. We have seen that Matthew was, at the moment, his most congenial friend. Matthew was a reader and, what was very alluring to Keats, dabbled in verse. Keats had a hunger for literary companionship, and Matthew supplied the best to be had at the moment. His merit as a poet was singularly small, but Keats, who lived so much in books, had, by a natural process of idealization, raised it into a considerable talent, and decided that they two were destined for a poetical brotherhood akin to that of Beaumont and Fletcher.

Keats's burrowings had somehow led him to the not-too-well-known poems of Michael Drayton, a copy of one of Smethwick's editions of Drayton's *Poems* is listed in the catalogue [1] of the books in his possession at the time of his death. That Drayton influenced him a great deal, we shall see over and over again. The epistle was a favourite Elizabethan form, it is true, but Drayton's epistles were probably those which made the greatest impression on Keats.[2] The fact that Drayton wrote epistles in verse to his intimate friends and fellow poets, Henry Reynolds, George Sandys, William Brown, and William Drummond of Hawthornden, must have been peculiarly intriguing to

[1] Woodhouse Book. Morgan Library.

[2] *Shakespeare and Keats*, by Claude L. Finney. A Thesis Submitted to the Faculty of Arts and Sciences in the Division of Modern Languages of Harvard University in Partial Fulfillment of the Requirements for the Degree of Doctor of Philosophy. April, 1922.

Keats, in whom poetry and friendship were so closely allied. It required only a slight effort of the imagination, and a little youthful blindness, to work Matthew up to the rôle of worthy recipient.

The opening lines of Drayton's *Epistle to Henry Reynolds* are:

> "My dearly loved friend, how oft have we,
> In winter euenings (meaning to be free,)
> To some well chosen place vs'd to retire,
> And there with moderate meats and wine and fire,
> Haue past the howres contentedly with chat,
> Now talk'd of this, and then discours'd of that,
> Spoke our owne verses 'twixt ourselues; if not,
> Other men's lines, which we by chance had got,
> Or some Stage pieces famous long before,
> Of which your happy memory had store."

Keats's *Epistle to George Felton Matthew* begins in this wise:

> "Sweet are the pleasures that to verse belong,
> And doubly sweet a brotherhood in song;
> Nor can remembrance, Matthew! bring to view
> A fate more pleasing, a delight more true
> Than that in which the brother Poets joy'd,
> Who with combined powers, their wit employ'd
> To raise a trophy to the drama's muses.
> The thought of this great partnership difuses
> Over the genius loving heart, a feeling
> Of all that's high, and great, and good, and healing."

The Beaumont and Fletcher note is struck at the outset, and there is also a very distinct resemblance to the tone of Drayton's poem. The Drayton parallel is even more exact a little farther on, where Keats says:

> ". . . O Matthew lend thy aid
> To find a place where I may greet the maid —
> Where we may soft humanity put on,
> And sit, and rhyme, and think on Chatterton."

The "maid" is, of course, the poetic muse, and the gist of the poem is that Keats finds his surroundings and occupations inimical to the writing of poetry. Apparently Matthew is in no such difficult situation, for Keats exclaims:

> ". . . fain would I follow thee
> Past each horizon of fine poesy;
>
> . . . . .
>
> But 'tis impossible, far different cares
> Beckon me sternly from soft 'Lydian airs,'
> And hold my faculties so long in thrall,
> That I am oft in doubt whether at all
> I shall again see Phœbus in the morning:
> Or flush'd Aurora in the roseate dawning!
> Or a white Naiad in a rippling stream;
> Or a rapt seraph in a moonlight beam;
> Or again witness what with thee I've seen,
> The dew by fairy feet swept from the green,
> After a night of some quaint jubilee
> Which every elf and fay had come to see:
> When bright processions took their airy march
> Beneath the curved moon's triumphal arch."

The last line of the passage is the finest he had yet written on the moon. But, indeed, the whole poem is an advance in poetical description over anything done before. Immediately after this passage comes the second misery which gnaws at his aching mind:

> "But might I now each passing moment give
> To the coy muse, with me she would not live
> In this dark city."

There is the rub, the "dark city." The lack of time is a great drawback, but the city hangs over him like a pall. Yet his very fighting against it turns up by contrast scenes and moments that he remembers, places that make one want to write, where thought is the outcome of environment. It is the old story of frustrated longing and the vividness of baffled recollection. Poking about in his imagination, Keats finds a spot

"Where the dark leav'd laburnam's drooping clusters
Reflect athwart the stream their yellow lustres,
And intertwin'd the cassia's arms unite,
With its own drooping buds, but very white.
Where on one side are covert branches hung,
'Mong which the nightingales have always sung
In leafy quiet: where to pry, aloof,
Atween the pillars of the sylvan roof,
Would be to find where violet beds were nestling,
And where the bee with cowslip bells was wrestling."

At the very moment, then, when Keats says he cannot write, we find him writing better than he ever has before. Which is not so strange a paradox in poetry as it might appear. "I have nothing to say," exclaims the poet, "I am dry, empty, drained of all emotion and utterly useless," and at once proceeds to write things of the greatest importance to mankind. Keats follows the usual line of march very closely, and with the usual ignorance that he is doing so.

The poem is interesting as showing his familiar reading at the time. He wants to talk to Matthew, not only about Chatterton, but about Beaumont and Fletcher, Shakespeare, Milton, and Burns, to say nothing of the beloved *Examiner* and its opinions in his desire to discourse "Of those who in the cause of freedom fell," choosing as examples, King Arthur, William Tell, and William Wallace. Lacking such scenes and such conversation, how is it possible for him to write:

"Felton! without incitements such as these
How vain for me the niggard Muse to tease:
For thee, she will thy every dwelling grace
And make 'a sunshine in a shady place.'"[1]

[1] Spenser's *Faerie Queene*.

Matthew is the chosen of Diana (her first appearance in Keats's poetry, by the way), he is destined for great things, and Keats waxes literary and a thought dull in depicting what Matthew may be expected to do some day, and which, of course, he never did.

Yet, notwithstanding that it is, on the whole, the best poem Keats had yet written, the note of discouragement in it is only too evident, and the discouragement is based upon incontrovertible fact. There was no time. It was a gruelling thing to work at medicine as he was doing and be in a constant fever to practise his ever increasing gift of poetry. No wonder he felt driven and at his wits' end. Matthew, who knew the circumstances, took serious alarm. He sat down and wrote Keats a series of verses [1] which, poor enough though they be, have a value quite apart from their merit.

The first two stanzas run:

"Oh thou, who delightest in fanciful song,
  And tellest strange tales of the elf, of the fay;
Of giants tyrannic, whose talismans strong
  Have powers to charm the fair ladies astray.

Of courteous knights, of high-mettled steeds,
  Of forests enchanted and marvelous streams,
Of bridges, and castles, and desperate deeds,
  Of magical curses, and fair ladies' screams."

In this tone, the poem continues, until Matthew begins to assure his friend that his gift is not due to his being in any particular place: "It is not the climate, nor nature around," to which Keats owes "the song that thou lovest to sing":

"Oh! no, 'tis the Queen of those regions of air,
  The gay fields of fancy thy spirit has bless'd;
She cherish'd thy childhood with fostering care
  And nurtured her Boy with the milk of her breast."

[1] Woodhouse Book. Morgan Collection.

Evidently the friends had decided that the moon was Keats's tutelary goddess, which, in good sooth, she was, all through his early years.

The most important part of the poem to us is the last two stanzas:

"When evening shall free thee from Nature's decays,
 And free thee from studies severest controul,
Oh! warm thee in Fancy's enlivening rays,
 And wash the dark spots of disease from thy soul.

Oh! let not the spirit of poesy sleep;
 Of fairies and Genie continue to tell;
Nor suffer the innocent deer's timid leap
 The wild bee to fright from her flowery bell."

Woodhouse remarks that the first and last lines of the penultimate stanza refer to "Keats's then profession of surgeon," and that the last two lines of the last stanza are an allusion to the *Sonnet to Solitude*. These last two lines are exactly what lead me to place the sonnet before the *Epistle*, and the *Epistle* is specifically dated in the *Poems* 1817, "November, 1815." Woodhouse thinks that these verses of Matthew's were in answer to the poem about the shell sent Keats by his (Matthew's) cousins, but despite their Tom Moore metre, they are so obviously an answer to the *Epistle*, that I am quite sure that Woodhouse is in error in considering them as a reply to the earlier poem. The *Sonnet to Solitude* is clearly written from London, because of the reference to the "murky buildings," and as Keats did not reach London until late September, and was not out of humour with his surroundings until some weeks later, as fogs are the product of Autumn and Winter, and "murky" undoubtedly a synonym for "foggy," and as people are not picking up shells at the seaside on November days, it seems quite certain that the shell was sent some months previous to the writing of the sonnet, and that therefore, if Matthew's poem were an answer to the shell verses, it could not have contained an allusion to the sonnet. What the fairy tales were of which Matthew speaks, we can have no idea. Either they have perished, or they existed merely in conversation, or they are a heightened allusion to the shell poem. For it seems extremely unlikely that the *Induction* and *Calidore* were even conceived in 1815, and, although knights and ladies appear in them, there are no fairies, nor giants, nor "genie." The *Sonnet to Solitude* and the *Epistle to George Felton Matthew* make a perfect sequence of emotion placed in this new order, which, after much cogitation, I believe to be the right one.

By this time, Keats's old friend, Cowden Clarke, was also in London. Clarke says that he cannot remember the precise time when he and Keats separated, nor which of the two first went to London. But it was while Keats was living in Dean Street that he discovered that Clarke was with his brother-in-law, a Mr. Towers, in Warner Street, Clerkenwell. The earliest of Keats's letters which has come down to us is the one written from Dean Street to Clarke, containing the description of the Borough which I have quoted. The return of Clarke upon the scene probably dimmed Matthew's lustre not a little. Matthew's chief attraction for Keats must have been that he wrote poetry, for, as far as sheer sympathy is concerned, Keats had abundance of that from his brothers. The innumerable transcripts of John's poems by both George and Tom prove their enthusiasm as nothing else could.

Not even the brilliant lectures of Astley Cooper could wean Keats from poetry. But he must have seemed to the great doctor as not in the best frame of mind for study. Probably Astley Cooper knew nothing of his preoccupation with studies other than medical, probably what he saw was a young fellow with marked ability working under that ass, Lucas, who had no idea how to bring out his latent powers. The boy needed contact with his profession out of hours, he needed some fillip to bring him into the ring, as it were. How could Astley Cooper know that the whole College of Surgeons were as nothing against that native bias which led Keats unerringly toward his destiny. They were a puff of mist obscuring a crimson sunrise, that was all. Keats himself had no inkling of the truth, he tried to take an interest in his hospital work, and was very likely grateful when Astley Cooper recommended him to the care of his own dresser, George Cooper. If Astley Cooper suggested that his assistant should actually take Keats under his wing, we are not told, but evidently George Cooper decided that Keats would whip into shape better if he were moved out of his solitary lodging. Whether the initial suggestion of the change came from him, or from Keats, it was undoubtedly pure kindness of heart on Cooper's part which led to Keats's removal to the lodgings which Cooper shared with two other medical students, a certain George Wilson Mackereth, and one Henry Stephens, the latter well known in after years as the inventor and proprietor of an excellent ink. For posterity, whatever fame he may have gained as a surgeon has been blotted out by the greater fame of his ink, but with that we have no concern here. These young men had rooms over the shop of a tallow-chandler in St. Thomas's Street.

The proposal seems to have met with the approval of all concerned. Keats was a very sociable fellow in these early years, and very popular with all and sundry. Everyone had liked him at school, he was a delightful companion and sensitive to the rights of others. The faculty of getting on with people was one of his very marked qualities. When the removal to St. Thomas's Street took place is not certain, but it was probably in either December 1815 or January 1816.

Sir Sidney Colvin quotes a long account of Keats at this time, written by his fellow medical student, Henry Stephens. The passage, Sir Sidney states, is made up of extracts from papers in the Houghton collection and reminiscences of Stephens's conversation by Sir Benjamin Ward Richardson published in the *Asclepiad*. Although these remarks are not to be believed in too blindly, being long-after remembrances by a man who appears quite incapable of understanding Keats, they are the best picture of Keats's student days which we have, and we know that Keats thought well enough of Stephens to look him up in 1818 when passing through Redbourne, where Stephens was then living, on his way to Liverpool. I quote the passage with a few omissions:

> [1]"Whether it was in the latter part of the year 1815 or the early part of the year 1816 that my acquaintance with John Keats commenced I cannot say. We were both students at the united hospitals of St. Thomas's and Guy's, and we had apartments in a house in St. Thomas's Street, kept by a decent respectable woman of the name of Mitchell[2] I think . . . John Keats, being alone, and to avoid the expense of having a sitting-room to himself, asked to join us, which we readily acceded to. We were therefore constant companions . . . His passion if I may so call it, for poetry was soon manifested. He attended lectures and went through the usual routine but he had no desire to excel in that pursuit . . . He was called by his fellow students 'little Keats,' being at his full growth no more than five feet high . . . In a room, he was always at the window, peering into space, so that the window-seat was spoken of by his comrades as Keats's place . . . In the lecture room he seemed to sit apart and to be absorbed in something else, as if the subject suggested thoughts to him which were not practically connected with it. He was often in the subject and out of it, in a dreamy way.
>
> He never attached much consequence to his own studies in medicine, and indeed looked upon the medical career as the career by which to live in a workaday world, without being certain that he could keep up the strain of it. He nevertheless had a consciousness of his own

[1] Colvin.

[2] Another account gives the name as Markham. Colvin.

powers, and even of his own greatness, though it might never be recognized . . . Poetry was to his mind the zenith of all his aspirations: the only thing worthy the attention of superior minds: so he thought: all other pursuits were mean and tame. He had no idea of fame or greatness but as it was connected with the pursuits of poetry, or the attainment of poetical excellence. The greatest men in the world were the poets and to rank among them was the chief object of his ambition. It may readily be imagined that this feeling was accompanied with a good deal of pride and conceit, and that amongst mere medical students he would walk and talk as one of the Gods might be supposed to do when mingling with mortals. This pride exposed him, as may be readily imagined, to occasional ridicule, and some mortification.

Having a taste and liking for poetry myself, though at that time but little cultivated, he regarded me as something a little superior to the rest, and would gratify himself frequently by showing me some lines of his writing, or some new idea which he had struck out. We had frequent conversation on the merits of particular poets, but our tastes did not agree. He was a great admirer of Spenser, his 'Faerie Queene' was a great favourite with him. Byron was also in favour, Pope he maintained was no poet, only a versifier. He was fond of imagery, the most trifling similes appeared to please him. Sometimes I ventured to show him some lines which I had written, but I always had the mortification of hearing them condemned, indeed he seemed to think it presumption in me to attempt to tread along the same pathway as himself at however humble a distance.

He had two brothers, who visited him frequently, and they worshipped him. They seemed to think their brother John was to be exalted and to exalt the family name . . .

Whilst attending lectures he would sit and, instead of copying out the lecture, would often scribble doggrel rhymes among the notes of Lecture, particularly if he got hold of another student's syllabus. In my syllabus of chemical lectures he scribbled many lines on the paper cover. This cover has long been torn off, except one small piece on which is the following fragment of doggrel rhyme:—

> 'Give me women, wine and snuff
> Until I cry out, "hold! enough."
> You may do so, sans objection,
> Until the day of resurrection.'

. . . He was gentlemanly in his manners and when he condescended to talk upon other subjects he was agreeable and intelligent. He was quick and apt at learning, when he chose to give his attention to any subject. He was a steady quiet and well behaved person, never inclined to pursuits of a low or vicious character."

I have omitted a reference to a young man named Newmarch who, Stephens insists, ridiculed Keats's poetry and made broad fun of his brothers for their admiration of it. The reason for my omission is that I do not believe in the existence of Newmarch. Stephens says that "he came often" having formerly been intimate with Keats. But Keats was the last man in the world to permit anyone who was rude to his brothers to come even once again. A man who has been the best fighter of a school for years does not suffer himself to be the object of "mortifying" tactics, such as Henry Stephens declares Newmarch's were. I feel very sure that Stephens is either thinking of some one else, or has mistaken his facts. The portrait of Keats, however, if we remember that we are seeing it through Stephens's eyes, is very vivid and illuminating. It was a good trick to write his nonsense in somebody else's note-book; the one of his own which we know is properly and seriously kept. Keats was always full of fun, a somewhat rollicking fun at times. But what a likable fellow he was! Who cares for his arrogance? Arrogance is inevitable when a young man is head and shoulders above his comrades. Keats did not study, and he did not listen to lectures, therefore how could he learn? That was the itching question these embryo medicos asked themselves, and it was not a little galling to them that he did learn. The attitude can be plainly read between the lines of Stephens's memoir, and it appears again in the communication of another student who says,[1] "even in the lecture room of St. Thomas's I have seen Keats in a deep poetic dream; his mind was on Parnassus with the Muses." As evidence of this, he gives the *Alexander Fragment*,[2] that odd little tale, written in a Chattertonian attempt at Middle-English, which may have come from here, there, or anywhere, and is chiefly interesting for the first mention we know of the great blowing pine, Milton's "tallest pine hewn on Norwegian hills," which creeps into Keats's poems on more than one occasion. Probably Sir Sidney Colvin is right in conjecturing that G. L. Way's translation of Le Grand's *Fabliaux ou Contes*, published in 1800, is the chief source of the tale. Keats's interest in Chatterton gives the language, while his combined spirits of experiment and mischief give the tone and the place of composition. There is a great deal about Alexander in the *Historical Library* of Diodorus Siculus, which Keats certainly read during either 1816 or 1817, as we shall presently see, but no Indian maid. The worthy Way produces her, however, neatly clad in couplets:

> "At the first glance all dreams of conquest fade
> And the first thought is of his Indian maid."

The whole fragment is plainly a joke, and a joke which the dreams in Dean Street amply account for.

It does not seem as though the experiment of lodging with Cooper, Mackereth, and Stephens can have been altogether successful, yet we have no word that it was not. All youngsters are more or less one-ideaed; doubtless the young medical gentlemen preferred to talk their own particular shop to that which was fast becoming Keats's. Keats worked at surgery because it was his business to do so, but he evidently did not care to talk about it. He

[1] Colvin.
[2] Quoted in full in Sir Sidney Colvin's *Life of John Keats*.

seems to have performed his duties as dresser satisfactorily, but he never got to the point of taking an interest in science. We have no record of his having been caught indulging in any scientific curiosity. I have a strong feeling that, had he lived, this would have come. Keats was keenly intelligent, and, after all, science and art are only the slightly sundered halves of a whole. They may be likened to the octave and sestet of a sonnet, obliquely different in attack, but related by a common emotion. Also, there are his speculations on the effects of different kinds of soil on health, set forth in a letter to Taylor, written from Winchester in 1819. But at the time he lodged in St. Thomas's Street, scientific research was a task to be got through as quickly as possible and then forgotten. We must remember, too, that Keats could command more stimulating intercourse than that provided by Messrs. Cooper, Stephens, and Co., and this they may have resented. It speaks much for the sweetness of Keats's disposition that, in spite of so many reasons why he and the others should quarrel, they do not seem to have done so. They lived together for nearly a year and appear to have parted, if without regret, at least in perfect amity and good will.

There is something pathetic and prophetic in the vision of "little Keats," perched on the window-seat of the sitting-room which was only one quarter his, peering through the window into space. It calls up the thought of a caged animal, or a bird; we are irresistibly reminded of Sterne's starling, repeating over and over, "I can't get out." But we must not make the mistake of supposing that Keats gave an impression of pathos to his friends. He was much too full of life for that, and they were far less likely to look for causes and effects beneath a surface than we are to-day.

It is the biographer's business to pry beneath surfaces, and pathos lurks behind Keats's words and actions too plainly and too constantly to be ignored. But I must caution my readers not to let a knowledge of what was to come hide for them what, at any given present, was — at least in appearance.

Mrs. Meynell has very wisely deplored[1] the fact that to most people the accounts of Keats's last days and death have overshadowed his life. This should not be. A man's life is more important than his death. Keats's life was short, but he lived it with enormous zest and avidity. Brown, in a letter to Fanny Brawne[2] written in 1829, already sees this danger:

> "Leigh Hunt's account[3] of him is worse than disappointing. I cannot bear it; it seems as if Hunt was so impressed by his illness, that he had utterly forgotten him in health. This is a great mistake."

What sort of an impression did Keats make upon his contemporaries? We have seen what a not very sympathetic fellow-student has to say. Now let us go farther and find out what kind of idea he left in the mind of his fellow "genius loving heart," his co-partner in the "brotherhood of song," George Felton Matthew. Matthew is writing thirty years after the event, and we shall probably not be wrong in thinking that the verses I have quoted represent a more contemporary judgment. Still we can glean not a little from Matthew's account, one thing being the why of Keats's drifting away from him. The priggish egotism he reveals shows him to have been a true blood cousin to the egregious Caroline. He may not have been such a silly fellow in 1816, but the germs of it must have been in him. He writes:

> [4] "Keats and I though about the same age, and both inclined to literature, were in many respects as different as two individuals could be. He enjoyed good health — a fine flow of animal spirits — was fond of company — could amuse himself admirably with the frivolities of life

[1] *Keats Memorial Volume.* [2] Dilke Collection. [3] *Lord Byron and his Contemporaries*, by Leigh Hunt. 1828. [4] Colvin.

— and had great confidence in himself. I, on the other hand was languid and melancholy — fond of repose — thoughtful beyond my years — and diffident to the last degree. But I always delighted in administering to the happiness of others: and being one of a large family, it pleased me much to see him and his brother George enjoy themselves so much at our little domestic concerts and dances . . . He was of the skeptical and republican school. An advocate for the innovations which were making progress in his time. A faultfinder with everything established. I, on the contrary, hated controversy and dispute — dreaded discord and disorder — loved the institutions of my country . . . But I respected Keats's opinions, because they were sincere — refrained from subjects on which we differed, and only asked him to concede with me the imperfections of human knowledge, and the fallibility of human judgement: while he, on his part, would often express regret on finding that he had given pain or annoyance by opposing with ridicule or asperity the opinions of others."

This is certainly Keats, in spite of the blue goggles of a middle-aged Matthew, struggling under the combined loads of an infinitesimal income and twelve children. There are things here that we must make fast in our minds: Keats was as healthy as any one need be — his spirits were of the liveliest — he liked company, and frankly enjoyed all the small pleasures which came in his way — he was full of confidence in himself. But even Matthew saw farther:

"A painter or a sculptor might have taken him for a study after the Greek masters, and given him 'a station like the herald Mercury, new-lighted on some heaven-kissing hill.'"

Yet Matthew was shrewd:

[1] "The eye of Keats was more critical than tender and so was his mind: he admired more the external decoration

[1] *Life, Letters, and Literary Remains of John Keats*, by Richard Monckton Milnes. (Lord Houghton.)

than felt the deep emotions of the Muse. He delighted in leading you through the mazes of elaborate description, but was less conscious of the sublime and the pathetic. He used to spend many evenings in reading to me, but I never observed the tears in his eyes nor the broken voice which are indications of extreme sensibility. These indeed were not the parts of poetry which he took pleasure in pointing out."

This is at direct variance with Clarke's account of the effect which a passage of *Cymbeline* had on him, as we shall do well to remember. Keats was always much moved by the great moments of poetry, but I do not think we need find these two opinions contradictory. When Matthew knew him, Keats was several years older than when he and Clarke read *Cymbeline* together in the arbour at Enfield. Keats had probably learnt a measure of self-control in the interval, and what he permitted himself to do with Clarke, he very likely carefully avoided doing with the less sympathetic Matthew. Matthew's sensibility appears to have been of the kind which abuses expression, and nothing is so dampening to real feeling as its over-pronounced simulacrum.

But we know that Keats loved imagery, even Stephens saw that, and he loved description. He delighted in pictures made out of words, and he adored the words themselves. Lord Houghton says:

"If he met with a word anywhere in an old writer that took his fancy he inserted it in his verse on the first opportunity."

What did Keats look like? Like "Mercury on a heaven-kissing hill" says Matthew, and we need not smile, for I think there is more than a touch of truth in the suggestion. Keats must have been a singularly attractive young man. He was very short (five feet and three quarters of an inch, Severn meticulously states), but broad-shouldered and athletic in build, with a good strong face and a very firm mouth. It is foolish to wonder whether this or that portrait resembles him, for there is, in the National Portrait Gallery, London, a life-mask which must look exactly like him. The face of the mask is, of course, in repose, and the hair is covered, but the features are there, and the mask is in excellent condition, or was, when I saw it twenty years ago. In thinking of Keats, one should think always of the life-mask and eschew all the pathetic caricatures which Severn, in his life-long devotion, never ceased to produce. A single one of these adoring and unable portraits seems, in comparison with the mask, in the least like, and that is the sketch made during one of the long night watches of Keats's last illness. There Severn rose beyond himself into real tenderness and truth. Two silhouettes, cut by Brown, are, I believe, excellent likenesses; they give something of the strength and buoyancy which the Severn portraits lack. And there is much to be learnt from a little-known source. This is the large, abortive painting of *Christ's Entry into Jerusalem*,[1] by B. R. Haydon. Haydon, following the custom of the old masters, introduced the heads of various of his friends and acquaintances among the attendant crowd, Keats's included. Hazlitt says that the head of Wordsworth was the most like of these portraits, and certainly the one of Keats reproduces neither the shape of his head nor the form of his features, but it does give a fire, and life, and verve, which is to be found nowhere else. The young man in the crowd is shouting with excitement, and looking at him one catches a spark of Keats's vivacity at certain moments, of which all his friends speak. His face was evidently one which lit up to an extraordinary degree under emotion. To know what Keats looked like, this picture must be taken into account. But certainly the most important portrait of Keats (next to Severn's sketch made during his last illness) is the recently discovered

[1] Now in the Cincinnati Art Museum.

drawing by Brown,[1] sent from New Zealand by his granddaughter to Sir Sidney Colvin and given by him to the National Portrait Gallery, London. Done at Shanklin, when Keats was already ill, it is sterner and quieter than the silhouettes. The man in the drawing is tired, but it is the fatigue of indomitable mental and moral strength. Brown was not a professional portrait painter, but he knew Keats in his last years as no one else except Fanny Brawne knew him. The features are those of the life-mask, the feeling of the drawing in perfect harmony with all we know of Keats. The discovery of this picture is of the utmost importance, adding so much as it does to our knowledge of Keats's appearance.

There has been a great deal of discussion as to the colour of Keats's hair. Evidently the word "red" had a comic connotation in the ears of his contemporaries. They have called it everything but its true colour. Only Mrs. George Keats, characteristically sensible, clear, and honest, gives its real colour. In her copy of Lord Houghton's *Life*, opposite the description of Keats's appearance, she wrote:[2] "His eyes were dark brown, large, soft, and expressive, and his hair a golden red." That this is the exact colour can be easily proved. There are locks of Keats's hair in the Dilke, Morgan, and Day collections. The Morgan Library possesses the least faded of these, and the colour is simply marvelous. Such a red I think I never saw before, no words can exactly describe it. It is lighter than the shade known as "Titian red," yet with no suggestion of the hue called "carrot." A red sunset comes nearest to the colour. The man with such glorious hair must have been striking in the extreme.

Keats's eyes were extremely brilliant, they impressed everyone. Mrs. Proctor wrote that they appeared to her "as those of one who had been looking on some glorious

[1] See Frontispiece to Vol. II.

[2] *Letters and Poems of John Keats,* edited by John Gilman Speed.

sight"; Bailey bears witness to their "fiery brightness"; Severn speaks of the "eagle" appearance of Keats at times, and says he could never forget the "wine-like lustre" cf his eyes. That, despite their brilliance, they were never metallic, Mrs. George Keats's words testify. Bailey also says that "the form of his head was like that of a fine Greek statue: — and he realized to my mind the youthful Apollo, more than any head of a living man whom I have known." We can see, from all this, that Keats lacked only height to be a man of very remarkable beauty. He seems never to have given his looks a thought, except to realize, rather bitterly, that he was very short. In a letter to Bailey, written in 1818, in which he discusses his attitude toward women, he says: "After all I do think better of womankind than to suppose they care whether Mister John Keats five feet high likes them or not."

We have seen Keats under various aspects indoors, but to see him outdoors we must turn to Severn. It takes an artist's perception to notice certain things, and luckily for us an artist was at hand. In Mr. William Sharp's biography of Severn, is a delightful description of Keats on holiday, compiled from Severn's notes:

> [1] "Severn was astonished by his companion's faculty of observation. Nothing seemed to escape him, the song of a bird and the undernotes of response from covert or hedge, the rustle of some animal, the changing of the green and brown lights and furtive shadows, the motions of the wind — just how it took certain tall flowers and plants — and the wayfaring of the clouds: even the features and gestures of passing tramps . . . the furtive animalism below the deceptive humanity in many of the vagrants, even the hats, clothes, shoes, wherever these conveyed the remotest hint as to the real self of the wearer . . . Certain things affected him extremely particularly when 'a wave was billowing through a tree,' as he described the uplifting surge of air among swaying masses of chestnut or oak

[1] *Life and Letters of Joseph Severn,* by William Sharp.

> foliage or when, afar off, he heard the wind coming across woodlands. 'The tide! the tide!' he would cry delightedly, and spring on to some stile, or upon the low bough of a wayside tree, and watch the passage of the wind upon the meadow-grasses or young corn, not stirring till the flow of air was all around him, while an expression of rapture made his eyes gleam and his face glow."

He loved to watch the wind running upon a field of barley. "From fields of oats or barley," Severn declared once, "it was almost impossible to allure him." Unlike Matthew, who does not seem to have noticed them, Severn remarks upon Keats's rapid changes of mood:

> "Even when in a mood of joyous observance with flow of happy spirits, he would suddenly become taciturn, not because he was tired, not even because his mind was suddenly wrought to some bewitching vision, but from a profound disquiet which he could not or would not explain . . . The only thing that would bring Keats out of one of his fits of seeming gloomful revery — when he would answer with cold, almost harsh brevity, or not at all, although his eyes would have no hardness . . . was the motion 'of the inland sea' he loved so well."

Keats's temperament was rather a difficult one to manage — for its possessor, I mean. That, in spite of the dashes of chilly gloom which swept over him on occasions, he should have been such a pleasant companion, shows how very hard he tried to hold on to himself. If, when he was enduring one of his blue fits, he answered coldly or not at all, we may be sure that the blithe, shallow, not too tactful Severn brought this on himself by teasing enquiries.

The faculty of observation which Severn remarks upon comes out again and again in his letters. I am almost inclined to call Keats the first of the colour writers, certainly no one before his time was so impressed by pure colour as he. But he had also another sense, the feeling for line simply as line, witness the interest with which he watched the curve of wind over a grainfield, or the linear bend and recoil of plants in a breeze. However subservient he may have made these things in his poems, thus unconsciously following the trend of his time, it was primarily as themselves that he saw them. Think of the descriptions of scenery in Shelley's letters, for instance; setting aside the manner in which they are written, they are not even observed as a man of to-day would observe them.

Now take Keats: Cowden Clarke tells of his describing a sunset over Loch Lomond, with the lake deep blue and in shadow, and at the further end "a slash across it of deep orange." The last words are quoted from Keats, and illustrate what I mean. His letters are full of such touches. Writing to Tom from Scotland, near Ben Lomond, he says, "The water was a fine Blue silvered and the Mountains a dark purple, the Sun setting aslant behind them." Here we have abundant colour, and the "aslant" gives all his feeling for line. From Winchester, he writes: "From the Hill at the eastern extremity you see a prospect of Streets, and old Buildings mixed up with Trees." That is at once a painter's vision, and a modern's expression. Again: "We went to tea at Mrs. Millar's, and in going were particularly struck with the light and shade through the Gateway at the Horse Guards." The interesting thing here is that it is not the gateway, with its light and shade, which interests him; not the light and shade composed into the picture of a place; but these by themselves, all unrelated, the gateway is subsidiary. He speaks of the sun "coming upon" the snow. Exactly the right expression, but I do not think he would ever have dreamt of using it in a poem; it would not have suited the poetical diction of the age, which even he could not quite shake off. For Keats is much more modern in his letters than in his poems. A man cannot jump a century at one fell swoop, and we know that what he did do gave the critics ample cause for concern. Think of the passage in *I Stood Tip-toe upon a Little Hill:*

> "... the moon lifting her silver rim
> Above a cloud, and with a gradual swim
> Coming into the blue with all her light."

"Gradual swim" is certainly a challenge to posterity. Less modern in expression, but so exact in observation as to be vivid as a thing seen, is

> "The rocks were silent, the wide sea did weave
> An untumultuous fringe of silver foam
> Along the flat brown sand."

There is perfect realism in his "keen, fitful gusts," or "Small busy flames play through the fresh-laid coals," or

> "The city streets were clean and fair
> From wholesome drench of April rains,"

or "The stars look very cold about the sky." Keats is generally called a romantic, and a romantic he certainly was; but he was also a realist, and that has not been so usually noticed.

How Keats's observation and love for poetry combined, is shown by the passages he marked in the books he read. There are enough books owned by Keats in existence to enable us to follow the workings of his mind very closely. One of these books dates from the period we are considering. It is the first volume of a set of Spenser [1] which came from the library of George Keats. When Keats acquired the book, there is no means of ascertaining. He certainly did not own it at the time he borrowed the *Faerie Queene* from Clarke. The title-page bears the inscription, "George Keats, 1816." John's name does not appear. A hieroglyph in the corner is supposed to be his initials, but I confess I doubt it, as they bear no resemblance to his usual way of

[1] Author's Collection.

writing them. My theory is that John, having fallen in love with Spenser after his reading of Clarke's copy, set about getting a copy for himself as soon as possible, and that, having read, marked, learned, and inwardly digested it, passed it on to George. The volume is heavily underscored in innumerable places,[1] and annotated, evidently by John, since his is the only handwriting which appears in the margin. But this is not the only evidence that the volume was much used by, in fact probably belonged to, John. Mr. James Freeman Clarke, who was Unitarian minister in Louisville from 1833 to 1839, knew George Keats well, and in an article quoted in Buxton Forman's Library Edition he says that George told him that John used this Spenser as a boy. The other five volumes of the set were lost before the descendants of George Keats parted with this one, but in it we have twelve cantos of the *Faerie Queene*. The book has been read and re-read, marked and over-marked. A few of these scored passages will suffice to show how often Keats was attracted by descriptions of colours, by pictures appealing directly to one or more of the senses.

He has underlined:

> "... His glistring Armour made
> A little glooming Light much like a Shade."

Again, he singles out the words "uncouth light," and the last half of the line: "And turning fierce, *her speckled tail advanced*," in which it was evidently the "speckled" which caught his fancy. Another little bit picked out of a stanza is:

> "All in a Kirtle of discolour'd Say
> He clothed was, ypainted full of Eyes."

He has marked the whole of the thirty-fourth stanza of the First Canto, which begins: "A little lowly Hermitage it was." And of course he has singled out the description of

[1] See Appendix C.

152 The Fairy-Queen. Book I.

XL.

The fourth appointed by his Office was,
Poor Prisoners to relieve with gracious Aid,
And Captives to redeem with Price of Brass,
From Turks and Sarazins, which them had staid;
And tho they faulty were, yet well he weigh'd,
That God to us forgiveth every hour,
Much more than that why they in Bands were laid
And he that harrow'd Hell with heavy Stowr,
The faulty Souls from thence brought to his heavenly Bower.

XLI.

The fifth had charge sick Persons to attend,
And comfort those in point of Death which lay;
For them most needeth Comfort in the end,
When Sin, and Hell, and Death do most dismay
The feeble Soul departing hence away.
All is but lost, that living we bestow,
If not well ended at our dying Day.
O Man! have mind of that last bitter Throw;
For as the Tree does fall, so lies it ever low.

XLII.

The sixth had charge of them now being dead,
In seemly sort their Corses to engrave,
And deck with dainty Flowers their bridal Bed,
That to their heavenly Spouse, both sweet and brave,
They might appear, when he their Souls shall save.
The wondrous Workmanship of God's own Mould,
Whose Face he made all Beasts to fear, and gave
All in his hand, even dead we honour should.
Ah dearest God me grant, I dead be not defoul'd.

XLIII.

The seventh, now after Death and Burial done,
Had charge the tender Orphans of the Dead,
And Widows aid, lest they should be undone:
In face of Judgment he their Right would plead,
Ne ought the Power of mighty Men did dread
In their Defence, nor would for Gold or Fee
Be won their rightful Causes down to tread:
And when they stood in most necessity,
He did supply their Want, and gave them ever free.

XLIV.

Cant. 10. The Fairy-Queen. 153

XLIV.

There when the Elfin Knight arrived was,
The first and chiefest of the Seven, whose care
Was Guests to welcome, towards him did pass;
Where, seeing *Mercy*, that his Steps up-bare,
And always led, to her with Reverence rare
He humbly louted in meek Lowliness,
And seemly welcome for her did prepare:
For, of their Order, she was Patroness,
Albe *Charissa* were their chiefest Founderess.

XLV.

There she awhile him stays, himself to rest,
That to the rest more able he might be;
During which time, in every good behest,
And godly work of Alms and Charity,
She him instructed with great Industry:
Shortly therein so perfect he became,
That from the first unto the last degree,
His mortal Life he learned had to frame
In holy Righteousness, without Rebuke or Blame.

XLVI.

Thence forward, by that painful way they pass
Forth to an Hill that was both steep and high;
On top whereof, a sacred Chappel was,
And eke a little Hermitage thereby,
Wherein an aged holy Man did lie,
That Day and Night said his Devotion,
Ne other worldly Business did apply;
His name was heavenly *Contemplation*;
Of God and Goodness was his Meditation.

XLVII.

Great Grace that old Man to him given had;
For God he often saw from Heaven's height,
All were his earthly Eyen both blunt and bad,
And through great Age had lost their kindly Sight,
Yet wondrous quick and pierceant was his Spright,
As Eagle's Eye, that can behold the Sun.
That Hill they scale with all their Power and Might,
That his frail Thighs, nigh weary and fordone,
'Gan fail; but by her help the top at last he won.

H 5 XLVIII.

Milton

SPENSER'S "FAIRY QUEEN" OWNED BY KEATS

Author's Collection

Morpheus's bed in stanza forty-one. Among the colour annotations is:

> "Now when the rosy-fingered Morning fair,
> Weary of aged Tithon's saffron Bed,
> Had spread her purple Robe through dewy Air."

And again:

> "A goodly Lady clad in scarlet Red,
> Purfled with Gold and Pearl of rich assay,
> And like a Persian Mitre on her Head
> She wore, with Crowns and Owches garnished,
> The which her lavish Lovers to her gave:
> Her wanton Palfrey was all overspred
> With tinsel Trappings woven like a Wave,
> Whose Bridle rung with golden Bells and Bosses brave."

One picture which he liked was:

> ". . . two goodly Trees, that fair did spred
> Their Arms abroad, with grey Moss over-cast;
> And their green Leaves trembling with every Blast,
> Made a calm Shadow far in compass round."

Shadows always intrigued him; here is another, quite different in shape and effect:

> "Whereas that Pagan proud himself did rest,
> In secret Shadow by a Fountain side."

Happy descriptive epithets charm him. For instance in the two lines:

> "She is ybrought unto a paled Green
> And placed under stately Canopy;"

he has only underlined the first. The "stately canopy" seemed not to call for notice, but he could not resist "paled Green." Remember what I have said of his feeling for realism, and observe that he marked this:

> "When I awoke, and found her place devoid,
> And naught but pressed Grass where she had lyen."

These are visual things, but he has also scored:

> "A shrilling Trumpet sounded from on high,"

and again the line:

> "With Shaumes, and Trumpets, and with Clarions sweet."

His own lines in the *Eve of St. Agnes:*

> "The silver, snarling trumpets 'gan to chide"

is finer than either of these, but probably owes its birth to them. There are other passages which find an echo later in the *Eve of St. Agnes*. Two lines which he has not only underscored, but put three marginal marks against, are:

> "Silly old Man, that lives in hidden Cell,
> Bidding his Beads all day for his Trespass."

Have we not here an ancestor to the ancient Beadsman? Also he has carefully noticed:

> "They bring them wines of Greece, and Araby,
> And dainty Spices fetch'd from furthest Ind'."

Keats liked the word "Ind." He has underlined this also:

> "As he had travell'd many a Summer's Day,
> Through boiling Sands of Araby and Ind'."

He tried his own hand at it in the sonnet *To J. R.*:

> "O to arrive each Monday morn from Ind!
> To land each Tuesday from rich Levant!"

The only place in the volume where anything has been written, refers to the following passage, which has not only been underlined throughout, but Keats has drawn two lines beside it and annotated it, "Milton." It runs:

> "Great Grace that old Man to him given had;
> For God he often saw to Heaven's height.

All were his earthly Eyen both blunt and bad,
And through great Age had lost their kindly Sight,
Yet wondrous quick and pierceant was his Spright,
As Eagle's Eye, that can behold the Sun."

This preoccupation with what I may call "images of effect" he never lost. Some time during 1819 or 1820, probably the former year, Keats borrowed from Taylor a copy of Southey's translation of the old Spanish romance, *Palmerin of England*, and with the charming irresponsibility of the born borrower filled it with appreciative scorings. Through the courtesy of the present owner,[1] I have been enabled, not only to examine, but to transcribe all the passages in the four volumes of *Palmerin*[2] marked by Keats. It is evident from them that his love for certain qualities in literature underwent no change from first to last. Among the passages which he marked are: "a fair and clear river, . . . so clear that whosoever walked on its banks might count the white stones at the bottom." A giant's body tumbling is like the "fall of a tower," which is promptly underscored. Tilting knights come to the ground with their "saddles between their legs." Under trees "there was a delicate shadow, and of such quality and nature, that in the hottest calm of summer they always moved with the wind." In one place, a spire of many-hued tiles is so arranged that "one colour gave beauty to another," which excellent description Keats pounced upon at once. "The waters of the river mournful both in colour and sound" is double scored. He notes the giants on a field of battle "their harnesses and helmets flashing over the field far away, as the sun shone on them." A great many passages describing the colours and devices of armour are marked: "A knight mounted on a mulberry courser" who wears "green armour"; white armour with "golden fruit of the arbutus in a green field on their

[1] Lucius Wilmerding, Esq., of New York. [2] See Appendix C.

shields"; armour "black and yellow with grey griffins thereon"; "armour red, with black joints." Images of effect are by no means the only things which Keats noticed in the books he read, but it is his colour sense and his faculty of observation which I wish to lay stress upon here. Later, when we come to consider Keats's intellectual habit at its full growth, and his attitude toward poetry in general and his own in particular, as well as his method of writing, I shall have occasion to quote scorings and annotations of quite a different character. But side by side with these, to the very end, we may witness his constantly recurring delight in words and phrases which convey a tactile, aural, or visual sensation with the swift economy of genius.

At the beginning of 1816, then, Keats is living in St. Thomas's Street, a conundrum to his fellow-students, a perturbing pleasure to Matthew, a petted protégé to Clarke, a flame-winged phœnix to his brothers, and a jolly good fellow to the rest of his small circle. Since to understand Keats, one must know his friends, I shall stop a moment to consider each as he comes along. Devoted as Keats was to the friends he made, it was usually George who found them for him. "I know not how it is," writes Keats in 1818, "but I have never made any acquaintance of my own — nearly all through your medium, my dear Brother."

I think these Keats boys were rather remarkable young fellows really, and I am leaving genius out of count entirely when I say this. George we know was not a genius, Tom we cannot suppose would have turned out one. Thomas Keats's wish that his sons should rise in the world they realized in every thing they did; in their tastes, points of view, and choice of friends. And they were totally without their father's consciousness in the matter. They moved inevitably from one class to another, because it was in them to do so. A natural refinement characterized all three of them. They had been to a good school, but that alone would not account for their very genuine simplicity and distinction. It was in them from the start, and probably Thomas Keats and his excitable wife knew in some obscure way that it was in *them*, too, handicapped as they were, to realize their ideals. When Nature sets out to make a gentleman she knows how to do it, no matter what the world may think. James Freeman Clarke, who knew George in middle life, judged him at his true value:

> [1] "He was one of the most intellectual men I ever knew . . . Joined with this energy of intellect was a profound intellectual modesty . . . George Keats was the most manly and self-possessed of men — yet full of inward aspiration and conscious of spiritual needs. There was no hardness in his strong heart, no dogmatism in his energetic intellect, no pride in his self-reliance."

The style of this appreciation is a little high-flown, it was written in 1843 and conforms to the taste of the day, but it clearly proves George Keats to have been an unusual man, and Dr. Clarke was no mean judge of men, the last person in the world to idealize a cypher.

Of Tom Keats, we know very little. He walks like a shadow across his brothers' letters, and we have only four of his own. He was almost always an invalid, with a sweet, affectionate, clinging disposition. Like his brother John, and his mother, he craved affection. George also may have inherited this trait, but in his case the craving was satisfied very early; even now, in 1816, he was surely and steadily falling in love with Georgiana Wylie.

It was probably in the late Autumn of 1815, or very early in the following year, that Keats, through the medium of the hospitable Wylies, met a young man named Haslam, by whom he was introduced to another young

[1] Buxton Forman. Library Edition. Vol. IV. First published in the *Dial*, April, 1843.

man, a painter, Joseph Severn. We know practically nothing about William Haslam, except that he was a few months older than Keats and a solicitor. For some perfectly inexplicable reason, I think of him as a large, burly man, but there is no justification for any such idea. I suppose it comes from the fact that Haslam was such a dependable creature; Severn speaks of him as "our oak friend." It is almost impossible to measure the degree of intimacy between intimate friends. He was one of Keats's inside circle, but not, I think, one of the closest of them. We have only one short letter to him from Keats, but that may be simply because other letters to him are lost. He was a very intimate friend of Severn's, whom he brought to the Wylies' where Keats must often have met him. Haslam's good will was unbounded, he appears to have been willing to do anything, and to have done it well.

Of Severn, there would be almost no need to speak, were it not that certain false notions in regard to him have become current. The fact that he went to Rome with Keats, nursed him during his last illness, and spent the rest of his life painting Keats from memory and talking and writing about him, has given him the position of inseparable companion in the minds of most people. As a matter of fact, until the journey to Italy, he stood in no such relation to Keats. One of the most widely circulated errors of the Keats legend is just this, and it is most important that it should be corrected. Severn also was one of the circle, but several other members of it knew Keats better than he. The great fact of his life was that he, and he alone, had been with Keats during the last terrible months. It is unpleasant to feel, as we must, that although his love was undoubtedly sincere, he made capital of it. It was his only claim to fame. It is true that in the years immediately following Keats's death, when Keats himself had little or no public beyond the boundary of his friends, Severn did his best to champion him; but, as the years went on and

Severn, the painter, saw only too clearly that he was a failure, he tended to rely with ever increasing insistence upon his rôle of Severn, the friend of Keats. In considering Severn's later life, the unpleasant truth is forced upon us that what began as genuine admiration ended as advertisement. He arrogated to himself a place in Keats's life which he never occupied, the accident of illness alone was responsible for a relation which would not have existed otherwise. He knew this, and yet he did everything in his power to foster the legend. Severn was a weak and a vain man, which is all the excuse that he can claim. He did not desert his post in Rome, that is his unique virtue, and that, of course, he knew.

Joseph Severn was the son of a music teacher. He was apprenticed to an engraver, but he had such a desire to paint that, in spite of his father's anger, he managed to attend the Royal Academy schools. Abandoning engraving, he started as a miniature painter, at the same time trying his hand at historical painting. Whatever disappointment and age made of Severn, as a young man he was hard-working and courageous. With practically no money, and only a moiety of tuition, he dared to compete for the Royal Academy's gold medal, offered in 1817 for a painting on some subject taken from Spenser. To get the materials for his picture, he was obliged to sell his watch and books, but when, in December 1819, the competing canvasses were exhibited, he won the medal. From the first, Keats seems to have inspired him to extra exertion. A little shred of justification for his permitting the world to think of him as the *fidus Achates* of Keats, may be found in the fact that he regarded Keats with wondering admiration, and, knowing the warmth of his own feelings, gradually attributed a like warmth to the feelings of Keats. Severn could instruct Keats about pictures; Keats could do the same for him with regard to books. That was the tie between them in 1816. It was Keats's enthusiasm for poetry which led Severn to choose Hermia and Helena from the *Midsummer Night's Dream* as the subject of his first oil painting, and Keats again whose devotion to the *Faerie Queene* induced him to compete for the Spenser prize. When Severn, struggling to keep going and painting, encountered Keats, the latter's contagious love for all forms of art put new life into him. Severn was impressionable, with a pleasant social gift; he was easy, light, and gay. He never fathomed Keats, but he enjoyed him, and in the sequel came to love him profoundly. Severn seems to have been a little teasing in his demands upon his friend's interest, but as a cicerone to picture galleries and a pointer toward things artistic he was invaluable. Keats liked him, but not to the extent that he liked Keats. He seems to have been one of those unfortunate people who are at once importunate and diffident. Keats's letters to him are always a little cool. George calls him "the complaining Severn," and on one occasion when Severn had been declaring that he feared he was not wanted, he writes to him a little sharply:

> [1] "Have the goodness never to complain again about being forgotten. How many invitations have you received from me? How many have you answered? To the former question may be answered 'a dozen'; to the latter, not one! . . . John will be in town again soon. When he is, I will let you know and repeat my invitation."

On another occasion, George writes:

> [2] "What a most unconscionable fellow you must be for fearing my Brother has forgotten you without knowing the 'how' — and the 'why' — take my assurance he has not."

The attitude on Severn's part which these letters imply is not an endearing one. Yet Severn was honest, and his obvious delight in Keats's company, together with the

[1] *Life and Letters of Joseph Severn*, by William Sharp.
[2] *Ibid.*

admiration he exuded at every pore, was an unpleasant pleasantness. Keats laughed with him, joked with him, took long walks with him, discussed painting and poetry with him, and put him off gently whenever he became a bore. Keats did not see his prize picture, the *Cave of Despair*, until it was hung at the Academy, which does not argue the daily intercourse that Severn in his reminiscences always infers. Yet, even in the reminiscences, Severn gives away his position. He tells how he used to go to Well Walk to finish his miniatures, nominally because he wanted backgrounds for them, but really to be with Keats. "They were my excuse for obtruding my miniature self upon his superior society," are the words in which he makes his confession. Severn was a likeable fellow, but not strong enough intellectually to attract Keats. Keats once told him that he was "the most astonishingly suggestive innocent," a characterization which Severn, panting for crumbs, seems to have regarded as a compliment. It was a compliment up to a point, but no farther. Where Keats was, by turns, in a fury of good spirits or overwhelmed in gloom, Severn was gently playful or querulously miserable. His temperament could not compass the swing of Keats's, poor fellow, and it is one of life's little ironies that Fate should have bound them together. Seymour Kirkup's drawing of Severn,[1] made in 1822, a year after Keats's death, although smoothed and prettified in the artist's best manner, tells us all we need to know. The eyes have a dreamy, and still mildly penetrating, look, but the regular nose and the weak mouth and chin proclaim the sentimentalist. Yet were it not for his careful tending of the legend, it would be pathetic to realize how keenly he gauged the truth in the end. Just before his death, he said to a friend:

> "I may say that of all I have done with brush or pen, as artist and man, scarce anything will long outlast me . . . yet through my beloved Keats I shall be remembered."

[1] *Life and Letters of Joseph Severn*, by William Sharp.

I have outstripped chronology, as I see I shall be forced to do again and again. We know more of Keats's friends than Keats did at the time of his meeting them, and by this very knowledge we can follow his relations with them, and their effect upon him, as we could not do otherwise. There are always many influences at work in the growth of a poet, and among the most important are the influence of books and the influence of personal contacts. To study an artist's work is to study his psychology, and that we can only do by concerning ourselves with the objects of his thought. There are men on whom the influence of environment is as potent as these I have mentioned, but such men are rare, and do not belong among the intellectual geniuses. That nature had its hand in the making of Keats, we very well know, but not to the extent of books and people.

The first poem of 1816, so far as we can tell, was the trochaic couplets *To Georgiana Augusta Wylie*, whose name, in the *Poems*, 1817, is represented by asterisks. The printed version is an alteration of a valentine which Keats composed for his brother George to send to his inamorata. The original valentine [1] was far simpler than the poem intended for the public gaze. The whole middle portion, from line 3 to line 34, was added later. For instance, the original lines:

"Like light in wreathed cloudlets nested
Thy hair in gilden casque is rested,
From the which four milky plumes
Like the fleur de Luce's blooms,
Springing from an Indian vase."

are much better than those which took their place:

"Like sunbeams in a cloudlet nested
Thy locks in knightly casque are rested:
O'er which bend four milky plumes
Like the gentle lilly's blooms
Springing from a costly vase."

[1] Woodhouse Commonplace Books.

"From the which" was, of course, bad, but the greater vividness and circumstantialness of the original cannot be denied. The more artificial character of the printed poem is, we fear, the result of friendly criticism, almost always a hindrance to Keats. It is certainly a horrible taste which permitted the abominable diction of:

> "Saving when, with freshening lave
> Thou dipps't them in the taintless wave."

Keats's indebtedness to Spenser in this poem has been pointed out by Professor de Sélincourt, but I think the verbiage of these two lines comes straight from Pope. Keats rhymes "Thalia" with "higher," which shows how shaky he was on the pronunciation of classical names. Even three years later he was not sure of them. The proof-sheets of *Lamia* contain a list of such names and their pronunciations, written, probably, by Woodhouse, for Keats's guidance. There is no hint in the *Poems*, 1817, that these lines were intended as a valentine, but the original is quite conventionally explicit on the subject, ending with all the frill of laced paper:

> "Ah, me! whither shall I flee?
> Thou hast metamorphosed me:
> Do not let me sigh and pine,
> Prythee be my Valentine!"

That there was much rejoicing in the house of Wylie on St. Valentine's Day, is obvious, and much foolish and delighted praise for the poet.

George availed himself of this Cyrano-like method of wooing again, and the result was the cheerful little bit of twaddle which begins "O Come dearest Emma," a euphemism for Georgiana. This youthful trifle mates Moore's metre and an eighteenth-century diction in a manner to set one's teeth on edge. The last lines are so excruciatingly bad that I think Keats, in his worst moments, never outdid them:

"So smile acquiescence, and give me thy hand,
With love-looking eyes, and with voice sweetly bland."

Doubtless Miss Wylie was pleased, but even Keats knew better than to include the verses in his book. The copy which Georgiana Wylie had, we may feel assured, made no mention of any Emma, instead it probably began: "O Come Georgiana," but as Woodhouse's transcripts read "Emma," I am afraid Keats liked what he had done well enough to hand it round among his friends, although carefully keeping George and Georgiana out of it.

The two recently recovered poems,[1] *Apollo and the Graces*, and *You Say You Love*, probably belong to this same period. Both of them are quite worthless. I unhesitatingly reject *Stay, Ruby-Breasted Warbler, Stay* from the list of Keats's poems. A transcript of the poem made by George Keats is carefully signed "G. K." [2] That Woodhouse was misinformed in attributing this poem to John, seems evident, for it is the height of folly to suppose that George did not know his own poem. *Stay, Ruby-Breasted Warbler* has an interest quite apart from the question of its authorship, because Woodhouse annotates it: "Written off in a few minutes at the request of some ladies who wished for fresh words to sing to their tune," and this leads to the supposition that it is the poem confused with a sonnet, *The Poet*, found in the Morgan Library Woodhouse Book, which bears practically the same inscription.[3] That the *Ruby-Breasted Warbler* was written for the Misses Matthew to sing at their "little domestic concerts" is a guess that we may very well hazard. *Apollo and the Graces* has for sub-title "Written to the tune of the air in 'Don Giovanni,'" which probably places it as owing its existence to another of these occasions. A strange thing, however, is that Woodhouse received *Apollo* and *You Say You Love* from Miss Reynolds,

[1] Woodhouse Commonplace Book. (*Poems II.*) Crewe Collection.
[2] *The Poems of John Keats*, edited by E. de Sélincourt, 4th edition.
[3] See Vol. I, p. 62.

who possessed the originals, which would seem to point to their being treasured in the Keats circle, or written later in the year, for Keats did not meet the Reynolds family until the Autumn of 1816. I am inclined to believe the former of these two alternatives, as Keats was doing so much better work by the Autumn. Still it is a fact that Keats was always prone to lapses in the quality of his poetry, and he is known to have written words to airs played to him on the piano by Charlotte Reynolds. But the particular kind of badness which these poems display so lavishly never appears again; the only song we know definitely to have been written for Charlotte Reynolds is of a totally different calibre.

While we are on the subject of bad poetry, let me mention an undated set of verses, the manuscript of which was given, many years later, by George Keats to John Howard Payne. Payne published them in a New York paper, the *Ladies Companion*, in 1837. They can, I think, belong only to this period. There is no doubt of their authenticity, for I have seen the manuscript.[1] As they have never been reprinted, I insert them here:

"Hither, hither, love —
  'Tis a shady mead —
Hither, hither, love!
  Let us feed and feed!

Hither, hither, sweet —
  'Tis a cowslip bed —
Hither, hither, sweet!
  'Tis with dew bespread!

Hither, hither, dear,
  By the breath of life,
Hither, hither, dear! —
  Be the summer's wife!

[1] Owned by Dr. Roderick Terry, Newport, R.I.

Though one moment's pleasure
In one moment flies —
Though the passion's treasure
In one moment dies; —

Yet it has not passed —
Think how near, how near! —
And while it doth last,
Think how dear, how dear!

Hither, hither, hither
Love its boon has sent —
If I die and wither
I shall die content!"

On March 3rd, as we have already seen by the Guy's Hospital register, Keats put himself down for another twelve months' term of tuition. He does not seem to have changed his surgeon, for again Mr. Lucas appears as his immediate chief. Evidently Keats still considered surgery as his destined profession. But the poetry was going on in a continually increasing flow. In this same March, Keats wrote a sonnet: *On an Engraved Gem of Leander*. Woodhouse [1] says that the "gem" was the gift of Miss Reynolds. This, I am sure, is another of Woodhouse's slips, for the same reason that applies to the two other poems of this period which Woodhouse obtained from her. A letter [2] from the third of the sisters, Charlotte Reynolds, written after Keats's death, may or may not throw some light on the situation. In this letter, Miss Reynolds asks for the return of an album which Woodhouse had taken away in order to write something in it, she also asks Woodhouse to send back a letter of Keats's which he had borrowed. Another letter from a Mrs. "Colonel" Green, whom I suppose to have been the future mother-in-law of Marianne Reynolds, written to Woodhouse [3] in 1819, speaks of her intention to rally Keats upon "a great *mistake*" com-

[1] Houghton Mss. Crewe Collection. Colvin.
[2] Woodhouse Book. Morgan Collection. [3] *Ibid.*

mitted by him "in the Book of trifles," whatever that may have been. Albums and Books of Trifles point to the preserving of effusions, and Keats may possibly have contributed poems to be copied into these repositories along with the songs written for Charlotte Reynolds to sing. The "gem" which gave rise to the sonnet was undoubtedly one of the innumerable coloured paste reproductions of antique and pseudo-antique cameos and intaglios made by James Tassie, who stole the idea of these reproductions from Wedgwood. Keats was very fond of "Tassie's gems," they keep cropping up in his letters; at one time he even thought of making a collection of them.[1] It is impossible to identify the particular "gem" which produced the sonnet. Tassie's catalogue gives over sixty [2] of which Leander is the subject.

The Leander sonnet is in so entirely different a key from the poems which immediately preceded it, and in so much more advised a diction than anything Keats had previously done, that I confess to a doubt as to whether Woodhouse's date be the correct one. Lord Houghton prints this sonnet after the one *On the Sea* which was written in April, 1817. By that time, Keats knew the Reynoldses well enough for one of them to have given him the "gem," and it would have been quite natural to give him a present when he was starting for the Isle of Wight to begin *Endymion*. Then again why, if the sonnet were written in March, 1816, was it not printed in the *Poems*, 1817? It is quite as good as some of the sonnets printed in that volume. But, lacking more evidence, Woodhouse's definite date must stand.[3] It is not a bad sonnet, in spite of some floridness of wording. It creaks a little with age to-day, but there is a sense of drama which is struck immediately in the dignified opening line:

"Come hither all sweet maidens soberly."

[1] Colvin. [2] *Ibid.*

[3] A holograph of this sonnet in the Bemis Collection is dated "March" and some year, but the last figure of the year date is undecipherable.

The sestet, with Leander's drowning, is full of vivid action.

The sonnet form was especially delightful to Keats in his early years. It held just about as much as he was prepared to say. It was dignified and serious, and he found it, as most poets do, an extremely sympathetic medium. Again during March, Keats wrote another, this time a tribute to all past poets dead and gone. It is not a particularly good poem, but the subject is illuminating. It shows how Keats was haunted by his reading. A fact to which the many "steals" and forgetful borrowings in all his early work vigorously testifies. The sonnet has no title, it is known by its first line, *How many bards gild the lapses of time*. Speaking of them, Keats declares

> ". . . I could brood
> Over their beauties, earthly, or sublime:
> And often, when I sit me down to rhyme,
> These will in throngs before my mind intrude."

It took him years to get them into the background.

Hunt, in his *Examiner* review of the *Poems*, 1817, criticized the first line of this sonnet for its see-saw rhythm, saying that "by no contrivance of any sort can we prevent this from jumping out of the heroic measure into mere rhymicality." Dr. Robert Bridges, on the other hand, regards "the inversion of the third and fourth stresses as very musical and suitable to the explanatory form of the sentence." The truth is that both of these critics are right. Nothing can prevent the first line from taking on a rhythm utterly unlike the traditional five-stressed iambic rhythm of the sonnet, and in any line but the first this might well have given a musical effect, but not in the first, since the first line of a short poem invariably sets the tune. The merry little lilt of this line starts the sonnet, not only clumsily for a sonnet, but unfortunately in regard to the total effect; it implies an attitude absolutely at variance with the mood of the poem as a whole. Cowden Clarke remembers [1] that Horace Smith, on hearing the sonnet read aloud by Hunt exclaimed, in reference to the thirteenth line: "What a well-condensed expression for a youth so young!" The thirteenth line is:

"That distance of recognizance bereaves."

Smith's comment is interesting as an illustration of the change of taste which a century has brought about, for it is just this sort of verbal torturing that the modern ear most deplores in Keats, and that he learnt more and more to eschew.

Keats's reading, diversified as it may appear at a casual glance, was really very much along a line. The line was, naturally, poetry, poetry old and new. History, travels, were all so many glosses to the old poetry; since the new needed no glosses, he gave it none. Modern writing, outside of poetry, he seems to have had no interest in. Novels, later than those of Smollett and Fielding, he seldom attempted to read, and when he did, he did not like them. He was, of course, too young to savour the delicate irony of Jane Austen's books, besides being entirely unacquainted with the class of society she portrayed, and the same thing, with differences, applies to Miss Edgeworth; but Scott was just beginning to take the world by storm, everybody was speculating on the identity of the author of these extraordinary romances except Keats. The second of them, *Guy Mannering*, appeared in 1815. Keats did not read it. The *Antiquary* came out in 1816, but although Keats did read it some time, it was probably not until later. He was intrigued with the bluff days preceding his own, and his critical acumen was not to be fooled by Scott's "big bow-wow style," as Scott himself called it. Writing to George Keats in 1818, he gives his reasons for his point of view:

[1] "*Recollections of Writers*," by Charles Cowden Clarke.

> "You ask me what degrees there are between Scott's novels and those of Smollet. They appear to me quite distinct in every particular, more especially in their aim. Scott endeavors to throw so interesting and romantic a colouring into common and low characters as to give them a touch of the sublime. Smollet, on the contrary, pulls down and levels what with other men would continue romance. The grand parts of Scott are within reach of more minds than the finest humours in 'Humphrey Clinker.' I forget whether that fine thing of the Sargeant is Fielding's or Smollet's,[1] but it gives me more pleasure than the whole novel of 'The Antiquary.'"

In other moods, Keats did full justice to Scott's power of interesting the public. In the journal letter to George and his wife, written at intervals from some time in December, 1818, to January 4, 1819, he remarks:

> "We have seen three literary kings in our Time — Scott — Byron — and then the Scotch novels."

This does not, I imagine, mean that Keats thought that Scott, Byron, and the anonymous novelist, were kings of literature in the sense of being head and shoulders above the rest of the contemporary writing world, since the modern writers he cared most for at the time were Coleridge and Wordsworth, but that he considered them as literary kings, their books being more in the public eye than anybody else's. In other words, they had a "corner on literature," and his "literary kings" is analogous to our "coal barons." Scott here is obviously the Scott of *Marmion* and *The Lady of the Lake*, not the author of the "Scotch novels." Something seems to have shaken Keats's belief of the year before that Scott was clearly the mooted author. He, like all the world at the time, vacillated from person to person in the endeavour to hit upon the right man.

If Keats did not read *Guy Mannering* and Miss Austen's *Emma*, he certainly did read Coleridge's *Christabel*,

[1] It is from Fielding's *Tom Jones*.

Shelley's *Alastor*, and John Hamilton Reynolds's *Naiad*. *Christabel* was to have its innings later on, but there was one book published early in 1816 which he read and fairly doted upon. He could not have enough of it. It got into his blood and started him off in fervent imitation. This epoch-making book was the little parlour-table volume, the *Story of Rimini*, by Leigh Hunt.

Keats was all prepared to worship anything Hunt did. Cowden Clarke admired him, and was his personal friend. Keats had been a sympathetic reader of the *Examiner* for years. He had probably read and admired Hunt's unimportant squib, the *Feast of the Poets*. Having elected Hunt into the chair of prophet and arbiter, Keats was ready to find *Rimini* a masterpiece. Then, too, it had a Preface which, to Keats, must have appeared the very voice of oracle. This Preface set forth Hunt's theories of versification, and poetry in general, with didactic precision. His thesis is the repudiation of Pope and his school, and the substitution of the freer style of Dryden, Spenser, and particularly of Chaucer. "I suppress a good deal that I had intended to say on the versification of the poem," he begins, but he continues, "I do not hesitate to say however, that Pope and the French school of versification have known the least on the subject, of any poets perhaps that ever wrote. They have mistaken mere smoothness for harmony; and, in fact, wrote as they did, because their ears were only sensible of a marked and uniform regularity." But he adds in fairness: "In speaking of such men, I allude, of course, only to their style in poetry, and not to their undisputed excellence in other matters."

Hunt was quite right in contending that a rigid metrical verse can be written by persons without the slightest sense of rhythm, where he went astray was in the insistence that there is a right and wrong in poetic styles. He refused to admit that, in poetry at least, what is one man's fault may be another man's virtue. Following these opinions, he goes on:

"With the endeavour to recur to a freer spirit of versification I have joined one of still greater importance, — that of having a free and idiomatic cast of language. There is a cant of art as well as of nature, though the former is not so unpleasant as the latter, which affects non-affectation. But the proper language of poetry is in fact nothing different from that of real life, and depends for its dignity upon the strength and sentiment of what it speaks. It is only adding musical modulation to what a fine understanding might actually utter in the midst of its griefs or enjoyments. The poet therefore should do as Shakespeare or Chaucer did, — not copy what is obsolete or peculiar in either, any more than they copied their predecessors, — but use as much as possible an actual, existing language, — omitting of course *mere* vulgarisms and fugitive phrases, which are the cant of ordinary discourse."

Hunt got most of these opinions from the "Advertisement" to Wordsworth's *Lyrical Ballads*, published eighteen years before, in 1798. There was, then, nothing particularly new about them. But so slowly did fashions change a century ago, that they had by no means won current acceptance. Hunt's whole theory was excellent, the fault lay in his practice. Wordsworth was possessed of an innate dignity which Hunt was without. Wordsworth's mistakes in illustrating his theories, when he made mistakes, led to nothing worse than dullness of diction and puerility of theme; Hunt's mistakes in *Rimini* were due to his total conception, or rather misconception, of his story, and the result was a miserable, cheap form of expression which ended by smothering his poem in an atmosphere of coquettish vulgarity.

How incapable Hunt was of comprehending Dante's purpose or achievement in the *Inferno*, can be seen by another glance at his Preface. Speaking of the subject of his poem he says:

"The following story is founded on a passage in Dante . . . The passage in question — the episode of Paolo and

Francesca — has long been admired by the readers of Italian poetry, and is indeed the most cordial and refreshing one in the whole of that singular poem the Inferno, which some call a satire, and some an epic, and which, I confess, has always appeared to me a kind of sublime nightmare. We even lose sight of the place, in which the saturnine poet, according to his summary way of disposing both of friends and enemies, has thought proper to put the sufferers; and see the whole melancholy absurdity of his theology, in spite of itself, falling to nothing before one genuine impulse of the affections."

We need only that expression, "the affections," to give us the clue to Hunt's manner of treating his theme. A few quotations will suffice to show it in all its trite commonplace.

Francesca is introduced in this manner:

"What need I tell of lovely lips and eyes,
A clipsom waist, and bosom's balmy rise,
The dress of bridal white, and the dark curls
Bedding an airy coronet of pearls?"

We are also told that she had "stout notions on the marrying score." Paolo fares no better:

"A graceful nose was his, lightsomely brought
Down from a forehead of clear-spirited thought;
Wisdom looked sweet and inward from his eye;
And round his mouth was sensibility."

The meetings between the pair are conducted along the lines of fashionable country-house intercourse:

"He read with her, he rode, he went a hawking,
He spent still evenings in delightful talking."

But the worst of all these colloquial trivialities occurs in the scene in which Paolo and Francesca read the fatal book together. Francesca is sitting in a Summer-house, reading the romance of Lancelot of the Lake:

> "So sat she fixed; and so observed was she
> Of one, who at the door stood tenderly, —
> Paolo, — who from a window seeing her
> Go straight across the lawn, and guessing where,
> Had thought she was in tears, and found, that day,
> His usual efforts vain to keep away.
> 'May I come in?' said he: — it made her start, —
> That smiling voice; — she coloured, pressed her heart
> A moment, as for breath, and then with free
> And usual tone, said 'O yes, — certainly.'"

This is tragedy depressed to the level of coloured illustration.

All the poem is not so bad as these passages which I have chosen to quote. There are scattered bits of description which are quite charming, but the tone of the tale is that of these various lines.

And Keats admired this poem! Which shows the state of his mind at the time as well as any of his own poems show it. But in spite of cockneyism and immaturity, there was already another side to Keats, and it did not take him long to outgrow *Rimini*, as we shall see.

Hunt's treatment of his poem as story is one thing, his treatment of it in the matter of versification and English is another. But, even in this latter aspect, the poem fails for want of taste. The freer treatment of the couplet was a move in the right direction; succeeding generations have upheld Hunt in the use of feminine rhymes, triplets, and run-on lines. The death of the close couplet was in the air, and Hunt was certainly one of its murderers. But no one can defend his lax rhymes and his grammatical liberties. It is very trying to have "look" rhymed with "smoke," and "emerging" with "Virgin." Londoners of Keats's class and time evidently dropped their "g's," but no educated man — and Hunt was an educated man — permits the mispronunciations of daily life to appear in his writing. Hunt did, which proves him either lazy, or so dyed-in-the-wool a cockney that all his reading had not modified him. And there are worse infractions against good English than these. His vocabulary was so limited that he permitted himself to coin another to save himself the trouble of consulting a dictionary. He pushed past participles into adverbs, forced nouns to do duty as adjectives, put one part of speech when he should have put another — in short he made a higgledy-piggledy of grammar and countenanced it as freedom. The truth is that he sacrificed everything for one object, which was that his poem should be readable, and this in a measure he achieved, but not to anything like the extent to which he achieved it in prose. I know few essays more delightful to read than Hunt's. His poetry never reached their level.

It may seem incredible that Keats should have found beauty in the trivial little piece of tawdry sentiment which is the *Story of Rimini*. But such a sweeping condemnation is really beside the mark. It gives me pause to remember that, at the age of fourteen or fifteen, I, too, found it both beautiful and absorbing. Let us admit at once that, with all its absurdities, with all its weakness, false rhymes, and impossible grammar, the *Story of Rimini* has a certain life to it. It is not, at any rate, dull. At least it is not dull to romantic and unsophisticated youth. Its imagery is sensuous and full of colour. There is a real bustle and activity in its crowds. The gardens and pleasances are skillfully painted, and to a young person unacquainted with the story itself, or with Dante's telling of it, there is both romance and tragedy. I confess that reading it to-day, thirty years after my last reading, the only things that strike me as even passably good are the procession in the First Canto, the ride to Rimini, and the description of the gardens. But the early nineteenth century was an age of sentimentalism. Keats was steeped to his eyes in it, as we know. The influence of *Rimini* is over all his early work, especially the *Induction to a Poem*, *Calidore*, and parts of

Sleep and Poetry. There is everything in the poem to attract him, and we may thank Haydon, probably, and tough old Chapman, for so soon lifting him out of the point of view which could delight in it. But when Keats first read *Rimini*, Haydon and Chapman were still over the horizon. There was nobody to show him its shallowness. He simply tumbled into it head first, and there and then determined to write a poetic romance as much like this wonderful new model as possible.

There was, however, an awkward difficulty to be overcome, he had not the slightest idea what to write about. When he thought of a story, he saw a picture. He had been reading and marking his Spenser with diligence not long before. By dint of long acquaintance, Spenser's scene was more familiar to him than any other. It is quite natural, therefore, that this tale to be, presented itself to his mind in the form of an image culled from the age of chivalry. The title was evidently invented after the poem had failed to come off as intended, it is: *Specimen of an Induction to a Poem.*

The opening lines are a delightfully simple expression of his visual inspiration:

> "Lo! I must tell a tale of chivalry;
> For large white plumes are dancing in mine eye."

A few lines later his visual imagination adds to this:

> "Lo! I must tell a tale of chivalry;
> For while I muse, the lance points slantingly
> Athwart the morning air."

This is as vivid and reticent as a Japanese print. We have the exact atmosphere: the faint blue of the sky; the fresh, rather damp air; the silver, not the golden, sun. It is admirable, done with the greatest economy of means. Only slightly less good is this, of the lance:

> "Sometimes, when the good Knight his rest would take,
> It is reflected, clearly, in a lake,

> With the young ashen boughs, 'gainst which it rests,
> And th' half seen mossiness of linnets' nests."

That was what Keats saw and wanted to stamp into a picture; and that was, I think, all he saw. He might have made a sonnet upon it, and rested it there. To-day we should call it an "image" and attempt no more with it. One feels the charm, light gaiety, and Spring-like quality of the picture. But Keats knew nothing of "images," Chinese and Japanese poetry were unknown in their original forms in his day. A picture was not enough. It was not enough to suggest a tale of chivalry, he must tell it; and he had no tale to tell. A lady is thrust into the poem, a distressingly commonplace lady, whom the poet's best efforts to make real only make tasteless. Wordsworth and Hunt had failed to marry theory with practice in the matter of every-day speech in poetry, each through lack of taste. Keats, swallowing the theory with hearty good will, went equally astray. He tells us that the lady's "tender feet" are so cold that she cannot feel them, a realistic touch certainly, as she is standing on the top of a battlement open to all the four winds, but in this case an irrelevant one, so irrelevant that the stating of it breaks the mood. Hunt's unhappy influence is again seen in the pretty-prettiness of the line:

> "Wraps round her ample robe with happy trembling."

In the first place, used in this way, "trembling" is a noun, and the article is left out; in the second, the expression is altogether too trivial, a kind of triviality aping the highly affecting, to which we must, I fear, apply the epithet "tawdry."

One of the lines of the poem has a sort of biographical interest, for from it we may guess at several things. The line in question:

> "Oh, wherefore comes that steed so proudly by?"

contained a misprint when the poem appeared in Keats's first volume, *Poems*, 1817. The word "knight" was substituted for "steed." Keats has carefully corrected this in ink in all the copies given to his intimate friends that I have seen. But, oddly enough, the correction was not made in the copy given to the Misses Reynolds,[1] nor in the one given to Wordsworth.[2] The explanation for the first of these omissions probably lies in the fact that Marianne and Jane Reynolds were "girls," and not to be taken too seriously; but at first sight it does seem strange that Keats did not correct what is obviously a blunder in a volume given to a poet whom he admired so much as he did Wordsworth. The Wordsworth copy is inscribed "To W. Wordsworth with the Author's sincere Reverence." Another puzzling thing about this copy, and one which baffled me for a long time, was why no letter from Wordsworth acknowledging the book had ever turned up, not even so much as a reference to such a letter in any of Keats's letters, or the letters of his friends, which we have. Wordsworth found the contents so little to his liking that he never took the trouble to cut open most of the book, which fact led me to conclude that he simply ignored it and never wrote to the author at all. But the discovery of a long and carefully critical letter to John Hamilton Reynolds, acknowledging a presentation copy of Reynolds's *Naiad*, published a year earlier than Keats's *Poems*, made this seem improbable. At last what I believe to be the truth flashed upon me. Undoubtedly Keats gave Wordsworth the book one day at Haydon's studio. On the end-paper of the front cover is a drawing of a man kneeling, which may very possibly have been jotted down by Haydon for some purpose. It is well known that Haydon was fond of giving Keats's poems away. No less than four copies of *Endymion* given by Haydon to various people are in existence to-day.

[1] Author's Collection. [2] Day Collection.

I imagine that, the talk having fallen upon Keats's book on some occasion when both Keats and Wordsworth happened to be in the studio, Haydon may have produced a copy, and there and then, egged on by Haydon's enthusiasm, Keats may have written the inscription and given the book to Wordsworth. We can easily conceive that, in the flustered state in which Keats would most certainly be at such a moment, he either forgot the alteration to be made in the *Induction*, or, with a kind of pride, found the making of an alteration under the circumstances to smack of pedantry. All this is mere supposition, of course, but supposition which such facts as we know seem to point to, and it offers a reasonable explanation for a series of rather odd occurrences.

I have been forced into a long digression, now let me return with all haste to Keats writing his poem. Beyond his original image, he cannot go. A rather confused passage of the lance in war, at a tournament, and at a banquet, and the poet again exclaims, almost desperately: "Yet I must tell a tale of chivalry," but breaks off immediately to invoke the aid of Spenser through the intercession of Hunt, "thy lov'd Libertas," and here the poem ends. As it is, it is a picture spoilt, and a story never begun. Aware of its inadequateness, Keats calls it *Specimen of an Induction to a Poem*, and lets it go at that. It is an illustration of the psychology of the poet, for in it we see his constant early attempt to write, not as he wanted, not as his genius dictated, but as the canons of art as he knew them demanded. It is the first clear example of much of the tragedy of his writing life.

We have seen Keats in the Autumn, alone in Dean Street, comforting his longing for woods and fields by reading Wordsworth, and here, in spite of his immediate submission to Hunt, is a reminiscence of that reading, for line 51:

"And always does my heart with pleasure dance"

is amusingly derivative from Wordsworth's daffodils:

> "And then my heart with pleasure fills
> And dances with the daffodils."

Keats's first romance ended in failure, yet a rather nice failure, he thought, since he included it in *Poems*, 1817. But he was not satisfied, he must get out a story somehow. He promptly set to upon *Calidore*.

Calidore does not start with a picture, and not really with a story, but with the necessity of telling a story. Here we have merely description, not sight. The scene is something thought of, not viewed. For instance:

> ". . . and shadowy trees that lean
> So elegantly o'er the waters' brim
> And show their blossoms trim."

"Elegantly" and "trim" are cockney, if anything ever was. They are Keats in the sad moments when the subconscious goes on strike.

Keats's effort to do something very fine leads, in *Calidore*, to his doing something very silly. The poem begins: "Young Calidore is paddling o'er the lake," which announcement gives the poet an opportunity to beg the question of story for two pages. These two pages he devotes to description. But Keats is intent on the fine thing he is about to do, and he forgets to think himself back into fact — not a usual fault with him, by the way. Lacking any clear vision of the scene, he makes it up out of words only. There could hardly be a greater number of factual errors, all contained in a few lines, than there are in this passage:

> "Green tufted islands casting their soft shades
> Across the lake; sequester'd leafy glades,
> That through the dimness of their twilight show
> Large dock leaves, spiral foxgloves, or the glow
> Of the wild cat's eyes, or the silvery stems
> Of delicate birch trees, or long grass which hems

A little brook. The youth had long been viewing
These pleasant things, and heaven was bedewing
The mountain flowers, when his glad senses caught
A trumpet's silver voice."

Because an island is tufted, is no reason for it to cast a "soft shade." Foxgloves are not spiral. Wild cat's eyes can scarcely have been "pleasant things" to observe staring at one. Heaven does not bedew flowers, and why these should be "mountain flowers" when there is no mountain, is a mystery. In the next stanza appears a most unhappy metaphor, which is quite out of the picture. *Calidore* sees a castle on one of the islands to which he rows, and the nick of time which he takes to get to it is illustrated in this way:

"Nor will a bee buzz round two swelling peaches,
Before the point of his light shallop reaches
Those marble steps that through the water dip."

The metaphor is bad because, instead of heightening the description of the action, it presents a perfectly alien picture to the mind. We instantly see the hanging peaches and the bees buzzing round them, and this brings with it the sense of glittering sunlight. Calidore's twilight, Calidore himself, the island, the castle — all vanish, and we get them back with difficulty.

Yet there are good things in these two pages, and a hint of what Keats will do later on with scenes. The steps dipping into the water are well conceived.

At this point, Keats is forced to start on his story. Calidore mounts the steps:

"... Over them he goes with hasty trip,
And scarcely stays to ope the folding doors:
Anon he leaps along the oaken floors
Of halls and corridors."

Few things in poetry are worse than this grasshopper-like entrance of Calidore into the castle. Keats could hardly have chosen a series of more infelicitous words. And he continues in the same strain, with a true love scene out of Hunt's laboratory. It is too long to quote, and yet I will quote it, for no one who has not read it can appreciate what Keats had to outgrow, and the extraordinary speed with which he did it:

> "Delicious sounds! those little bright-eyed things
> That float about the air on azure wings,
> Had been less heartfelt to him than the clang
> Of clattering hoofs; into the court he sprang,
> Just as two noble steeds, and palfreys twain,
> Were slanting out their necks with loosened rein;
> While from beneath the threat'ning portcullis
> They brought their happy burthens. What a kiss,
> What gentle squeeze he gave each lady's hand!
> How tremblingly their delicate ankles spann'd!
> Into how sweet a trance his soul was gone,
> While whisperings of affection
> Made him delay to let their tender feet
> Come to the earth; with an incline so sweet
> From their low palfreys o'er his neck they bent:
> And whether there were tears of languishment,
> Or that the evening dew had pearl'd their tresses,
> He feels a moisture on his cheek, and blesses
> With lips that tremble, and with glistening eye,
> All the soft luxury
> That nestled in his arms. A dimpled hand,
> Fair as some wonder out of fairy land,
> Hung from his shoulder like the drooping flowers
> Of whitest Cassia, fresh from summer showers:
> And this he fondled with his happy cheek
> As if for joy he would no further seek;
> When the kind voice of good Sir Clerimond
> Came to his ear, like something from beyond
> His present being: so he gently drew
> His warm arms, thrilling now with pulses new,
> From their sweet thrall, and forward gently bending,
> Thank'd heaven that his joy was never ending;

> While 'gainst his forehead he devoutly press'd
> A hand heaven made to succour the distress'd;
> A hand that from the world's bleak promontory
> Had lifted Calidore for deeds of Glory."

Comment fails before that passage. The saccharine sentimentality of it is astounding, and no parody could exceed the ghastly rhodomontade of the last two lines.

Before Calidore and the ladies, stands a knight, to whom are given the two best lines of the poem:

> "So that the waving of his plumes would be
> High as the berries of a wild ash tree."

The knight greets Calidore, and the whole company go into a "pleasant chamber" and sit down, and we are told that

> "The sweet-lipp'd ladies have already greeted
> All the green leaves that round the window clamber."

This is certainly a most cordial houschold, where the very vines come in for a share of the abundant largess of the ladies' kisses. They compose themselves to ease:

> "Sir Gondibert has doff'd his shining steel,
> Gladdening in the free, and airy feel
> Of a light mantle."

This is the first time that Keats's favourite "feel" as a noun appears in his verse, and here it seems peculiarly objectionable. The poem ends with everybody sitting about comfortably and chatting, with moonlight, and the scent of lime flowers, and the song of the nightingale, and the sound of a distant trumpet, all coming in through the window. The poem breaks off in the middle of a line and closes with asterisks, as though Keats knew very well that he had not finished it.

A more disappointing "tale of chivalry" can scarcely be imagined. What attracted Keats to the period was not so much its spirit as its trappings. He loved the forests, the meads, the rivers, and islanded lakes. He loved the stuffs, the wrought devices on armour, the colours of banners and harness, the sound of trumpets in a bright and open air. All this ceremonial of pageant and banquet, all this gentle and courteous advance into love, with the paraphernalia of "bowers," "tapers," "silken couches," "goblets of sparkling wine," "moonlight on embroidered vestments," enchanted his imagination. Intrigued as he was by the purely external side of the age of chivalry, he could by no means give it a soul. *Calidore* is maudlin just because he found it luscious. Its fundamental badness, a badness quite apart from all its other faults, is that it is a product of intellect plus sensation, and is without an ounce of real feeling. He felt the plumes and the lance in the *Induction*, he felt nothing whatever in *Calidore*.

But we must not be too hard on Keats, nor shall we be if we remember the circumstances: the distasteful medical studies, the long hours by hospital beds, the uncongenial young men with whom he lodged, the part of London he lodged in. He was in love with beauty, and because he grasped it most easily through material things is far from meaning that he did not feel it in those of deeper significance. The stuff and nonsense of *Calidore* reveals more than a striving after picture-book literature, it reveals a spirit starved of those essentials to its health — love and beauty. Within the sentimental expression lies a sincere craving. These two poems are evidence of

> "The large-eyed wonder, and ambitious heat
> Of the aspiring boy,"

to quote from *Calidore*. We may ridicule — who could help it? We may even feel distinctly ashamed for Keats. But it is a poor analysis which does not comprehend the particular why of Keats's delight in the *Story of Rimini*, and the impulses, other than literary, from which the *Induction* and *Calidore* sprang.

Meanwhile an event was approaching which was to have an enormous effect upon Keats, was, in fact, to change his whole life. That the change would have come soon, at any rate, cannot be doubted, but this particular event brought it about more immediately than could otherwise have been the case. Cowden Clarke decided to show some of Keats's poems to Leigh Hunt.

Hunt, after leaving prison in 1815, had sojourned for a while at Maida Vale, but in the following Autumn had returned to Hampstead and early in 1816 was definitely settled in a little house in the Vale of Health. Hunt possessed the happy faculty of sociability. His house, even when it was a prison, became a meeting-place for his friends, and these friends were the chief writers, poets, artists, musicians, of the period — of all such, at least, as sympathized with Hunt's point of view. It was a sort of high class Bohemia, meeting between the four walls of a perfectly domestic home. Hampstead, in those days, was really country, but country only a little removed from town. It could be reached on foot easily enough, and Hunt's house was the ideal goal for a long walk; it could be reached by stage more easily still, with plenty of margin for strolls, chats, and tea. Clarke was a frequent visitor, and one fine day he carried with him a few of Keats's poems to see what Hunt thought of them. Horace Smith happened to be there also (it was the occasion on which he made the remark I have already quoted about the last line of *How many Bards*[1]), and the two men were much struck by the poems. Even Clarke's enthusiasm was "not prepared for the unhesitating and prompt admiration which broke forth before he [Hunt] had read twenty lines of the first poem." If the first poem consisted of twenty lines or more, it must have been the *Epistle to George Felton Matthew*, the *Induction*, or *Calidore*, for Clarke would certainly not have taken any of the earlier long things, and

[1] See Vol. I, p. 117.

it speaks volumes for Hunt's insight that he could deduce so much promise in the poems shown him. Hunt was a very good critic of everybody's work but his own. Along certain lines, he has never been surpassed. His own account of the incident shows clearly just what he felt and how much:

> [1] "I shall never forget the impression made upon me by the exuberant specimens of genuine though young poetry that were laid before me."

If we stop a moment to realize what, at this time, Keats had written, we shall be astonished at Hunt's acumen. We cannot doubt that Keats's sonnet on Hunt's leaving prison was in Clarke's bundle, and it argues much for Hunt's perspicacity that he rejected this, and the obvious imitations of his own style — the *Induction* and *Calidore* — and settled upon the *Sonnet to Solitude*, the most reticent poem of the lot, to print in the *Examiner*. For that is what he did, good fellow, he took the sonnet for his paper. Hunt was shrewd, however, and he had enjoyed a large experience with poetical aspirants. He would not commit himself to an interview without being sure of his man. Clarke reports his attitude without a hint of humour:

> "After making numerous and eager inquiries about him personally, and with reference to any peculiarities of mind and manner, the visit ended in my being requested to bring him over to the Vale of Health."

Keats being reported "dependable" in a social sense, Hunt characteristically flung his door open to him. He was not a man of half measures in friendship, at least not if he could help it. Hospitality was no theory with him; it was a sound, practical fact. In asking Clarke to bring Keats to see him, he was prepared, if circumstances warranted, to offer him the immediate freedom of his house.

[1] *Lord Byron and his Contemporaries*, by Leigh Hunt.

tions after MONMOUTH's enterprise: or, to adopt the case properly mentioned by Sir FRANCIS BURDETT, from the miscreants, clothed in ermine, who murdered those martyrs and ornaments of their age, RUSSELL and SYDNEY. Mr. LAW's legal reading and knowledge of history and facts must be miserably defective if he does not see a necessity for the fear he deprecates, and if he does not recognize in Parliament a court holding jurisdiction over every other court, capable not only of investigating judicial proceedings, but also of sending to impeachment and chastisement every Judge in the kingdom. Judges, like other men, are fallible; and we have seen that even the voice of conscience, and the solemnity of oaths, have yielded to the baleful influence of bad circumstances. What then remains but the fear of public opinion and Parliamentary inquiry? Has Mr. LAW to be told, that if fear takes away the judgment, so do flattery of and fawning on the Great. Let us suppose a Judge the constant attendant at levees, the haunter of palaces, a man of aspiring ambition, anxious to aggrandize himself and family,—take away the fear of Parliamentary enquiry from such a Judge and he may become the compliant sycophant and mere tool of power, eager to stretch royal prerogative and invade public right, the partaker of indecent orgies, and the minister of vengeance on such as denounce despotism and its vices—the base prototype of Cambyses' Judges, who when their approbation was demanded by the Prince to some illegal measure, said that though there was a written law, the Persian Kings might follow their own will and pleasure.

"Our suspicions respecting Sweden were not without foundation. A war between that country and Denmark is hinted at in the French papers. The journey of the Ex-King to the North is doubtless connected with this state of affairs, and we should not be at all surprised to see M. BERNADOTTE follow the example of the other Potentates whom the French Revolution raised from obscurity to thrones."—*Sun.*

Besides Count TORRENO, five or six other Spaniards have been arrested at Paris. It is also said, that all the Spanish refugees in France, who reside in Provinces adjoining to Spain, have been ordered to retire into the interior of the kingdom.

They write from the Hague, that the French Refugees have received orders to retire to the towns situated in the northern parts of the Netherlands.

The republic of letters has just sustained a loss by the death of Sir HERBERT CROFT, who lived in France for the last 15 years.

An Extraordinary Gazette of the Government of Lima, dated the 23d of December, 1815, contains a dispatch from PEZUELA, the General in Chief of the army of Upper Peru, in which he boasts of having obtained a complete victory over RONDEAU, who commands the army of the Buenos Ayres rebels, as they are called.

On Friday a Special Court of Common Council was held at Guildhall, when Mr. Alderman BIRCH moved an Address to the PRINCE REGENT, congratulating him on the Marriage of the Princess CHARLOTTE with the Prince of COBOURG: another Address of a similar nature to the QUEEN; and the compliments and congratulations of the Court to the Princess CHARLOTTE, and to the Prince of COBOURG, separately. The motion was unanimously agreed to.

A letter has appeared, Signed "JOS. JACKSON," relative to the West India Colonies and the Appointment of Agents in this country. Upon this letter, and upon Colonial affairs in general, we shall shortly have something to communicate, which will abundantly prove, that the system now established is founded in deception, corruption, and injustice.

Some foreign Papers have alluded to a Note, addressed by the Court of Rome to the Minister Plenipotentiary of the King of the Netherlands, approving the conduct of the Belgic Prelates, in refusing to accept certain Articles of the new Ecclesiastical Constitution.

A letter dated Verona, April 10, speaking of the death of the Empress of AUSTRIA, says, "One cannot make too public the noble and affecting scene that the last moments of the Empress presented. This august Princess desired to see successively, in private, all the persons of her household; she addressed to each of them words of kindness and consolation. She expressed some satisfaction that the Archduchess BEATRICE, her mother, was accidentally at a distance from a scene which would have too deeply affected her heart.—"The road to the tomb," said the dying Princess, "is that of truth; all illusions cease; there is no more flattery, there is no more grandeur; it must be forgotten that I have been Empress and Queen. I wish that people may retain of me sentiments honourable to my memory." Her MAJESTY desired to embrace the Ladies who approached the nearest to her, and the following were the last words that could be collected:—"Happiness is in a good conscience: I feel this soothing sentiment much more in death than upon the Throne.—Adieu! my friends! my children! Adieu!"—She ceased to breathe."

To the City Address respecting the French Protestants, the PRINCE REGENT has returned the following "most gracious" Answer:—

"The just sense entertained by his Majesty's subjects of the value and importance of Religious Toleration is necessarily calculated to excite in their minds strong feeling of uneasiness and regret at any appearance of the want of it in other nations of the world.—In such feelings, when called for and justified by the occasion, I shall ever participate: and, whilst I lament the circumstances which led to your Address, I derive great satisfaction from the persuasion that they are in no degree to be attributed to an indisposition on the part of the Government of France to afford to the freedom of Religious Worship the benefit of its promised protection and support."

A letter has been forwarded to us respecting the death of a soldier, named *Hegg*, belonging to the 3d regiment of Guards. The Writer asserts, that the Sister of the deceased, on visiting him in the hospital, was told by him, that he had received an injury in his arm, and that he should not see her any more. He died soon after. Previous to this, he had complained of severe pain in his arm, which he attributed to the extent of the incision made when he was bled, which is described in the letter as being large enough to admit the first joint of the little finger. The Writer says, it has been given out that hard drinking occasioned Hegg's death; but this he strongly denies; and he adds, that the Sister of the deceased was refused admittance to see the remains, till the body was so changed that she with difficulty recognised it to be her brother's, and the blood was then oozing through the shroud.

TO SOLITUDE.

O SOLITUDE! if I must with thee dwell,
Let it not be among the jumbled heap
Of murky buildings;—climb with me the steep,
Nature's Observatory—whence the dell,
Its flowery slopes—its rivers crystal swell,
May seem a span: let me thy vigils keep
'Mongst boughs pavilioned; where the Deer's swift leap
Startles the wild Bee from the Fox-glove bell.
Ah! fain would I frequent such scenes with thee;
But the sweet converse of an innocent mind,
Whose words are images of thoughts refin'd,
Is my soul's pleasure; and it sure must be
Almost the highest bliss of human kind,
When to thy haunts two kindred spirits flee.

J. K.

PAGE OF THE "EXAMINER" CONTAINING KEATS'S SONNET "TO SOLITUDE"

From the collection of Louis A. Holman, Esq.

When the meeting took place exactly, we do not know, but Hunt has clearly stated[1] that when he printed the *Sonnet to Solitude* he had not yet met Keats personally. The sonnet appeared in the *Examiner* of May fifth, 1816, and the inference of Hunt's paragraph is that the meeting occurred directly afterwards.

What the suggestion of such an interview must have meant to Keats, we can easily imagine. When Clarke told him that Hunt was to print his sonnet, the news must have been overwhelming. To be really in print is an enormous step for any man who cherishes designs on literature. I believe that those fourteen lines in actual type were the determining factor in Keats's decision to give up surgery; but the idea was still in embryo, for it was only two months since he had entered himself for another year's term at the hospital. The idea once in his head, he began coquetting with it, and the coquetting gradually became a convinced purpose. Yet I do not believe his abandoning surgery was so much because he disliked that profession as that he liked poetry a great deal better. Keats, entirely apart from his poetic faculty, was a decidedly able man. After all, a sensible man breaks with some reluctance from a calling he has pursued for five years. Keats never played the poet. He was no precocious youngster vapouring about the artist's *milieu*. Hitherto he had simply considered it impossible for him not to be a surgeon. The printing of the sonnet revealed to him a hesitating doubt. Suppose — suppose — and that, I think, was as far as he dared to go, for he wisely did nothing at the moment, not until he had got his diploma.

They went, then, Clarke and Keats, to call upon Hunt. Clarke has described Keats's looks and attitude on the occasion:

> "That was a 'red-letter day' in the young poet's life, and one which will never fade with me while memory

[1] Review of Keats's *Poems* in the *Examiner*, July 9, 1817.

> lasts. The character and expression of Keats's features would arrest even the casual passenger in the street; and now they were wrought to a tone of animation that I could not but watch with interest, knowing what was in store for him from the bland encouragement, and Spartan deference in attention, with fascinating conversational eloquence, that he was to encounter and receive. As we approached the Heath, there was the rising and accelerated step, with the gradual subsidence of all talk. The interview, which stretched into three 'morning calls,' was the prelude to many after-scenes and saunterings about Caen Wood and its neighbourhood; for Keats was suddenly made a familiar of the household, and was always welcomed."

It has been the fashion of recent years to belittle Hunt, to patronize him as a man of small account, and Keats's admirers and biographers have outdone one another in denouncing him as the instigator of all that is worst in Keats's poetry. But this is a myopic view. A man of no account does not persist in living for a hundred years as a personality to be reckoned with, even to the extent of cursing, to continually succeeding generations. Hunt was not a great creator certainly, but he was a great introducer. His peculiar quality was that he considered poetry as an art, not as a rag-bag for inconsequential erudition. Would that a score of Hunts could be dotted round among our colleges; it would do us a world of good. I can never forget that it was his *Imagination and Fancy* which first taught me what poetry was. There is no better text-book for the appreciation of poetry than that volume. He had what I may call a touch-stone mind; he knew instinctively what was good and never feared to proclaim it. His limitations are plain enough, and became only too plain to Keats later on. But that he stimulated Keats to increasing effort, no one can fail to see. The books by which we know him best were none of them written in Keats's day, but the man who wrote them was there in his conversation.

Forget that he perpetrated *Rimini*, and then notice what an immeasurable advance *I Stood Tip-toe Upon a Little Hill* is over the *Induction* and *Calidore*. If his influence had been entirely baneful, Keats would not have improved so much in a few short months as the comparison of these poems shows that he did. Hunt was suggestive; that was, and is, his secret. He may be outgrown, but at a certain stage he is invaluable, and Keats encountered him at just that stage. He was that rare thing, a constructive critic; he knew how to instruct without dampening. Where he erred was in being too kind. But give Keats half a chance and he could not help learning, he learnt so fast that he outlearnt his teacher in a short time, but that is only to say that Keats was a genius and Hunt was not. That Hunt did not gauge the difference quite soon enough, merely argues Hunt's very natural slowness when brought into contact with so swift a mind as Keats possessed. It is, after all, the incident of the hen who hatched a duckling, all over again; but the duckling would have been in very poor case at one stage without the hen.

Let us see for a few moments what Hunt's contemporaries thought of him — not the men of a later period, who doled pence into his dripping pockets and gave him odd literary jobs to keep his old age going, with a gentle compassion, indeed, but also with a good deal of condescension. He outlived his time. The youth of his old age was tuned to another key. He had faults in plenty; he borrowed of everyone and never returned a copper. Many faults always, but marked virtues too, and the chief of these were sincerity and a kindly good nature which he never outgrew. The men who knew him in daily intercourse all attest his charm. To Charles Lamb, he was "one of the most cordial-minded men I ever knew, a matchless fireside companion." Hazlitt, in a half-humourous, wholly complaining, letter to Hunt, says: "I have said you were one of the pleasantest and cleverest persons I ever knew, but that you teased any one you had to deal with out of their lives," both of which facts are undoubtedly true. Crabbe Robinson calls Hunt "an enthusiast, very well intentioned"; he describes the impression of one meeting by saying: "There was a glee about him." Robinson's summing up of Hunt is very pertinent: "He loves everything, he catches the sunny side of everything, and excepting that he has a few polemical antipathies, finds everything beautiful." The exuberant Haydon says practically the same thing, if we make allowance for his usual garishness of expression. He writes to Wilkie on October twenty-seventh, 1816:

> "I have been at Hampstead this fortnight for my eyes, and shall return with my body much stronger for application. The greater part of my time has been spent in Leigh Hunt's society, who is certainly one of the most delightful companions. Full of poetry and art, and amiable humour, we argue always with full hearts on everything but religion and Buonaparte, and we have resolved never to talk of these . . . Though Leigh Hunt is not deep in knowledge, moral, metaphysical, or classical, yet he is intense in feeling, and has an intellect forever on the alert. . . . As a poet, I think him full of genuine feeling. His third canto in 'Rimini' is equal to anything in any language of that sweet sort."

We see by this last sentence how the Hunt circle took *Rimini*. Small wonder, therefore, that Keats should have been its dupe for a while. Later Haydon quarrelled with Hunt over the non-return of some spoons borrowed by Mrs. Hunt, but even after that Haydon could not resist Hunt's perennial attractiveness, he records that

> "Accidentally meeting him at a friend's, he was so exceedingly delightful I could not resist the dog. We forgot our quarrels and walked away together, quoting, and joking and laughing as if nothing had happened."

Hunt's faults estranged his friends; his charm and perfectly sincere warm-heartedness held them; one and all, they fell in and out with him over and over again, and in the end they all have a good word to say. With his enemies, it was a different matter; both his literary canons and his radical political opinions raised up for him a host of bitter enemies. He was pursued, in these early years, driven, tormented, by the adherents of a Tory government, yet he stood firm. His host of enemies alone is enough to disprove the theory of his being a man of no importance. So much ink is not spilled over a nonentity. He cooled down into a gentle and tolerated old man — true; but he had had a fiery youth, and when Keats met him he was in his heyday.

Apparently Keats did not meet any of Hunt's more intimate friends during the early Summer of 1816; or, if he did meet them, the meetings led to no consequences. Hunt himself was a vastly stimulating, but possibly a somewhat awe-inspiring, companion, in the beginning of their acquaintance. Keats was anything but a hero-worshipper in actual life, he held his own with perfect dignity and independence always, but it would have been very strange if he had not considered himself lucky beyond reason in being permitted to stroll and talk with Hunt. The hail-fellow-well-met days of their companionship do not seem to have begun until the Autumn. Keats was a very busy man in May and June, his examinations were coming on in July and he had no intention of failing in them. If he coquetted with the idea of giving up everything for poetry, as I have suggested, he did so with admirable common-sense. An apothecary's diploma once his, he was prepared for any eventuality. He would get it, and what he did afterwards was his own affair. Besides, Abbey was still in the background, and Keats would not come of age until the very end of the next October. But no matter how hard he had to study, no matter how often he stole time to run out to Hampstead, he went right on writing poetry. The most important poem of this period is *I Stood Tip-toe Upon a Little Hill.*

Sir Sidney Colvin thinks that *I Stood Tip-toe* was written in the following Autumn or Winter. I am compelled to disagree with him. That the poem was not *finished* until the Winter, we know, for in a letter to Charles Cowden Clarke, postmarked December 17, 1816, Keats says: "I have done little to 'Endymion' lately — I hope to finish it in one more attack." *Tip-toe* was first called *Endymion*, but was eventually published in *Poems*, 1817, without a title, presumably because, before the book was printed, Keats had begun to plan his long poem of that name. My reasons for differing from Sir Sidney are, first, Hunt's distinct statement:[1] "This poem was suggested to Keats by a delightful summer's day, as he stood beside the gate that leads from the Battery on Hampstead Heath into a field by Caen Wood." Professor de Sélincourt, who makes no attempt to date the poem, after recording Keats's letter, does say however: "But the earlier part of the poem at least reads more like a summer rhapsody than a mere winter's reminiscence." To be sure it does, and so much so that, without Keats's letter, the poem would date itself automatically. It is scarcely likely that Keats, all keyed up as he must have been by his intercourse with Hunt, should not have felt impelled to write something. The exuberance with which the poem overflows points to some particular excitement over and above the Summer's day. My second reason, then, is just this, the evidence of the lines themselves. My third reason is the entire difference of attitude and tone in this poem and in *Sleep and Poetry*. *I Stood Tip-toe* is delightfully unpremeditated, it is a perfect burst of enthusiasm; *Sleep and Poetry* is premeditated throughout. Keats worked over *I Stood Tip-toe* with great care, as we can see by a fragment of the first draft[2]

[1] *Lord Byron and his Contemporaries*, by Leigh Hunt.
[2] Widener Library. Harvard University.

which is still extant, he may even have written the much less good last part in the Autumn and Winter, but that it was begun immediately after the walk which fathered it seems abundantly evident.

I Stood Tip-toe is the first thoroughly characteristic poem which Keats wrote. The days of his "juvenilia" are definitely over. However many poor poems he afterwards composed, and they were not a few, they were mere lapses, for, in *I Stood Tip-toe*, Keats struck the vein which was eminently and absolutely his. The poem is less a completed work of art than the *Odes*, for instance, but there are passages in it which he never surpassed. The whole beginning is magnificent, I do not know that Keats has anywhere done better descriptions.

I Stood Tip-toe is so well known that there is no need to quote it; but there is some need to examine it in detail, I think, if we would follow Keats's development as man and poet.

To begin with, we must postulate conditions. Keats is in a perfect fury of delight. Life is teeming with interest, the world is extraordinarily beautiful. His happiness is so great that everything he sees is brighter, finer, lovelier, than anything has ever been before. When we think of Keats's life as "painful," we must not forget to balance that thought by the recollection of his absolute rapture in moods like this which produced *I Stood Tip-toe*.

Keats heads the poem with a motto from the beloved Rimini: "Places of nestling green for Poets made." The beginning of the poem, although it does not contain any of its best lines, is so important that I must quote it:

"I stood tip-toe upon a little hill,
The air was cooling, and so very still,
That the sweet buds that with a modest pride
Pull droopingly, in slanting curve aside,
Their scantly leaved, and finely tapering stems,
Had not yet lost those starry diadems

> Caught from the early sobbing of the morn.
> The clouds were pure and white as flocks new shorn,
> And fresh from the clear brook; sweetly they slept
> On the blue fields of heaven, and then there crept
> A little noiseless noise among the leaves,
> Born of the very sigh that silence heaves:
> For not the faintest motion could be seen
> Of all the shades that slanted o'er the green."

There is much food for thought in that passage, for it mingles two perfectly distinct types of poetry, an old and a new; and two opposed forms of expression, a stereotyped and an original. Much of it is artificial, much is *cliché*. As illustrations of the former, there is the "modest pride" of the buds, the "sobbing of the morn," and "morn" itself; for the latter, there is the old metaphor of clouds as sheep, only relieved by the fancy of their having just come out of a fresh brook, and the other ancient figure of the sky as a blue field. Keats was dogged by this kind of thing in his early work. His literary life was one long effort to escape from it and remain poetic. Again and again he fell back, always to make a new start toward freedom. But there is the second type of poetry to be considered, and the second form of expression. The "modest pride" of the buds is unfortunate — granted, but what could be better as observation, more true to fact, than that they

> "Pull droopingly, in slanting curve aside,
> Their scantly leaved, and finely tapering stems,"

and what originality of expression the "slanting" shows, a modern touch, which was then only modern because it was indubitably Keats. We see the same thing in the "shades that slanted o'er the green." We regret "o'er" because it is a contraction which present-day poetry has agreed to drop, but naturally it did not trouble Keats's ear, intent upon the slants of light, shade, and tint. The "noiseless noise" is absolutely perfect, and what a strange thing that this effect of Summer calm should have been noted by Dorothy Wordsworth in the very same words. In her Alfoxden Journal for January twenty-third, 1798, she speaks of "That noiseless noise which lives in the summer air." Keats could not possibly have known this, the duplicate expression is mere coincidence, but it goes to show how minutely careful both Keats and Dorothy Wordsworth were in recording natural impressions. Lovers of nature, the two of them. After this beginning, Keats is much more himself. The whole first part thereafter, until the entrance of the maiden, is free of both artificiality and unobservant figure. It is a marvel of first-hand writing.

A few lines farther on there is a perfect description of the how and the why of the poem:

> "I gazed awhile, and felt as light, and free
> As though the fanning wings of Mercury
> Had played upon my heels: I was light-hearted
> And many pleasures to my vision started;
> So I straightway began to pluck a posey
> Of luxuries bright, milky, soft and rosy."

We may take the poem, then, as being simply a series of "luxuries." The first stanza represents the scene he saw; the succeeding stanzas, the scenes he imagines.

Keats was very sensitive to three kinds of beauty: beauty of natural objects, beauty of story, beauty of phrase. At this period, he was not awakened to the beauty of human passion, that developed later.

Evidently *I Stood Tip-toe* was a favourite poem with Keats and with his friends. We happen to know just what they thought about it. In a copy of the *Poems*[1] given by Keats to his brother George, many of the lines are underscored. For instance, in the passage:

> "A filbert hedge with wild briar overtwined,
> And clumps of woodbine taking the soft wind

[1] Author's Collection.

> Upon their summer thrones; there too should be
> The frequent chequer of a youngling tree"

the lines

> "... clumps of woodbine taking the soft wind
> Upon their summer thrones"

is not only scored, but double-scored, while the far more beautiful "chequer of a youngling tree" is not marked at all. The superb passage beginning:

> "Open afresh your round of starry folds
> Ye ardent marigolds!"

is marked, and the splendid short line double marked. The sweet-pea passage is scored, and "on tip-toe for a flight" double-scored. The minnows and goldfinches are scored, but not double-scored. The rising moon is scored, and the excellent word "swim" approved by double-scoring. The apostrophe to the moon, "O maker of sweet poets" is double-scored, but one cannot think that this was so much for its wording as for what the boys undoubtedly believed to be its truth.

The sentimentality of the time and the environment creeps in too, in the double-scoring of the "nips" which Cupid and Psyche "gave each other's cheeks," in the double-scoring of the four lines which begin "Poor nymph, — poor Pan," and which end with the horrible "balmy pain," and in the friends who, beholding the recovery of those sick, are "nigh foolish with delight." But it is only fair to add that the beautiful line, "Full in the speculation of the stars," is also double-scored.

Let us see what Keats has put into his "world of blisses" as he calls it in line 49. A bush of May flowers full of bees; a "lush laburnam"; moss; violets; a filbert hedge overgrown with sweet-briar; a brook, its banks covered with blue-bells; marigolds, hot and burning; sweet-peas, so perfectly *felt*, so entirely presented, that the passage *is* sweet-peas forever after to any one who has read it. This is a catalogue of things that Keats likes. It is foolish to seek an allegory beneath the words, none is needed. This is a portrait of John Keats aged twenty, recorded in a list of "luxuries."

Leaving flowers, Keats, started by his "spring-head of clear waters," bethinks him of a brook he knows. Cowden Clarke says that Keats told him that this brook passage was a recollection of walks taken together, when they [1]"frequently loitered over the rail of a foot-bridge that spanned . . . a little brook in the last field upon entering Edmonton." What better description is there in literature of the smooth flowing of a deep brook than "How silent comes the water round that bend"? One can almost smell the dampness of it. But, even here, Keats is caught in the net of his reading. How could he lug in Shakespeare so crudely! And he did not better the passage in *As You Like It:*

> "Find tongues in trees, books in the running brooks,
> Sermons in stones, and good in everything"

with his

> "To where the hurrying freshnesses aye preach
> A natural sermon o'er their pebbly beds."

The goldfinches, his next "luxury," may have been borrowed from Chaucer's *The Floure and the Lefe:*

> "Therein a goldfinch leaping pretile
> Fro bough to bough, and as him list he eet
> Here and there of buds and floures sweet,"

as Woodhouse thinks, but that would go to prove Cowden Clarke's memory at fault in believing that Keats had not read Chaucer until the following February, when he found a volume of that poet in Clarke's room. Clarke is very

[1] *Recollections of Writers*, by Charles Cowden Clarke.

careful to state that he is not absolutely certain that this was Keats's first introduction to Chaucer, but Woodhouse has the true student's love of tracing sources. After all, what need had Keats for Chaucer's goldfinches when he had the birds themselves to remember? In spite of Woodhouse, it seems more likely that he took his picture from real goldfinches often seen. At any rate, this is not borrowing, but metamorphosing, and is open to no such objection as the stealing of Shakespeare's "sermons."

The next "bliss," not unnaturally in a youth of twenty, is a woman, but Keats was not happy in drawing women. We may dismiss this lady of the "locks auburne" as having nothing very attractive about her except the rustle of her dress "fanning away the dandelion's down." The lady, having crossed the bridge and departed from the poem, Keats exclaims "What next?" And the "next" is perhaps the most beautiful passage in the whole poem:

> ". . . A tuft of evening primroses,
> O'er which the mind may hover till it dozes;
> O'er which it well might take a pleasant sleep,
> But that 'tis ever startled by the leap
> Of buds into ripe flowers; or by the flitting
> Of diverse moths, that aye their rest are quitting;
> Or by the moon lifting her silver rim
> Above a cloud, and with a gradual swim
> Coming into the blue with all her light."

Lord Houghton notes a variant reading of the last two lines of this passage:

> "Floating through space with ever-living eye,
> The crowned queen of ocean and the sky."

Here we have it — artificiality and *cliché*, both at once. We may thank the power of growth in Keats which caused him to strike them out and substitute the daring originality of the lines as they stand.

Immediately following upon this passage is an invocation to the moon, Keats's tutelary goddess. The genesis of Keats's peculiar love for the moon appears in it, the moon which meant to him something so illusive and beautiful, so mystical and pure, so inciting and satisfying, that, despite his many attempts, he was never able to express the full complexity of his feeling in words. The moon, to Keats, was both itself and a symbol; its shining was peace, the glimmer and smoothness of its light and shade were the ever baffled search of an ideal leading through mystery to imagined truth. There is no aspect of the moon, seen, or experienced in the penumbra of dreaming, with which Keats was not familiar. He dwelt with her in his heart. She was his rapture, his torment, his provocation to a bold and achieving life, his comforter, his pride. Only later, when life grew imperative and anxious, did Keats lose his preoccupation with the moon.

The invocation begins:

> "O Maker of sweet poets, dear delight
> Of this fair world, and all its gentle livers;
> Spangler of clouds, halo of crystal rivers,
> Mingler with leaves, and dew and tumbling streams."

But *I Stood Tip-toe* is not *Endymion*. Keats has not yet reached a full understanding of what, to him, is involved in the moon. Here the moon's chief glory is to

> "... smile on us to tell delightful stories,"

and he goes on to picture these stories with the peculiar scene which each sort of tale suggests. The finest and simplest of these scenes is that contained in the lines:

> "In the calm grandeur of a sober line,
> We see the waving of the mountain pine."

It is perhaps worth while to notice another reminiscence of his reading in the "mountain pine." A pine, a pine on a mountain — it is a delightful thought, the essence of lonely, elevated grandeur, just the sort of thing Keats never failed to observe. This mountain pine is full of connotations to the imaginative mind. Keats had never seen a mountain when he wrote *Tip-toe*, but he had seen pines and he had read in *Cymbeline* of

> "... the rud'st wind
> That by the top doth take the mountain pine,"

and in the *Merchant of Venice* that

> "You may as well forbid the mountain pines
> To wag their high tops and to make no noise,
> When they are fretted with the gusts of heaven."

Not only the pine, but the wind taking the pine, intrigued him. We have seen how the flight of wind and its effect upon foliage had always intrigued him. In this very poem he has remarked the wind blowing across a clump of woodbine. Knowing this, we can feel the appropriateness of his "waving of the mountain pine." He conceives it standing alone, bending to a high air, and, contemplating it so, what better illustration could he have for the "calm grandeur of a sober line"! When Keats uses his reading in this way, he is not copying, but recording an experience, none the less real because it is vicarious, engendered in his imagination. The mountain pine stayed with him, as intense experiences always do. We find it again in *Endymion* in the Hymn to Pan:

> "By every wind that nods the mountain pine."

The moon leads Keats to mythology, and he proceeds to detail the "luxuries" of legend: Cupid and Psyche; Pan and Syrinx; Narcissus; and finally Endymion, whose love for the moon makes him a particularly sympathetic hero to Keats. It must be admitted that, in spite of lines of much beauty, the telling of these legends is too much touched with sentimentality to keep them on a level with the first part of the poem. They are, in fact, boyish, a lapse backward in technique. The sure touch of the earlier descriptive passages is not in them.

The poem ends on a wide leap of the imagination. One might almost call it a spiritually autobiographic leap. Keats conceives that from the love of Diana and Endymion a poet is born. What poet is in kinship of spirit nearer to these two than himself? He does not quite say so, but there is little doubt that he dallied with the idea — playfully in seeming, but unquestionably in his own heart with a much deeper significance. He laughed with himself at the idea, and yet he cherished it. Both the humour and the significance of this bold thrust of fancy are in the last four lines:

> "Cynthia! I cannot tell the greater blisses,
> That follow'd thine, and thy dear shepherd's kisses:
> Was there a Poet born? — but now no more,
> My wand'ring spirit must no farther soar."

No holograph of *I Stood Tip-toe* was known to Keats's early editors, or, at least, no holograph of a first draught. A fair copy of a part of the poem (lines 96 to 182) was in the Rowfant collection and is now in mine. In his Complete Edition, Buxton Forman has noted its variant readings from the printed text. They are few and unimportant. The single sheet on which Keats copied the passage has an inscription in Haydon's handwriting written sideways in the margin: "Given me by my Dear Friend Keats — B. R. Haydon." Two fragments of the first draft are extant, however, one beginning with line 38 and ending with line 48, and the other, which is merely the reverse of the sheet, consisting of twelve lines starting with line 53. This scrap, evidently cut from the full manuscript, was given to James T. Fields, the Boston publisher, by Charles Cowden Clarke, and is now in the Widener Library. Its obverse side was reproduced by Mrs. Fields in *Scribner's*

Magazine for March, 1888, and again, later, in her volume, *A Shelf of Old Books*, published in 1895. It is therefore a little odd that Buxton Forman should have failed to incorporate its readings in the text of his Complete Edition, published in 1900. Apparently he knew nothing of it, and only came across it in time to print it as an "addendum" to the first volume of that edition. Professor de Sélincourt ignores it completely, so I suppose that he is not yet aware of its existence.

This first fragment is particularly interesting as showing Keats working and reworking, even in the heat of composition, and clearly reveals why a poem conceived in Midsummer took months to finish. Keats often had several poems going at once, and worked at whatever one he felt in the mood for at any given time, which is the reason that his poems remained in a half-finished state so long.

The line "The frequent chequer of a youngling tree" was at first not that at all, but began: "The delicate ash," and "delicate" was originally something else, a word I have been unable to decipher. However, this beginning was immediately cancelled in favour of the line as it now stands, except that "a" was originally "some." The next line began "Of beechen green," which gave place at once to "That shoots with many of its light green peers." Then "shoots" was struck out and "sprouts" substituted. Finally, all this was scratched out, and the line as it is now was written underneath. The forty-first line read first: "Round which is found the spring-head of a stream," which was soon changed to the present "Round which is heard a spring-head of clear waters." The daughters of the stream were first "blue eyed," then "fragrant," then "fairest," and finally "blooming," the text reading of "lovely" is evidently the result of a later revision; and they were "woodland hyacinths" to start with, but this was abandoned as soon as written and "Spreading blue bells" boldly begins again the unfinished line, which is at once carried to a triumphant conclusion. The marigold passage is illuminating. It originally began "Come ye bright Marigolds," and there the line stops, whether because Keats cancelled what he had written before finishing the line, or whether he at first intended to begin the passage with a short line instead of ending it so, it is impossible to tell. The forty-seventh line starts off: "Open afresh your congregated," but before he writes "folds" Keats decides against the adjective and puts above it "crowns," immediately completing the line with "of starry folds." Nevertheless, "crowns" does not entirely satisfy him and he deletes it in favour of "cinques," but again writes above, "round," although without scratching out "cinques," leaving the two words as alternatives to be decided upon later. "Ye ardent marigolds" came at once in all its glorious perfection, but minus the exclamation point. Keats's punctuation is largely of the type which is put in afterwards.

The use of short lines is particularly interesting in view of what Keats did with them afterwards in the various songs in *Endymion*. Professor de Sélincourt thinks that he caught the trick of them from Spenser's nuptial *Odes*, or from Milton's *Lycidas* — very probably, and both together.

The second fragment contains a discovery. It begins, as I have said, with line 53; but the line following line 60 is not, as we should expect, 61, but 107. After this, the fragment continues substantially as we know it, ending with line 110. This looks as though the fifty lines which tell of the minnows and goldfishes and the auburn-haired maiden were an afterthought due to revision. Unfortunately, since we have no more of the first draft, this discovery leads to nothing more definite than a query.

How much of *I Stood Tip-toe* was done in the Summer, we can only guess. If there were any actual break, I should suppose it to have occurred just before the invocation. What is more probable is that Keats wrote most of the part preceding this in his first heat and roughly sketched the course of the second section in his mind, and that he kept tinkering on the whole poem constantly until it was done.

I Stood Tip-toe does not represent all the poetry that Keats wrote during May and June. There are three fugitive sonnets which we know of. His impending examination only troubled the rim of his mind, evidently, although it must have taken up a good deal of valuable time.

Among Keats's friends was a certain Charles Wells, who had been a schoolfellow of Tom's though not of his brothers. Wells was a red-haired, snub-nosed, blue-eyed, little fellow,[1] full of boisterous spirits, and with an irrepressible fondness for practical jokes. Keats liked him very well, until his tendency towards practical joking led him to play a cruel prank on Tom Keats which John never forgave. He is known to posterity as the author of a now defunct poem, *Joseph and his Brethren*, published some years after Keats's death. This poem had a recrudescence, many years after its appearance, owing to the surprising admiration of Rossetti, but has long faded out of sight. In 1816, Wells was a boy of fifteen, and for some reason he was moved to send Keats a bunch of roses. Buxton Forman, who got his information from Horne, thinks that the roses were in the nature of an apology from Wells for having offended Keats in some way. At any rate, he sent them, and Keats replied with a sonnet. *To a Friend who sent me some Roses* is a pleasant, though not particularly good, sonnet, but it shows Keats's reading at the time. Yes, the short lines in *I Stood Tip-toe* may very well have come from *Lycidas*, for here is *Lycidas* again in the second line of the sonnet. "What time the sky-lark" is just "What time the grayfly" of Milton's poem. Keats unblushingly

[1] Colvin.

changes his live-stock and considers the expression his. I cannot dismiss this sonnet without noting Keats's fanciful way of producing atmosphere. He wanders in the fields "what time the sky-lark" etc., but also

> ". . . when anew
> Adventurous knights take up their dinted shields,"

which is surely one of the most Spring-like things ever written, although one would be puzzled to say why.

Some time earlier in the month, the far better sonnet, *To one who has been long in city pent*, was composed. George Keats wrote on a transcript he made of the poem: "Written in the Fields — June, 1816." The "fields" were undoubtedly Hampstead Heath and its environs. Did Keats not notice, or did he not care, that he was indebted to *Paradise Lost* for his first line? Milton's line which, consciously or unconsciously, Keats copied is:

> "As one who long in populous city pent."

The last three lines of Keats's sonnet are an amusing bit of self-revelation:

> "Fatigued he sinks into some pleasant lair
> Of wavy grass and reads a debonair
> And gentle tale of love and languishment."

No better characterization of *Rimini* could be given, and without a doubt it was *Rimini* that he read "in the fields."

A third sonnet seems to date from this time: *Oh! how I love, on a fair summer's eve*. It is a sort of companion piece to the *City Pent* sonnet, but greatly inferior. So like are the two, that it is very interesting to compare them line by line, but there is no space for that here. It is probable that *Oh! how I love* was written first, and that Keats, realizing it was a failure, used the subject over again. Both the sonnet to Wells and the *City Pent* sonnet were printed in *Poems*,

1817; *Oh! how I love* was not printed at all in Keats's lifetime,[1] which seems to prove Keats's opinion of it.

We have no record of any poems written in July. Clearly Keats was obliged to buckle down to his medical studies during that month. On July twenty-fifth, 1816, came the fateful examination, and Keats went up and — passed. No wonder his fellow students were dumbfounded, but so it was. A page of the Register of Apothecaries' Hall, printed as a form to be filled in, reads as follows:[2]

"*July 25th 1816.*

189 Mr. *John Keats of full age* — CANDIDATE for
a CERTIFICATE to practise as an APOTHECARY in *the Country.*
An APPRENTICE to Mr. *Thomas Hammond of Edmonton*
APOTHECARY FOR *5* Years
TESTIMONIAL from *Mr. Thomas Hammond* —

LECTURES.

2 COURSES on ANATOMY and PHYSIOLOGY.
2 — THEORY and PRACTICE OF MEDICINE.
2 — CHEMISTRY.
1 — MATERIA MEDICA.

HOSPITAL ATTENDANCE.

6 MONTHS at *Guy's and St. Thomas's* —

as

MONTHS at

168 Examined by Mr. Brande & approved."

Evidently Mr. Hammond bore Keats no ill-will, for he came forward with the necessary testimonial. The "six months," which were really nine, at Guy's and St. Thomas's would not have been allowed as adequate preparation for admission to the examination if the four years' apprentice-

[1] It was first published by Lord Houghton in his *Life, Letters, and Literary Remains of John Keats.* 1848.

[2] *Literary By-Paths in Old England*, by Henry C. Shelley, contains a photograph of the original page.

ship to Mr. Hammond had not been added to them. This is quite evident from the entries in the Minute Book of the Court of Examiners of the Society of Apothecaries,[1] the first of which is: "John Keats attended and produced testimonials to the satisfaction of the Court, and was admitted to Examination," and the second, "Mr. Keats was examined by Mr. Brande, and the Court granted him the certificate for which he had applied." Everard Brande was one of the Court of Examiners of the Society of Apothecaries. He is not to be confused with the noted chemist, William Thomas Brande, who was, however, the Society's professor of chemistry and superintending chemical operator. William Thomas Brande was considered the best chemistry teacher in London. If Keats had been unlucky in serving under Mr. Lucas, he was eminently lucky in having, for two of his teachers, Astley Cooper and William Thomas Brande.

Here was Keats, then, licensed to practice as soon as he pleased. I am very sure, however, that by this time he was fully determined to do no such thing. He did not communicate his decision to Abbey until later, as we shall find out, but there was no need to take that step yet. Even Abbey could see the advisability of a vacation, and afterwards he would be so nearly of age that the placating of Abbey would not matter. His immediate concern was to put his diploma in his trunk and promptly forget all about hospitals and hospital studies. So Keats bade good-bye to his fellow students at Guy's and St. Thomas's, and went off to Margate, so far as we know, alone.

[1] Letter from William Wale, formerly Wills Librarian, Guy's Hospital, in the London *Times* for Tuesday, January 10, 1918.

CHAPTER III

THE CRYSTALLIZING OF INTENTION

It is usually supposed that Keats's decision to give up surgery dates from the late Autumn of 1817. A careful study of his mental outlook at Margate, and on his return to London, leads me to believe that the time should be advanced as I have stated in the last chapter. That his mind was fully made up long before he spoke to Abbey on the subject, an anecdote related by Abbey to Taylor and recorded in the letter so often quoted seems to prove. This anecdote will be given in due course.

Keats, at Margate, is all agog with the idea of being a poet. A poet with the whole strength and force of his energy, not merely a man who writes poetry. A man's chief interest must be in his vocation, not in his avocation. Keats believed himself to have sufficient ability to make his devoting himself to poetry worth while; he felt sufficient security in his financial affairs not to experience any qualms on the score of earning nothing. There he was grossly in error, as he would have known at once had he taken the trouble to ask a few questions. He had been spending steadily for five years without earning a penny. To meet the expenses of his surgical education, Abbey had been obliged to encroach upon his capital. A perfectly justifiable proceeding, had Keats lived up to his guardian's expectations and begun to practice as soon as he was qualified to do so. In that case, by Abbey's calculation, he would be able to pay himself back by degrees. The matter assumed a totally different complexion if there were to be no paying back. When Keats refused to fulfill what Abbey considered his obligations, that startled merchant either would not, or could not, make his financial prospects clear to Keats. To this lack of understanding on Keats's part is due much of the misery of his later years.

Money affairs were as far from Keats's mind as surgery during his sojourn at Margate. Poetry was everything, he thought of nothing else. Margate was the brightest kind of experience, all shimmered over with beautiful words and beckoning visions. He did not yet know enough of the poetic life to consider its laboriousness and constant strain. At this juncture, he saw only the happiness of achievement. To be quit of surgery, able to give all the time he liked to receiving impressions and pouring them out in verse, there was joy greater than any he had ever known. He savoured it to the full, and with it came again the heightened sense of beauty and of personal contacts he had felt when he wrote the beginning of *I Stood Tip-toe*. At other times, before, he had known the fret of barrenness, had been afraid that his creative faculty had flown, but not now — now he can even comment on such moments, being filled with convincing purpose.

I am not imagining this, it is all given in his *Epistle to my Brother George*, which he wrote at Margate. But I cannot help thinking that, in point of time, his sonnet: *To my Brother George* precedes the *Epistle*. The sonnet is simpler and seems to voice a first reponse to his change of environment, whereas in the *Epistle* we are made aware of much cogitating, he has had time to do a deal of thinking about the high calling to which he is now dedicated. I will suppose that my theory of precedence is correct, and take the poems in order.

The sonnet is quite charming in its simplicity. It is just an expression of a mood, the mood of escape from drudgery, the mood of delighted impression. A transcript by George Keats is dated: "Margate, August, 1816," but through the poem itself we can add some details to the mere bald date. It is sunset, and Keats is sitting looking at the ocean. Just to one side of the flaming sky, just beyond the edge of its fire, a little sickle moon is growing into light. It is all so beautiful that Keats immediately wishes that George were there to see it with him, and the wish is so strong that he writes the sonnet. He is not thinking of being a poet at that moment; he is thinking how magnificent the sky and sea are, and noticing the delicate touch given to the scene by the little faint moon. The sonnet begins:

> "Many the wonders I this day have seen,"

and one feels that this is the clue to his feeling — wonder. Keats's observation is extraordinarily sure in this poem, and his words equal it. The sonnet is keen with the perfect combination of these two qualities. How excellent "feathery gold" is for sunset clouds! How thoroughly satisfactory his sea:

> "The ocean with its vastness, its blue green,
> Its ships, its rocks, its caves, its hopes, its fears, —
> Its voice mysterious."

The remarkable thing about this passage is that it not only paints the actual sea, but suggests all that the sea stands for to humanity, and this with no effect of overloading and spoiling the picture. It is admirably done. As an inherent colourist, Keats was much impressed by the colours of the sea. Here he has "its blue green"; better still is

> "Ocean's blue mantle streak'd with purple and green"

in the *Epistle to George Keats*.

The sonnet is a sort of prelude to his sonnet *On the Sea*, written in the following year. The later poem is better, stronger, more serious and penetrating, but the *naïveté* of this earlier poem is very attractive. The moon passage is tinged with fancy:

"Cynthia is from her silken curtains peeping
So scantly, that it seems her bridal night."

No clumsy artificiality here; merely the faintest flush of artifice. The wistfulness of the last two lines is scarcely even that, the slightest whiff of nostalgia playing over the remembrance of understanding companionship:

"But what, without the social thought of thee,
Would be the wonders of the sky and sea?"

His brother George came nearer to filling up the gap in Keats's heart than any of his friends ever did. The separation of the brothers, when George emigrated to America, tore the scheme of Keats's existence from end to end. By the time he had learnt to do without George, he was a different man.

The *Epistle to my Brother George* is again dated by George Keats, "Margate, August, 1816." The opening of the poem speaks of the depression induced by a period of unproductiveness. This is the characteristic poetic temper which Keats possessed in the extreme. It proves him as having considered himself apprenticed to the business of poetry for some time. But the depression is reminiscent, the immediate present holds no such feeling:

"But there are times, when those that love the bay,
Fly from all sorrowing far, far away;
A sudden glow comes on them, nought they see
In water, earth, or air, but poesy."

He goes on to tell of the visions beheld by poets in creative trances. To heighten his effect, Spenser and Hunt are again brought in in juxtaposition, somewhat as they are in the *Induction*, and again Hunt is "Libertas." The imagery of the poet's trance is very much that of *Calidore*, but this of the *Epistle* is distinctly more imaginative. For instance, the conception of sheet-lightning as being the opening of the portal of a knightly castle in the sky is an original and pleasant fancy.

Two lines in the poem gave rise to an illuminating example of the limitations of critics:

> "And, when upheld, the wine from each bright jar
> Pours with the lustre of a falling star."

Leigh Hunt found fault with this simile, which proves his lack of observation and Keats's discernment, also possibly Keats's good eyesight and Hunt's bad. For in August (the month of falling stars) one can often see a wake behind the dropping star.

Keats's preoccupation with the poetic life appears in a long passage put into the mouth of a dying poet, the gist of which is that no other life is half so important to the world and satisfying to the individual. This passage is really the voicing of his own ambition, and he goes on in his proper person:

> ". . . Ah, my dear friend and brother,
> Could I, at once, my mad ambition smother,
> For tasting joys like these, sure I should be
> Happier, and dearer to society.
> At times, 'tis true, I've felt relief from pain
> When some bright thought has darted through my brain:
> Through all that day I've felt a greater pleasure
> Than if I'd brought to light a hidden treasure.
> As to my sonnets, though none else should heed them,
> I feel delighted, still, that you should read them."

"Sonnets" may have been put in for the metre, or it may be that he cared particularly for his sonnets. This may seem odd when we remember that the only ones written at that time were *To Byron*, *On Peace*, *To Chatterton*, *On Leigh Hunt Leaving Prison*, *To a Young Lady who sent me a Laurel Crown*, *Sonnet to Solitude*, *On an Engraved Gem of Leander*, *Oh! how I love*, *To a Friend who sent me some Roses*, and *To one who has been long in city pent*, not one of which ranks with his best sonnets. But, after all, think of the other poems done before August, 1816. Does one of them equal *Leander*, *City Pent*, or the *Sonnet to Solitude?* Keats was right, his best work up to this time, with the exception of *I Stood Tip-toe*, which was not finished, was in his sonnets.

It will be noticed that it is the autobiographical content of the *Epistle* which I have emphasized, not the poetical. I have done so because it is not until the end of the poem, where Keats describes the actual scene before his eyes as he writes, that the *Epistle* becomes poetically interesting. This description is among Keats's best, and it is important in another connection also, for here is the scenery which Keats was living with at Margate:

> "E'en now I'm pillow'd on a bed of flowers
> That crowns a lofty clift, which proudly towers
> Above the ocean-waves. The stalks, and blades,
> Chequer my tablet with their quivering shades.
> On one side is a field of drooping oats,
> Through which the poppies show their scarlet coats;
> So pert and useless, that they bring to mind
> The scarlet coats that pester human-kind.
> And on the other side, outspread, is seen
> Ocean's blue mantle streak'd with purple, and green.
> Now 'tis I see a canvass'd ship, and now
> Mark the bright silver curling round her prow
> I see the lark down-dropping to his nest,
> And the broad-winged sea-gull never at rest;
> For when no more he spreads his feathers free,
> His breast is dancing on the restless sea."

In spite of its inexpertness in several places, that passage is in the new, direct manner which Keats was just learning how to manage, the manner so well exemplified in the first part of *Tip-toe*. The chequering of his paper with the shadows of grass-blades is a repetition of the "youngling tree" in the earlier poem. Or was the "youngling tree" a result of tinkering, owing its existence to the grass-blades?

No one can read this *Epistle*, I think, without realizing whither Keats was tending, and agreeing with my contention that surgery was now quite a thing of the past, an ancient nightmare dissolved and blown away.

Because of Keats's constant brooding over the career of poetry, I am emboldened to hazard a guess as to the date of an unpublished poem in the Woodhouse Book in the Morgan Library. Woodhouse says it was written "About 1815/6." 1815 it cannot be, on the face of it. Keats wrote in no such style in that year. I scarcely think it can have been written later than 1816, it is too youthful in expression. It must have been done early in Keats's writing life — the slight touch of bombast at the end proves that, also it does not fit with any of the remarks on poetic psychology given in his letters, and still less is it a companion piece in feeling or wording to *Where's the poet?* which, although we do not know where it should be placed, has the ironic flash Keats learnt to play with only much later. There seems every reason to suppose that this last poem was written about the time of Keats's letter to Woodhouse of October twenty-seventh, 1818, the tone of it is in perfect keeping with that letter, which the tone of this sonnet emphatically is not. *The Poet* has little merit, but in connection with the *Epistle to George Keats* it gains a certain reality and importance which it would otherwise lack:

"THE POET.

At Morn, at Noon, at Eve, and Middle Night,
He passes forth into the charmed air,
With talisman to call up spirits rare
From plant, cave, rock, and fountain. — To his sight
The hush of natural objects opens quite
To the core: and every secret essence there
Reveals the elements of good and fair;
Making him see, where Learning hath no light.

Sometimes, above the gross and palpable things
Of this diurnal ball, his spirit flies
On awful wing; and with its destined skies
Holds premature and mystic communings:
Till such unearthly intercourses shed
A visible halo round his mortal head."

The poem appears never to have been finished, for the word "sphere" is written above "ball," and the word "earth" is written below. "Earth" is scratched out, but "sphere" is left as a possible alternative. Also, in the last line, a choice is given between "mortal" and "living." These may quite well be Woodhouse's emendations and not Keats's at all, for Woodhouse was fond of trying his hand at such improvements.

The line:

"Making him see where Learning hath no light"

may reasonably refer to the heavy and uninspiring tomes on anatomy, chemistry, etc., which Keats had ached through for many a long year. To my mind, that line is fair evidence for placing the poem as written during the Margate sojourn. If this be the case, Keats was well advised in not allowing it to strut into the pages of the *Poems*, 1817. It would certainly have given the impression of an over-weening egotism on Keats's part that he was very far from feeling. Keats believed in his destiny as a poet, but not with his hat put on sideways and his nose in the air. If ever a man pursued his course with humble confidence, that man was John Keats. He never identified himself with the poet of this sonnet, obviously; this poet was a generality, the ideal practicant of the noblest of all arts, which was what Keats conceived the great masters to have been. But a censorious world would assuredly have read the poem otherwise, and *Blackwood's* would have had another handle to twist upon.

We have no exact data as to how long Keats stayed at

Margate, but in a poem written to Charles Cowden Clarke and subscribed "September, 1816," he speaks of it being "some weeks" since he last saw the steeples of London reflected in the Thames. Although we have no definite knowledge that Keats wrote more at Margate than the sonnet and *Epistle* to his brother George, there is no reason to suppose that he left it for any other place before returning to town. By this calculation, the *Epistle to Charles Cowden Clarke* ranks as a Margate poem, and allowing the placing of *The Poet* in this category, gives us four poems done during August and September, or, at least, during a part of those months. He may have been away a month in all, he may have been away two. However long he was at Margate, I do not believe that these four poems represent all the work he did there. Of those poems which we know to have been written in 1816, a few give no hint as to the month we should ascribe them to; none of these, however, seem to fit in with the Margate vacation. Yet it is reasonably certain that Keats was intermittently at work all the time he was at Margate. Probably he was revising the much-worked-over *I Stood Tip-toe* and adding little pieces to it, and he may very likely have been altering the *Induction* and *Calidore*. But we must also suppose that he was doing an immense amount of mere day-dreaming. There was a great deal to think about; for instance, there was the inevitable conversation with Abbey, which was undoubtedly rehearsed again and again, with "He will say" and "I will say" in a never ending chain of repetitions and in every possible shade of tone on Keats's part, running the gamut from persuasion through indifference to defiance. There were also innumerable castles in Spain to build, in which Keats saw himself as the author of another *Faerie Queene*, or another *King Lear*; and there were long hours of reading, of course, with the books and the dreams all muddled up together. It can scarcely have been otherwise. Keats was an introspective man, he tried to know himself, and finally in a great measure succeeded.

All this soul searching and castle building was fatiguing, and there is evidence of fatigue in the *Epistle to Charles Cowden Clarke.* Fatigue of spirit, that is, for as an autobiographic and psychologic record we can trust it implicitly. The more Keats goes over his past life, the greater he feels his debt to Clarke to be, and it becomes a kind of duty to write something specifically addressed to the friend who has done so much for him. The poem is a catalogue of boons received. He can hardly write to Clarke in the same strain of egoistic enthusiasm which he permits himself with his brother. Clarke is his friend; but he is also, in many ways, his mentor. If the eight years between them are dwindling, still he cannot think of Clarke without being conscious of how very far he is from realizing his own dreams as yet. Besides, September is not August, and the self-communings have shorn away a good deal of his colt-let-out-in-a-meadow sort of excitement. His awareness of his own shortcomings in the beginning of the poem is very touching. The *Epistle to Clarke* starts clumsily enough with a simile of a swan striving to save the drops of water he spatters upon his feathers, and Keats exclaims:

> "Just like that bird am I in loss of time
> When e'er I venture on the stream of rhyme
> . . . . .
> Still scooping up the water with my fingers,
> In which a trembling diamond never lingers."

Never lingers! That sounds uncommonly like depression. Has Keats been having a little encounter with his abiding blue devils? No, I think they have no more than fanned him with their bat-like wings here in Margate, but reaction from the high tension of August was inevitable.

Following the swan simile, Keats proceeds to relate it:

> "By this, friend Charles, you may full plainly see
> Why I have never penn'd a line to thee:
> Because my thoughts were never free, and clear,

> And little fit to please a classic ear;
> Because my wine was of too poor a savour
> For one whose palate gladdens in the flavour
> Of sparkling Helicon."

The inference is not that his thoughts are now clear, for I suppose they had seldom been more confused, but that he can no longer delay this duty of obligation. Helicon leads to a literary catalogue which is interesting only because it shows the kind of books with which Keats had become familiar, largely through Clarke. They are Tasso, Spenser, Shakespeare, and Milton. Sandwiched in between Shakespeare and Milton is Hunt, who is ushered in in the worst tea-table verse:

> "One, who, of late, had ta'en sweet forest walks
> With him who elegantly chats, and talks —
> The wrong'd Libertas, — who has told you stories
> Of laurel chaplets, and Apollo's glories;
> Or troops chivalrous prancing through a city,
> And tearful ladies made for love, and pity."

Keats had no thought of irony when he wrote these lines, but no malicious pen-driver could have stumbled on a more apt and damning description of Hunt than Keats's "him who elegantly talks." To a man who, like Clarke, has communed with all these great ones, what can there be in his, Keats's, poetry — that is the gist of the passage. Nor would Keats address him now

> "But that I've known you long;
> That you first taught me all the sweets of song."

And he proceeds to describe the various kinds of poetry in a manner which proves that, whatever Clarke taught, Keats had *learnt* a great deal. Here is his happy delineation of Spenser's style:

> "Spenserian vowels that elope with ease,
> And float along like birds o'er summer seas."

There is no better description of the "wind-back" sonnet than:

> "Who read for me the sonnet swelling loudly
> Up to its climax and then dying proudly."

No wonder his friends believed in his future, a boy so sensitive as this to poetic *nuances*! This man has an intellect, he can not only feel, he can analyze his sensations and put the causes of them under a microscope. This is inspirational criticism, there is no other word for it.

Ode, epigram, epic, follow next, and then comes this passage:

> "You too upheld the veil from Clio's beauty,
> And pointed out the patriot's stern duty;
> The might of Alfred, and the shaft of Tell;
> The hand of Brutus."

Notice that the patriots, King Alfred and William Tell, are the same as in the *Epistle to George Felton Matthew*, and that William Wallace, in the first poem, has given place to Brutus in the last; whereas Sydney, Russell, and Vane are the patriots in *Lines on the Anniversary of Charles II's Restoration*, while Sydney is again mentioned in connection with "patriotic love" in the sonnet *Oh! how I love.*

Up to line 84, the poem has been a *tour de force*, something he wanted to write from a grateful sense of duty. Here is the circumstance in a nutshell:

> ". . . When many lines I'd written,
> Though with their grace I was not oversmitten,
> Yet, as my hand was warm, I thought I'd better
> Trust to my feelings, and write you a letter.
> Such an attempt requir'd an inspiration
> Of a peculiar sort, — a consummation; —
> Which, had I felt, these scribblings might have been
> Verses from which the soul would never wean."

So we see that he had been writing "many lines" at Margate; we also see that, in spite of the passage on poetry, he was not in vein — was, in fact, tired.

With the eighty-fourth line, Keats begins to describe the country he is living with. It is not so good a description as that in the *Epistle to George Keats*, but it is important as proof of what I have said was his state of mind. He was simply aching for just the type of scenery to be found at Margate. He had to get it. He went to Margate in a kind of thirst, and satisfied himself with the sights, the sounds, the smells, all the things which London, even Hampstead, could not give him. These bursts of desire for a particular kind of place were usual with Keats throughout his life. Sensitiveness to atmosphere was one of his most marked traits. Here is the story:

> "Some weeks have pass'd since last I saw the spires
> In lucent Thames reflected: — warm desires
> To see the sun o'erpeep the eastern dimness,
> And morning shadows streaking into slimness
> Across the lawny fields, and pebbly water;
> To mark the time as they grow broad, and shorter;
> To feel the air that plays about the hills,
> And sip its freshness from the little rills;
> To see high, golden corn wave in the light
> When Cynthia smiles upon a summer's night,
> And peers among the cloudlets jet and white,
> As though she were reclining in a bed
> Of bean blossoms, in heaven freshly shed.
> No sooner had I stepp'd into these pleasures
> Than I began to think of rhymes and measures:
> The air that floated by me seem'd to say
> 'Write! thou wilt never have a better day.'
> And so I did."

Note the observation of the morning shadows "streaking into slimness," and his marking the time by their growing broader and shorter. Note the moon among black and white clouds; here is Keats the colourist in full swing. I can recall no other line in poetry where the black and white of moon clouds is given. At this period, in passages like these, Keats is boyish, but all himself.

The end of the poem is a reminiscence of his school-days and the years at the Edmonton surgery.

It seems strange that, with all the writing which Keats says he has done, so few poems appear to have been written. A possibility is that both the *Induction* and *Calidore* were written at Margate, but I reject this idea for the reason that the manner of those poems is not the manner of the ones we know to have been done there. Except for the one passage in the *Epistle to George Keats* which I have already pointed out, there is no suggestion of either the imagery or the diction of the *Induction* and *Calidore* in any of them. On the contrary, they approach much more nearly to the style of *I Stood Tip-toe*.

The countryside had done its work. Already, in the Cowden Clarke poem, we feel that Keats is through with it, and not averse to the change back to town. When he left Margate is uncertain, but probably we shall be right in concluding that it was not later than the middle of September.

Where did Keats go on his return to London? That has recently become a mooted question owing to the researches of Mr. Louis A. Holman. Clarke is the authority for the belief that Keats left St. Thomas's Street to lodge with his brothers in the Poultry. Clarke describes these lodgings with some minuteness. They were, he says, "on the second floor of a house in the Poultry, over the passage leading to the Queen's Head Tavern, and opposite to one of the City Companies' halls — the Ironmongers, if I mistake not." Mr. Holman has recorded[1] that no place answering to this description can be found in the Poultry, but that it is quite accurate for a certain part of Cheapside. The Keats brothers did live in Cheapside, but the removal there cannot have taken place much before the twentieth

[1] The Boston *Transcript*.

of November, as in a letter to Haydon of that date Keats puts as a postscript: "Removed to 76 Cheapside." Mr. Holman's argument is as follows:

> "What Clarke intended to say was 'rooms in *Cheapside*, over a passage leading to the Queen's *Arms* Tavern.' This is evident from his further statement that the lodgings were opposite 'one of the City Companies' Halls.' Opposite the entrance to the Mercers' Hall we find Bird-in-Hand Court, Cheapside, leading to the Queen's Arms Tavern. Clarke further shows that he had confused the Poultry with Cheapside, when a little later he has Keats remove directly from these lodgings, which he again speaks of as being in 'the Poultry,' to Hampstead."

Mr. Holman would seem to have made his point that Clarke had the Cheapside lodging in mind when he wrote, and his argument is greatly strengthened by the fact that Mercers' Hall is at the corner of Ironmonger Lane; but, even so, that does not prove that there was not an earlier lodging in the Poultry.

Cheapside runs into the Poultry, and that a person re collecting over thirty years later should have confused the two is not surprising. Cornelius Webb wrote in a copy of the *Poems*, 1817, which he says was given him by Keats, that, at the time the book was published, Keats was living "in lodgings near the Poultry," and we know that when the *Poems* came out Keats was living at 76 Cheapside. Still I do not think that that disposes of a possible Poultry lodging entirely. On the contrary, I am inclined to adopt the usually accepted view that there were two lodgings. To explain my reasons for this belief, I must shift the ground of the argument.

George Keats, writing to Dilke in 1824,[1] says: "Between the time of John's leaving the surgeon and his coming of age he and Tom (who had been with Mr. Abbey and left

[1] Author's Collection. Quoted by Buxton Forman, Library Edition. Vol. IV.

him) spent 3 times their incomes." As Tom was not yet sixteen at the time of Keats's move from Edmonton to London, he cannot have been long in Abbey's employ. Suppose that he left school when he was fifteen, as John did, or even, following George's example, when he was fourteen, he went directly to Abbey's. The later age is more likely than the earlier, for we know that it was ill health which caused him to leave, and he could scarcely have found out that he could not stand the confinement of a desk under some months' trial. Where did he go? In one of George Keats's letters to Dilke,[1] George speaks of Abbey's advancing money to Tom "when Tom went to Lyons." We know nothing of this journey except this single mention, but it seems very probable that it occurred just at this time. Tom's going there was undoubtedly due to an impression that Lyons, being so far South of Paris, would be warm. Supposing that Tom tried Lyons, his stay there was evidently of the shortest, yet even a short sojourn would account for a certain period after he had left Abbey's and before John had quitted the hospital. This supposition is the more plausible, because for Abbey to have permitted a ward of fifteen or so to go into lodgings all by himself seems ridiculous. Also, would John have left Tom alone for the better part of a year while he himself lived with a set of none-too-congenial fellow students in another part of the town? I think not. The Poultry was not such an everlasting distance from the Borough as to make it impossible for John to have reached the hospital with a little effort. Owing to these considerations, we are undoubtedly right in assuming that, after Tom's departure from Abbey's counting-house, he went to Lyons, from whence he returned in the Spring or early Summer of 1816. That by this time Tom was "on his own" and in constant need of money, is shown by a draft of a letter

[1] Author's Collection.

to Abbey in a pocket-book [1] which Tom used at this time:

> "John lent me 5£ on the 4th inst. according to your desire for which I am much obliged. I have only 1£ this morning I shall soon want more at your convenience I will thank you to give some to George for me and he will enclose it. I hope Mrs. and Miss Abbey are well I beg my respects to them and my love to Fanny."

This letter tells us many things. First, that George was still living at Abbey's business quarters in Pancras Lane which he left not long after; second, that Abbey was unequal to the sacrifice of having Tom at his Walthamstow house; third, that Tom was seeing John constantly; fourth, that Tom needed a good deal of money, presumably chiefly to pay his keep. The letter is not dated, but it is jotted down only one item removed from a copy of Keats's sonnet to George from Margate. The item which divides them has some importance because of its date. It is: "2 shirts, 4 cravats, 2 pair socks, 1 P.N.H. Hank, 1 Flannel Waist." Is this a washing-list? Possibly, but for whom? It also may be a memorandum of things to put into a valise. The date is July twenty-fourth and Keats's examination was on the twenty-fifth. Is this note — washing-list or memorandum — preparation for the trip to Margate? If so, it looks as though Keats were already living with Tom, and that may have been the case. I notice that Professor de Sélincourt, on what authority I do not know, puts Keats's removal to the Poultry as occurring in either June or July. My only reason for disbelieving this is that it appears improbable that Keats would make such a change with his examination so short a time away and with the Margate excursion in view. A question obtrudes itself — why did not he take Tom with him? The answer may be that Tom's finances were not

[1] Day Collection.

equal to such a jaunt. As to his leaving Tom alone, I can only say that he left him alone when he went on his Scotch tour, and Tom was a very sick man in the Summer of 1818. In 1816, he was probably not sick at all, merely too frail to continue in his position with Abbey. It may pertinently be asked why I think Tom was not with him at Margate. The answers to this question are two. The first of them is to be found in the last two lines of his sonnet *To my Brother George*:

> "But what, without the social thought of thee,
> Would be the wonders of the sky and sea?"

If Tom were with him, he would not need to invoke a "social thought" for an absent person, his nostalgia for George would have been expressed differently. The "wonders of the sky and sea" need companionship to complete them, and such companionship is not at hand, as it would have been had Tom been there. The second answer is the evidence of a letter written to Hunt in May 1817, in which he speaks of his Margate quarters as "my old lodging" not "our old lodging."

The final reason on which I base my conclusion that Tom was alone, or with a friend, until after Keats's return from Margate, is just the removal to Cheapside in November. For may not that change of lodging be due to the fact of George's joining his brothers? Possibly the Poultry quarters were not big enough for three. If John had gone back to St. Thomas's Street on returning to London, would he have stayed there a whole month after he came of age and was his own master? Nobody has ever suggested this, and I think it most improbable. The Cheapside move was not made until late November. If Keats were still at St. Thomas's Street, his sending the sonnet on Chapman's *Homer* to Clarke in Clerkenwell in time for Clarke to receive it at ten o'clock, when the two had only parted at "day-spring," would have been a distinct feat.

Whereas, although quick work, if he only had to go to the Poultry there would be ample time for him to walk "composing as he went, and to commit his draft to paper and send it to Clerkenwell by ten o'clock."[1]

A long digression, this, but I fear a necessary one. It has, perhaps, proved nothing; but it does, at least, throw a very strong weight on the probability that when Keats returned from Margate he returned to the Poultry and to Tom.

Coming back to London meant coming back to Clarke and the rest of his friends. It also meant the resumption of the Hampstead walks, and the eager, fortifying talks at Hunt's house in the Vale of Health. Keats threw himself into these pleasures with an ardour which could not have left much room for the pursuit of his medical studies. Probably he resumed his hospital and lecture attendance in a fitful way, Abbey would have seen to that, for it was still a full month before he was to come of age. His distaste for surgery can have been no secret to his friends for some time, however successfully he may have concealed it from Abbey. Cowden Clarke relates a conversation which he had with Keats before his examination. Clarke, seeing Keats so absorbed by poetry, enquired how he was going to make such absorption fit with the practice of surgery. Keats promptly answered that he disliked the study of anatomy as a main pursuit, and that, feeling so, he was unsuited to be a surgeon. In illustration of his attitude, he said, "The other day, for instance, during the lecture, there came a sunbeam into the room, and with it a whole troop of creatures floating in the ray; and I was off with them to Oberon and fairy-land."

It was quite customary for holders of an apothecary's certificate to return to the hospital and resume both their duties as dressers and their attendance at lectures. The twelvemonth's term for which Keats had entered himself

[1] Colvin.

in the previous March was still in operation, and Abbey was too thrifty a soul to wish Keats to part with his money and not get his money's worth. So Keats bided his time, and mum was the word as far as Abbey was concerned.

Some time in October, Keats had an experience. He was booked to spend the evening with Clarke, and accordingly wended his way to Clerkenwell. He found Clarke in high good humour over the loan of a book. It was Chapman's translation of Homer in the folio edition of 1616. Keats was a true booklover, delighting almost as much as Lamb in old calf-bound folios. Later, in 1818, we find him rejoicing over the purchase of a black-letter Chaucer. The 1616 Chapman's *Homer* is a sumptuous volume, with one of the engraved architectural title-pages so dear to the heart of the seventeenth century bibliophile. This particular copy had been lent to Clarke by a Mr. Alsager who conducted the money-market department in the *Times*. Alsager was one of Hunt's admirers, and he and Clarke had made each other's acquaintance while dancing attendance upon their idol in the Horsemonger Lane prison.

Neither Clarke nor Keats had ever read Chapman's translation of Homer; what knowledge they had of both the *Iliad* and the *Odyssey* was derived from Pope. Down they sat, says Clarke, and turned to the "'famousest passages' . . . for instance, that perfect scene of the conversation on Troy Wall of the old Senators with Helen, who is pointing out to them the several Greek Captains." The description of these old senators is just the kind of passage which Keats would be likely to be struck by:

"All graue old men; and soldiers they had bene, but for age
Now left the warres; yet Counsellors, they were exceeding sage.
And, as in well-growne woods, on trees, cold spiny Grasshoppers
Sit chirping, and send voices out, that scarce can pierce our eares

For softness and their weak faint sounds; so, talking on the tower,
These seniors of the people sate."

This is only the beginning, the whole scene is too long to quote. Clarke especially mentions "the Senator Antenor's vivid portrait of an orator in Ulysses":

"But when out of his ample breast he gaue his great voice passe,
And words that flew about our eares, like drifts of winter's snow;
None thenceforth, might contend with him; though naught admird for show."

Another passage cited by Clarke is that of "the shield and helmet of Diomed, with the accompanying simile":

"From his bright helme and shield, did burne, a most vnwearied fire:
Like rich Autumnus golden lampe, whose brightnesse men admire,
Past all the other host of starres, when with his chearefull face,
Fresh washt in loftie Ocean waues, he doth his skies enchase."

And still another, called by Clarke, "the prodigious description of Neptune's passage to the Achive ships":

"But this security in Ioue, the great Sea-Rector spied,
Who sate aloft on th' vtmost top, of shadie Samothrace,
And viewd the fight. His chosen seate, stood in so braue a place,
That Priams cittie, th' Achiue ships, all Ida did appeare,
To his full view; who from the sea, was therefore seated there.
He tooke much ruth, to see the Greeks, by Troy, sustaine such ill,
And (mightily incensed with Ioue) stoopt straight from that steepe hill;
That shooke as he flew off: so hard, his parting prest the height.
The woods, and all the great hils neare, trembled beneath the weight

Of his immortall mouing feet: three steps he onely tooke,
Before he far-off Ægas reacht; but with the fourth, it shooke
With his drad entrie. In the depth, of those seas, he did hold
His bright and glorious pallace built, of neuer-rusting gold;
And there arriu'd, he put in Coach, his brazen-footed steeds,
All golden man'd, and pac't with wings; and all in golden
weeds
He cloth'd himself. The golden scourge, (most elegantly
done)
He tooke, and mounted to his seate: and then the God begun
To driue his chariot through the waues. From whirlpits
euery way
The whales exulted vnder him, and knew their king: the Sea
For ioy did open; and his horse, so swift, and lightly flew:
The vnder-axeltree of Brasse, no drop of water drew.
And thus, these deathlesse Coursers brought, their king to
th' Achiue ships."

This whole picture must have been a breathless excitement to Keats. Hitherto Pope had been all he knew of Homer. Chapman's version is concrete, Pope's is general. Keats did not love the general. No man ever gloried in minute descriptions more than he. There was tonic and healing to him in the sweeping vigour of Chapman. Careless of finicky niceties, relying only upon an infinite gusto, this honest, swaggering, extraordinarily masculine kind of poetry must have been like a great puff of wind swishing across a room full of trifling knick-knacks, knocking them off the tables, twisting them about, swirling the pictures from the walls, and filling the stagnant, scented air with a rush of inconsequence. Something was needed to tip *Rimini* off the table of Keats's mind — *Rimini*, and the false beauty it stood for. Virile old Chapman was the very one to do it. Not all at once, but gradually. If any one would have a grateful task, let him track Keats's indebtedness to Chapman's *Homer*. There is an ample field and practically unexplored.

Before I leave these passages which Clarke says gave

Keats particular pleasure, I must quote the last. Clarke recalls it in these words: "One scene I could not fail to introduce him to — the shipwreck of Ulysses, in the fifth book of the 'Odyssies' where Ulysses is cast up on the shores of Phæacia, and I had the reward of one of his delightful stares upon reading the following lines":

> "Then forth he came, his both knees faltring; both
> His strong hands hanging downe; and all with froth
> His cheeks and nosthrils flowing. Voice and breath
> Spent all to vse; and downe he sunke to Death.
> The sea had soakt his heart through: all his vaines
> His toiles had rackt, t'a labouring woman's paines.
> Dead weary was he."

Clarke italicizes "the sea had soakt his heart through," as though it were just as he read those words that Keats stared. Clarke says that on an "after-occasion" he showed Keats the corresponding passage in Pope's version:

> "From mouth and nose the briney torrent ran,
> And lost in lassitude lay all the man."

Keats probably recollected this comparison when he wrote of the

> ". . . musty laws lined out with wretched rule
> And compass vile"

a few months later, in *Sleep and Poetry*.

All night long, these enthusiastic young persons read, and it was nearly dawn before Keats could tear himself away. We can imagine Clarke's surprise, therefore, when at ten o'clock the next morning he received a note from Keats which turned out to be a sonnet, *On First Looking into Chapman's Homer*.

Two manuscripts of this sonnet are in existence, one [1] is evidently a first draft, the other [2] is probably the copy

[1] Author's Collection. [2] Morgan Collection.

sent to Clarke. In the draft, Keats has drawn lines down the side to remind himself where the rhymes came. Homer is "low-brow'd," not "deep-brow'd"; Cortez's eyes are not "eagle," but "wond'ring"; and the seventh line reads: "Yet could I never tell what men could mean," which Clarke says he eventually changed because he considered it "bald and too simply wondering." This may have been one reason, but there were probably three others: first, the repetition of the word "could"; second, the awkward effect of the consonants — too many "n's" — and the reiteration of the short "e" in "never," "tell," and "men"; and still a third, the sameness of the rhyme sound in "demesne" and "mean." The substituted line, as everybody knows, is:

> "Yet did I never breathe its pure serene."

A most interesting suggestion in regard to the curious expression "pure serene" has recently been made by Mr. Paget Toynbee. His remarks, in part, I will give in his own words:

> [1] "The phrase 'pure serene,' which is not to be found in Shakespeare, Milton, Dryden (so far as I am aware), or Pope, occurs in Cary's translation of the 'Paradiso' . . .
>
> '*Lumé non è, se non vien dal sereno*
> *Che non si turba mai*' —
>
> which Cary renders:
>
> '. . . Light is none,
> Save that which cometh from the pure serene
> Of ne'er disturbed ether."
>
> It will be noted that Cary's epithet 'pure' has no equivalent in the original . . .
>
> Cary's 'Dante' had been published in January, 1814, in

[1] Letter from Paget Toynbee in the London *Times Literary Supplement*, June 16, 1921.

On the first looking into Chapman's Homer

Much have I travell'd in the Realms of Gold,
And many goodly States, and Kingdoms seen;
Round many Western islands have I been,
Which Bards in fealty to Apollo hold.
Of one wide expanse had I been told,
Which ~~low~~ deep brow'd Homer ruled as his Demesne;
Yet could I never judge what Men could mean,
Till I heard Chapman speak out loud, and bold.
Then felt I like some Watcher of the Skies
When a new Planet swims into his Ken,
Or like stout Cortez, when with wond'ring eyes
He star'd at the Pacific, and all his Men
Look'd at each other with a wild surmise —
Silent upon a Peak in Darien —

FIRST DRAFT OF THE SONNET "ON FIRST LOOKING INTO CHAPMAN'S HOMER"

From the original manuscript in the possession of the author

> the diminutive edition in three volumes, a copy of which Keats carried in a corner of his knapsack on his tour in the north in the summer of 1818.
>
> If my surmise is correct Keats's acquaintance with Cary's 'Dante' must have begun at a somewhat earlier date than is usually assumed."

It has hitherto been supposed that Keats's introduction to Dante came through Bailey. But, even if that were virtually the case, it is quite possible that Hunt has read him a passage or two out of Cary before. Certainly there is more than coincidence in Keats's repetition of Cary's exact words. I think it extremely likely that he came across Cary's phrase after writing his sonnet, and during the time that he was puzzling his head how to better his erring seventh line.

The simile in the sestet is a reminiscence of a passage in Robertson's *History of America*, which Clarke has told us was in the school library at Enfield. This book seems to have interested Keats very much, we find him reading it again in April, 1819. Keats confused Balboa with Cortez, as Tennyson pointed out to Palgrave, but Keats's friends do not seem to have noticed the mistake. Hunt, in *Imagination and Fancy*, refers to Titian's portrait of Cortez, and says "his 'eagle eyes' are from life, as may be seen by Titian's portrait of him." Keats may have known the portrait, or not, but at any rate he put Cortez, probably by accident. It is no matter. The passage in Robertson which gave him his picture is this:

> "At length the Indians assured them, that from the top of the next mountain they should discover the ocean which was the object of their wishes. When, with infinite toil, they had climbed up the greater part of that steep ascent, Balboa commanded his men to halt, and advanced alone to the summit, that he might be the first who should enjoy a spectacle which he had so long desired. As soon as he beheld the South Sea stretching in endless prospect below

him, he fell on his knees, and lifting up his hands to heaven, returned thanks to God, who had conducted him to a discovery so beneficial to his country, and so honourable to himself. His followers, observing his transports of joy, rushed forward to join in his wonder, exultation, and gratitude."

The late Dr. Richard Garnett suggested as another source for Keats's simile a note in Wordsworth's *Excursion.*[1] It was taken from the notes to a poem by William Gilbert called the *Hurricane:*

> "A man is supposed to improve by going out into tne *World*, by visiting *London*. Artificial man does; he extends with his sphere; but, alas! that sphere is microscopic; it is formed of minutiæ, and he surrenders his genuine vision to the artist, in order to embrace it in *his ken* . . . The reverse is the Man of Mind . . . he would certainly be swallowed up by the first *Pizarro* that crossed him. But when he walks along the river of Amazons; when he rests his eye on the unrivalled Andes; when he measures the long and watered savannah; or *contemplates, from a sudden promontory, the distant vast Pacific*, — and feels himself a freeman in this vast theatre and commanding each ready produced fruit of this wilderness, and each progeny of this stream — his exaltation is not less than imperial."

The use of the word "ken" in this passage, and in the sonnet, is the striking thing here. Keats knew the *Excursion* well, and he may have read the notes, but even so, there is no such vivid flash to this picture as there is to Robertson's. And Robertson's mention of Balboa's followers, so carefully preserved by Keats, seems to make his passage the far more likely original of Keats's lines, although the suggestion in the note that it was the "Man of Mind" who was exalted by these things must have been a taking one to Keats. The truth is, probably, that the

[1] *The Poems of John Keats*, edited by E. de Sélincourt. 4th Edition.

initial idea came from Robertson, touched up and augmented by a recollection of the note in the *Excursion.* Keats's passage has another debt — to Shakespeare, for his lines in the *Rape of Lucrece:*

> "Enchanted Tarquin answers with surmise
> In silent wonder of still-gazing eyes."

Perhaps poor old Bonnycastle's *Astronomy*, Keats's prize book for 1811, may have been responsible for the planet.

Few poems show more clearly than this sonnet how the creative faculty works. Even after the thunders of Chapman, Keats cannot quite forego a taste of fancy, the mythological fancy so dear to him. A man does not change his form of speech in one night. Hunt's lily-handed ladies and sighing wooers are tipped off the table for the nonce, but Apollo comes back from an earlier period to take his neophyte by the hand. Cary's phrase, being an afterthought, we may dismiss; but at this point in the poem in strides Chapman himself in the words, "loud and bold." The simile of the Pacific is lying in Keats's mind, waiting for use, and the Sea-Rector's journey, bringing the ocean up before him, lets it loose; while Bonnycastle may (and not too imaginatively reckoned so, I think) have been lying on his table and happened to catch his eye, although, considering that he has been walking home with the dawn stars paling over his head, he scarcely needed anyone's astronomy to father the thought of a planet.

Out of whatever bits and tittles of thought and memory Keats made his sonnet, he made a superb thing. The whole poem is so much more mature and finished in its execution than anything which had preceded it that the difference is astonishing. The success it met with in the Keats circle must have clinched his resolve to free himself from surgery without delay.

The birthday came and passed, and Abbey began to think with a certain concreteness of the future. Keats's paid twelvemonth would be up in March, and it behooved a careful guardian to look about and see what could be done in the way of establishing his ward in a practice. If Abbey were no longer a legal guardian, he was, and would remain for a considerable time, a trustee. His enquiries on John's behalf produced an opening at Tottenham. The tale of the upsetting of his plans is the pleasantest passage in his revelations to Taylor.[1] I will give it exactly as Taylor wrote it to Woodhouse:

> "John was apprenticed to a Surgeon at Edmonton, who did not however conduct himself as Mr. A. conceived he ought to have done to his young Pupil,[2] and partly to punish him by the Opposition, — partly because Mrs. Jennings was known and respected in the Neighborhood, on which account her Grandson had a better Introduction there than elsewhere, it was Mr. Abbey's advice that John commence business at Tottenham as a Surgeon. He communicated his Plans to his Ward, but his Surprise was not moderate, to hear in Reply, that he did not intend to be a Surgeon. Not intend to be a Surgeon! why what do you mean to be? I mean to rely upon my Ability as a Poet — John, you are either Mad or a Fool, to talk in so absurd a Manner. My Mind is made up, said the youngster very quietly. I know that I possess abilities greater than most men, and therefore I am determined to gain my living by exercising them, Seeing nothing could be done Abbey called him a Silly Boy, and prophesied a speedy Termination to his inconsiderate Enterprise. — He brought in not Long after, says that worthy man, a little Book which he had got printed. I took it and said that I would look at it because it was his writing, otherwise I should not have troubled my head with any such Thing. When we next met I said, Well John I have read your Book, and it reminds me of the Quaker's Horse which was hard to catch, and good for nothing when caught. So your Book is hard to understand and good for nothing when it is understood.

[1] Abbey Memoir. Author's Collection.
[2] This seems to have been an error, see Vol. I, p. 154.

Do you know, says the old Man, I don't think he ever forgave me for uttering this Opinion, which however was the Truth."

Keats's determination to live by his abilities, and his certainty of being able to do so, must have seemed the merest rhodomontade to the prudent coffee merchant; and Keats, quiet though he may have been, undoubtedly met Abbey's suggestions with a square-jawed obstinacy which nothing could move. Keats was as far as possible from being a boastful fellow, but he knew he had powers and he would have been a fool if he had not known it, also, a sneering opposition is of all others the very thing to produce a corresponding self-assertion. Granting every possible allowance for the annoyance which a man who has done his best and sees his plans frustrated naturally feels, Abbey certainly expressed himself with a tactlessness which, if not caused by downright stupidity, was unkind to the point of brutality. It was not so much a case of Keats never having forgiven him. The relations between the two men were shattered past any question of forgiveness by Abbey's attitude. By temperament, training, and natural abilities, they were as far asunder as two men can be. I think it is fair to say that Keats loathed Abbey from that moment, if, in fact, he had not done so before. And Abbey misunderstood and distrusted Keats, even going so far as to fear his influence for his young sister Fanny. As Abbey's trusteeship would not terminate until Fanny Keats came of age, or not until eight years later, in 1824, he and John were kept in constant communication, an intercourse calculated to renew their mutual irritation every so often, particularly as John only wrote or called to ask for advances of money or request some indulgence for his sister which Abbey was loath to grant.

An experience which Keats did not tell Abbey had clinched his resolve to abandon surgery. One day Keats was called upon to open a man's temporal artery. He performed the operation skilfully, but with a wandering mind. "I did it with the utmost nicety," he told a friend later, "but on reflecting on what had passed through my mind at the time, my dexterity seemed a miracle, and I never took up the lancet again."

About this time, another unpleasantness in regard to the Keats children and Abbey occurred. Abbey had a junior partner named Hodgkinson. All that we know of him is that on some occasion he behaved with insolence to George Keats, or, at least, George thought he did, and his brothers adopted his view. So long after as the Summer of 1819, John tells Fanny that he cannot bear even to write Hodgkinson's name. This was extreme, of course, but all Keats's reactions were extreme, and particularly those contingent upon any rudeness to his brothers. George was a high-spirited fellow, a little over much so, in fact; he and his brothers called it pride, a more worldly-wise and less prejudiced person might have called it folly. The rise from one class into another is not accomplished without some loss. The Keats boys had done well for themselves socially, but there is evidence, here and there, that at times they had got a little above themselves, as the homely saying is. This was so in these early years, at any rate.

What Hodgkinson did or said is nowhere stated, but out George flounced, hugging his pride and putting all his chances for life in jeopardy. Yet his action brought about no such break with Abbey as Keats suffered. Abbey seems to have sat on the fence in the matter. He did not sever his partnership with Hodgkinson, and he did not force George, who was still under age, to remain in his employ. George left, and the three brothers moved to new lodgings at 76 Cheapside. The move was already accomplished by the twentieth of November, as we have seen.[1]

[1] See Vol. I, p. 171.

Keats, meanwhile, was in the first flush and heyday of life and spirits. He made friends easily, and thoroughly enjoyed them. Indeed, there was something winning about the man which has persisted even across the gulf of death. His publisher, Taylor, when sending a copy of *Endymion* to Sir James Mackintosh, apologizes for telling him so many details of the poet's life, but adds, "If you knew him, you would also feel that odd personal interest in all that concerns him." Any one who comes near Keats feels it even to-day, as the list of searchers into the details of all his doings bears witness.

The passage I have quoted from the Abbey Memoir relates two conversations occurring some time apart. What Abbey speaks of as "a short time" was really some months. I am persuaded, however, that the first conversation occurred very soon after Keats's first meeting with the Olliers, his first publishers, which took place in November. The second conversation must have been early in March. The Memoir itself is dated "20 April 1827," and was undoubtedly written immediately after the talk between Taylor and Abbey which it records and while Abbey's words were fresh in Taylor's mind. At that time, Taylor and Woodhouse were collecting materials for a brief biography of Keats, a plan which fell through.

I presume, for how could it have been otherwise, that Keats, having turned down the proposition of the Tottenham surgery, turned down with it his lingering connection with the hospitals and his fellow students at those institutions. What most of his friends guessed, and some of them knew, everybody was now to witness. Good-bye to the dingy Borough and all it signified. That was the end of that. But Keats had made some warm, if now necessarily to be abandoned, friends at St. Thomas's Street. Henry Stephens cared enough about him to copy the whole of his *Poems*, 1817 into a blank book. To him we owe two bits of doggerel, *Wine, Women and Snuff*,[1] scribbled by Keats in

[1] See Vol. I, p. 88.

one of Stephen's note-books, and a joke sonnet, *Before he went to feed with owls and bats*. Since we have no clue to what the sonnet refers, we lose the joke; but I cannot help thinking that it is connected with Keats's giving up his career as a surgeon. Doubt has been cast upon the authenticity of this sonnet, but as Woodhouse refers[1] to it in an account of a conversation which had taken place at a dinner at a Mr. F. Salmon's, the doubt may be laid.

Keats, then, is no longer at the parting of the ways, where he has been lingering in fact, if not in fancy, ever since receiving his diploma; he has at last turned definitely down the road to poetry. The stuff of his life is now to be, to outward seeming, friendship and all that friendship may bring; the inner fibre is to be poetry, books, and the thousand answerless questions which were always proposing themselves to his brain.

His circle of friends was increasing almost daily, and as Keats had the happy faculty of amalgamating one set of friends with another, he was not teased by psychological dislocations. First, there were the friends he had derived from his brother George either directly or indirectly. Second, there was the Hunt contingent, and, in the late Summer and Autumn of 1816, these were far the most important.

The intimacy with Hunt had been steadily growing ever since Keats's return from Margate. Fun and fancy, frolic and earnest, with endless readings and discussions — Hunt's intimates ran the gamut of these. Keats was enchanted with the whole atmosphere, and was constantly running out to Hampstead to enjoy it. Hunt's house was small, and overflowing with his family, but his hospitality was such that he could always stretch bed and board to take in a friend. Sometimes, when the evening chat had prolonged itself to a very late hour, Keats would spend the night in an improvised bed made up on the sofa in Hunt's

[1] Woodhouse Book. Morgan Collection.

LEIGH HUNT'S HOUSE IN THE VALE OF HEALTH, HAMPSTEAD

From a photograph by Louis A. Holman, Esq.

study. Hunt, although eleven years Keats's senior, had not outgrown a certain youthfulness of attitude. Woodhouse relates an innocent prank in which he and Keats were actors. Says Woodhouse:

> "As Keats and Leigh Hunt were taking their wine together after dinner, at the house of the latter, the whim seized them (probably at Hunt's instigation) to crown themselves with laurel after the fashion of the elder bards. While they were thus attired, two of Hunt's friends happened to call upon him. Just before their entrance Hunt removed the wreath from his own brow, and suggested to Keats that he might as well do the same. Keats, however, in his mad enthusiastic way, vowed that he would not take off his crown for any human being; and he accordingly wore it, without any explanation, as long as the visit lasted. He mentioned the circumstance afterwards to some of his friends, along with his sense of the folly (and, I believe, presumption) of his conduct. And he said he was determined to record it by an apologetic ode to Apollo on the occasion. He shortly after wrote this fragment."

The fragment is the *Hymn to Apollo*. The *Hymn* was written as a joke, but it has a magnificent movement, and the refrain "O Delphic Apollo" is really superb. It is a pity he did not build up another, serious poem to Apollo on this movement.

Two other poems, sonnets, owe their inception to the laurel prank: *On Receiving a Laurel Crown from Leigh Hunt* and *To the Ladies who Saw me Crowned*. It looks as though these sonnets were written as a competitive pastime with Hunt, for Hunt also wrote two sonnets commemorating the event. Hunt's opinion of the whole performance appears in the first lines of his second sonnet:

> "It is a lofty feeling, yet a kind,
> Thus to be topped with leaves."

Hunt, who, for some reason, missed laurel and got only

ivy, took the thing quite casually and turned out a couple of florid sonnets which he thought well enough of to publish later. Not so Keats; for all his apparent bombast, the play had an undercurrent of seriousness to him, but his sonnets are poor, particularly the last. The first is in a half-mocking vein, and Keats is so openly boyish in his desire to write a fine thing while he has the laurel crown on, and so evidently disappointed when the best thought he can muster is only a rehash of Hunt's political creed, that one cannot help smiling. He knew the sonnet was a failure and did not include it in the *Poems*, 1817, but he cared enough about the thing he had wanted to say in it to write it in Reynolds's copy of that volume. What shows that the sonnet was only half-heartedly humourous is that he took parts of it later for his *magnum opus* — as he felt it to be — *Endymion*. Later on, he was rather severe with himself upon the subject of the crowning, overdoing the severity, of course.

When the crowning came off is not known exactly, but it was probably some time during this Autumn or Winter. It is hardly possible that it could have happened before Keats went to Margate, he was so much less intimate with Hunt then, and so taken up with his examination. Professor de Sélincourt thinks that it took place in 1817, just before his visit to Oxford, but this is clearly not so, as Keats refers to it in a letter to George written in the Spring of that year.

Hunt loved nature in a degree only second to Keats. At this unfledged epoch of Keats's life, the two were rarely congenial. It was not long before Hunt dubbed his young friend with the inescapable soubriquet of "Junkets." The odd thing is that none of his other friends seem to have taken it up. Jolly good fellow as Keats was (he himself appears to have had no objection to this telescoped edition of his name; in one of his letters to Hunt, he signs himself "John Keats alias Junkets"), there was something about him which precluded nicknames. "Junkets" simply would not stick. He was "Keats" to his friends, and, strangely enough, to Fanny Brawne also, just "Keats."

The most important consequence of Keats's frequent visits to the cottage in the Vale of Health was to bring him into contact with Hunt's friends. Haydon had spent some weeks in October at Hampstead, seeing much of Hunt,[1] and while there he must have heard a good deal of Hunt's new protégé. The result appears to have been an invitation to Clarke to bring Keats to his studio. Haydon says[2] that he met Keats at Leigh Hunt's, but Keats's letter to Clarke seems to prove that this was not the case.

Haydon was a very singular man. Born in Plymouth, the son of a bookseller, he had from his earliest years a perfect passion for drawing. Coming up to London when he was only nineteen, he worked with such indefatigable zeal, chiefly drawing from plaster casts, that he ruined his already impaired eyesight which never afterwards entirely recovered. His ambition was to become a great historical painter. With every aptitude of genius except its inspiration, he continued for years painting huge canvases which were too large to be comfortably housed in any private dwelling. In order to keep himself in paint, canvases, and models, he borrowed of everyone, rich and poor, always believing that success would come when the particular picture he had in hand was finished. His belief in himself was almost a mania, nothing could shake it. If he were not appreciated, it was because people were dolts, not because he was a bad painter. A group of enthusiastic and ignorant friends fanned the flame of his self-adulation. A few years of questionable notoriety was the fullest mead of recognition he was ever to know, and in the end, worn down by the hopeless fight and the load of debts which

[1] See Vol. I, p. 138.
[2] *Haydon's Biography and Journals,* edited by Tom Taylor.

there was no prospect of discharging, he cut his throat and shot himself at the age of sixty.

But if Haydon over-estimated himself as a painter, he was nevertheless a very extraordinary man. His fecund mind was constantly on the alert, devising schemes for the advancement of art. He longed to see the principal public buildings of England decorated with immense wall paintings of historic scenes, and proposed plan after plan to succeeding committees on the subject. Unfortunately, his manner towards his opponents was so violent that where he should have won friends he made enemies. It was impossible for him to see clearly in human relations. Haydon was an egotist of so extreme a type that he may be considered as practically a megalomaniac. A little real success would have been good for him, but his blindness to his own demerits made such a thing impossible. He fought with the Royal Academy, he fought even with his patrons. But he sacrificed himself unsparingly in the cause of art. His unending labours to make the British Nation purchase the Elgin Marbles have earned him his chief fame. For years, he button-holed painters, patrons, ministers, members of the House, committee-men, always to force them to listen to his views on the worth of the Marbles. He pamphleteered for them, he brought down upon himself obliquy and derision. He kept on; the Marbles were bought. It was a triumph, almost his only one.

This hectic, unbalanced, passionately devoted, passionately irreconcilable man was thirty years old and enjoying a simulacrum of success when Keats first encountered him. The Elgin Marble controversy had ended in a victory for Haydon, the Marbles being actually acquired by the Nation in 1816. His first picture, *Joseph and Mary resting on the Road to Egypt*, which was of moderate size, had been hung on the line at the Academy and sold at once; but his next two, *Dentatus* and *Macbeth*, had failed to create the interest he had expected for them. His third picture,

HAYDON'S "CHRIST'S ENTRY INTO JERUSALEM"
From a photograph of the original painting taken by Louis A. Holman, Esq.

however, the *Judgement of Solomon* — a painting nearly thirteen feet long and over ten feet high — when it was exhibited in 1814 had really been acclaimed, and loudly. The directors of the British Gallery decided to buy it at Haydon's price, seven hundred guineas, but they were too late, the picture had been bought by a private person. Haydon was now engaged on a more pretentious subject than any he had yet undertaken, *Christ's Entry into Jerusalem*. He was at work on this picture during the whole time that Keats knew him.

The *Jerusalem* is a very large picture. The centre of the canvas is occupied by the figure of Christ riding on a donkey, and all round, about, and behind him press a crowd of agitated spectators. Among them are one or two who can be recognized, for Haydon, following the custom of the early painters, did not scruple to introduce portraits of real people here and there. Voltaire is put in to represent skepticism, but this flight of fancy troubled Haydon not a little, he read Voltaire carefully to be sure of the justness of his idea of him, he prayed for guidance, and in the end Voltaire remained. But Haydon was too audacious to stop at Voltaire; he went on to add the heads of various of his friends, among them Wordsworth, whose portrait Hazlitt declared to be the best likeness of the lot. Haydon worked and worked over this picture. He painted his Christ in and out seven times, and left him in the end a failure. "Mr. Haydon," said Samuel Rogers, when the picture was finally finished and on exhibition, "your ass is the Saviour of your picture." A cruel, but painfully just, criticism. The faces of the crowd, however, are strikingly done. Various and curious, they cannot fail to attract attention. The *Entry into Jerusalem* took six years to paint. When it had been doing for a year, in 1815, Haydon was so elated with it and with himself that he described his feelings in a letter as follows: "Never have I had such irresistible and perpetual urgings of future greatness. I have been like a man with air-balloons under his armpits and ether in his soul."

Haydon took to Keats at once with all the florid ardour of his disposition. He says in his *Autobiography*:

> "About this time I met John Keats . . . and was amazingly interested by his prematurity of intellectual and poetical power.
>
> I read one or two of his sonnets and formed a very high idea of his genius. After a short time I liked him so much that a general invitation on my part followed, and we became extremely intimate. He visited my painting-room at all times and at all times was welcome."

This was written many years later, his contemporary expression is more vivacious. His journal for March, 1817, contains this note, written shortly after the appearance of Keats's *Poems*, 1817:

> "Keats has published his first poems and great things indeed they promise . . . Keats is a man after my own heart. He sympathizes with me, and comprehends me. We saw through each other at once, and I hope are friends forever. I only know that, if I sell my picture, Keats shall never want till another is done, that he may have leisure for his effusions; in short, he shall never want all his life while I live."

Fine words, Mr. Haydon, but how did you live up to them? Very badly indeed, as we shall discover.

Keats, constantly in the midst of a group of Haydon enthusiasts, was all prepared to find the painter a second Michael Angelo. On October thirty-first, he dispatches a note to Clarke, in which he says:

> "I will be as punctual as the Bee to the Clover. Very glad am I at the thought of seeing so soon this glorious Haydon and all his creation."

This looks very much as though Keats were anticipating an initial meeting, and in the painting-room, where Haydon will be surrounded by "all his creation." Haydon's

DETAIL OF HAYDON'S PICTURE: "CHRIST'S ENTRY INTO JERUSALEM." SHOWING THE HEADS OF KEATS, WORDSWORTH, AND VOLTAIRE

From a photograph of the original painting taken by Louis A. Holman, Esq

statement that he met Keats at Leigh Hunt's is undoubtedly the trick of a faulty memory. But Haydon's *Autobiography* can never be taken as gospel in its details; he jumbles events and places, telescopes one year into another, and generally confuses the issue. For general knowledge, it is admirable; for particular knowledge, it must be edited with some care and much reference to other sources of information.

Another sentence in this note to Clarke is arresting, for Keats continues:

> "I pray thee let me know when you go to Ollier's and where he resides — this I forgot to ask you."

What does this mean — Ollier's? The Olliers were the publishers of the *Poems*, 1817. Why, that a publication was in the wind, to be sure. I judge this by the fact that, although Keats asks where Ollier resides, he is clearly not referring to any specific engagement like a party. As he did not at the time know either of the Olliers, his going to see either of them was probably for business, not social, reasons. It had evidently been decided by Hunt and Company that Keats had enough poems for a volume; at any rate, that it would do no harm to consult a publisher. The brothers Ollier, Charles and James, were publishers of the lesser type, the kind who encourage youthful talent and gamble on its success. They had issued Shelley, and were personal friends of Leigh Hunt, at least one of them was, for they were sharply divided in their interests. James was the business member of the firm; Charles, who was musical and dabbled in verse, probably ran the literary end. That Keats asks Clarke where the Olliers live, must mean that he counts shortly upon going there. Of when he went, and what was said, no record remains. But we can imagine, in the light of future events, that a book was agreed upon, to be brought out for the Spring season, thus giving Keats an opportunity to add to his sheaf any poems written between the Autumn and the time the manuscript must go to press, which would probably be about January or February. As a matter of fact, nothing written after December appeared in the volume.

Probably it was the *Chapman's Homer* sonnet which fired the train leading to publication. Hunt's delight in Keats's work, and particularly in that sonnet, was being constantly justified by the attitude of the various friends to whom he read the poems. He speaks of one occasion when

> [1] "having the pleasure of entertaining at dinner Mr. Godwin, Mr. Hazlitt, and Mr. Basil Montague, I showed them the verses of my young friend, and they were pronounced as extraordinary as I thought them. One of them was that noble sonnet on first reading Chapman's *Homer*, which terminates with so energetic a calmness, and which completely announced the new poet taking possession."

We must thank Hunt for the excellent expression, "so energetic a calmness"; it is perfect.

These joyful days! — gay with hope, and crowded with new acquaintances! Another intimate of the Hunt circle, another fledging swan of the Hunt brood, was John Hamilton Reynolds. Reynolds was a most attractive young man, a year younger than Keats, but already the author of three books of poetry. He was the only son, and fourth child, of the head writing master, who was also mathematical master, of Christ's Hospital. The family, as Keats knew it, consisted of the father and mother, two sisters — older, respectively, by two and three years than their brother — and a younger sister. Marianne and Jane, the older sisters, became great friends of Keats's for a time. The elder, Marianne, afterwards married a Mr. Green; the younger, Jane, became the wife of Thomas Hood. Charlotte, the third sister, was a girl of fourteen when Keats was intro-

[1] *Lord Byron and his Contemporaries*, by Leigh Hunt.

duced to the family. Her piano playing at a little later date was a source of much enjoyment to Keats. There was still another member of this interesting family, Eliza, the oldest of all, but she had married a Mr. Longmore of Chelmsford, Essex, before Keats's advent into the family circle. He met her, on one occasion at least, when he wrote the sonnet *On Spenser* at her request, at her father's house, where she was probably making a brief visit; circumstances, however, caused her to remain merely a casual acquaintance, a little known member of a family with whom he was intimate.

John Hamilton Reynolds was born at Shrewsbury on September ninth, 1796. Part of his boyhood was spent at Sidmouth, but on his father's receiving the appointment to Christ's Hospital the family moved to London and occupied one of the houses reserved for the masters of that school, No. 19 Lamb's Conduit Street, Little Britain. They were a gay and intelligent group, these Reynoldses, with a lively interest in literature and a taste for the society of literary people; Mrs. Reynolds is said to have been quite equal to taking her part in the talk at Charles Lamb's evening parties.[1] The elder Reynolds was a bluff and hearty personage, if we can judge by a sketch of him made by his son-in-law, Thomas Hood,[2] but there is no mention of him in Keats's letters, whereas allusions to Mrs. Reynolds abound.

John Hamilton Reynolds was educated at St. Paul's School. At the time when Keats met him, he was a clerk in the Amicable Insurance Company, but he, and everyone else, believed that his destiny was literature. Reynolds possessed a precocious talent, which, like the majority of such talents, withered in the promise. In 1814, when he was only eighteen, he had published two books: *Safie, an Eastern Tale,* an imitation of Byron, to whom it was de-

[1] Colvin. [2] *Literary By-Paths in Old England,* by Henry C. Shelley.

dicated; and a pamphlet entitled *An Ode*. Reynolds sent a copy of *Safie* to Byron. Byron replied at length, praising the poem and predicting a shining future for the poet. In 1816, Reynolds brought out another volume of verse, the *Naiad*. This new book he sent to Wordsworth, who answered with much politeness, tempering a very judicious criticism by his manner of expressing it. Reynolds's best known book, the *Garden of Florence*, did not come out until after Keats's death, in 1821, and then under the pseudonym of "John Hamilton." The interval between the *Naiad* and the *Garden of Florence* saw the appearance of a parody of Wordsworth's *Peter Bell*, a burlesque of pugilism, published anonymously under the title of *The Fancy: A Selection from the Poetical Remains of the late Peter Corcoran*, and a farce, *One, Two, Three, Four, Five; by Advertisement*. In 1818, Reynolds, it is supposed at the instigation of the young lady, a Miss Drew, to whom he was engaged, decided to become a solicitor, but he continued to write occasional pieces for the magazines and provided the comedian, Charles Matthews, with words for several of his monologues; he was, besides, joint author with his brother-in-law, Thomas Hood, of a little anonymous book, *Odes and Addresses to Great People*. In the end, however, he was successful in neither literature nor law, and at last retired, a disappointed man, to the Isle of Wight, where he held the post of assistant clerk of the County Court of Newport. At the end of his life, he took to drink, and gradually sank in the social scale. He died at Newport in 1852.

No one could have foreseen this sad and abortive career in the days when Keats and Reynolds met in 1816. Reynolds was brilliantly clever, so every one thought, full of fun, a captivating companion, just the type to attract Keats. Hunt and Haydon were wonders, but they were much older; Reynolds was another youngster. Nothing could be better. And Reynolds brought with him a friend,

James Rice, a young solicitor, who seems to have been an unusually fine fellow in every way. Rice does not appear to have done anything particular outside his law; he just *was*, and everybody who knew him drifted rapidly under the spell of his kindness and his combination of wit and wisdom. Keats relied much upon his judgment, "Rice would not make an immature resolve," is one of his remarks about his friend, and again he writes to George in 1819, that Rice is "the most sensible and even wise man I know. He has a few John Bull prejudices, but they improve him." Dilke speaks of Rice as "dear, generous noble James Rice — the best, and in his quaint way one of the wittiest and wisest men I ever knew"; and Reynolds, to whom Rice had given over his entire practice, and who had made ducks and drakes of it — Reynolds, even after that, wrote to Lord Houghton, "He was a quiet true wit — extremely well read — had great taste and sound judgment. For every quality that makes the sensible companion — the valuable Friend — the gentleman, and the Man — I have known no one to surpass him."

Yet Rice was no prig, as all this might lead one to think. He was not averse to getting a little tipsy on occasion, as in those days was a common enough thing, he liked to kiss a pretty girl when circumstances threw one in his way, he did not shy from reading tales of a singular breadth of humour. He was, in short, good for play, and pre-eminently good for earnest. Rice seems not to have been strong; he was always ailing, but coming "on his legs like a cat," Keats says.

Others of the Hunt circle whom Keats met in the Autumn or early Winter of 1816 were Shelley, Hazlitt, the brothers Horace and James Smith, authors of *Rejected Addresses*, and Charles Lamb, but with none of these men did he ever become really intimate. He did not like Shelley. Poor, iconoclastic, circumstance-baffled Shelley! In December, 1816, his first wife, Harriet Westbrook, committed suicide, and three months later Shelley was deprived of their children by order of Court. These were unfortunate months in which to meet him for the first time, undoubtedly; but really there was too little in common between Keats and Shelley for them ever to have found much pleasure in each other's society. Shelley took his three years seniority as sufficient excuse to advise Keats not to be in a hurry to publish. Considering how the Hunt circle were beginning to feel about Keats, this must have been an unexpected and bitter drop to swallow. Shelley, apart from his poetry, was, as Max Beerbohm so succinctly puts it, "a plain, unadulterated crank." Keats did not like Shelley's type of poetry, and he was farther from being a crank than from any other thing one can name. Keats had an excellent mind, the kind of mind which is well spread out, not the kind which is all squeezed together into one little spot in an otherwise empty cranium. Shelley's opinions on practical affairs were worth nothing; on politics, ethics, and social economics, he talked and acted like a fractious, unreasonable child. Keats, on the other hand, was a perfectly logical, straightforward, and unprejudiced thinker. His emotions might run away with him; his ideas, never. His genius was above and beyond his mind, yet it did not impoverish it, as does the unbalanced genius of poets of lower rank. Shelley's mind was sucked and dwindled by his poetical faculty; Keats's was nourished and energized by his. Read the letters of the two men. When Shelley is neither poet nor crank, he is a pleasant, well-informed gentleman, seeing the world agreeably and mentioning what he sees in quite the usual manner of the early nineteenth century traveller; Keats is Puck, Paracelsus, even Paul Pry, perhaps. He is here, there, everywhere, with his tentacular mind poking into everything. Haydon, who always saw obliquely, thinks that Keats disliked Shelley because of his rank. But after all, a baronetcy only recently created is not a dazzling rank.

Keats was something of a snob, as we have seen, and he loathed being patronized with all his heart, but I think it more probable that Shelley's advice induced the fear of patronage than that the fact of his father's being a baronet did. The long and the short of it is that they did not get on, and never could have, each being what he was. Seeing that Keats was firmly under the spell of Chaucer and the Elizabethans at just that time, how could he have been expected to relish the kind of poetry which Shelley wrote? Keats was very young, and youth is not eclectic. It is only age, which having gone through much retains a little of all, that can be tolerant.

Keats never became intimate with Hazlitt for quite other reasons. Age and opportunity were against it, and it is a fact that Hazlitt did not care much for Keats's poetry — Haydon complained that it was only after Keats's death that he was able to get Hazlitt to acknowledge his genius — but he liked the man, and he liked the man's mind, or he would not have given him the manuscript of one of his books to read before the book came out, as we shall see that he did later. In these early days, he simply counted out the poetry; yet how justly he came to regard it finally can be seen by his *Select British Poets*, published in 1824. Here he says of Keats: "He gave the greatest promise of genius of any poet of his day. He displayed extreme tenderness, beauty, originality and delicacy of fancy." Hazlitt's selections from Keats's poems consisted of several passages from *Endymion*, the whole of the *Eve of St. Agnes*, *Fancy*, *Robin Hood*, and an extract from *Hyperion*. This was the first reprint of any of Keats's poems, preceding the Galignani reprint by five years. The reason this reprint has been so entirely overlooked by biographers is probably because the book was suppressed almost as soon as issued, for copyright reasons, and the better known edition of the following year omitted all the poets subsequent to Cowper. When we think of Keats and Hazlitt, we must remember that, after all, there were seventeen years between them. A pleasant, casual kind of acquaintance was all that their intercourse ever amounted to, in spite of Keats's warm admiration for Hazlitt's critical acumen.

Keats seems to have seen Charles Lamb only a few times, and there is no reason to suppose that he was ever at any of Lamb's famous evenings. Horace Smith appears to have asked him to dinner occasionally, and the two kept up a desultory intercourse while Keats remained in England. So it was with others of the Hunt group, pleasant acquaintances all of them, but Reynolds and Haydon were the only two with whom casual contact ripened into close friendship.

Keats's note of October thirty-first to Clarke gives the impression that Clarke is to take Keats to Haydon's and that the visit is by appointment. This idea is confirmed by another, hitherto unpublished, note to Clarke [1] which seems to announce the postponement of this very visit. The note reads:

> " To C.C.C. greeting
> Whereas I have received a Note from that worthy Gentleman Mr. Haydon, to the purport of his not being able to see us on this days Evening for that he hath an order for the Orchestra to see Timon ye Misantrophas, and begging us to excuse the same — it behooveth me to make this thing known to you for a manifest Reason.
> So I rest your Hermit — JOHN KEATS."

Why I believe this note, although undated, to refer to the visit already planned on October thirty-first, is the simple fact that Timon of Athens was on at Drury Lane for the ten days beginning on Monday, October twenty-eighth, and ending with the performance of Wednesday, November sixth. Clarke being concerned in the meeting in both

[1] Day Collection.

letters goes far toward proving my supposition. That the postponed visit came off soon after Haydon's evening at Drury Lane is probable. The mutual pleasure of the poet and painter on that occasion led almost at once to the most cordial of relationships which, in turn, warmed into a friendship productive of much stimulation on both sides.

The sonnet, *Addressed to Haydon*, is confused by Professor de Sélincourt with the second sonnet to Haydon. The two followed one immediately upon the other in the *Poems*, 1817, and the second is simply entitled *Addressed to the Same*. In Keats's letter to Haydon of November twentieth, he enclosed the second sonnet only, and that is the one to which Haydon replied on the same day suggesting that he send the poem to Wordsworth. The first sonnet is so general in character that it may well have been written before Keats had actually met Haydon, and he quite evidently did not send it to Haydon or that insatiable battener upon compliments would certainly have lost no time in acknowledging it, and have duly recorded the acknowledgement in his journal. Haydon's share in the Elgin Marbles controversy was known to everyone, and when Haydon won, and the Marbles were actually the possession of the British Nation, enthusiasm ran riot. Haydon's son, in his Memoir of his father,[1] describes the furor with which Haydon's pamphlet was greeted, and continues:

> "Nor did his own circle of private friends behave less absurdly. They appear to have written sonnets in turn. Leigh Hunt in the character of a 'bard' led the way. He 'approves and blesses.' Miss Mitford 'sheds tears.' Reynolds apostrophises him as the 'savior of art.' Somebody else sends him to heaven as a modern Raphael and Michael Angelo rolled into one. Another adds the qualities of Leonardo to his credit, and calls upon Europe to build

[1] *Benjamin Robert Haydon: Correspondence and Table Talk.* With a Memoir by his son, Frederick Wordsworth Haydon.

him a palace and endow him with riches. Wordsworth and Keats were the only two who kept their judgment and wrote something sensible."

There is no record of Keats's having written anything at the time of the pamphlet's appearance, and it seems quite evident from Keats's reply to Haydon's letter about sending the second sonnet to Wordsworth that Haydon had received but one. Keats enclosed only one, and in his answer he speaks of "it" not "them." Under these circumstances, I cannot help thinking that the first Haydon sonnet, which is clearly addressed to Haydon as the champion of the Marbles, precedes the second, and that, in the interval between the two, Keats paid his first visit to Haydon's painting-room. The second sonnet as clearly refers to both an impression and a conversation, indeed Keats says as much in the accompanying letter. "Last evening wrought me up," so Keats expresses himself. If the first sonnet had been written after he had seen "this glorious Haydon and all his creation," would the creation have figured as nothing, and Haydon himself merely as the unselfish devotee of "the cause of steadfast genius"? The difference in feeling between the two sonnets is another proof. There is a cool aloofness about the first sonnet, Keats was not the man to glow at the vision of abstract virtue, he needed the personal touch to spark him into flame. There is little choice between the sonnets as sonnets; there is a world of difference between them in feeling. They are neither of them among his best work in the sonnet form, but the second holds us by its evident fire, the first leaves us cold.

Keats had removed to Cheapside before November twentieth, but how immediately before is not known. That he was already there on the eighteenth is certain, for his sonnet, *To my Brothers*, is obviously written when they are all together. It is in Keats's most satisfying vein. The whole tone of it is Keats — Keats, one of the most affectionate and domestic men who ever lived. Here he is at home. This is a quiet, comfortable evening with the brothers, who, after all, are nearer to him than any of his fine new friends. In Tom Keats's copy-book, the sonnet is headed *Written to his brother Tom on his Birthday*, and dated "Nov. 18, 1816." Tom was seventeen. There is so much of stress and turmoil in Keats's life that it is not only pleasant to see him at peace, it is absolutely necessary to give us a perspective and to make us realize how bitter the stress and turmoil were. With such an abiding love of home, such a craving for a home, as Keats had, the fact that he lost all semblance of one so soon takes on a great significance. The loss cannot be rightly gauged as a factor in his life until we understand this quality of his nature.

Because Keats can describe the scene far better than I, and because the scene is so important, I will quote the sonnet, well known though it is:

"TO MY BROTHERS.

Small, busy flames play through the fresh laid coals,
And their faint cracklings o'er our silence creep
Like whispers of the household gods that keep
A gentle empire o'er fraternal souls.
And while, for rhymes, I search around the poles,
Your eyes are fix'd, as in poetic sleep,
Upon the lore so voluble and deep,
That aye at fall of night our care condoles.
This is your birth-day Tom, and I rejoice
That thus it passes smoothly, quietly.
Many such eves of gently whisp'ring noise
May we together pass, and calmly try
What are the world's true joys, — ere the great voice,
From its fair face, shall bid our spirits fly."

We, who know the future in store for these boys, who know how few "such eves" there were to be, cannot help feeling the deep pathos underlying the peace. And for them, too, it was here; for Keats rejoices that Tom's birthday is passing smoothly and quietly. An odd boon to be thankful for on a youngster's seventeenth birthday. Nothing could show better the storm and rack which these Keats boys had gone through — blow after blow, change upon change, loneliness, instability of circumstance, they were used to these, so used that a momentary lull was cause for gratitude.

How modern and realistic are the first two lines! Keats puts "cracklings," not "crackling," observe. This sonnet is somewhat reminiscent of Wordsworth's series of sonnets entitled *Personal Talk*. Wordsworth's "flapping flame" multiplies into many "Small, busy flames" whose "faint cracklings" are "like whispers." The word "voluble" is found in the third sonnet of Wordsworth's series, in which he also refers to the reading of books. Many years later, Hunt pilfered from Keats's lines:

> ". . . the household gods that keep
> A gentle empire o'er fraternal souls"

for his *Rainy Night:*

> "Stormy love's abroad and keeps
> Hopeful coil for gentle sleeps."

To my Brothers is a curious mixture of Hunt, Wordsworth, and pure Keats.

But moods change, and Keats was of moods compact. Authentic and deeply personal as was the mood of *To my Brothers*, Keats had other moods, many of them, quite as authentic and personal. On Monday, Keats is happy just to be at home with his brothers; on Tuesday, he is off and away to Haydon's to sit and gaze at all the paraphernalia of art in the making and talk his head off. It was the gayest kind of excitement and delight. These were heroic paintings: huge, virile sketches of heads, studies of muscles straining up from taut arms, charcoal drawings of torsos done from the Elgin Marbles, rough smudges of attitudes and expressions. The room was full of memoranda flung about in every direction, and on the great easel glowered the half-finished picture of the *Entry into Jerusalem*, with the crowd in every state of completion, but the Christ, it is more than probable, a mere blank, undergoing one of its periodical washings-out. In the midst of this creative confusion, seeming to Keats like a god who has but to wave his arm to bring forth multitudes, was Haydon, Haydon flaming back to Keats's fire of admiration, burning from Keats's spark, wakened to an even more impulsive ardour than usual by the presence of an evident disciple. For, in these early days, Keats was very much that to Haydon. He swallowed Haydon's theories, he listened to Haydon's ideas, he talked to Haydon's talk, and Haydon was wise enough to know that here was a young man whom it was well worth while to ignite.

This was certainly a night, a night to produce effects. Quite a different sort of night from that spent with Chapman's *Homer*, but none the less one of those occasions which rank as experiences. Keats went home in a furor of energy and purpose, and wrote the second sonnet to Haydon. The note which contained it, despatched on Wednesday, the twentieth, is short and very much to the point:

> MY DEAR SIR —
>
> Last evening wrought me up, and I cannot forbear sending you the following. [Here he copies the sonnet.]
>
> Yours unfeignedly
>
> JOHN KEATS."

Haydon is still "My dear Sir," but things are moving. In view of how far they moved, we may consider this sonnet as more momentous than itself.

Haydon records the receipt of the sonnet in his *Autobiography* as follows:

> "One evening (19th November, 1816) after a most eager interchange of thoughts I received from Keats the sonnet beginning, 'Great spirits now on earth are sojourning.'"

Haydon answered Keats at once, and in his answer suggested sending the sonnet to Wordsworth. This proposition amazed and astounded Keats. His reply of Thursday afternoon declares that Haydon's letter has filled him "with a proud pleasure." He adds the significant sentence: "I begin to fix my eye upon one horizon." But Wordsworth — Wordsworth! This is Keats's reaction to Haydon's proposal: "The Idea of your sending it to Wordsworth put me out of breath — you know with what Reverence I would send my Well-wishes to him."

Haydon, unlike most painters, was a reader and a genuine lover of poetry. He was, besides, a fair critic. In his letter, he suggested a daring alteration in one of the lines of the sonnet, the thirteenth, which originally read:

> "Of mighty workings in some distant Mart?"

Haydon had the temerity to urge Keats to drop the second part of the line and leave it short:

> "Of mighty workings?"

Keats was too good a critic himself not to see at once how great an improvement this was. His answer is emphatic: "My feelings entirely fall in with yours in regard to the Ellipsis, and I glory in it." The change was made at once and for all time. The copy of the sonnet which Haydon pasted into his journal has the thirteenth line truncated, and so it was printed in the *Poems*, 1817.

The "great spirits" of Keats's sonnet appear a little quaint to us to-day. Wordsworth, of course, but Hunt and Haydon! Lord Houghton reminds us that, in 1816, Wordsworth's position was far from secure and that it was "something for so young a man to have torn away the veil of prejudice then hanging over that now-honoured name." Odd, indeed, are the inscrutable laws which govern changes of taste! Wordsworth is the only one of Keats's three supermen whose name does not seem out of place. But even in Keats's day, opinions differed. Woodhouse remarks of Hunt's inclusion in the sonnet, "He is introduced here to much better company than his merits entitle him to keep." Now, one hundred years later, Hunt is far better known than Haydon. Hunt is still read, but no one cares a fig for Haydon's pictures.

When Keats, descending from his "great spirits," referred to the still nameless men who constituted the hope of the future in the lines:

> "And other spirits there are standing apart
> Upon the forehead of the age to come"

he ran foul of the critics, who chose to consider such a statement as "a piece of personal conceit."[1] An evidence of quiet confidence in his own generation, these lines certainly were; but of conceit, no. Keats's metaphor here is reminiscent of *Lycidas:*

> "Flames in the forehead of the morning sky,"

and of *Troilus and Cressida :*

> "So rich advantage of a promised glory
> As smiles upon the forehead of this action."

In spite of the precedents for "forehead," it is not happily placed here. One cannot help seeing a phylactery of geniuses standing upon an immense forehead in the manner of a frieze to a Greek vase. The expression immediately brings in a grotesque element which is out of key and far from the author's intention.

In Haydon's *Autobiography*, he refers to his letter acknowledging Keats's sonnet by saying simply, "I thanked

[1] *The Poems of John Keats,* edited by E. de Sélincourt.

him." But really he did much more than that — he ran round to Reynolds and showed him the sonnet. And he must have done this on the very next evening after he had received it, for Reynolds's reaction was prompt. His letter is dated: "Lamb's Cond^t Street Friday morning 10 o'Clock," so we know everything except the important facts of month and year, but the context so evidently supplies these that we can very well do without them, particularly as November twenty-second, 1816, was a Friday. Here is the letter:

"MY DEAR HAYDON,

As you are now getting 'golden opinions from all sorts of men,' it was not fitting that One who is sincerely your Friend should be found wanting. Last night when you left me — I went to my bed — And the Sonnet on the other side absolutely started into my mind. I send it to you, because I really *feel* your Genius, and because I know that things of this kind are the dearest rewards of Genius. It is not equal to anything you have yet had, in power, I know; — but it is sincere, and that is a recommendation. Will you, at my desire, send a copy to Mr Keats, and say to him, how much I was pleased with his.

Yours affectionately,
J. H. REYNOLDS."

Reynolds's sonnet we need not consider; it is both fulsome and feeble. The letter is important as showing that Reynolds and Haydon were already intimate, but that Keats was still a comparative stranger to both of them. With Haydon, a step had been taken; with Reynolds, the step was to come. Keats must have thought better of Reynolds's sonnet than we can possibly do, for it seems to have been the entering wedge to their friendship, although this could not have been long delayed in any case. Keats's social life was getting into its stride, if I may so put it. The little mutual admiration society which constituted Keats's world at this period was running on oiled wheels. Nothing was lost, everything was gained. To the delightful meetings at Hunt's cottage in the Vale of Health, Hampstead, were added the equally delightful meetings in Haydon's painting-room in Great Marlborough Street. The talk at both places was endless, and in both places, also, there were pictures, casts, books of engravings, a host of interests to stimulate Keats's thinking faculties, at the same time that the perpetual discussions of technique roused and coloured his poetic dreams. The surface Keats was living on air; the profounder heart of the man was being watered, fecundated, rowelled up, stamped down, offered a hundred changing contours to the face of life. His friends were witnesses of the airy walk; only his brothers knew of the ferment in his soul. Wherever he went, he was welcomed; and indeed he was a most companionable fellow during the Winter of 1816–17. He was happy, that is the salient fact. His happiness, and the reasons for it, are all to be found in his sonnet *Keen, fitful gusts are whisp'ring here and there* which describes a night walk when he is coming home from Hunt's. The realistic and perfectly modern description in the first three lines is notable:

> "Keen, fitful gusts are whisp'ring here and there
> Among the bushes half leafless, and dry;
> The stars look very cold about the sky."

The coldness of Winter stars seems to have made a great impression on Keats. We have this effect again in a line in *What the Thrush Said*, written in 1818:

> "... the black elm tops 'mongst the freezing stars."

Keen, fitful gusts is an excellent sonnet, and completely in the new manner which I have often spoken of, and this makes it almost impossible to believe that it preceded *On Leaving some Friends at an Early Hour*. Yet Clarke says positively that it did. But Clarke's memory sometimes played him false in the matter of dates, and this last sonnet is so strained and jejune, so overladen with weak ornament, so smothered beneath clap-trap prettinesses, that I should unhesitatingly place it as written in the Spring, at the time when Keats first met Hunt, were it not for some unfortunate passages in *Sleep and Poetry* which we know to have been written during the Autumn. I am scarcely convinced, yet without more evidence I feel obliged to retain Clarke's chronology.

The matter of the sonnet is as bad as its diction. The poet craves a golden pen, with which, while lying on "heap'd up flowers," he may write on a tablet whiter than a star or the hand of a "hymning angel" seen through the strings of a "heavenly harp." A pearly car is to glide by, in which he espies a glorious confusion of pink robes, wavy hair, flashing diamonds, and keen glances. While this is going on, music is to "wander round his ears," at "each delicious ending" of which he is to write down "a line of glorious tone, and full of many wonders of the spheres." At this point, he exclaims!

> "For what a height my spirit is contending!"

For what a height! For what a depth. This boarding-school-miss kind of nonsense is not to be tolerated. It is a pity that some one was not there to say, "My dear fellow, tear that stuff up at once. It is rubbish." But his friends liked it apparently, for he printed it.

On Sunday, December first, there appeared in the *Examiner* a little article entitled, *Young Poets*. The article was in the nature of an editorial, for, though unsigned, it conveyed the impression of carrying the weight of the paper behind it. Hunt, of course, was its author. The article began with Hunt's favourite thesis, the rise of a new school of poetry. Harping on this everlasting theme in the manner of the preface to *Rimini*, Hunt proclaims:

> "... there has been a new school of poetry rising of late, which promises to extinguish the French one that has

> prevailed among us since the time of Charles 2nd. It began with something excessive, like most revolutions, but this gradually wore away; and an evident aspiration after real nature and original fancy remained, which called to mind the finer times of the English Muse. In fact it is wrong to call it a new school, and still more so to represent it as one of innovation, its only object being to restore the same love of Nature, and of *thinking* instead of *talking*, which formerly rendered us real poets, and not merely versifying wits, and bead-rollers of couplets."

Having set his stage, Hunt proceeds to introduce his actors:

> "The object of the present article is merely to notice three young writers, who appear to us to promise a considerable addition of strength to the new school."

These three poets are Shelley, Reynolds, and Keats. Hunt calls Shelley "a striking and original thinker," and excuses himself for not quoting any of Shelley's poems by confessing that he has mislaid some which were sent to him. He speaks of an intention to read Shelley's published books soon, from which we must suppose that he knew Shelley's work very little at this date. Reynolds is praised and blamed in about equal measure, and a passage of twenty-seven lines from the newly published *Naiad* is quoted. Keats, for whom is reserved the honour of being the climax of the article, is dealt with as follows:

> "The last of these young aspirants whom we have met with . . . is, we believe, the youngest of them all, and just of age. His name is JOHN KEATS. He has not yet published anything except in a newspaper, but a set of his manuscripts was handed us the other day, and fairly surprised us with the truth of their ambition, and ardent grappling with Nature. In the following Sonnet there is but one incorrect rhyme, which might be easily altered, but which shall serve in the mean time as a peace-offering to the rhyming critics. The rest of the composition, with

> the exception of a little vagueness in calling the regions of poetry 'the realms of gold,' we do not hesitate to call excellent, especially the last six lines. The word *swims* is complete; and the whole conclusion is equally powerful and quiet."

At this point, Hunt quotes *On First Looking into Chapman's Homer*, which, with half a dozen lines of peroration, concludes the paper.

Hunt's wisdom in choosing just that sonnet to quote, cannot be sufficiently extolled, and his criticism of the poem is both apt and just. The false rhyme is, of course, "demesne" and "mean," which proves that up to December first, six weeks after he had written the poem, Keats had not fallen in with Cary's "pure serene." By the time his book went to press, however, which cannot have been later than early in February, the line had been altered to its present form.

Things were going well for Keats, but the effect of all this boosting was to make him itch to do something a little bigger. Haydon's colossal figures and colossal talk were producing an effect, and, on the whole, it was not a bad effect. Haydon was a believer in huge canvases, and, as opposed to Hunt, was like one of his own pictures placed side by side with a Spode tea-pot. Keats vacillated manfully between the two. Then there was the Wordsworth influence, remote and shadowy, but fruitful in the suggestion that poetry should be more than a beautiful surface. Chaotic as Keats's mind was in its effort to digest so many diverse new impressions, he yet felt the need of saying something at first hand, of slipping some definite idea beneath a superstructure.

How long he pondered this, there is no possible way of knowing; but the desire was not new to him when, some time during the Autumn, he passed a sleepless night with his surging confusions on the sofa in Hunt's study. This was a congenial place enough in which to have them assail him. The room was lined with low bookcases on which stood busts, and the walls were crowded with pictures. Hunt says that this study was no bigger than "an old mansion's closet," and we can imagine the kind of literary and artistic jumble it was. These pictures, and books, and busts, merely carried on the talk of the evening. The silence must have buzzed with suggestion to Keats's excited ears. Atmospheres must have flowed into, and superseded, one another with the swiftness of kaleidoscopic patterns, as his mind lighted upon one object or another of the many by which he was surrounded. Above him were the effigies of the great masters, whose voices pealed and thundered from the shelves. These men had known how to leap the breach of death, and Keats longed with all his soul to capture this one overwhelmingly important secret — how not to die. He would spend himself to the pith to rise from the ruck of perishing men through the agency of an imperishable work of which he was the author. Poetry! Poetry! That was at once his sword and the world it should conquer. But how still the room was, how breathlessly quiet and concentrated! How softly the night wrapped itself about him, how possible darkness made his wildest dreams! Then the other men, all those writing hosts that had preceded him, those who had done well, those who had done ill — he speculated upon them in the teeming blackness. So the night went, wide-eyed and exhausting; but the impression remained and out of it grew *Sleep and Poetry*.

When *Sleep and Poetry* was written, we do not know exactly. But probably not earlier than November, 1818. The poem, as printed in the *Poems*, 1817, was headed with a most appropriate motto from Chaucer's *The Floure and the Lefe*. If Cowden Clarke's recollection be right, Keats's first introduction to Chaucer was when he read the *Floure and the Lefe* at Clarke's in February, 1817. But, as Keats's book was already entirely printed by the second of March, when he wrote his *Dedication* sonnet which is dated on that day, it must certainly have been in press a month or so earlier. To insert a motto of five lines in a book after it was set up, would mean changing all the succeeding pages, an annoyance which few publishers would be willing to undergo for a young author with his first book. It is possible that the call at Clarke's may have occurred very early in February, and that the book may have taken less than a month to print, but this is pushing possibilities rather far. My own opinion is that Keats had read Chaucer before the day at Clarke's, and that the *Floure and the Lefe* sonnet was not an extempore piece of work, as Clarke thought. But of that later. The point here is that, although the motto may have been given to the poem after it was finished, *Sleep and Poetry* is long and must have taken a good while to write. Keats always took a long time with long poems; we have seen him taking several months to finish *I Stood Tip-toe.* I think, therefore, that in assigning *Sleep and Poetry* to November and December we shall not be far wrong.

Sleep and Poetry is certainly Keats's most ambitious attempt up to that time. Because it is in some ways a poem he set himself to write, it lacks the exuberant beauty, the flash, of *I Stood Tip-toe.* The poem begins with an invocation to sleep. The first line is charming:

> "What is more gentle than a wind in summer?"

but the next line spoils everything:

> "What is more soothing than the pretty hummer"

even the next two explanatory lines:

> "That stays one moment in an open flower,
> And buzzes cheerily from bower to bower?"

do not help it. These inequalities in the technique of Keats's early poems are very interesting, showing, as they do, the disabilities under which he laboured. In this case, he was floored by the rhyme. No man ever worked harder to bring his technique into line with his thought than did Keats; a study of his first drafts is a liberal education in the art of writing poetry, as it is also an illuminating pointer to the psychology of the creative mind.

Some of Keats's similes on sleep in this invocation are very happy:

> "What is more tranquil than a musk-rose blowing
> In a green island."

He goes on to "the leafiness of dales," and "a nest of nightingales," then he suddenly catches sight of an engraving of Cordelia, or, if it is too dark to see it, recollects it, and promptly adds:

> "More serene than Cordelia's countenance?"

No one has yet traced the source of Keats's interest in an ash-tree full of berries, but somewhere, somehow, in fact or literature, Keats had met such an ash-tree and he could not forget it. I think he read of it, for he connects it with mountains, and at that time he had never seen a mountain. In *Calidore*, he speaks of plumes waving

> "High as the berries of a wild ash tree,"

here he has

> "Fresher than berries of a mountain tree."

This line stands at the opening of a new stanza, for now, across his thoughts of sleep, filtering through them, dominating them, come other thoughts, "awful, sweet, and holy." Sometimes they are "like fearful claps of thunder," sometimes

> ". . . like a gentle whispering
> Of all the secrets of some wond'rous thing
> That breathes about us in the vacant air."

These are thoughts of poetry, that high thing to which he is aspiring. He likens it to the sun bursting through clouds, and says that any one who has seen this and has

> "... felt his bosom clean
> For his great Maker's presence, but must know
> What 'tis I mean."

This is a boy's utterance, a boy who is still content to be taught, to learn, whose individual opinions are no opinions at all, only feelings; who feels nature, but accepts philosophies, yet who is beginning dimly, ever so dimly, to formulate a creed, mostly at present of other men's designing, but still the stray beginnings of a creed.

Another invocation follows, and this time it is to poetry:

> "O Poesy! for thee I hold my pen
> That am not yet a glorious denizen
> Of thy wide heaven — Should I rather kneel
> Upon some mountain-top until I feel
> A glowing splendour round about me hung,
> And echo back the voice of thine own tongue?"

Unfortunately the "echoing back" was resorted to only too often. It was not until very near the end of his writing life, and not entirely even then, that Keats learnt to eschew the echo. In fact, with all his originality, he permitted himself echoes to an extent which might almost be termed plagiarizing.

"Stop and consider! life is but a day," he exclaims, in a line destined to live in familiar speech on account of its apposite quotability. Life is a dew-drop falling from a tree, the sleep of an Indian whose boat is rushing toward a cataract. (Here is Robertson's *America* again, for the cataract is the Fall of Montmorency.) But, after all, his youth asserts:

> "Life is the rose's hope while yet unblown;
> The reading of an ever-changing tale;

> The light uplifting of a maiden's veil;
> A pigeon tumbling in clear summer air;
> A laughing school-boy, without grief or care,
> Riding the springy branches of an elm."

The last three lines are the essence of careless happiness. Keats at this time was indeed a laughing school-boy, riding the springy branches of an elm, and in this case the elm was that life of stimulating friendships and intellectual excitement opening before him. It is his very soul which cries out

> "O for ten years, that I may overwhelm
> Myself in poesy; so I may do the deed
> That my own soul has to itself decreed."

How young and immature he still was, is seen in his plea for ten years. Ten years is a monstrous long time when one is very young. And yet thirty-one is scarcely the period of completion in most men's lives. Viewing the expanse of life with a child's eyes, he thought it would suffice. Poor boy! He had only four years and a fraction, and to his own thinking the deed was never done; but what he did accomplish has been sufficient to put him "among the English poets" as long as the language lasts, one supposes. These lines are particularly important, for in them the poet expresses his determination of direction. We must note them carefully, for we never cease to hear the same cry while we have to do with Keats.

Keats's point of view was not formulated in prose. It was not in a condition to state, but still he was already vaguely conscious of it; he could circle round it in symbols, although he was utterly incapable of intellectualizing it, even to himself. We shall realize this more fully when we come to consider *Endymion*. A year and a half later, writing to Reynolds on May third, 1818, he has crystallized it into a statement. In this letter, Keats is discussing Wordsworth's *Tintern Abbey*, and he may have had *Tintern Ab-*

bey in mind when he wrote *Sleep and Poetry*, for in it, he, like Wordsworth, sketches the differing phases of childhood, youth, and manhood. But how unlike is the attitude of the two poets. Wordsworth passes over his childhood without a trace of either interest or sentiment. He has lost all tenderness for the little fellow he once was, whose erstwhile joys appear to him merely as

> "The coarser pleasures of my boyish days
> And their glad animal movements."

That is all he has to say on the subject, his manner towards his childish self is avuncular and distant. Keats, on the other hand, looks very kindly at the boy he has so recently been. The springy branches of the elm are a recent and alluring memory.

The second state, youth, not only shows the difference in age of the two men at the time each wrote, but the difference in temperament. It is not a fair comparison, for Wordsworth is at his best in the passage in *Tintern Abbey* where he describes his youthful love of nature, and Keats is at his worst in the corresponding passage in *Sleep and Poetry*. Wordsworth looks back upon his youth with the sympathy he denies his boyhood, but still his description is in retrospect. It is, as he says, "what I then was." The description of natural objects in *I Stood Tip-toe* would be a juster counterpart to this passage of Wordsworth. The account of the period of youthful joys, of the pleasures of nature and imagination during it, in *Sleep and Poetry*, is among the most unfortunate things which Keats ever wrote. It is superficial, trivial, and forced; it is cheap and materialistic. It does not do justice to Keats's own temperament. He is thinking up a list of pretty pleasures of the Huntian type, but outdoing Hunt in silliness. In *I Stood Tip-toe*, Keats is recording what he really loves; in this passage in *Sleep and Poetry* he is writing verse for effect. Its poverty is evident in every line. It is exactly this passage which makes me hesitate to put *On Leaving Some Friends at an Early Hour* back in the Spring. Any versifying folly is possible to a man who could perpetrate such miserable stuff as this, and insert it in a poem of avowedly serious intent. Keats did himself a great wrong in these lines, and the melancholy part of it is that undoubtedly his mentor, Hunt, and probably his other friends, praised him for them.

The comparison of Wordsworth and Keats in the last stage, manhood, can scarcely be properly made. Wordsworth was speaking of what he had experienced, Keats was guessing and his guess-work blew off in picture. Although the comparison is hardly just, it is interesting to set these two passages side by side, partly to make more evident what Wordsworth had and Keats had not, partly to prove Keats's growth in comprehension a year and a half later when he wrote to Reynolds. I shall quote the letter when we reach the period to which it belongs. Soberly, without exuberance, Wordsworth sets down the fundamental concept of his maturity:

> "... For I have learned
> To look on nature, not as in the hour
> Of thoughtless youth, but hearing oftentimes
> The still, sad music of humanity,
> Not harsh nor grating, though of ample power
> To chasten and subdue. And I have felt
> A presence that disturbs me with the joy
> Of elevated thoughts; a sense sublime
> Of something far more deeply interfused,
> Whose dwelling is the light of setting suns,
> And the round ocean, and the living air,
> And the blue sky, and in the mind of man,
> A motion and a spirit, that impels
> All thinking things, all objects of all thought,
> And rolls through all things. Therefore am I still
> A lover of the meadows and the woods,
> And mountains; and of all that we behold

From this green earth; of all the mighty world
Of eye and ear, both what they half create,
And what perceive; well pleased to recognize
The anchor of my purest thoughts, the nurse,
The guide, the guardian of my heart, and soul
Of all my moral being."

Wordsworth's passage, fine and serious though it is, is marred by didacticism, a fault into which Keats never fell. Keats's manhood in this poem is mere vision:

"And can I ever bid these joys farewell?
Yes, I must pass them for a nobler life,
Where I may find the agonies, the strife
Of human hearts: for lo! I see afar,
O'ersailing the blue cragginess, a car
And steeds with streamy manes — the charioteer
Looks out upon the winds with glorious fear:
And now the numerous tramplings quiver lightly
Along a huge cloud's ridge; and now with sprightly
Wheel downward come they into fresher skies,
Tipt round with silver from the sun's bright eyes.
Still downward with capacious whirl they glide;
And now I see them on a green-hill's side
In breezy rest among the nodding stalks.
The charioteer with wond'rous gesture talks
To the trees and mountains; and there soon appear
Shapes of delight, of mystery, and fear,
Passing along before a dusky space
Made by some mighty oaks: as they would chase
Some ever-fleeting music on they sweep.
Lo! how they murmur, laugh, and smile, and weep:
Some with upholden hand and mouth severe;
Some with their faces muffled to the ear
Between their arms; some, clear in youthful bloom,
So glad and smilingly athwart the gloom;
Some looking back, and some with upward gaze;
Yes, thousands in a thousand different ways
Flit onward — now a lovely wreath of girls
Dancing their sleek hair into tangled curls;
And now broad wings. Most awfully intent

> The driver of those steeds is forward bent,
> And seems to listen: O that I might know
> All that he writes with such a hurrying glow.
>
> The visions all are fled — the car is fled
> Into the light of heaven, and in their stead
> A sense of real things comes doubly strong,
> And, like a muddy stream, would bear along
> My soul to nothingness: but I will strive
> Against all doubtings, and will keep alive
> The thought of that same chariot, and the strange
> Journey it went."

Was ever a more unsatisfactory statement of intention put into words? Keats realizes that to be a great poet he must find "the agonies, the strife of human hearts," but he has so little idea of how this is to be done that all he can think of is to conjure up a fairy-tale of a charioteer whirling over a world of mysterious visions, the most concrete of which is "a wreath of girls." That the figure is intended to mean a poet descending from the cloudy heights of imagination to mingle with humanity, needs no stressing. It is not the idea which is at fault, that is commonplace enough, in all conscience; it is the expression of it. Keats meant a great deal more than he had the power to think out. What he wanted to say was that descriptions were all very well, but he must learn to get nearer the poignance of life and infuse his poetry with it. Yet, even as he says this, or, at least, approaches to saying it, his fancy gets the better of him, and he swirls off in an aurora of patternless colour, committing the very blunder he swears to eschew. Curious psychological evidence of a bugbear — it is no more, no less. The interesting thing is that he knows it, and yet cannot escape — cannot, indeed, more than half want to escape — as yet.

Leaving the three ages of man, Keats turns to poetry, and the many talks he has had with Hunt and Hunt's friends about the new movement. Keats's chief antipathy was, quite naturally, the poetry of the eighteenth century. Every age revolts against its immediate predecessor. The eighteenth century was over, the *Lyrical Ballads* had started a new era. It did not need Hunt to show him his direction; he inherited his bias by the mere fact of being born at the proper moment. Keats was all agog with the new movement; and, with the intolerance of youth, he hated the formal, unlyrical school of Pope. His new acquaintance with Chapman had shoved Pope still farther into the discard. With a charming arrogance, he declared of the group that

> ". . . with a puling infant's force
> They sway'd about upon a rocking horse,
> And thought it Pegasus."

He shouted that "the winds of heaven blew, the ocean roll'd." He even caught up Wordsworth to help him and announced that

> ". . . The blue
> Bared its eternal bosom,"

so borrowing from Wordsworth's sonnet, *The world is too much with us*, the line:

> "The sea that bares her bosom to the moon."

"Beauty was awake," cried Keats to the shades of eighteenth century masters peacefully sleeping in the comfortable cerements of fame:

> "Why were ye not awake? But ye were dead
> To things ye knew not of, — were closely wed
> To musty laws lined out with wretched rule
> And compass vile: so that ye taught a school
> Of dolts to smooth, inlay, and clip, and fit,
> Till, like the certain wands of Jacob's wit,
> Their verses tallied. Easy was the task:
> A thousand handicraftsmen wore the mask

> Of Poesy. Ill-fated, impious race!
> That blasphemed the bright Lyrist to his face,
> And did not know it, — no, they went about,
> Holding a poor, decrepit standard out
> Mark'd with most flimsy mottos, and in large
> The name of one Boileau!"

This is a splendid, ingenuous diatribe. A good wholesome blast of invective. The fact that Keats did not know what he was talking about when he called the sharp-edged, epigrammatic couplets of Pope, the carefully pruned, skilful, exquisite verses of Gray, easy, shows that he had never tried to write anything of the sort. Poetry has many mansions and one of them is verse; but probably the passing world, see-sawing back and forth from opinion to opinion as it moves on, records in ever increasing ratio its conviction that verse, however witty, satirical, and keen, is but an outhouse in the domain of poetry after all.

The poem rises out of the chaos of half-realized sensation in a perfect drum-rattle of protest and scorn. In this passage, Keats writes himself down a true modern and a man of his time.

From the Boileau passage, Keats goes on to picture the spirits of the older poets hovering round the scenes they knew, perhaps to give a welcome to the poets of whom he approves, who are, this time, Chatterton, Wordsworth, and Hunt, with a somewhat troubled reference to Byron at the end. There follows an idyllic vision of future poetry, in the midst of which Keats is suddenly seized with a most characteristic diffidence in regard to himself:

> "Will not some say that I presumptuously
> Have spoken? that from hastening disgrace
> 'Twere better far to hide my foolish face?
> That whining boyhood should with reverence bow
> Ere the dread thunderbolt could reach?"

But if he should hide, he exclaims, it would be in poetry.

No, he will not despair, for

> "... there ever rolls
> A vast idea before me, and I glean
> Therefrom my liberty; thence too I've seen
> The end and aim of Poesy ...
>
> . . . . .
>
> An ocean dim, sprinkled with many an isle
> Spreads awfully before me. How much toil!
> How many days! What desperate turmoil!
> Ere I can have explored its wildnesses.
> Ah, what a task! upon my bended knees,
> I could unsay those — no, impossible!
> Impossible!
> For sweet relief I'll dwell
> On humbler thoughts."

Keats's ambition knew no bounds, but, even as he cherished it, he began to fear its immensity. His mind during this Autumn and Winter is in a constant tumult over his great paradox. To do, and yet how possibly to do, that is his question. Again and again he must have turned from it in exhaustion. We see him doing this here. He begins to muse on his friends, particularly, we can imagine, on Hunt, in whose house he is, on the delight of their reading poetry together, on the pleasure of talking over books read before, and so he drifts into a fanciful description of the pictures hanging about him in the study. The poem ends by stating that

> "... The morning light
> Surprised me even from a sleepless night;
> And up I rose refresh'd, and glad, and gay,
> Resolving to begin that very day
> These lines; and howsoever they be done
> I leave them as a father does his son."

Was ever so boyish and inconsequential an ending? Here we have it, a scrap-book of Keats's mind at the time, but scarcely a very successful poem. It does not compare in beauty to *I Stood Tip-toe.* It cannot match the chiselled serenity and completeness of *On First Looking Into Chapman's Homer.* It has few lines that stick in the memory, or that one wants to remember. Why, then, did not only his contemporaries, but those critics who succeeded them, even down to the present day, unite in declaring it the high-water mark of the 1817 volume? For the simple reason that it opened doors to a great many interesting thoughts and speculations. It is a grand failure, full of potentialities. Every one of the stages of Keats's career was marked by some splendid and fructifying failure. Having taken a step and laboriously brought his work up to the stage he had reached, he invariably took another step, and the new stage was again marked by a failure and various successes. He was too genuine a poet to be unwilling to dare; he was too brave a poet to remain within the limits of any achieved perfection; he was too honest a man to wrap himself in the cloak of an outdistanced knowledge. Four great failures punctuate his life, and they are among the most interesting things in it, from the psychological point of view. They are: *Sleep and Poetry*, *Endymion*, *Otho the Great*, and *Hyperion* — the poem so-called, I mean. For the *Vision*, that is a different matter; it teems with potentialities, and it is only the slightest of fragments.

There are three lines in the passage on the end and aim of poetry which I did not quote in their context for the reason that I wished to emphasize them particularly by themseves. They are:

> ". . . Therefore should I
> Be but the essence of deformity,
> A coward, did my very eye-lids wink
> At speaking out what I have dared to think."

We cannot enter fully into Keats's attitude when he wrote *Sleep and Poetry* unless we realize that the poem was intended as a sort of confession, and more than a confession, a very signing of a poetical thirty-nine articles. He has worked himself up to the idea that it is encumbent on him to state his position. Regarding the creation of poetry as the most ideal activity to which a man can devote his life, he finds it a necessity that any one so dedicated should proclaim the fact, be the consequences of such proclamation what they may. Vague as his conceptions on the subject are, he must, nevertheless, say that he has them. No longer do we see the joyous excitement which imbues the poems done at Margate. At Margate, he was intoxicated with the idea of being actually a poet and nothing else; now the same thought is sobering. He has gazed long and ardently at his purpose, he has even fathomed something of the meaning of what he has undertaken. He knows vaguely, but with a reasonable speculation, how great will be his task. Tremulous, yet undaunted, he burns his ships, and in *Sleep and Poetry* we see the waving of the torch which ignites them. He has stated his case before the world, as he feels in bounden duty to do.

This was a challenge as it stood, but Keats had no idea how much of a challenge it was, and he flew directly in the face of destiny when he not only publicly signed himself poet, but left no doubt as to the kind of poet he was going to be. The early nineteenth century was not so tolerant to the utterances of youth as is the early twentieth. For one thing, the middle-aged to-day can scarcely point with pride to the results of the system into which they were born and which they are doing their best to continue. The cry of "Patience! Patience!" is not listened to gladly by boys who believe that they are the dupes of a want of prevision in their elders. It was very different in Keats's day. The powers that were could wave complacent hands toward the banners of Waterloo and Napoleon shut up at St. Helena. They could point out what they had done and command that it be thought good, and the majority were on their side. It was an age of precedent, and precedent with deeds to back it. Poetry was breaking its chains and beginning to run with a mighty freedom, but the critics were not yet aware of an unsteady footing, or at least only so much aware of it as to stand firmer than ever. Keats threw in his lot with the new men; he could not possibly have done anything else, and it is quite characteristic of him that, instead of merely holding an opinion and acting on it, he must needs come out with it slapdash before everybody. It was foolish, of course, but a rather magnificent foolishness, after all. And he would have expected just what he got if he had been more experienced. It seems surprising that Hunt and Hunt's friends did not prepare him. I am afraid that they were too pleased with the annexation of so brilliant a young adherent to the movement to warn him as they should.

One curious thing about Keats's work is that, with all his infinite pains, he was often strangely careless. Many copyings by hand are probably partly responsible, and Keats seems to have been a wretched proof-reader, so we may put something down to those causes. The two short lines in *I Stood Tip-toe* are on purpose, of course, but equally of course the line in *Sleep and Poetry:*

> "Or the low rumblings earth's regions under"

must be a mistake, unless Keats thought of "rumblings" as having three syllables, as he may have done, since he makes the same blunder in

> "The dazzling sun-rise: two sisters sweet."

This very matter of pronunciation tripped him more than once. It overset him again in

> "Perhaps to see shapes of light, aerial limning"

when he certainly read the first word "p'raps." But I do not think

> "Ere the dread thunderbolt could reach? How!"

is a mistake. I believe it to have been intentional, an effort to introduce a rest into a line for the effect of the pause before the exclamation "How!" Keats was more rhythmically daring than any poet of his time except Blake, and I believe this to be an instance of his attempting to impose a degree of variance into conventional prosody which that prosody will not, even to this day, contentedly bear.

Hunt and Haydon — these were the dual influences, as far as human contacts were concerned, which ruled Keats's intellectual life during this Autumn and Winter. Hunt appears to have replaced Cowden Clarke as mentor; Clarke, being himself largely derived from Hunt at this period, began imperceptibly to take a more equal place in Keats's estimation. For were not he and Clarke on a par where admiration of Hunt was concerned? Meanwhile the intercourse with Haydon was fast growing into intimacy. Keats was now not so much a vistor, as a frequenter, of Haydon's studio at 41 Great Marlborough Street. It was there, I am convinced, that a little incident of considerable importance to posterity must have occurred some time between the twentieth of November and the seventeenth of December. This incident is the making of the life mask.

It is not known for a fact that Haydon was the perpetrator of the mask, but that is the legend. And, in the cold light of reason, who else would have been likely to do it? Haydon was an adept at making plaster casts. He had obtained permission to take what casts he pleased of the Elgin Marbles, and had abundantly availed himself of the opportunity. In July, 1815, he had made a cast of his friend, the painter, David Wilkie's face. He records the affair with gusto:

> "Never had such fun, as Wilkie lay on the ground looking like a Knight Templar on a monument. We quizzed him till we roared. We gave him leave to laugh if he could;

all he could do was to clasp his hands to express his participation in the fun."

Keats was just the fellow for an artistic lark of this kind. He admired Haydon's taste, and if Haydon wanted a cast of his face, that in itself was a subtle flattery. On December seventeenth, he wrote to Clarke:

> "You may now look at Minerva's Ægis with impunity, seeing that my awful Visage did not turn you into a John Doree. You have accordingly a legitimate title to a Copy — I will use my interest to procure it for you."

It is not known whether Clarke ever did get a copy, but Reynolds certainly had one, which is quite natural, as Reynolds was more intimate with Haydon at this time than either Keats or Clarke. The Reynolds cast descended to his sister, Miss Charlotte Reynolds, by whom it was given to the National Portrait Gallery, London, in 1883. The legend which attributes the mask to Haydon also has it that it was made in 1816; so does our problematical evidence swing full circle. Buxton Forman says that Keats's sister, Señora Llanos, considered it "a more satisfactory representation of her brother than any of the portraits."

Keats was extremely industrious all through the month of December. He must have been overhauling his manuscripts preparatory to printing them. We know that he was still working on *I Stood Tip-toe*, and, as I have already shown, *Sleep and Poetry* must have been on the stocks, but, besides these activities, he found time to write five sonnets. Two of these seem to owe their existence to Hunt's surroundings and Hunt's conversation. For where should Keats have got his passing preoccupation with Italy if not at Hunt's? The sonnet, *Happy is England*, is simply the expression of a sort of nostalgia for the Italy of — what? *Rimini?* A little perhaps, but more likely of some romantic engraving in Hunt's parlour. It is not a good sonnet, although the "tall woods" of England "with high romances blent" are pleasant. The sonnet is merely one of Keats's youthful flights of fancy, and his desire to float "about the summer waters" with "beauties of a deeper glance" than are common in England, relates it to the "wreath of girls" passage in *Sleep and Poetry.* At just this period, Keats was intermittently occupied with visions of vague and nameless damsels disporting among Utopian scenes. Punctually to certain moods, they reappeared, precisely as one might have recourse to a box of sugar-plums.

The second of these Hunt-begotten sonnets is that *To Kosciusko* which Hunt printed in the *Examiner* for February 16, 1817, where it is signed "J. K." and dated "Dec. 1816." The Polish patriot, who had not only fought for the integrity of his own country against a rapacious Russia in vain, but, after a voluntary banishment, had returned and headed another national movement against Russia and Prussia combined, who had been defeated, wounded, and thrust into prison, had also, in the beginning of his career, gone to America and joined the revolutionary army there. Such a man could not fail of becoming an idolized hero in the eyes of the Liberals of the period. It was surely talk of Kosciusko among the Hunt set which caused Keats to fall into his old patriotic stride and indite a sonnet to the man of the moment in Huntian discourse. Kosciusko's name is to stand with Alfred the Great's, but here he is not followed by any others of Keats's favourite heroes, his usual naming of them gives place to the comprehensive: "the great of yore." The poem is uninteresting, and, indeed, one begins to tire of Keats's dutiful echoes of Hunt's political opinions. The truth is that, at this early date, Keats had not begun to think of the subject at all. He took his politics ready-made from the group which attracted him for quite other reasons.

Exactly when George Keats's attachment to Georgiana

Wylie became a recognized engagement is nowhere recorded. But there is perhaps an inkling that the engagement was considered definitely as such by the end of 1816 in the fact that one of these December sonnets is openly addressed "To G. A. W." and written in Keats's own person and not as the mouth-piece of his brother. In the manuscript, the sonnet is entitled *To Miss Wylie*; in a transcript in Tom Keats's copy-book, it is called *Sonnet to a Lady*. Evidently a compromise between the obvious and the obscure was hit upon for the book. The initials told his friends what there was no longer any need to hide, and the public remained decorously in the dark.

As an evidence of Keats's love and admiration for Georgiana Wylie, the sonnet is most interesting; as a sonnet, it is one of the unfortunate things which date. Try as we will, to twentieth century ears its obsolescent diction hides the charm of its conception. The first line:

"Nymph of the downward smile, and sidelong glance,"

should be a delightful characterization, but it is spoilt by "Nymph." Time may bring this style of writing back to us, as time usually does in the long run; at the moment, it cannot be savoured. Yet the poem is a document of great value, not only because it reveals Keats's feeling for his future sister-in-law, but because, in spite of its florid technique, it proves what a singularly attractive person Miss Wylie was. That she was a very rare woman in many ways, there can be no doubt, but here we discover that she was also a very charming one.

On Sunday, December twenty-second, Keats wrote a sonnet which is so little known that I am going to quote it here:

"WRITTEN IN DISGUST OF VULGAR SUPERSTITION.

The church bells toll a melancholy round,
Calling the people to some other prayers,
Some other gloominess, more dreadful cares,

More hearkening to the sermon's horrid sound.
Surely the mind of man is closely bound
In some black spell; seeing that each one tears
Himself from fireside joys, and Lydian airs,
And converse high of those with glory crown'd.
Still, still they toll, and I should feel a damp, —
A chill as from a tomb, did I not know
That they are dying like an outburnt lamp;
That 'tis their sighing, wailing ere they go
Into oblivion; that fresh flowers will grow
And many glories of immortal stamp."

Tom Keats wrote in his copy-book, "Written by J. K. in fifteen minutes," which rapid writing shows how strongly he felt his invective. Tom dates the sonnet "Sunday evening, Dec. 24, 1816," but Christmas Eve in 1816 fell on a Tuesday, not on a Sunday, and it was evidently for the Sunday church-going that the bells were tolling, not for any Christmas festival. Tom could not have mistaken the day of the week, the subject of the sonnet proves that, but it is equally evident that he blundered over the day of the month, not an uncommon error with all three of the brothers, John himself is often very vague as to the date on which he is writing.

In this poem, we get at Keats in a surprising and effective way. He is beginning to think and probe for himself, to cast off the trammels of convention. It is true that he had been seeing Shelley, and had heard not a little of Shelley's atheistic talk; but Shelley's atheism was of the eighteenth century brand, as was Godwin's, and this kind of skepticism made no appeal whatever to Keats's type of mind. His own disbelief, when it came, was of a totally different sort. It reached him through no angry and spectacular revolt, but through the slow churning of thought within him. It made no difference to his actions as regards his life as a human being among human beings. His unbelief comforted itself with no rhodomontade, he never paraded it, it simply settled upon him as an undeniable conviction, quite without the sphere of ethics. Ethical, Keats always was. Duty was his watchword; duty to his art, and to his personal relations. Keats could never have got into the sort of mess which Shelley fell into with Harriet Westbrook, and, having married her in a spurt of good feeling, have brutally deserted her. Shelley's whole spiritual nature was inimical to that of Keats. Realizing this, it seems extremely unlikely that either Shelley's braggadocio, or Hunt's gay impiousness, ever influenced Keats. There were parts of himself which he gave into no one's keeping.

It was no agnostic who wrote *Written in Disgust of Vulgar Superstition*, but a man who will not brook hypocrisy, and who dares see the false insistence of unhappy dogmatism.

The sonnet is good because it is straightforward and fraught with genuine feeling. The fact that it really ends in the middle of the penultimate line is, of course, a technical error; the rest of the line and the last line were tacked on because the form required it, and the result is anticlimax. "Lydian airs" is unfortunate; the diction of Milton's *L'Allegro* does not fit well with the forthright speech of this poem. "Converse high of those with glory crown'd" is Thomson's "hold high converse with the mighty dead" in *The Seasons*, *Winter*, but it is sufficiently disguised.

This was one of the home days, reading by the fire. In a note, from which I have already quoted,[1] in the Woodhouse Book in the Morgan Library, Woodhouse speaks of this sonnet as having been written "on the bells which disturbed him at his lodggs. at No.   Cheapside." The incongruity of the gloomy bells, and all that they stood for, breaking in on his peace, that peace which meant so much in certain moods, roused Keats to a sudden hatred

[1] See Vol. I, p. 188.

of the grim ugliness they represented. A religion without beauty was a misnomer. It could not be; it was not. So far had he got and no farther — yet. This is a flicker in the wind which we must note at its relative value.

The sonnet is not a finished composition, but it conveys itself with swiftness and feeling, and the first four and a half lines of the sestet are really fine. Evidently Keats thought nothing of it, which is a proof of how hard it was for him to believe that a poem written in natural language could have merit. It may have been for this reason that Keats did not include it in his forthcoming book, more likely he thought, or some of his friends thought, that it would be considered a shocking performance. The manner of it can hardly have pleased the Hunt circle, and the vociferously religious Haydon, if he ever saw it, which I doubt, would have instantly begun a course of argument and prayer. So the poem vanished away, not to reappear for thirty-two years, when Lord Houghton printed it in his edition, from a copy probably, as he gives it the erroneous sub-title, *Written on a Summer Evening*.

Christmas came and passed; but with whom it was spent, we do not know. The stream of letters which gives us so many of the details of Keats's life does not become continuous until the following Spring.

We owe to Clarke the account of an evening spent at Hunt's very late in the year. It was, to be exact, on Monday, December the thirtieth, that Clarke and Keats went out to Hampstead. Clarke recounts that the talk having got upon crickets, "the cheerful little grasshopper of the fireside — Hunt proposed to Keats the challenge of writing then, there, and to time, a sonnet 'On the Grasshopper and Cricket.' No one was present but myself, and they accordingly set to . . . I cannot say how long the trial lasted. I was not proposed umpire: and had no stop-watch for the occasion. The time, however, was short for such a performance, and Keats won as to time."

Hunt was fond of these competitions, but his sonnet in this instance is execrable. We come at the two men so excellently in these poems that I will give them both. Hunt's sonnet shall precede:

"THE GRASSHOPPER AND THE CRICKET

Green little vaulter in the sunny grass
Catching your heart up at the feel of June,
Sole voice that's heard amidst the lazy noon,
When ev'n the bees lag at the summoning brass;
And you, warm little housekeeper, who class
With those who think the candles come too soon,
Loving the fire, and with your tricksome tune
Nick the glad silent moments as they pass;
Oh sweet and tiny cousins, that belong,
One to the fields, the other to the hearth,
Both have your sunshine; both though small are strong
At your clear hearts; and both were sent on earth
To sing in thoughtful ears this natural song, —
In doors and out, summer and winter, Mirth."

This is Keats's sonnet:

"ON THE GRASSHOPPER AND THE CRICKET

The poetry of earth is never dead:
When all the birds are faint with the hot sun,
And hide in cooling trees, a voice will run
From hedge to hedge about the new-mown mead;
That is the Grasshopper's — he takes the lead
In summer luxury, — he has never done
With his delights; for when tired out with fun
He rests at ease beneath some pleasant weed.
The poetry of earth is ceasing never:
On a lone winter evening, when the frost
Has wrought a silence, from the stove there shrills
The cricket's song, in warmth increasing ever,
And seems to one in drowsiness half lost,
The Grasshopper's among some grassy hills."

Hunt must have perceived how much better Keats's

sonnet was than his own, but the generosity of the man was sincere and unflinching. Clarke testifies to the "unaffected generosity and perfectly unpretentious encouragement" with which he greeted Keats's poem. Clarke mentions "his sincere look of pleasure at the first line," which he called "Such a prosperous opening!", and tells how, when he came to the lines about the frost, he exclaimed "Ah! That's perfect! Bravo Keats!" What Hunt does not seem to have noticed is the excellent pattern weaving of the poem: the sestet beginning with a variant replica of the first line of the octave; the careful keeping of the grasshopper in the octave; the condensed and yet ample characterization of the cricket; the return of the grasshopper in the last line, welding the two sections together and rounding out the conception with a satisfying completeness. This sonnet proves that Keats, careful reviser though he was, could on occasion improvise very well indeed. We have no first draft of the poem, so how much it differed from the printed version it is impossible to tell. Keats included this sonnet in *Poems*, 1817, and, in spite of the book's being, by that time, out, Hunt printed it in the *Examiner* on September twenty-first, 1817. It was so appropriate to the season that I suppose he could not resist it, particularly as he printed his own corresponding sonnet in the same number. There was also another reason, of which I shall have occasion to speak later.

The odd part of Clarke's tale is the end, where he remarks: "With all the gratifying things that were said to him, Keats protested to me, as we were afterwards walking home, that he preferred Hunt's treatment of the subject to his own." It would be interesting to know what Keats really said. Did he mean the conception of the subject or its execution? There is a great difference here. Keats's treatment is certainly far more original than Hunt's, but it is possible to like Hunt's approach to the subject; I do not think it possible to like Hunt's execution of it. If Keats really did, then young, wondering friendship is blind, like love.

Keats's sonnet, although not up to his best, is a delightful thing. The opening is an excellent picture, vivid and suggestive; one can see it, feel it, and smell it. The frost, as Hunt pointed out, is perfect; and the return of the grasshopper in the end, as being recollected through the sound of the cricket, well managed. This end is not only beautiful as regards the technical pattern, as I have said, it is so in regard to what I may call the mental pattern as well.

Two more sonnets belong to 1816, but we have no more exact date for them than the year. One, *As from the darkling gloom*, may be dismissed with its mention. Keats rejected it for his forthcoming book, and he was perfectly right. The other, *Had I a man's fair form*, reads as though it belonged to the preceding Spring, since there appear in it a "knight," a "foeman," and a "cuirass." It is a love-poem, of no value as poetry, and only interesting because the first words, "Had I a man's fair form," seem to refer to a momentary and painful realization of his diminutive stature, which he conceives as a hindrance to any woman's loving him. This, and his mention of his size in the letter to Bailey I have already quoted,[1] make us aware that, in spite of the advantages of his appearance in other ways, his lack of height worried him a good deal at times. That George Keats stood quite five feet ten and was already a successful lover, is probably the clue to this first line. There is no hint to whom the sonnet was addressed. In Tom Keats's copy-book it is simply called, *Sonnet.* I believe it to have been merely one of those periodic gestures toward a vague and ideal eroticism which we have already observed occurring from time to time.

When Keats looked back on what had been accomplished during the year, I think he must have rubbed his eyes. He had got his apothecary's certificate, and imme-

[1] See Vol. I, p. 96.

diately after had let fall the aim of five hard-working years to take up another of most precarious possibility. True, fortunes were being made in poetry. The popularity of Byron, Moore, and Scott testified to this, but Keats could hardly have supposed that his kind of work would lead to any such golden future. Still, he had lined out his path and was stepping along it — that was a great wonder. A year ago, he had been a struggling medical student, knowing only a few obscure people; now, many of his friends were important men, men who were acknowledged masters in their kind, and he was taken in among them on equal terms, or, at least, on terms as equal as the difference between promise and achievement admits. But the most remarkable thing of all was that he had a book coming out. Dear me! What changes! And all to the good in his eyes, for not for one moment did he regret the loss of the sure subsistence which the practice of surgery would have brought him. The body of work that he had done, so much greater than ever before, justified his action. He must have felt sure of this, and regarded the future with considerable confidence. Probably he was happier just at this time than he was ever destined to be again. His woes, when he had them, were personal and artistic. For the nonce, the miseries of inevitable event were quiescent. The extent of Tom's illness was realized by nobody. There seemed to be plenty of money for all current needs. He sincerely liked the girl to whom George was engaged. When the church-bells tolled for the New Year, theirs can have been no sinister sound; hearing them, he must have felt a good deal like Dick Whittington resting by the milestone.

CHAPTER IV

A PET LAMB IN A SENTIMENTAL FARCE

THE heading of this chapter is Keats's subsequent expression of the rôle he was playing at this period.[1] That he came to regard it so, is significant of his power of growth. Petted he certainly was, and to a degree which falls to the lot of few young men, even those who give promise of marked genius. He enjoyed it, of course, and it took him some time to get his bearings and wrench himself away, but it speaks volumes for his just apprehension of facts and his naturally affectionate disposition that even when he had learnt to see the triangle of his friends, his work, and himself in a truer relation, these same friends, in differing degrees, continued a part of his life. No longer a child in leading strings, he took them on another plane; but it was their fault, not his, when change, however subtly, altered the circumstances of their intercourse with him.

We shall see all this happening in due time. The sentimental farce was in full swing during the Winter of 1816–17. After all, although the sentimentality cannot be gainsaid, farce is perhaps too strong a word. It applies very well to Hunt, whose attitude toward life was chiefly one of pleasant buoyance — on very shallow grounds, indeed, but this a series of unnecessary and thriftless misfortunes were unable to make him aware of. In the case of Haydon, the farce takes on the dourness of satire. He was sincere enough, but like a man catching at phantoms in a game of blind-man's-buff. Unlike his friend, Wilkie, who knew what he could do and did it to the best of his ability, at the same time carefully eschewing what was beyond his power,

[1] See *Ode on Indolence*; also letter to Miss Jeffrey of June 9th, 1819. Buxton Forman. Complete Edition.

Haydon persisted against all sense in believing himself a giant, and ended as the veriest pigmy of them all. John Hamilton Reynolds, less assured, and with reason, than Hunt and Haydon, takes his place in the farce more pathetically. We are not tempted to see satire in his failure so much as tragedy. As to Keats himself, the word farce applies only to the extent of his admiration for men so far his inferiors. What would have been the effect upon him had Haydon been Turner, Hunt been Coleridge, and Reynolds been Shelley? This brings in the question of whether genius is best fostered by genius. I think we can safely answer "no." Genius goes its own way, and is usually only hampered by too close an intercourse with other correspondingly great geniuses. Is there a case, except that of Goethe and Schiller, where one genius has been cordially and profitably intimate with another? I cannot think of one. At this stage in his career, Keats needed admiration and stimulus. The admiration could not be overdone for his good, provided the time allotted to it were short. The kind of stimulus which Hunt, Haydon, Reynolds, etc. gave him was just enough. He could assimilate it and pass on. There was no danger of its holding him; he was bound to outdistance it, and, when this was accomplished, follow his own trend unconfused by any rival issue. On the whole, he was considerably indebted to the farce, a fact which he never clearly understood.

Among other things which genius is, a genius is a man with the power of growing beyond other men in particular directions. For this reason, to a man of genius, friendships, events, atmospheres, must, to a great extent, be merely stepping-stones. The air he breathes at certain periods of his life is uncommonly likely to stifle him at others. Everything must be lived through with zest, and very nearly everything must be sloughed off in due course. We can see this process taking place in Keats's life, short though it was, with remarkable clarity. Already, by this

New Year of 1817, the sloughing had begun. Where were Keats's schoolmates? We know that he was popular at school, and there must have been fellows there whom he considered as friends, but not one of these appears to have followed him even so far as the Edmonton surgery. Henry Stephens and the medical students had gone, and even George Felton Matthew seems to have dropped away, for we hear nothing of him henceforward. Matthew may have married. He must have done so young, as thirty-odd years later, in 1848, he was the father of twelve children. In the case of these early friends, it is not necessary to probe into the whys and wherefores of their disappearance from the scene of Keats's life. For his later, more important, friendships, we shall see them arriving and departing, or, if not departing, remaining with altered psychological contours as far as their position in the scheme of Keats's life is concerned. And we shall see the same thing with regard to books, art, and life in general. With Keats, things moved swiftly, and when we consider that, starting from this January of 1817, four years completes the span of his life, we shall realize the incredible speed of his development.

Among the most salient events of this time was Keats's rapidly growing intimacy with John Hamilton Reynolds and the whole Reynolds family. The two friends were extremely congenial. Their tastes and aims were the same, and their characters fitted to a T. Marianne and Jane Reynolds quickly became almost like sisters to Keats. The fact that they were older than their brother brought them into just the right relation with his friend. Keats was not in the frame of mind to fall in love, except with theoretical nymphs in fairy grottoes, but he was very much in the frame of mind to appreciate older sisters. It is significant that a year and a half before, when he was seeing much of the Matthew family, both the Miss Matthews were much older than himself. I have already spoken of his need of being mothered. With women older than himself, such a relation might be imperceptibly assumed. It was to the thinness of their natures that the Matthew girls owed their inability to mean more to Keats than they did. The better endowed Reynoldses gave what the Matthew ladies could not, and for some years they were very important to Keats.

In spite of the fact that George Keats was the younger of the two brothers, he was far more self-sustaining and mature than John. This is perfectly in keeping with nature's usual procedure. Since John was to develop much farther than George, he had, perforce, to go more slowly. George's nature was all that had to grow; in John's case, his genius had to grow as well. It was quite on the cards that George should fall in love with a girl younger than himself, and feel perfectly comfortable and capable in the position of accepted lover. John was neither able to bring about, nor did he desire, any such condition for himself. His unique demand of the women to whom he was attracted was that they should be as much as possible like sisters; unless they were going to be suitable to him in that capacity, they were quite useless. He made a delightful brother; as an admirer, his time had not yet come.

It is a pathetic thing that Keats never found just the woman he needed to act as mother, confidant, playmate, and wise and sympathetic counsellor, a woman fitted to see him through his difficulties and enthusiasms with unwearying sympathy, and hand him over to the inevitable girl who was sure to come, when the time arrived. Even Marianne and Jane Reynolds were not of a kind to do all this. His intercourse with them seems to have been affectionate, playful, and sincere, but not to have reached very far below the surface. Still they did quite well for the time, and Keats was very fond of them.

Considering how profoundly Keats admired his future sister-in-law, Georgiana Wylie, who was in his estimation "a glorious human being," it may at first sight seem not a little strange that he could not find in her just what he needed. But a moment's reflection will show where the hitch came. In the first place, Georgiana Wylie was, at the moment, only fifteen; in the second, she was engaged to his brother. Now, however dear a sister may be, even a favourite brother is not the recipient of the best she has to give in the early days of her engagement. If Keats corresponded with Miss Wylie before her marriage, there is no evidence of it, while he did correspond with Marianne and Jane Reynolds. He grew to love Georgiana with the most devoted brotherly affection, but she belonged uniquely to George. There can be no doubt that, had she and George remained in England, John would have come to rely upon her more and more. Just at this time, she was too young, and too completely occupied with George.

We have seen what Keats looked like, and we have probed a good way into his heart and mind through the medium of his poems. We know how he appeared to Stephens and Matthew when he first arrived in London. But a year had passed, and the year had been full of action and growth. What manner of man did he seem to his new friends? What kind of impression did he make upon those who knew him in the flush of his early ambition, walking happily about the narrow world of his daily routine? Lord Houghton, whose opinion being based on the accounts of eye-witnesses may be taken as almost first-hand evidence, depicts him as follows:

> "... his society was much sought after, from the delightful combination of earnestness and pleasantry which distinguished his intercourse with all men. There was no effort about him to say fine things, but he did say them most effectively, and they gained considerably by his happy transition of manner. He joked well or ill, as it happened, and with a laugh which still echoes sweetly in many ears; but at the mention of oppression or wrong, or

at any calumny against those he loved, he rose into grave manliness at once, and seemed like a tall man. His habitual gentleness made his occasional looks of indignation almost terrible."

Cowden Clarke says much the same thing:

"I never knew one who so thoroughly combined the sweetness with the power of gentleness, and the irresistible sway of anger, as Keats. His indignation would have made the boldest grave; and they who had seen him under the influence of injustice and meanness of soul would not forget the expression of his features — 'the form of his visage was changed.'"

Bailey, who came into Keats's orbit a few months later, recording his impressions, which exactly tally with those of Clarke, writes:

[1] "I was delighted with the naturalness and simplicity of his character, and was at once drawn to him by his winning and indeed affectionate manner towards those with whom he was himself pleased . . . His brother George says of him that to his brothers his temper was uncertain; and he himself confirms this judgement of him in a beautiful passage in a letter to myself. But with his friends, a sweeter tempered man I never knew. Gentleness was indeed his proper characteristic, without one particle of dullness, or insipidity, or want of spirit. Quite the contrary . . . He was pleased with everything that occurred in the ordinary mode of life, and a cloud never passed over his face, except of indignation at the wrongs of others.

His conversation was very engaging. He had a sweet-toned voice, 'an excellent thing' in *man* as well as 'in woman . . .' He had a soul of noble integrity: and his common sense was a conspicuous part of his character. Indeed his character was in the best sense manly."

From this quotation from Bailey's memoranda, we see that George Keats was right in saying that John did not

[1] Colvin.

trouble his friends with his moods and vexations until after Tom's death and George's departure for America.

The charm of his conversation seems to have impressed everybody except Haydon. Writing in his journal after hearing of Keats's death, he has many things to say, among them:

> "In fireside conversation he was weak and inconsistent, but he was in his glory in the fields. The humming of a bee, the sight of a flower, the glitter of the sun, seemed to make his nature tremble."

It is amusing to note what sides of Keats's character struck which of his friends. The painters, Severn and Haydon, are observant of his powers of perception, and the effect which natural objects made upon him; his literary friends remark upon his keen critical sense, his aptness of expression and beauty of phrase, his likes and dislikes in regard to books. No one sees him entire; it is only posterity, looking through many eyes, who can approach to that.

In this posthumous description of Keats, Haydon, who had wronged him and thereby lost the treasure of his complete esteem, is a trifle malicious, or, if not that by intention, at least he is inclined to exaggerate facts and misconstrue actions. Yet, in spite of this tendency, his account is both more complete and more illuminating than most of the others. That his praise was just and his understanding keen, is shown by his opening declaration in regard to Keats, which is that "a genius more purely poetical never existed!" Continuing from the part I have already quoted, here is Haydon's account, from which I have deleted a few redundancies and one or two grossly misrepresenting passages:

> "He was haughty, and had a fierce hatred of rank; but he had a kind gentle heart, and would have shared his fortune with any man who wanted it. His classical know-

> ledge was inconsiderable, but he could feel the beauties of the classical writers. He had an exquisite sense of humour . . . He had no decision of character, and having no object upon which to direct his great powers, was at the mercy of every petty theory Hunt's ingenuity might start.
>
> One day he was full of an epic poem; the next day epic poems were splendid impositions on the world. Never for two days did he know his own intentions.
>
> He began life full of hopes, fiery, impetuous, and ungovernable, expecting the world to fall at once beneath his powers."

It is not difficult to separate the true from the false in Haydon's statement. The last sentence, indeed, is a far better characterization of Haydon himself than of Keats. Keats was extremely fiery, and his ambitions were as far-flung as ambitions can be, but he was no fool; on the contrary, he was a particularly modest and hard-working man. Impetuous, of course he was, but ungovernable principally in being determined to work out his own salvation. It is a big man who will let a disciple go his own way when he is ready to travel alone, and neither Haydon nor Hunt were of sufficient calibre to permit their neophyte to escape their clutches without recrimination. But Haydon, while misinterpreting the reasons completely, has hit upon something important when he says that Keats had "no object upon which to direct his great powers." I wish to go into this later, but not here. This is not the place to expatiate upon a fact which no one who has written upon Keats except Haydon seems to have realized. I shall return to this when we reach the time when Keats himself began to be aware of it. He was not aware of it in 1817, and neither was Haydon; indeed, as a fact, it had not then begun to exist.

Of course it is nonsense to say that Keats had no decision of character. Few men have had so much. Haydon mistook immaturity for indecision, that is all. We must always remember that Haydon lacked the sense of shading. Things were, or they were not, to him. A poorer psychologist never lived, he could see only what was patent at a glance, to causes and motives he was deaf and blind. As to Keats's vacillating from one point of view to another on matters of detail, how could it be otherwise with a man so excited, delighted, confused, and exhausted with the furious onslaught of new impressions as Keats was at this period. Haydon and Hunt, both of whom he admired to an absurd degree, were each pulling him different ways, and he, poor boy, bounced between them with perfect good will, but with the obvious appearance of changing goals.

Both Hunt and Haydon speak of Keats's hatred of rank, so I suppose he must somehow have exhibited this quality. It does not appear in his letters, and we have merely their word for it. If Keats had this trait, it could have come out only in conversation, a poor guide where a very young man is concerned. Since he never, during his whole life, met any one possessed of any rank whatever save what native wits could supply, he can scarcely have shown his feeling by action. The republican Hunt, who rather loved a lord than otherwise when he chanced to encounter one, was probably largely responsible for any utterances on the subject which Keats may have made, and Haydon, who sought patronage and then failed to deserve it, doubtless roused Keats's indignation against those aristocratic connoisseurs of art by means of whom, and solely by means of whom, painters of that day could earn a living.

It has become somewhat the fashion of late years to decry Keats's sense of humour. How any one can read his letters and fail to perceive his inexhaustible sense of fun, it is beyond my powers of comprehension to conceive. Exquisite, as Haydon says, his humour was. It bubbled out of him in a sparkling effervescence. Perfectly natural, unsophisticated, prankish humour it is, running all the way from the keenest wit to the sheerest kind of nonsense, the sort of nonsense which Edward Lear has made so famous. His wit is ever present, it even infuses those passages in his letters where it is without intention. It is high, and it is contagiously low; at times it descends to a rollicking verbal horse-play, and then again it is the slenderest thread of playfulness which we lose and follow and find again across the stuff of serious things. He can be a very clown upon occasion, or he can touch with the lightest hand some foible, some gesture, of a person carelessly met, but stamped in this way to a perpetual grotesqueness. Toward the end, his humour became shuttled with irony. The *Cap and Bells* proves what he might have done with satire had he lived. Here is a description of three bores, so brightly and inevitably sketched, so shrewdly differentiated, that it could in nowise be bettered. Comedy of a high order, indeed! He flings it off in a letter written to his sister-in-law in January, 1820:

> "I know three people of no wit at all, each distinct in his excellence — A, B, and C. A is the foolishest, B the sulkiest, C is a negative. A makes you yawn, B makes you hate, as for C you never see him at all though he were six feet high. — I bear the first, I forbear the second, I am not certain that the third is. The first is gruel, the second ditch-water, the third is spilt — he ought to be wiped up. A is inspired by Jack-o'-the-clock, B has been drilled by a Russian serjeant, C, they say, is not his mother's true child, but she bought him of the man who cries, Young lambs to sell."

For the benefit of a generation who have no recollection of even Punch and Judy, who used to parade the London streets of my youth, it may be well to state that toy lambs were carried round on trays, the cry of the vendor being "Young lambs to sell."

As to Keats's nonsense, that can wait until we come to the letters written to his little sister Fanny. His puns may,

I think, be left unrecorded. Punning was rife in the Keats circle; it was the fashion of the time. A notable thing about Keats is that, even when he indulges in a very bout of slapstick fun, he is not vulgar. There are only two instances throughout the whole of his correspondence which overstep the bounds of permissible joking, and this is not a little remarkable when we reflect that a pleasant hoax of the period was the passing round at a party of a dish of medicated bon-bons. It was the era of the practical joke and the unbridled tongue, when ladies were not present.

Keats was an extraordinarily many-sided man. One of his chief charms was his perfect freedom from affectation. It is safe to say that the greater the man, the more natural he is. Again Haydon sees Keats clearly when he says:

> "Keats was the only man I ever met with who seemed and looked conscious of a high calling, except Wordsworth. Byron and Shelley were always sophisticating about their verses: Keats sophisticated about nothing. He had made up his mind to do great things, and when he found that by his connection with the Examiner clique he had brought upon himself an overwhelming outcry of unjust aversion he shrunk up into himself; his diseased tendencies showed themselves, and he died a victim to mistakes on all hands, alike on the part of enemies and friends."

Once more Haydon is a perfect reporter and a poor interpreter. It is extremely important to have the testimony of one who knew Keats well to the fact that he never sophisticated about anything. If he gave the effect of being conscious of a high calling, we know from his letters that bumptiousness can have had no part in it. He was quietly sure, but without the least taint of cocksureness. For the last part of the passage I have quoted, it is sufficient to say that Haydon did not know of how many misfortunes Keats was a victim.

Haydon is responsible for an impression which was prevalent for some time. Namely, that Keats was inclined to periods of dissipation. Haydon even tells a story to prove Keats's super-sensuality in drinking. That this tale was bandied about and discussed at length, that it proved a real stumbling-block toward a true comprehension of his character, is one of the most amusing bits of evidence against the England of good Queen Victoria. Let me say emphatically, what no one now needs to be told, that Keats was not at any time in his life a drunkard. He drank, of course, everybody did; the idea of total abstinence had not then dawned upon the human race, with the exception of that part of it which professed Moslemism. Everybody drank, and most people drank too much. It meant nothing at all to be "a little so-soish," as the slang of Keats's day called getting tipsy. Keats went with his world, but within sensible limits. As Lord Houghton says: "A strictly regulated and abstinent life would have appeared to him pedantic and sentimental." None of the Keats set were drunkards, and he himself seems to have kept well on the margin of any form of dissipation. His taste was for claret, which alone proves how mild his alcoholic tendencies were. It takes a great deal of drinking to get drunk on claret, and there is no reason to suppose that Keats was in the habit of consuming enough bottles to reach that stage. In fact, as Lord Houghton points out, he speaks of having drunk too much on one occasion as a rare piece of joviality. His own description of claret is more poetical than convivial. Here it is, set forth in a letter to George of February, 1819:

> "I never drink now above three glasses of wine — and never any spirits and water. Though by the by, the other day Woodhouse took me to his coffee house and ordered a Bottle of Claret — now I like Claret, whenever I can have Claret I must drink it, — 'tis the only palate affair I am at all sensual in. Would it be a good spec. to send you some vine roots — could it be done? I'll inquire. If you could

make some wine like Claret, to drink on Summer evenings in an arbour! For really 'tis so fine—it fills one's mouth with a gushing freshness — then goes down cool and feverless — then you do not feel it quarrelling with your liver — no, it is rather a Peacemaker, and lies as quiet as it did in the grape; then it is as fragrant as the Queen Bee, and the more etherial Part of it mounts into the brain, not assaulting the cerebral apartments like a bully in a bad-house looking for his trull and hurrying from door to door bouncing against the wainscot, but rather walks like Aladdin about his enchanted palace so gently that you do not feel his step. Other wines of a heavy and spirituous nature transform a man into a Silenus: this makes him a Hermes — and gives a Woman the soul and immortality of an Ariadne, for whom Bacchus always kept a good cellar of claret — and even of that he could never persuade her to take above two cups."

Does that sound like a confirmed wine-bibber? The idea is absurd. How little he knew of wine is proved by his suggestion that George try vine-growing in Louisville, Kentucky. Haydon's tale is that Keats "once covered his tongue and throat as far as he could reach with Cayenne pepper, in order to appreciate the 'delicious coldness of claret in all its glory.'" Well, suppose he did, where is the harm? It was clearly done as a waggish experiment. But even if he had always drunk his claret so (which he did not, as the letter to George proves), what would it signify? Simply that his mucous membrane was as tough as a cowhide boot, which again it was not, or the letter to George would never have been written. Haydon was a gentleman of oblique vision, given to profuse statement. In this case, the false emphasis he has laid, and wilfully laid, upon a boyish prank, is something one finds it hard to forgive. "If you want to make a man your enemy, lend him money," that proverb is the cue to Haydon's attitude in these posthumous recollections.

One fact about Keats cannot be too strongly insisted

upon. This is the entire absence in his letters of any loose mention of women. We hear of wine-parties and card-parties, but there is no mention of any women being present at these entertainments. Keats writes everything to his brothers, he gives them a complete account of his doings. The slips in taste I have mentioned occur in letters to them. Yet not once do we hear of any equivocal adventure. What immoralities Keats perpetrated, if any, were evidently not a subject for mirth or comment. Manners were lax in the early nineteenth century. Every reader of the *Farrington Diary* must be struck with the numbers of "natural" children of noblemen whose parentage was perfectly well known, but who enjoyed all the privileges of rank notwithstanding. Aristocratic damsels with a bar sinister were apparently quite as eligible for marriage as their more conventionally born sisters. Kept mistresses, if the connection lasted any time, enjoyed quite an enviable status, while cheaper and more transient immoralities were as popular as they always have been. The middle-classes were a good deal sounder morally than the peerage, but a young man could do pretty much as he pleased without animadversion. Evidently Keats pleased to live a decidedly clean and strenuous life. We may say, with something like certainty, that we know everything he did; for which reason, it is safe to assume that what we do not know of, he did not do. He had a good healthy liking for the broad speaking of sixteenth and seventeenth century writers, and was quite capable of relishing a lively, animal pleasantry, but the painful and cynical making of mud-pies which is the principal preoccupation of our modern novelists was as far from his attitude as it was from that of Congreve, for example.

It is curious to realize in this day and age that Keats and his friends took snuff. This habit, inherited from the eighteenth century, had not yet universally given place to smoking. Everybody snuffed, from the Prince Regent down. Captain Gronow tells an amusing story of the famous surgeon, Astley Cooper, warning him against cigar smoking, to which he was addicted, declaring that it would shorten his life.[1] Keats several times mentions taking snuff; he never mentions smoking. Keats does not seem to have danced, although he occasionally went to dancing-parties. His chief indoor recreation undoubtedly was talking, but he also played cards, and speaks with glee of having won ten shillings and sixpence. It was a mild form of gambling, for his greatest loss appears to have amounted to no more than ten pounds, and this was a rare event. Vingt-et-un is mentioned, but what other games the Keats circle played can only be surmised from our knowledge of the card games then in fashion.

Among other amusements was what Keats calls "playing a concert." This consisted in everyone's impersonating some instrument and then setting to with its appropriate sound. This innocent pastime greatly irritates Sir Sidney Colvin. Why, I cannot conceive. Probably these young fellows produced the most horrible cacophony, but that need hardly tease the ears of any one a hundred years afterwards. Had these boys been music students, they might have made these concerts quite pleasant. They were not, but I cannot find the "playing a concert" so silly an affair as Sir Sidney would have it. At any rate, it kept them out of mischief.

Keats had a great love of the theatre, which was cheap enough, for, if out of funds, he could go to the shilling gallery. His taste seems to have led him to the classic and modern serious drama at Drury Lane. He did go to pantomimes, and what were called private theatres, but never seems to have cared much for either. His musical knowledge was slight, although he enjoyed listening to the piano, but on the whole he preferred painting and sculpture to music. He positively haunted picture galleries,

[1] *The Reminiscences and Recollections of Captain Gronow*, 1810–1860.

yet, in spite of Haydon and Severn, he never seems to have acquired much technical insight into either art.

There was one type of amusement which was very prevalent in Keats's day. This was boxing. Keats, as an old boxer, liked to see a "mill" now and again. In 1820, Reynolds wrote a poem entitled *The Fancy*, under the pseudonym of "Peter Corcoran." This has given rise to the idea that Reynolds was a constant frequenter of sparring matches. Perhaps he was, certainly Woodhouse enjoyed them. In a preface to a recent reprint of *The Fancy*, John Masefield has described a typical evening at a sporting establishment so pleasantly that I cannot do better than insert it here. It represents a scene with which Keats was familiar. Masefield is speaking of Reynolds, exaggerating the frequency of his attendance at such places, I think, but that is no matter:

> "Night after night, when the London lamps were lit, he was to be seen sauntering down to the Five's Courts, or to Jack Randall's in Chancery Lane, to meet the bloods and the sports and to watch some sparring. There, in the great shed-like building, in an atmosphere of cigar-smoke, heavy-wet, and deady, he would jest with the leading pugilists, or with the great Pierce Egan, or with Captain Barclay, the leading amateur, who had trained Tom Cribb for his fight with Molyneux. Every now and again they would pause to watch the sparring; for in both resorts there was a ring on a raised stage where the game sports stripped and sparred. Reynolds and his set were not mere on-lookers, content to watch while the mufflers padded on the flesh. They were fond of the sport for its own sake; and often put on the gloves and had a rattling good rally with really good boxers, such as the Davises or Randall himself."

The Fives Court was the great place for rackets, the precurser of our modern tennis, but Keats did not, apparently, play, although we know that on one occasion he met Hazlitt going there for a game and went along with him part of the way.

Sparring matches and prize-fights are all very well, but it is a little disconcerting to modern taste to find Keats going to a bear-baiting. Yet he did. Clarke describes the impression left on him, which seems to have been principally a matter of drama with no particular awareness of cruelty attached to it. It is the dramatic sense in Keats which Clarke emphasizes:

> "He once described to me his having gone to see a bear-baiting, . . . his concurrent personification of the baiting, with his position — his legs and arms bent and shortened till he looked like Bruin on his hind legs, dabbing his fore paws hither and thither, as the dogs snapped at him, and now and then acting the gasp of one that had been suddenly caught and hugged — his own capacious mouth adding force to the personation, was a remarkable and as memorable a display."

Clarke however adds these pregnant words to his account:

> "The partaking in such exhibitions did not for one moment blunt the gentler emotions of his heart, or vulgarize his inborn love of all that was beautiful and true. He would never have been a 'slang gent,' because he had other and better accomplishments to make him conspicuous . . . Had he been born in squalor he would have emerged a gentleman."

Perhaps Keats's sensibility increased as he grew older, perhaps the sporting element in the bear-baiting obscured to him its horrible cruelty, for some time later he had a stand-up fight with a person whom Clarke calls "a butcher boy," George Keats, "a fellow in livery," and Keats himself, simply "a brute," who was tormenting a kitten. Keats battered his antagonist to good purpose, although he was much the lighter and slighter of the two, and bore away the victory and a black eye.

The gist of all these quotations is that Keats was a very human sort of man, and a perfectly healthy and virile one.

If he did not play rackets or cricket, he did take immensely long walks, and probably kept his hand in with a little boxing. One side of his character relieved another, and all together kept him mentally and physically alert. I think nothing describes him so well, at this period, as the slang term "a regular fellow." We must not forget that the friends with whom he went to boxing-matches, and bear-baitings, and sat up playing cards till day-spring, were none of them idle, brainless fellows; all were working hard at something, and not a few of them were artists. Reynolds, and his brothers, were probably his companions at the sporting events, for we can scarcely imagine Hunt and Haydon being partakers in them.

Haydon has left us one little glimpse of Keats which rounds out a whole story: "I have enjoyed Shakespeare with John Keats," he says, "more than with any other human creature."

All this time, there is no mention of ill health. And certainly Keats must have been extremely robust to have stood the wear and tear of the previous Winter, torn between his medical studies and poetry. Matthew especially states that "he enjoyed good health," and during the Winter of 1817 this same good health seems to have been universally taken for granted, for no one mentions it. One little circumstance, however, should not be overlooked. Leigh Hunt records [1] that Keats would look at his hand, "which was faded, and swollen in the veins, and say it was the hand of a man of fifty." But as Hunt gives no date to this proceeding, it may refer to a subsequent period.

To all these pen-portraits, I wish to add one of another kind that is particularly charming. In Tom Keats's notebook [2] — which seems to have been a sort of catch-all, used indiscriminately by both John and Tom for any random jotting, from drafts of poems and letters to lists of one

[1] *Lord Byron and his Contemporaries*, by Leigh Hunt.
[2] Day Collection.

PENCIL DRAWING OF KEATS IN A NOTE-BOOK WHICH BELONGED TO HIS BROTHER TOM

From the original drawing in the possession of F. Holland Day, Esq.

kind and another and even rough sketches — appears a drawing. This drawing is evidently intended for John. Who is responsible for it, we do not know, but that it represents John Keats reading one of his favourite big books is evident from the attitude of the figure. At the end of his paper on Keats,[1] Clarke says:

> "There is one of his attitudes during familiar conversation which at times (with the whole earnest manner and sweet expression of the man) ever presents itself to me as though I had seen him only last week... The attitude I speak of was that of cherishing one leg over the knee of the other, smoothing the instep with the palm of his hand."

Somebody, perhaps Tom, perhaps Severn, has caught Keats as he sat reading in this most characteristic position, and thereby given us a glimpse of him as he appeared constantly to all his friends. Through the courtesy of Mr. F. Holland Day, who owns the original, I am enabled to reproduce this drawing for the first time.

Knowing Keats as well as we must by this time, it is not difficult to imagine his daily life during the early months of 1817, although we have no letters from him between December and March. Haydon tells of a dinner party where were present the Hunts, the Shelleys, Miss Kent (Hunt's sister-in-law), Hill, Haydon, Horace Smith, and Keats. At this dinner, Shelley attacked Haydon on the subject of Christianity; Haydon vociferously defended himself and Christianity together, feeling, he says, "like a stag at bay"; Hunt egged on first one disputant and then another, always inclining to Shelley's point of view; and Keats remained outside the discussion entirely. Buxton Forman says that Haydon's son told him that this dinner took place in January, but we know that the Shelleys were in London during the first weeks of February and were much at Hunt's. Mary Shelley's diary speaks of Keats drop-

[1] *Recollections of Writers*, by Charles Cowden Clarke.

ping in two or three times. On one of his visits, Reynolds was with him, so that Hunt's three "young poets" were actually together in the same room at least once. Shelley did not take to Reynolds, and as Keats and Reynolds were already on terms of the closest and most sympathetic friendship this circumstance probably added its quota to Keats's indifference to Shelley, while Haydon's cordial dislike of him after the quarrelsome dinner may possibly have also had its influence upon Keats.

During January, Keats was undoubtedly busy with the final revision of his poems for publication. By February, the book had gone to press and proofs were being corrected. Revising is an arduous task and so is proof-reading, and Keats had these excuses for writing nothing, or practically nothing, for one sonnet written on January thirty-first is his sum total of poetry for that month. This is perfectly natural. The creative faculty works by bursts, unless it be engaged in bringing some considerable conception into existence. Keats needed a creative rest. He had been composing at a great rate for months; it was a necessity for him to lie fallow.

The January sonnet, *After dark vapours*, refers to the sudden appearance of a warm day in the midst of Winter, with the thoughts which such a day engenders. It is one of the Huntian group of poems, and rather curious in that the atmosphere, in Keats's imagination, seems to take on the "feel," not only of May, as Keats has it, but of Summer and Autumn as well, the whole cycle of the year's fruitfulness in short. This makes the sonnet seem more of a literary poem than a poem spontaneously sprung from the experience of a change in the weather. The last line:

"A woodland rivulet, — a Poet's death"

bears out the theory. Hunt printed this sonnet in the *Examiner* on February twenty-third.

Some time in February, in all likelihood during the last

two weeks of that month, the sheets of Keats's book were ready for binding. Clarke recounts how one evening, when he and various other friends were at Keats's lodgings, the last proof-sheet was brought in, with the intimation that, if there were to be a dedication, the printers must have it at once. Keats "withdrew to a side-table," relates Clarke, "and in the buzz of a mixed conversation . . . he composed and brought to Charles Ollier, the publisher, the Dedication Sonnet to Leigh Hunt." Clarke is convinced that this sonnet was conceived then and there, but this I very much doubt. It is hardly likely that Keats had not pondered over the question of a dedication. Hunt had been very kind to him, printing his poems in the *Examiner*, smoothing the path to publication, encouraging him in every way; in common courtesy, if the volume were to be dedicated to any one, it must be to Leigh Hunt. I cannot say exactly why, but the poem reads to me too trippingly to have been hurried off with the printer's devil waiting at the door. It may have been written down then, in all the hubbub, but certainly it gives the impression of being well considered and carefully planned. Clarke is fairly possessed with his idea of Keats as a rapid writer, but we have little proof of this. The *Grasshopper and the Cricket* sonnet was certainly done at speed, but, as I have pointed out, we have no knowledge of the first draft.

Whether the *Dedication* sonnet were written at the moment, or copied from a slip of paper in Keats's pocket, or set down as an end to considerable previous cogitation, it is a good sonnet. I have said that Keats was more or less obliged to dedicate the sonnet to Leigh Hunt. That is true, but he evidently felt no reluctance in so doing. Far from it, the whole tone of the sonnet is sincere and threaded through with abiding admiration. Whatever Haydon may have felt on the subject, it is quite clear that Hunt's star is still in the zenith. The last five lines are perfect Hunt and Keats mixed:

"And I shall ever bless my destiny,
That in a time, when under pleasant trees
Pan is no longer sought, I feel a free,
And leafy luxury, seeing I could please
With these poor offerings, a man like thee."

Hunt was, not unnaturally, delighted with this tribute, which he acknowledged in an answering sonnet. This, however, does not seem to have been written immediately, or at least it cannot have been communicated to Keats for some time, for, in the copy of the *Poems*, 1817, given by John to his Brother George,[1] George has carefully copied on the half-title both of Hunt's "crowning" sonnets, heading them "Sonnet on Receiving a Crown of Ivy from my brother John. By Leigh Hunt," but there is no sign of this new sonnet.

Hunt's reply sonnet is as follows:

"TO JOHN KEATS.

'Tis well you think me truly one of those,
Whose sense discerns the loveliness of things;
For surely as I feel the bird that sings
Behind the leaves, or dawn as up it grows,
Or the rich bee rejoicing as he goes,
Or the glad issue of emerging springs,
Or overhead the glide of a dove's wings,
Or turf, or trees, or, midst of all, repose.
And surely as I feel things lovelier still,
The human look, and the harmonious form
Containing woman, and the smile in ill,
And such a heart as Charles's, wise and warm, —
As surely as all this, I see, ev'n now,
Young Keats, a flowering laurel on your brow."

The gist of this sonnet proves that Leigh Hunt, for all his silliness, had a great deal of insight and knew genius when he saw it. So far, so good; but, in spite of its insight, Hunt's sonnet is a cloying thing. Here is the sentimental farce

[1] Author's Collection.

rampant, and Keats, the pet lamb, led along with a garland of roses. No wonder that Keats, when his eyes were once fairly open, turned away from this sort of thing in disgust. Compliments paid in such a tone of voice fail of their object. They are tasteless and disillusioning. The pet lamb had to turn, or be a pet lamb to the end of his days.

Hunt put this reply sonnet into his book, *Foliage*, published a year later, in 1818. But, by that time, Keats's change of heart was complete. In the copy of *Foliage* which Hunt gave him,[1] he has not deigned to make a single annotation or score a solitary line. He gave the book later to Fanny Brawne, but the gift seems to have been a casual one, for the pages remain unmarked and there is no fresh inscription.

The period of Hunt's supremacy in Keats's eyes was nearing its term, but as yet not even Keats was aware of any such approaching alteration of his views. It is for this reason that I put the sonnet, *On the Story of Rimini*, as belonging to this time. Lord Houghton dates the poem "1817," but that alone would not seem conclusive, as Keats's friends may quite possibly have been in error in giving Lord Houghton that date, for, on the face of it, we should expect the sonnet to have been written during Keats's preoccupation with Hunt's book the year before. There is, however, stronger evidence for giving 1817 as the year of its composition. This is the internal evidence of the poem itself. The style of it is that of 1817, not 1816. There is no getting away from this cogent fact. What brought Keats back to *Rimini*, we do not know, but that he was brought back is evident. A little later, and Keats is off the Hunt track altogether, as far as his interests go at least, so the poem must have been written early in the year. I attribute it to February because, before the first ten days of March had gone by, Keats had seen the Elgin

[1] Author's Collection.

Marbles and started off in a new direction. Early in 1817 *Rimini* is still "that sweet tale"; by May of the same year he is "not in humour" with either Hunt's poetry or his own.

The *Rimini* sonnet, while by no means great, is quite a pleasant little thing. The mention of the moon:

> "Or Moon, if that her hunting be begun"

is a pointer to his already crystallizing project of writing a poem on the story of Endymion.

Keats's next poem, also a sonnet, we know to have been written in February. Sir Sidney Colvin dates it February twenty-seventh, but he gives no authority for this, and I cannot find it in any of the records to which I have had access. This is not to say that February twenty-seventh is an incorrect date, but merely that I have been unable to verify it. It is quite clear from the sonnet's not appearing in the *Poems*, 1817, that it was written too late to be incorporated in that volume. But I am doubtful of Sir Sidney's date for the simple reason that Reynolds's *Sonnet — To Keats. On Reading his Sonnet Written in Chaucer* is dated by Woodhouse on that very day.

Clarke tells a pretty tale of the circumstance, as he believes it, which induced the composition of *Written at the end of "The Floure and the Lefe."* I may as well give it in his words:

> "Another example of his promptly suggestive imagination, and uncommon facility in giving it utterance, occurred one day upon returning home and finding me asleep on the sofa, with a volume of Chaucer open at 'The Flower and the Leaf.' After expressing to me his admiration of the poem, which he had been reading, he gave me the fine testimony of that opinion in pointing to the sonnet he had written at the close of it, which was an extempore effusion, and without the alteration of a single word. It lies before me now, signed 'J. K. Feb., 1817.' If my mem-

ory do not betray me, this charming out-door fancy scene was Keats's first introduction to Chaucer."

Clarke is writing many years after the event, and there are several reasons for thinking that his supposition that this was Keats's first introduction to Chaucer is a mistake. In the first place, there is the motto of *Sleep and Poetry*, taken from this very poem of Chaucer's. Of that, I have already spoken.[1] Then there is Keats's statement that he had been reading the poem. Clarke, in recollection, refers this to an immediate reading, but it is quite as likely to have been a general statement, meaning that he had been reading the poem lately. This was probably so, at any rate, for there is the motto; moreover, Sir Sidney Colvin points out that a dream within a waking sleep is both Keats's and Chaucer's *mise en scène*. The parallel between *Sleep and Poetry* and *The Floure and the Lefe* ends here, of course; but, as far as it goes, it exists. A third, very cogent reason, has been exploited by Buxton Forman, who, in a pertinent note as to the extemporaneousness of the sonnet, says:

> "As Clarke seems to have been asleep when it was written, we are justified in construing the word *extempore* with a certain latitude. It was certainly most unusual for Keats to write a sonnet without a single erasure; and it is likely that he jotted this one down in pencil in a note-book that he certainly carried at that time and did draft sonnets in. In any case he probably had ample time and quiet, while Clarke was sleeping, to elaborate the two highly finished quatrains in his mind; the third quatrain and the couplet are of inferior merit, and might well be extempore."

Buxton Forman is quite right in saying that the first eight lines of the poem are the best; he is also right as to the unlikelihood of Keats's writing a poem "without the alteration of a single word." What was there to prevent

[1] See Vol. I, p. 215.

Keats from copying an already composed sonnet into Clarke's volume of Chaucer while Clarke was asleep? He did just this with the *Bright Star* sonnet in a copy of Shakespeare's *Poems* which he had recently given to Severn, when the two were on their voyage to Italy in 1820.

The chief inference of this examination is that Keats already knew Chaucer's *The Floure and the Lefe* before the day of Clarke's call; but there is also a by-product here which is of importance. If Sir Sidney Colvin's date for Keats's sonnet be correct, then, in all probability, Reynolds had seen it before Clarke did, in which case the sonnet in Clarke's Chaucer is a copy and not a first draft; if, on the other hand, Clarke is right as to the sonnet's having been composed on the day of his call at Keats's lodging, then Sir Sidney's date must, it would seem, be incorrect. It would be quick work for Keats to run to Reynolds and show him his sonnet, and for Reynolds to reply with another, all on the same day, and less than half a day at that. On the whole, I am inclined to believe the first of these alternatives, particularly as Keats signed Clarke's copy with no date but the year. If the sonnet had been composed on the spot, does it not seem likely that Keats would have put down the day of the month as well? If he had forgotten it, as he often did, Clarke was there to prompt him.

The octave of Keats's sonnet is a beautiful thing. The sestet falls badly. But, autobiographically, the line

"I that forever feel athirst for glory"

is interesting, once more proving Keats's consuming ambition at this time. The last couplet with its rhyme of "sobbings" and "robins" really ruins the poem. Keats's authority for this was probably his own false pronunciation. Did the middle classes of those days habitually drop their "g's," as did the "swells" of the 'eighties? Probably also Keats leant on Wordsworth for justification, for in Wordsworth's *The Redbreast and the Butterfly*, in his *Poems* of 1807, are these lines:

> "Art thou the Bird whom Man loves best,
> The pious Bird with scarlet breast,
> Our little English Robin;
> The Bird that comes about our doors
> When Autumn winds are sobbing?"

Keats's new sonnet was enthusiastically received by the little circle of his friends. Hunt printed it almost immediately, in the *Examiner* of March sixteenth. He prefaced it with characteristic enthusiasm:

> "The following exquisite sonnet . . . is from the pen of the young poet (Keats) . . . who may already lay true claim to that title: —
>
> '. . . the youngest he
> That sits in shadow of Apollo's tree.'"

Reynolds rushed into verse, and the sonnet he wrote is among his best things. I print it here, partly to show what Reynolds's verse was like, partly as evidence of the quality of his feeling for Keats and his generosity in regard to him:

[1] "SONNET — TO KEATS.

ON READING HIS SONNET WRITTEN IN CHAUCER.

Thy thoughts, dear Keats, are like fresh-gathered leaves,
Or white flowers pluck'd from some sweet lily bed;
They set the heart a-breathing, and they shed
The glow of meadows, mornings, and spring eves,
Over the excited soul. Thy genius weaves
Songs that shall make the age be nature-led,
And win that coronal for thy young head
Which Time's strange hand of freshness ne'er bereaves.
Go on! and keep thee to thine own green way,
Singing in that same key which Chaucer sung; —

[1] Woodhouse Commonplace Book, in the possession of Sir Sidney Colvin. Quoted by Buxton Forman. Complete Edition.

> Be thou companion of the Summer day,
> Roaming the fields and olden woods among:—
> So shall thy Muse be ever in her May;
> And thy luxuriant Spirit ever young."

Reynolds's sestet is not a bad criticism of Keats. It is amusing to observe that the last line of the octave is a sort of back-hand echo of the penultimate line of Keats's sonnet *How many bards:*

> "That distance of recognizance bereaves."

Reynolds, in his triple rhyme in this octave, employs exactly the same words, with one exception, that Keats had used in the sestet of that sonnet.

Reynolds wrote his sonnet on a Thursday, and he probably read it or sent it to Keats on Friday or Saturday. Is the note which Keats wrote to him and dated simply "Sunday Evening," an answer to it? Yes, and no. Part of the note seems to refer to the sonnet, part to be an answer to something which Reynolds had either said or written about his forthcoming book. Keats writes:

> "Your kindness affects me so sensibly that I can merely put down a few mono-sentences — your criticism only makes me extremely anxious that I should not deceive you.
>
> Its the finest thing by God — as Hazlitt would say. However I hope I shall not deceive you. — There are some acquaintances of mine who will scratch their Beards and although I have, I hope, some Charity, I wish their nails may be long."

The acquaintances who are to scratch their beards are undoubtedly Abbey and his friends. The conversation in which Abbey derided the idea of Keats adopting poetry as a life career rankled not a little, naturally. The book is to set everything right, it is proof positive that Keats had not mistaken his vocation. Yet he is too wise to trust entirely to the prejudiced enthusiasm of his friends; he hopes they may not be deceived. Here is the natural delight of a boy in his first book, but also the diffidence of a man who sees considerably farther into possibilities than do most young aspirants to fame. It is just this modesty which gauges Keats's calibre, and perhaps it was this very trait in him quite as much as the promise in the poems he had then written that led Hunt, and the rest of the more experienced of his circle, to count so surely upon his future.

The *Poems*, 1817, is usually said to have been published early in March. Sir Sidney Colvin is more definite, he gives the date of publication as March third. Once again he does not give the source of his information, but circumstantial evidence bears him out. March third, be it remembered, was a Monday, a very proper day of the week on which to have the book appear. There exists a copy of the *Poems* which seems to have been the property of Charles Ollier; in it, some one, presumably Ollier, has written a sonnet to Keats. This sonnet is dated the second of March, 1817. Of course it is possible that the sonnet was written on that date and copied into the book later, but if the book were Ollier's (and no one appears to doubt it) there is good reason to suppose that the date given was that of the sonnet's composition, and that the book was bound and ready some days earlier. Ollier, being the publisher, would have a copy as soon as the volumes came from the binder, of course. If the book were to be issued on Monday, the edition must have been ready a day or two before. A few copies were probably given out to Keats, one of which went to Reynolds. Every one who has to do with writing knows that a book is a totally different thing from its manuscript, or even its proof. Reynolds, with the finished volume fairly in his hands, sees and thinks many things, and these he promptly communicates to Keats — if in conversation, Keats mulls over them and sends a note; if in writing, Keats replies. With Ollier's sonnet and Keats's note, both written on a Sunday, which, in Ollier's case, we know to have been March second, and, by inference, may suppose the same date for the note, I think we can be certain that the book was issued to the public on Monday, March third.

Ollier's sonnet is so decidedly in the farce, and Keats is so unquestionably the pet lamb, that for both historical and biographical reasons it seems worth while to quote it here:

> "Keats I admire thine upward daring Soul,
> Thine eager grasp at immortality
> I deem within thy reach; — rejoic'd I see
> Thee spurn, with brow serene, the gross controul
> Of circumstance, while o'er thee visions roll
> In radiant pomp of lovely Poesy!
> She points to blest abodes where spirits free
> Feed on her smiles and her great name extol. —
> Still shall the pure flame bright within thee burn
> While nature's voice alone directs thy mind;
> Who bids thy speculation inward turn
> Assuring thee her transcript thou shalt find.
> Live her's — live freedom's friend — so round thine urn
> The oak shall with thy laurels be entwin'd."

For a publisher to break into poetic eulogy of a client is so very strange an occurrence that this fact alone must have given Keats every assurance of a good reception for his book. The firm was evidently lavish in allowing Keats copies to give away. Hunt, Haydon, and Clarke must each have had one; Reynolds's is still in existence, and one copy was not enough for the Reynolds family, Marianne and Jane had theirs;[1] also, if my memory holds good, I have seen one to Mrs. Reynolds somewhere. George had his special copy,[2] so we may presume that Tom and Fanny had each another. Georgiana Wylie was given one,[3] punctiliously presented by both John and George.

[1] Author's Collection. [2] *Ibid.*
[3] In the possession of Lucius Wilmerding, Esq., of New York.

Severn's [1] contains the merry inscription: "The Author consigns this copy to the Severn with all his Heart." Charles Wells even was not forgotten, but he is gently reminded that he is but a young thing, for Keats writes in it "From J. K. to his young friend Wells." [2] It is not my purpose to draw up a list of all the presentation copies of Keats's three books known to-day. It would, I think, form quite a large catalogue. But there is one other copy of the *Poems* [3] which I must mention. The inscription in it reads "From the author to his Friend, Thos. Richards." Written into the book are Hunt's sonnets on the ivy crowning, and the sonnet which has been attributed to Ollier. The Hunt sonnets are carefully stated to be by him; no name is given in connection with the supposed Ollier poem. This may have some bearing on the authorship of the sonnet in question or it may not. Here are the facts. First: nothing is known about this Richards. A certain C. Richards was the printer of the book, therefore Thomas Richards may have been his son, or his brother, more likely the former. By this token, Ollier and Richards were known to each other and connected in business. Second: several copies of the *Poems* given by Keats to his intimate friends have Hunt's sonnets written in them, but, if I recollect rightly, it is only in the Ollier and Richards copies that this particular anonymous sonnet appears. Third: Keats seems to have known this Thomas Richards well and treated him as a contemporary, whereas Ollier was presumably somewhat older. Four: the Hunt sonnets were known to everybody; the anonymous sonnet to nobody. If Richards had written it, would he not have been likely to show it to Keats, in which case would George not have transcribed it with Hunt's in his book? On the other hand, if Ollier wrote it, might he not have shown it to his printer, but forbidden him to pass it round? The date is

[1] Bemis Collection. [2] *Ibid.*

[3] In the possession of William M. Elkins, Esq., of Philadelphia.

the same in both copies, which looks as though there were collusion. This is all the weakest kind of evidence; what it boils down to is that presumably either Ollier or Richards wrote the sonnet, and probability weighs a little heavier on Ollier's side. I dislike to count guesses as facts, but, after considering everything, I have decided to let the text stand as above. If Ollier did not write the sonnet, he agreed with its sentiments well enough to put it into his copy, always supposing the volume in question to have been his copy. I have not seen it, but Buxton Forman, while not stating Ollier's ownership of it as a proven fact, appears to have no doubt of it.

The actors in this sentimental farce either lost their heads completely, or, with unpardonable cruelty, led their pet lamb directly to the slaughter without a word of preparation. True, Keats must have known that Hunt was the perpetual butt of Tory criticism, and that in dedicating a book to Hunt he was sealing his own doom at the hands of its servants. But to know a thing and to realize it are two very different matters. The glamour of praise blinded his eyes; the cotton-wool of praise dulled his ears. Without being in the least over-weening in his hopes, he did expect fair play. It was just on this point that he should have been warned. The small end of the wedge which apprized the Tory press of his annoying existence had been driven by Hunt himself in his article on the *Young Poets*. In that article, Hunt had quoted the *Chapman's Homer* sonnet. Were Messrs. Lockhart, Wilson, and Company blind that they saw nothing in that poem? Blind and purblind, wound about in the cocoon of a professional war. Poetry is one thing, the politics of poetry quite another, and poor Keats, through his association with Hunt, was immediately and heavily thrown into the very centre of the political arena. But although this article of Hunt's drew the critics' attention and animadversion down on his young poets, the blow did not fall until more than a year and a half later.

The *Poems* came out and — nothing happened. Scarcely a flutter stirred the literary air. The choleric and cocksure reviewers of the *Quarterly* and *Blackwood's* were silent. They were biding their time, as we are now aware. Keats was known to be a friend of Leigh Hunt, poems of his had been published in Hunt's paper, the *Examiner*, but not one of Hunt's ferocious enemies gave tongue as yet, nor did they turn their nefarious pens on Keats until the appearance of *Endymion*. *Blackwood's*, indeed, was in its pre-Lockhart, pre-Wilson, stage, being merely, at the moment, an unsuccessful bantling struggling for existence. Its days of influence were a half a year away.

Clarke has expressed the situation on the publication of the *Poems* clearly and decisively:

> "Every one of us expected (and not unreasonably) that it would create a sensation in the literary world . . . Alas! the book might have emerged in Timbuctoo with far stronger chance of fame and approbation. It never passed to a second edition; the first was but a small one, and that was never sold off. The whole community, as if by compact, seemed determined to know nothing about it."

A pleasant state of things truly, for both Keats and his disappointed friends. It must have been some amends to have known the why of the matter, as every one of them did. Impressions were made, but *sotto voce*, as it were, by private persons at their own firesides. For the press, the book was virtually ignored. One small notice in the *Monthly Review* for April was all the attention accorded to it, but this notice, in spite of its extreme brevity (a bare nineteen lines in all), was good. It compared Keats, not unfavourably, with the Elizabethans, and added by way of peroration: "There is in his poems a rapturous glow and intoxication of the fancy — an air of careless and profuse magnificence in his diction — a revelry of the imagination and tenderness of feeling, that forcibly impress themselves on the reader." The *Monthly Review* was a standard periodical, but even so, its short, if kindly word, could hardly do more than point the general silence. Months later, the *Poems* was noticed at some length in both Constable's *Edinburgh Magazine* and the *Eclectic Review*, a paper devoted to the interests of nonconformity. The *Eclectic Review*, in its September number, led the way. It admitted a moiety of merit to some of the sonnets, of which *Chapman's Homer* was not one, and allowed "considerable taste and sprightliness" to parts of *I Stood Tip-toe*, but declared that the author of *Sleep and Poetry* was "indeed far gone, beyond the reach of the efficacy either of praise or censure, in affectation and absurdity," and continued with a prophecy so ludicrous to our ears as to be almost amusing, were it not also tragic: "Seriously, however," cries the irritated journalist, "we regret that a young man of vivid imagination and fine talents, should have fallen into so bad hands, as to have been flattered into the resolution to publish verses, of which a few years hence he will be glad to escape from the remembrance." The *Edinburgh Magazine* for October, 1817, praised Keats for modelling much of his work on Spenser, and admitted that this was done with some skill. With unexpected insight, it singled out "the moon lifting her silver rim" passage in *I Stood Tip-toe*, calling it "a glorious and Virgilian conception." It waxed magnificently pompous, however, in a grave warning anent "the appalling doom which awaits the faults of mannerism or the ambition of a sickly refinement," and ended with a dig at Hunt and Hazlitt by announcing that "if Mr. Keats does not forthwith cast off the uncleanness of this school, he will never make his way to the truest strain of poetry in which, taking him by himself, it appears he might succeed." The fact that there was a grain of truth in all this did not make it more palatable. The advice might have been given more gently, but gentleness was not the order of the day in book-reviewing at that time. Blunderbusses for gnats was the motto of the craft.

Newspaper criticism may wound an author, but it seldom influences him. The real danger in these belated reviews was their effect on the publishers. As to the public, that misty, yet vitally important, entity could scarcely be more indifferent than it was already. Hunt was past wincing; Keats was annoyed, but determined; the others fulminated and consoled. So matters stood; but, before anything of this had happened, something else had come to pass of great importance to Keats.

On a day early in March — probably, indeed, March first — Haydon took Keats to see the Elgin Marbles, already housed in the British Museum. Seeing that Haydon's insight and Haydon's enthusiasm had been the chief factors leading to the acquisition of the Elgin Marbles by the British Nation the year before, no better guide than he for a first visit to them could have been found in all England. Certainly no one knew them half so well. For years he had been studying them, copying them in groups and in detail, he had even made casts of them. They had become an artistic creed to him. Keats was fortunate in his *cicerone*.

The effect of this view of the Marbles was to leave Keats in a state of mind bordering upon stupefaction. Here was a totally different art from any he had known. He had seen Haydon's casts, but casts are to sculpture what translations are to poems. We get in them merely a hint, a teasing possibility, an attempted sketch of a lost impression. The Marbles themselves brought confusion, like a blow on the head. Chapman had invigorated him; the Marbles were too much, they overbore him entirely. He wrote two sonnets on them, or rather, one sonnet on the Marbles and one on Haydon in his rôle of paterfamilias to them. This sonnet *To Haydon, with a sonnet on seeing the Elgin Marbles* is practically worthless. After declaring that he (Keats) is not of "ample strength" to praise the Marbles, he breaks out in an overdressed tribute to Haydon. If, he says, he could write of them as he wishes,

"... all those numbers should be thine;
Whose else? In this who touch thy vesture's hem?
For when men star'd at what was most divine
With browless idiotism — o'erwise phlegm —
Thou hadst beheld the Hesperean shine
Of their star in the East, and gone to worship them."

This is wretched poetry, and it is a flagging imagination which could represent the Parthenon frieze under the metaphor of the Star of Bethlehem. The truth was, he had said all he could of the Marbles in the other sonnet, which was probably written first, although Haydon puts them the other way about in his journal. A characteristic bit of evidence to the fact that Haydon was more interested in Haydon than in even the Marbles.

The sonnet *On Seeing the Elgin Marbles for the First Time* is much better. The opening passage has the poignance of prophecy, seen as we cannot help seeing it:

"My spirit is too weak — mortality
Weighs heavily on me like unwilling sleep,
And each imagined pinnacle and steep
Of godlike hardship, tells me I must die
Like a sick Eagle looking at the sky."

Keats was not weak; but no foreknowledge of the facts could have found a better expression for his last struggle with disease than does his fifth line.

After so stern and solemn a beginning, the sixth line:

"Yet 'tis a gentle luxury to weep"

comes like a slip into soft mud, with the splash and subsequent jolt. Keats, who loathed mawkishness a little later, had a hard time to rid himself of it. He had to find out its banefulness all by himself, the sentimental farcists were unable to help him here for the simple reason that they liked the very type of expression which he learnt to detest. Three lines pertaining to the gentle luxury of weeping, I will skip. The end of the sonnet is equal to, and in some ways surpasses, the beginning:

> "Such dim-conceived glories of the brain
> Bring round the heart an indescribable feud;
> So do these wonders a most dizzy pain,
> That mingles Grecian grandeur with the rude
> Wasting of old Time — with a billowy main —
> A sun — a shadow of a magnitude."

"A shadow of a magnitude" is one of the finest and most startling expressions in all poetry. Beautiful, too, is

> ". . . the rude
> Wasting of old Time."

The passage is much injured by "billowy main"; not because the sea is out of place here, but because both "billowy" and "main" are poetic words, jargon words, stock euphemisms of an artificial speech much employed by such "elegant" poets as the Swan of Lichfield and Keats's early admiration, Mrs. Tighe.

"A most dizzy pain" is perfect realism, it is just what Keats felt, but good as it is, I think it was an afterthought. There are signs in this sestet that the first parts of it to be composed were "mingles Grecian grandeur with the rude wasting of old Time" and "a shadow of a magnitude." Thus he saw the Marbles, these phrases were to him absolute description. "Dizzy pain" did, I think, come next, and the rhyme is to blame for "main." Starting the actual writing of his sestet with "So," he completed the last four lines and then went back and worked out the first two. The rather forced word "feud" is another rhyme-impulse, the employment of it gives his progression away. This is, of course, carpentry, but carpentry necessitated by inspiration. Faultless inspiration in his conception; carpentry, unfortunately, of not too high a grade, not nearly so high as Keats often achieved. All poetry consists of flashes of the subconscious mind and herculean efforts on the part of the conscious mind to equal them. This is where training comes in. The more expert the poet, the better will he fill in the gaps in his inspiration. Revising is the act of consciously improving what has been unconsciously done. Sometimes, but rarely, the subconscious comes to the rescue of the reviser. We have seen this happening in the marigold passage in *I Stood Tip-toe*. In this sestet, Keats filled in rather perfunctorily. He seems too tired for expression. The Marbles gave him a couple of superb epithets, and after them he has nothing to say. Yet his epithets are too good to perish, he must make a sonnet as a frame for them. The octave came easily enough, because in it he does not deal with the actual Marbles at all, but with himself. The weariness of it shows that he has been puzzling his brains over the work, for he knows that his two epithets must end the poem, not begin it; there are, therefore, some twelve lines to be done before he can arrive at them. The first five lines of the octave he does well by begging the question entirely; the next three are time-keeping merely; the sestet is as we have seen.

Haydon was, of course, enchanted with both sonnets; although, in spite of the personal praise in the one especially written to him, he seems to have had the sense to realize that the other was the better poem. In his enthusiasm, he at once sat down and wrote to Keats about them. His letter, as printed, is dated "March, 1817," but Buxton Forman says that it appears from the manuscript copy in Haydon's journal to have been written on March third. There is no mention of the book in it, undoubtedly because the book had not yet reached him. Whoever had advance copies, he does not seem to have been among the number.

Haydon's letter is full of his usual rhodomontade. After thanking Keats for his "two noble sonnets," he flames out: "I know not a finer image than the comparison of a poet unable to express his high feeling to a sick eagle looking at the sky, where he must have remembered his former towering amid the blaze of dazzling sunbeams, in the pure expanse of glittering clouds" etc. etc. We need not follow his eloquence farther; he himself is so much in love with it that he ends the letter without referring to Keats's tribute to himself. One line, however, carefully edited out by his son,[1] speaks volumes; it is,[2] "You filled me with fury for an hour, and with admiration for ever." Here follows a postscript: "I shall expect you and Clarke and Reynolds to-night." But a twinge of conscience assails him and he begins again:

> [3] "My DEAR KEATS —
> I have really opened my letter to tell you how deeply I feel the high enthusiastic praise with which you have spoken of me in the first Sonnet — be assured you shall never repent it — the time shall come if God spare my life — when you will remember it with delight —
> Once more God bless you
> B. R. HAYDON."

We see, by this, that in whatever order the sonnets were written, Keats was canny enough to send them to Haydon with the one written to him as the first.

Keats must have had a delightful time that evening with Haydon and Reynolds and Clarke. It is probable that he brought Haydon's copy of the *Poems* with him, and the talk about it must have been a joy to his ears. Then there were the new Elgin Marble sonnets to be read aloud and discussed, with the casts of the Marbles lying round in the painting-room to refer to. Writing years later, Haydon

[1] *Benjamin Robert Haydon: Correspondence and Table-Talk.* With a Memoir by his Son, Frederick Wordsworth Haydon.
[2] Buxton Forman. [3] Buxton Forman.

says that he thinks that Reynolds was with them when he took Keats to see the Marbles;[1] if such were the case, the comparison of notes must have come in, first impressions weighed against second, familiarity tallied up with the onslaught of a first view. But whatever they talked of, we can imagine that the conversation was forever veering back to the excitement of the new book which was to set the Thames on fire forthwith.

It was a charming little volume, this new book. Just the right slimness to slip easily into a pocket, pleasantly bound in cool-looking drab boards, with "Keats's Poems. Price 6s." on the back label, for all the world as though Keats were somebody already. In the middle of the title-page was a head of Shakespeare, and above it a motto from Spenser's *Fate of the Butterfly*:

> "What more felicity can fall to creature,
> Than to enjoy delight with liberty."

It was only out that day, and nothing had as yet reached Keats's ears but the chorus of praise with which his friends showered him. Hunt, we may suppose, had an advance copy; at any rate, Keats carried the book to Hunt himself. Hunt parenthetically and pleasantly tells of this event, and the placc where it occurred. This is what he says:

> [2]"It was in a beautiful lane, running from the road between Hampstead and Highgate to the foot of Highgate Hill, that, meeting me one day, he gave me the volume. If the admirer of Mr. Keats's poetry does not know the lane in question, he ought to become acquainted with it, both on his author's account and on its own. It has been also paced by Mr. Lamb and Mr. Hazlitt, and frequented like the rest of the beautiful neighbourhood, by Mr. Coleridge; so that instead of Milfield Lane, which is the name it is known by 'on earth,' it has sometimes been called Poets' Lane, which is an appellation it richly deserves. It divides

[1] From an unpublished letter in the Bemis Collection.
[2] *Lord Byron and his Contemporaries*, by Leigh Hunt. 1829.

MILLFIELD LANE

From a photograph taken by F. Holland Day, Esq.

the grounds of Lords Mansfield and Southampton, running through trees and sloping meadows, and being rich in the botany for which this part of the neighbourhood of London has always been celebrated."

All days are not first days, unhappily, and as the days drew into weeks it became increasingly evident that the book was about as far from being a success as anything could be; it was, in fact, a flat failure. The copies would not go off. There they sat on the booksellers' counters, gathering dust and hard opinions. All unbeknownst to Keats and his group, however, the book was making friends. A clever young solicitor, who was a friend of the senior partner of a firm of publishers, and also the firm's reader, read it and liked it so much that he wrote a sonnet about it. The sonnet was not published, and has only recently come to light. It is poor stuff, but the fact that Richard Woodhouse cared enough for the *Poems* to write it, makes it of epochal importance in Keats's life. Here it is:

"TO APOLLO.

Oh thou, whose unimaginable lay
  Wraps in charm'd silence the celestial crew
  Of powers Olympian; who didst an old few
After Troy's fall make tuneful; nor the lay
To our own sires didst scant in happier day;
  But with rich strains high fancies didst imbue.
  And taught'st them makings, such as ever woo
The vacant ear, and will not pass away;—
Have these thy glories perish'd? or in scorn
  Of thankless man hath thy race ceased to quire?
Oh no! thou hear'st! for lo! the beamèd morn
  Chases our night of song: and, from the lyre
Waking long dormant sounds, Keats, thy last born,
  To the glad realm proclaims the coming of his sire."

In the Woodhouse Book in the Morgan Library, this sonnet is dated "4 Mar. 1818," so I may be wrong in supposing it to belong to the previous year. But Woodhouse is often guilty of errors of date, and the sonnet bears such evident reference to Keats's battle-cry in *Sleep and Poetry* that I believe it to have been inspired by the *Poems*. Sir Sidney Colvin, indeed, definitely so states, and he has printed the poem, and derived his information, from a totally different source.[1]

Another admirer was Joseph Ritchie, a young surgeon with strong literary tastes. In 1813, he had been House Surgeon at the Lock Hospital, Grosvenor Place. In the Spring of 1814, he took his apothecary's diploma. In 1817, in Paris, he met Humboldt, and soon after was recommended to the British Government as a man qualified by his scientific abilities to head an exploring expedition to the Nigritian Soudan. He died at Murzuk, in Fezzan, before achieving the object of his journey, in November, 1819. We shall hear of Ritchie again. Our immediate concern with him is a passage from an unpublished letter[2] to his intimate friend, the Reverend Richard Garnett, father of Dr. Richard Garnett, for many years librarian of the British Museum. Ritchie's remarks, had they seen them, would have been honey-balm to Keats, Hunt, and the other adherents of the anti-Popean school. This is what he says:

> "If you have not seen the Poems of J. Keats a lad of 19 or 20 — they are worth your reading. If I am not mistaken he is to be the great poetical luminary of the age to come. How vastly glad I am that we are in so fair a train of getting clear of the trammels of French taste & French Criticism & that we may still look forward to seeing in our writers some portion of that manly force and originality which characterizes the men who graced the earliest and best periods of our Literature. Every thing appears to me to show a tendency in the public taste at the present moment to revert to what is truly great & national in our literature & Philosophy — the artificial & unnatural System imported from France by the Writers of Charles II & Anne's Time seems fallen never to rise again."

[1] From *New Notes on Keats,*" by Sir Sidney Colvin. London *Times Literary Supplement.* February 19, 1915.

[2] Day Collection.

Ritchie was sanguine; Keats, as a martyr to the cause, could have enlightened him. Perhaps he did, later.

Still another man we know of came under the spell of Keats's *Poems*. This was Benjamin Bailey. Bailey played so large a part in Keats's life for a short period, that I shall reserve any description of him until we reach the time when he and Keats became friends. Suffice it to say here that he was an Oxonian, a friend of Reynolds's, and at the moment, or not long after, paying court to Reynolds's sister, Marianne. Reynolds recommended Keats's *Poems* to Bailey, and Bailey was so much struck with them that, on running up to London for a brief few days, he took pains to make the acquaintance of the author. So Keats and he met for the first time, but the sequel was not yet.

The indifference of the public, and the Elgin Marbles, together acted as irritants to Keats's self-esteem. They stung him to start again, to be up and doing. Already the idea of writing a poem on the story of *Endymion* had been buzzing in his head. We have noticed the fact that even so recently as the middle of December he had spoken of *I Stood Tip-toe* as *Endymion*.[1] But when the poem went to press, the name had been cancelled. Therefore we know that by February, at least, the germ of the longer *Endymion* was fulminating. Medwin relates that Shelley and Keats agreed to write a long poem each during the ensuing Summer. Shelley's was to be *Laon and Cythna*, Keats's to be *Endymion*. This may be true, but Medwin's memory is a vague and unreliable quantity. Yet nothing is more likely than that both these young poets aired their projects sufficiently openly. I should suppose that all the Hunt set knew perfectly well what each was meditating.

Disappointment acts differently upon different natures. With Keats, its effect was to make him itch to be up and at the indifferent public and the silent reviewers with something more imposing. Here was Haydon's chance, his

[1] See Vol. I, p. 140.

opportunity to filch Keats from under Hunt's wing. What he said just at this time, we do not know; what he said a little later will be quoted in due course; what he did was first to write Keats a letter, and second to give him a book.

The letter begins on the usual excitable note. "Consider this a sacred secret," he abjures his correspondent. The secret is a confidence to the effect that when he sits by his fire musing on his work, he is visited by visions of the "mighty dead," whereupon he sinks down and prays the "great Spirit" to make him "worthy to accompany those immortal beings in their immortal glories." At this, each floating ghost smiles upon him and nods its head in "awful encouragement." We can clearly see that here Haydon, while indulging to the full the delights of self-revelation, is also hinting an encouragement to Keats. He continues:

> "My dear Keats, the Friends who surrounded me were sensible to what talent I had, — but no one reflected my enthusiasm with that burning ripeness of soul, my heart yearned for sympathy, — believe me from my soul, in you I have found one, — you add fire, when I am exhausted, and excite fury afresh — I offer my heart and intellect and experience — at first I feared your ardour might lead you to disregard the accumulated wisdom of ages in moral points — but the feelings put forth lately have delighted my soul — always consider principle of more value than genius — and you are safe — because on the score of genius, you can never be vehement enough. I have read your "Sleep and Poetry" — it is a flash of lightning which will rouse men from their occupations, and keep them trembling for the crash of thunder that *will* follow.
>
> God bless you! let our hearts be buried on each other.
>
> B. R. Haydon."

This letter has no date save "March 1817," but it is evident that it was written fairly early in the month. Cruel fact had not yet disproved Haydon's hopes for his friend. There are sentences here the meaning of which is as clear as day. Haydon has been alarmed lest Keats was succumbing to Hunt's and Shelley's religious theories. He cannot bear to see this promising neophyte revolving in Hunt's orbit, either morally or intellectually; he offers the tale of the visions to introduce the efficacy of prayer. This was no hypocrisy on Haydon's part. He did, and often did, just what he has here stated. That he mistook the type of Keats's mind is shown in every line of the letter; but no matter, he did what he could to wrest Keats away from that part of his daily life which did not include himself. He meant well, and, on the whole, did well, at this juncture.

The book which was to stamp his precepts, to rouse a heroic mood, the mood of the Marbles, and fit Keats for great deeds, was Goldsmith's *History of Greece*. The first volume bears the inscription, "To John Keats, from his ardent friend, B. R. Haydon, 1817." I have no absolute proof that Haydon gave the book to Keats at exactly this time, but circumstances and the similarity of tone between the letter just quoted and the inscription make it, I think, obvious.

If Haydon's ardour were undiminished, it was growing increasingly clear that that of the publishers was not. Their enthusiasm was visibly cooling. The chill of the book's non-sale was seriously affecting their tempers. Like all inexperienced authors suffering the smart of failure, Keats seems to have considered that the fault lay in the publishers' methods. The book was not being handled properly; the Olliers were not pushing it. This is the old cry of disappointed authorship echoing down the generations. The seasoned authors of Keats's acquaintance were in a quandary. If they told him that a book was far less at the mercy of the firm which published it than might appear, they were simply adding an extra drop of poison to Keats's inflamed sensibilities; besides, they had predicted success, and its failure to arrive reflected somewhat adversely on their powers of divination. They seem to have sat on the fence as regards the publishers' share in the matter. But Keats had all the sympathy he wanted on this score from his brothers and Reynolds. Reynolds, who had already undergone the experience of changing publishers and had found his new firm obliging, energetic, and cordial, was ready with a suggestion. Why should not Keats make a change? He was meditating a new poem which the Olliers must certainly not issue. Keats must follow his example, and give his new book to Messrs. Taylor and Hessey, of 93 Fleet Street. These gentlemen had, the year before, brought out Reynolds's *Naiad*, and he was on the pleasantest terms with them.

Who introduced Keats to Taylor and Hessey has been a much discussed question. Sir Sidney Colvin suggests that Bailey was the connecting medium. This may be so, I am not convinced of it. Sir Sidney bases his theory on the fact that Bailey was a friend of Taylor's, but so was Reynolds, and Reynolds's letters to Taylor are far more intimate in tone than Bailey's, still that may be because Bailey was a rather formal person and Reynolds was quite the opposite. It is possible that Bailey introduced Reynolds to Taylor in the first place, or it may have been the other way round. Reynolds, who was already an old hand at publishing, and who moved in a literary set, might have met Taylor in various ways. The letters I have seen to Taylor from both Bailey and Reynolds are of a later date than 1817, when there had been ample time for acquaintance to ripen into friendship. If methods of address and signature are of any significance, Reynolds either begins "Dear Taylor" or "Dear John" and signs himself "Ever yours" or "Yours ever most truly"; Bailey varies his form of address from "My dear Taylor" to "My dear Sir," he never uses Taylor's Christian name, but he signs himself "Yrs Affectly," "Your affectionate friend," "Yours most faithfully," indeed he signs himself in almost any manner, even down to "Yours very truly." Personally, I think the lack of the Christian name speaks more loudly than the "affectionately." Let us grant, then, that it is a mooted question whether Reynolds owed his introduction to Taylor to Bailey or Bailey his to Reynolds; but, admitting that, by the Spring of 1817 Reynolds had known Taylor certainly more than a year, was on the spot, and was the obvious person to bring Keats and Taylor together. Bailey might have acted as intermediary on the occasion when he was in town, but where would have been the need of him with Reynolds constantly there? The circumstances of the case point so much more sensibly to Reynolds that I cannot doubt that he was the actual introducer.

In meeting Taylor, Keats took one of the most fortunate steps in his life. From that moment, his publishing affairs became a bed of roses. Taylor seems to have been a shrewd enough man in his ordinary course of business, but his attitude toward Keats was positively Utopian. We may lay this to the fact that his intimate friend and confidential adviser was Richard Woodhouse. It was not long after the connection between Keats and the firm of Taylor and Hessey was formed that the firm became in some sort Keats's bankers. Advance payments to Keats were frequent, and loans upon an indefinite security, and it was ten to one that these loans, although nominally emanating from Taylor, drew their substance from the purse of Woodhouse. I shall refer to this later, and quote a letter from Woodhouse to Taylor substantiating a fact which has, I believe, not been known hitherto.

Before continuing the story, I must act the part of Reynolds and introduce these three excellent men, Taylor, Hessey, and Woodhouse, to the reader.

John Taylor was born at East Retford, Nottinghamshire, in July, 1781. He was, therefore, a man of thirty-five when Keats made his acquaintance. Somewhere about 1806, he had come up to London and formed a partnership with a certain James Augustus Hessey, under the firm name of "Taylor and Hessey," for the publishing and retail selling of books. Taylor was a man of high character, his tastes were scholarly, and he was the originator of the theory that Sir Philip Francis was the author of the famous *Letters of Junius*. In support of his opinion, he published in 1813 a book entitled *A Discovery of the Author of the Letters of Junius*, this was followed, in 1816, by *The Identity of Junius with a distinguished Living Character Established*, and, in 1817, by *A Supplement to Junius Identified*. He was interested in philology, as various letters to him from Woodhouse and Reynolds show,[1] although he does not seem to have written anything on the subject. The firm published Hazlitt, Reynolds, John Clare, etc. and were, at the time of Keats's connection with them, a well-to-do and rising house. In 1821, Taylor and Hessey bought the *London Magazine*, of which Taylor constituted himself unannounced editor, with Thomas Hood as sub-editor. At the same time, the business plant was divided, the publishing department, and the offices of the magazine, moving to Waterloo Place, while the retail shop, under Hessey's superintendence, remained in Fleet Street. In later years, Hessey retired from the partnership, and the firm became "Taylor and Walton," and under this name acted as official publishers to the University of London.

Taylor, whose younger brother James was a banker at Bakewell, was much exercised over the currency question, strongly advocating a return to bimetallism; on this subject, he wrote voluminously. In later life, he devoted himself to classic and Biblical studies. He never married, but lived a long and busy life among his books, not dying until 1864. Taylor seems always to have been more interested in scholarship than in literature, but his warm friendship with Richard Woodhouse corrected this tendency so far as his publishing was concerned. The two men seem to have made an excellent working combination, although there is no sign that Woodhouse was ever even a sleeping partner in the firm. He was, however, its chief,

[1] Woodhouse Book. Morgan Collection.

CHARLES BROWN. BUST MADE BY ANDREW WILSON IN 1828

From a photograph of the original bust, in the possession of Louis A. Holman, Esq.

JOHN TAYLOR

From a photograph of an oil painting, in the possession of F. Holland Day, Esq.

if not its only, reader, and very likely drew a salary for acting in that capacity. It is usually assumed that Taylor lived "at the business" in 93 Fleet Street. But this appears to be an error. After examining the contexts and addresses on a number of letters to him from various people, I am certain that it was Hessey who lived in Fleet Street, and that Taylor lived, or had rooms, at 91 New Bond Street. Even Hessey writes to him there in a letter which, though undated, is evidently written from the Fleet Street shop. Bailey, whose letters are not on business, almost always addresses them to New Bond Street. On one occasion, when Taylor is taking a vacation in the country, Woodhouse writes: "You are probably at this moment (N.B. 1/2 p. 6 P.M.) engaged in deep chat with the very individual, who has been beaming looks of benignity from his canvas over Hessey, Mrs. H., your humble, and a cold leg of mutton." [1] Half-past six P.M. means after dinner, and the obvious usualness of the occasion seems to indicate that the Hesseys were eating at their own accustomed dinner-table, even though the portrait of Taylor's father hung upon the wall. On another occasion, writing from Fleet Street, Woodhouse remarks: "I am taking tea with Hessey." [2] Henry C. Shelley in *Literary By-Paths in Old England* says that "the shop and the storerooms of the publishing business were in front," the living rooms being at the back. But this seems not to have been so, for Woodhouse speaks of people "book-buying in the back shop." I think the likeliest supposition is that the back rooms served as both shop and living apartments. I have gone into this so minutely because the Fleet Street premises, both shop and living rooms, quickly became one of Keats's chief haunts. The firm not only published and sold current books, it dealt in second-hand books as well. It seems to have been altogether an energetic and money-making concern. Taylor, it appears, ran the publishing end, while Hessey attended to the retail business.

[1] Woodhouse Book. Morgan Collection. [2] *Ibid.*

Of James Augustus Hessey, we know very little. Taylor has been considered of sufficient importance to be included in the *Dictionary of National Biography*; Hessey is nowhere to be found. Our information concerning him is extremely slight, consisting of very little beside the facts that he was born in 1785 and died in 1870, and that he was married. Lord Houghton, who applied to Reynolds for information about him, learned only that he managed the firm's retail business, and that, in Reynolds's words, "he was a very respectable man — but of no moment in the memoir" of Keats. He must have been a nice person, for Keats nicknamed him "Mistessey," and one does not nickname a man unless he is a good fellow. He had a son, who afterwards became Archdeacon Hessey. There our knowledge of him practically ends. But it is quite plain from the correspondence that, without any of Taylor's varied attainments, he was a gentle, friendly being, devoted to his wife and his work. He is never of the sociable gatherings which Taylor and Woodhouse frequented. Taylor and Woodhouse, both being bachelors, were freer of foot than he. We read of card-parties at Brown's, when Keats lived with him, at which both Taylor and Woodhouse were present, but there is never any mention of Hessey. His relations with Keats and Reynolds seem to have been purely those of business, although the letters to Taylor invariably contain kind messages to him. It is probable that when he and Taylor dissolved their partnership, the book-selling end of the business was acquired by Hessey, who continued to run it under his own name. Even so early as 1827, Taylor's name had disappeared from the shop, although it is evident from his title-pages of the period that he still retained an interest in it. In 1830, Hessey gave up bookselling and became a "Book & Print and Picture Auctioneer"[1] and in 1835 he "took a large

[1] Letters from Taylor to Clare in *New Sidelights on Keats, Lamb, and Others. From Letters to J. Clare,* by Edward Blunden. The *London Mercury,* June, 1921.

old school at Hampstead," but whether with a view to becoming school-master or merely as a place of residence I have not been able to find out.

So much for Keats's publishers, as for Taylor's running mate, the important, unofficial fifth wheel of the partnership, Richard Woodhouse, there is, unhappily, very little to say. In spite of marked abilities, Woodhouse never distinguished himself sufficiently to gain admittance to any encyclopædia. What is known of him has been gleaned by the painstaking efforts of Lord Houghton, Buxton Forman, and Sir Sidney Colvin, to which accounts I am able to supplement information contained in a letter from a niece, written to Mr. W. van R. Whitall, who has given me permission to make what use I please of it. From these various sources, I learn that Richard Woodhouse was descended from an old Herefordshire family. Who or what his father was, no one says, except that he was owner, or part owner, of the White Hart Inn at Bath. Whether this proprietorship absorbed all Mr. Woodhouse Senior's energies, or was merely one of several properties, I have not been able to discover, but it is known that the family had business relations with Spain and Portugal. At the time we are speaking of, he lived at 8 Duke Street, Bath. Richard Woodhouse was born in 1788, the oldest of a family of fourteen children. How this large family was divided as to boys and girls, is not stated, but eight of the brothers lived to grow up. Of these, one became a Lieutenant in the Royal Navy, one a Church of England clergyman, three were wine merchants, and the next to the youngest was called to the bar, although he never practised. The career of the eighth brother is obscure. Richard himself was educated at Eton, but did not go on to a University; instead, he became a solicitor, with chambers at Kings Bench Walk, Temple. Woodhouse was deeply interested in literature; he dabbled in verse, but does not seem to have published anything in either verse or prose. He appears to have had some means, but whether this money was inherited, or was in the nature of an allowance from his father, or was derived from his law practice, is not clear. Neither do we know how he and Taylor came to be so intimate, nor for how many years Woodhouse had been reader to Taylor before the Spring of 1817. From the very first moment of his reading the *Poems*, 1817, Woodhouse seems to have been firmly convinced of Keats's future. Very shortly after Keats's connection with the firm, Woodhouse began to make, and keep, transcripts of his poems, and to collect whatever stray matter concerning him he could lay his hands on. I have already quoted [1] a remarkable note made by Woodhouse in one of his transcript books,[2] which shows how thoroughly he believed in the permanent value of Keats's work. Woodhouse was a good judge of general effect, hence his value as a publisher's reader, but he was an extremely poor critic of detail. He was prone to make suggestions, and tried his hand at several would-be improvements in Keats's poems with the utmost complaisance. It is needless to say that his emendations were invariably failures. Woodhouse had a useful reading knowledge of French, Spanish, and Italian; indeed, he seems to have been an eclectic devourer of books in all these tongues as well as his own. He was also a keen appreciator of the new schools of poetry of his day. Because of this bias, he was able to temper Taylor's classical leanings to the extent of making the firm progressive as well as solid. In later life, he was one of the founders of the Law Life Insurance Society. That Woodhouse was a level-headed man, is proved by the fact that, much as he loved literature, he did not himself attempt to write for publication. The impression we get of him is that, in spite of a good deal of sentimentality, and a weak critical sense in regard to technical detail, he was a kindly, wise, and upright man.

[1] See Vol. I, p. 61. [2] Woodhouse Book. Morgan Library.

RICHARD WOODHOUSE AS A BOY

From an oil painting in the possession of W. van R. Whitall, Esq.

I cannot find out that he ever married. He died of pulmonary tuberculosis,[1] in September, 1834, at the comparatively early age of forty-six.

When Reynolds suggested to Taylor that his firm take on the author of that fine failure, the *Poems*, recently issued by the Olliers, we stand aghast at his temerity. One does not usually introduce a client to a publisher with the inducement of a perfectly unsaleable book. But the faith of Keats's friends seems to have been profoundly oblivious to all common-sense rules. Keats was not selling, therefore Taylor must take him on. The odd fact is that this Quixotic proposition does not seem to have staggered Taylor. Perhaps he had already heard Woodhouse's opinion of the book. We need no double-barrelled eye-glasses to see that Woodhouse was responsible for Taylor's surrender. He and Reynolds could point triumphantly to the Elgin Marble sonnets, published in the *Examiner* of March ninth, and to *The Floure and the Lefe* sonnet, which was printed in the same paper a week later, on March sixteenth. Taylor, accustomed to rely on Woodhouse, seems to have raised no objection to this gambling proposition; so here was Keats, duly installed as one of Taylor and Hessey's authors, under contract to give them his next book as soon as might be, with no syllable of that book yet written.

Along with the proof-reading, publishing, and scant writing of the Winter, there had been a good deal of gadding. Too many card-parties, reunions, long exciting talks leading to sleepless nights. It was all beginning to tell a little on Keats's nerves. Haydon saw this, and was troubled. That great long poem which Keats was committed to, how was it ever going to be written in the midst of this well-meaning social hurly-burly? Everything had conspired — Chapman's *Homer*, the Elgin Marbles, the ob-

[1] Letters from Taylor to Clare in *New Sidelights on Keats, Lamb, and Others. From Letters to J. Clare,* by Edmund Blunden. The *London Mercury,* June, 1921.

livious reviewers — to force upon Keats the necessity of producing a poem of some length which should carry the weight of a real achievement. "Go away," urged Haydon, "leave everybody and everything. Go off somewhere alone, where you will have leisure to look into your own mind and see what you can get out of it." I am not quoting, I am imagining; but something like this Haydon must have said, for Keats writes to Reynolds, in an undated letter which Buxton Forman, for some reason best known to himself, attributes to "March, 1817," as follows:

> "My Brothers are anxious that I should go by myself into the country — they have always been extremely fond of me, and now that Haydon has pointed out how necessary it is that I should be alone to improve myself, they give up the temporary pleasure of living with me continually for a great good which I hope will follow. So I shall soon be out of Town. You must soon bring all your present troubles to a close, and so must I, but we must, like the Fox, prepare for a fresh swarm of flies. Banish money — Banish sofas — Banish Wine — Banish Music; but right Jack Health, honest Jack Health, true Jack Health — Banish Health and banish all the world."

The last passage here is a parody of Falstaff's speech in the second act of Shakespeare's *Henry IV*. This is important to note, because it shows that Keats had Shakespeare on the tip of his tongue. He seems, at the moment, to be absolutely feeding upon Shakespeare. Throughout his life, he is given to quoting Shakespeare, whom he appears to have known almost by heart; but during this Spring, Shakespeare seems to have been hardly out of his mind a single instant.

We can make no guess as to what determined Keats on where to go. The South coast had done him a great deal of good the Summer before, that may have been the reason for his deciding on it again. But he was curious enough to want to try a new place, and he seems to have gone off rather in the dark as to where he should finally fix.

If Buxton Forman's date to the Reynolds letter be correct, Keats did not start on his *villeggiatura* immediately. Yet he was anxious to be off, the type of social distraction which Hunt calls "one of our old evenings joco-serio-musico-pictorio-poetical" was beginning to bore him a little. Hunt himself did not seem either so stimulating, or so wise, as he used to be. Keats was becoming dimly aware of the farce, and was fretting against it and his position in it. On Wednesday, April ninth, he was at Hunt's, probably to bid him good-bye. To this period seems to belong a little undated scrap of a note,[1] directed simply "Messrs. Taylor & Hessey." Keats's new publishers appear to have given him some standing invitation, or offered him some privilege, of which, under the circumstances, he was unable to avail himself. The collective and formal address shows that Keats's acquaintance with the members of the firm was a very recent thing, it is therefore this journey to which the note must refer.

> "My dear Sirs
>
> I am very unfortunate for I am just going out and have not a sheet of paper handy — so I can only beg pardon for this scrap — and thank you for your kindness which will be of little use for I will steal out of town in a day or two — excuse this shabby affair
>
> Yours
>
> John Keats."

On Monday, April fourteenth, he booked an outside seat for Southampton on the Lymington and Poole Mail, leaving the Bull and Crown Inn, Holborn, at half-past seven on that very evening. Shortly after three in the morning, the mail clattered through the little village of Chawton,

[1] Not before published. Author's Collection.

past a small cottage standing directly beside the road. In this cottage lived a widow lady, Mrs. George Austen, and her two daughters, Cassandra and Jane. Did Jane Austen wake just as day was breaking on that Tuesday morning and listen to the mail going by? I wonder.

Four hours later, at seven o'clock, the mail drew up before the door of the Coach and Horses Inn at Southampton. Almost the first thing that Keats did on arrival was to sit down and write to his brothers. This letter shows so much of him — his observation, his descriptive faculty, his poetry withal — that I shall quote it at some length:

> "I am safe at Southampton — after having ridden three stages outside and the rest in for it began to be very cold. I did not know the Names of any of the Towns I passed through — all I can tell you is that sometimes I saw dusty Hedges — sometimes Ponds — then nothing — then a little Wood with trees look you like Launce's Sister 'as white as a Lilly and as small as a Wand' [1] — then came houses which died away into a few straggling Barns — then came hedge trees aforesaid again. As the Lamplight crept along the following things were discovered — 'long heath broom furze' — Hurdles here and there half a Mile — Park palings when the Windows of a House were always discovered by reflection — One Nymph of Fountain — N.B. Stone — lopped Trees — Cow ruminating — ditto Donkey — Man and Woman going gingerly along — William seeing his Sisters over the Heath — John waiting with a Lanthorn for his Mistress — Barber's Pole — Doctor's Shop — However after having had my fill of these I popped my Head out just as it began to Dawn — *N.B. This tuesday Morn saw the Sun rise* — of which I shall say nothing at present. I felt rather lonely this Morning at breakfast so I went and unbox'd a Shakspeare — '*There's my Comfort*' [2] — I went immediately after Breakfast to Southampton Water where I enquired for the Boat to the Isle of Wight as I

[1] Shakespeare's *Two Gentlemen of Verona.* Very likely the trees were silver birches. [2] Shakespeare's *Tempest.*

intend seeing that place before I settle — it will go at 3. So shall I after having taken a Chop."

Of the town, he says:

"I know nothing of this place but that it is long — tolerably broad — has by streets — two or three Churches — a very respectable old Gate with two Lions to guard it — the Men and Women do not materially differ from those I have been in the Habit of seeing — I forgot to say that from dawn till half past six I went through a most delightful Country — some open Down but for the most part thickly wooded. What surprised me most was an immense quantity of blooming Furze on each side the road cutting a most rural dash . . . You, Haydon, Reynolds, &c. have been pushing each other out of my Brain by turns — I have conned over every Head in Haydon's Picture[1] — you must warn them not to be afraid should my Ghost visit them on Wednesday . . . I hope one of you will be competent to take part in a Trio while I am away — you need only aggravate your voices a little and mind not to speak Cues and all[2]. . . Remember me particularly to all my Friends — give my love to the Miss Reynoldses and to Fanny who I hope you will soon see. Write to me soon about them all — and you George particularly how you get on with Wilkinson's plan."

We see more than a little homesickness here. This is not at all the mood of the Margate vacation. Keats had not more than half wanted to go away. He had itched to get into the mood to write his poem, but the mood has not found him yet. If he were bored and a little impatient of his surroundings while still in town, these same surroundings look immensely pleasant in recollection. His preoccupations are abundantly evident here, and it is clear that Hunt is not one of them. It is also worth remarking that Georgiana Wylie receives no direct message, which bears out my contention about Keats's attitude toward

[1] *Christ's Entry into Jerusalem.*
[2] Shakespeare's *Midsummer Night's Dream.*

her at this date.[1] His asking George how he gets on with Wilkinson's plan probably refers to some new business venture which George had started upon. The letter is addressed to "Mr. G. Keats, No. 1 Well Walk, Hampstead, Middx.," so that the Keats brothers must have moved there before John started on his trip, or George and Tom may have moved out on the very day that John set off for Southampton. It was undoubtedly this removal which determined the date of John's journey.

At three, went the boat to the Isle of Wight, and in it went John Keats, bound ostensibly for Cowes, but in reality for solitary contemplation, and the beginning of that great work already determined upon, and already christened *Endymion*.

The sixteen miles of water from Southampton to Cowes is minutely described in a guide-book to the Isle of Wight, the second edition of which was published in 1811. If Keats fell in with this beguiling volume when he was deciding where to spend his country sojourn, we cannot wonder at his choice. "The air has long had the character of salubrity," declares this entrancing book, and as a proof cites the fact that "the longevity of the inhabitants is well known." Among other bits of valuable information the reader is informed that "the *sheep* annually shorn have been rated at 40,000; and not less than 5,000 lambs have been sold in one year to the London butchers. The cows are principally of the Alderney breed, though mixed with others of English complexion." Sportsmen are assured that "hares, partridges, and pheasants . . . may be termed plentiful," while less actively inclined souls are told that "The Isle of Wight has not infrequently been styled the *garden of England*." The little volume goes on to enumerate hills, dales, woods, chines, and prospects, in a manner which few travellers could resist. In spite of the presence of some of the oddest looking "gentlemen's seats" that

[1] See Vol. I, p. 245.

ever graced a countryside, the Isle of Wight was, in those days, a rural, peaceful, simple, and lovely place, how simple may be gathered from this statement, "the roads are very indifferent, and in some parts absolutely impassable for carriages except in the finest weather." No wonder that Keats wanted to see it before determining on where to settle.

Arrived at Cowes, Keats took coach for the five miles to Newport. The mail road, as it is called in our guide-book, although not a turnpike for "there are no turnpikes throughout the island," ran from Cowes to Newport. Among other objects of interest on the way, was a building called the "House of Industry," a charming spot containing "a chapel, a pest house, a house for the smallpox, cells for delinquents, and a place of internment." We may hope that this dismal reminder of disease and death was unremarked by Keats; but a still more sinister sight which he did remark were the barracks, standing just on the edge of Parkhurst Forest. Our guide-book tells us all about them: "They are a depôt for recruits, such as formerly used to be at Chatham; whence they easily escaped by means of the river Medway, and effectually concealed themselves in the overgrown metropolis of the British Empire. Twelve hundred feet by seven hundred is the extent of ground occupied by the barracks, which have every possible accommodation. Near it on the North is the *hospital*, containing a number of convenient wards."

Keats is so modern a man in his outlook on life that we are apt to overlook some of the special aspects of his time. The England of Keats's day was full of contradictions, and one of them was the cynical disregard of individual claims where the army and navy were concerned. What a melancholy state of things our guide-book opens up! The barracks are set here precisely in order that the miserable recruits — poor ignorant country yokels, lured by drink and the glisten of the King's shilling to join the colours —

may not be able to run away. Here they suffered a misery they had never dreamed possible, where "a number of convenient wards" were necessary to keep them from dying outright before having smelt the smoke of a single battle. Keats hated a red coat, and all it stood for, with a holy hatred. We have already had a hint of this in his Epistle to my Brother George.[1] The sight of these barracks dismayed him. Writing two days later to Reynolds, he says:

> "On the road from Cowes to Newport I saw some extensive Barracks which disgusted me extremely with the Government for placing such a Nest of Debauchery in so beautiful a place. I asked a man on the coach about this — and he said that the people had been spoiled. In the room where I slept at Newport, I found this on the Window — 'O Isle spoilt by the Mil*a*tary!'"

The day following Keats's arrival at Newport, he spent running over the island trying to decide where he should settle down. He relates his doings in the letter of April seventeenth, from which I have just quoted, so much better than I can do, that I give them in his own words:

> "Ever since I wrote to my Brothers from Southampton, I have been in a taking, and at this moment I am about to become settled, for I have unpacked my books, put them into a snug corner, pinned up Haydon, Mary Queen of Scots, and Milton with his daughters seated in a row. In the passage I found a head of Shakespeare, which I had not before seen. It is most likely the same that George spoke so well of, for I like it extremely. Well — this head I have hung over my books, just above the three in a row, having first discarded a French Ambassador — now this alone is a good morning's work. Yesterday I went to Shanklin, which occasioned a great debate in my mind whether I should live there or at Carisbrooke. Shanklin is a most beautiful place; sloping wood and meadow ground reach round the Chine, which is a cleft between the Cliffs of the depth of nearly 300 feet at least. This cleft is filled

[1] See Vol. I, p. 162.

with trees and bushes in the narrow part, and as it widens becomes bare, if it were not for primroses on one side, which spread to the very verge of the Sea, and some fishermen's huts on the other, perched midway in the Balustrades of beautiful green Hedges along their steps down to the sands. But the sea, Jack, the sea — the little waterfall — then the white cliff — then St. Catherine's Hill — 'the sheep in the meadows, the cows in the corn.' Then, why are you at Carisbrooke? say you. Because, in the first place, I should be at twice the Expense, and three times the inconvenience — next that from here I can see your continent — from a little hill close by, the whole north Angle of the Isle of Wight, with the water between us. In the 3rd place, I see Carisbrooke Castle from my window, and have found several delightful wood-alleys, and copses, and quick freshes.[1] As for primroses, the Island ought to be called Primrose Island — that is, if the nation of Cowslips agree thereto, of which there are diverse Clans just beginning to lift up their heads. Another reason for my fixing is, that I am more in reach of the places around me. I intend to walk over the Island — east — West — North — South. I have not seen many specimens of Ruins — I don't think however I shall ever see one to surpass Carisbrooke Castle."

Keats lodged at a Mrs. Cooke's, New Village, Carisbrooke, less than a mile out of Newport. One reason for his fixing there, we may assume, knowing his habits, to have been the presence of what our guide-book calls "one of the brightest ornaments of this town," namely "a permanent public library." "The most respectable gentlemen in the island are among its members," declares that enthusiastic store-house of information, and goes on to say that its frequenters "are also accommodated with newspapers, the principal reviews, and other periodical publications of the day. It is conducted on the most liberal principles, and has a considerable collection of books in various languages."

[1] Shakespeare's *Tempest.*

The newspapers and periodicals may well have been an inducement to so homesick a man as Keats was at the moment. How homesick, can be seen from another passage in this same letter:

> "The wind is in a sulky fit, and I feel it would be no bad thing to be the favourite of some Fairy, who would give one the power of seeing how our Friends got on at a Distance. I should like, of all Loves, a sketch of you and Tom and George in ink which Haydon will do if you tell him how I want them."

Loneliness is beginning to prey upon him. Each day is age long. "Ever since I wrote to my Brothers from Southampton." Ever since! It is only two days. The truth is that neither Keats nor his friends had the slightest idea what the weight of complete solitude means during the strain of creation. When one has worked all one can for the moment, and the brain is hot and agitated and incapable of relief from itself, something, some one, must be there to ease it off into quiet. Keats was in the habit of talking himself free from whatever worried him. Here he was alone, with nothing to do when he had got through his daily stint but think about what he had written and what he would write. Even in walking one can think, in reading one must use one's mind, and Keats had only walking and reading to relieve him from work. The result was, of course, that the rest times were more restless and fatiguing than the working ones. During the first days at Carisbrooke, he was not writing, he was considering what to write, or rather, how to enclose in verse the chaotic magnificence which was surging in his mind. It is more difficult to plan a poem than it is to write it when the plan is formed. Keats was totally ignorant of how such planning is done. A long poem was a new departure for him. He felt that it was time for him to make such an attempt, but he dreaded it as well. I do not suppose that any one not a poet can realize the agony of creating a poem. Every nerve, even every muscle, seems strained to the breaking point. The poem will not be denied, to refuse to write it would be a greater torture. It tears its way out of the brain, splintering and breaking its passage, and leaves that organ in the state of a jelly-fish when the task is done. And yet to have no poem to write is the worst state of all. Truly a poet's life is not a happy one. Broken and shattered when creating, miserable and void when not creating, urged always to a strain which cannot heal except through immense pain, peaceful only in the occasional consciousness of a tolerable achievement — certainly the poor creature must be born to his calling, for no man would take on such an existence willingly. This is just the difference between the poet and the poetaster, I think. Does a man create with his blood and sinews, and suffer in so doing? If he does not, give no heed to his works, they are still-born.

Keats says it all in his letters at this time; they are a very mine to the psychologist who would study the workings of the creative faculty. In the letter to Reynolds so often quoted, but under the new date of April eighteenth, is this passage:

> "I find I cannot exist without Poetry — without eternal Poetry — half the day will not do — the whole of it — I began with a little, but habit has made me a Leviathan. I had become all in a Tremble from not having written anything of late — the Sonnet over-leaf did me good. I slept the better last night for it — this Morning, however, I am nearly as bad again."

"Over-leaf," on April seventeenth, he had written out the sonnet on the sea, *It keeps eternal whisperings.* He prefaces it by saying: "From want of regular rest I have been rather *narvus* — and the passage in *Lear* — 'Do you not hear the sea?' has haunted me intensely." The haunting passage is this:

"Hark, do you hear the sea? . . .

. . .

Come on, Sir; here's the place: stand still. How fearful
And dizzy 'tis, to cast one's eyes so low!
The crows and choughs that wing the midway air
Show scarce so gross as beetles: half way down
Hangs one that gathers samphire, dreadful trade!
Methinks he seems no bigger than his head:
The fishermen, that walk upon the beach,
Appear like mice; and yond tall anchoring bark,
Diminish'd to her cock; her cock, a buoy
Almost too small for sight: the murmuring surge,
That on the unnumber'd idle pebbles chafes,
Cannot be heard so high. I'll look no more;
Lest my brain turn, and the deficient sight
Topple down headlong."

It is strange, in Keats's sonnet, to note where it follows Shakespeare and where Keats's own experience is the sole guide. Since this cannot be done without comparison, I will give the whole sonnet here:

"ON THE SEA.

It keeps eternal whisperings around
Desolate shores, and with its mighty swell
Gluts twice ten thousand Caverns, till the spell
Of Hecate leaves them their old shadowy sound.
Often 'tis in such a gentle temper found,
That scarcely will the very smallest shell
Be mov'd for days from where it sometime fell,
When last the winds of Heaven were unbound.
Oh ye! who have your eye-balls vex'd and tir'd,
Feast them upon the wideness of the Sea;
Oh ye! whose ears are dinn'd with uproar rude,
Or fed with too much cloying melody—
Sit ye near some old Cavern's Mouth and brood
Until ye start, as if the sea-nymphs quired."

Curiously enough, the effect of the sea seen from a height, which is the very essence of Shakespeare's lines, and which was an actual daily vision to Keats from the cliff-edges of the Isle of Wight, has no part in his picture here. The sonnet is less a picture than a synthesis. Its added depth and seriousness, its awareness of the ocean's vast, majestic indifference, of the consolation offered by the view of this resistless force and overwhelming elemental grandeur, show how far Keats had moved since the year before, when he was at Margate. Admirable as was his sea picture in the sonnet, *To my Brother George*, written there, cogent as were its suggestions, it cannot be compared to this new sonnet, so greatly does the last poem surpass the first.

Shakespeare's lines serve as a text rather than a starting-point. Keats's "shell" is Shakespeare's "pebbles," that is the nearest approach to a parallel to be found, although the "eye-balls" were probably suggested by the long impression of sight in the *Lear* passage, combined with the recollection of Gloucester's being blind. Weary eye-balls soothed by the sea's immensity, is a flash of revelation into Keats's state of mind. So tired, so strained, so tossed was he by the fever of his imagination, and here was a peace beyond his seeking, a magnitude the contemplation of which was rest. "Cloying melody"—he must get away from that; in those words and their context the sentimental farce is snuffed out like a candle-wick between his fingers. Here, beyond Chapman's *Homer*, beyond even the Elgin Marbles, is the healing wonder of the mighty, law-abiding, everlasting sea.

The first lines of the sonnet seem to take colour from the scenery of the *Tempest*, the rest is pure synthetic imagination. The only awkwardness throughout the poem is that the order of the rhymes in the sestet is a little uncouth and teasing, and that "quired" for "choired" is odd, and a questionable rhyme for "tir'd."

This sonnet is one of Keats's best, as he must have known; but, successful though it was, it could not quiet him because *Endymion* was pressing to be done. Keats was fully alive to the immensity of the task he had set himself, and in many ways he felt that he was not ready for it. But he realized also that fugitive pieces would not do forever, that he must strive after something bigger. Already he had planned at least the length of his poem, and that alone was sufficiently formidable. In an undated letter to George, he says, "It will be a test, a trial of my powers of imagination and chiefly of invention by which I must make 4000 lines of one bare circumstance and fill them with poetry." Keats was wise enough to understand that the fugitive pieces of men capable of great work have in them, perforce, the quality of their creators, a quality which can never imbue the fugitive pieces of lesser poets. To make even his sonnets of value, he must be able to grasp and secure more extended conceptions. It is not the size of a poem which counts; it is the calibre of the man who writes it. His acquaintance with this truth is evident from some remarks in this same letter:

> "As to what you say about my being a Poet, I can return no Answer but by saying that the high Idea I have of poetical fame makes me think I see it towering too high above me. At any rate, I have no right to talk until *Endymion* is finished . . . Did our great Poets ever write Short Pieces? I mean in the shape of Tales."

After something like a week, Keats found that he could not stand the loneliness, so he left Carisbrooke and went to Margate, at the same time sending for Tom to join him there.

Biographers differ as to whether Keats began *Endymion* at Carisbrooke, or not until he reached Margate. I am convinced from the evidence in hand that he began it in the Isle of Wight. This evidence is as follows: At the end of the letter to Reynolds, the second part of which is dated "April 18th," he says: "I shall forthwith begin my Endymion." He wrote to Hunt on May tenth, from Margate, speaking of his wearing himself out with thinking at Carisbrooke: "In a week or so, I became not over capable in my upper stories, and set off pell-mell for Margate"; and again, "I began my poem about a fortnight since, and have done some every day, except travelling ones." The "travelling ones" are, of course, those days spent in going from Carisbrooke to Margate. A "fortnight since" would take him back to April twenty-sixth, but he only says "*about* a fortnight." A week at Carisbrooke would take him to April twenty-third, but he only says "a week or so." He tells Haydon, on May tenth: "I was there but a Week." On May sixteenth, he writes Taylor and Hessey: "I went day by day at my poem for a Month . . . was obliged to give up for a few days." Taking all these remarks into consideration and tallying one with another, the fact that Keats began *Endymion* at Carisbrooke seems perfectly clear, and that the day of his beginning was somewhere between the eighteenth and the twenty-third of April.

The letters from Margate tell the tale of the Carisbrooke weeks. "I went to the Isle of Wight," he says, in the letter of May tenth to Leigh Hunt, "thought so much about poetry, so long together, that I could not get to sleep at night . . . Another thing, I was too much in solitude, and consequently was obliged to be in a continual burning of thought, as an only resource."

At Margate, Tom's presence was a help, but Keats was in a fever of work and kept at it, and at it, until he forced himself into a real depression, almost a doubt of himself. "I have asked myself so often," he writes in this same letter to Hunt, "why I should be a poet more than other men, seeing how great a thing it is, — how great things are to be gained by it, what a thing to be in the mouth of Fame, — that at last the idea has grown so monstrously beyond my seeming power of attainment, that the other day I nearly consented with myself to drop into a Phaeton. Yet 'tis a disgrace to fail, even in a huge attempt; and at this moment I drive the thought from me . . . Perhaps I may have done a good deal for the time, but it appears such a pin's point to me that I will not copy any out. When I consider that so many of these pin-points go to make a bodkin-point . . . and that it requires a thousand bodkins to make a spear bright enough to throw any light to posterity, I see nothing but continual up-hill journeying. Now is there anything more unpleasant . . . than to be so journeying and miss the goal at last? But I intend to whistle all these cogitations into the sea."

Keats's ingenious reason for not sending any of his poem to the man whose meddling, if kindly, finger he does not wish to see streaked across his new pie is very illuminating. At the end of the letter, Keats turns whimsical, as was his wont, and covers his feelings under a sort of rueful joke:

> "Does Shelley go on telling strange stories of the deaths of kings? Tell him there are strange stories of the deaths of poets. Some have died before they were conceived . . . Does Mrs. S. cut bread and butter as neatly as ever? Tell her to procure some fatal scissors, and cut the thread of life of all to-be-disappointed poets."

Then comes the bane of over-work, the true hell reserved for over-zealous artists. His work seems bad, all faults until — the great until! — he compares it with work of another kind, and takes heart again in the realization that at least his aim is all right. In the letter of May tenth to Haydon, he says:

> "I have been in such a state of Mind as to read over my Lines and hate them. I am one that 'gathers samphire, dreadful trade' [1] — the Cliff of Poesy towers above me — yet when Tom who meets with some of Pope's Homer in Plutarch's Lives reads some of those to me they seem like Mice [2] to mine. I read and write about eight hours a day."

[1] See Vol. I. p. 304. [2] *Ibid.*

Toward the end of his letter, he adds: "I never quite despair and I read Shakespeare—indeed I shall I think never read any other Book much . . . I am very near agreeing with Hazlitt that Shakespeare is enough for us." The letter finishes with a blessing perfectly adapted to his correspondent's taste: "So now in the name of Shakespeare, Raphael and all our Saints, I commend you to the care of heaven!"

A little incident which testifies to Keats's charm occurred on his departure from Carisbrooke. His landlady insisted on giving him the picture of Shakespeare which he liked so much. "I was there but a Week," he tells Haydon, "yet the old woman made me take it with me though I went off in a hurry. Do you not think this is ominous of good?"

I have already spoken of Keats's preoccupation with Shakespeare at this time. He was reading the plays over and over again evidently. In the letter to Reynolds from Carisbrooke, is a significant passage on the kind of way he was going over them. Not merely reading, but marking, learning, and inwardly digesting them to the smallest detail of poetry and meaning. This is what he says:

> "I'll tell you what—on the 23^d^ was Shakespeare born. Now if I should receive a letter from you, and another from my Brothers on that day 'twould be a parlous good thing. Whenever you write say a word or two on some Passage in Shakespeare that may have come rather new to you, which must be continually happening, notwithstanding that we read the same Play forty times."

The gift of Shakespeare's picture is "ominous of good"; to receive a letter on Shakespeare's birthday "would be a parlous good thing"; now, in the May tenth letter to Haydon, he goes farther: "I remember your saying that you had notions of a good Genius presiding over you. I have of late had the same thought, for things which [I] do half at Random are afterwards confirmed by my judgement in a dozen features of Propriety. Is it too daring to fancy Shakespeare this Presider?" Shakespeare, so dwelt upon and brooded over, takes on something of an oracular quality to Keats's heated imagination. What has he to say of Christianity, that already mooted subject to Keats? It is not to Haydon, naturally, that he dares suggest a pro and con, but to Leigh Hunt, whose views he finds interesting, although he is not quite able to accept them for himself. The Margate letter to Leigh Hunt contains the following:

> "I ought to have said a word on Shakespeare's Christianity. There are two which I have not looked over with you, touching the thing: the one for, the other against: that in favour is in *Measure for Measure*, Act II, Scene 2,
>
> *Isab*. Alas, alas!
> Why all the souls that were, were forfeit once;
> And he that might the 'vantage best have took,
> Found out the remedy.
>
> That against is in *Twelfth Night*, Act III, Scene 2,
>
> *Maria*. For there is no Christian that means to be saved by believing rightly, can ever believe such impossible passages of grossness."

Keats ends the subject with this quotation. He leaves it, in fact, unsolved. Indeed, I suspect that the subject was still in solution in his mind at this time. He seems still to believe in Deity, but to have reached the point of questioning Christianity.

Keats's letter to Haydon seems to be a reply to one from Haydon to him, misdated in Haydon's journal as of May eleventh. Haydon has heard of Keats's depression from his letters to his brothers, and he writes to cheer him up, characteristically exhorting him to "Trust in God with all your might, my dear Keats," and again referring to the consolation of prayer. In his answer, Keats ignores this suggestion of Haydon's explicitly, but in a totally different connection does speak of "our Creator."

Haydon, having succeeded in removing Keats from Hunt — geographically, at least — cannot resist reinforcing his action in this wise:

> "Beware, for God's sake, of the delusions and sophistications that are ripping up the talents and morality of our friend! He will go out of the world the victim of his own weakness and the dupe of his own self-delusions, with the contempt of his enemies and the sorrow of his friends, and the cause he undertook to support injured by his own neglect of character."

This is pretty stiff speaking, but Haydon knew that his leaven was working. Keats has listened and is beginning to acquiesce with Haydon's views. To this remark of Haydon's he replies:

> "I wrote to Hunt yesterday — scarcely know what I said in it. I could not talk about Poetry in the way I should have liked for I was not in humour with either his or mine. His self delusions are very lamentable — they have enticed him into a Situation which I should be less eager after than that of a galley Slave — what you observe thereon is very true must be in time.
>
> Perhaps it is a self delusion to say so — but I think I could not be deceived in the manner that Hunt is — may I die to-morrow if I am to be. There is no greater Sin after the seven deadly than to flatter oneself into an idea of being a great Poet . . . how comfortable a feel it is to feel that such a Crime must bring its heavy Penalty? That if one be a Self-deluder accounts must be balanced?"

Poor Hunt! No longer will ropes of roses suffice to lead his pet lamb whither he will. He is no more the headmaster, glorious and invincible chief; he is a man replete of faults and foibles even as other men, and so Keats never afterwards fails to consider him.

While this psychological drama was going on at Margate, Keats's affairs in London were moving at an unfortunately rapid rate. George Keats, whether by John's authority or on his own initiative we do not know, had undertaken to express his views to the Olliers regarding their management of the sale of the *Poems*. The answer vouchsafed him was not one calculated to soothe rasped nerves. Under the date of "29th April, 1817," the publishers wrote:

"SIR, —

We regret that your brother ever requested us to publish his book, or that our opinion of its talent should have led us to acquiesce in undertaking it. We are, however, much obliged to you for relieving us from the unpleasant necessity of declining any further connection with it, which we must have done, as we think the curiosity is satisfied, and the sale has dropped. By far the greater number of persons who have purchased it from us have found fault with it in such plain terms, that we have in many cases offered to take the book back rather than be annoyed with the ridicule which has, time after time, been showered upon it. In fact, it was only on Saturday last that we were under the mortification of having our own opinion of its merits flatly contradicted by a gentleman, who told us he considered it 'no better than a take in.' These are unpleasant imputations for any one in business to labour under, but we should have borne them and concealed their existance from you had not the style of your note shewn us that such delicacy would be quite thrown away. We shall take means without delay for ascertaining the number of copies on hand, and you shall be informed accordingly.

Yours most &c.

C. & J. OLLIER."

That is a nasty letter. What can George have said to call down such sheer abuse? I fear that this is another instance of George's "pride." Whatever it was, there was a flat end to the Olliers. Probably it was James, the business brother, who wrote the letter, for Keats seems to have remained on pleasant terms with the verse-dabbling Charles to the end of the chapter. What became of the unsold remainder of the first edition, I have not been able certainly to discover. From this letter, it would look as if

George had intimated that he was prepared to take it over. But did he? The Olliers continued to publish Hunt and Shelley, but, as this firm did not advertise its publications in the back of its books, I cannot check the *Poems*, 1817, in either Shelley's *Revolt of Islam* or Hunt's *Foliage*, both of which volumes were issued in 1818, where such an advertisement would naturally appear. Taylor and Hessey did print such lists in the back of their volumes, and I have consulted a number of them. *Endymion* appears, and so, in 1820 and after, does *Lamia*, but not the *Poems*. Taylor and Hessey seem to have taken Hazlitt's *Characters of Shakespeare's Plays* over from the Olliers, and an advertisement of it is duly printed in the back of the *Lectures on the Comic Writers*. It certainly looks, therefore, as though the *Poems* were not taken over; on the other hand, there are occasional references in Woodhouse's letters which lead to the inference that they sometimes sold them.[1] Could the Keats brothers command a sum sufficient to buy out the edition? It does not seem likely, and what would Abbey have said at being asked for money for such a purpose. We must leave the question unanswered, I fear. One little hint there is that George had contemplated buying the books, possibly because of some sort of an assurance that Taylor and Hessey would handle them in the way of retail business. This hint is in the shape of a word to John that the money from their grandfather's main estate could not be touched because of the dragging Chancery suit.[2] At least we can infer that this was the gist of George's communication to John, mentioned in the letter to Haydon. The mention is a little ambiguous as to the exact facts, probably because Haydon knew all about them. In the second half of the letter, written on May eleventh, Keats says:

"This Morning I received a letter from George by which

[1] Since writing the above, I have found an advertisement of the *Poems* in the back of Clare's *Village Minstrel*, published by Taylor and Hessey in 1821.

[2] See Vol. I, p. 27.

it appears that Money Troubles are to follow us up for some time to come — perhaps for always — these vexations are a great hindrance to one — they are not like Envy and detraction stimulants to further exertion as being immediately relative and reflected on at the same time with the prime object — but rather like a nettle leaf or two in your bed. So now I revoke my Promise of finishing my Poem by the Autumn which I should have done had I gone on as I have done — but I cannot write while my spirit is fevered in a contrary direction and I am now sure of having plenty of it this Summer. At this moment I am in no enviable Situation — I feel that I am not in a Mood to write any to-day; and it appears that the loss of it is the beginning of all sorts of irregularities. I am extremely glad that a time must come when every thing will leave not a wrack behind. You tell me never to despair — I wish it was as easy for me to observe the saying — truth is I have a horrid Morbidity of Temperament which has shown itself at intervals — it is I have no doubt the greatest Enemy and stumbling block I have to fear — I may even say that it is likely to be the cause of my disappointment."

Keats was certainly in a disagreeable position. Not only did *Endymion* tease to be written because it must, there was still another complication to trouble him. He had contracted for the poem with a new firm of publishers, and the poem would not get itself written. It was awkward. Not that Messrs. Taylor and Hessey urged him, they seem to have been perfectly comprehending and sympathetic, and never to have dreamt of hurrying him, but his own conscience hurried him. He was the author of a most unsuccessful book of poems, the unsaleable copies of which the publishers were most anxious to throw back on his hands, and yet he had found another firm who were willing to venture on a new poem by him, and a long one at that. And he was under still greater obligations to this extraordinary pair of partners. By the terms of his agreement with them, he was to receive an advance payment of twenty pounds.[1] This money, probably at George's solicitation, they sent to him at Margate. We can imagine George arriving at 93 Fleet Street with the dismal news that, far from being able to buy back his books, John was in actual need of money. It seems likely that this was the way of it, for, if John had written, doubtless his letter would have been preserved along with the others. His acknowledgement, written on May sixteenth, we have.

Keats's letter to Taylor and Hessey shows that already he was on the most friendly terms with them. After a somewhat pathetic attempt at playful joking, he adds, with characteristic frankness:

> "I went day by day at my poem for a Month — at the end of which time the other day I found my Brain so overwrought that I had neither rhyme nor reason in it — so was obliged to give up for a few days. I hope soon to be able to resume my work — I have endeavoured to do so once or twice; but to no purpose. Instead of Poetry, I have a swimming in my head and feel all the effects of a Mental debauch, lowness of Spirits, anxiety to go on without the power to do so, which does not at all tend to my ultimate progression."

Keats calls Margate a "treeless affair," and perhaps the sea had woven itself too closely into his depression. It was not like the Summer before, when he had hankered after just the scenery which was to be found at Margate. His mood is utterly different now from what it was a year earlier, and Margate does not suit it. He wants — trees. Already, by May tenth, he had told Hunt: "I fancied that I should like my old lodging here, and could contrive to do without trees . . . Tom is with me at present, and we are very comfortable. We intend, though, to get among some trees." As a postscript, he adds: "You shall hear where we move." Six days later, he has decided where to go. He tells Taylor and Hessey: "This evening I go to

[1] Colvin. From information supplied by a great-niece of Taylor's.

Canterbury, having got tired of Margate. I was not right in my head when I came. At Canterbury I hope the remembrance of Chaucer will set me forward like a Billiard Ball."

On Friday, May sixteenth, then, Keats left Margate, seeking, as so many poets have done, an atmosphere which will put him into the frame of mind necessary for his work. The portmanteaux are hoisted in, the cloths are pulled off the horses, the whip cracks, the horn blows, and John and Tom Keats, and some hundreds of lines of *Endymion*, rattle away to Canterbury.

I have been in something of a quandary as to just how to deal with *Endymion* in the matter of time. It took Keats seven months to write the poem, and during those months he was moving from place to place, and his mind was in a constant flux and flow. To weave the poem in with his daily existence, as I have been trying to do with his poems hitherto, was manifestly impossible, if any continuity in the poem itself were to be preserved. It has seemed to me best, therefore, to abandon the strict chronological sequence in this instance, and devote a chapter to *Endymion* alone. Of course, in doing this, I have been obliged to make such reference to events, and to Keats's continual growth of thought, as have to do with the poem, reserving, however, the narrative proper for a succeeding chapter. How much Keats had written by the time he left Margate, we do not know. But it is clear that he had advanced a good way with the First Book. His life and mental experiences in Carisbrooke and in Margate are so much of a piece that no break could well be made between them. Now, however, we come to a pause, a pause because we have no letters to fill a gap of a month. That Keats wrote no letters for a month, it is impossible to conceive, but it is a fact that none have come to light. Here, then, seems the logical place to take up the long, and very difficult, poem which is *Endymion*.

CHAPTER V

ENDYMION

It is not hard to understand why Keats chose the story of Endymion for the subject of his contemplated long poem. Possible subjects for long poems fall roughly into five groups. These groups we may classify as mythological, historical, satirical, allegorical, and narrative pure and simple. If modern poetry were in question, another group might be added, the psychological, but psychology was unknown to science until very recently, and, however much psychology there was in the poetry of an earlier day, it worked under the cover of narrative or drama. Purely psychological poems such as Edwin Arlington Robinson's *Avon's Harvest* or *Roman Bartholow*, for instance, are a product of modern scientific thought. Taking these five groups one by one, we shall quickly see upon which Keats's choice was predestined to fall.

Historical poetry requires much knowledge and considerable research, and Keats, at this period, had neither the knowledge nor the patience necessary to hunt facts and laboriously combine them into an artistic whole. His reading had always been of the impressionistic order; to receive impressions, not to tabulate facts, was his aim, and it is the wisest aim for a budding poet. Not until the poetical view-point is so firmly fixed as to become a dependable habit, can youth engage in a long, conscious preparation of detail before starting to write. It may sound paradoxical, but it is a truth that Keats had to write, it would have been an ill-judged move on his part to have held off from actual writing for any preparation whatsoever. Time for that later on. We see, therefore, that a subject taken from history was out of the question.

For satire, a poet needs experience, experience of events

and persons. He also needs the possession of a certain state of mind. Keats's experience was of the slightest, and his state of mind was as far removed from the satirical as could well be. Satire is not a lover's tool, and Keats was fairly in love with poetry. Beauty and poetry were synonymous to him; it took years, and the flint of disappointment, to strike the spark of satire in his soul.

As to allegory, that was completely foreign to Keats's nature. There is no trace of allegory to be found anywhere in his works. The ingenious efforts of commentators to find allegorical meanings in *Endymion* and *Hyperion* have led to a great deal of interesting writing; but these tracts, as I may call them, are quite beside the mark, since they are invariably based upon the supposition that Keats was a type of man which any intimate study of his character proves that he was not. In the following analysis of *Endymion*, I have endeavoured to show how Keats really wrote the poem, basing my explanations entirely on his own statements and upon the known facts of his life and personality.

In speaking of narrative as a category by itself, I mean that kind of tale in verse which is concerned with men and women such as the poet may possibly have encountered in the flesh. Chaucer's *Canterbury Tales* comes under this heading, and so do many of Wordsworth's poems. Crabbe is an uninspired exemplar of the *genre*, as, in our own day, but with the quality of poetry added, are John Masefield and Robert Frost. One would suppose that Keats, while visiting Dr. Hammond's patients in Edmonton, or walking the London hospitals, must have come across scores of people whose lives would have given him abundance of material for just this sort of thing. The material may have lain before him as thick as hoar-frost on an Autumn morning, but it was not in him to react to it. Poetry, to Keats, was a thing of zest and glamour. Realist though he was, his realism confined itself to detail; it was realism vitalizing romance, for Keats is one of the great romantics of literature. His dislike of Wordsworth's rural episodes was absolute and irrevocable. In a review of Reynolds's skit on *Peter Bell*, published in the *Examiner* in 1819, Keats says of the then anonymous author: "The more he may love the sad embroidery of the *Excursion*, the more he will hate the coarse samplers of Betty Foy and Alice Fell." Nobody can dislike Chaucer, but it was the great, sincere, straightforward and penetrating poet whom Keats admired, rather than the teller of tales. It is significant that the one poem of Chaucer's on which he was moved to compose was the apocryphal *Floure and the Lefe*. Besides, the centuries had invested Chaucer's everyday characters with a romantic aura.

Counting out the four groups of history, satire, allegory, and domestic narrative, we see that the only one of our five divisions which Keats could cope with in the Spring of 1817 was the mythological. Mythology had captivated him even in his school-days. There was Lemprière, which Clarke thinks he knew almost by heart. He was familiar with Sandys' translation of Ovid from the same early period, and the Elizabethan poets he had delved into were full of mythological allusions and suggestions. Since mythology was the only possible source from which he was fitted to draw inspiration for the poem he wished to write, the choice of the legend of Endymion was a foregone conclusion. I have already spoken of his peculiar and transcendental feeling for the moon. Realizing this, it is evident that the Endymion myth must have a peculiar attraction for him, and that he would undoubtedly attempt to write it as soon as he felt able to do so. It is also obvious that the Endymion drama was capable of becoming the expression of just those ideas which he had, somewhat haltingly, tried to express in *I Stood Tip-toe* and *Sleep and Poetry*. His little essay of it in the first of these two poems points clearly to his direction.

There are many books in which Keats may have read the legend. It is told, or referred to, in Spenser's *Epithalamium*, Shakespeare's *Merchant of Venice*, Ben Jonson's *Masque of Oberon*, Marlowe's *Ovid's Love Elegies*, Beaumont and Fletcher's *Faithful Shepherdess* and the *Maid's Tragedy*. But, in all this goodly array, there was only one Elizabethan poet who let his fancy really play over the subject, and that was Michael Drayton. Drayton wrote two long poems dealing with the myth of Endymion and Diana. These poems are *Endimion and Phœbe* and the *Man in the Moone*.

Sir Sidney Colvin is as convinced as everybody else that Keats, in constructing his plot, was much indebted to the *Man in the Moone*, which was included in Smethwick's edition of Drayton; but he is also stoutly convinced that, in spite of the far closer parallels between Keats's *Endymion* and Drayton's *Endimion and Phœbe*, Keats could never have seen that work. This interesting question did not seem to me solved by a mere statement of impossibility, and I set out to find what reasons for and against could be discovered. The result of my search has been to convince me, in my turn, that Keats could, without difficulty, have seen the poem, and that, taking into consideration the many passages in *Endymion* which almost duplicate passages in *Endimion and Phœbe*, he certainly did see it, and, in fact, took one of the most important episodes in his poem directly from it.

Before considering the important questions of where and how Keats could have met with Drayton's little known work, *Endimion and Phœbe*, I wish to point out the evidence in the two poems which makes it conclusive that one is derived from the other. Even Sir Sidney does not deny this evidence, but he considers it due to coincidence, an opinion which becomes untenable when the impossibility of Keats's ever having seen Drayton's poem is explained away.

Drayton's *Endimion and Phœbe* is so scarce a book that only two copies are known to exist to-day. It has been my good fortune to trace the present whereabouts of both these copies, and to find out enough of the history of one of them to disprove Sir Sidney's contention. Drayton published the book in 1594, and he never reprinted it. Why, no one knows, but such is the case. One may, however, conceive the reason to have been pique. Shakespeare's *Venus and Adonis* had appeared in 1593, and already, in 1594, it had attained to a second edition, and a third was called for in 1596. Marlowe's *Hero and Leander* was being widely and successfully circulated in manuscript. *Endimion and Phœbe* fell upon indifferent ears. For some reason, it was not fancied, and Drayton, in view of his comparative failure in a style of work so pleasantly received from the pens of Shakespeare and Marlowe, not improbably determined that his poem should disappear; and disappear it did, from the knowledge of scholars, at least, for two hundred and sixty years. There is an almost exact parallel here to the case of the Dutch painter, Vermeer, with this difference: Vermeer's pictures were known and attributed to various other painters, but his existence was entirely forgotten; Drayton was well known, but this particular poem was not only lost, all knowledge that he had ever written such a poem was lost with it. To be sure, eighteen extracts from the poem were printed in *England's Parnassus* in 1600, but, as the name of the poem from which they came was not mentioned, these quotations could not serve any purpose of identification.

To realize how greatly Keats drew on Drayton's poem, it is necessary to compare various passages from it with corresponding passages in *Endymion*. There are two modern reprints of *Endimion and Phœbe*, dating from a period more than thirty years subsequent to Keats's death. These reprints were privately issued for the Roxburgh Club of London, but since both are long out of print and difficult to obtain, I shall give these passages in full. Let me say at the start that, although I have worked with the originals before me, my task has been greatly facilitated by reference to an unpublished manuscript in the Widener Library, which the author, Mr. Claude L. Finney, has kindly given me his permission to make use of.[1]

Before starting on the comparisons, there is one stumbling block which must be cleared up. In the first edition of *Endymion*, the lines are carefully numbered, but this numbering is entirely out of accordance with proper metrical usage. The poem is written in heroic couplets — that is, the lines are iambic pentameter with each pair rhyming, rarely there are three rhymes in succession. Whenever Keats wished to make a division in his poem, he dropped his next line down one space, and when these divisions happened to occur in the middle of a line, he followed the same procedure with that part of the line belonging to the new section. The line, however, being always of five feet, was not metrically altered by this form of printing, but Keats, or his publishers, in defiance of both logic and strict metrical custom, counted every divided line as two. Buxton Forman, very naturally, preferred to adhere to precedent and consider these sundered lines as undivided, reading as one line what Keats read as two, and in this he has been followed by Professor de Sélincourt. The result is, obviously, extremely confusing, for it means that Keats's numbering and this later numbering become more and more at variance throughout each book of the poem. Plainly, then, when Keats, in his letters, mentions a line by its number, only those happy possessors of the first edition can know which line he means without the necessity of carefully re-counting all the lines by his method from

[1] *Shakespeare and Keats*, by Claude L. Finney. "A Thesis Submitted to the Faculty of Arts and Sciences in the Division of Modern Languages of Harvard University in Partial Fulfilment of the Requirements for the Degree of Doctor of Philosophy. April, 1922."

the beginning of the particular book in which the line stands. Since first editions are scarcely plentiful, I have been forced, for the convenience of readers, to adopt Buxton Forman's plan. Whenever, in allusions to statements in the letters, I have been obliged to use Keats's numbering, I have said so in the text. Unless otherwise stated, therefore, the line numbers throughout this chapter correspond to those in Buxton Forman's and Professor de Sélincourt's editions.

The verbal correspondences between *Endimion and Phœbe* and *Endymion* begin with the sixty-fourth line of *Endymion* and the twenty-second of Drayton's poem. The openings of the two poems are quite unlike. *Endimion and Phœbe* opens directly by telling the reader that on Mount Latmus, the favourite resort of all the sylvan deities, but especially dedicated to the vestal rites of Diana, there lives a young shepherd named Endimion. At this point, Drayton describes the mountain as follows:

> "Vpon this Mount there stood a stately Groue
> Whose reaching armes to clip the Welkin stroue,
> Of tufted Cedars, and the branching Pine,
> Whose bushy tops themselues doe so intwine,
> As seem'd when Nature first this work begun
> She then conspir'd against the piercing sun:
> Vnder whose couert."

Keats's description in *Endymion* is extraordinarily like Drayton's:

> "Upon the sides of Latmos was outspread
> A mighty forest; for the moist earth fed
> So plenteously all weed-hidden roots
> Into o'er-hanging boughs, and precious fruits.
> And it had gloomy shades, sequestered deep,
> Where no man went; . . .
>
> . . . . .
>
> . . . Who could tell
> The freshness of the space of heaven above,
> Edg'd round with dark tree tops?"

Continuing the description, Drayton goes on:

> "Out of thys soyle sweet bubling Fountains crept,
> As though for ioy the sencelesse stones had wept,
> With straying channels dauncing sundry wayes,
> . . .
> Which breaking forth the tender grasse bedewed."

This picture is condensed in *Endymion* to:

> ". . . Cold Springs had run
> To warm their chilliest bubbles in the grass."

On the banks of these streams, says Drayton, grow many sorts of flowers; and nightingales, ousels, and blackbirds sing. Marble steps lead up to the grove at the top of the mountain, and here Phœbe, in the form of a nymph arrayed in an "Azur'd Mantle," discovers herself to Endimion as he is fishing by a river-side. This "Azur'd Mantle" is one of the parallels between *Endimion and Phœbe* and *Endymion.* And here let me say that Keats's verbal correspondences with Drayton's poem by no means follow in Drayton's order. They skip about here and there wherever Keats found them of use. That I may not duplicate my quotations, however, I give them where they fall in this outline of the plot of Drayton's *Endimion.* The mantle is given in Drayton thus:

> "An Azur'd Mantle purfled with a vaile,
> Which in the Ayre puft like a swelling saile,
> Embosted Rayne-bowes did appeare in silk,
> With wauie streames as white as mornings Milk;
> Which euer as the gentle Ayre did blow,
> Still with the motion seem'd to ebb and flow."

When Keats's Endymion first sees his goddess, this same blowing blue mantle forms part of his vision:

> ". . . The wind out-blows
> Her scarf into a fluttering pavillion;
> 'Tis blue, and over-spangled with a million

Of little eyes, as though thou wert to shed,
Over the darkest, lushest blue-bell bed,
Handfuls of daisies."

Later, in the *Man in the Moone*, into which Drayton rewrote some of the passages of *Endimion and Phœbe*, this mantle passage is altered and greatly enlarged, an enlargement which Keats paraphrases in his account of Glaucus's cloak in Book III. But, in the *Man in the Moone*, the mantle is not specifically blue, on the contrary, it is described as being "of sundry Colours"; also, the *Man in the Moone* mantle is not spangled. In Diana's scarf, Keats carefully preserves both the blue and the spangles; even when he comes to Glaucus's cloak, he makes it blue.

To continue with Drayton's plot, when Phœbe comes upon Endimion fishing, she at once enters into conversation with him and proceeds to make love forthwith. But Endimion is unmoved, stating that he is the sworn servant of Diana and vowed to chastity. Phœbe persisting, he threatens her with Diana's wrath should that goddess observe them, telling the supposed nymph that "Diana came that way" upon occasion. The wooing continues, and Endimion remains obdurate until Phœbe has gone, when he would fain recall her, having fallen in love during the parley. Night comes on. Endimion sits on a moonlit bank, longing for the vanished nymph. This scene, in Drayton's words, is as follows:

"Now fast by Latmus neere vnto a Groue,
Which by the mount was shadowed from aboue,
Vpon a banck Endimion sat by night,
To whom fayre Phœbe lent her frendly light;
And sith his flocks were layd them downe to rest,
Thus giues his sorrowes passage from his brest.

. . . .

And lifting now his sad and heauy eyes
Vp towards the beauty of the burnisht skies,
Bright Lamps (qd.he) the glorious Welkin bears,

Which clip about the Plannets wandring Sphears,
And in your circled Maze doe euer role,
Dauncing about the neuer-moouing Pole:

[Here follows a prayer to the constellations and planets to shed their beneficent influences]

Vpon Endimion pyning thus in loue."

At dawn, Phœbe, being, as it were, off duty, descends once more to earth. The moon is no longer in the sky,

"But her sweet Latmus, which she lou'd so much,
No sooner once her dainty foote doth touch,
But that the Mountaine with her brightnes shone,
And gaue a light to all the Horizon:
Euen as the Sun, which darknes long did shroud,
Breakes suddainly from vnderneath a clowd."

These two passages together evidently suggested to Keats his far more beautiful lines:

"... Methought I lay
Watching the zenith, where the milky way
Among the stars in virgin splendour pours;
And travelling my eye, until the doors
Of heaven appear'd to open for my flight,
I became loth and fearful to alight
From such high soaring by a downward glance:
So kept me steadfast in that airy trance,
Spreading imaginary pinions wide.
When, presently, the stars began to glide,
And faint away, before my eager view:
At which I sigh'd that I could not pursue,
And dropt my vision to the horizon's verge;
And lo! from opening clouds, I saw emerge
The loveliest moon, that ever silver'd o'er
A shell for Neptune's goblet: she did soar
So passionately bright, my dazzled soul
Commingling with her argent spheres did roll
Through clear and cloudy, even when she went
At last into a dark and vapoury tent —

> Whereat, methought, the lidless-eyed train
> Of planets all were in the blue again."

In this correspondence, the parallel is one of idea rather than of words. In each case, Endymion is lying on the grass, gazing at the stars. In each, the brilliance of the stars is remarked. Phœbe's shining when she steps on earth at dawn, in Drayton's poem, is duplicated in Keats's by her appearance at the horizon's edge. In both, the horizon is mentioned. In Drayton, darkness shrouds the sun; in Keats, the moon goes into a dark and vapoury tent. In Drayton, the sun breaks suddenly through a cloud; in Keats, the outshone planets appear once more twinkling brightly in the sky.

Again to return to Drayton's story: Phœbe finds Endimion asleep, which reminds us of Book II of *Endymion* where Diana finds Endymion, if not actually asleep, at least preparing to fall asleep and dream. But the subsequent proceedings are not immediately the same. Drayton recounts how Phœbe calls her nymphs, who hang garlands about Endimion, anoint his body, and after kissing him solemnly one after the other withdraw and leave him alone with the goddess. Phœbe, having prepared him for the sight of her divine self, undisguised, by infusing into his soul "the fiery nature of the heauently Muse," wakes him up. At first he is overcome by her dazzling presence. Yet he still thinks of her only as a nymph, not yet knowing her for the goddess. Presently he finds courage to make love to her. This episode is duplicated in the Fourth Book of *Endymion*, where Endymion makes love to the Indian Maiden; but there is also a close parallel of idea here, which Keats employs in quite a different place. The passage in Drayton is this:

> "Be kind (quoth he) sweet Nymph, vnto thy louer,
> My soules sole essence, and my senses mouer,
> Life of my life, pure Image of my hart,

Impressure of Conceit, Inuention, Art!
My vitall spirit receues his spirit from thee,
Thou art that all which ruleth all in me:
Thou art the sap and life whereby I liue,
Which powerfull vigor doost receiue and giue;
Thou nourishest the flame wherein I burne,
The North whereto my harts true tuch doth turne."

In Book III of *Endymion*, Keats, without exactly copying a single metaphor, perfectly reproduces Drayton's conception:

"And as I grew in years, still didst thou blend
With all my ardours: thou wast the deep glen;
Thou wast the mountain-top — the sage's pen —
The poet's harp — the voice of friends — the sun;
Thou wast the river — thou wast glory won;
Thou wast my clarion's blast — thou wast my steed —
My goblet full of wine — my topmost deed: —
Thou wast the charm of women, lovely Moon!
O what a wild and harmonized tune
My spirit struck from all the beautiful!"

The love passage which follows Drayton's apostrophic lines is more keenly visualized in Book II of *Endymion* than it is in *Endimion and Phœbe*, but the content is the same.

Here I must go back a little to Phœbe's dawn descent to earth, for Drayton relates that the gods and goddesses of Olympus, horrified at this proceeding, consider what they can do to restrain her, and come to the conclusion that, as she is mistress of tides and circumstances, they can do nothing. This episode is much amplified in the *Man in the Moone*, and it is the *Man in the Moone* version which seems to have influenced Keats most.

Following upon the love scene in *Endimion and Phœbe*, the goddess reveals herself to Endimion. Having told him that she is, in truth, Diana, she clothes herself in all the glory of her celestial light and, wrapping Endimion in a fiery mantle, carries him up to the skies. Drayton describes how Phœbe bears Endimion through the "starry firmament" and shows him the "Twynns" the "heauenly archers," the "Lion," the "Bear," the "tear-distilling mournful Pliades," and other members of the zodiac. There are two flights in Keats's *Endymion*; one in Book I, the other in Book IV. Drayton duplicates the flight in his first poem in his second, the *Man in the Moone*, where Keats, of course, read it; but, although Drayton's flights have a distinct resemblance, it is important to note that details in the *Endimion and Phœbe* version do not reappear in the *Man in the Moone*, while these same details are reproduced by Keats. A very slight and unimportant one is the "starry firmament," which, in *Endymion*, becomes the more pictorial "Where falling stars dart their artillery forth." This is in the First Book. The second flight, in the Fourth Book, contains a much closer and more important parallel. In this second flight, Endymion falls asleep and so fails to hear a "pinioned multitude" who sweep by him singing the pre-nuptial song of Diana. In this song, the signs of the zodiac, the Lion, the Bear, Castor and Pollux (Drayton's "heauenly archers"), and the Centaur, are mentioned.

Having by this airy journey "impt the wings of his desire," Phœbe returns Endimion to earth and vanishes. From this moment, fortune and the Muses attend upon Endimion; his flocks prosper; bees bring him honey; when he would hunt, the nymphs bear him company.

As the time approaches when Phœbe intends to honour Endimion, she sends Mercury to summon the sylvan deities to the solemn celebration which she has obtained Phœbus's consent to hold. They come: Fauns, Satyrs, Oreads, Dryads, Hamadryads, even the Naiads "vpon Sea-horses." The gist of this passage is repeated in the song of the "multitude" in Book IV of *Endymion*, where the lesser gods, goddesses, sylvan deities, and constellations, all gather for "Dian's feast" on "her marriage night." In *Endymion*, the actual solemnity is supposed to take place after the close of the poem. Keats leaves Endymion and Diana flying to the heavens to be ready for it. Drayton has devised a different ending. In *Endimion and Phœbe*, Phœbe arrives in a "Christall Coach" in the pomp of all her titles, and wafts Endimion to the top of Mount Latmus. On reaching this, her favourite spot on earth, she lays him "vnder a bushie Lawrell's pleasing shade," where she may easily descend to sport with him daily. Here, for thirty years, Endimion rests, "Remayning ever beautiful and yong." The poem ends with a sort of epilogue, addressed particularly to Spenser and Lodge, in which Drayton invokes the protection of these poets for his poem.

The most important point in which Drayton's *Endimion and Phœbe* influenced Keats is the device by which Diana, in the guise of a nymph, steals Endimion's love from her true self, the goddess. This is a striking episode, so striking, and so absolutely without parallel in all the other versions of the legend, whether of classic original or Elizabethan follower, that it is most improbable that Keats reinvented it. Such a coincidence would be so remarkable that it is almost out of the bounds of possibility. Keats could not have found it in the *Man in the Moone* for nothing of the sort occurs there. If there were no other resemblance between Drayton's and Keats's poems, this alone would be sufficient evidence that Keats had read *Endimion and Phœbe*. But there are other evidences, as we have seen. The complete table of Keats's indebtedness to *Endimion and Phœbe*, I paraphrase from Mr. Finney's excellent summary.[1] It is as follows:

1. The invention of Phœbe's assuming the guise of a nymph, and the result of her so doing. Although this is paralleled

[1] *Shakespeare and Keats*, by Claude L. Finney.

in various places throughout *Endymion*, the chief of these parallels is the episode of the Indian maiden in Book IV.

2. Certain details in the description of Mount Latmus.
3. Endimion lying on the grass and gazing at the starry sky while he pines for his vanished lady, who, in both poems, is the goddess, supposed by him to be a nymph.
4. Endimion's expression of the influence which the moon has upon him.
5. Details and colour of Phœbe's mantle used by Keats in description of Diana's scarf, colour re-employed in Glaucus's cloak.
6. Certain details of Endimion's flight in the air, particularly the mention of the signs of the zodiac.
7. The marriage gathering at the end, to which come the lesser and sylvan deities.

These particular points are none of them duplicated in Drayton's second attempt at the subject, the *Man in the Moone*.

Since the *Man in the Moone* is perfectly accessible to inquiring readers, I shall do little more in referring to it than state those places where Keats evidently borrowed from it. That Keats knew the poem well, there is no doubt. At the time of his death, he owned a copy of John Smethwick's edition of Drayton's Poems. Of course this by no means proves that the book was in his possession in 1817, but both the 1619 and the 1636 editions of Smethwick's collection were obtainable. Any of his friends might have had a copy, or he could have read it at the British Museum, to the reading room of which we know that Haydon, at some time, procured him a ticket.

Both the *Man in the Moone* and *Endymion* begin with the yearly festival to Pan. In both, the shining of the moon serves as introduction to the story of Endymion; but in the *Man in the Moone* a shepherd, Roland, relates the tale, while in *Endymion* it is the theme of the poem itself and not a story told by one of the characters. On this account, the festival of Pan, which, in the *Man in the*

Moone, is merely an introductory setting, is, in *Endymion*, the first scene of the main action of the poem. In this we see that Drayton diverged from the direct relation of his earlier poem, while Keats kept to it.

In the *Man in the Moone*, Roland tells how Endimion

> "... vs'd to ly,
> All the long night contemplating the sky
> At her hie beauties."

This is a paraphrase of the more vivid description of Endimion's sky-gazing and longing for the nymph in *Endimion and Phœbe*, but here Endimion is and knows he is, in love with Diana; there is no assumption of any disguise in the *Man in the Moone*, as there is in the earlier poem and in *Endymion*. Keats, as we have seen, followed Drayton's first version in the details of the grass and the stars, but the expression "her hie beauties" very likely suggested "the loveliest moon," and all that goes with it, in *Endymion*. Again, in his original rewriting of the legend, Drayton makes the gods and goddesses much shocked at Phœbe's behaviour, but in the later poem he adds a little humour to the episode by having her descend to earth, not only by day, but by night:

> "That oft her want vnto the world was strange,
> Fearing that heauen the wōted course wold change
> And Phœbus her oft missing did inquire,
> If that elsewhere she borrowed other fire."

It is certainly this more distinctly human passage which suggested Keats's lines in Book II, where Venus tells Endymion that she has heard that he loved

> "Some fair immortal, and that his embrace
> Had zoned her through the night. There is no trace
> Of this in heaven: I have mark'd each cheek,
> And find it is the vainest thing to seek;
> And that of all things 'tis kept secretest."

Another passage in the *Man in the Moone* tells how, when Endimion fell in love with the goddess, he forsook

"All the delights which shepheards doe prefer,"

and pursued Phœbe to "the groues and springs." This Keats follows in making Endymion neglect his duties and sports, and wander mournfully through the woods seeking to recapture his vision.

Phœbe comes first to Endimion in a totally different manner in the *Man in the Moone* from the way she comes in *Endimion and Phœbe* or in *Endymion.* In the *Man in the Moone*, she appears riding upon a bull. Her mantle is again mentioned; but, as I have already pointed out, it is not blue. The description in this new version is infinitely more detailed, so detailed, in fact, that the account of it takes up seventy-six lines of the poem. This description Keats borrows for Glaucus's cloak, in the Third Book of *Endymion*, but condenses it from seventy-six lines to seventeen.

Again there is a flight, and this sky journey is a good deal like that in *Endimion and Phœbe*, but it lacks the signs of the zodiac. However, the later poem is undoubtedly responsible for Endymion's wanderings in the woods, the sea, and in the air, for to these Phœbe flies with Endimion. Endymion's earth journey seems to have been Keats's own invention, for I cannot agree with Mr. Finney that "since Phœbe was supposed to have power in heaven, earth and hell, what was more natural than that Keats should send Endymion in pursuit of her through those regions that she ruled?" [1] There is nothing in the least suggestive of Hell in Endymion's earth rambles, and I believe them to have been merely a natural corollary when sea, woods, and mountains had been suggested to him.

The end of the *Man in the Moone* is not at all

[1] *Shakespeare and Keats*, by Claude L. Finney.

poetical. There is no such beautiful apotheosis for Endimion as in *Endimion and Phœbe*. No imaginative possibilities are opened to the reader as in *Endymion*. The *Man in the Moone* ends in a complete and rather base realism. Nothing could be more unlike the whole feeling of the close of *Endymion* than the finish of the *Man in the Moone*. Yet, with all its unlikeness, there is the parallel of antithesis here, for Drayton's last two lines are as follows:

> "The early Larke soon summoned the Day,
> When they departed every one their way."

while *Endymion* ends in this wise:

> ". . . Peona went
> Home through the gloomy wood in wonderment."

From this brief analysis, we cannot fail to see that, although Keats evidently took some few particulars for his poem from the *Man in the Moone*, he was far more deeply influenced by *Endimion and Phœbe*. What he got from the *Man in the Moone* is as a raindrop to an ocean compared with what he got from *Endimion and Phœbe*. It behooves us, then, to look closely into the subject of where and how he could have come across this extraordinarily rare volume.

Some time prior to 1837, Payne Collier, critic, bibliophile, and Shakespearian forger, stumbled upon a copy of the unique edition of Drayton's *Endimion and Phœbe*. Where he met with it, he was very careful not to say; presumably he picked it up on some bookstall, for he stated quite clearly that he "procured it." His first mention of it was in his catalogue of the Bridgewater Library, where he described it as the only copy known. This copy lacked the title and the succeeding leaf, or, in bibliographical language, leaves A2 and A3. Afterwards, Collier discovered another, perfect, copy, the whereabouts of which his love of mystery counselled him to conceal. When, in 1856, he edited a new collection of Drayton's poems as one of a series of privately printed volumes issued for the members of the Roxburgh Club, he included *Endimion and Phœbe*, saying of it: "Only two copies of 'Endimion and Phœbe' have been brought to light, one formerly the property of Camden, and the other in the hands of the editor of the present volume." In a reprint of his collection, made some years later, he confused the issue to the best of his ability by announcing that "the perfect copy is also in a private collection." By the expression, "a private collection," we may charitably suppose that Collier considered all collections not owned by the British Government to be private, for private in any other sense the collection which contained the only perfect copy of *Endimion and Phœbe* certainly was not.

Now what was there for a seeker to go upon? Merely the facts that Collier had owned an imperfect copy of the book, and that a perfect copy existed which had once been Camden's. Having discovered so much, I wrote to Mr. George Watson Cole, librarian of the Henry E. Huntington Library, to ask if any other exemplars of the book were known. Mr. Cole was so good as to direct his assistant, Mr. Cecil K. Edmonds, to look into the matter, and tell me what he could discover. Mr. Edmonds's information, scanty though it perforce had to be, set me on the right track, for, among other things, he suggested that I inquire of Mr. W. A. White of Brooklyn, who was the owner of an imperfect copy, which might, or might not, have been Collier's.

Mr. White is always kindness itself to collectors and scholars. He instantly replied to my query by telling me that his book had once belonged to Collier, that it lacked pages A2 and A3, that he had bought it at the sale of the Rowfant Library, and that the book contained a note by Collier to the effect that the one perfect copy known to him was in "a collegiate library." A glance at the Rowfant

Library Catalogue proved that Locker-Lampson had bought the book directly from Collier. Here was Collier's copy traced up to date, but its inverse progression was a dead wall, nothing to be learnt of it previous to Collier's ownership. On that copy, I had drawn a blank. I turned to the other.

What did I know of it? Next to nothing, and contradictory evidence at that. The book had belonged to the antiquary and historian, William Camden. It was in a private collection. It was in a collegiate library. The matter looked hopeless, but there was a clue. The *Dictionary of National Biography* supplied it by recording the fact that by Camden's will, proved in 1623, all his books that were not claimed as borrowed from his friend, Sir Robert Cotton, were bequeathed "to his successors at Clarenceux," but that, by a legal quibble, Dr. John Williams, Bishop of Lincoln and Dean of Westminster, had seized upon them for the library of the Dean and Chapter of Westminster Cathedral. Sir Robert Cotton's library is in the British Museum, but even the fanciful Collier could scarcely call the British Museum either a private collection or a collegiate library. Clearly, then, my next step must be Westminster, and here success rewarded me. On my asking for information as to whether a copy of *Endimion and Phœbe* were in the library, the librarian, the Rev. Dr. Leigh H. Nixon, most kindly, courteously, and immediately, replied that it was. Here was one copy traced at last to the place where it had been in Keats's day.

One more link and my chain of possibilities was complete. Following another suggestion of Mr. Edmonds's, I consulted Washington Irving's essay on *The Mutability of Literature* in the *Sketch Book*. I found that in Keats's time the Westminster library must have been accessible to the public on application to a verger. Irving, in his essay, describes the library, to which he was admitted in this casual way. It is quite evident from his narration that

Irving used no literary nor personal pull to gain admittance; he probably accomplished this by a ready exchange of coin, an honoured custom, perfectly understood by vergers. Irving speaks of his visit as due to the idle thought of a moment, leaving no impression of having been accorded an unusual privilege. What is more, he seems to have been allowed to take down and read such volumes as he pleased, and even to have been left alone with the books until the verger came back to tell him it was closing time.

Here, then, is the case as, with this new knowledge, we may consider it. All this detective work leads to the following deductions. Collier's copy was knocking round somewhere before he found it in 1837, and therefore it is not impossible that Keats may have come across it on some bookstall; but this, if not impossible, at the best is only a coincidental guess. What is also a guess, but with much probability behind it, is that Keats saw the copy in the Westminster Library. Suppose that he had drifted in on some occasion when he was in the Abbey, suppose him to have happened on the *Endimion and Phœbe* there, he might have copied parts of it for his own pleasure, or, with his singularly retentive memory, he might merely have been so impressed by the book that parts of it remained in his consciousness. In time, this memory would merge into his own conception, and when he came to write he may have been quite oblivious to the plagiarism in certain of his lines. Plagiarism did not trouble Keats very seriously, as we know, therefore, even if he remembered where he got his impulse, it is unlikely that he would check the flow of his lines on that account. That Keats did not immediately rush round to his friends and proclaim the discovery of this unique book, was undoubtedly because he had not the slightest idea that it was unique. The fact that Smethwick's edition of Drayton's *Poems* did not contain *Endimion and Phœbe*, meant nothing. He was used to old editions of old poets varying in content.

Again, even if he told his friends, it is extremely doubtful if the bibliographical knowledge of any one of them, even Hunt, was of an extent which would have meant a realization of Keats's discovery. Readers of Keats's day were largely dependent upon chance encounters with old books in shops and on stalls. Browsers have no place at the British Museum, one must know what one wants before one can ask for it. And how could one ask for Drayton's *Endimion and Phœbe* when no one had the least notion that such a book existed? Running across it somewhere, and not inconceivably in the Westminster Library, Keats read and assimilated it, happy in its discovery for himself, totally ignorant of its rarity and its importance to scholars on that account.

A natural supposition for any one not aware of all the facts, would be that Keats found the quotations from *Endimion and Phœbe* in *England's Parnassus*, which he could have read at the British Museum, or in *Helicona*, published in 1814, which contained a reprint of the *Parnassus*. But this supposition is untenable, because, of the eighteen extracts from Drayton's poem in the *Parnassus*, only two are among those which compose the sum of Keats's borrowings from that work as already tabulated.[1] These two are the description of Mount Latmus, and the beginning of Endimion's flight through the air.

There is still a third possibility, which is that the two copies of *Endimion and Phœbe* known to Collier were not the only ones in existence, and that somewhere, somehow, Keats had access to another. But this seems the slimmest sort of speculation, since to-day, with the agents of multimillionaire book-collectors combing every hole and corner for lost books and paying fabulous prices for any such that turn up, it is most unlikely that a third should not have been found if there be one. True, over a hundred years have elapsed since Keats wrote *Endymion*, plenty of time

[1] See Vol. I, pp. 330–331.

for a book to be burnt or torn up for waste paper, but we need not stretch our theoretical guesses so far, I think. It is enough to realize that it is by no means impossible for Keats to have read Drayton's *Endimion and Phœbe*, and, in view of the internal evidence of Drayton's poem and Keats's *Endymion*, the event becomes not merely probable, but a certainty.

Having dutifully examined the dry and dusty question of source, we may now take up the far more interesting subject of the poem itself. For this, it is necessary to go back to Keats's sojourn at Carisbrooke. I have already given my reasons for believing that Keats began *Endymion* at that place on some day between April eighteenth and April twenty-third.[1] In the letter from there to Reynolds, after saying "I shall forthwith begin my Endymion," Keats continues "which I hope I shall have got some way with by the time you come, when we will read our verses in a delightful place I have set my heart upon, near the Castle." Of course, it is the merest fancy to suppose that Keats really did begin his poem in this delectable nook; he may, or may not, have done so. But if we do not know the whereabouts of his first actually putting something down on paper, we do know, at least, that it was at Carisbrooke, and we also know what sort of thoughts had been singing through his brain for some time past. Chapman's *Homer*, the Elgin Marbles, the everlasting myths of antiquity — these shreds of beauty enduring out of a vanished world were very part and parcel of his daily communings and speculations, whip-lashes and trumpets goading him on.

I propose to consider *Endymion*, Book by Book, as Keats wrote it; and, for the purpose of clarity, I have put each Book into a separate division. All that has been said so far is in the nature of an introduction; from now on, the poem will be dealt with directly.

[1] See Vol. I, pp. 306–307.

Book I.

So Keats, sitting down at Carisbrooke, either indoors or out, began his poem:

"A thing of beauty is a joy forever."

The next line came afterwards — after the briefest of intervals perhaps, but still afterwards. The first line is a full thought by itself; it was at once a statement of fact, a creed, and a whistling to keep up his courage, for it is a fearsome thing actually to write down the first words of a long poem, much brooded over and considered upon. Those first words are like the shove which separates a boat from the safe wharf of mere speculation, and starts a voyage across an unknown sea, full of hardship, and peril, and strain, toward a destination which may never be reached. The opening lines of *Endymion* meant the untarnished and ever-renewing splendour of the moon; the glory of old legend; they were a proud challenge to those who count the moon and legend stale; a comforting conclusion that, however the poet may fail, his theme is worthy and unassailable.

There is a tale that Keats composed this first line when he was living in St. Thomas's Street with his fellow medical students, Cooper, Mackereth, and Henry Stephens. This tale has it that the first version was "A thing of beauty is a constant joy," and that, upon criticism by Stephens, Keats altered the line to its present form. Sir B. W. Richardson, recollecting a conversation with Stephens many years later, is the authority for this statement, and it may be true. It does not matter either way, but personally I doubt it. So good a line would surely have got itself into one of the poems of 1816; it could easily have found a place in *I Stood Tip-toe*, for instance, while its perfect applicability to his state of mind at the time of his going to the Isle of Wight seems to date it more probably from then or shortly before. Sir Sidney Colvin thinks that the first twenty-four lines of *Endymion* belong to the *I Stood Tip-toe* period. I disagree with him. They catalogue beauties, it is true, but they are the beauties all about him at Carisbrooke.

This is a Spring world; *I Stood Tip-toe* was a world in the full flush of Summer. There, there were violets, bluebells, sweet peas, even marigolds; here are trees just leaving out, daffodils, clear brooks, sheep, and, with a leap forward as to season, musk-roses coming into bloom. But here too is the loneliness and passion he has been going through, for these excellent natural things wreathe

> "A flowery band to bind us to the earth,
> Spite of despondence, of the inhuman dearth
> Of noble natures, of the gloomy days,
> Of all the unhealthy and o'er-darkened ways
> Made for our searching; yes, in spite of all,
> Some shape of beauty moves away the pall
> From our dark spirits."

This is as far as possible from the attitude of *I Stood Tip-toe* and the other poems of that period, and is a direct reflection of the "continual burning of thought" he has been going through.

It is, of course, extremely dangerous to assume that a poet is actually among the scenes he describes. But there seems no doubt that, in this beginning to *Endymion*, Keats is painting an exact picture of his surroundings at the moment of writing. He will "trace the story of Endymion" now, while

> ". . . each pleasant scene
> Is growing fresh before me as the green
> Of our own vallies: so I will begin
> Now while I cannot hear the city's din;
> Now while the early budders are just new,
> And run in mazes of the youngest hue

About old forests; while the willow trails
Its delicate amber; and the dairy pails
Bring home increase of milk."

Mr. Mackail, in a most interesting paper in the *Keats Memorial Volume*, points out that the "old forests" probably refers to Parkhurst Forest, which, he says, "still retained its oaks notwithstanding the heavy drain of naval timber from it during the Napoleonic wars." Mr. Mackail is also probably right in believing that lines 201–203 of this First Book:

"Swelling downs . . .
. . . where prickly furze
Buds lavish gold"

comes directly from the "blooming furze" of his coach ride to Southampton, and that the letter to Reynolds about Shanklin Chine and St. Catherine's Hill turns into the passage beginning with line 74, of Book II:

". . . one track unseams
A wooded cleft, and, far away, the blue
Of Ocean fades upon him."

These are fascinating speculations, and *Endymion* is particularly rich in such, but we must not linger too long with them. What is very strange about this opening of *Endymion* is the expression of the rigid time allowance which Keats set himself, and the fact that it was strictly adhered to. Following immediately upon the dairy pails, Keats continues:

". . . And, as the year
Grows lush in juicy stalks, I'll smoothly steer
My little boat, for many quiet hours,
With streams that deepen freshly into bowers.
Many and many a verse I hope to write,
Before the daisies, vermeil rimm'd and white,
Hide in deep herbage; and ere yet the bees

> Hum about globes of clover and sweet peas,
> I must be near the middle of my story.
> O may no wintry season, bare and hoary,
> See it half finished: but let Autumn bold,
> With universal tinge of sober gold,
> Be all about me when I make an end."

He finished *Endymion* on November twenty-eighth, 1817, just seven months after beginning it.

So far, so good, he has written a very beautiful opening, but it is not so different from descriptions he has done before. It is, after all, chiefly a lyrical outburst as it stands. Fifty-seven lines down on paper and no real beginning made! One more shiver of fear, a little more whistling to his courage in the lines

> "And now at once, adventuresome, I send
> My herald thought into a wilderness:
> There let its trumpet blow, and quickly dress
> My uncertain path with green, that I may speed
> Easily onward, thorough flowers and weed."

This is a decided tumble from the lyrical passage which precedes it, but it serves clumsily to leap a gap, and Keats let it stand — let it stand even after revision, which was a blunder, but by the time revision came the poem had been going on so long that he let many things stand.

After this halting peroration, Keats plunges with firm determination into his story. He is fairly off, and the poem is begun.

The true beginning of *Endymion*, then, is at the sixty-third line. It starts with a description of Mount Latmos, which is again the Isle of Wight made grander and bolder, with mountains instead of rolling hills, and deep gullies, wolf-haunted, taking the place of its chines. Paths wander through fern and ivy banks all leading to an open space which Keats infelicitously, even if with Elizabethan precedent, calls a "wide lawn." In the midst of this clearing stands an altar. It is sunrise, which we may regret that Keats chooses to speak of as "Apollo's upward fire," but, forgetting that artificiality, nothing could better give the brightness of the sun than

> "The lark was lost in him; cold springs had run
> To warm their chilliest bubbles in the grass."

Suddenly a throng of children bursts into the clearing, followed by maidens carrying baskets of flowers and, after them, shepherds. Behind the shepherds walks an aged priest, bearing wine and sweet herbs. Another crowd of shepherds, and in the midst of a multitude, on a car harnessed to three dappled horses, a youth is drawn into the circle. He is dressed as a chieftain, with a silver bugle and a boar-spear. A goodly fellow, but evidently a prey to some secret trouble.

The whole company, ranged in a circle about the altar, is addressed by the old priest, who tells them of the bounties which Pan has heaped upon them, ending with this charming bit of perfect realism:

> "... The merry lark has pour'd
> His early song against yon breezy sky,
> That spreads so clear o'er our solemnity."

Those lines set the scene with admirable succinctness. Having finished his exordium, the priest lays the herbs on the altar, sets fire to them, and pours the wine upon the ground, and, while the pyre burns, the whole multitude sings a hymn to Pan.

This *Hymn to Pan* is one of the finest things that Keats ever wrote. It is remarkable for the way in which the emotion soars up and up to the very last line. Technically, it is a perfect example of variation within a pattern. No stanza is exactly like another, yet all have a similar music slightly changed. The short last line is a fine touch, but in one stanza the short line is the third from the end instead of the last. In stanza two, the broken lines are simply delightful, but Keats knew too much to repeat so bold a device again. There is here the flavour of Beaumont and Fletcher's *Faithful Shepherdess*, that touch so indubitably English and Elizabethan, and yet Keats, keeping it, has at the same time altered it so that it becomes at once modern and undateable. He has taken his models and made them over in his own image, for who but Keats would write

> "And gather up all fancifullest shells
> For thee to tumble into Naiads' cells."

The movement is most satisfying, the poem breaks into a music of its own which the introduction of tone could only mar. How happy the epithets (and never one duplicated!) given to Pan; how daring the desertion of Pan in the last line of the first stanza; and how unexpected the rhyme which makes of the last line the crown and glory of Pan himself, although he is not mentioned! The sheer volume of noise in the last three lines is astounding:

> "And giving out a shout most heaven rending,
> Conjure thee to receive our humble Pæan,
> Upon thy Mount Lycean!"

Many elements go to make up this immense volume of sound, among which we should not overlook the rhyme of "out" and "shout" in close juxtaposition. Never were a finer series of effects than Keats has hit upon in this *Hymn*. One would like to know where and when it was written, and under what circumstances Keats was so thoroughly overwhelmed by his own subconscious self. Nowhere else in the whole of *Endymion* is Keats so taken possession of and carried away by the flood of his own creative power.

When, months afterwards, Keats read the *Hymn to Pan* to Wordsworth, the older poet's comment was "a pretty piece of Paganism," which touch of superciliousness must have been a trifle dampening. And we can but smile at

Wordsworth's orthodoxy taking fright, for anything less Pagan can hardly be imagined. It is no more Pagan than the whole of *Endymion* is Greek. Keats never had the slightest knowledge or comprehension of the true Greek spirit. What is beautiful in *Endymion* comes from itself, without any necessary reference to Greece or anywhere else.

As if exhausted by the effort which produced the *Hymn to Pan*, the next hundred lines of *Endymion* are of an almost insupportable dullness. Two little tricks of technique relieve the outset of the passage: the displaced accent of "abrupt thunder" which is almost onomatopœic in its effect; and the whole series of displaced accents in line 313, whereby the stately march of the iambic line is shattered to bits and we seem to be all at once whirled away into the blythe dance rhythm of

> "Young companies nimbly began dancing."

What happens in these hundred lines is simply a description of the breaking up of the multitude, released from the unity of emotion in which the *Hymn to Pan* had held them, into relaxed and cheerful groups pursuing various forms of amusement. Some dance, some watch the quoit players or the archers, some listen to stories, some dream of ancient legend, which gives Keats a chance to bring in various classic myths that are a weariness to read as he has told them here. About Endymion and the old priest, a group gathers, whose conversation takes on a sober tinge as, one by one, each imagines himself in Elysium and relates who among the departed he wishes most to meet. Endymion, however, says nothing, and no one is a whit the wiser as to the sorrow which, as all can plainly see, is his chief preoccupation. This passage contains one of the carelessnesses which were so oddly left in the published version of the book: line 335 lacks a syllable. It runs:

> "Branch down sweeping from a tall ash top."

Buxton Forman suggests that Keats intended "the heavy monosyllable 'Branch' to do duty for a whole foot or time-beat," which would be all very well if there were any reason for so weighting the word. But the words to be dwelt upon in the line are "down sweeping," the branch is of no importance except for its down sweeping movement. It seems more likely that Keats meant to write "downward sweeping" and in the hurry of composition left out half the word. It is important to remember that this First Book was corrected as it stood and no fair copy made, and that Keats was a wretched proof-reader. It is, however, but fair to say that in a letter to Taylor of February twenty-seventh, 1818, Keats, who is reading the proof, refers to this line and says it should have no comma, but does not mention the lost syllable. He quotes it, with the two words immediately preceding, all in one line, "the raft branch down sweeping from a tall ash-top," which probably is where the confusion of ear occurred. After all, a false foot can be borne, but one cannot bear the horrible line that follows:

> "Call'd up a thousand thoughts to envelope
> Those who would watch."

This is one of the places where one shudders and tries to forget.

To return to the story. While Endymion is lost in melancholy dreams, he hears a voice close beside him. It is his sister Peona, who persuades him to leave the assembly and go away with her. The name Peona seems to have been an invention of Keats's, as indeed was her existence, she has no place in legend or poetry until Keats gave her one. Sir Sidney Colvin says that her name was perhaps suggested "by that of Pæana in the fourth book of the *Faerie Queene*, or by the Pæon mentioned in Lemprière as a son of Endymion in the Elean version of the tale, or by Pæon, the physician of the gods in the *Iliad*, whom she resembles in her quality of healer and comforter; or very probably by all three together." I think the *Iliad* a little too remote in connection here, and personally I am willing to stake my faith on Lemprière. At any rate, it is a charming name, and we may thank Keats for suppressing the diphthong.

The two steal away from the throng and wander

> "Along a path between two little streams . . .
> . . . to where these streamlets fall,
> With mingled bubblings and a gentle rush,
> Into a river, clear, brimful, and flush
> With crystal mocking of the trees and sky."

In the interleaved copy of *Endymion* which Woodhouse had bound up for his own use, he has underlined "mocking" and written against it in the margin "for reflection." This amusing meticulousness must have been a little galling to Keats on the occasions when his sage friend undertook to criticize him, which seem to have been many.

At the confluence of these streams, Endymion and Peona find a little boat, into which they get, and steered by Peona reach a small island and disembark in "a shady, fresh, and ripply cove." This is a favourite retreat of Peona's, for here is

> ". . . an arbour, overwove
> By many a summer's silent fingering;
> To whose cool bosom she was used to bring
> Her playmates, with their needle broidery
> And minstrel memories of times gone by."

We may be very sure that Keats owed this picture to Shakespeare. To trace Keats's indebtedness to one or another poet would need a volume to itself, for Keats was a handy borrower, he recognized no law of *meum et tuum* in the matter of writing. I shall note only such cases as tend to throw light on his thoughts or doings at the moment of setting them down, or which reveal some hint of his psychology. Peona's playmates embroidering and singing are taken directly from the *Midsummer Night's Dream*, where Helena says:

> "We, Hermia, like two artificial gods,
> Have with our needles created both one flower,
> Both on one sampler, sitting on one cushion,
> Both warbling of one song, both in one key."

Keats's mind was stuffed with quotations from Shakespeare, but what probably put this one into his head was the fact that Severn had just completed a picture of this scene, which was then on exhibition at the Royal Academy. The picture was entitled *Helena and Hermia* and had this very quotation as a superscription.[1] George Keats, in a letter to Severn postmarked "May 22, 1817,"[2] speaks of having written about it to John, who was then at Canterbury. The line about Peona's playmates is 434 of Book I. It seems hardly likely that Keats had written so little by the end of May, but, of course, we do not know how long before writing to Severn George had sent his letter to John. The picture had been a-painting for some time, and its appearance at the Academy, and where it would be hung, was undoubtedly a frequent subject of speculation among the friends, which must have brought it intermittently to Keats's attention. If we cannot determine the date of the passage from George's letter, we can, at least, see — to appropriate Mr. de la Mare's well known line about Miss T — how everything that Keats did and read turned at once into Keats.

In this arbour, Peona induces Endymion to lie down and rest. He falls asleep while she watches. So quiet is it that

> ". . . a whispering blade
> Of grass, a wailful gnat, a bee bustling
> Down in the blue-bells, or a wren light rustling
> Among sere leaves and twigs, might all be heard."

[1] See Vol. I, p. 108.

[2] *Bulletin of Keats-Shelley Memorial*, Rome. No. 1. *Life of Joseph Severn*, by William Sharp.

The melancholy effect on Keats of the sound of gnats buzzing is interesting. Here he calls a gnat "wailful"; in the ode *To Autumn*, the "small gnats mourn."

This pleasant, quiet scene is followed by an invocation to sleep, which is, on the whole, much better than that of the year before in *Sleep and Poetry*. Keats copies in some sort the sleepy images of Spenser's bed of Morpheus in the *Faerie Queene*. Not that he chooses the same images, Keats's are at once splendid, confused visions such as come on the margin of sleep, and auditory hallucinations of soothing sounds. Sleep is the

> ". . . great key
> To golden palaces, strange minstrelsy,
> Fountains grotesque, new trees, bespangled caves,
> Echoing grottos, full of tumbling waves
> And moonlight; aye, to all the mazy world
> Of silvery enchantment."

I think that few people have noticed the excellent psychology of this invocation. The comparative reasonableness of the "golden palaces" gives way to a music already somewhat "strange," which ushers in fountains with a touch of the grotesque about them. The trees are unlike those of the waking world, "bespangled caves" gives points of glittering light playing over darkness, the music sounds mellow and far, it repeats itself and echoes, ceases to be music, becoming instead the continued roar of waves, while the sparkling scintillations change to a broad and serene light, the sleeper is in a "mazy world" where contours merge and fade and all that remains is a silver efflorescence flooding a dazed feeling of delight. Then comes forgetfulness. Keats must have experienced just this sort of falling asleep a thousand times, as we all have, if we stop to think of it.

Endymion wakes refreshed and very grateful to Peona for her care, and, as a proof of his affection for her, vows to stop grieving and take up his normal life again. Peona receives this information in a singular manner, she takes her lute and sings. Keats makes use of the music to bring in a fine alliterative effect in the last line of the passage:

> ". . . 'Twas a lay
> More subtle cadenced, more forest wild
> Than Dryope's lone lulling of her child."

The irritating trick of accenting a past participle on its silent last syllable — cadencéd — a trick constantly employed throughout *Endymion*, is overlooked by the reader in the sad, wistful, crooning sound of "lone lulling." And the couplet to which this line belongs was a correction! It took the place of six not particularly effective lines. One can only wish that Keats had revised the whole of *Endymion* with a greater energy, for where he makes corrections they are invariably an improvement.

Endymion is melted into a communicative mood by the song, and Peona, seeing this, and having spurred her courage by the music, lays her lute aside and begins to question him. What has happened? Has he offended the gods in any way? Has he shot a Paphian dove, or wounded one of Diana's deer-herds; has he perhaps caught sight of Diana herself on some occasion, a sight which he knows no mortal may live after seeing?

Endymion suddenly notices that she, too, is troubled, and divines that it is on his account. A ghastly passage in the original draft is here altered into the innocuous reading of the printed text. These colourless lines are relieved by a broad and virile image in

> "I, who still saw the horizontal sun
> Heave his broad shoulder o'er the edge of the world."

It is no matter that Keats probably got this from Thomson's *Seasons*, where, in *Winter*,

> ". . . The horizontal sun,
> Broad o'er the south, hangs at his utmost noon."

Keats has much improved upon Thomson, which is the only justification needed for a literary theft.

Endymion declares that his ambition does not sleep, but that what he longs for is nothing that years or effort will bring him, that

> "... with so deadly gasp
> No man e'er panted for a mortal love."

He is resolved to unbosom himself now to Peona, and he straightway tells her how when the sun's chariot

> "Its beams against the zodiac-lion cast,"

which Woodhouse carefully informs us is "in July," he lay beside a stream watching the sunset, when suddenly a bed of ditamy and poppies bursts into bloom beside him. At this, he marvelled greatly, and began teasing his mind to guess the cause.

> "... Thus on I thought,
> Until my head was dizzy and distraught.
> Moreover, through the dancing poppies stole
> A breeze, most softly lulling to my soul;
> And shaping visions all about my sight
> Of colours, wings, and bursts of spangly light;
> The which became more strange, and strange, and dim,
> And then were gulph'd in a tumultuous swim:
> And then I fell asleep."

The resemblance of this sleep passage to the invocation to sleep a hundred lines before is very striking. The same changing visions, the same growing confusion, the same impressions of sparkling light dimming into oblivion. Keats was evidently so struck with the truth of his description of the on-coming of sleep that he thought he could not better it, and gave it over again, with only the slightest of differences.

Once asleep, Endymion dreams that he is gazing at the Milky Way:

"When, presently, the stars began to glide,
And faint away, before my eager view:
At which I sigh'd that I could not pursue,
And dropt my vision to the horizon's verge;
And lo! from opening clouds, I saw emerge
The loveliest moon, that ever silver'd o'er
A shell for Neptune's goblet: she did soar
So passionately bright, my dazzled soul
Commingling with her argent spheres did roll
Through clear and cloudy, even when she went
At last into a dark and vapoury tent—
Whereat, methought, the lidless-eyed train
Of planets all were in the blue again."

"Loveliest moon" was a daring thing to say. It might so easily have been mawkish, and it is not. Modern taste could dispense with "Neptune's goblet," but Keats's catalogue of beauties emphatically included classic allusion, which we must remember constantly throughout the poem, and certainly

". . . she did soar
So passionately bright"

brings back the reality and vividness of actual sight and takes away the chill of erudite metaphor.

The moon being for a moment shadowed by cloud, the dazed youth once more looks upward, and sees "a bright something, sailing down apace" which resolves itself into a vision that would tax any poet's invention to describe. Keats does it both well and ill.

"Hast thou a symbol of her golden hair?
Not oat-sheaves drooping in the western sun"

is very well. But the rest is not so good. Keats wished to outdo himself here, of course, but it must be admitted that the particular bugbears of his early verse got the better of him. There is sentimentality, not sentiment, in his description, and there is a most unhappy confusion of feature in

"Her pearl round ears, white neck, and orbed brow;
The which were blended in, I know not how,
With such a paradise of lips and eyes,
Blush-tinted cheeks, half smiles, and faintest sighs,
That, when I think thereon, my spirit clings
And plays about its fancy."

Undoubtedly Keats's fancy gave his spirit something quite worthy of being clung to; but for the reader, who has only what he *says* to go upon, not what he *saw*, the result is somewhat pudding-like and produces, not wonder, but a smile. A quite indulgent smile, however, for Keats is very young and terribly in earnest. He set himself a task which only age and much technical experience could carry through, and he had neither. He is much happier when he leaves direct description for indirect, as in

". . . The wind out-blows
Her scarf into a fluttering pavillion;
'Tis blue, and over-spangled with a million
Of little eyes, as though thou wert to shed,
Over the darkest, lushest blue-bell bed,
Handfuls of daisies."

That is imagination functioning in absolute ease and content even if he did get his idea from Drayton, as we have seen.

The vision approaches Endymion, touches him, lifts him in her arms and rises with him into the air. But he feels

". . . not fearful, nor alone,
But lapp'd and lull'd along the dangerous sky."

Here Keats again makes use of alliteration with excellent effect, and finds the surprising and perfect adjective "dangerous" for the sky. It is interesting to note that these lines also are an afterthought, come upon in revision.

It has often been objected that the love passages in *Endymion* are sentimental; some critics have gone so far as to pronounce them vulgar, which is the last thing they are. They are sensuous — and are not all love scenes so fundamentally? Again I say, the real and unique trouble with them is that Keats was flustered by them. He wanted to say so much that he ends by saying very little. He essays to touch the core, but so blunderingly that he remains always at the circumference. Love and beauty were his creeds, out of them in combination he fashioned what he called "truth." Love to him was both fact and its own symbol. He believed in its sensual side as all idealists do; what shocked commonplace and vulgar-minded contemporaries like Bailey was that he saw purity in the approaches to the great miracle of life where they saw only indecent dalliance. Keats was, above all, no hypocrite; that which he believed to be beauty, he set down — "the principle of beauty in all things," he calls it. If Endymion can be taken as allegory at all, the allegory is just here. That to the pure all things are pure. That Nature is wise and to be trusted, and that there is a beauty of the senses which is "the outward and visible sign of an inward and spiritual grace." Why Keats failed in making himself understood was that his vocabulary was insufficient, and that he had not lived long enough to pass from the easier business of describing scenery and flowers to the far more difficult one of presenting human passions. Keats was on fire with love — physical, mental, spiritual — when he wrote of Endymion flying through the air in his goddess's arms, but he cannot rise out of his own heat sufficiently to crystallize it for us in terms which give its essence. He stutters and talks wildly like a boy making his first declaration of love:

> "I was distracted; madly did I kiss
> The wooing arms which held me."

It is pitifully weak, because it would be so strong. He simply could not do this sort of thing at the time *Endymion* was written, and his friends were not of the kind to help him to realize what was wrong. Some of them delighted in his sentimental overstatement; some chid him for daring to state such things at all. Keats was far ahead of his time, as we shall see again and again.

The flight ends upon a flowery alp, in one of Keats's characteristic nature scenes:

> "... Sometimes
> A scent of violets, and blossoming limes,
> Loiter'd around us; then of honey cells,
> Made delicate from all white-flower bells."

A pretty conceit — even if quite untrue — that white flowers give the most delicate honey!

Endymion, much against his will, falls asleep, and wakes from the dream to find himself once more by the stream-side in the chilly dawn. The revulsion of feeling is too great, and Keats records it with a grotesque touch he seldom employs, but which he evidently well understood how to manage:

> "... all the pleasant hues
> Of heaven and earth had faded; deepest shades
> Were deepest dungeons; heaths and sunny glades
> Were full of pestilent light; our taintless rills
> Seem'd sooty, and o'er-spread with upturn'd gills
> Of dying fish; the vermeil rose had blown
> In frightful scarlet, and its thorns out-grown
> Like spiked aloe."

Peona finds the cause unworthy of the brooding, for neither he nor she have the slightest idea that Endymion's experience is other than a dream, or that the dream lady, although obviously not a mortal, is the goddess Diana. She chides her brother for forsaking the reality of life to dote wearily and wistfully on a dream. She does this at some length in a manner that is neither particularly good nor particularly bad. The poem lets down at this point. One feels that Keats himself is not much interested in what Peona has to say, but he has vowed to write a thousand lines to a Book and he is only at a bare eight hundred. Also he must have some sort of a plausible ending. He finds it in what is, if not the best poetry, at least the most moving bit of personal revelation in the whole of this First Book. Here is Keats's creed, his longing, his hope and dedication. For *Endymion* is at once Keats's criticism of life and his escape from it. Without reading into *Endymion* allegory as a whole, we may, without too much difficulty, disentangle those parts in which Keats speaks in his own person. Ambitious as he is, declares Endymion, it is no mere idle dream which could so disrupt his life. "Wherein lies happiness?" he asks, and answers himself that it is "a fellowship with essence." This is "the clear religion of heaven." When the beauty of nature, close mingled with the beauty of history and legend, moves the heart

> . . . that moment have we stept
> Into a sort of oneness, and our state
> Is like a floating spirit's."

This is man joined to nature by the mere beauty of earth, joined to the past of his race through the consideration of its history and its wealth of legendary lore. The passage goes on:

> ". . . But there are
> Richer entanglements, enthralments far
> More self-destroying, leading, by degrees,
> To the chief intensity."

The "self-destroying" here is a little difficult. I take it to mean that, insignificant as a contemplation of nature may make the individual man seem, unimportant as his particular life may appear measured against that of the race, personal emotion and personal contact are even more capable of dissolving his ego and producing in him a sort of ideal, selfless personality. For the knowledge of his own selflessness causes him to realize his dependence on others for the very self that he loses both by and for them. Losing himself, he yet creates the world.

The "crown" of these entanglements, says Keats,

> "Is made of love and friendship, and sits high
> Upon the forehead of humanity.
> All its more ponderous and bulky worth
> Is friendship, whence there ever issues forth
> A steady splendour; but at the tip-top,
> There hangs by unseen film, an orbed drop
> Of light, and that is love: its influence,
> Thrown in our eyes, genders a novel sense,
> At which we start and fret; till in the end,
> Melting into its radiance, we blend,
> Mingle, and so become a part of it, —
> Nor with aught else can our souls interknit
> So wingedly: when we combine therewith
> Life's self is nourish'd by its proper pith."

This is both a creed and a confession. Keats speaks as a very young man filling the emptiness of his soul by the invention of an ideal love story. It is vicarious fulfillment to solace a perfectly conscious ache. But it is more than that. The vicarious satisfaction is not all. This passage is an absolutely clear statement of a position, the position that the beauty of love in all its aspects is the highest good mankind can know. What other, differently built, minds get out of religion, Keats got out of this conception of the oneness of beauty and love. His writing *Endymion* was, I think, to him what the vigil of watching his armour was to a young knight in the Middle Ages. He sees it as a stupendous task to be undertaken as a necessary part of his initiation to poethood. He has nothing to guide him through it but the belief that somehow he must embue it with his cherished idea. And here, at the end of his First Book, just at the point where his inventiveness as a story-teller dies down, he feels his poem as a dedicated labour all the more strongly because dramatic incidents for his tale, as tale, are, for the moment, lacking. So this passage, put into the mouth of his hero, serves at once to fasten the legend more firmly to his somewhat vague main theme, and also to remind himself of the vital importance of keeping himself true to that main theme in his art and in his life. The passage ends with a serious restatement of the old proverb "'Tis love that makes the world go round":

> "Just so may love . . .
>
> . . . . .
>
> Produce more than our searching witnesseth:
> What I know not: but who, of men, can tell
> That flowers would bloom, or that green fruit would swell
> To melting pulp, that fish would have bright mail,
> The earth its dower of river, wood, and vale,
> The meadows runnels, runnels pebble-stones,
> The seed its harvest, or the lute its tones,
> Tones ravishment, or ravishment its sweet
> If human souls did never kiss and greet?"

This is not good poetry, not nearly so good as the beginning of his creed statement. But Keats meant something basic in it, he was passionately in earnest about it, but again his vocabulary is inadequate; he cannot say just what he means, because in truth his idea is inchoate, not yet formed into a direct proposition. He *feels* what he means, but gropes in the expressing of it. We must not let that throw us off, however. We must realize through the words, as it were; but also we must not permit ourselves to formulate where Keats did no such thing. I do not think that Keats, in writing *Endymion*, had any more definite plan than I have tried to detail. In the rejected Preface, he distinctly says: "Before I began I had no inward feel of being able to finish; and as I proceeded my steps were all uncertain." I am perfectly sure that *Endymion* was a product of day by day imagination, meandering where it would, or could, with no guide but the "principle of beauty in all things" and supereminently in sexual love. Later, that very Autumn, he had progressed in thinking to a point where he could put his vague, apprehended creed into something like a succinct statement, but not in May, when he was writing this First Book. Still, if we keep in mind the fact that he scarcely knew it himself, only came upon it gradually as he wrote — and lived — this statement, in a letter to Bailey, written on November twenty-second, 1817, may be taken as the key to *Endymion*, and the sole and only key:

> "I am certain of nothing but the holiness of the Heart's affections, and the truth of Imagination. What the Imagination seizes as Beauty must be Truth — whether it existed before or not, — for I have the same idea of all our passions as of Love: they are all, in their sublime, creative of essential Beauty. In a Word, you may know my favourite speculation by my first Book."

Keats makes another commentary on this creed passage in a letter to Taylor on January thirtieth, 1818. He is either reading the proof of this book, or, more likely, he writes merely after a conversation with Taylor. After making a textual change at the beginning, he goes on,

> "The whole thing must, I think, have appeared to you, who are a consecutive man, as a thing almost of mere words, but I assure you that, when I wrote it, it was a regular stepping of the imagination towards a truth. My having written that argument will perhaps be of the greatest service to me of anything I ever did. It set before me the gradations of happiness, even like a kind of pleasure thermometer, and is my first step towards the chief attempt in the drama. The playing of different natures with joy and Sorrow."

By this we see that Keats was not quite prepared to open the whole truth to Taylor as he had done to Bailey. Nothing in this account controverts the other; indeed, as far as the imagination stepping toward truth is concerned, the two are identical; but evidently, by the time this letter was written, Keats had armed himself with a good dramatic reason for the poem in general and this passage in particular. The only trouble with it is that it fits nothing and nowhere, and must therefore be regarded as camouflage. Obviously, the real theme touched him so nearly that he could not be expected to wave it as a banner, even to the kind and "consecutive" Taylor.

As though the very contemplation of his essential theory had served to whet his imagination afresh, Keats takes up his narrative with renewed energy after this semi-digression. Endymion proceeds to tell Peona of two more mysterious happenings, how he has seen the lovely face of his dream in the calm, reflecting waters of a well, and how once, having wandered near a grotto, he heard the soft voice he remembered calling him. What occurred within the grotto is suggested in a lament for the fleeing of "those swift moments." But Endymion assures Peona that he will cease to pine for what has been unrepeated since that day. He will live calmly, steadily — even as Keats will calmly and steadily work at his poem — without fever, he hopes. In a homely little touch, Endymion suggests that, if they return to the mainland, some kind neighbour may have brought his "car" to take them home. At this, they re-embark and the Book closes.

What shall we think of this First Book? That it shows a great advance in sustained composition over anything that Keats had hitherto attempted. That it is weak in narrative power, and fills out the slimness of incident with a good deal of padding. That there are many lines of so striking a beauty they never fail to seduce our judgment from the execrable writing of other parts. That in the *Hymn to Pan* Keats reached a height which he had before reached only in *On Looking into Chapman's Homer*. That the book is slovenly in many ways like a beautiful, undusted room. That horrible rhymes, wrongly accented words, and lines — two — left rhymeless, not for effect but through sheer carelessness, are unforgivable faults. All these things are true, and altogether they make a good "try," but not a finished work of art. Never mind, the thing has magic — and life. Vigour — no; but life. Something moves here, more like a bird not yet chipped from its egg perhaps, but it is not still-born, it lives. Keats had no great reason to be proud of himself on finishing it, I think, and no reason at all to despair. I fear, at this point, he was a little too satisfied with what he had done. Haste killed the poem, but haste is attendant upon youth. Of course Keats had to go on and erect his structure before he could arrange its detail. The trouble was that he did not work over the detail enough after the job of mere building was done. It was nothing short of impertinence never to copy this First Book, but to make what corrections he did make up and down the margins of the paper. He did copy the other three Books, but at no time, when he was preparing the volume for the press or even in reading the proof, did he contemplate, consider, revise, or correct enough. He was amply aware of this in the end, but he was also aware that the poem had gone stale on his hands. A sentence in the rejected Preface states his position clearly:

> "In duty to the Public I should have kept it back for a year or two, knowing it to be so faulty; but I really cannot do so, — by repetition my favourite passages sound vapid in my ears, and I would rather redeem myself with a new Poem should this one be found of any interest."

He was simply sick of it, longing for something new. He should have kept it back; but, if he had, it would still have been unrevised. It embodied a period in his life, and where he had passed he would never go again. To bother with the thing any more probably gave him almost a sensation of physical illness. He himself had changed so materially during the year in which he had been concerned with it, that it was practically impossible to touch it farther.

It is not my purpose to enter upon the question of Keats's use of words; better philologists than I have been writing on that subject for years. I think, myself, he has justified his verbal inventions and his archaisms by making poetry of them. When he does not make poetry, but is content with verbiage, posterity does not read. For which reason, this First Book will always be to most people the *Hymn to Pan*, the moon pictures, and the various lyric bits scattered through the pages. Endymion and Peona are not characters, but shapes of opalescent mist. The moon alone has personality and a loveliness which Keats, above all poets, has been able to suggest. Moonlight floods this whole First Book, and, in the final count, proves both its reason and symbol. For moonlight renders nothing clearly, but infuses magic into everything. And no one can deny that this most faulty of poetic attempts is, at least, possessed of a sort of silvery magic. Here, for the moment, we may leave it.

Book II

Is it, or is it not, wise to break a narrative with personal reflections? From the point of view of our more swiftly moving age, I think the answer would be a flat negative. Keats, following his Elizabethan models, thought otherwise. Each of the four Books of *Endymion* begins aside from the story. The first three start with statements of opinion, philosophical speculations; in the last, statement is disguised under an invocation to the poet's muse. This method does slow up the narrative; but, considering these passages otherwise than æsthetically, they clarify the poem for us, and bring us into the closest contact with Keats's mind at the time of his writing them. Had more attention been paid to them as they stand, and no effort made to twist them into the rôle of annotated chapter-headings, the poem had been better understood. I refuse to be led away from the plain text as so many critics have been. Poetry is best comprehended by taking it to mean what it says. If literature has been kept alive by scholars, as is often averred, it has been quite as often killed by them. Ingenious theories cloud the issue; what a poet means, that he sets down, and we should beware of thrusting ourselves into a scene designed to make its effect without us.

The Second Book begins with a perfectly straightforward declaration of Keats's point of view.

> "O sovereign power of love!"

Keats exclaims. And has not the First Book already proclaimed the same thing? What are wars, what is history, tales of heroes and omens — is not love more important than these?

> ". . . Juliet leaning
> Amid her window-flowers, — sighing, — weaning
> Tenderly her fancy from its maiden snow,
> Doth more avail than these: the silver flow
> Of Hero's tears, the swoon of Imogen,
> Fair Pastorella in the bandit's den,
> Are things to brood on with more ardency
> Than the death-day of empires."

Well, is he not right? If we have the courage to look matters squarely in the face, and observe the universe with the unprejudiced eye of science instead of the sentimental one of conventional and conventual religion, shall we not come to the same conclusion? Sexual love is the most stupendous fact of the universe, and the most magical mystery our poor blind senses know. To Keats it signified the penetralia of religion, the purity and grandeur of Godhead. He approaches it with awe and reverence, but also with rapture. He shudders at the task that he has undertaken, so great it seems as he envisions it:

> "... Fearfully
> Must such conviction come upon his head,
> Who, thus far, discontent, has dared to tread,
>
> . . . . .
>
> The path of love and poesy"

he cries. But, undaunted, continues

> "... But rest,
> In chaffing restlessness, is yet more drear
> Than to be crush'd, in striving to uprear
> Love's standard on the battlements of song."

Perhaps, but more men than he have found the world too coarse-minded to listen with ears tuned to just this message. In Keats's case, commentator after commentator, shocked and uncomprehending, has tried to torture this idealization of sexual love into something else: the soul striving toward a pallid, celibate heaven, or man rising out of his individuality into a cheerless, humanitarian vacuum. Keats meant none of these things. He meant the love of man for woman, as being both his physical and spiritual fulfillment. It is the proper attitude of youth. As life cools, other conceptions take the place of this; other aspects of the central mystery impinge upon us. We imagine more universal heavens, and dare conceive of the individual as lost in a multitude of souls. So does aging humanity cloak itself in mist, because we are ourselves dissolving into the desireless emptiness of death. To suspect Keats at twenty-one of holding the soul's mission to be anything so vague and solitary is to misunderstand him completely, and to misread his obvious intention throughout *Endymion*. But it is more, it is to cast a slur upon the workings of that universe which we are afraid to trust, of those natural laws we have the temerity furtively to condemn.

How long a time elapsed between Keats's finishing the First Book and beginning on the Second, we have no means of knowing, but we see by the brevity of this introduction compared to that of Book I that he is no longer afraid to begin on his story.

Before I take up the tale, however, I cannot resist quoting a note in Woodhouse's interleaved copy. The good Woodhouse was certainly not over-gifted with imagination. Like most commentators, he missed the essential in searching for the collateral. Two lines in this introduction read:

> "Yet, in our very souls, we feel amain
> The close of Troilus and of Cressid sweet."

Here Woodhouse, puzzling his head over whether the allusion is to Chaucer's or to Shakespeare's "work under this title," loses the significance of the lines entirely. But Woodhouse, whatever his limitations, was an honest man, he adds to his note as follows: "I have since learned that the author meant *embrace* by the word *close*." One can imagine Keats's amusement when called upon to explain his meaning.

Starting once more upon the story: In spite of his brave promises, Endymion still mopes. One day, as he sits idly dabbling his fingers in a brook, he notices a rose-bud hanging from a tree over his head. He picks it and dips its stalk into the water. The flower breaks at once into full bloom, and a yellow butterfly hidden within it opens its wings, on which Endymion seems to discern a message, and flutters away. Endymion follows

> "Through the green evening quiet in the sun,"

which, by the by, is one of the most modern lines that Keats ever wrote. The butterfly, with Endymion after it, flutters down into a glen where a fountain splashes by the side of a cave. The butterfly drops down upon the water, but disappears at the very instant that it seems to touch it. Endymion wanders about perplexed, shaking the flowers, and seeking everywhere for the butterfly. At last he gives up the quest and flings himself down by the fountain. Suddenly a nymph rises through the water and tells him that she has led him here out of pity. She declares, in lines full of colour, but unsatisfactory in everything else, that she would give all she has to be able to help him, yet she can do nothing except commiserate his plight.

Keats's old habits betray him in this passage to the commission of a most unfortunate false accent:

> "... all my clear eyed-fish,
> Golden, or rainbow-sided, or purplish."

If Woodhouse, instead of seeking possible sources for lines which need none, had pointed out a few of these infelicities he would have done Keats a greater service.

The nymph continues by telling Endymion that he

> "... must wander far
> In other regions, past the scanty bar
> To mortal steps, before thou cans't be ta'en
> From every wasting sigh, from every pain,
> Into the gentle bosom of thy love."

This is one of the passages which have been seized upon in the interests of allegory. Yet it requires none. Endymion is avowedly in love with an immortal, in short with an ideal. So is Keats. Endymion must become able to bear the sight and touch of his goddess on equal terms, as a mortal he cannot so join with her. Has not Peona said that to a mortal the sight of Diana is death. Keats again must grow and change to be worthy of his own conception of love, but also he must endure through struggle to the achievement of his poem. For the symbol here seems to be double. Endymion's love for Diana is both Keats's story, merely as story, and Keats's own life and work, especially his work on this poem.

The nymph vanishes, and Endymion sits down

> "Holding his forehead, to keep off the burr
> Of smothering fancies."

Excellent lines, and excellent conception, whether Keats meant "burr" in the sense of sound, or as a husk to cover him, or as the bright halo encompassing, and making edgeless, the sun or moon.

He muses upon the ever onward-moving range of imagination, and here we have an evidence that the lines left blank in *Endymion* were so by accident. For where the published text reads:

> "... Whoso encamps
> To take a fancied city of delight,
> O what a wretch is he! and when 'tis his,"

Keats originally wrote:

> "... Whoso encamps
> To take a fancied city of delight,
> O what a wretch is he: 'tis in his sight."

In changing the last line to its present reading, Keats failed to notice that it did not rhyme, and left it rhymeless. This is careless, of course, but not nearly so careless or unfortunate as rhyming "vile" and "toil" a few lines farther on. Keats's ear was often faulty, and his pronunciation frequently wrong, but is it possible that he pronounced "toil" "tile"? I do not believe it. I think he simply thought the rhyme would do as it was. Another instance where Woodhouse might have been of service had he had a finer perception and troubled his mind less with unimportant erudition.

Life, thinks Endymion, is but struggle after struggle. At each bourne attained, man yearns beyond it, and so is led always on to something else. But, he considers, this is human, this is life. These very desires and efforts

> "... are still in the air, the subtle food,
> To make us feel existence, and to shew
> How quiet death is."

But, for himself, Endymion can see nothing worth doing. Yet he would rather

> "... stand upon this misty peak,
> With not a thing to sigh for, or to seek,
> But the soft shadow of my thrice-seen love,
> Than be — I care not what."

Here Keats is speaking again in *propria persona.* For surely he would rather be ploughing through the tangles of his great poem, be that striving, persistent creature, a poet, than anything else whatever.

So Endymion, having arrived at this point in his meditation, begins to call on his love. He begs Cynthia to send down to him one little clouded moonbeam. No, rather would he beg wings to fly to her. He feels himself bursting the bars of his mortality. Verily he believes that he is again sailing with her through the sky. He feels himself above the world, but it is too much. He cries in anguish

> "... my spirit fails —
> Dear goddess, help! or the wide-gaping air
> Will gulph me — help!"

As he stands trembling, with outstretched arms, a voice from the cave speaks. The voice tells him to enter the cavern and

> "... descend where alleys bend
> Into the sparry hollows of the world!"

He is never crowned with immortality who fears to follow where airy voices lead, he is told. The injunction ends with a beautiful solemnity:

> "... so through the hollow,
> The silent mysteries of earth, descend!"

In an instant Endymion plunges into the cavern.

These wanderings of Endymion in the underworld,

must, I think, be taken purely in the light of baroque fantasy. In recounting them, Keats, the functioning poet, breaks away from Keats, the dedicated neophyte. He simply loses himself in the exuberance of his imagination. This part of the poem is perfectly described by a sentence in the old romance, *Guzman d'Alfarache*, which Keats himself has underlined. Not, be it said, in any connection with *Endymion*, probably Keats did not read *Guzman* until a year later. Still, at some period, he did mark the passage, and it is singularly pertinent to this middle part of Book II, which is indeed a "rapsodie of things hudled one on the neck of another." It is amazing what a gusto of invention Keats exhibits in these underground scenes. For instance:

> "... Dark, nor light,
> The region; nor bright, nor sombre wholly,
> But mingled up; a gleaming melancholy;
> A dusky empire and its diadems;
> One faint eternal eventide of gems."

Following a vein of gold studded with jewels, "with all its lines abrupt and angular," Endymion hurries forward. This golden stratum is sometimes above, sometimes below him. It widens over him into a vast roof; it glitters beneath him so that "it seems an angry lightning." He proceeds past silver grottoes, sapphire columns. Far off, he sees "an orbed diamond"

> "... like the sun
> Uprisen over chaos."

On he goes, and reaches "a mimic temple" where, at the far end of "a long pillar'd vista," stands a statue of Diana. Around and about searches Endymion, exploring "courts and passages," until, weary with wandering, he sits down at the entrance to a "wide outlet" and gives way to a sensation of utter loneliness, well called by Keats "the deadly feel of solitude." Keats knew whereof he wrote, had he not been alone at Carisbrooke? But what had solaced him in some measure in the Isle of Wight had been the hills and valleys, the woods just leaving out, the primroses, the distant vari-coloured sea. Endymion, on the other hand,

> ". . . cannot see the heavens, nor the flow
> Of rivers, nor hill-flowers running wild
> In pink and purple chequer, nor, up-pil'd,
> The cloudy rack slow journeying in the west,
> Like herded elephants; nor felt, nor prest
> Cool grass, nor tasted the fresh slumbrous air."

This reads like realistic remembrance of late afternoon walks at Carisbrooke, when his work was over for the day and he got what comfort he could from nature. For Endymion, lacking these things, such loneliness is not to be endured. He asks himself why he should remain in that place, and, retracing his way to the temple, importunes Diana's effigy to let him return to earth. Nothing in his address to the statue gives any reason to suppose that he identifies his dream goddess with Diana. And yet, in his cry to Cynthia before entering the cavern, he imagines himself sailing with her through the "dizzy sky," and exclaims "How beautiful thou art!" He does not imagine himself sailing with any other goddess, so he must have considered that his dream-flight in Book I, of which he is evidently thinking when he longs for another, was made in company with the same being. It is certainly confusing to unravel what Endymion did, and did not, think. Probably Keats meant such confusion to exist because it existed in Endymion's own mind. At moments, he believes that it is, in truth, the great goddess Diana with whom he has been in communion; at other times, he scarcely credits this, and Diana disentangles herself from his dream lady to become again the remote and worshipped goddess of his youthful upbringing.

His prayer ended, "obstinate silence came heavily again," and poor Endymion, completely discouraged, bows his head. But not for long. Suddenly leaves and flowers begin to push up through the marble floor. Keats has a nice touch here to describe the rustle they make in coming, he says:

> "... the floral pride
> In a long whispering birth enchanted grew
> Before his footsteps."

Barring "floral pride," this is good, but better is the ensuing simile which shows Keats's keen observation and his power of transmuting it into words. The steady growth and spreading of the flowers is

> "... as when heav'd anew
> Old ocean rolls a lengthened wave to the shore,
> Down whose green back the short-liv'd foam, all hoar,
> Bursts gradual, with a wayward indolence."

Completely regaining his self-possession at the sight of flowers and green leaves, Endymion starts again on his journey, and now, as he proceeds, he hears a strain of music, a "sleepy music" which forces him to "walk tiptoe."

This music incites Woodhouse to the expression of an extraordinary opinion. Beside these lines:

> "For it came more softly than the east could blow
> Arion's magic to the Atlantic isles;
> Or than the west, made jealous by the smiles
> Of thron'd Apollo, could breathe back the lyre
> To seas Ionian and Tyrian"

Woodhouse, in his interleaved copy, has written:

> "The delicate character which the Imagination is here taught to give to this music, wafted so long a distance, exceeds that suggested by the admired lines of Shakespeare

on the same subject at the beginning of his 'Twelfth Night':

> 'That strain again! It had a dying fall.
> Oh, it came o'er my ear like the sweet South,
> That breathes upon a bank of violets,
> Stealing and giving over.'

It is also more complete in itself, for the comparison can be judged by the ear, & does not appeal to another sense."

That any one with the slightest pretence to poetic appreciation could prefer Keats's lines in this instance to Shakespeare's, is incredible. Apparently the word "violets" in Shakespeare's lines affected Woodhouse so strongly that he felt them and saw them and forgot the music in so doing. And what about Arion and Apollo, and the Atlantic isles, and the Ionian and Tyrian seas, do they carry no pictures, no thought of ancient myth? Are they so vague to the reader that the music sweeps over them as though they were not? To me, at least, they clutter up the lines and destroy the musical effect entirely. Keats would have done better to have left the passage at "tiptoe." Excellent, heavy-footed Woodhouse! The wonder is how Keats went on growing poetically in the face of such criticism as his friends supplied him with. Again, here, Keats leaves a line blank, and again through inattention. For "lyre" had a mate originally in the word "Dire," which followed "Tyrian." Noticing that the line was long enough without it, Keats deleted it, and, quite forgetting that a rhyme was needed to the line above, proceeded at once to change the whole passage to give a rhyme to "Tyrian." This he found, and carelessly left "lyre" forever unmated. Apart from the classical allusions, the passage does not exist. There is nothing in it to suggest music or even a sound. It is florid and empty, inappropriate and uninteresting.

The music banishes Endymion's momentary content, his absorption in the adventure as such. It brings him back to himself and to the thought of his lost love, which so overwhelms him that he would surely, so the poem tells us, have fallen over some precipice had not a "heavenly guide" led him through a grove of myrtle trees, where the brushing of the branches against his head rouses him once more to a sense of reality. Before him is a light, somewhat oddly described as "panting." Keats likens it to sunset, peeping into a wood, so we may suppose that he intended to convey the fact that the light flickered as though it came through blowing leaves. But "panting" seems altogether bad in this connection, and one of Keats's failures. Continuing on his way toward the light, Endymion passes cupids sleeping on the grass and "after a thousand mazes overgone" he finds himself in a myrtle-walled chamber. The chamber is

> "Full of light, incense, and tender minstrelsy,"

which line gives the key to the whole passage that follows — a passage in Keats's most voluptuous and feeble vein.

In the middle of the chamber is a couch, and on the couch a sleeping youth, the description of whom is cloyingly oversweet and effeminate. Only in the colours of the covers on the couch is Keats at all happy. But his colour sense is unimpeachable; these coverlids are

> ". . . gold-tinted like the peach,
> Or ripe October's faded marigolds."

The youth disposed of, as far as portraying him goes, Keats turns his attention to the bower of flowers in which he lies, but only one of these lines reaches the poet's usual felicity of phrase in such passages. It is

> "The creeper, mellowing for an autumn blush."

Three successful lines out of forty in what was meant to be a scene of rare loveliness is a poor proportion. He tried hard, but the thing eluded him. How hard he tried, and the reason why he failed, can be seen by a note of Woodhouse's. Keats, in the midst of his description of the slumbering youth lying all relaxed upon the couch, speaks of

> ". . . the tenting swerve
> Of knee from knee."

Woodhouse, not unnaturally, could make nothing of the expression, but he records that Keats told him it meant "in the form of the top of a tent." By which we are expected to see raised knees somewhat divided, I suppose. But we see nothing of the kind, and there is no reason why we should. A sleeping person relaxes, and therefore the knees would fall unless something underneath held them up. For once Keats's realism fails, his observation is at fault. Not only is the expression laboured to the last degree, the effect it seeks to give is untrue to nature.

Having gazed at this strange scene, Endymion approaches one of the watching cupids with the intention of asking an explanation. But before the question is uttered, the cupid informs him that he is the recipient of the highest honour which the gods can bestow on man, for he has been permitted to enter a sacred bower. Offering Endymion a banquet of fruits, a banquet so far inferior to the supper which Porphyro spreads for Madeline in the *Eve of St. Agnes* that one is not tempted to quotation, the cupid proceeds to relate the story of Venus and Adonis. As poetry, this relation is uninteresting enough, what is interesting is the way in which Keats mingles the various versions of the myth which he has read, and adds a picturesque touch of his own.

Keats, as we know, was familiar with Sandys' translation of Ovid's *Metamorphoses*. He was also deeply read in the *Faerie Queene*, and Shakespeare he knew almost by heart. Now Ovid, Spenser, and Shakespeare all tell the story of Venus and Adonis, and all three versions differ slightly from one another.

In Ovid, Venus falls in love with Adonis, who is the son of Myrrha and her father, Cyneras. Venus urges Adonis to hunt deer, hares, and such like animals, but to leave the fierce beasts of the forest alone. Adonis disobeys and pursues a wild boar, who turns on him and kills him. Venus finds Adonis dying, and as a memorial of her grief and love turns him into a fragrant flower.

In the Third Book of the *Faerie Queene*, Spenser gives a paraphrase of the tale as related by Ovid, but, in the sixth canto of the same Book, he departs from Ovid's ending by inventing a "Garden of Adonis" in which Adonis, restored to life, exists forever as Venus's lover.

Shakespeare, in his *Venus and Adonis*, borrows an episode from the legend of Salamis and Hermaphroditus in the Fourth Book of the *Metamorphoses*, by making Adonis reluctant to yield to Venus's advances.

Keats takes his main theme from Ovid, but adds to it Shakespeare's reluctant Adonis and Spenser's conclusion, wherein Adonis, restored to life, is given immortality. But that is not all. By a happy start of inspiration, Keats sends Venus, after Adonis's death, to Jove to plead for clemency. Jove, moved by her tears, grants Adonis half her plea. He decrees that every Winter Adonis is to lie in a tranced sleep, but, with the return of Summer, he is to wake again into life.

The narration ended, Adonis stirs, the sleeping cupids rouse themselves and rub their eyes, and far aloft appears a dove-drawn car which swiftly approaches. It is Venus, who has come for her lover's awakening. The first embraces are scarcely over, before Endymion begins to pour out his misery to the goddess. Venus tells him that she too has suffered, and in the same way. In a speech which seems sometimes addressed to Endymion, sometimes to Adonis, she explains

> "That when through heavy hours I us'd to rue
> The endless sleep of this new-born Adon',

> This stranger ay I pitied. For upon
> A dreary morning once I fled away
> Into the breezy clouds, to weep and pray
> For this my love."

The horrible shortening of Adonis to Adon', although not without classic precedent, Keats probably justified to himself by deciding that Venus would very likely have some pet nickname for Adonis. That would be a thoroughly Keatsian way of reasoning; in a cancelled passage in Book IV, Peona addresses Endymion as "Dear Endy." Nothing is more curious in Keats's early poems than his supreme taste in some instances and his utter lack of it in others.

Venus goes on to tell him that she has seen him wandering in a wood, and in listening to his mutterings has discovered that he loves, and has had intercourse with, an immortal, but who this immortal is she cannot discover, for

> "... There is no trace
> Of this in Heaven."

Feeling sure, therefore, that secrecy is needful, she will not take him up to Olympus. With this, Endymion has to be satisfied. Venus and Adonis disappear in the dove-drawn car, and Endymion is left alone in a sudden twilight.

For what purpose did Keats introduce the myth of Venus and Adonis into this Second Book? Explanations have been many, varying with the particular allegory favoured by the commentator. The reason perhaps is not so far to seek. Keats was a little put to it to fill his allotted thousand lines. He did not fear digressions, he welcomed them. I have said that his fancy ran riot in this Second Book. The springing of the flowers is a most fanciful touch, and this circumstance very probably brought to Keats's mind sundry myths of the return of Summer. There was Proserpine and Ceres, for example, but that could hardly be fitted into his tale as, to chime with its general tenor, love and Spring must be synonymous. Hence his hitting on the legend of Venus and Adonis and inventing a Spring awakening for his hero. Again, Keats has been revelling in the beauties of things seen throughout this book, now, for a change of direction, he introduces the beauty of ancient mythology. He has been doing so all along in fragmentary bits; it is quite in keeping that he should do so once in a while more at length. There may have been a number of other reasons, due to his reading, or a conversation, or a picture. He liked the story and — it filled two hundred lines. He did not write it very well, none of this Second Book is so well written as parts of the First, but I doubt whether he was in a state of mind to know that. He just went on, wherever fancy led. Observe, I say this Book is not *written* so well as the First; as far as sheer invention goes, his wanderings in the cavern are amazing.

To have someone else believe in the reality of what he scarcely credits himself, was naturally very cheering to Endymion, and that his immortal lady kept her secret inviolate seemed to prove how dearly she cherished it. It is therefore with "unusual gladness" that Endymion resumes his journey. A certainty of future happiness banishes all thought of loneliness from him, in spite of the disappearance of Venus, Adonis, cupids, even of the bower itself. The underworld resumes its earthy magnificence. He passes

> "Through caves, and palaces of mottled ore,
> Gold dome, and crystal wall, and turquois floor,
> Black polish'd porticoes of awful shade,
> And, at the last, a diamond balustrade,
> Leading afar past wild magnificence."

Sometimes the way leads through zigzag tunnels; again, the diamond path crosses "enormous chasms" where streams "all foam and roar" rush beneath him; then he finds himself overlooking

> ". . . the silvery heads
> Of a thousand fountains."

He dashes the waters with his spear and

> ". . . those spouting columns rose
> Sudden a poplar's height, and 'gan to enclose
> His diamond path with fretwork."

The waters change their shapes continually through a passage of great beauty and even greater inventiveness. After watching them altering, resolving, dissolving into new forms and contours for a long time, Endymion reluctantly turns away. He passes queer gaping caves, and jutting rocks "half seen through deepest gloom." So weird is it, that Endymion's high spirits ooze away, yet the mere adventuring amid such strangeness constantly revives him. All of a sudden, he catches sight of the earth goddess issuing forth from a rugged arch beneath him. Keats imagines and describes this well:

> ". . . in the dusk below,
> Came mother Cybele! alone — alone —
> In sombre chariot; dark foldings thrown
> About her majesty, and front death-pale,
> With turrets crown'd. Four maned lions hale
> The sluggish wheels; solemn their toothed maws,
> Their surly eyes brow-hidden, heavy paws
> Uplifted drowsily, and nervy tails
> Cowering their tawny brushes. Silent sails
> This shadowy queen athwart, and faints away
> In another gloomy arch."

All at once the diamond path ends, and ends at nothing. There is nowhere to set his foot, his way is lost in air. Seeing no hope, Endymion calls on Jove for help, and an eagle appears flying towards him. Endymion flings himself upon the eagle's back and they drop — down — down — until the sweet smell of flowers rises up to them

> "... where little caves were wreath'd
> So thick with leaves and mosses, that they seem'd
> Large honey-combs of green."

The eagle sets him on the ground and flies away, and Endymion finds himself in

> "... a jasmine bower, all bestrown
> With golden moss."

A strange elation comes over him:

> "... His every sense had grown
> Ethereal for pleasure; 'bove his head
> Flew a delight half-graspable."

The suspense, infused with a vague expectation, is excellently done. It is the essence of realism and romanticism fused together. It is also drama, and Keats can so seldom manage the dramatic that the point here should not be missed. It is heightened and continued by Endymion's most human cry:

> "... will all this gush of feeling pass
> Away in solitude?"

This is strong, full of emotion; it is suggestion revealing unuttered things. Unfortunately, from this moment, the dramatic effect lessens. Suggestion gives way to statement, and the poignance of the beginning disappears. The passage is continued in Keats's usual form of narrative soliloquy. Yet it has a story interest, for it seems to prove that Endymion has now at last decided that he does not know who his goddess is. He implores her in this wise:

> "... O my love,
> My breath of life, where art thou? High above,
> Dancing before the morning gates of heaven?

> Or keeping watch among those starry seven,
> Old Atlas' children? Art a maid of the waters,
> One of shell-winding Triton's bright-hair'd daughters?
> Or art, impossible! a nymph of Dian's,
> Weaving a coronal of tender scions
> For very idleness? Where'er thou art,
> Methinks it now is at my will to start
> Into thine arms; to scare Aurora's train,
> And snatch thee from the morning; o'er the main
> To scud like a wild bird, and take thee off
> From thy sea-foamy cradle; or to doff
> Thy shepherd vest, and woo thee mid fresh leaves."

The last line here makes up in simplicity and sharpness for the rather mediocre rest.

Endymion, in despair, decides that what he cannot have in the flesh he will seek in a dream. He goes along

> ". . . a dim passage, searching till he found
> The smoothest mossy bed and deepest, where
> He threw himself, and just into the air
> Stretching his indolent arms, he took, O bliss!
> A naked waist: 'Fair Cupid, whence is this?'
> A well-known voice sigh'd, "Sweetest, here am I."

It is the merest prudery which denies beauty to Keats's conception in this place. The lover's words are not what they should be, any one can see that; but Endymion suddenly finding his empty, uplifted arms clasped about a naked waist is a beautiful flight of imagination, astringently, absorbingly expressed. No one is more aware than Keats himself that such scenes as this require a master poet for their portrayal. He breaks off his story to say as much:

> ". . . Helicon!
> O fountain'd hill! Old Homer's Helicon!
> That thou wouldst spout a little streamlet o'er
> These sorry pages . . .
>
> . . . . .

> . . . but all is dark
> Around thine aged top, and thy clear fount
> Exhales in mists to heaven. Aye, the count
> Of mighty Poets is made up; the scroll
> Is folded by the Muses."

Yet he feels he must not shirk his high task of announcing the love which is all things. But he is no such fool as to force theory into drama. He will set down what is, to the best of his ability, and trust that what also is, but hidden, will penetrate his reader as it has penetrated him. He has spoken his meaning, in a different connection, in his criticism *On Edmund Kean as a Shakesperian Actor*, published as current theatrical criticism in the *Champion* newspaper for Sunday, December twenty-first, 1817. In this paper, he is speaking of poetry, but it serves equally well for his attitude toward love:

> "A melodious passage in poetry is full of pleasures both sensual and spiritual. The spiritual is felt when the very letters and points of charactered language show like the hieroglyphics of beauty; the mysterious signs of our immortal freemasonry! 'A thing to dream of, not to tell!'"

We may use Keats's own words to illustrate his failure in the love scene which follows the lines I have quoted. The letters and points of his language here are not equal to the strain put upon them. They are too flat, too pale to contain the hieroglyphics of beauty. They give the sensual aspect, but their lustre is too weak for the spiritual to shine through except to the most determined of observers. It is, however, a vulgar criticism which can call this scene vulgar. There are many foolish words in it, many inadequate expressions, but not in any place is it in the least vulgar. It is even, considered aside from its verbal infelicities, done with considerable skill. For the passion of the lovers is always the passion of love, not lust. A fine instinct is required to make the distinction, and a delicate touch is needed to keep it, and Keats has both the instinct and touch, however much he blunders in other ways. Dramatically, the scene is excellent, vivid, true to life. Yet verily Keats was inexperienced. How could any one write of such a scene to the length of one hundred and fourteen lines! I can think of no other poet who has attempted such a feat. It was not wise so to challenge fate, and fate, in the persons of many erudite but unimaginative and gross-minded chroniclers, has slain his very intention here, again and again. Only youth, uncontaminated by the jeers of the critics, has in the inmost recesses of its heart understood. How many boys and girls have found solace and joy in this passage! As Keats did, to be sure. He knew he had not done what he set himself to do, yet he could not bear to forbear. He could not tear himself away from his own creation, for he saw what he has not given us to see. We may admire his heroism, even while smiling a little sadly at the result. Keats never quite outgrew his inability to escape from the sentimental into the wide simplicity of sentiment, in direct allusion. With indirect, as we have seen, it is quite different. Following this love scene, Keats has written lines of a more perfect beauty, a poetry stronger and more magical, than can be found anywhere else in this Second Book. These lines are so well known as not to need quoting, yet I will quote them here:

> ". . . Ye who have yearn'd
> With too much passion, will here stay and pity,
> For the mere sake of truth; as 'tis a ditty
> Not of these days, but long ago 'twas told
> By a cavern wind unto a forest old;
> And then the forest told it in a dream
> To a sleeping lake, whose cool and level gleam
> A poet caught as he was journeying
> To Phœbus' shrine; and in it he did fling
> His weary limbs, bathing an hour's space,
> And after, straight in that inspired place
> He sang the story up into the air,
> Giving it universal freedom."

We may indeed pity; it is only the prurient who, knowing Keats's mind, have any wish to condemn.

Once more Endymion sleeps, and once more he wakes alone, but this time there is no fierceness in his regret. He is too weary with emotion for that:

> "No, he had felt too much for such harsh jars:
> The lyre of his soul Æolian tun'd
> Forgot all violence, and but commun'd
> With melancholy thought."

He takes up his quest again, but without any sense of adventure, without any sense at all except that of loss. Before, he had been eagerly observant of everything about him, now he is the most careless of travellers, entirely absorbed in reviewing his past life. He realizes that everything must be changed with him henceforward. That nothing will ever interest him again if he cannot be with his Beloved:

> "Now I have tasted her sweet soul to the core
> All other depths are shallow."

As he meditates, he is aware of a distant murmur which seems to be echoing his thoughts. He listens, roused to attention, and immediately two streams gush out of the rock beside him. One seems pursuing, the other retreating, and the murmur alters to voices, one imploring, the other replying. It is the nymph Arethusa, changed into a stream, fleeing the river god Alpheus. Of all Keats's stories within the story, this is the best done and the one most closely interwoven with the initial tale. For Arethusa longs to yield, but fears the wrath of the virgin goddess Diana. This finely touched irony gives the poem a fresh poignance, for we know that the high and chaste Diana is even as her fearful nymph, deeply in love; but, as Arethusa dreads her wrath, she dreads that of the other gods and goddesses. It is fear of shame that keeps Diana from acknowledging her love for Endymion. This particular angle of his story is as though Keats were declaring once more that basic truth of all religions: that mortal must put on immortality, and immortal must share the weakness and need of humanity, to make a perfect whole of heaven and earth. I do not think that Keats thought this out; it is a sort of atavistic gloss over his gospel of love.

The irony is nicely given in a speech of Arethusa's:

> "... Cruel god,
> Desist! or my offended mistress' nod
> Will stagnate all thy fountains: — teaze me not
> With syren words — Ah, have I really got
> Such power to madden thee? And is it true —
> Away, away, or I shall dearly rue
> My very thoughts: in mercy then away,
> Kindest Alpheus, for should I obey
> My own dear will, 'twould be a deadly bane.
> O, Oread-Queen! would that thou hadst a pain
> Like this of mine, then would I fearless turn
> And be a criminal."

Alpheus replies:

> "... Those fitful sighs
> 'Tis almost death to hear: O let me pour
> A dewy balm upon them! — fear no more,
> Sweet Arethusa! Dian's self must feel
> Sometimes these very pangs."

But Arethusa still fears:

> "What can I do, Alpheus? Dian stands
> Severe before me: persecuting fate!
> Unhappy Arethusa!"

The streams plunge "adown a fearful dell," and Endymion hears no more than a faint echo of "Arethusa" floating back to him. The scene touches him very nearly. He weeps, and prays to Diana, whom he seems at last to recognize as the goddess of his love:

"'. . . I urge
Thee, gentle Goddess of my pilgrimage,
By our eternal hopes, to soothe, to assuage,
If thou art powerful, these lovers' pains;
And make them happy in some happy plains.'

He turn'd — there was a whelming sound — he stept,
There was a cooler light; and so he kept
Towards it by a sandy path, and lo!
More suddenly than doth a moment go,
The visions of the earth were gone and fled—
He saw the giant sea above his head."

So ends the Second Book, on an infinitely higher plane than that on which it was begun.

I have said that the poetry in this Second Book does not reach the level of that in the First, for there is nothing in Book II to equal the *Hymn to Pan* or some of the purely lyric passages in Book I. But, for all that, the Second Book is in some ways an advance in composition over the First. It is not so fragmentary and disconnected. Keats shows that he has a firmer hold upon his medium; he is not so much at the mercy of momentary inspiration. His sense of the dramatic has gained enormously, and his inventive faculty has reached out in every direction and taken on a far greater originality. The First Book has more charm, but there are more potentialities in the Second.

This underworld of Keats's, as Sir Sidney Colvin has pointed out, seems to have no particular symbolic meaning. It is not Hell, nor the place of departed spirits. It is as devoid of occult suggestion as Jules Verne's *Journey to the Centre of the Earth.* Its advantage to the story is that it gives a chance for new imagery. We can see this at once if we conceive of Endymion wandering over and over the world through four Books which, however differentiated topographically, would in that case be all very much the same. Since Keats had wisely ordained that his hero's trials should be psychological, not physiological, some change of scenery was necessary to take the place of startling episode. For think how Keats has amplified the tale as told by Drayton, Fletcher, Marlowe, Shakespeare, to say nothing of those shorter allusions found in so many of the Elizabethan poets. Whatever Keats has not done in *Endymion*, he has written a psychological piece of no mean significance. Not allegorically, I am certain of that, but humanly. Endymion is Keats, is any young man, full of life, natural desire, and an idealistic habit of mind. In this Second Book, for all its rich imaginings, the chief subject is the processes of Endymion's thought. The Endymion of the First Book is a child's sketch to the Endymion of the Second. The man who steps along the sandy path and finds the sea above his head is a person. We have been inside his mind, and we know how he feels and how circumstance affects him. He claims our interest quite apart from the poem. I do not think that the Second Book is easy reading. There are not so many passages which can be picked out of their contexts and delighted in as there are in the First Book; but, if we can win through the Second Book consecutively at all, we are the gainers by finding ourselves in possession of an analysis of a state of mind which is, indeed, very well done.

We have no idea what caused this perfectly new departure in Keats. We have no Canterbury letters and only two from Hampstead, neither of which throws any light on the matter. But we can almost certainly say, from the Oxford letters, and from the very intimate knowledge we have of the rest of Keats's life, that this new departure was due to no external circumstance. That it must be the result of thinking, reading, pondering, and dissecting himself. We can be reasonably sure that Keats thought out this Second Book of *Endymion* by a constant reference to himself. This is how he had felt in such and such a case, this is how he would most assuredly feel in another. It was really great fun to do, like exploring a new country. Keats did not know that he had it in him, he had never approached it before. So he goes up to Oxford, and the tone changes again, as we shall see.

BOOK III.

Keats reached Oxford on a visit to his friend Bailey about the second or third of September. The first two Books of *Endymion* were finished, or rather the first drafts of them were. Keats had left Endymion under the sea. It was therefore the sea, and Endymion's wanderings in it, which were now to be described.

By the extraordinary law of paradox which all poets know well, Keats, having left it, is obsessed by the sea. This had begun at Hampstead. By a perfectly natural reaction, Keats, returned to London in Midsummer, begins to look parchingly back to the Isle of Wight and Margate and Hastings. The Isle of Wight as valley, down, and wood, with the sea as incidental vision, had given him the scene for his First Book. The earth journey of Book II seems to have been sheer fancy, unless, and it is a tenable theory, the columned nave and transepts of Canterbury Cathedral had been the suggestive influence. One can easily imagine it. Stone is of the earth, and fretted arches and pillared porticoes, to say nothing of underground vaults and narrow stairways leading from crypts to bell-lofts, may readily become the inciters to just such scenes as Keats invented for his Second Book. But back at Hampstead he was not surrounded by anything which could be utilized in his poem. The hot, dusty streets, the heavily-leaved trees, the smells and noises assailing him through open windows, turned his mind longingly back to the sea. So under the sea goes Endymion, and Keats is at the opening of another book.

Since the scheme of *Endymion* required an introduction to each book, Book III must have one. Nothing pertinent seems to have suggested itself, however, and the introduction written is really twisted unmercifully to make it take on a semblance of leading into anything to do with the story. Woodhouse records that "Keats said, with much simplicity, 'It will be easily seen what I think of the present ministers, by the beginning of the Third Book.'" That may be true, for Keats probably did think quite as badly of them as the introduction states, but what had the "present ministers" to do with *Endymion?* Nothing, of course. Let us do a little more guessing and suppose that Keats, in turning over his unpublished manuscripts, happened on the sonnet *On Receiving a Laurel Crown from Leigh Hunt*, and was struck with the "turbans and crowns" passage. He thought well enough of this sonnet to write it on a blank page in Reynolds's copy of the *Poems*. Here was a cue to go on with, and in lieu of a better he took it. The Tory government becomes a fine, bombastic generality, which floats, be it a little awkwardly, into the "throned seats unscalable" of cosmic powers; and, once arrived at that point, the cosmic powers melt without much difficulty into the Olympian gods of Keats's tale. Here, having circled back to mythology, Keats breaks off and calls it a day. Opposite line 41 in the draft, Keats has written "Oxford, Sept. 5." As Bailey has told us that this Third Book was written at the rate of fifty lines a day, and that if Keats fell short of his quota one day he would make it up the next, we may reckon this as his first day's work.

This introduction, although it fits nothing, is not bad in itself. It sounds well, yet, to speak truth, it has more sound than sense. It starts off with considerable dignity:

> "There are who lord it o'er their fellow-men
> With most prevailing tinsel: who unpen
> Their baaing vanities, to browse away
> The comfortable green and juicy hay
> From human pastures."

The first two lines here are so good that they have passed into current allusion, and while the figure of the nibbling sheep is something of a drop in sentiment, it is a striking figure. Bailey found fault with "baaing," but Bailey would. The nonsense begins with the lines:

> "Who, through an idiot blink, will see unpack'd
> Fire-branded foxes to sear up and singe
> Our gold and ripe-ear'd hopes."

The "idiot blink" is bad enough, but when we come to the unpacking of the foxes nonsense is fairly on the rampage. The foxes, to anyone unfamiliar with their Biblical origin in the *Book of Judges*, are a difficulty, but "unpack'd" is an outrage. We will suppose Keats's meaning to be that each pair of foxes runs round on its own hook, that the pack is scattered; but can he have imagined that a pack of foxes ever advances in a serried order like a regiment of troops on parade? And, if we assume another possible meaning, what an odd, inadequate word to describe the loosing of foxes caught and fastened tail to tail by fire-brands! No, it would appear that "unpack'd" was put in for the rhyme; but the preceding line ends with "O torturing fact," and we can hardly believe Keats to have found this exclamation so necessary that he had to preserve it to the extent of forcing in a ridiculous word to rhyme with it. Bailey, quibbling over "baaing," which in spite of its cacophony is quite an illuminating epithet, seems to have overlooked the inanity of unpacking the foxes entirely. We have "blear-ey'd nations" proudly mounting to their "spirits' perch"; "far majesties" who with "gorgeous pageantries enrobe our piece of heaven" (what enrobes the other pieces we are not told); all sorts of windy foolishnesses which are best expressed by the slang term "hot air." Keats had an idea, however far fetched in its context, but he descended to the trick of mere vapid sonority in presenting it. The amount of it is that he had an off day, and, realizing it, stopped nine lines short of his prescribed stint. And the thing bored him so that he never altered it, a proceeding quite characteristic of his methods with *Endymion*, but most unfortunate.

Beginning his second day's work, Keats exhibits a quality which is too often overlooked by critics of this long, unequal poem; this is his sense of construction. In spite of the waywardness and irrelevance of much of the narrative, Keats, again and again, by some sudden turn, brings it back to its path. Remember that Keats in *Endymion* sees the moon under a dual aspect: as the most beautiful thing in nature, and as the highest peak of love that man can know. In the First Book, the two halves of this aspect are pretty well mixed; as I have said, the whole of Book I is flooded with moonlight. In Book II, the moon, as moon, is in abeyance; it is the moon as Diana that is insisted upon. But Keats does not wish to lose either half of his conception in the other. The magic of moonlight must not be allowed to disappear from his poem. It was, with perfect propriety, excluded from the Second Book, partly because Endymion was underground, partly, and chiefly, because in that Book it was the love motif which Keats wanted to emphasize. The introduction gave the tone at the outset, and Keats followed it through the Book without deviation. Now, however, Keats's constructive sense tells him that it is high time to get back to the moon, the moon floating in the heavens and casting silvery light upon the world. He does it rather neatly by calling Apollo to witness that of all the "thousand powers" who

> ". . . keep religious state
> In water, fiery realm, and airy bourne"

Diana is the "gentlier-mightiest." So he leads up to one of the loveliest moon passages in the poem. There are a few artificial words in it, but not enough to mar the whole:

"O Moon! the oldest shades 'mong oldest trees
Feel palpitations when thou lookest in:
O Moon! old boughs lisp forth a holier din
The while they feel thine airy fellowship.
Thou dost bless everywhere, with silver lip
Kissing dead things to life. The sleeping kine,
Couched in thy brightness, dream of fields divine:
Innumerable mountains rise, and rise,
Ambitious for the hallowing of thine eyes;
And yet thy benediction passeth not
One obscure hiding-place, one little spot
Where pleasure may be sent: the nested wren
Has thy fair face within its tranquil ken,
And from beneath a sheltering ivy leaf
Takes glimpses of thee; thou art a relief
To the poor patient oyster, where it sleeps
Within its pearly house. — The mighty deeps,
The monstrous sea is thine — the myriad sea!
O Moon! far-spooming Ocean bows to thee,
And Tellus feels his forehead's cumbrous load."

Thus Keats returns to the moon, and to his immediate obsession, the sea.

It is worth while to note here Keats's feeling for sound and its suggestions, that onomatopœic sense he had so strongly. He says "spooming," not "spuming," because the double "o" sound is more open than the "u," and more capable of suggesting the wide surge and wind-rush of an immensity of breaking waves. After the quiet sylvan scenes which had preceded, he wanted to give the moon's effect over a vast area. He has precedent for his spelling in Beaumont and Fletcher and in Dryden. That this spelling was intentional here for the reasons I have stated, seems evident, as in line 655 of this same Book, where no such reasons existed, the word is written "spume."

Keats heightens this moon effect by juxtaposing to it the melancholy desolation of the ocean floor, strewn with those objects which wrecked and decaying vessels disgorge. It has been pointed out by many editors that a passage in Shakespeare's *King Richard III* was probably in Keats's mind when he wrote his. Let us compare the two, for a reason which I will state in a moment. Shakespeare's description is at the beginning of the fourth scene of the First Act:

> "What dreadful noise of waters in mine ears!
> What ugly sights of death within my eyes!
> Methought I saw a thousand fearful wrecks;
> Ten thousand men that fishes gnaw'd upon;
> Wedges of gold, great anchors, heaps of pearl,
> Inestimable stones, unvalued jewels,
> All scatter'd in the bottom of the sea:
> Some lay in dead men's skulls; and, in those holes
> Where eyes did once inhabit, there were crept,
> As 'twere in scorn of eyes, reflecting gems,
> Which woo'd the slimy bottom of the deep,
> And mock'd the dead bones which lay scatter'd by."

Keats's lines are :

> ". . . Far had he roam'd,
> With nothing save the hollow vast, that foam'd,
> Above, around, and at his feet; save things
> More dead than Morpheus' imaginings:
> Old rusted anchors, helmets, breast-plates large
> Of gone sea-warriors; brazen beaks and targe;
> Rudders that for a hundred years had lost
> The sway of human hand; gold vase emboss'd
> With long-forgotten story, and wherein
> No reveller had ever dipp'd a chin
> But those of Saturn's vintage; mouldering scrolls,
> Writ in the tongue of heaven, by those souls
> Who first were on the earth; and sculptures rude
> In ponderous stone, developing the mood
> Of ancient Nox; — then skeletons of man,
> Of beast, behemoth, and leviathan,
> And elephant, and eagle, and huge jaw
> Of nameless monster. A cold leaden awe

> These secrets struck into him; and unless
> Dian had chaced away that heaviness,
> He might have died."

Shakespeare's passage is so infinitely superior to this that no comment is needed on that score. But, if we study the technique of the two descriptions, the reasons for this superiority are abundantly clear; so clear that nothing could better serve as an illustration of the weakness of Keats's verse along certain lines. Shakespeare's sentences are as direct as though he were writing prose. He is, it is true, employing blank verse, which obviates the necessity of rhyme; but it does not take away the need for poetry. Poetry, the highest type of poetry, is never once departed from, yet it requires no fine figures of speech, no metaphors, no interpolated allusions, to make itself felt. The pound, pound, pound, of statement only adds to it. The force of simplicity, the vividness of short, sharp, actual speech, carries an emotion with it that can be got in no other way. The precision of Shakespeare's utterance is nothing less than marvellous. And then the economy of it! Shakespeare says in twelve lines what it took Keats twenty merely to approach, and yet Shakespeare seems to have given the fuller picture.

Now take Keats. Inversions, extraneous details, ancient gods called in to help out short lines or lend a circumstance to tag a rhyme. Unnatural archaisms such as the ponderous stones of Nox, or behemoth and leviathan, which come directly from Milton and should have been left there, or at least reserved for some more appropriate occasion. Cheap expressions, again in the cause of rhyme, as in the revellers who had never "dipp'd a chin." Preposterous suggestions, as that of elephants and eagles at the bottom of the sea. We might be gazing at the wreck of Noah's ark. The mind is led away from the scene in almost every line by some impertinent interpolation.

But none of these things is the reason for which I have made this comparison. The reason is deeper. It lies in the fact that Keats's description is soothed and succoured out of all semblance of horror. Shakespeare feared no horror; he saw plainly and truly. Keats tricked out his lines; Shakespeare left his stark. This inveterate desire to soften what is inevitably harsh, we shall have occasion to come back to later. Keats tells us that, seeing these things, his hero might have died were it not for the consoling moonbeam, therefore we must think that Keats intended them to be dreadful; but in his soul Keats hated horror, and this tendency of his to gentle and smooth is very much in evidence here.

Now that we have seen what Keats did not do in this passage, let us observe that the idea of it, coming in where it does, is good. It makes the moon even more important than it would otherwise have been, for it becomes the saviour, the comforter, and at the end we see it once more sailing above all these tokens of death, pouring its rays down upon them through translucent water.

Having fairly set the moon once more in the sky, Keats proceeds to mingle his two aspects. For he will not have his readers forget that love is the undercurrent of his theme; also, he must return to the telling of his tale. Cynthia pines as one sorrowful; she is changed and woe-begone:

> "She dies at the thinnest cloud; her loveliness
> Is wan on Neptune's blue: yet there's a stress
> Of love-spangles, just off yon cape of trees,
> Dancing upon the waves, as if to please
> The curly foam with amorous influence."

Can we not see that cape of trees, black against the scattered brilliance of the moon-touched water? In the matter of word-painting, Keats has done nothing better than this. He has not merely observed the effect, it has soaked into his very bones. "Amorous influence" is a blot, he learnt a wiser diction later, but the purely descriptive lines have no flaw.

Moon-rays cannot shine through the earth, which is the very excellent reason why, in the Second Book, they do not do so. But moonlight can pierce water; therefore Endymion, wandering along under the sea, is comforted by a shaft of silver radiance falling upon him through the waves. Cheered by this stray moonbeam, he lies down in his usual manner and waits until morning to continue his journey. Starting forth again, he meditates on the extraordinary effect which the moon has always had upon him. We may take it as Keats speaking again of himself when Endymion says:

> " What is there in thee, Moon! that thou shouldst move
> My heart so potently? When yet a child
> I oft have dried my tears when thou hast smil'd."

This passage is too long to quote entire. It is interesting to observe the divided strands of Keats and Endymion in it, for Keats does not forget the agricultural pursuits of Endymion in which he himself could have had no share. But it is clearly Keats in the voice of Endymion who cries

> " Thou wast the mountain-top — the sage's pen —
> The poet's harp — the voice of friends — the sun;
> Thou wast the river — thou wast glory won;
> Thou wast my clarion's blast — thou wast my steed —
> My goblet full of wine — my topmost deed: —
> Thou wast the charm of women, lovely Moon!"

To Keats, the moon is more than the most beautiful of the heavenly bodies, more than the cause of magical effects of light, she is an almost mystical influence. Keats was no mystic, he had not an iota of mysticism in him; but moonlight evidently moved him strangely, and let loose those subconscious promptings which are the genesis of all poetry.

For some reason, Endymion seems again confused as to the identity of his goddess. For he says that all his devotion was to Diana until "my strange love came." We might suppose that he meant merely that his worship had changed to love, were it not that he continues:

> "She came, and thou didst fade, and fade away —
> Yet not entirely; no, thy starry sway
> Has been an under-passion to this hour."

And again:

> ". . . Dearest love, forgive
> That I can think away from thee and live! —"

It is quite obvious that Keats means to show that, without knowing it, it is always Diana whom Endymion loves. But certainly, at this moment, Endymion does not know it himself. And it is quite possible that I am wrong in thinking that Keats ever meant him to seem confused on the subject. The passage in the beginning of Book II can be read either way, or, more likely, Endymion is, as it were, in love with both his dream-goddess and Diana at the same time and can scarcely himself disentangle the two sensations.

In the midst of his invocation to Diana, Endymion looks up and, with a start, sees in front of him an old man. The old man is Glaucus, and the rest of Book III is concerned entirely with a Keatsian version of the story of Glaucus and Scylla. Keats is ingenious in welding it into Endymion's travels, yet, by its style, it remains apart. For Bailey and Oxford are having their effect. We hear no more of the moon, and the sea ceases to flash with authentic observation; it turns literary in vision and expression. We can perfectly see why. Oxford is not a place that can go unremarked, but no excuse could be found for Oxford in the depths of the ocean. It obliterated the sea as present vision, and gave nothing which could be utilized as such. Because of this, Keats is thrown back upon association, literary association. The interminable literary discussions between the two friends, which Bailey has taken pains to preserve, turned Keats's mind even more toward books than it usually was, if that were possible. Bailey was the last man to become excited over the moon. By Bailey's count of lines, it took just four days to wean Keats away from her. Tale within tale was already quite the habit of the poem, but not before had Keats dwelt so long upon an interpolated story. Bailey could perfectly sympathize with Glaucus, particularly in the manner in which Keats, sitting in Bailey's study in Magdalen Hall with Bailey at his elbow, presented it. Even as it was, Bailey had some qualms, as we see in a letter written to Taylor on August twenty-ninth, 1818.[1] In this letter, he says he cannot defend the moral part of the poem:

> "There are two great blotches in it in this respect. The first must offend anyone of proper feelings; and indelicacy is not to be borne; and I greatly reproach myself that I did not represent this very strongly to him before it went to the press — not that I apprehend that it would have had any great effect; but it would have been some self-satisfaction. The second book, however, was concluded before I knew Keats. The second fault I allude to I think we have noticed. The approaching inclination it has to that abominable principle of Shelley! — that sensual love is the principle of things. Of this I believe him to be unconscious, & can see how by process of imagination he might arrive at so false, delusive & dangerous conclusion."

From this we notice how little Bailey had understood Keats's explanation of his theme in *Endymion* in the letter sent from Burford Bridge on November twenty-second, 1817.[2] This letter to Taylor hardly does Bailey complete justice, however, for, in other letters, he says that he greatly admires the Second Book, and we know that he

[1] Woodhouse Book. Morgan Collection.
[2] See Vol. I, p. 360.

defended *Endymion* with loyalty and asperity; but it does show the bent of his mind, and in such close association as he and Keats were during Keats's Oxford visit this bent naturally had some effect upon Keats. That Bailey did have a great effect upon Keats, we shall see presently. At the moment, it is only necessary to observe this influence in the abrupt alteration of subject and manner which occurs at line 187 of Book III.

How completely in sympathy Bailey was with Keats's new method, can be seen by the fact that, thirty years after the event, Bailey's recollection of Keats's reading of a passage at the beginning of the Glaucus story is still quite fresh. He says:

> [1] "I remember very distinctly, though at this distance of time, his reading of a few passages; and I almost think I hear his voice, and see his countenance. Most vivid is my recollection of the following passage of the fine and affecting story of the old man, Glaucus, which he read to me immediately after its composition:—
>
> 'The old man raised his hoary head and saw
> The wilder'd stranger — seeming not to see,
> The features were so lifeless. Suddenly
> He woke as from a trance; his snow-white brows
> Went arching up, *and like two magic ploughs*
> *Furrow'd deep wrinkles in his forehead large,*
> *Which kept as fixedly as rocky marge,*
> *Till round his wither'd lips had gone a smile.*'
>
> The lines I have italicised are those which then struck me as peculiarly fine, and to my memory have 'kept as fixedly as rocky marge.' I remember his upward look when he read of the 'magic ploughs,' which in his hands have turned up much of the rich soil of Fairyland."

That Bailey liked this passage, stamps Bailey. For it is very poor, imitative stuff. If Keats liked it, he was fooled by the heat of creation. It is quite usual for creative

[1] Bailey Memoranda. Colvin.

writers to be particularly pleased in the beginning with work which they afterwards see is bad. What strikes most at first, frequently turns out to be feckless. Did Keats continue to like this passage? It would be interesting to know. Eyebrows in the semblance of magic ploughs wrinkling a forehead is a detestable simile, for ploughs connote cutting. "Arching up" is a steal from Sandys and none the less good on that account, but the mixed metaphors at the end are Keats's own. We have the ploughs furrowing the forehead, which remains as fixed as a "rocky marge." But how can even a magic plough draw a furrow through rock? And, if we grant that the forehead may have undergone petrifaction after the furrowing was done, still what has it to do with a marge? Why the word "marge," which is decidedly out of place? There are many pertinent things that could be rocky, but marge means margin, an edge, and to liken a forehead to an edge in any material is far-fetched indeed. It looks as if the only reason for "marge" is that it rhymes with "large." Then the lips round which "had gone" a smile. Now "had gone" distinctly suggests movement and progression. Try as we will, we cannot help seeing the smile begin at one end of the lips and steal stealthily round them until it reaches its starting place, a very strange way for a smile to behave. I have said that this is imitation, and so it is; but it is spurious imitation, brummagem instead of ore. If Keats's models had done no better than that, he would not have read a line of them and neither would anybody else.

This quotation has a little outdistanced the place at which we left the poem. To return, Glaucus is described and his cloak, which, as we have seen, Keats paraphrased from Drayton, and did so with a skill that makes the passage admired of Bailey following immediately upon it the more amazing in its ineptitude.

Glaucus hails Endymion with the solemn announcement: "Thou art the man!" Now, he says, he will regain his lost youth, his life will be changed, and much more to the same purport. Endymion is somewhat taken aback by this. He sees himself sacrificed in a hundred dreadful ways. But Glaucus weeps, and Endymion finds him no longer sinister, only pitiful, and kneeling down begs forgiveness with tears. Glaucus reassures him, and tells him he knows he loves "an unknown power," that he, Glaucus, is a friend to love and that Endymion has been

> ". . . Commission'd to this fated spot
> For great enfranchisement."

After this, the two move on together. As they walk, Glaucus tells his story, and here Keats follows Ovid's version, merely dressing it up with a few pictorial touches, but these are so far beneath what Keats could do in this line when he was in the vein that they are not memorable. Having sketched his early life, Glaucus relates how he plunged into the sea. Keats departs from Ovid in this by making Glaucus's reason for this desperate act a desire to have, what we may call, the "freedom of the ocean." Keats suppresses the herb by means of which Glaucus is suddenly cast into the sea, also there is no suggestion that Glaucus has changed into a sea creature. He returns to Ovid, however, in the meeting of Glaucus with Scylla, but generalizes it, whereby it loses its vividness and zest. The diction of this part of the tale is not only cold and unillumined by the flashes of verisimilitude by means of which Keats usually keeps his narrative fresh and clear, it descends to such cheerless banalities as, when Glaucus decides to invoke Circe's help:

> ". . . So above the water
> I rear'd my head, and look'd for Phœbus' daughter."

This time it is Glaucus who sleeps, and we may wonder that Keats allowed himself to use this same device so many times in one poem. His invention during the writing of this part of *Endymion* lags badly. Circe's arrival on the scene of Glaucus's narrative is not so different from Diana's many arrivals, only not so good as any of them. Circe is of a "coming-on" disposition. She tells how she has wept thinking Glaucus dead, and she tells this in a manner almost worthy of Pope, if Keats had stopped to think of it, for she has shed "an urn of tears," and, now that Glaucus is alive, she assures him that she

> ". . . will pour
> From these devoted eyes their silver store."

To give an idea of the irresistible *allure* of her speech, Keats informs us that

> ". . . she link'd
> Her charming syllables."

Poor Keats! Poetry is not written at a table sitting opposite another man who is cramming for an examination. The best that can be done under such circumstances is verse, and there is abundance of mere verse in this Third Book.

Let us realize, nevertheless, that there was a reason for this drop in the poetic temperature quite apart from Bailey's ill-advised taste. Whatever Bailey may have been on the poetical side, he was a scholar; and Keats was not simply a poet, but a man of very keen intellect with only a mediocre education. He positively gulped down Bailey's conversation. He could not have enough of this new point of view. It took him clean out of the *Endymion* mood. His thinking faculty was growing up at a great rate. All sorts of ideas were knocking at his perception; he wanted, and needed, to give way to them, but he had to get on with *Endymion*. The best he could do with it was to retell a tale he knew by heart with only a minimum of change in it, just enough to fit it into his frame. His imagination was taken up with other things. His state of mind was a good deal like that of a sleepy man who tries to keep himself at a task; but, in Keats's case, instead of the clouding over of the mind by sleep, it was the sweeping over it of a host of new impressions. He kept on writing, but only half his faculties were on the job. It must have been at just about this time, calculating by his fifty lines, that he wrote to his sister Fanny, on September tenth:

> "I have been writing very hard lately, even till an utter incapacity came on, and I feel it now about my head."

Had he been wise, he would have left *Endymion* alone until he felt like going on with it, but I suspect he had an inkling that if he stopped for a day that would be the end of the poem altogether. Keats was a man of character and he would not be beaten.

In taking up the thread of the Glaucus episode, we shall lose nothing if we hurry over this part of the tale and let "billows rude" and "haunts umbrageous" and "antler'd deer" sufficiently suggest how it is told.

Unlike Ovid, Keats permits Glaucus to succumb to Circe's blandishments, but one day he finds her torturing her crew of animals, men made such by her enchantments. He flees in horror and hides in a wood, only to be found after three days by Circe, and Keats rises to something like force in the witch's speech of bitter invective in which she curses Glaucus and sets a spell upon him. He is to return to the ocean and take on the appearance of a feeble old man. This shape he must keep for a thousand years without dying; at the end of that time, he will be allowed to die if fate so decrees.

Having cast her spell, Circe disappears, in as perfect a simile as Keats ever invented. But it must be given in its context. The dramatic irony of her last words is admirably conceived, for, after cursing Glaucus in a sort of hideous glee, dwelling on the miseries which he will undergo, she bids him good-bye with a refinement of brutal savagery quite in keeping with her nature. To gain the full effect of this climax and the simile which follows it, we must go back a few lines and quote the end of Circe's curse as Glaucus recounts it to Endymion:

> " 'Disabled age shall seize thee; and even then
> Thou shalt not go the way of aged men;
> But live and wither, cripple and still breathe
> Ten hundred years: which gone, I then bequeath
> Thy fragile bones to unknown burial.
> Adieu, sweet love, adieu!' — As shot stars fall,
> She fled ere I could groan for mercy."

These lines prove succinctly that Keats is regaining his equilibrium. He is more in the poem in this curse of Circe's than he has been since Glaucus came on the scene, except in the single instance of the description of Glaucus's cloak. From now on, Keats, to a great extent, returns to his own natural manner.

What delivered him from books and Bailey, from Oxford and conversation? What gave him back himself? Nothing more startling than that first impressions were wearing off, I think. Like all men of extreme sensibility, Keats was extraordinarily quick to receive impressions, and be imposed upon by them; but again, like all powerful creative minds, he was equally sudden in returning to himself. No outside influence could keep its ascendancy long, none could turn him for more than a moment from his path. He took them up, assimilated what he needed of them, and discarded the rest. Witness his delight in mountain scenery at the beginning of his Scotch tour, and his admission to his brother Tom at the end of it that he has seen enough. It took him scarcely an instant, as life goes, to gather in mountains, rocks, and waterfalls, and store them up for possible use; as to these objects in actual fact, he was soon through with them. So here in Oxford. He had been completely bowled over by his impressions at first, he could not even write like himself. But ten days sufficed to dull the sharpness of their appeal. Not that they held no farther interest for him. Bailey's conversation had not lost its charm, and we know by his letters for a twelvemonth to come how much he relied upon Bailey's character and Bailey's judgment. But it is evident by the renewed vigour in this part of Book III that his creative faculty was beginning to dominate him again. The end of the Third Book is far better than the middle. From line 187 to line 555 the poem is principally filling space, as we have seen.

While Glaucus, having regained his element, the sea, and not yet feeling the effects of Circe's curse, is swimming, he comes upon the dead body of Scylla. Then, indeed, does he realize the full extent of Circe's wrath. It is noteworthy how Keats leaves Ovid from this point on. With his returning submergence in the poem, he begins to invent for himself, and the mere act of invention seems to bring with it his own personal diction. I have already remarked how seldom Keats employs the grotesque. Harsh and violent things always seem to repel him. There is a sort of wild power from which he seems to turn voluntarily away. He liked smooth edges and soft surfaces, if one can so put it without any intention of meaning the terms literally. He thought Haydon the greatest of living painters, even before he knew him, but never once does he mention Turner; he must have read Blake, the *Daisy's Song* is so close to Blake's manner in the *Songs of Innocence*, but there is no evidence to show that he ever read Blake's symbolic books, although Dilke was a Blake collector. Possibly Dilke did not begin his collection until after Keats's death, but it is more than likely that he knew of the prophetic books, and, if he did, undoubtedly Keats did too. In changing the horrible fate allotted to Scylla by Ovid, Keats may have merely had the interests of his story in mind, but it also seems likely that the loathsome horror of a woman with her lower extremities turned into dogs disgusted him. Far otherwise is the fate of Scylla in his version, and from now on there is no question of Ovid.

Glaucus carries the beautiful dead body of his former love to a grotto

> "Ribb'd and inlaid with coral, pebble, and pearl."

We need no plainer evidence of Keats's return to himself than the way in which Glaucus tells how

> "Headlong I darted; at one eager swirl
> Gain'd its bright portal, enter'd, and behold!
> 'Twas vast, and desolate, and icy-cold."

He leaves the body in a niche and flees; but, even as he goes, his fate comes upon him, and

> ". . . these limbs became
> Gaunt, wither'd, sapless, feeble, cramp'd, and lame."

As Oxford grew familiar through daily association, Keats began to think again of the sea. In a letter to Jane Reynolds, written on the fourteenth of September, a perfectly healthy letter of fun and fancy, Keats, moved thereto by the fact that his correspondent is at the seaside village of Little Hampton, speaks of the profound effect which the sea has upon him:

> [1] "I have found in the ocean's music, — varying (though self-same) more than the passion of Timotheus, an enjoyment not to be put into words; and 'though inland far I be,' I now hear the voice most audibly while pleasing myself in the idea of your sensations . . . But don't you think there is something extremely fine after sunset, when there are a few white clouds about and a few stars blinking — when the waters are ebbing, and the horizon a mystery? This state of things has been so fulfilling to me that I am anxious to know whether it is a favourite with you."

[1] Corrected from the original letter. Author's Collection.

By the inevitable calculation of lines, this seems to have been written a day or so before the Circe speech; and now, as Glaucus, skipping quickly over the passage of some hundreds of years, begins to tell of a shipwreck, all at once, for the first time after reaching Oxford, Keats writes again realistically and naturally of the sea.

Glaucus begins the story in this manner:

> ". . . On a day,
> Sitting upon a rock above the spray,
> I saw grow up from the horizon's brink
> A gallant vessel: soon she seem'd to sink
> Away from me again, as though her course
> Had been resum'd in spite of hindering force —
> So vanish'd."

That is clearly remembered experience, so brightly imagined that the words are inevitable, suddenly they are there. No one who has watched a ship rise slowly out of the ocean from masthead to hull can fail to appreciate the perfect realism of "grow up from the horizon's brink." She comes, she goes, *sinking* down and disappearing. The rest of the shipwreck is good, but not so good as this.

The vessel gone down and the crew lost with it, Glaucus sits mournfully regarding from his rock the now empty ocean. All at once, through the water beneath him, there rises the hand of an old man holding a scroll and a wand. Glaucus reaches down and seizes the hand, trying to pull it farther up the rock, but the body below is too heavy, and the hand tears from his grasp and sinks, leaving the scroll and wand with Glaucus. This scroll, when Glaucus opens it, appears to refer to him. It tells of a poor, bewitched wretch dwelling in the sea, whose doom it is to live for a thousand years and then die alone. But yet, it says, he shall not die, if he will learn "the meanings of all motions, shapes, and sounds," and explore them to "their symbol-essences." Besides this, he must salvage the bodies of all drowned lovers and lay them side by side until, at a given time, a youth shall appear whom

"... he shall direct
How to consummate all."

The youth chosen must do this thing, or both he and Glaucus will be destroyed.

Endymion cheerfully accepts this unrevealed destiny, and Glaucus leads him to the grotto where he sees thousands of dead lovers laid in rows and reverently cared for.

Glaucus wishes to fulfill the decree at once, and starts by tearing up the scroll. He then takes off his cloak and binds it round Endymion, after which he strikes the air with his wand nine times. Glaucus next gives Endymion a thread as fragile as a spider's web and bids him wind it "to a clue," whatever that may be; I fear that once again Keats was governed in his choice of word by the need of a rhyme. Endymion next receives a shell on which he is told that something is written, although Glaucus says it is "pearly blank" to him. Endymion apparently deciphers the writing, for Glaucus is overjoyed and declares that they are safe. He next commands Endymion to break the wand against a lyre which is standing on a pedestal. The wand broken, music gushes about them, and Glaucus, reaching the final charm, orders Endymion to strew upon him some of the leaves of the torn scroll. No sooner have the "minced leaves" touched Glaucus's face than he stands transformed. Age has dropped from him, he is a young man crowned with a coral diadem — a youthful god, in fact. Glaucus, the altered Glaucus, at once turns to the corpse of Scylla, which he touches, weeping. Scylla sighs, and revives. One by one, Endymion, following the directions of Glaucus, resuscitates the other dead lovers by strewing upon them the remaining leaves of the scroll. When all are risen up, Glaucus shouts that they must away to pay their respects to Neptune. Out of the grotto they rush, "pouring" down the marble steps "as easily as hour-glass sand," and on emerging behold another multitude coming to greet them. These are the mates of those lovers who have suffered the misfortune of drowning while separated from their loves. The joined hosts move on to Neptune's palace.

The similarity of these episodes to many in the *Arabian Nights* has often been pointed out. A hand rising from the sea, holding something of huge importance, is a very common occurrence in Arabian and Persian tales. But we need not go so far to seek it, if we remember King Arthur and the way in which he received his sword, "Excalibur." The whole rigmarole of the rites performed in the grotto is familiar to any reader of folk-tales in any language. Usually it is some enchanted liquid which is sprinkled to wake the dead to life; but, as a liquid in a liquid realm seems to lose its significance, Keats has happily substituted fragments of the scroll. There is very little originality in this whole episode, as far as the facts of it are concerned. Keats is content to take various old charms and ceremonies which he finds lying round in his brain from his multifarious readings. I think it futile to seek their sources, for I doubt if Keats remembered them himself. He gets a bit here, a bit there, he even goes back to Ovid for the number of times that Glaucus beats the air with his wand. But it is important to notice that the scene is told in Keats's own idiom, that curious idiom, so packed with quotations, and so completely personal in spite of them. It is not his idiom at its best, but it is better than he had been doing before the passage where Circe curses Glaucus. Small wonder, therefore, that he was pleased with it. And he was. It — the poem — marched, as the French say. On September twenty-first, he writes to Reynolds in high enthusiasm:

> "I am getting on famous with my third Book, — have written 800 lines thereof, and hope to finish it next Week. Bailey likes what I have done very much. Believe me, my

dear Reynolds, one of my chief layings-up is the pleasure I shall have in showing it to you, I may now say, in a few days."

Eight hundred lines carries the poem to the moment when all the lovers have come to life and are just quitting the grotto. It should be remembered that Keats speaks according to his own numbering of lines. As I have already pointed out,[1] Buxton Forman numbers the lines differently from the numbering of the first edition.

Nothing could have been more unwise than Keats's determination to make every Book consist of a thousand lines. He stuck to it, or nearly so. By his own count of lines, the First Book has 993; the Second, 1026; the Third, 1043; and the Fourth, 1020. This is a remarkable evidence of holding to a principle, but he injured his poem in so doing. Now here, at the eight hundredth line, the story of his Third Book was ended, or rather, a few lines only were needed to end it, by no means the two hundred that his scheme demanded. He fell back upon fancy, sheer fancy, to supply the want of logical action.

We are taken to Neptune's palace, which is described in much the same style as the underground descriptions in Book II. The account of the palace is good, but the analogous parts of Book II are better. Yet some of his imaginings are very striking, as, for instance, this, in Neptune's Hall, where

> ". . . there did spring
> From natural west, and east, and south, and north,
> A light as of four sunsets, blazing forth
> A gold-green zenith 'bove the Sea-God's head."

After the description of the palace, which takes up fifty lines, the action of the story starts again. Triton blows his horn, the Nereids dance, the Sirens sing, and Venus,

[1] See Vol. I, pp. 322–323.

"the ooze-born Goddess," enters upon the scene. She appears surprised that Endymion is "still wandering in the bands of love," for, she tells him

> ". . . Since the hour
> I met thee in earth's bosom, all my power
> Have I put forth to serve thee."

She had expected that already he would have "escap'd from dull mortality's harsh net." But she counsels patience and tells him that it will not be long now. Very prettily she comforts him, a nice touch on Keats's part:

> ". . . Pr'ythee soon,
> Even in the passing of thine honey-moon,
> Visit now my Cythera."

The last line of the above reads, in both the finished manuscript and the first edition, "Visit my Cytherea." But the draft has the reading I have printed, and Buxton Forman and Professor de Sélincourt have adopted it, since the island is correctly spelt "Cythera." Buxton Forman even believes that the spelling in the printer's copy is an error of transcription. I do not think so; I think the change was intentional owing to the greater beauty of sound in "Cytherea." One of the many names given to Venus was Cytherea, as Keats knew, since he speaks of Venus as "goddess Cytherea" in the *Hymn to Neptune* a little farther on. Knowing the name to be derived from the island, he evidently confused the difference between the spellings and supposed them interchangeable.

A "glorious revelry" begins, and some of the description so nicely illustrates one of Keats's marked characteristics that it will be well to pause and consider it. I refer to his habit of borrowing other poets' words and even, at times, other poets' contexts. In this instance, the last is more by implication than actual fact, but the suggestion of Keats's lines is evidently the outcome of his reading of the following passage of Shakespeare. In the first scene of the Third Act of *Much Ado About Nothing*, he found:

> "And bid her steal into the pleached bower
> Where honeysuckles, ripen'd by the sun,
> Forbid the sun to enter . . .
> . . . . .
> So angle me for Beatrice, who even now
> Is couched in the woodbine coverture."

Here two words and a connotation give him a pregnant scene for his revelry:

> "And plunder'd vines, teeming exhaustless, pleach'd
> New growth about each shell and pendant lyre;
> The which, in disentangling for their fire,
> Pull'd down fresh foliage and coverture
> For dainty toying."

A hymn strikes up. This *Hymn to Neptune* is evidently modelled upon the *Hymn to Pan* in the First Book; it reproduces the short line, and even attempts to vary it with the same sure rhythmic felicity. But nothing of the inevitable excellence of the *Hymn to Pan* is here. This is a faded effort to regain a lost emotion. Keats cannot work himself up, the *Hymn* is a dead thing throughout. Endymion begins to feel dizzy, the palace whirls about him. He calls on Venus for help, asks where his unknown goddess is, and falls at Neptune's feet insensible. Keats's custom of rendering his hero unconscious whenever some important event is about to happen, has been remarked upon before. Apparently Keats's dramatic sense could think of no other method of bringing about an alteration of scene or emotion, for he employs it in either instance.

As Endymion is carried away, he hears in his mind a well-known voice reassuring him:

> "Dearest Endymion! my entire love!
> How have I dwelt in fear of fate: 'tis done —

Immortal bliss for me too hast thou won.
Arise then! for the hen-dove shall not hatch
Her ready eggs, before I'll kissing snatch
Thee into endless heaven. Awake! Awake!"

Endymion regains consciousness, and as he does so "a placid lake" comes "quiet to his eyes." An expression better than this to express his slowly growing sense that he is looking at a lake can scarcely be imagined. It is perfect realism; it is also perfect poetry. A forest spreads about him, and in its freshness, and the realization that he is once more upon the earth, he tastes a comforting happiness, and the Third Book closes.

Opposite the last line in the draft, Keats wrote: "Oxf: Sept. 26." This date proves how very accurate Bailey was in his recollection that Keats wrote fifty lines a day, for the whole 1043 lines (Keats's reckoning) were done in twenty-one days. But the last two hundred and forty-three lines had exhausted him. They were a *tour de force*, and although some of them are very good, two hundred of them at least could have been dispensed with. He is no longer in the triumphant mood of his letter to Reynolds of the previous week, when, on September twenty-eighth, he writes to Haydon:

> "You will be glad to hear that within the last three weeks I have written 1000 lines — which are the Third Book of my Poem. My Ideas with respect to it I assure you are very low — and I would write the subject thoroughly again — but I am tired of it and think the time would be better spent in writing a new Romance which I have in my eye for next summer — Rome was not built in a Day — and all the good I expect from my employment this summer is the fruit of Experience which I hope to gather in my next Poem."

He had finished the Third Book two days before this letter was written, and two days is ample time to gain a perspective. Also, the experience he hoped to gather was already partly his, and its effect was to ruin his pleasure in what he had done. He went too far, of course; to his weary and disappointed mind, the First and Second Books went down with the Third. His discouragement was largely due to strain and overwork, no doubt; he had been keyed up to an unnatural pitch, now the reaction had set in. But beneath the strain and the reaction lay experience. Keats did not merely feel — he knew; and he never ceased to know afterwards. Although he regained some measure of self-approbation over his work in the poem later, he is never quite so exuberant about it again. He had not our knowledge of what was to come, and what an immense amount the writing of *Endymion* had taught him. He lingered on at Oxford for a week or ten days after finishing the Third Book, during which time he and Bailey went on an excursion to Stratford-on-Avon, but, with excellent sense, he made no attempt to begin the Fourth.

The Third Book has been so completely analyzed already that no particular summing up seems necessary. To lovers of Keats's most personal and unique type of poetry, it offers less than the rest of the poem. The moon passages are its greatest allurement. The story of Glaucus interpolated into the narrative of Endymion's quest irritates a reader who has begun to take a real interest, not only in what we may call the plot of the poem, but in Endymion himself as an individual. There is not the slightest hint of psychology in the Third Book. Humanity gives way to ancient legend, told with very little inspiration and a minimum of originality. Because this interpolation never quite justifies itself, commentators have beaten their brains to find the reason for its intrusion. I am profoundly certain that there is none other than I have stated.

The usual explanation for poetry, any poetry, is far less complex than most people think. Consider the Browning societies, and how they have tangled a very simple meaning. Keats has escaped the societies, but he has not escaped the lucubrations of critics. It were well to ponder him a while as he was and not as he might have been, only so shall we avoid building up a man who never existed. Allegories have been, and will be, written, poems have been devised on the principle of cipher writing, but not by boys of twenty-one, in love with the sensuous in nature and letters, and who make no secret of their predilections. He who runs may read, if he will look about him and not bury his nose in a theory, as is the common way.

Sir Sidney Colvin's ingenious key to the story of Glaucus, after Keats's departure from the myth related by Ovid, would be worth more consideration if the action were not that of hundreds of legends in every language. Expiation for some fault or misfortune by the performance of a noble and difficult deed is mere stock in trade with all such tales. It was an obvious ending to the story, since Keats did not find himself disposed to adopt Ovid's far more original ending. I cannot, therefore, see any reason for supposing Keats to have given it an altruistic undercurrent, and this opinion I firmly hold to after many readings of the poem and much study of Keats's statements in his letters, and those of his friends, on the subject of *Endymion*. The prevalence of Ovid in this Third Book, beginning with the introduction of the Glaucus episode, not only in the story itself, but in innumerable details drawn from other parts of the *Metamorphoses* to which I have had no space to allude — a prevalence far greater than we see in any of the other Books — leads to the supposition that Keats, already familiar with Sandys' translation, came across it while ferreting among Bailey's books and read it over again, then and there.

BOOK IV.

We know that Keats did not begin the Fourth Book

until after his return to Hampstead, because he writes to Bailey from there some time in October as follows:

> "I don't suppose I've written as many lines as you have read volumes, or at least chapters, since I last saw you. However, I am in a fair way now to come to a conclusion in at least three weeks, when I assure you I shall be glad to dismount for a month or two; although I'll keep as tight a rein as possible till then, nor suffer myself to sleep. I will copy for you the opening of the Fourth Book, in which you will see from the manner I had not an opportunity of mentioning any poets, for fear of spoiling the effect of the passage by particularizing them."

Here we observe several things. In the first place, that the poem has been going very slowly. No fifty lines a day now. Keats's first letter to Bailey after leaving Oxford, in which he tells of his return journey, was written on October eighth. In this second letter, Keats says that he has been confined a fortnight or more at Hampstead, so we can safely say that it was not begun before October twenty-second, and a full fortnight is a tolerable length of time in which to have written only a few lines. The letter from which I have quoted is undated, but Buxton Forman considers it to have been written in November, and puts it before another letter to Bailey post-marked November fifth. I think he may be right as to the second half of the letter, but Keats, in the second paragraph, began the letter afresh, a fact which Buxton Forman did not know. I shall state the source of my knowledge later. Keats had done much more than the introduction by the time the second paragraph was written. In the second place, we see that the introduction to Book IV had been talked over with Bailey. Bailey's was the mind of a scholar, and evidently the introduction as planned was to be a nutshell history of the progress of poetry from the earliest times, enriched by lists of poets ancient and modern. Keats came back from Oxford thoroughly tired, and more in the mood for gadding than for writing. He was, moreover, ill and discouraged. Pondering upon this introduction, with no enthusiastic Bailey at his elbow, he becomes less and less enamoured of it. He writes it, as agreed, probably because he could think of nothing better, but shortens it to a mere twenty-nine lines; it is the shortest introduction in the poem. Sensible of the disappointment which Bailey was sure to feel, Keats explains, qualifies, almost apologizes, and apparently sends off only the introduction, which we know was not all that he had written of the Fourth Book when he posted the letter; but, with the introduction, Bailey and Ovid both vanish from the poem. Evidently Keats had either refreshed his memory with a re-reading of *Endimion and Phœbe* or had been keeping the episode of Diana in mortal guise all along as matter for his last Book.

We need not greatly trouble ourselves with this introduction; it is forced, obscure, and uninteresting. Woodhouse notes that line 10 refers to Hebrew poetry, line 11 to Greek poetry, and line 15 to Roman poetry. But so vague and florid are these allusions, that even so staunch an admirer as Buxton Forman is moved to remark: "The references to the Hebrew, Greek, Roman, and Italian literatures are scarcely as clear and pointed as might have been expected from Keats."

The gist of the introduction is that, during the times of the Hebrews, Greeks, and Romans, there was no English poetry, England being still in a state of barbarism. Yet her turn came, and her poetry, after long delaying, burst out in great magnificence. Now, however, the great days of English poetry are over; the poets of the present cannot compare with their predecessors. They are crushed, confined, and fretted, a prey to despondence; they lead "dull, uninspir'd, snail-paced lives." Keats refers to various of his poems, notably to his *Epistle to my brother George*, and also to the introduction to *Sleep and Poetry*, in the lines:

> "Long have I said, how happy he who shrives
> To thee! But then I thought on poets gone,
> And could not pray: — nor could I now — so on
> I move to the end in lowliness of heart."

One cannot help pitying the boy, so out of love with his poem and himself, and yet so rigidly determined to finish it, willy-nilly.

The introduction ends with the lines just quoted, and Keats begins his Fourth Book by plunging at once into a scene without a beginning. A voice is speaking — a woman's voice, lamenting that she has ever left her native land, which, as she mentions the Ganges, we perceive must be India. She bewails her solitary lot and tells how she thirsts for love. This passage lacks the passionate zest of the earlier love speeches; it shows poverty of emotion, a writing from the brain and not from the heart; it is not felt, only thought. Keats is clearly not in cue.

A sort of invocation to Endymion follows, in which he is advised to "vanish into air" rather than observe the maiden's charms, for, says the poet, "Is Phœbe passionless?" But if he must look, behold the maiden!

The voice continues its plaint, begging for love:

> "Ye deaf and senseless minutes of the day,
> And thou, old forest, hold ye this for true,
> There is no lightning, no authentic dew
> But in the eye of love: . . .
>
> . . .
>
> . . . there's not a breath
> Will mingle kindly with the meadow air,
> Till it has panted round, and stolen a share
> Of passion from the heart."

Keats is trying, desperately trying, to bring back the mood of his First and Second Books. It will be remembered that never once throughout the Glaucus story has he been tempted to speak his own sentiments through the mouth of his characters. The First and Second Books are quite as much Keats as Endymion, but in the Glaucus episode Keats is the writer, not the partaker. Suddenly, here, we have Keats again, crying out for his lost interest in his poem — and, a little, in his life too at the moment — with the voice of the Indian maiden. The Glaucus mood is not to end the poem, that is positive; Keats knows, with a rightness of judgment he had not been capable of at Oxford, that he must get back to a sensuous presentation of his story or the whole poem will lose its point and no one will be less pleased with it than he. But still he feels nothing, he only hopes that feeling will come as he goes on.

Endymion, with an immediacy which Keats must have envied, falls in love at once. But this is not, in his case, a matter of rejoicing, for he is ashamed at his own fickleness. He has become reconciled to loving the moon and his unknown goddess at the same time, soothing his soul by considering that, in the case of Diana, his love can be translated as worship. Now here he goes and falls in love with a mortal, which cannot be translated into anything; it is, and he sees it, sheer betrayal. His bewildered mind takes stock of the event accurately enough, and Keats infuses into Endymion's words a considerable degree of surprised, and rather horrified, passion:

> "Goddess! I love thee not the less: from thee
> By Juno's smile I turn not — no, no, no —
> While the great waters are at ebb and flow. —
> I have a triple soul! O fond pretence —
> For both, for both my love is so immense
> I feel my heart is cut in twain for them.
>
> And so he groaned as one by beauty slain."

One can perfectly understand why Keats sent Bailey only the introduction.

With what I consider an unwarrantable high-handedness, Buxton Forman, followed by Professor de Sélincourt, has altered the next to last line of the above quotation. In both the corrected printer's copy and the first edition the line is as I have given it, and rhymeless. Although this is probably another instance of Keats's carelessness, I do not think Buxton Forman's excuse that he found his altered reading, "I feel my heart is cut for them in twain," written in pencil on the margin of the manuscript, a valid reason for adopting it. Keats was not in the habit of correcting his manuscripts with a pencil. I think it far more probable that Woodhouse, who loved to tinker with what he considered infelicities in Keats's poems (witness his rewriting of the last stanza of *In Drear-Nighted December*[1]), is responsible, or even some other friend or later owner. If editors permit themselves such liberties, the result must be a series of garbled texts, of no use to students and thoroughly misleading to general readers. An author's text should be inviolate, and secure from the tampering of no matter how well-meaning an editor.

Endymion's struggle with himself does not last long. A moment more and he springs out of his hiding-place, and with startling abruptness tells the maiden that she has stolen

"... the wings wherewith
I was to top the heavens."

That she is his executioner, since he feels that love and hate, misery and happiness, will "in a few short hours" be nothing to him, that his whole story will be simply that passion has slain him. Amusingly colloquial is his prayer for favour:

"Do smile upon the evening of my days."

The maiden, even while weeping, does not fail to encourage him, very prettily, and very certainly. She asks, and answers herself:

[1] See Vol. I, p. 534.

"Why must such desolation betide
As that thou speakest of? Are not these green nooks
Empty of all misfortune? Do the brooks
Utter a gorgon voice? Does yonder thrush,
Schooling its half-fledg'd little ones to brush
About the dewy forest, whisper tales? —
Speak not of grief, young stranger, or cold snails
Will slime the rose to-night. Though if thou wilt,
Methinks 'twould be a guilt — a very guilt —
Not to companion thee, and sigh away
The light — the dusk — the dark — till break of day."

We should, in passing, note the pregnant condensation of the last line.

Endymion, so urged, immediately declares that he loves her, and that his "days will never last." But, as he is surely about to die, he implores her to speak to him that he may have music in dying, he desires no greater happiness. Then, for a reason which appears to be simply that Keats wants an excuse for the song which follows, Endymion asks the maiden if she had not spoken of India. She replies to this opening with the long song known as the *Ode to Sorrow*, or the *Indian Maiden's Song*. This song is so important, both as poetry and for the many discussions as to its sources, that I must digress from the story a moment to consider it.

In the first place, when was it written? We cannot say exactly, but it was certainly written at Hampstead, since we know that Keats lacked only five hundred lines to complete his poem when he went to Burford Bridge, and, according to the numbering of lines in the first edition, the song begins on line 143. There is also proof in a letter to Jane Reynolds which, as it has never before to my knowledge been published, I will give in full: [1]

"My dear Jane,
When I got home the other night there was a letter from Bailey — and so very kind a one after all my indolence

[1] From a transcript of the original holograph in the Day Collection.

that I felt a very repentence — and finished my letter to him immediately. I hope you are getting well quite fast. I send you a few lines from my fourth Book with the desire of helping away for you five minutes of the day —

O Sorrow
Why dost borrow
hue
The natural ~~line~~ of health from vermeil lips?

To give maiden blushes
To the white rose bushes?
Or ist thy dewy hand the daisy tips?

O Sorrow
Why dost borrow
The lustrous passion from a Lover's eye?

To give the glow worm light?
Or on a moonless night
To tinge on syren shores the salt sea spray?

O Sorrow
Why dost borrow
The mellow dities from a mourning tongue?
To giv't at evening pale
Unto the nightingale
That thou may'st listen the cold dews among?
O Sorrow
Why dost borrow
Hearts lightness from the merriment of May
A lover could not [1] [tread]
A cowslip on the head,
Though he should dance from eve till peep of day —
drooping
Nor any ~~sacred~~ flower
Held sacred for thy bower
Wherever he may sport himself and play.
To Sorrow

[1] In the transcript, the next word is omitted. The published version puts the word "tread" at the end of the line.

I bad good morrow
And thought to leave her far away behind
But cheerly cheerly
She loves me dearly –
She is to me so constant and so kind
I would deceive her
And so leave her
But ah! She is too constant and too kind!

Give our love to Marianne

Yours sincerely
JOHN KEATS."

This letter has neither date nor address, but nevertheless it can be timed with some accuracy. That it was written from Hampstead is certain, as Keats sends "our love," which means his and his brothers', they were, therefore, all together when the letter was written, and, by the twenty-second of November, Keats was at Burford Bridge and his brothers on the point of leaving for Devonshire. Then he says that he has received a letter from Bailey so kind that he finished his own letter to him immediately, and we may be fairly sure that the letter he finished was the one in which he enclosed the introduction to the Fourth Book, as, shortly after speaking of the introduction, he begins a new paragraph by saying, "Thus far had I written when I received your last." How long the letter had been waiting to be finished, we cannot, of course, tell. I think it not unlikely that a week or more elapsed between the two parts of it, which would date this letter to Jane Reynolds as written, probably, during the first week of November. Two additional proofs of this are to be found at the end of the letter to Bailey, for Keats says: "You must forgive, although I have only written three hundred lines; they would have been five, but I have been obliged to go to town," and again: "Yesterday I called at Lamb's." Lamb's is Lamb's Conduit Street, where the Reynoldses lived, and Keats goes on to speak of Jane Reynolds. This last sentence shows clearly that the letter to Jane, where he speaks of the call as having taken place "the other night," was written a day or two after the finish of the letter to Bailey. That the three hundred lines refer to *Endymion* is certain, because the *Indian Maiden's Song* ends, according to Keats's count, on line 288. A bare three hundred lines, then, constituted all that he was able to do in the month after leaving Oxford.

Why did Keats send only the first part of the *Indian Maiden's Song* to Jane Reynolds? Because the whole was too long, or because he thought that the first part would be the one most liked by a young lady? Either supposition is plausible, both may have been true, yet there is another — that he composed the song in sections, and that he had not definitely decided to blend this section with the rest when he wrote his letter. The erased words seem to indicate that the part quoted was still in process of construction at this time. Internal evidence is in favour of a break just at this point, for the style of the song definitely changes here.

One would suppose, on first thoughts, that any consideration of the sources from which Keats got his inspiration for the second part of the song, the *Triumph of Bacchus*, was unnecessary, the legend in all its detail being so well known. True, on first thoughts, but second thoughts lead us a little farther. First and foremost among sources is, of course, Lemprière. Woodhouse, in his interleaved copy so often referred to, repeats the story almost word for word from Lemprière, merely abridging it. But Lemprière gives only the sheerest outline of the legend, naming, however, all the authors whom he has consulted. Now I do not for a moment imagine that Keats first determined to write of Bacchus, and then set to work to hunt the legend down through a score of volumes more or less difficult to obtain. That was not Keats's way. Something had to start him going, and succinct, meticulous Lemprière can hardly have done that. It is generally taken for granted that Ovid was responsible, and we know that Keats had been much occupied with Ovid during the writing of the Third Book; but there are certain things in Keats's lyric which he cannot have found in Ovid, because they are not there. Some of these lie buried in the pages of Rabelais, but only a few. Naturally we must allow Keats the full measure of his imagination; yet when we realize how often, how very often, the initial cause of his inspiration came from his reading, we cannot ignore suggestions apposite to his lines or points of view when we find them in books with which we know he was familiar. The case is altered, and its interest greatly augmented, when we find such suggestions in books which he might have read, but which we have no certain knowledge that he did read. Such a case exists in the *Historical Library* or Diodorus Siculus. Professor John Livingston Lowes first pointed it out to me, as he also did Keats's indebtedness to Rabelais in this connection. Unhappily, his detailed study of the matter[1] has not yet been published, nor have I seen it, but he has courteously permitted me to follow up his suggestions and print the resulting discoveries here. Another reason for thinking that Keats had read Diodorus, I will give in a later chapter, and we shall find still others when we come to consider the sonnet *To the Nile* and the *Ode to a Nightingale*, but, as these belong to a later period than that with which we are now dealing, I shall not touch upon them until they properly arrive. I do not wish to anticipate the chronological progression which I have adopted in telling the story of Keats's life. As I stated at the end of the last chapter, it has seemed best to treat of *Endymion* as a whole, even though, by so doing, I am obliged to outdistance events.

For the reasons which I have referred to, I believe, not only that Keats had read the *Historical Library*, but that

[1] A paper read before the Modern Language Association in December, 1922.

he had read it before he went to Oxford, and been much impressed by the descriptions of exotic countries contained in it. So much impressed, indeed as to resolve to make use of some of them whenever a suitable opening presented itself. If we grant that the episode of Diana wooing Endymion in mortal guise was kept on purpose for the last Book of the poem, we can understand why no trace of anything connected with that episode appears in the Third Book. Keats may have read Diodorus before, after, even during, the composition of the Third Book, but the plan of that book effectually excluded any reference to him.

Diodorus was not a difficult book to get in 1817. On the contrary, it was probably an extremely easy one. Keats, with his inveterate habit of borrowing, may have come across Booth's translation in the folio of 1699 at somebody's house, or he may have read it in the British Museum, since, as I have already said, we know that at some period of his life Haydon procured him a reader's ticket, but the folio is an unlikely possibility, principally because there is no need for it. So recently as 1814, there had appeared a reprint in two octavo volumes which could be bought anywhere. Keats may never have owned it himself — what he owned is the merest fraction of what he read — but again there were the handy collections of his friends, and Diodorus was the kind of book that Keats's set read. We talk about what Keats owned and did not own too much as though we knew the facts. It should never be forgotten that the list given in the Woodhouse volume of transcripts[1] was undoubtedly one made either just before, or just after, Keats's death, for purposes of identification of ownership and to tally lent copies. Keats not only borrowed and lent, he gave away books, and any complete list of his library from first to last would certainly show many more titles than are in the Woodhouse catalogue.

The first great question as regards the disguise Diana chose to assume is: Why an Indian maiden? Why India?

[1] Woodhouse Book. Morgan Collection.

Nothing in *Endymion* hitherto had suggested India — for I believe Bacchus to be the result of India, not India of Bacchus. Diana owes the nationality of her impersonation, I am firmly convinced, to Diodorus. That work abounds in fascinating, apocryphal descriptions of India. According to the imaginative Sicilian, it is a land of enchantment. This mighty, fragrant, and impossible India had the advantage of presenting the poem with a new *mise en scène*; it opened possibilities which Keats only half realized at first; the very name of the place intrigued him, coloured over as it was with the marvellous pictures of Diodorus. An excellent place to languish for, indeed, viewing it through the old historian's eyes. (It is just possible that Diodorus, with his constant mention of Alexander, sent Keats's mind harking back to the little fragment he had written in the lecture room at St. Thomas's, and connotatively to Way's translation of Le Grand's *Fabliaux ou Contes* and his couplet on the Indian maid,[1] but I rather doubt it. It seems too remote.) After India, came Bacchus, though how he was to be brought in Keats did not at once see. Ovid does not emphasize India over the other lands which Bacchus belligerently and triumphantly marched through; Diodorus does, and so does Rabelais — but of that, later.

Now Diodorus gives three separate accounts of Bacchus, or rather, gives an account of the three separate heroes of that name. He is much more exhaustive than Ovid, even than Sandys' commentary on Ovid, and much more interesting. Keats takes the third Bacchus, the son of Jupiter and Semele, for his hero, but mixes him up with the first, who is really Osiris, as is commonly done.

Here is Diodorus, describing, not India in this particular passage, but a mythical island off the coast of Greece:

> "The first entrance into the island runs up a long vale, shaded all along with high and lofty trees, so thick, that

[1] See Vol. I, p. 89.

only a dim and glimmering light passes through; but the fiery beams of the sun enter not in the least to offend the passenger. In passing along, issue many sweet and crystal springs."

The *Triumph of Bacchus* begins:

> "Beneath my palm trees, by the river side,
> I sat a weeping: in the whole world wide
> There was no one to ask me why I wept, —
> And so I kept
> Brimming the water-lilly cups with tears
> Cold as my fears.
>
> Beneath my palm trees, by the river side,
> I sat a weeping: what enamour'd bride,
> Cheated by shadowy wooer from the clouds,
> But hides and shrouds
> Beneath dark palm trees by the river side?"

The scene is that of Diodorus, the "lofty trees" have turned into appropriate palms, often spoken of in the *Historical Library*, the "crystal springs" have widened into a river, the "glimmering light" has given the "shadowy wooer." But Diodorus is not uncompanioned in reminiscence in these two stanzas. There is a hint of *Lycidas* in the brimming lily cups, and more than a dash of Coleridge's peculiar touch of weird suggestion in the last three lines. We are irresistibly reminded of the "woman wailing for her demon lover" in *Kubla Khan*. Keats was reading Coleridge at just this time. In a letter addressed to "My dear Dilke, Mrs. Dilke, or Mr. Wm. Dilke" and dated "this Wednesday morning of Novr. 1817," he asks the loan of *Sibylline Leaves*. *Kubla Khan* was not in the *Sibylline Leaves* volume; it had been printed a year earlier, in 1816, in a little paper-covered pamphlet, together with *Christabel* and the *Pains of Sleep*, so that Keats was already familiar with it, he may even have owned it, certainly many of his friends did.

With the beginning of the third stanza, Diodorus comes markedly to the fore. It starts:

> "And as I sat, over the light blue hills
> There came a noise of revellers: the rills
> Into the wide stream came of purple hue —
> 'Twas Bacchus and his crew!
> The earnest trumpet spake, and silver thrills
> From kissing cymbals made a merry din —"

The "light blue hills" might perfectly well be actual remembrance of a real scene, were it not for the fact that Keats had never been anywhere where he could have seen hills high enough to make a blue horizon. Margate, Hastings, the Isle of Wight, Oxford, Stratford-on-Avon, London and its suburbs — these were the only places he had been to before this Autumn of 1817, unless, indeed, the Lulworth Cove suggestion [1] be of any importance, in which case the coast of Dorsetshire and the road thereto should be added to the list. He had probably read of distant blue hills all his life, but he must have met them again in the Third Book of Diodorus where they are admirably sketched, although without absolute colour, in this passage:

> "This coast has very few harbours in it, by reason of the many vast mountains that lie all along as they sail; from whence is presented to the view such variety of colours, that they afford a most wonderful and delightful prospect to the passengers at sea as they sail along."

Keats's "rills" are, of course, the "springs" of the "lofty tree" passage already quoted, and the stream coming "of purple hue" is taken almost bodily from this same Third Book, where Diodorus, relating that the Teians believed their city to be the birthplace of Bacchus, says:

"The Teians, for confirmation of what they say, bring

[1] See Vol. I, p. 7.

> this argument, that there is a spring in their city, which at certain times streams forth most rich and fragrant wine."

When it comes to the instruments, Keats both follows and leaves Diodorus, for Diodorus distinctly states that "in the heat of battle he made use of timbrels and cymbals; the trumpet being not at that time found out." This seems plain enough; but what does exact archeology matter to a poet, particularly when his instructor is anything but exact himself? In Sandys' translation of Ovid, the instruments are given as sac-buts and timbrels, and to the latter Keats much preferred Diodorus's cymbals, and naturally so, considering that he promptly married them to the happy adjective, "kissing." But Keats wanted trumpets, and the sac-buts gave him a sufficient excuse; an even better one added its weight, for Rabelais makes Bacchus's army advance to the sound of "cornets." The rest of the stanza is simply derived from general accounts of the legend, and particular excursions of Keats's own for the sake of bringing in the maiden.

In the next stanza comes Bacchus, and this is the Bacchus of Keats:

> "Within his car, aloft, young Bacchus stood,
> Trifling his ivy-dart, in dancing mood,
> With sidelong laughing;
> And little rills of crimson wine imbrued
> His plump white arms, and shoulders, enough white
> For Venus' pearly bite."

Ovid accosts his Bacchus in this wise:

> ". . . Still dost thou injoy
> Unwasted youth; eternally a Boy!
> Thou'rt seene in heaven; whom all perfections grace;
> And, when unhorn'd, thou hast a Virgin's face."

This is Sandys rendering Ovid, of course, and Woodhouse's catalogue of Keats's books shows him to have owned Ovid both in translation and in the original Latin, but he was much more familiar with the former. This Bacchus, joint production of Latin poet and English translator, is a very pale and staid personage compared to Keats's Bacchus. Far more lively and wanton, a much better prototype for this Bacchus of Keats, is that of Diodorus. "Being," says Diodorus, "a very beautiful young man, he spent the time of his youth in dancing, plays, and all manner of sports and pastimes." And later Diodorus describes him even more vividly:

> "They say, likewise, that the son of Semele . . . was of a slender and delicate shape of body, and most comely feature, exceeding amorous, and addicted to the sports of Venus."

This is a laughing, dancing, sporting, and rather lascivious young Bacchus, as is Keats's, but he is slender. Where did Keats get the idea of the plump shoulders then? Out of Rabelais, to be sure. For Rabelais's Bacchus "looked as young as a child . . . He was as red as a cherry, or a cherub, which you please, and had no more hair on his chin than there's in the inside of my hand."

The stanza ends with an emasculated picture of Silenus who, instead of "reeling still" and weakly hanging upon his ass, as Ovid has him — the abominable old drunkard of Diodorus and Rabelais — is pelted with flowers, and his actions in his cups are refined to the fact that he is "tipsily quaffing." In this we see another illustration of Keats's desire to smooth. It is even more in evidence in the next stanza, which describes the Mænads. In Ovid, they are "light Baccides," which is simply to beg the whole question; Sandys in his commentary is not so squeamish. He describes the Bacchic orgies of the Theban women imitating the Mænads with a forthright hand. There is no joy in his account, the ladies are very certainly the victims of "the furious effects of wine." Even Diodorus, whose

Mænads are "excellent singers," exceedingly merry, "armed with lances, and adorned with garlands of flowers," is obliged to admit that their descendants, the women of the Bacchanalia, ran about "like furies, hallooing and setting forth the praises of the god." How tame are Keats's Mænads in comparison with these! They seem agreeable young persons, lured but recently from their embroidery frames, starting out on a picnic. But they are gay, contagiously gay:

> "Whence came ye, merry Damsels! whence came ye!
> So many, and so many, and such glee?
> Why have ye left your bowers desolate,
> Your lutes, and gentler fate? —
> 'We follow Bacchus! Bacchus on the wing,
> A conquering!
> Bacchus, young Bacchus! good or ill betide,
> We dance before him thorough kingdoms wide:—
> Come hither, lady fair, and joined be
> To our wild minstrelsy!'"

But the minstrelsy is not so very wild after all. The stanza is a mere sugar-plum affair, tricked out with a little gilding and tied with a pink sash. This is confectionery, quite attractive confectionery, but not poetry. Yet it must be admitted that it is swift with movement, and that is an effect worth achieving. One interesting thing about it is that the Mænad's cry, "Bacchus on the wing" proves conclusively that Keats had Rabelais in his mind when he was writing the song. Of course, the obvious meaning is Bacchus on the march, Bacchus flying from country to country; but, although Keats probably meant this, he also meant much more. In the Fourth Book of Rabelais, he had most certainly come across this:

> "Formerly the Amycleans worshipped the noble Bacchus above all other gods, and gave him the name of Psila, which in the Doric dialect signifies wings; for, as the birds raise themselves by a towering flight with their wings

> above the clouds, so, with the help of soaring Bacchus, the powerful juice of the grape, our spirits are exalted to a pitch above themselves, our bodies are more sprightly, and their earthly parts become soft and pliant."

The Mænad's cry, read in the light of this passage, goes far to redeem the stanza.

The Satyrs, in the sixth stanza, are the conventional ones of every retailer of the legend. Ovid speaks of them as "skipping satyrs." Diodorus enlarges upon their sprightliness:

> "The satyrs, who are naturally inclined to skipping, dancing, and singing, and all other sorts of mirth, were taken in as part of the army."

This is in the First Book; in the Fourth, he mentions them again:

> "They say, likewise, that he carried satyrs along with him, who by their dancing and skipping in his sports and plays, made the god exceeding merry."

Keats's satyrs only "skip" by implication. By following the very words of the preceding stanza in the first two lines and again in the last two, he gives the effect of a dance with its necessary repetitions; both Mænads and Satyrs dance the same measure, first one group passes by and then the other. But these Keatsian Satyrs are chiefly remarkable for their kinship to the Satyr in Beaumont and Fletcher's *Faithful Shepherdess*. The country they have left is none of those through which Bacchus marched; if we are to judge it by its flora, it must be England. This is a cheerful geographical anachronism. Keats, knowing nothing about India pertinent to the Satyrs, gives them heath, mushrooms, and broom, which is probably not so much due to reading as to some walk over Hampstead Heath to Caen Wood.

The seventh stanza is so interesting for its derivations that I must quote it entire:

"Over wide streams and mountains great we went,
And, save when Bacchus kept his ivy tent,
Onward the tiger and the leopard pants,
    With Asian elephants:
Onward these myriads — with song and dance,
With zebras striped, and sleek Arabians' prance,
Web-footed alligators, crocodiles,
Bearing upon their scaly backs, in files,
Plump infant laughers mimicking the coil
Of seamen, and stout galley-rowers' toil:
With toying oars and silken sails they glide,
    Nor care for wind and tide.
Mounted on panthers' furs and lions' manes,
From rear to van they scour about the plains;
A three days' journey in a moment done:
And always, at the rising of the sun,
About the wilds they hunt with spear and horn,
    On spleenful unicorn."

According to Diodorus: "Osiris, being come to the borders of Ethiopia . . . Thence he passed through Arabia, bordering upon the Red sea as far as to India." (It was in Ethiopia, Diodorus says, that "a company of Satyrs were presented to him.") All these countries and many more, such as Egypt, Abyssinia, etc. are exhaustively described by Diodorus. Truly, to read him is to pass over "streams and mountains" galore, and these descriptions added many a touch to this *Triumph of Bacchus.* For instance, Diodorus, coming to Arabia, speaks of "lions, wolves, and leopards, out of the deserts"; Arabia, too, gave Keats the connotative idea of the "sleek Arabians." The tigers come from Sandys' commentary of Ovid's Fourth Book, where they are called "Gangetic tygres," but it is noticeable that Ovid states that Bacchus's chariot was drawn by lynxes, and Keats eschews the lynx. He does not mention specifically what sort of beasts drew Bacchus's car, but he had plenty of choice, for Rabelais sends the god into battle with leopards, and marches him triumphantly away harnessed to elephants — those "Asian elephants," gloriously given a line all by themselves! Ovid has no elephants, but they tramp up and down the pages of Diodorus in herds: India affords "plentiful pastures for multitudes of mighty elephants"; "India breeds the largest, most courageous, and strongest elephants of any other place"; Bacchus "was the first in triumph mounted upon an Indian elephant"; Osiris "addicted himself much to hunting of elephants." There is a wonderful account, which Keats must have delighted in, but which space forbids me to quote, of the method employed by the Ethiopians to kill elephants. Keats chose to take his elephants from Asia, doubtless because of the sound of the word "Asian," but that is a trifle. Keats invents the zebras, as he also does the alligators, but these last owe their existence to the crocodiles, who come directly from Diodorus, for the old historian assures us that "there are crocodiles and river-horses in Egypt," and that "the river Nile breeds many creatures of several forms and shapes . . . the crocodile . . . its skin is covered all over with scales of an extraordinary hardness." Note that the "infant laughers" ride on the "scaly backs" of crocodiles. This episode refers to the legend that Bacchus had once been taken prisoner by the Thuscan pirates. Given the legend, and given the crocodiles — but what, if anything, gave the infants on their backs? Again it is Rabelais. In his Fifth Book, shortly after the description of the Bacchus pictures, we read:

> ". . . round the body of the crystal lamp there was carved in cataglyphic work a lively and pleasant battle of naked boys, mounted on little hobby-horses, with little whirligig lances and shields that seemed made of vine-branches with grapes on them; their postures generally were very different, and their childish strife and motions were so ingeniously expressed that art equalled nature in every proportion and action."

The "whirligig lances and shields" and the "childish strife and motions" are responsible for

> "... the coil
> Of seamen, and stout galley-rowers toil"

mimicked by Keats's "infant laughers." Of no great importance, except that we happen, for the moment, to be tracing these things, is the parallel between Keats's "Nor care for wind and tide," and Coleridge's line "Withouten wind, withouten tide," in the *Ancient Mariner*, published in *Sibylline Leaves*.

Continuing with Keats's menagerie, the "panthers' furs" are obvious, for the panther was sacred to Bacchus; but the unicorn brings us back to Rabelais, whose "cornets" again figure in the "horns" to the notes of which Bacchus's army went a-hunting. These unicorns are "a curst sort of creatures" declares Rabelais, and he ought to know as he saw "two and thirty" of them, "out of each of their foreheads sprouts out a sharp black horn, some six or seven feet long; commonly it dangles down like a turkey-cock's comb. When a unicorn has a mind to fight, or put it to any other use, what does it do but make it stand, and then 'tis as straight as an arrow." It is evident that such an animal deserves the adjective "spleenful."

Coming to the eighth stanza, Professor de Sélincourt thinks that "Osirian Egypt" is taken from Milton's *Ode to the Nativity*. It may be; but, considering the number of pages devoted to Osiris in Diodorus, I think it a most natural expression without any necessity to look elsewhere for it. Nor need we seek Milton's "heathen deities vailing their might before the infant Christ," to quote Professor de Sélincourt, in Keats's "parch'd Abyssinia," "old Tartary," "kings of Inde," "Brahma," etc. falling under the yoke of Bacchus. This is part and parcel of the legend specifically amplified by imagination. Abyssinia is again from Diodorus, even the word "parch'd" appears in one of his descriptions, although it is connected with Ethiopia, not Abyssinia. These transpositions are all in the poet's, any poet's, way of working. The passage runs:

> "By reason of the scorching heat, and want of both spring and river water, the grass is parched up, and none to be had."

This resemblance might seem far-fetched if it stood by itself, but when we find Keats so often leaning upon, and paraphrasing, Diodorus, it is not unreasonable to assume that in reading this sentence he was struck by the word "parched," so vividly illustrated by Diodorus, and made use of it here.

At the end of the stanza, the Indian maiden tells how she strayed away from Bacchus's company and wandered alone until the meeting with Endymion.

Three final stanzas return to the metre and sentiment of the beginning of the poem.

Titian's picture, *Bacchus and Ariadne*, in the National Gallery, London, is commonly supposed to have been Keats's chief source of inspiration in the *Triumph of Bacchus*. An idea which I do not subscribe to at all. In the first place, Keats does not mention Ariadne, who, indeed, belongs to a subsidiary myth. In the second place, the mood of the picture is quite different from the mood of Keats's poem. Sir Sidney Colvin's contention that Keats was more often moved to poetry by things he saw than by things he read, cannot, I believe, be substantiated. He saw the *Grecian Urn*, but he read Chapman's *Homer*; he heard the *Nightingale*, but he read of Endymion; he walked out of Winchester on an Autumn day, but he was extremely familiar with Boccaccio; the *Eve of Saint Agnes* is pure, digested, etherealized folk-lore, so is the *Eve of Saint Mark*; *Lamia* was read of, so was *Hyperion*; *Meg Merrilies* is a book tale at second hand, *La Belle Dame Sans Merci* sprang from library shelves.

In spite of Keats's extraordinary powers of observation, and his delight in certain pictures, if it be the initial inspiration which Sir Sidney refers to, I think the palm goes to reading. The sources of the *Triumph of Bacchus* do, indeed, the more carefully we examine them, boil down to Ovid, Diodorus Siculus, and Rabelais.

Speaking of this *Indian Maiden's Song*, Dr. Robert Bridges makes an amazing statement.[1] He declares it to be "unmatched for life, wide motion, and romantic dreamy Orientalism." I find none of these things in it, except the motion. It is too artificial to contain much life. The procession is an amusing picture, but it is not in the least Oriental. I wish I knew what Dr. Bridges means by "romantic, dreamy Orientalism." Dreamy romance is certainly not a quality of Greek literature, and one may search the Bible, that great storehouse of Hebrew texts, without finding anything to qualify; Egyptian literature has no trace of it, and never once in my delvings into the literatures of China and Japan have I come across anything to which the term might fitly be given. The Hindu may supply us with mysticism, even, perhaps, if one chooses to call it so, romance, but scarcely, I think, of the type to which "dreamy" would apply. Persian literature comes the nearest, but the romantic dreams of Persia are so entirely based upon eroticism that any comparison between them and Keats's lyric simply cannot be made. Keats knew nothing of any Oriental state of mind; to most English speaking people, the Bible is not a study for comparative literature, but a document of faith, and there is no evidence that Keats ever escaped from this point of view and read it as a book like other books. After all, how could the song be Oriental, considering that the legend on which it is based reached Keats through the medium of a Roman, a Sicilian, and a Frenchman? All that is dreamy in the poem are the first two stanzas of the *Triumph of Bacchus* section, and this is Coleridge's dream, which is *Kubla*

[1] *John Keats. A Critical Essay*, by Robert Bridges. 1895.

Khan, derived from old travellers' tales of the Orient, it is true, but changed and transmuted by Coleridge into universal beauty.

If we examine the song, we are immediately struck by the fact that there are two breaks in it; one, which I have already pointed out, following immediately upon the *Ode to Sorrow* section, and one after the first two stanzas of the *Triumph of Bacchus* section. That the *Ode to Sorrow* was originally intended to be a song by itself seems most probable, particularly as we know that Keats copied it, and it alone, in the letter to Jane Reynolds already quoted. After it comes so decided a change in the temper of the song that I feel certain the stanzas immediately following it represent an entirely new beginning. Keats had been reading Coleridge, and these two new stanzas have so much of the flavour of Coleridge in them that I think, in all likelihood, Keats jotted them down while the mood induced by Coleridge was strong upon him. I doubt whether he knew how the poem so begun was to go on. He was under the spell of Coleridge, and tried his hand at the same sort of thing. Two reasons must have brought him up short; the first, the difficulty of doing Coleridge's type of thing as well as Coleridge did it; the second, the unwisdom of doing it at all. With a determined round-about-face, Keats took up the Bacchus theme which he had already decided was to go in somewhere. He took his cue from the scene he had found in Diodorus and lit with Coleridge's sun, and continued the poem in an entirely different key.

Here then, is a poem, an unrelated poem; he likes it and wonders where he can fit it in. The plot of his Fourth Book is already fairly well laid down — as to episode, at any rate — and this seems the only place where the Bacchus lyric can possibly go; so he hitches it, rather awkwardly, to the *Ode to Sorrow* and adds the last three stanzas to make the hitching plausible. It is an ingenious bit of literary cabinet work, but, for all his efforts, the song remains two distinct poems.

Probably some time elapsed between the writing of the *Ode to Sorrow* and the final blending of it with the *Triumph of Bacchus*. Each represents a lyric mood. Keats is getting on badly with *Endymion*, he is in a fever to follow those various hints and suggestions which are forever flowing into a poet's mind. It was a relief to write the *Ode to Sorrow*; but another mood seizes him and again it is a relief to do the *Triumph of Bacchus*, which represents a rebound from an abortive Coleridge mood. The poem, then, is psychologically interesting as showing Keats utterly weary of sticking to his last, represented by *Endymion*, but teeming with desires leading to other things. The *Ode to Sorrow* is poor, he cannot quite get his stride, much as he wants to write it. He dashes at Coleridge and knows he is baffled, and falls upon the *Triumph of Bacchus* in a kind of "well-if-I-can't-do-that-I-can-do-this" state of mind. And he does it, and feels infinitely better afterwards.

The Bacchus lyric has been extravagantly praised, rather out of proportion to its merits, I fear. What is chiefly interesting in it is its rhythm. Luckily for Keats, this new rhythm makes an excellent foil to that of the *Ode to Sorrow*. Again Keats tries the occasional, irregularly repeated short line, and succeeds admirably with it. When we consider that the metre is exactly that of the *Hymn to Pan*, differentiated only by the use of more short lines and a slightly irregular rhyming scheme, we shall be forcibly struck with how great a change of movement Keats has managed to bring into it. Metres do not always determine rhythms, and rhythmically the *Triumph of Bacchus* is as far from the rhythm of the *Hymn to Pan* as can well be. What Keats did not do in the *Hymn to Neptune*, he has done triumphantly here. It is not only variation within a pattern; it is the taking of an excellent pattern, full of its own variations, and so altering it, and varying it from the alteration, that the result is a feat of technical skill.

As a poem, however, the *Triumph of Bacchus* is not in the same class with the *Hymn to Pan*. Keats is master of his medium in the Bacchus; the *Hymn to Pan* masters him. In one case, he is possessed and transcended; in the other, he remains outside and guides. Poems consciously composed may reach a very high plane, but never so high a one as poems subconsciously composed. It may be said that Keats wrote the *Triumph of Bacchus*; but that the *Hymn to Pan* wrote itself. I am not taking into consideration corrections made after the heat of composition is over, because, strange as it may seem, they have almost nothing to do with whether the original draft is done subconsciously or not. A common reason for them is that the subconscious mind dictates too fast for the poet to follow; again, the connection between the subconscious and the conscious minds may break, here and there, leaving holes which the poet must fill as best he can. It is, nevertheless, a fact that Keats made many more corrections in the *Triumph of Bacchus* than he did in the *Hymn to Pan*.

The Bacchus poem is, apart from its rhythm, a marvellous achievement in condensation. If any one will take the trouble to read Ovid, Diodorus, and Rabelais with an attention to detail, and then turn to this poem and see how much of this detail Keats has been able to force into service in his eight stanzas, that person will, I think, be amazed. It is this extraordinary wealth of detail, doubtless, which has confused Dr. Bridges into declaring the poem "unmatched for life." It is not life which is here, but literature; and what raises it from verse well done to poetry, is, uniquely, its rhythm.

The line immediately following the song is:

"O what a sigh she gave in finishing."

At which we cannot help smiling. For the sigh is evidently

autobiographical. The song did Keats good; it set him on his feet once more, and started him going at a swifter rate than had been possible to him for some time.

I have analyzed the *Triumph of Bacchus* at so great a length, because no other poem shows with equal clarity how Keats worked when he was writing to a theme. Usually, many as are the echoes he permits himself, he does not adhere as strictly as this to his sources. I do not mean that his treatment in this poem is not original; it is, very. But his method here is somewhat akin to the old game, where, given a word and a question, each player must write a poem bringing in the word and answering the question. Another important motive for the long survey I have made of this particular poem is that no previous biographer has noted its connection with the works of Diodorus and of Rabelais, and Professor Lowes's study, not being yet in print, is for the time being inaccessible.

Keats resumes his narrative with the weary and wistful line I quoted a moment ago. The Indian maiden is utterly exhausted by the account of her miseries. Endymion, speechless, listens to

> ". . . the wind that now did stir
> About the crisped oaks full drearily,
> Yet with as sweet a softness as might be
> Remember'd from its velvet summer song."

These lines are in Keats's most charming outdoor manner, and we see in them his inveterate tendency throughout *Endymion* to make the seasons of the poem coincide with the seasons in which he is writing. It was Spring when he began the poem, and it is Spring and early Summer during the whole of the First Book. The rose and butterfly of the Second Book give us Summer a little more advanced, and the moon passages of the Third Book are obviously August pictures. Now it is Autumn, and the Fourth Book reflects the first touch of Autumnal change.

Endymion rouses himself to speak to the maiden, and proceeds to make love in what is easily the worst love passage of the poem. How bad it is can be inferred by the expression, "thine other softling" in speaking of one of the lady's hands. In spite of his fervent love making, he is troubled with qualms of conscience, and he begs the maiden not to let him think. Suddenly the words "Woe to that Endymion! Where is he?" echo through the forest. The lovers clasp each other trembling:

> "... when lo,
> Foot-feather'd Mercury appear'd sublime
> Beyond the tall tree tops; and in less time
> Than shoots the slanted hail-storm, down he dropt
> Towards the ground."

No one, comparing this descent of Mercury with the departure of Circe in the Third Book, can fail to be astonished by the excellence of the figures employed to describe the different effects of movement which Keats wished to convey.

Mercury, veering down to earth, delays only long enough to touch the ground with his wand and instantly darts up again and disappears. Immediately two black horses spring out of the turf, Endymion places the Indian maiden on one, vaults upon the other himself, and they are off on the skyey flight which Keats, as we saw at the beginning of this chapter, borrowed from Drayton. Through the "sleepy dusk" they fly. They meet Sleep, drowsily floating toward heaven "to hear the marriage melodies" of a goddess with a mortal. At his approach, the horses spread their wings on the mist and fall asleep, and outstretched upon these same wings Endymion and the Indian maiden also slumber. In his sleep, Endymion dreams that he is in heaven, surrounded by the gods and goddesses, walking and talking among them. The Seasons appear and join in a dance with the Hours. They demand of one another who this mortal may be, and answer one another that it is the beloved of Diana. "Lo," they cry, "she rises crescented." Endymion looks,

> ". . . 'tis she,
> His very goddess: good-bye earth, and sea,
> And air, and pains, and care, and suffering;
> Good-bye to all but love!"

Apparently, at the sight of Diana, Endymion realizes at last that she and no other is the goddess he has loved so long and sought through earth, ocean, and sky. He springs toward her and awakes, but to his astonishment he finds himself still among the whole company of gods and goddesses. Diana bends to him; but, as she does so, Endymion is aware of the Indian maiden sleeping at his side. He feels himself cruelly torn between his two loves. His heart surges toward Diana "as to its rightful throne," yet the Indian maiden is so beautiful he cannot refrain from kissing her. He craves forgiveness of his bright goddess, and immediately kisses the Indian maiden again. At this last kiss, the goddess weeps and melts into the air. Endymion, distracted, cries to her to stay, to search his heart. The cry ends with the despairing words:

> ". . . Is there nought for me
> Upon the bourne of bliss, but misery?"

Endymion's cry wakes the Indian maiden, and while he insists that they must leave "this murky phantasm" because it would be a horrible thing if she were to die from his "heart-treachery," she weeps. He longs to be "whole in love" as is she, and yet he assures her that he feels perfectly innocent. He can see no end, only his spirit flitting solitary through the dark. In an agony of confusion and shame at his divided loyalty, he arouses the horses, who carry the lovers on across a sky fading from sunset into night.

The work had been going fairly well since the beginning of the *Triumph of Bacchus*, but at this point there was another break; Keats went to Burford Bridge. Things had not been altogether peaceful at Hampstead. Hunt had lectured him about his poem, Tom Keats's health had become a subject of anxiety, and there were other things to tease and distract. I will not anticipate; all these worries will appear in due course in the next chapter. I merely allude to them here as a cause for Keats's decision to seek solitude and change of scenery. The exact spot in the poem at which this break occurred is determined by a couple of sentences in letters written to Reynolds and Bailey just after his arrival at Burford Bridge. To Bailey, he writes:

> "At present, I am just arrived at Dorking — to change the Scene — change the Air, and give me a spur to wind up my Poem, of which there are wanting 500 lines."

Line 497 of this Fourth Book, by Keats's reckoning, immediately precedes one of those divisions in the narrative which serve to indicate a change of some sort; they may, indeed, be considered in the light of stanzaic pauses. As it seems most likely that Keats would delay a journey, the date of which was unimportant, until some such pause was reached, it is probable that this particular pause represents what of the Fourth Book was written before he went to Burford Bridge. "Five hundred lines" was approximate, not actual, for obviously no one would say "There are wanting five hundred and three lines to finish my poem," particularly if the number of lines to be completed were also approximate as, in this case, they naturally were. But there is a farther proof which makes it certain that the break was just here. The letter to Reynolds tells a very important piece of news, for in it Keats says, quite casually:

> "I like this place very much. There is Hill and Dale and

a little River. I went up Box hill this Evening after the moon — 'you a' seen the Moon' — came down, and wrote some lines."

Now the next lines after the pause are these:

> "Full facing their swift flight, from ebon streak,
> The moon put forth a little diamond peak,
> No bigger than an unobserved star,
> Or tiny point of fairy scymetar;
> Bright signal that she only stoop'd to tie
> Her silver sandals, ere deliciously
> She bow'd into the heavens her timid head."

How many the "some lines" were, we do not know. They seem to have been a good many, for he quotes to Reynolds from the wedding song of the multitudes, beginning at the line, "Crystalline brother of the belt of Heaven" to "Haste, haste away." But we may be certain that the moon, drifted over by clouds through which it partially emerges with an extreme of shining every now and then, was the moon seen from Box Hill on that twenty-second day of November, 1817.

Keats might not have mentioned these lines to Bailey in any case, but a very cogent reason for not mentioning them is that they were not written at the time he wrote. Buxton Forman puts the letter to Reynolds before the letter to Bailey in his editions, but I think he is in error, because of these two passages. I believe that Keats wrote his letter to Bailey either the day before, on November twenty-first, or in the morning or afternoon of the twenty-second, for I own this letter, and the postmark is "Leatherhead, 22 NO. 1817." The letter itself is undated, Buxton Forman dates it from the postmark alone. But Leatherhead was evidently the post town, for Burford Bridge was merely a hamlet at that time, and it is scarcely likely that a letter written in the evening would be postmarked at a town three miles distant on the same night, even though the mail did not go out until after eleven. That it must have been written in the evening if it were written after the letter to Reynolds is clear, as in the letter to Reynolds Keats says, "I went up Box hill this Evening." The Reynolds letter is dated "Leatherhead, 22 November, 1817," which is to give Reynolds his postal address, of course, as Reynolds, who had been seeing him constantly in London, must have known where he was staying. Buxton Forman gives no postmark, and I have not seen the holograph, but undoubtedly the letter was sent the next day and so would have been postmarked November twenty-third.

Many have been the speculations by both readers and critics as to which were the lines that Keats wrote after coming down from Box Hill that evening, but no one hitherto, apparently, has thought of the simple expedient of counting lines and gauging probabilities. I offer my argument and its results for what they are worth.

Coleridge crops up again in the little diamond moon peak, "No bigger than an unobserved star," for one of the most vividly imagined pictures in the *Ancient Mariner* is the one where

> "All in a hot and copper sky
> The bloody sun, at noon,
> Right up above the mast did stand,
> No bigger than the moon."

At the sight of the moon sailing through the clouds, Endymion looks to see if the Indian maiden has noticed its wonderful beauty, and, to his horrified eyes, her body seems to be fading. He seizes her wrist and finds that it is his own hand which he is grasping. This line is another of the mateless ones scattered all through the poem. That the loss of the companion line was unintentional, would seem proved by the cacophony of this, which reads:

> "And, horror! Kiss'd his own — he was alone."

Buxton Forman is surely correct in his surmise that the line "was condensed from a roughly drafted couplet in which 'own' rhymed with 'alone.'"

The lady vanished, her steed "dropt hawkwise to the earth." Not so Endymion's charger, who still bears him on through the sky. Here follows a passage of great beauty in which Keats, under a figure, exemplifies the old adage that it is always darkest before dawn. He describes the soul, tormented with grief, falling into a deep sleep. In this sleep, all miseries are forgotten, there is only the consciousness of a vague sense of well-being. This passage is certainly not autobiographical, except in a general sense. Keats was not unhappy at this time, and he was very far from being numb. I mention this as so many passages in *Endymion* have reference to Keats's state of feeling and being at the time of writing; this one, however, has no such significance. He is either remembering some state of mind experienced long before, or merely projecting his imagination into a possible one.

Endymion, asleep or entranced, it is not quite clear which, fails to notice a multitude which passes him singing. But if he does not see, he does, it seems, hear, for the song ends abruptly, because

> ". . . More
> Endymion heard not."

The beginning of this song is quite charming, with its catalogue of flowers and herbs written in that simple, effective style which is so peculiarly English, to be copied by no other nation whatsoever. It has persisted in English poetry ever since the days of Chaucer, and is one of the chief delights of the Elizabethans. It seems almost a property of the soil, for expatriated Englishmen soon lose the touch, and as to poets of other countries, I can think of no single instance in which one has captured it. The song, which is an epithalamium for Diana, proceeds with a long allusion to the signs of the zodiac and their actions on this auspicious night. The signs of the zodiac, it will be remembered, constituted one of the parallels between Keats's poem and Drayton's *Endimion and Phœbe.* This song is in the same metre as the two *Hymns* and the *Triumph of Bacchus,* yet again it has a totally different effect, although this time the result seems to be chiefly a lack of effect. We are not struck with its rhythm; it is without any defined movement other than an unruffled, continuous flow, and in this very fact we see another evidence of Keats's skill in the use of the form.

As the song ceases to be heard, Endymion's horse sweeps down with him

> "Prone to the green head of a misty hill"

which is, of course, Box Hill, seen from Norbury Park or some other place where Keats had been in his walks.

The touch of the earth beneath his feet arouses Endymion, but it also brings back to him the memory of his lost mortal love, the Indian maiden. All at once, he hears her voice, and sees her lying on the grass. The exaltation of his flight is gone, once more he pines for the human contact he believes he has enjoyed with her. If only she will return to him he will be satisfied and give up forever his heavenward aspirations. Very well conceived are his words:

> ". . . I have clung
> To nothing, lov'd a nothing, nothing seen
> Or felt but a great dream."

This again is drama, as is the whole passage, which is also poetically excellent, although, in spots, a bit florid and Watteau-like. One the whole, however, this is one of the successful passages of the poem. The companionship of woods, fields, and streams, always set Keats off, to use his own expression, "like a cannon-ball." This is plainly Autumn at Box Hill:

"... Under the brow
Of some steep mossy hill, where ivy dun
Would hide us up, although spring leaves were none;
And where dark yew trees, as we rustle through,
Will drop their scarlet berry cups of dew?
O thou wouldst joy to live in such a place."

Keats was certainly "joying" in just such a place himself when he wrote that.

Following what now seems his desire, Endymion declares that he will seek "cloudy phantasms" no more. He bids them good-bye:

"... Caverns lone, farewell!
And air of visions, and the monstrous swell
Of visionary seas! No, never more
Shall airy voices cheat me to the shore
Of tangled wonder, breathless and aghast."

He will devote himself henceforward to his Indian maiden, yet not without a slight pang of regret for the goddess of his dream:

"... Although so vast
My love is still for thee. The hour may come
When we shall meet in pure elysium.
On earth I may not love thee."

He will make offerings to Diana if only she will shine on, and bless, his other love. He then turns to the pleasures he will contrive for the Indian maiden, and it is the account of them which brings Watteau to mind. Dainty conceits, these, in an eighteenth century vein, as where he says:

" I will entice this crystal rill to trace
Love's silver name upon the meadow's face."

Hearing him, the Indian maiden again weeps, although happiness shines in her eyes, a cheering omen which Endymion fails to discover. She answers him in a way that must have been fairly distracting, since she speaks partly as Diana, partly as the Indian maiden. Hitherto she has been herself and her disguise by turns, but now she mingles both these personalities in what she says. The game of hide and seek which Diana plays all through this Fourth Book, popping in and out of her assumed personality, is decidedly intriguing, although it needs close attention on the part of a reader to follow her changes of individuality. Now she calls on Eros, declaring him cruel to her. She cries out that she has always believed in his kindness and that he would befriend her, but she finds herself bitterly wronged. She informs Endymion that she may not be his; it is forbidden. But from whom this prohibition emanates, she is very careful not to say. They might embrace and die, to be sure, the victims of an obscure vengeance, but she prefers to bless and leave him.

Endymion takes this baffling speech in good faith, it seems, and never guesses that again he has to do with the goddess. Beaten by her assurance that they must part, he has nothing to say, and the two wander on dolefully. After a while, Diana cannot bear his gloom. In a cryptic utterance, she announces that "felicity has been thy meed for many thousand years," and hints that he is now more than mortal. That Diana is merely teasing him with her declaration that all is over for them, is quite evident, since heaven is already agog with her approaching marriage. By this time, the lovers have arrived at the very stream-side where Endymion had "his first soft poppy dream," but he is too miserable to recognize it. He does not even observe that Diana is smiling. Then he sees that someone else is there, and this someone is staring at him. It is his sister Peona.

Peona is greatly distressed at the sight of Endymion's sorrow, particularly as he is "hand in hand with one so beautiful." Are the two of them, perhaps, "too happy to be glad?" She begs them to "feel as if it were a common day," which is perfect psychology, finely expressed, even if Keats did cull "common day" from Wordsworth's *Ode to Immortality*, as Professor de Sélincourt thinks. She tells the Indian maiden that she shall be the queen of the shepherd folk and that to-night there is to be a festival to Diana; Endymion has been believed dead, and his return will bring a great rejoicing.

Endymion, in another line of intimate psychological perception on Keats's part,

> "Bent his soul fiercely like a spiritual bow,
> And twang'd it inwardly."

The upshot of the matter is that he accepts his fate. He does not tell Peona this, as she knows nothing about what has passed, but he declares that he would have Peona his only friend, the only person he sees, for he is resolved to be a hermit, and asks her to allow the Indian maiden to live with her henceforward. Diana pretends to be very grateful for the suggestion which gives her a home at last, and says that she will become a priestess of Diana, and that

> ". . . this very night shall see
> My future days to her fane consecrate."

They are all a little confused, except possibly Diana. They try to keep up their spirits by talking as though these remarkable suggestions were perfectly natural and in the due course of things. Endymion is the first to realize that an end must precede a beginning. He bids them goodbye, and Peona, with the disguised Diana, walks "dizzily away." They have no sooner been lost to sight in a cypress grove than Endymion calls after them. But it is too late; they have gone.

Endymion can endure no more. Down he lies, as he always does in any crisis, but this time he is unvisited by either dream or vision. So he remains

"All the long day; save when he scantly lifted
His eyes abroad, to see how shadows shifted
With the slow move of time, — sluggish and weary
Until the poplar tops, in journey dreary,
Had reach'd the river's brim."

How briefly and surely Keats has caught the shadows of the high poplars stealing imperceptibly upon the still sunny river!

Evening having come, Endymion starts off for the temple. He had shouted into the cypress wood for Peona and the Indian maiden to meet him there that he might take a last farewell of his beloved, but, as no answer was vouchsafed him, he is ignorant of whether they heard or not.

It is a beautiful evening of early Autumn. Endymion notices all its loveliness as he goes along, thinking what a wonderful time it is for his last meeting with his Indian lady. He considers that he will, that very night, die; meaning, I suppose, that bidding good-bye to all that means life to him is, in fact, death. Rather unfairly, he persuades himself that he has been a searcher after the lighter aspects of love and that he is justly paid. This cruel judgment of himself acts as a sort of flagellation and exalts him to a pitch of hysterical happiness; Keats calls it a "sort of deathful glee." It pleases him to imagine that this bright evening is a fitting end to a life inordinately stirred by beauty. Yet, beneath this, he feels an impious rage at having been abandoned by the very loveliness he has worshipped, which is a euphemism, presumably, for the goddess of the moon to whom his life from a child has been dedicated.

So absorbed is he in his rebellious revery that he does not observe the approach of Peona and the Indian maiden. Peona asks what it is he wants. Endymion replies that his desire, if only heaven would permit, is to command all their fates. Amazingly, at this, Diana tells him that "By

Cupid's dove," he shall! Whereupon, in front of him, she changes from the black-haired Indian maiden to the golden-haired Diana. He knows her at last as she is, his only love. She explains:

> "... Drear, drear
> Has our delaying been; but foolish fear
> Withheld me first; and then decrees of fate;
> And then 'twas fit that from this mortal state
> Thou shouldst, my love, by some unlook'd for change
> Be spiritualiz'd."

Endymion, so addressed, kneels before her while she blesses Peona, and promises many future meetings. The lovers vanish, and Peona goes

> "Home through the gloomy wood in wonderment."

So the poem, the effort of seven long months of labour, ends. On the last page of the draft, Keats wrote: "Burford Bridge. Nov. 28, 1817—" It was done, the interminable vigil was over. We can imagine the sense of relief with which he recorded the place and date of his emancipation.

We, who read *Endymion* a hundred years after its publication, need not be disturbed by its departures from the strict form of the couplet, as were contemporary critics. Run-on lines and displaced accents are not disagreeable to twentieth century ears. Poetry has widened its prosodiac boundaries just as music has its harmonic ones. Neither art has stood still, and what were daring innovations once have become usual even to staleness. Modern readers are more troubled by past participles scanned as two syllables except where they are purposely abbreviated; and to present-day taste coined words are not more irritating than obsolete words, the precedents for which have sunken out of memory.

Critics of the generations preceding mine have ticketed

and tracked Keats's verbal surprises with indefatigable zeal. I shall have nothing to say of them here, they may be exhaustively read about in so many books that to discuss them again would be an act of supererogation. I wish to be both simpler and more profound, if possible, by seeking the essence through the means. *Endymion* has persisted for a hundred years in spite of every sort of microscopic investigation, and when a book does that, there is some inherent reason which we shall do well to search for. It may be said that *Endymion* is read because Keats, in his later poems, set himself in such a position that all his work merits study; but I believe that *Endymion* deserves more than this. It does, indeed, seem probable that *Endymion* would still be a poem to be reckoned with had Keats never written another line.

Shelley has made the shrewdest criticism on it that has yet been written when he says:

> "Much praise is due me for having read it, the author's intention appearing to be that no person could possibly get to the end of it. I think if he had printed about fifty pages of fragments from it, I should have been led to admire Keats as a poet more than I ought, of which there is now no danger."

A poem, of which even fifty pages of fragments tempted Shelley to admire the poet more than he ought, is no negligible thing. Let us admit, with Shelley, that to read the poem through is a hard task, and yet most people who are fond of poetry do manage to get through it once in their lives, if they are lucky enough to have read nothing about it beforehand. Having read it, however, most of us promptly forget all but a few passages, but these stick so close in the mind that they are never forgotten, and we go back to them from time to time with constantly renewed appreciation. For, with all its faults, obscurities, and digressions, *Endymion* is the spirit of youth rampant.

Its adolescence is irresistible; to read it is to touch the day-spring of life.

First and foremost, let us brush away the dusty cloud of extraneous meanings with which the Victorian critics have well-nigh smothered its brightness. *Endymion* is no allegory. Keats's mind was not of the kind which works in parables. He was as clear as daylight in thought and expression, with his feet planted firmly on the good round earth, and his eyes busy beholding the beauties of a material universe which includes friendship, love, and all sorts of human intercourse as well as clouds, trees, sea, flowers, and moonlight.

Keats was concerned with poetry as an art, not as a tract. As Mr. Finney, to whose interesting paper[1] I have referred so often at the beginning of this chapter, well says: "Keats did not love the 'Faerie Queene' for its allegory or 'Paradise Lost' for its religious purpose; but he loved them for their 'sweets of song.'" Yet when I say that Keats never could have wished to write an exact allegory, I do not mean to imply that his poetry is all surface with no bottom. Keats was a man of keen intellect, a thinker as well as a poet. His poetry means a great deal beneath what it says, which is only to state that, like all real poetry, it is full of suggestion. But suggestion is as far from allegory as a page of Emerson is from the Athanasian creed.

Endymion is one of the most suggestive poems in English literature, but apart from the basic theory that love is the principal of all things and "creative of essential Beauty," the suggestions in it are as fleeting and unrelated as a Summer day-dream.

Also, we must not forget that during the seven months of its composition Keats was in the eager, receptive state of mind of a very young man to whom the world is opening wider every day, challenging him to a thousand new

[1] *Shakespeare and Keats*, by Claude L. Finney.

thoughts, upheaving and altering ideas in a myriad ways, breaking, upbuilding, making over that very tough and fragile thing, a personality.

Endymion is chaotic because Keats was chaotic at the time he wrote it. The First Book is the most charming, because it is the most boyish. The Second Book is chiefly interesting because it is so imaginative, the rush and zest of the First Book is calming down, but it is replaced by such a huge fervour of imagery that we are carried along on its flood of pictures in a breathless hurry of pleased perception; it is also psychologically the most significant in the poem. The Third Book, after the nostalgic and rather wistful splendour of the moon passages, becomes heavy and laboured, since Keats himself was weighed down under the new sensations which pressed upon him through his intercourse, for the first time in his life, with that questionable benefit to a poet, the mind of a scholar. Keats had intellect enough to rate scholarship at its true value, and pierce through the pedantic vestibule of learning to the columned courts which lie beyond, had he been given time. Plenty of poets have done this; in modern times, Browning is the noticeable example. But Keats had a better mind than Browning, and where Browning, competent scholar and magnificent poet though he was, remained as an original thinker almost a child, we may be sure, from the evidences of his letters and criticisms, that Keats would eventually have stamped on jejune points of view and kept his thought and poetry to an equal level. I do not say that Keats would ever have been as great a poet as Browning; I think that is extremely doubtful. What I mean can best be expressed under a figure — for Browning may be likened to a man driving a tandem, of which the leader is his poetry and the wheeler his thought; while Keats would surely have driven his thought and poetry harnessed side by side, a well-matched pair, both up in the collar and pulling for all they were worth.

The Fourth Book is a little weary, in spite of all Keats can do, yet it is a more thorough and tempered piece of work than any of the others. It hangs together better, is calmer, and more integral in structure. But it has neither the sparkle of the First Book, the psychological importance and imaginative wealth of the Second, nor the beauty of the moon passages in the Third. It does gather up the threads of the poem to a plausible ending, nevertheless. I can imagine someone reading it first and alone; and, should anyone do so, I am convinced it would appear as a perfectly logical ending to a poem which might have preceded it.

It will be remembered that, in my analysis of the First Book, I quoted from the letter written to Bailey from Burford Bridge on November twenty-second. I said that what in the beginning was felt rather than thought became in the end a conscious expression of opinion. Off by himself at Burford Bridge, Keats had a chance to range his new ideas and sensations into some sort of order, and out of this order he evolved what he wrote to Bailey. Yet the Fourth Book is less suggestive in this respect than the First. He was more conscious of his direction; but the direction and the narrative, as he had conceived it out of Drayton, did not jibe. Failing to find an end so good as the one he had planned but which would better fit his thought, and in a desperate hurry to finish, Keats laid philosophy aside and ended with pure story. There is no necessity to see symbolism in the skyey ride, as the allegorical critics have done, when we remember that it is in Drayton, and also that it joins the poem to the dream flight in the First Book and the longing for a second flight in the Second Book. The letter to Bailey was written when the Fourth Book was only half done, and it is a noticeable fact that nothing of his speculations gets into the lines written subsequently. Bailey kept all Keats's letters, so we may be fairly sure that he was not written to again while Keats was at Burford Bridge. We have no record of any more letters from Burford Bridge to anybody. Keats wrote the last five hundred lines in a week, which was fast writing, only the less good Third Book seems to have been done at the unvarying rate of fifty lines a day. The moon and nature wrested him away from philosophical probings, and gave him back to his first love — the beautiful, unglossed moon.

It is unfortunate that this letter to Bailey should have led so many critics astray. They have read into it far more than it says, and developed *Endymion* into a complete allegory, which, I repeat, it is not. It has not occurred to them to measure theory with fact and study Keats not only as a poet, but as a man. Because of this allegorical bias, most of what has been written about the poem is ingenious, but lacks perception. Of these allegories, the best, because the simplest, is probably Sir Sidney Colvin's; the worst, because in the light of Keats's age and character it is nothing short of absurd, is that of Professor H. Clement Notcutt of Stellenbosch University, South Africa. Dr. Bridges' interesting study need be considered in this connection only when he deserts his exact allegorical structure for a less positive description in which he comes far nearer the truth. I am willing to admit that "the poet was very sensible to the mysterious effects of moonlight, and felt the poetry of nature more deeply under that influence; and that mood being given, one step further only is necessary, which is that other ecstatic and poetic moods should be likened to it, and the conditioning cause of the first, which is known, be taken for a symbol of the other unknown causes, of that which is common to all." So viewed, Dr. Bridges thinks that "the poem becomes . . . readable as a whole, suggestive of meaning, and full of shadowy outlines of mysterious truth"; and with this last sentence I am in perfect accord.

Poetry is avowedly what one makes of it. A poem

should mean different things to different people. All good poetry has a double character. It is at once absolute, and "full of shadowy outlines of mysterious truth." Its absolute quality can be gauged and criticized; its "shadowy outlines" will vary with every reader. In so far as a poem is an organic entity, it changes its meaning, which is why it lasts to ever succeeding generations.

Keats was right in saying that *Endymion* was as good as he could make it; it was. But as a long poem, with a beginning, a middle, and an end, all working together for a total effect, it was a failure. He knew this perfectly well. Has he not spoken of "the slip-shod 'Endymion'"? But his epithet was not well chosen, or only in so far that he scanted his revision of the poem. In itself, it is not slipshod; it is merely not done. One man began it and another man ended it, that is all. Yet as a heap of fragments of marvellous beauty, it is an abiding solace and an enduring work of art; and as an illustration of poetic psychology, its value is incalculable.

CHAPTER VI

A HARD-WORKING SUMMER

We left Keats on Friday, May sixteenth, 1817, bowling along through the lovely Kent countryside on his way to Canterbury; Canterbury, where he hoped that the remembrance of Chaucer would set him "forward like a Billiard Ball." He started from Margate in the evening, but the fifteen miles or so to Canterbury cannot, at the longest, have taken much more than a couple of hours to traverse in one of the extremely efficient coaches of those days. England was approaching the height of her coach travel just at that time; steam-boats had made their appearance, it is true, but railroads had not yet come into being. Inland the coach carried him, where there was certainly no lack of the trees which he was seeking. Nothing could be more unlike Margate than the ancient city of Canterbury, with its great cathedral, and its memories of Thomas à Becket and Chaucer.

All his life, Keats seems to have experienced a remarkable stimulation at the thought of the older poets. He had the imaginative power of throwing round any place connected with a person whom he admired, or any object which such a person might have owned or touched, a bright halo of connotations. It was the fashion of the time to do so certainly. A year later we find Haydon nearly beside himself on reading in the paper of the finding of a ring in a field at Stratford which the credulous believed might have belonged to Shakespeare. The letter he writes to Keats on the subject is an idiotic extravaganza. Keats was never at any time, nor in anything, so silly as Haydon. Where one man plays the fool, the other is deeply and genuinely stirred. I do not know if, in this instance, Canterbury and the thought of Chaucer did set him forward like a billiard ball, for not a single letter from Canterbury, or record of any kind of his stay there, has yet been found. The nearest approach to it is the letter from George Keats to Severn, referred to in the last chapter,[1] in a postscript to which George says: "John and Tom are at Canterbury." Canterbury, therefore, is a blank. It is scarcely possible that Keats wrote no letters while he was at Canterbury, but why, if he did write, has no scrap of paper dating from there ever turned up? The question is unanswerable, of course, the only shadow of a reason is that he was set forward at such a rate in his work that he had no time for letters. The probabilities are that he finished the First Book of *Endymion* at Canterbury. By a little tabulating of facts — which must have been known to all his former biographers, but appear to have urged them to no inquiry — I seem to have discovered evidence of a brief but joyful reaction, the sort of reaction which every sensible poet indulges in when he reaches a natural pause in a sustained composition. It has long been known that, at some time in his life, Keats visited Hastings, but apparently not much effort has been made to find out when, it being blithely assumed that the Hastings trip occurred in the early years, before our more exact knowledge of Keats begins. Yet there is in existence another letter from George Keats to Severn, which I have already made use of in a different connection,[2] and this letter contains a pregnant sentence. After scolding Severn for his constant complaining, quite in the style of the letter of May twenty-second, George remarks: "John will be in town again soon. When he is, I will let you know and repeat my invitation. He sojourns at Bo Peep, near Hastings. Tom's remembrances."[3]

This letter is dated simply "Hampstead, Tuesday," but the tone of it, compared with that of the other letter,

[1] See Vol. I, p. 349. [2] See Vol. I, p. 108.
[3] *Life of Joseph Severn*, by William Sharp.

seems to place it as the last of the two, yet as following closely upon the first. It must have been written during the Summer of 1817, because, in 1816, the Keats brothers were not in Hampstead, and, in 1818, we know that, in the short time which elapsed between John's and Tom's return from Teignmouth and John's departure to Scotland, John went nowhere, being far too much occupied with George's marriage and immediate departure for America. It is barely possible that John and Tom returned to Hampstead after leaving Canterbury, and that John alone started off for Bo Peep. But this does not seem very likely, as, by that time, he was immersed in his Second Book; also it is rather far fetched to suppose that, having left the South coast, he would so soon run back to it again. What he probably did was to ship Tom back to London and betake himself to Bo Peep — of which he had doubtless heard from Haydon, with whom it was a favourite resort — in the holiday spirit induced by having brought his First Book to an end. Tom may have wanted to go home, being tired of travelling for the moment, since he was contemplating a trip to Paris later in the Summer. At any rate, it is quite clear that John went to Bo Peep alone.

If this reasoning be correct, George's second letter must have been written on either May twenty-seventh or June third, so that Keats would appear to have taken five or six weeks to write his First Book.

The little fishing village with the entrancing name of Bo Peep can be found on no map to-day, it has changed its character and its designation, the latter having been dropped in favour of the egregious, pretentious, and meaningless title of West Marina, for Keats's Bo Peep is now the extreme Western end of that popular watering-place, St. Leonards.

The only thing which Keats did at Bo Peep of which we have any cognizance was to kiss a lady. A very charming lady, we are led to suppose, but a perpetually anonymous one, for Keats never found out her name. He met her again in London, once "when going to the English opera," another time when taking a walk; indeed, she pops in and out of his letters two or three times, but always under the soubriquet of "the lady I met at Hastings." Their intercourse seems to have gone no farther than the kiss aforesaid, but the fact of it shows Keats in a happy and enfranchised mood, thoroughly enjoying the lull between the finish of his First Book and the start on his Second.

Keats, having little ready money except what Taylor and Hessey had sent him in May, spent freely and agreeably, but spent; and in less than a month, found it necessary to apply again to the same source. The note in which he did so is postmarked June tenth,[1] not July tenth as in Buxton Forman's editions. The re-dating of this letter from the original holograph is most important, as it proves that Keats was already back in Hampstead early in June. This is evident because, although Keats put nothing at the top of his paper but "Tuesday Morn," the letter is addressed merely "Fleet Street," which fact means that it cannot have been written from any distant place, for, in that case, he would have been obliged to add "London." Also, June tenth was a Tuesday, while July tenth was a Thursday.

The manner in which he asks assistance is, it must be admitted, distasteful in its cool bravado, or rather the cool bravado of its opening. Keats was embarrassed, as well he might be, and his embarrassment takes the not unusual form of jaunty jocularity. He begins "My Dear Sirs, I must endeavor to lose my maidenhead with respect to money Matters as soon as possible — and I will too — so, here goes!" What goes is that "a couple of Duns" are hounding him; he had expected them to let him be "till the beginning, at least, of next month (when I am certain to

[1] Author's Collection.

be on my legs, for certain sure)." However, to disabuse his publishers of the idea that he is extravagant, and to leave in their minds an impression of his diligence in regard to the book they are going to publish, he is careful to declare that he is "not desolate, but have, thank God, 25 good notes in my fob. But then, you know, I laid them by to write with and would stand at bay a fortnight ere they should grab me. In a month's time I must pay, but it would relieve my mind if I owed you, instead of these Pelican duns." At the end, comes the time-honoured formula of borrowers, "I am sure you are confident of my responsibility, and in the sense of squareness that is always in me." Keats assuredly meant to be square, but he permitted the corners of his squareness to be chipped on occasions when his financial obligations pressed. A man who cheerfully spends his quarter's allowance before it is due, and makes a practice of so doing, is not the best judge of rectangularity. It was eight months since he had attained his majority, and during that time he had been at no pains to acquaint himself with his financial position. This letter is the first of many, unhappily. That Keats should never have given a thought to the possibility that he might be straining the good will of his publishers too far, speaks volumes for their kindness and his extraordinary ignorance of the ways of the world.

On his return from Bo Peep, Keats joined his brothers in their new lodging in Well Walk, Hampstead. Exactly why the brothers moved there, no one says, but inference is not difficult. Tom was poorly housed in the thick of London smoke for a consumptive, for that he was a consumptive was becoming clearer every day; John found the peace and quiet of a suburb far better to write in than clattering Cheapside; George could reach the City without difficulty, although, as a matter of fact, he does not seem to have been obliged to reach it very long. The first letter to Severn implies that already, at the end of May, he had no daily engagement in town. George's "pride" does not appear to have accorded well with a clerkship in anybody's employ. Hence the subsequent departure to America, where a man had but to stand on his own feet with energy and perseverance to make a fortune! Oh, the innocence, the pathetic innocence of these boys! How sorely they paid for it!

The landlord of the Well Walk lodging was a postman named Bentley. Bentley, slightly as he is sketched in Keats's letters, gives the impression of having been a good, honest sort of man, and his wife, we are told, was a kind and motherly woman, but the children were a source of some annoyance to Keats. As I have already said, Keats does not seem to have cared much for children. On one occasion, the Bentley children "are making a horrid row"; on another, Keats speaks without enthusiasm of the smell of their damp worsted stockings.

Hampstead was an almost perfect place for Keats to settle in. To be sure, Hunt was no longer in the cottage in the Vale of Health, but, considering Keats's altered feelings toward Hunt, that was rather a boon than otherwise. But, if Hunt had left Hampstead, two friends of his, whom the Keats brothers had already met through him, remained, and both these friends were destined to become very intimate with Keats as time went on, one of them, indeed, to play almost the part of a brother during the last years of Keats's life. These men were Charles Wentworth Dilke and Charles Brown.

Just when Keats first met them is not known, but it was certainly some time during the Winter of 1816–17. There are references to a party at Mrs. Dilke's to which Keats could not go, in the letter which Keats wrote to Reynolds announcing his approaching departure from London in the Spring, but we hear nothing of Brown at that date, although Keats must have made his acquaintance at about the same time that he made Dilke's.

The Dilke family were somewhat higher in the social scale than most of Keats's friends. There were Dilkes of Maxstoke Castle in Warwickshire, and Charles Wentworth Dilke, the father of Keats's friend, was the head of a younger branch of the same family. They were descendants of a Sir Peter Wentworth, who was a member of the High Court of Justice, and of a still older Sir Peter Wentworth, who had married a sister of Sir Francis Walsingham, and was the leader of the Puritan opposition under Queen Elizabeth. Dilke's father, the elder Charles Wentworth, had been in the civil service; but, when Keats knew the family, he had retired to Chichester.

Charles Wentworth Dilke was a young man of twenty-seven when the Keats brothers moved to Hampstead. By profession, he was a clerk in the Navy Pay Office, but his tastes were literary. He had edited a series of volumes as a continuation to Dodsley's *Old Plays*, the books appearing at intervals from 1814 to 1816. Dilke was also something of an antiquary, and in politics a confirmed radical, which bias induced him to advocate the repeal of the corn laws in 1821. In 1830, he undertook the editorship of the *Athenæum*, which had been established two years before, but was, at the time, languishing. By his energy and fearlessness, he soon put the paper on its feet and gave it the prominent position it held for many years. Later, in 1846, he became manager of the *Daily News*. In 1862, he left London for Hampshire, where he died in 1864. Dilke was an indefatigable writer on his favourite subjects, but published no books other than his series of edited plays. It was not until ten years after his death that his fugitive essays were gathered together by his grandson, and issued under the title, *Papers of a Critic*.

Dilke had a tidy, but inelastic, mind. He wished to reduce everything to a system and dogmatize from a settled basis. Keats summed him up very neatly in a letter written to his brother George in 1819: "Dilke," he says, "is a man who cannot feel he has a personal identity unless he has made up his mind about everything . . . Dilke will never come at a truth as long as he lives, because he is always trying it." At another time, he calls him "a Godwin-perfectability man." In spite of their total unlikeness of character, Keats and Dilke enjoyed each other's company immensely. Dilke's knowledge of books and antiquities, combined with the genial hospitality of his nature, cannot fail to have made him a pleasant, as well as an interesting, companion, while his appreciation of Blake should have had more of an effect upon Keats than it did, unless, indeed, it dates from a period subsequent to Keats's death. At any rate, a man who could appreciate Blake certainly had much in him by which Keats could profit.

Dilke married early, his son being born in 1810. This boy, the idol of his father's heart, the Charley Dilke of the letters, was therefore only seven when Keats went to live at Hampstead.

Mrs. Dilke, for no account of Dilke is complete without mention of his wife, was evidently a very charming woman. Her enthusiasm about, and friendliness for, Keats duplicated her husband's attitude. But there must have been something about her which did not lure Keats quite as far as it might have done, for, cosily intimate as Keats was with her, she never fell into the place of confidant. Perhaps the fact that Keats encountered Fanny Brawne when his acquaintance with Mrs. Dilke was scarcely more than a year old, a year in which he was much away from Hampstead, may have been the reason, rather than any lack in Mrs. Dilke's character. Her friendship with Keats drifted into one with his sister Fanny, to whom she was very attentive after Keats's death, and this friendship with Fanny Keats she kept up for years. Mrs. Dilke had a little frailty which gives the memory of her a delightfully human touch; she was unpunctual, never ready when called for by

CHARLES WENTWORTH DILKE

From a photograph of an oil painting, in the possession of F. Holland Day, Esq.

appointment, no matter what the appointment were for. So we see the Dilke family: Dilke, Mrs. Dilke, and little Charley; a domestic *milieu* which was destined to crowd out that of the Reynoldses', quite as the Reynoldses' had crowded out the Matthews'.

Some time previous to 1817, Dilke, and a friend and schoolfellow of his, Charles Brown, had built a house together at the foot of John Street, Hampstead. It was of the sort which we should now call a "two-family house," each half quite separate from the other, but both covered by one roof. This double house stood — still stands,[1] in fact, although alterations have done away with its double character — in a garden of a comfortable size, where grew several fine trees, among them, a plum of no mean dimensions. This plum we shall meet again later on. The house and garden were named Wentworth Place, a proud little tribute paid by Dilke to the memory of his important ancestors.

Charles Brown, who occupied the lesser half of the structure dedicated to the glorious, but defunct, Wentworths, was a bachelor. And here let me say that Sir Sidney Colvin is quite right in declaring that the interpolated middle name of Armitage, which Brown adopted in later life, is absolutely out of place when speaking of him at this time. Charles Brown, he was, pure and simple, in those days, and for a long time after. How and why he became Charles Armitage Brown will appear presently. Considering that Brown was not, in himself, by any means a distinguished man, we really know a good deal about him. Even more than Severn, he lives for later generations solely because he was Keats's friend. It should, however, be remembered that of all his friends, Brown was the one to whom Keats clung most closely from the time of Tom Keats's death until his own. I do not think that Brown

[1] It has recently been acquired by the Keats Memorial Association and is to be kept in perpetuity as a Keats museum.

entirely justified Keats's love for him, I think he failed on more than one important occasion, but something in him drew and held Keats. Circumstance threw the two men into an intimate relation, and Keats, with his pathetic desire for relations, put Brown, as far as possible, into the place left empty by Tom's death and George's emigration to America.

Charles Brown was born in Lambeth in 1786. He was the sixth son of his father, a Scotch stock-broker settled in London. As sons were plentiful in the family and money was not, Brown found himself, at fourteen, perched upon a stool in a counting-house, earning forty pounds a year. An older brother, John, was in business as a "Russia merchant," as the term then was. The firm's activities consisted in the importation of Russian products to be sold in England. When Charles was only eighteen, John took him into partnership, and sent him to St. Petersburg to represent the firm at the Russian end. At first affairs went well with the brothers, but a large purchase of bristles fell dead on their hands owing to the great competition of split whalebone, then a newly invented substitute, and bankruptcy was the result. Brown returned to London, penniless, about 1810, and for some time was miserably poor. He is said to have existed on one meal a day, which he got for fourpence at an ordinary where the knives and forks were chained to the table.[1] But if one brother had failed him, another came to his rescue. This brother, James, was one of that corps of local "residents" set up by the East India Company in those various districts of India under its control. James, who had made good use of the opportunities of his position and acquired a reasonable competence, made Charles his London agent. Shortly after, James returned to England broken down in health, and, on his death a few months later, Charles found himself the possessor of the competence aforesaid. This meant,

[1] Unpublished Memoir by his son, C. A. Brown. Day Collection.

not riches, but comfort, if Charles spent carefully. He had no wish to embark again in business, the plethoric bristles were too fresh in his mind; he sat himself down to live on his means, which he eked out by contributing occasional papers to periodicals. One stroke of quasi-luck he did have, however. He wrote the libretto of an opera, the music of which was supplied by Braham and Reeve. *Narensky, or the Road to Yaroslaf* was performed at Drury Lane in 1814, with Braham in the title rôle. Braham's popularity carried the piece through several performances, which earned for Brown three hundred pounds and free admission to Drury Lane for life. But even Braham could not keep the opera on the boards; it disappeared promptly, and nothing more was to be hoped from it. Yet, as it was, Brown, who had a sturdy sense of humour, declared he had got more than his share of the thing was worth, and destroyed every copy of the libretto (it had been published) which he could lay his hands on. At the time that Keats met him, he was living the life of a dilettante writer, rather hoping to strike out something good, but with no particular expectation of doing so, and not really trying very hard for a prize he knew beyond his reach.

Brown's life in the years when he knew Keats is without external incident, except as regards one thing. In 1819, apparently without Keats's knowledge, he travelled to Ireland and married a young peasant woman named Abigail Donohue,[1] who, there is some reason to think, had been a servant in Brown's house. The marriage, being performed by a Catholic priest, was illegal, but the woman, who was a Catholic, was perfectly satisfied. Brown never seems to have had any intention of acknowledging the marriage, or of living with his wife, and we hear nothing of her making any objection to the arrangement of separate existences. A son was born to the couple in 1820, and for two years Brown left him with his mother. At the end of

[1] Unpublished Memoir by his son, C. A. Brown. Day Collection.

that time, he obtained possession of the boy, and immediately left for Italy, fearing, says his son, that the mother "might appeal to Chancery to give her legal custody of the boy, on the same grounds that Shelley had been deprived of his children." The marriage seems to have been an odd transaction altogether, and points to a kink in Brown's mind more in accordance with eighteenth century ideas than with those of his own day. Brown does not appear to have cared a snap for the woman, but he was devoted to his child, which certainly has the look of a preconcerted, scientific plan to provide himself with a son who should inherit intellectual ability from him, but who should also enjoy the advantage of strong, healthy peasant blood. Brown hoped to give him both brain and brawn by this means, but the experiment was not pre-eminently successful apparently, at least as regards the first of these qualities.

I can find no mention anywhere of what Brown's friends knew, suspected, or thought; but, from 1822 to 1834, Brown presented the strange spectacle of a middle-aged English gentleman wandering over Italy with a small boy attached to his coat-tails. Of course, this was after Keats's death; Keats himself, I am certain, never knew of Brown's marriage, or of the birth of his child.

The Italian years were pleasant ones for Brown, who was an excellent Italian scholar. He read, he wrote, he taught his son. He met Byron, and became intimate with Landor and Trelawny; indeed, he and Trelawny lived together for a while, and he re-wrote Trelawny's *Adventures of a Younger Son* and put it into shape for publication, a task that Mrs. Shelley had attempted and given up as impossible. In 1834, Brown returned to England and settled in Plymouth, in order that his son might have the benefit of a thorough-going British education before it was too late. In Plymouth, Brown continued to busy himself with desultory writing. He printed various of Keats's unpublished poems in his possession in the *New Monthly Magazine*, edited a Plymouth weekly paper, and lectured on Shakespeare and Keats. So long before as 1829, he had projected writing a life of Keats, but when he did finally write it in the abbreviated form of a short biographical sketch, it was rejected by both the *Morning Chronicle* and the booksellers. The only approach to it was an account of the first part of the Scotch tour which he and Keats had taken in 1818. This account he printed in several numbers of the *Plymouth and Devonport Weekly Journal* in 1840.

Brown's best-known work was a volume entitled *Shakespeare's Autobiographical Poems. Being his Sonnets clearly developed: with his Character drawn chiefly from his Works.* The book was published by Bohn of London in 1838, and on the title-page, Brown, for the first time, styled himself Charles Armitage Brown. His son's account of the reason for this is amusing: "He assumed the name of Armitage, a family name on the mother's side, when he published 'Shakespeare's Autobiographical Poems' — bearing in mind what Trelawny said to him, 'Brown, your name is that of a tribe, not a family.'" [1]

For various reasons, as time went on, Brown became dissatisfied with Plymouth and decided to emigrate to New Zealand, to which end he took up a government grant in New Plymouth, now Taranaki, North Island. Realizing that such a move ended all possibility of his writing a life of Keats, he made over his papers relative to the subject to Lord Houghton before he went, which papers Lord Houghton made good use of, and they have been a chief source of information to subsequent biographers. The land grant satisfactorily settled, Brown sent his son ahead to prepare the way, following himself a few months later, in 1841. At first, he rather enjoyed the change, but the lack of congenial society, and the dearth of newspapers

[1] Unpublished Memoir by his son, C. A. Brown. Day Collection.

and periodicals, soon discouraged him, and he made up his mind to return to England, a journey he was destined never to take. Before his arrangements could be completed, he had an attack of apoplexy in which he died in 1842. His grave, for many years lost, was discovered in 1921.

In 1817, Brown was an agreeable, rather full-fleshed, man of thirty-one, with a bald head, side whiskers, and spectacles. He was extremely active and robust, a large eater, and with a strong liking for the good things of this world. Although not without a streak of coarseness, Brown had a keen love for genuine poetry. He was an indefatigable copyist of Keats's poems, running Woodhouse hard in this direction. A warm friend, a genial companion, with immovable prejudices — "his odd dislikes," Keats calls them — there was much to like in Brown, and a good deal to deplore. He could be generous, he was scrupulously honest, but his honesty was of the kind which makes no allowances for others which he would not permit to himself. Sir Sidney Colvin has given us an admirable picture of him when he says: "a truly Scottish blend of glowing warm-heartedness and 'thrawn' prejudice, of frank joviality and cautious dealing."[1] He lent Keats money, and paid Keats's share of their joint housekeeping when Keats could no longer do so; but, after Keats's death, he came down on George for the entire sum plus interest, which item amounted to something like seventy-two pounds.[2]

Brown liked Keats at once, but he was not a man to push; his eminently tactful method of approach, as he told it to Lord Houghton, was this:

> [3] "I succeeded in making him come often to my house by never asking him to come oftener; and I let him feel himself at perfect liberty there chiefly by avoiding to assure him of the fact."

[1] Colvin.

[2] Note by Dilke in his copy of Lord Houghton's *Life of Keats*, quoted by Buxton Forman.

[3] Houghton Papers, quoted by Buxton Forman.

When we remember Hunt's method, Haydon's method, and recollect how recently Keats had flung himself out of the sentimental farce, we realize a good deal of why Brown's manner of acting worked as it did, and the reason of Brown's strong attraction for him. But Rome was not built in a day, and Brown was little more than a casual acquaintance in the Summer of 1817.

The Summer months of June, July, and August were busy ones for Keats. His Second Book must have absorbed a great deal of his energy, when we think what an exuberance of imagination he poured into it. The pleasure of being once more among his friends was undoubtedly very great, but we have neither letters nor notes to tell us so. The dearth of documents continues. Everybody whom he cared about was in London; but whatever engagements he may have made do not seem to have required epistolary confirmation. We gather more from this silence than would at first seem possible. Keats, in true Alice-in-the-Looking-Glass fashion, had jumped a square. He was in a totally different mood from the one he was in when, three months before, he had quitted London. His First Book had given him a considerable degree of confidence, and he had no desire to go back to the harness of leading strings.

It is largely this complete absence of letters which makes me certain that the Bo Peep sojourn occurred immediately after Canterbury and not later in the Summer. We know that he was alone at Bo Peep, and Keats was never alone very long without writing. Not to write for a few days' holiday is one thing; not to write on a journey undertaken for the purpose of work is another, and that Keats was working hard by Midsummer is evident.

One thing Keats did not do, he did not seek out Hunt. Hunt, having returned from some country jaunt, had settled at Maida Hill, Paddington. Thus he was farther away than at the Vale of Health certainly, but the distance was not so great after all. It had been easy enough to run out to Hampstead from Cheapside, a few months earlier, but now it was a difficult thing to go from Hampstead to Paddington. This is quite plain from a paragraph in a letter from Hunt to Cowden Clarke written on July first, when Keats had been back at Hampstead for nearly a month. Hunt's allusion to him is: "What has become of Junkets I know not. I suppose Queen Mab has eaten him." [1]

So much for Hunt. As to Haydon, who, so long ago as May, had begged Keats to come back to town in order that he, Haydon, might put Keats's head into his picture, he was at the old stand, painting as usual, but under difficult circumstances. I imagine that the sketch of Keats's head was begun at this time, although Haydon, in his journal, is a little obscure as to just when in 1817 he painted Keats as one of the shouting crowd gathered about the entering Christ. Now Haydon was in a stew this Summer. His eyes were in a shocking condition; he was looking for a new studio; he was in love, with no prospect of being able to marry; he was "in the clutches of the money-lenders." The studio was found at Lisson Grove, North, a street into which Hunt also moved very shortly. The throes of moving over, Haydon departed for Oxford, and it is significant that Keats does not seem to have written a line to him while he was gone. No, the people whom Keats appears to have frequented most during the three months that he was in town were the Reynoldses, for there he again met Bailey, *en route* to spend the first part of the long vacation with friends in the country.

Bailey was a new sensation. Keats was just in the mood for him. The men he had known hitherto, well read and devoted to literature though they were, were none of them scholars. Keats had begun to feel the advantage of well-grounded knowledge. His excellent mind, whipped to a great eagerness by the long effort of creation, was fumbling

[1] *Recollections of Writers* by Charles Cowden Clarke.

for coördination; it demanded a solid basis for its superstructure, and found itself lacking at every turn. The kind of impressionistic substitute for learning which was all he had to guide him was full of holes, and this he realized and keenly regretted. Not that exact knowledge could help the act of creation, but that, with knowledge as a springboard, imagination could leap with more certainty of aim. Then, too, Keats was groping after an ideal, something morally firm and stable, and he thought he discerned in Bailey a type of this solidity. Bailey was a serious-minded young man, preparing for holy orders, and the somewhat broad smear of pedantry that marked his character, which he noticed so little that he made no effort to rid himself of it, did not trouble Keats, because Keats was entirely concerned in delighting in Bailey's other qualities. When, in the sequel, Bailey turned out to be a brass idol with feet of clay, Keats could not forgive him. The truth being that, although Keats may never have reasoned it out to himself, Bailey's defection from the standard which Keats believed him to hold broke a cherished illusion of Keats's heart. If Bailey were not what he had seemed, Bailey was a chipped and useless thing. For another man, Keats could have made allowances, but not for Bailey.

Bailey, this Summer, was a godsend. His whole attitude was new and sustaining. Bailey's account of his and Keats's mutual pleasure in seeing each other is corroborative of this. They took to each other at once. Here is what Bailey says:

> [1] "At the commencement of the long vacation I was again in London, on my way to another part of the country: and it was my intention to return to Oxford early in the vacation for the purpose of reading. I saw much of Keats. And I invited him to return with me to Oxford, and spend as much time as he could afford with me in the

[1] Memoranda sent by Bailey to Lord Houghton, quoted by Sir Sidney Colvin.

silence and solitude of that beautiful place during the absence of the numerous members and students of the University. He accepted my offer, and we returned together."

Benjamin Bailey is the last of Keats's friends whom it is necessary for us to know much about. The sum of Keats's connections, except in one important case, that of Fanny Brawne, completes itself with Bailey. Casual, friendly folk arrive and pass; but Bailey is the last of those whose influence on Keats is marked. After this, Keats's eager receptivity in the matter of added friendships calms down. He already had more friends than falls to the lot of most men. In developing his relations with the men he knew, in solidifying with some, and drifting off with others, his personal life was as full as personal contacts, other than those of love, could make it. In saying this, I am carefully separating his personal, from his artistic, life; where his poetry was concerned, Keats never lost his avidity. In one sense, the two halves of himself were inseparable, and it is really those men who affected him artistically who deserve to rank as his friends. Yet there is another sense in which these two halves of Keats's personality can be divided, for, in the end, he was artistically beholden to no living person, but he never lost that wistful longing for affection which was one of the mainsprings of his character.

Bailey was the son of a Mr. John Bailey of Thorney Abbey in Cambridgeshire, at which place he was born in 1791. He seems to have been a most susceptible young man, falling in love at a rapid and continuous rate. He had wooed several young ladies before his affair with Marianne Reynolds.[1] Dilke states that, in the latter case, he was actually refused, but begged Miss Reynolds to reconsider her answer. She might have remained obdurate, but no chance of announcing her final decision was given her, for Bailey, who had gone on a visit to his friend Gleig's family

[1] See Vol. I, p. 283.

in Scotland in the Summer of 1818, promptly placed his volatile heart at the feet of Miss Hamilton Gleig, a daughter of his host, Bishop Gleig, and this time he was accepted. The Reynolds family seem to have taken Bailey's defection very hard, although there is no reason to suppose that Marianne herself was much troubled. At any rate, she later consoled her pride by becoming engaged to a Mr. Green. It was this behaviour of Bailey's which so upset Keats. His opinion on the matter will appear in due course.

Later in the same Summer of 1818, Bailey settled in a curacy near Carlisle. In 1819, he became vicar of Dallington, in Northamptonshire, a living which he held until 1822. For some years after this, his career is obscure, although we know that he was, at one time, private chaplain to Lord Hawke, and, at another, rector of Minster, Kent. The next authentic knowledge of him is as Senior Chaplain of the Island of Colombo, a post which he was filling in 1831. For twenty years, beginning in 1832, he was the Chaplain of St. Peter's Fort, Colombo, but a bitter disagreement with his bishop led to his return to England, where he died in 1853.[1]

Bailey was an omnivorous reader. Keats writes to him: "I should not like to be pages in your way; when in a tolerable hungry mood you have no mercy. Your teeth are the Rock Tarpeian down which you capsize epic poems like mad." Bailey's chief enthusiasm was for Milton, with Wordsworth as a close second.

It has been the fashion of biographers to speak highly of Bailey on very insufficient data. I have had the good fortune to read a number of his letters to Taylor in which he speaks of Keats,[2] and the impression left upon me by their perusal is not altogether pleasant. The pedant and

[1] This account of Bailey is partly derived from unpublished letters in the Day Collection.

[2] Woodhouse Book. Morgan Collection.

the prig are very much in evidence, and there is a touch of hypocritical prudery, a specimen of which I gave in the last chapter, that is not alluring. These letters cover a period of two years between February, 1818, and February, 1821. I shall give such bits of them as seem important when we reach the periods to which they belong.

I have said that there is a dearth of documents relating to this Summer. So there is, as far as letters are concerned, but for printed matter, it is another thing, as Leigh Hunt's belated criticism of the *Poems* suddenly began to appear. The first instalment was printed in the *Examiner* on June first, entitled *Poems by John Keats.* It begins by stating that the volume in question is by the author of the various sonnets signed "J. K.," which had appeared in the *Examiner* from time to time. Hunt next tells how, before he knew Keats, he had read some of his work, adding, mendaciously, that even earlier than this he had printed one of the sonnets. So much said, Hunt veers to his chief preoccupation: the immediate poetry revival. This first instalment is really only an introduction, done in much the same style as his opening in the article, *Young Poets*, of the previous December. Hunt grinds his favourite axe stoutly, but we need not reiterate his thrice-told tale, it has already been given in reference to *Rimini* and the December article. His diatribe in this introduction ends with this florid declaration:

> "The rich and enchanted ground of real poetry, fertile with all that English succulence could produce, bright with all that Italian sunshine could lend, and haunted with exquisite humanities, had become invisible to mortal eyes like the garden of Eden:
>
> 'And from that time those Graces were not found.'"

Here the article stops abruptly, without returning to Keats. Was this "pussy-footing" on Hunt's part? I do verily believe it was. Why did he wait so long to review the book of his cherished disciple? I cannot help thinking that, unkind as this delay in coming to Keats's rescue in print may seem, it was really prompted by the knowledge that no championing of his could do Keats otherwise than harm. Yet one cannot very well leave a satellite forever in the hands of despoilers, something to succour him must be done before long. It was a ticklish business, and I think Hunt shirked it as long as he could, and then came out with this oblique article in which nothing to the point was said. The paper breaks off with the formula: "To be concluded next week." But not the next week, nor, indeed, until five weeks had passed, did Hunt continue his review. A natural conjecture is that this resumption of an apparently abandoned theme was owing to the fact that he had heard nothing from Keats for months, as we have just seen, and very probably considered that this silence was in part due to his own obvious unwillingness to write any more of his article.

In the second instalment, which appeared on July sixth, Hunt plumps into his neglected train of thought as though his readers had dwelt with it all the while. Naïvely, then, considering the lapse of five weeks, he starts his second paper in this remarkable manner:

> "These Graces, however, are reappearing; and one of the greatest evidences is the little volume before us."

After enlarging somewhat, to point his argument, Hunt fairly begins his review by generalizing about Keats with insight and tact. This passage I give in full:

> "We do not, of course, mean to say, that Mr. Keats has as much talent as he will have ten years hence, or that there are no imitations in his book, or that he does not make mistakes common to inexperience; — the reverse is inevitable at his time of life. In proportion to our ideas, or impressions of the images of things, may be our acquaintance with the things themselves. But our author has all

the sensitiveness of temperament requisite to receive these impressions; and wherever he has turned hitherto, he has evidently felt them deeply.

The very faults indeed of Mr. Keats arise from a passion for beauties, and a young impatience to vindicate them; and as we have mentioned these, we shall refer to them at once."

These faults are, Hunt thinks, first a tendency to accord a disproportionate space to detail; and second, "a sense of the proper variety of versification without a due consideration of its principles."

We need not follow Hunt into his illustrations to his first proposition; they are more idiosyncratic than universal. For his second censure, he is content to cite one example: the first line in *How many bards*.

In coming to the beauties, Hunt is on better and surer ground for the exercise of his own particular critical gift. No more penetrating criticism of the excellencies of Keats's poetry could be made than this summary with which he starts his catalogue of "beauties":

"Their characteristics indeed are a fine ear, a fancy and imagination at will, and an intense feeling of external beauty in its most natural and least expressible simplicity."

Again, what shrewder paraphrase could be given of *I Stood Tip-toe* than "The first poem consists of a piece of luxury in a rural spot."

Following these generalities, Hunt sets down various illustrations, among them are the "noiseless noise," the "youngling tree," the marigolds, and the moon coming into the blue with a "gradual swim" — all from *I Stood Tip-toe*. It is amusing to note that every one of these selected "beauties," except the second, were underscored by George Keats in his copy of the *Poems*.[1] From *Calidore*, Hunt quotes:

[1] Author's Collection. See Vol. I, pp. 143–144, and Appendix C.

"... fir trees grow around,
Aye dropping their hard fruit upon the ground."

Of this passage, he says: "This last line is in the taste of Greek simplicity," which, curiously enough, for Keats is so seldom in the least Greek, it is. A few more quotations, not so happy as these, and Hunt ends his second section as abruptly as though his manuscript had been slashed into with a pair of scissors.

The third, and last, paper was published a week later, on July thirteenth. In it, Hunt reviews briefly the *Epistle to Charles Cowden Clarke*, glances at a sonnet or two, announces that "The best poem is certainly the last and longest, entitled *Sleep and Poetry*," from which he quotes fifty-five lines, and seizes the opportunity of Keats's verses on the subject of poetry to end, as he had begun, with animadversions on those poets whose ways are not his — this time, the Lake Poets. By this return to his ever-present irritation, we see that Hunt lost no means to advance his theories; and excellent and just though his review is, and handsome tribute as he certainly meant it to be, it smells of propaganda, and must be taken, for all its skilful criticism, as very much a piece of special pleading, which proves why it did not help Keats's reputation as it would have done had it been written by a critic with no personal interests to forward.

How Keats took this spasmodically printed review, we have no means of knowing. But there is a very broad hint of his attitude towards it in the fact that his recently written sonnet, *On the Sea*, was published in the *Champion* on August seventeenth. This was the first of Keats's poems to appear in any paper other than the *Examiner*, and the chances are that Keats took the poem to John Scott, the editor, for the best of all possible reasons, to free himself from Hunt's ægis, and advise the reading public that he did not exist solely in the shadow of Hunt's fostering wing. It is now fairly clear what induced Hunt to print the already published sonnet, *On the Grasshopper and the Cricket*, in the following September. We may take his doing so, apart from the reason I have already given [1] of providing a foil to his own sonnet on the same subject, as a sort of declaration of ownership. If he were in the slightest degree hurt at Scott's getting the opportunity to publish *On the Sea*, his friendship was, nevertheless, sincere; and it is no more than fair to see in his action a desire to keep his relations with Keats on the most cordial terms. Since he had nothing new of Keats's to use, he made this published sonnet serve a triple purpose.

The period of the year was now approaching when Londoners, if they can, go out of town. George and Tom purposed tripping to Paris, but John naturally did not want to break up his work on *Endymion* and so decided not to go with them. Shelley invited him to stay at Great Marlow, but Keats refused, "in order," he told Bailey afterwards, "that I might have my own unfettered scope." The truth is that Keats was feeling his way. His newly acquired conviction that Hunt had hampered him, made him certain that he had best go alone. He wanted sympathy, but he by no means wanted to be lectured. And there he was quite right; it was both too late and too early to give him advice. He was just at a point where he had, of necessity, to codify his recently discovered possibilities; he must weigh, retain, reject. He must seize the opportunities which farther seeing and clearer understanding were opening out before him. He must, in short, prove himself. He did not want to break what coherence *Endymion* had; and he felt, not without reason, that it did have some coherence, being all spun out of himself. But he knew himself too sensitive still to risk the effect of alien inquiries and suggestions. He must be in a congenial atmosphere or his little sproutling of a poem would shrink and shrivel.

[1] See Vol. I, p. 238.

With Bailey, he felt safe. Much as Bailey read, his writing was confined to a few mild literary essays and prospective sermons. Keats had nothing to fear from an impinging poetic personality. That Keats reckoned a little too wide of the mark in thinking that no personality save a poetic one could affect his work, we have seen in the last chapter. But, if Keats ever realized this, he certainly had no inkling of it when Bailey's invitation opened before him the pleasant alternative of Oxford to solitary lodgings in Hampstead.

It was probably on either September second or third that Keats and Bailey went to Oxford, going down by the Oxford and Cheltenham day coach "Defiance," which started from the Belle Sauvage, Ludgate Hill, at the pleasantly early hour of a quarter before eight in the morning and reached the Mitre Inn, Oxford, at three that same afternoon. No better time for a first sight of Oxford than three o'clock on a bright September afternoon could well be devised. Bailey's rooms were in Magdalen Hall, and here the two young men settled themselves forthwith to enjoy a few weeks of strenuous work and high companionship. Keats was excellently situated at Oxford. The town was slumbering in the quiet of the Long Vacation, and the absence of the usual throng of undergraduates saved him from feeling too much of an outsider. The beauty of the halls and colleges clustered among green trees solaced his eyes and his mind, and the atmosphere of leisure, books, wisdom, and security, gave him the sense of walking in a soothing and temperate air. He was abundantly happy. A couple of days after reaching Oxford, he writes a letter of bubbling nonsense to Marianne and Jane Reynolds, who had gone to the seaside village of Little Hampton for the usual Londoner's holiday. Here is Oxford, and Keats in it, so effervescing with good spirits that everything (on the surface) is sheer fun:

"... here am I among Colleges, halls, Stalls, Plenty of trees, thank God — Plenty of water, thank heaven —

> Plenty of Books, thank the Muses — Plenty of Snuff, thank Sir Walter Raleigh — Plenty of segars, — Ditto — Plenty of Flat country, thank Tellus's rolling pin — I'm on the sofa — Buonaparte is on the snuff-box."

So he races along, higgledy-piggledy, cloaking his impressions under a whirl of irresponsible gaiety. I have interpolated the little qualification, "on the surface," with intention. On the surface, Keats plays his joking banter right heartily; but all the time, underneath the surface, he was soaking in new sights, new thoughts, mellowing like a peach on a South wall. If Oxford soothed, it also startled. This was a city of the past. Along these tree-shaded paths, and in and out of these echoing halls, the poets of his predilection might have walked. Over these glorious, unimaginable buildings presided a dignity which his jostled, and rather ragged, life had never known. Not being able, by the exigences of his poem, to write of Oxford, he wrote of the moon, and the kinship between the two is not hard to seek, if we look into Keats's mind. Both moon and Oxford mean peace and supreme beauty.

A week after his arrival, he writes to his little sister Fanny, in a less rollicking strain than he had written to the Reynolds girls certainly, but much to the same purpose:

> "This Oxford I have no doubt is the finest City in the world — it is full of old Gothic buildings — Spires — towers — Quadrangles — Cloisters — Groves &c. and is surrounded by more clear streams than ever I saw together. I take a Walk by the Side of one of them every Evening, and, thank God, we have not had a drop of rain these many days."

No rain! A parlous thing for England, who had, the year before, experienced one of the worst seasons in her history, a season of cold and drought when there should have been warmth and showers, and cold and wet when the harvest was being reaped. This condition had raised the price of bread to a height which caused acute distress to the lower classes. Now, in 1817, the country needed the present harvest to be more than usually bountiful. But Keats never considered this, he considered only the great splashes of sunlight lying beyond cool doorways, the slants of sunlight catching ancient spires, the glitter of sun-touched water sparkling the faces of meadows. If the country needed grain, he needed sun, the bright sun of a cloudless sky, bewitching beautiful things to an even greater beauty. The rainless weeks made Oxford, to him, a veritable *Paradisus in Sole*.

The mood engendered by all these things was a sane, peaceful, and purposeful outlook on life. Keats seemed to himself lifted into a poetical sphere where art joins with intelligence to make a full-sided whole. In such a sphere, the old poets must have dwelt to write as they did. The flurry of modern artistic circles, fuming and fretting against this or that pettiness and themselves pettishly rebellious of misunderstanding and neglect, shrank to the merest wind-puff of dust particles when compared with the silent, stately, abiding eloquence standing in rows on the shelves of the Bodleian. Oxford was to Keats what the woods were to Emerson when he described them as looking down on a fussing, hurrying human creature with the comment: "So hot, my little Sir!" Just so did Oxford speak to Keats. Do I make use of a strange epithet when I say that Keats's mood was almost a domestic one? His surroundings turned him back to the innate, persisting things, things like the unalterable ties of blood, for instance. Seen in this light, it is most natural that the first of Keats's letters to his sister Fanny, that series of letters which show us what is perhaps the sweetest and most lovable side of him, should have been written from Oxford.

Bailey, in the Memoranda sent to Lord Houghton, testifies to Keats's preoccupation with his sister at this time, and inadvertently reveals that little Fanny was the innocent, childish thread of a dream woof of even more beautiful possibilities. Bailey's words are:

> [1] "He had a truly poetic feeling for women; and he often spoke to me of his sister, who was somehow withheld from him, with great delicacy and tenderness of affection."

The withholding was, in fact, only too true. Dull-witted Mr. Abbey had conceived the opinion that Keats was a bad influence for his sister. In Abbey's opinion, a man who could act as Keats had done, who could fling away his opportunity of becoming a member of a worthy and lucrative profession to follow the will-o'-the-wisp chances of poetry, was almost an abandoned character. He was too ignorant to know the reputations of the men whose society Keats frequented. Like many Britishers of the lower middle class during the last century, he shuddered at the name "artist," and experienced at the mere thought of men devoting their lives to such bagatelles as painting pictures or writing verses a kind of nameless fear. John was one of the crew, and therefore he was undoubtedly bad, if indeed, he were not mad; and it is probable that Abbey would have felt much easier in his mind could his recalcitrant ward have been proved hopelessly insane. That, at least would not have been blameworthy, or due to any error of his guardian's bringing up. Such intercourse as he allowed between Fanny and John was of the most meagre kind. But, at this period, he seems not to have objected to their exchanging letters, as he did later on.

In this first letter, Keats sets out his purpose clearly. It is that he and Fanny shall keep up a regular correspondence to make up, as far as may be, for the infrequence of their meetings. This is how he puts it:

> "Let us now begin a regular question and answer — a little pro and con; letting it interfere as a pleasant method of my coming at your favourite little wants and enjoy-

[1] Colvin.

> ments, that I may meet them in a way befitting a brother.
>
> We have been so little together since you have been able to reflect on things that I know not whether you prefer the History of King Pepin to Bunyan's Pilgrim's Progress — or Cinderella and her glass slipper to Moor's Almanack. However in a few letters I hope I shall be able to come at that and adapt my scribblings to your Pleasure. You must tell me about all you read if it be only six Pages in a Week and this transmitted to me every now and then will procure you full sheets of Writing from me pretty frequently. — This I feel as a necessity for we ought to become intimately acquainted, in order that I may not only, as you grow up love you as my only Sister, but confide in you as my dearest friend."

The wistfulness of Keats's suggestion is pathetic. Here again is the old story: that longing for a woman in whom he can confide; that need of a sister, one of the great, compelling needs of his life. Fanny is too young still, as he realizes (she was only fourteen), but he seeks to build up such a relation between them that, by the time she has developed to the point of understanding him, she will unconsciously have stepped into the empty place in his heart and be quite ready to function toward him in the capacity he so much desires. Now, at Oxford, this sister-need is imperious, and Fanny, just growing old enough to talk to — about some things, at any rate — is very much in his mind.

Toward the end of the letter, he comes back to his charge:

> "Now Fanny you must write soon — and write all you think about, never mind what — only let me have a good deal of your writing."

Fanny must have obeyed, for the "full sheets of writing" which he promises to send her "pretty frequently" in answer, she certainly got. The letters are constant with inquiries as to what she would like him to send her — books, pencils, drawing-paper, plants, even the advisability of a flageolet is discussed. He lets his fun run over in these letters, they fairly ripple with enchanting nonsense, and are full of a solicitous tenderness for the little girl and every small thing about her life.

Here I must abandon chronology for a moment and give a few excerpts from these letters to Fanny. They reveal a certain side of Keats as nothing else does, and without this side no portrait of him is complete. Keats regarded the Abbeys as a sort of ogres, and Fanny does not seem to have been happy with them. This Oxford letter is addressed to her at "Miss Kaley's School," which looks as though Keats preferred not to send his letters to Mr. Abbey's house. As the school was in Walthamstow, where Abbey lived, this method of address, even if Fanny were a boarder, seems odd without some such explanation.

Keats may not have cared for children in general, but he cared very much for Fanny, and he knew perfectly how to please her. In one of these letters he asks her a profoundly important question, as follows:

> "On looking at your seal I cannot tell whether it is done or not with a Tassie — it seems to me to be paste. As I went through Leicester Square lately I was going to call and buy you some, but not knowing but you might have some I would not run the chance of buying duplicates. Tell me if you have any or if you would like any — and whether you would rather have motto ones like that with which I seal this letter; or heads of great Men such as Shakespeare, Milton, &c. — or fancy pieces of Art; such as Fame, Adonis &c. — those gentry you read of at the end of the English Dictionary."

Keats often speaks of seals, and, as I have already mentioned,[1] he had a great affection for these Tassie "gems." There was a wide range for him to choose from, since the Tassie reproductions ran into thousands of specimens. Those letters of Keats which I have, in which

[1] See Vol. I, p. 115.

the seal impressions are not obliterated, show five different designs; there is a head of Shakespeare, two large heads of worthy gentlemen I cannot identify, a small square containing the torso of a boy, and a beautiful little lyre with two of its strings broken and the rather wistful motto: "*Qui me néglige me désole.*" [1]

Whatever goes to the making of an interesting man is interesting, therefore I feel no scruple for bringing in the seals, nor this most engaging bit in another letter to Fanny, written after waiting for a stage-coach to start:

> "I got to the stage half an hour before it set out and counted the buns and tarts in a Pastry-cook's window and was just beginning with the Jellies."

There the sentence ends and leaves us with our mouths watering.

One more quotation from these letters to his sister, I must give. Its quaintness and charm are, I think, irresistible. It is one of the best examples of this vein in Keats. He is writing from Winchester on an August day:

> "I should like now to promenade round your Gardens — apple-tasting — pear-tasting — plum-judging — apricot nibbling — peach-scrunching — nectarine-sucking and Melon-carving. I have also a great feeling for antiquated cherries full of sugar cracks — and a white currant tree kept for company. I admire lolling on a lawn by a water lillied pond to eat white currants and see gold fish: and go to the Fair in the Evening if I'm good. There is not hope for that — one is sure to get into some mess before evening."

After all this whimsey, comes the loving solicitude after Fanny's welfare, for the letter ends:

> "Have these hot days I brag of so much been well or ill for your health? Let me hear soon —"

[1] See drawing on title-page.

This pursuit of Keats's attitude toward his sister has taken us far afield from Oxford. I propose to scramble back forthwith, by giving Bailey's account of the manner in which the two friends spent their days.[1] Says Bailey:

> "He wrote, and I read, sometimes at the same table, sometimes at separate desks or tables, from breakfast to the time of our going out for exercize, — generally two or three o'clock. He sat down to his task, — which was about 50 lines a day, — with his paper before him, and wrote with as much regularity, and apparently as much ease as he wrote his letters . . . Sometimes he fell short of his allotted task, but not often: and he would make it up another day. But he never forced himself. When he had finished his writing for the day, he usually read it over to me: and he read or wrote letters until we went for a walk. This was our habit day by day."

We can supplement this meagre outline from a sketch in a letter written by Keats to Reynolds on September twenty-first. It is a far more brightly coloured picture:

> "For these last five or six days, we have had a Boat on the Isis, and explored all the streams about, which are more in number than your eye-lashes. We sometimes skim into a Bed of rushes, and there become naturalized river-folks, — there is one particularly nice nest, which we have christened 'Reynolds's Cove,' in which we have read Wordsworth, and talked as may be."

Bailey seems to have been under the impression (which, after all, is not likely to be very accurate, as he was writing thirty years later) that Keats wrote a great many letters while he was at Oxford. If he did so, few of them have descended to us. Two letters to Jane Reynolds, one to Jane and Marianne together, two to their brother, one to Fanny Keats, and one to Haydon, are all we have from Oxford, and, of these, one is a new discovery. In the last chapter,

[1] Bailey Memoranda. Colvin.

I quoted some passages from one of the letters to Jane Reynolds.[1] In that same letter, there is a pleasant little bit of fooling; which is not all fooling, to be sure. The passage runs:

> "Imprimis — I sincerely believe that Imogen is the finest creature, and that I should have been disappointed at having you prefer Juliet — Item — yet I feel such a yearning towards Juliet that I would rather follow her into Pandemonium than Imogen into Paradise — heartily wishing myself a Romeo to be worthy of her, and to hear the Devils quote the old proverb 'Birds of a feather flock together.'"

This mention of Juliet in the letter of September fourteenth, puts the new, undated letter as written after that. As to what it refers, we can only surmise that Jane Reynolds had been twitting Keats about his preference for Juliet. Through the kind permission of the present owner,[2] this letter to Jane Reynolds appears here for the first time in print:

> "My dear Jane:
>
> You must not expect that your Porcupine quill is to be shot at me with impunity — without you mean to question the existence of the Pyramids or rout Sir Thos. Newton out of his Coffin. If I did not think you had a kind of preference yourself for Juliet I would not say a word more about it — but as I know people love to be reminded of those they most love — 'tis with me a certain thing that you are much fishing for a little proing and conning thereon. As to your accusations I perhaps may answer them like Haydon in a postcript. If you go on at this rate I shall always have you in my imagination side by side with Bailey's Picture of Jeremy Taylor who always looks as if he were going to hit me a rap with a Book he hold[s] in a very threatening position.
>
> My head is always in imminent danger. However with

[1] See Vol. I. p. 406.

[2] Mrs. Roland Gage Hopkins, of Brookline, Mass.

the armour of Words and the Sword of Syllables I hope to attack you in a very short time more at length.

My love to Marianne.

Yours sincerely,

JOHN KEATS."

I should, perhaps, say that not only does the mention of "Bailey's Picture of Jeremy Taylor" prove that the letter was written from Oxford, there is also the fact that it is written on a doubling of a letter of Bailey's. For those of my readers who are not accustomed to the folded and sealed letter sheets of a hundred years ago, before the invention of gummed envelopes, I must explain that the "doublings" were the folded-under edges of the last sheet, by means of which the letter itself became an oblong packet, with a plain surface on one side for the address and a flap on the other for the seal.

It is amusing to observe that Keats's absence from Hunt, and also his absence from Haydon's animadversions in respect to Hunt, tend to weaken his dissatisfaction with his former idol. Writing to Reynolds on September twenty-first, he has this to say on the subject:

> "I think I see you and Hunt meeting in the Pit. What a very pleasant fellow he is, if he would give up the sovereignty of a room pro bono. What evenings we might pass with him, could we have him from Mrs. H. Failings I am always rather rejoiced to find in a man than sorry for; they bring us to a Level. He has them, but then his makes-up are very good."

This humourously tolerant attitude toward Hunt's "failings" is evidence that the sentimental farce is now so far behind that Keats is no longer even in the state of revolt and escape. As a free man, a member of no group and adherent of no school, he and Hunt are on a level, and Keats can afford to make allowances.

We have only to glance back a year, two years, to see how

immeasurably Keats has advanced in the time. Not only poetically; he is infinitely more mature, less open to pressure from without, more capable of judgement in every way. Think of the boy who came to London in September, 1815; think of the young fellow who, a year later, came back from Margate, full of an eager desire to renew his acquaintance with the author of *Rimini*; and think of him now, set fair toward poetry, a poetry of thews and muscle, of clarity and precision. Not that he had yet achieved it, but that he knew it was a thing he must achieve. His gradual growth can be minutely followed in his letters. No biography can do more than add marginal notes to them.

We cannot do better here than return to Bailey's Memoranda, which records various details of the interminable conversations the two young men indulged in during all that halcyon month. They are fragmentary, of course, just scraps which stuck in Bailey's mind, and probably somewhat coloured by Bailey's own opinions; but, even so, they are most important. The italics are Bailey's and refer presumably to those lines in the poems quoted which Keats admired.

[1]"Our conversation rarely or never flagged, during our walks, or boatings, or in the evening. And I have retained a few of his opinions on Literature and criticism which I will detail. The following passage from Wordsworth's Ode on Immortality was deeply felt by Keats, who however at this time seemed to me to value this great Poet rather in particular passages than in the full-length portrait, as it were, of the great imaginative and philosophical Christian Poet, which he really is, and which Keats obviously, not long afterwards, felt him to be.

> Not for these I raise
> The song of thanks and praise;
> But for those obstinate questionings
> Of sense and outward things,
> Fallings from us, vanishings;

[1] Bailey Memoranda. Colvin.

> Blank misgivings of a creature
> Moving about in worlds not realized,
> *High instincts, before which our mortal nature*
> Did tremble like a guilty thing surprized.

The last lines he thought were quite awful in their application to a guilty finite creature, like man, in the appalling nature of the feeling which they suggested to a thoughtful mind. Again, we often talked of that noble passage in the lines on *Tintern Abbey*: —

> That blessed mood,
> In which the *burthen of the mystery*,
> In which the heavy and the weary weight
> Of all this unintelligible world
> Is lightened.

And his references to this passage are frequent in his letters. — But in those exquisite stanzas,

> She dwelt among the untrodden ways,
> Beside the springs of Dove.

ending, —

> She lived unknown and few could know
> When Lucy ceased to be;
> But she is in her grave, and oh,
> *The difference to me.*

The simplicity of the last line he declared to be the most perfect pathos."

I am afraid we must take some of Bailey's statements in the foregoing passage with a grain of salt. It is quite evident that the young aspirant for clerical orders read into Keats's remarks some of his own predilections, and that the middle-aged clergyman who recollected them went even farther astray. Keats certainly preferred Wordsworth in his lyrical moods to Wordsworth philosophically inclined, although, under Bailey's tuition, he was beginning to probe a little deeper into the domain of philosophical speculation. But Keats's philosophizing, when he arrived at it, was of a totally different kind from Wordsworth's. Wordsworth was, as Bailey says, a Christian poet; Keats was only Christian in the sense that a man must be who has been brought up in a Christian country and habituated from his earliest years to the teaching of a Christian sect. In so far as Christianity has modified social laws and customs, Keats was a Christian, but in no other way. His gradual drifting away from the Christian religion, indeed from any religion, was in him an evolution, not a revolution. Wordsworth stood to him as a type of great poet and far-seeing man, the dogma in which Wordsworth encased his opinions, the idiom in which he presented them, were to Keats unimportant superfluities. It does not take a great deal of understanding to see that in the instance quoted by Bailey, Keats was criticizing Wordsworth's poetical content, Bailey his ethical. Keats saw in the lines italicized by Bailey a felicity of poetic expression, while to Bailey these same lines were fraught with the truths of religious faith. Man is a finite creature to the believer and the unbeliever alike; but he is a guilty finite creature only to the former. Nothing that we know of Keats permits us for a moment to suppose that he ever regarded mankind from this point of view. The last four lines of the first quotation given by Bailey translate too well into Keats's own state of mind, confronted by all the newly opened mental and imaginative vistas raying out before him, for us to ignore them in this connection. The same thing is true of the second quotation. "The burthen of the mystery" is excellent as phrase and description both; and, as both, Keats undoubtedly acclaimed it, but without any specific dogmatic significance. A little later, it became one of his favourite expressions, standing for its actual meaning shorn of all doctrinal bias.

It cannot be too much insisted upon that Keats was not a Christian poet, employing the word in its usual orthodox sense. His was a strongly religious nature, but the religion he harboured was a highly individualized form of satisfaction in ignorance. He believed in the "principle of beauty" and the wisdom of virtue, but beyond these shadowy outlines of truth he was content not to go. He was the type of man who holds to a visionary clue flung out from himself and projected into the unknown. To such a man, the ideal is a magnified essence of his own finest qualities; the difference between him and the devotees of creeds is that, where he is satisfied to leave everything vague and fluid, they must needs crystallize and announce an actuality.

Before long, we shall find Keats profoundly speculating on these things, and even using Wordsworth's *Tintern Abbey* to point his argument, but I do not wish to give these speculations a year earlier than he seems to have arrived at them. They belong to his mental attitude in 1818, not in 1817, although the germ of them was undoubtedly at work in the Oxford days. It is, however, precisely from these later expressed opinions of Keats that I have deduced his attitude toward religion.

That I am right in my supposition as to how and why Bailey misunderstood Keats's criticisms, is shown by the last quotation, where the underscored line is important in its dramatic sense alone.

Another conversation recollected by Bailey concerns the passage in Wordsworth's *Excursion* referring to Grecian mythology:

> ". . . Fancy fetched
> Even from the blazing chariot of the Sun
> A beardless youth who touched a golden lute,
> And filled the illumined groves with ravishment."

In Bailey's words, "Keats said this description of Apollo should have ended at the 'golden lute,' and have left the imagination to complete the picture, how he 'filled the illumined groves.'" In this criticism, we see how very well

Keats was beginning to understand the value of suggestion as a factor in poetry. Bailey also recalls that "Keats was an ardent admirer of Chatterton," and continues:

> [1]"Methinks now I hear him recite, or chant, in his peculiar manner, the following stanza of the Roundelay sung by the minstrels of Ella:—
>
> *Come with acorn cup and thorn*
> Drain my hertys blood away;
> Life and all its good I scorn;
> Dance by night or feast by day.
>
> The first line to his ear possessed great charm."

The first line charms for two reasons: one is that strange, elusive English presentation of sylvan things, a grace which cannot be analyzed; the other lies in the alternations of the "u" and "o" sounds, and the alliterative "c's" and "th's," the softness of the effect being relieved by the sharp "p" in the middle.

Apparently Bailey was the only one of Keats's friends who did much probing into his method of composition. In connection with Bailey's remembrance of Keats's pleasure in this line of Chatterton's, it is interesting to know that

> "One of his favourite topics of discourse was the principle of melody in verse, upon which he had his own notions, particularly in his management of open and close vowels... It was, that the vowels should be so managed as not to clash with one another, so as to hear the melody, — and yet that they should be interchanged, like differing notes of music to prevent monotony..."

There does not seem to be anything very remarkable about that. I think every respectable poet, since time was, has had the same theory, if such it deserves to be called. I have not had access to Bailey's manuscript myself, so I must

[1] Bailey Memoranda. Colvin.

take Sir Sidney Colvin's word for it that "Bailey here tries to reconstruct and illustrate from memory Keats's theory of vowel sounds, but his attempt falters and breaks down." [1] Lord Houghton has given us one more sentence, paraphrased from Bailey, to the effect that "all sense of monotony was to be avoided, except when expressive of a special purpose." But that idea also is universal. That Keats had a theory is evident, and it is equally evident, from what we know of Keats, that it was not the platitudinous stuff here recorded, but the most evident thing of all is that Bailey had forgotten everything about it except that it had existed. Lord Houghton's remarks on the results of Keats's practice of his theory are more conclusive than anything we know of the theory itself. They are:

> "Uniformity of metre is so much the rule of English poetry, that, undoubtedly, the carefully varied harmonies of Keats's verse were disagreeable, even to cultivated readers, often producing exactly the contrary impression from what was intended."

How hard, how desperately hard, is the way of the experimenter in art! How cruelly do those persons, whose blunt-edged senses cannot keep pace with his alert ones, treat such a man! Keats was, all his life, an experimenter. He knew his English public, but he changed his ways not a jot to placate them. Has he not said: "One of the great reasons that the English have produced the finest writers in the world is, that the English world has ill-treated them during their lives and foster'd them after their deaths." But this was after he had learnt to comfort himself with the wry smile of irony.

How did Keats write? What were his methods of composition? In what manner did his poems get themselves actually put down on paper? We have seen a little of his way of work, from time to time, but this seems a good place to consider the subject more in detail.

[1] Colvin.

I have in my possession a manuscript in Woodhouse's handwriting which I take to be one of the many notes on various aspects of Keats that he was forever jotting down. This paper is, in many ways, so untrue to fact that I cannot help thinking that when Keats gave him the data for it, as he seems to have done, he was, as the term is, gently "pulling Woodhouse's leg." It would not be an uncharacteristic gesture, where Woodhouse was concerned. Yet the paper has interesting things in it, and as I have never seen it anywhere, I believe it to be unpublished. I shall, therefore, quote it practically in full. It bears no title, nor date, and begins without any preamble:

> "These lines give some insight into Keats's mode of writing Poetry. He has repeatedly said in conversation that he never sits down to write, unless he is full of ideas, and then thoughts come about him in troops as though soliciting to be accepted and he selects (One of his maxims is that if Poetry does not come naturally it had better not come at all). The moment he feels any dearth he discontinues writing and waits for a happier moment. He is generally more troubled by redundancy than by a poverty of images, and he culls what appears to him at the time the best. — He never corrects, unless perhaps a word here or there should occur to him as preferable to an expression he has already used — He is impatient of correcting and says he would rather burn the piece in question and write another or something else. 'My judgment' (he says) 'is as active while I am actually writing as my imagination. In fact all my faculties are strongly excited and in their full play — and shall I afterwards, when my imagination is idle, and the heat in which I wrote has gone off, sit down coldly to criticize when in possession of only one faculty what I have written when almost inspired.' This fact explains the reason of the perfectness, fullness, richness and completion of most that comes from him. He has said that he has often not been aware of the beauty of some thought or expression until after he had composed and written it down — It has then struck him with astonishment and seemed rather the

> production of another person than his own. He has wondered how he came to hit upon it. This was the case with the description of Apollo in the 3rd book of 'Hyperion' . . . It seemed to come by chance or magic — to be as it were something given to him."

There is more, but nothing of importance, and we have enough to see both the substratum of truth and the over-work of nonsense of which it is composed. That Keats ever said the things here attributed to him, as they stand, it is ridiculous to suppose. Whatever Keats was, he was no prig. He certainly did believe that poetry which did not force itself to be written was valueless. In a letter to Taylor, written in February, 1818, he says:

> "In poetry I have a few axioms, and you will see how far I am from their centre.
>
> 1st. I think poetry should surprise by a fine excess, and not by singularity; it should strike the reader as a wording of his own highest thoughts, and appear almost a remembrance.
>
> 2nd. Its touches of beauty should never be half-way, thereby making the reader breathless, instead of content. The rise, the progress, the setting of Imagery should, like the Sun, come natural to him, shine over him, and set soberly, although in magnificence, leaving him in the luxury of twilight. But it is easier to think what poetry should be than to write it. And this leads me to
>
> Another axiom — That if poetry comes not as naturally as the leaves to a tree, it had better not come at all."

That is what Keats really thought, in his own words. He may have said that on reading a passage over it sometimes struck him as being better than he remembered, he probably did say that he never forced himself to write when not in the mood, but the sentimental tone of awe attributed to him by Woodhouse is absolutely foreign to his habit of thought. And that he wrote his poems out almost as they were to stand and seldom corrected them, is simply not so. Keats corrected and corrected. Not only at the moment of writing, but up to the last proof. All good poets correct, and Keats's corrections are a most important study for any one who is learning the art of poetry. He rarely blunders. Each new change is practically always an improvement. His early drafts are full of alterations done in the very heat of composition. I have several interesting examples of this in my own collection. For instance, I happen to own the first draft of the ode *To Autumn*; the copy of it made on the same day and sent in a letter to Woodhouse; and, of course, the first edition of the *Lamia* volume in which it appeared. There may have been other drafts, there is a transcript of a holograph manuscript in the British Museum, but these two holographs of mine, and the first edition, will serve us here.

Taking the first seven lines of the second stanza, here is the way Keats composed: He started, "Who hath not seen thee," with a question mark after it, and the line goes on, "for thy haunts are many." Then he scratched out the question mark and changed the end of the line to "oft amid thy stores," with the question mark at the end; then he drew a line through the "s" of "stores" and left "store." In the letter copy, written the same day, he reverts to "stores," but again cancels the "s" in the printed version which now reads "store." The second line in the first draft was first written, "Sometimes whoever seeks for thee may find," but "for thee "is deleted in favour of "abroad," and this correction is retained in the letter draft and in the first edition. The third and fourth lines are uncorrected, and read as in the printed version; but the fifth, sixth, and seventh gave him much trouble. For line five, he first wrote "While bright the sun slants through the barn," then, noticing that he is a foot short, he adds "bushy" before "barn," putting it above the line with a caret. But even so the line does not strike him as entirely satisfactory, and he cancels it at once for "or sound asleep in a half reaped field," cancels that, and writes over it "or on a half reap'd furrow sound asleep," which he follows in the next line with "Dosed with red poppies; while thy reaping hook;" this he lets stand and goes on with the seventh line, which begins "Spares from some slumbrous," but evidently feels at once the hum of the "m" sounds, so writes half way under the line, "minutes while warm slumbers creep." But, by this time, the manuscript is in an awful mess, so he criss-crosses out the three confused lines and begins to transcribe them clearly. Taking the line he has decided on, he writes it out fairly "or on a half reap'd furrow sound asleep," but already he has thought of a change for the sixth line, and he now writes it "Das'd with the fume of poppies while thy hook," and then the difficult seventh line begins to bother him again. He tries his first attempt, with one word altered, for the beginning, and adds a different end, making the line read "Spares for some slumbrous minutes the next swath," but again seeing that the hum continues in spite of the change of "from" to "for," draws his pen through the whole line and writes above "Spares the next swath and all its twined flowers." In the letter draft, these three lines remain as finally left in the first draft, but in the first edition the word "Das'd" has given place to "Drows'd."

The last line of the poem shows how he touched and re-touched his things. In the first draft, he begins "And new flock still," scratches it out, and puts underneath the full line "And gathering swallows twitter in the skies." In the letter draft, he changes to "gathered swallows," but reverts to his first reading of "gathering" in the first edition.

These are not the only changes in these three versions of the ode *To Autumn*, but they are enough to show how Keats worked. What is true of this poem is true of all his manuscripts which I have seen. The first draft of the *Eve of St. Agnes*, in my collection, is so altered and rewritten as to be almost unreadable. To follow variations from a text in notes at the bottom of a page, gives us the gist of what the poet was trying to do, but gives no clue as to how his mind really worked. To see the manuscripts is almost like getting inside his brain. I mean, of course, manuscripts which are first drafts, where the poet was not copying, but composing as he went along.

These, naturally, are verbal criticisms; criticisms of subject matter rarely appear in a manuscript. But Keats was no mere intuitive poet. He reflected constantly on his art, and the remarks about poetry scattered through his writings prove him to have possessed — beside, and quite apart from, his genius — a very acute and subtle mind. "The excellence of every art is its intensity" is one of his dictums, and it is absolutely true. Again, he speaks of "that trembling delicate and snail-horn perception of beauty," and if ever man had it, it was he. Once when George Keats had been making some comparison between him and Lord Byron, he answers in a letter: "You speak of Lord Byron and me. There is this great difference between us: he describes what he sees — I describe what I imagine. Mine is the hardest task." Writing to Reynolds in February, 1818, he points with a deft finger to the abiding fault of didactic poetry, where statement is permitted to oust suggestion, and maps the large gusto of the Elizabethans with an accurate eye, and all this in a passage of such nicely mingled common, and uncommon, sense that it is difficult to decide which predominates:

> "It may be said that we ought to read our contemporaries, that Wordsworth &c. should have their due from us. But, for the sake of a few imaginative or domestic passages, are we to be bullied into a certain Philosophy engendered in the whims of an Egotist? Every man has his speculations, but every man does not brood and peacock over them till he makes a false coinage and deceives himself . . . We hate poetry that has a palpable design upon us,

and, if we do not agree, seems to put its hand into its breeches pocket. Poetry should be great and unobtrusive, a thing which enters into one's soul, and does not startle or amaze with itself, but with its subject . . . Modern poets differ from the Elizabethans in this: each of the moderns like an Elector of Hanover governs his petty state, and knows how many straws are swept daily from the Causeways in all his dominions, and has a continual itching that all the Housewives should have their coppers well scoured. The ancients were Emperors of vast Provinces, they had only heard of the remote ones and scarcely cared to visit them."

It was not only in religion, but in poetry as well, that Keats was content to leave ultimate purpose unsolved. Witness this interesting bow-shot at a truth sent to his brothers at Teignmouth:

". . . it struck me what quality went to form a man of achievement, especially in literature, and which Shakespeare possessed so enormously — I mean *Negative Capability*, that is, where a man is capable of being in uncertainties, mysteries, doubts, without any irritable reaching after fact and reason. Coleridge, for instance, would let go by a fine isolated verisimilitude caught from the Penetralium of mystery, from being incapable of remaining content with half-knowledge. This pursued through volumes would perhaps take us no further than this, that with a great poet the sense of Beauty overcomes every other consideration, or rather obliterates all consideration."

Poetry was Keats's chief interest, but not his only interest, he brought his faculty of analysis to bear on anything he happened to be reading. There are keen criticisms of prose to be found in his letters, of which this is an example:

"You ask me what degrees there are between Scott's novels and those of Smollet. They appear to me to be quite distinct in every particular, more especially in their aim. Scott endeavours to throw so interesting and romantic a colouring into common and low characters as to give them a touch of the sublime. Smollet, on the contrary, pulls down and levels what with other men would continue romance. The grand parts of Scott are within the reach of more minds than the finest humours of 'Humphrey Clinker.' I forget whether that fine thing of the Sargeant is Fielding's or Smollet's,[1] but it gives me more pleasure than the whole novel of 'The Antiquary.'"

It is with great difficulty that I resist the temptation to multiply quotations such as these, but a book cannot be stretched indefinitely, and I have given enough to show with what diligent insight Keats's mind occupied itself with the art of writing. I have dealt here with poetry and prose, in the next chapter we shall see how Keats observed and considered plays.

Keats did a great deal of reading at Oxford, among other things he found on Bailey's shelves was the folio volume of the poems of Mrs. Katherine Philips, the seventeenth century lady better known as "the matchless Orinda." He was so struck by the verses this lady wrote to her friend "Mrs. M. A." or "Rossannia" (really Mary Awbrey) that he copied them in full to Reynolds in illustration of what poetry by a woman should be. This was after airing his views on "a set of devils," who are "a set of women, who having taken a snack or luncheon of Literary scraps, set themselves up for a tower of Babel in languages, Sapphos in poetry, Euclids in Geometry, and everything in nothing." So, to the banging of kettle-drums, he buries his early love for Mrs. Tighe. There was one woman of whom he had never heard, and whom it is doubtful whether he had the qualities to appreciate if he had, a woman who painted women as only Shakespeare has painted them. Keats was writing on September twenty-first, nine weeks before, on July eighteenth, Jane Austen had died at Winchester. But if Keats had never heard of

[1] Fielding's *Tom Jones*.

Miss Austen, Miss Austen had never heard of Keats. The slim little *Poems* does not seem to have reached Chawton, where she lived; nor Godmersham Park, where she visited; nor Winchester, where she died; and probably she would not have liked it at all had it drifted her way, for her favourite poet was Crabbe.

We have seen how Keats wrote of Oxford to the Reynolds girls and his sister Fanny. To John Reynolds, he bursts into a characteristic bit of fooling in rhyme. In an undated fragment of a letter, which Buxton Forman puts after the one I have just quoted, written on Sunday, September twenty-first, but which I think belongs to the beginning of his stay with Bailey, is this remark: "Wordsworth sometimes, though in a very fine way, gives us sentences in the style of school exercizes." Here Keats misquotes a couple of lines from Wordsworth's poem beginning "The cock is crowing," and continues: "Now, I think this is an excellent method of giving a very clear description of an interesting place such as Oxford is.

The Gothic looks solemn
The plain Doric column
Supports an old Bishop and Crosier;
The mouldering arch,
Shaded o'er by a larch
Lives next door to Wilson the Hosier."

There are three stanzas, and there may have been more, for the fragment ends after the third stanza. If Keats meant to do his poem "in a fine way," he certainly did not succeed. The rhyme to "crosier" wrecked him, he could think of nothing but "hosier," and, with the advent of the excellent Wilson, the poem's doom is sealed. Thereafter it never even peeps back at its departed "fine way"; it is joking pure and simple.

I cannot leave these first weeks at Oxford without giving one more excerpt from the letter of September fourteenth to Jane Reynolds. It will be remembered that it is in this very letter that Keats speaks of the sea, and I have already shown how the gradually diminishing effect of Oxford brought him back to his preoccupation with the sea, and to his own natural poetic speech. It almost looks as though Keats were conscious of this, and also partly aware that his mental home-coming is, in a way, a receding from Bailey. This receding he may have felt, half-consciously, to be a disloyalty, but he knows that, however his creative faculty may revolt from even the least intended influence, he himself is absolutely loyal to his friend. How loyal, we see from this passage:

> "To your brother John (whom henceforth I shall consider as mine) and to you, my dear friends, Marianne and Jane, I shall ever feel grateful for having made known to me so real a fellow as Bailey. He delights me in the selfish and (please God) in the disinterested part of my disposition. If the old Poets have any pleasure in looking down at the enjoyers of their works, their eyes must bend with a double satisfaction upon him. I sit as at a feast when he is over them, and pray that if, after my death, any of my labours should be worth saving, they may have so 'honest a chronicler' as Bailey. Out of this, his enthusiasm in his own pursuit and for all good things is of an exalted kind — worthy a more healthful frame and an untorn spirit."

Keats possessed to a very great degree the power of generous enthusiasm. He was no niggard of love. Where he gave affection and admiration, he gave with an unstinting hand. He was a man of friendships, because friendship to him was so tough and full-hearted a thing. Yet it is a melancholy fact that, warm and kindly as many of his friends were, in no single instance did he get back as good as he gave. The only exception is in the case of a man whom Keats certainly never rated as one of his inner circle. I mean Richard Woodhouse, for Woodhouse gave all that the relations between the two men permitted, and more than Keats ever knew. For the reasons that they never came closer together, we must look to those baffling laws which rule the circumstances of personal attractions.

By the time the Third Book was done, on that Friday when he wrote at the end of his finished manuscript, "Oxf. Sept. 26," Keats was dog tired. He needed what he always needed after a long bout of writing — a change. Constant change of scene was the miraculous draught of Keats's life. Change startled him into the creative mood, and braced up his flaccid nerves when he had been working too long. At this point, somebody had an inspiration, and I imagine it was Bailey. Why should they not both go on a little jaunt to Stratford-on-Avon, and see Shakespeare's house, and revel in the kind of dreams which Keats knew so well how to evoke? It was a simple journey from Oxford, a comfortable coach ride of just under forty miles, the only difficulty being that, as Stratford was on the way to various other places, the London coaches which they must have taken to reach it all passed through Oxford at night. A night to go, two days and a night at Stratford, a night to return — that was probably the itinerary followed by Keats and Bailey. We know that they were in Stratford on Thursday, October second, for their signatures appear under that date in the visitors' book of Holy Trinity Church.[1]

Keats, much as he must have been moved by Stratford — as he always was by places of literary association, and Stratford was certainly the cream of such to him — was in no mood for writing poetry, and under no necessity to write letters since he was going home so soon. Therefore it is to Bailey's account that we must look for Keats's impressions of the trip. They are exactly what one would suppose:

[1] Colvin.

[1] "We went of course to the house visited by so many thousands of all nations of Europe, and inscribed our names in addition to the 'numbers numberless' of those which literally blackened the walls. We also visited the Church, and were pestered by a commonplace showman of the place . . . He was struck, I remember, with the simple statue there, which, though rudely executed, we agreed was most probably the best likeness of the many extant, but none very authentic, of Shakespeare.

His enjoyment was of that genuine, quiet kind which was a part of his gentle nature; deeply feeling what he truly enjoyed, but saying little."

We may regard this, as far as it goes, as fact. Although Bailey gets his date wrong — recollecting the visit as having taken place before Keats finished his Third Book, which we see by the signatures and date in the visitors' book of Holy Trinity was not so. I think it very likely, however, that Bailey is right in saying that Keats returned with him to Oxford. Keats may well have thought that the long pull of ninety-three miles back to town would be better broken by a quiet night or two at Bailey's. They probably came back from Stratford on Friday night, for on Sunday, at the latest, Keats went up to town, going "from coach to Coach as far as Hampstead," he tells Bailey in his bread-and-butter letter written on the Wednesday following. At Hampstead, he found his brothers, returned from Paris; and so the Summer outings ended and the three boys settled down to life as they supposed it was going to be.

The first thing that John did the very next day after his arrival was to rush off and see everybody. First came the Reynoldses, then Haydon and even Hunt, the last two now living near each other in Lisson Grove. At Hunt's, he found Shelley, and in all three places he heard news of his set and gossip of not too agreeable a character. The next

[1] Bailey Memoranda. Colvin.

morning he went to Brown's and Reynolds came in, Reynolds "was pretty bobbish, we had a pleasant day." The very night that he is writing, the brothers are to dine at Brown's where Reynolds is also expected.

This is Keats to the life, just what we should expect. Violent reaction engendering a mood of lively sociability. He wants to see everybody, and see them all in a hurry, and hear about everything, and what he heard was none too grateful. There were a lot of sprightly little quarrels going on. Haydon's picture was at a dead stop, and Hunt was continually going to see him and criticizing it adversely; Horace Smith had become bored with Hunt. Haydon told Keats not to show Hunt his poem "on any Account" or Hunt would surely say that he had done half of it. Reynolds told him that, on his informing Hunt that Keats had completed nearly four thousand lines, Hunt had said that were it not for him they would have been seven thousand. These small grievances were warmed over and served piping hot to Keats in the pleasant way of friends. It was all pretty discouraging, and Keats retails it all to Bailey. The Bentley children and their noise bothered him, and he was not feeling very well. So the letter goes, but it is noticeable that Brown does not figure among the tale-tellers, which was another step forward for Brown's system.

A certain sentence at the end of the letter to Bailey has been seized upon by various biographers and pamphleteers and made to carry a sinister meaning. The sentence in question is this:

> "The little Mercury I have taken has corrected the poison and improved my health — tho' I feel from my employment that I shall never be again secure in Robustness."

W. M. Rossetti was, I believe, the first to read into this sentence the suggestion that Keats had contracted syphilis at Oxford. He based his theory, of course, on the fact that, in those days, mercury was generally employed in the treatment of that disease. But it is equally true that mercury was used in many other diseases, as, for instance, rheumatism, croup, cholera morbus, dysentery, and pulmonary tuberculosis. Keats was confined to the house for two weeks with some disorder very shortly after he got back to Hampstead, but this may have been due to any one of a number of ailments. For we must remember that he had been under a continuous creative strain for five months and was tired out and run down. His illness evidently attracted attention, for, writing to Bailey from Burford Bridge in November, he says:

> "The world is full of troubles, and I have not much reason to think myself pestered with many.
>
> I think Jane or Marianne has a better opinion of me than I deserve; for, really and truly, I do not think my Brother's illness connected with mine — you know more of the real Cause than they do; nor have I any chance of being rack'd as you have been."

This passage must be read carefully to dig out its meaning. Evidently Jane or Marianne Reynolds was afraid that Keats's recent ill-health pointed to consumption, and considered that he was taking it bravely. Bailey's being racked refers to the non-success of one of his love affairs. Keats thinks himself safe from ever being in Bailey's position, and he does not believe himself touched by tuberculosis. What it all seems to point to is that Keats feared he might have contracted syphilis, but felt that the mercury had cured him since certain symptoms his medical training had taught him to expect did not appear. It is, however, possible that the disease may have struck in and increased his hereditary tendency to tuberculosis. All this may have been true, but it should never be forgotten that none of it is needed. Keats not only inherited a very strong tendency to tuberculosis, he was living intimately with a man who had it, his brother Tom. The sanitary precautions against catching tuberculosis, with which all the world is now familiar, were unknown in his day. The brothers eat together and lived in poorly ventilated rooms. A run-down condition would greatly increase the danger of infection, and Keats, on his return from Oxford, was clearly run-down and in no state to resist any infection to which he might be exposed. The tuberculous throat, which made its appearance definitely in the following Summer, was, without doubt, an effect of long germination in the lungs. How strong the tendency to tuberculosis was in the Keats family is shown by the fact that, in the four generations which we know of, it regularly appeared. Keats's mother died of it, as did two of her sons; of George Keats's children, two became its victims, and two grandchildren also developed it. The fifth generation seems to have outgrown the tendency, also the improved methods of treatment to-day have made curable what was once hopeless. I have not, naturally, written all this without taking medical advice on the subject, and carefully examining the facts of Keats's health as we know them with this advice in mind.

Dr. John B. Hawes, 2nd,[1] for whom I compiled a health history of Keats taken from his letters and those of his friends, writes as follows:

> "I have been over Miss Lowell's manuscript giving the history of Keats's life and death and I can say that in checking it up, it is not inconsistent with pulmonary tuberculosis and laryngeal tuberculosis. Although not typical of the latter, I have seen not a few cases of laryngeal tuberculosis that have acted in just the way this one

[1] Chief of the Pulmonary Clinic. Massachusetts General Hospital. Chief of the Non-Surgical Tuberculosis Clinic. Massachusetts General Hospital. Consultant in Pulmonary Cases for the Veterans' Bureau of Massachusetts. Formerly Secretary of the Tuberculosis Hospital Board of Massachusetts.

> has done. There have been periods when the throat condition has been very severe with hoarseness, and pain, and then for some unknown reason there would be equal periods when practically all symptoms would disappear except a slight hoarseness.
>
> While syphilis, therefore, may have been a factor in this case, I do not feel that such would necessarily be the case, but I do feel that tuberculosis would explain everything."

As to the testimony of the mercury, a letter from Dr. Abner Post,[1] who also examined the "health history" with great care, proves it most unstable evidence. Dr. Post says:

> "There was a long period during which mercury, in a number of forms, was used in medicine very freely and, as it seems today, almost recklessly. Syphilis was only one of the many diseases for which it was used, and it is impossible to know what the disease was, simply because mercury in some form was used in its treatment. The first third of the nineteenth century was included in this period of mercurial infatuation."

Dr. Post goes on to cite a number of authorities in regard to the diseases in which mercury was commonly employed, and to these appends a list of such diseases, which runs to the considerable figure of nineteen. It is from this list that I compiled the much abbreviated catalogue already given.

In view of the opinion of these eminent specialists, my conclusion is that although it is possible that Keats did contract syphilis, there is no proof whatever that he did, since his symptoms, so far as we can tell, are perfectly attributable to tuberculosis alone. Probably, had Keats lived to-day, consumption in his case could have been prevented. He seems to have had a strong constitution apart from his one weakness, although we must not forget that the exactions of an emotional temperament such as his were a handicap. Living when he did, he was in constant

[1] Professor Emeritus of Syphilis. Harvard Medical School.

peril from the moment that he began to over-exert himself, and his close association with the dying Tom left him no loop-hole of escape. The beginning of his illness is usually dated from his return from Scotland in August, 1819. I think that is an error; and, in the light of modern medical research, I am strongly inclined to believe that we must date it, the faint indications of it, from the Autumn of 1817. He was, we remember, very tired and nervous in March, before he went to the Isle of Wight, and since then six months had passed, a period during which he had worked with indefatigable zeal, and suffered to the full the alternations of excitement and depression. The two weeks of illness at Hampstead we must take as a sort of break-down, and a break-down undergone in the close proximity of a tuberculous brother. If we realize this, we shall marvel at the constitution and will which kept him going so long, and not wonder, as some of his earlier biographers have done, that he went so quickly at the end.

The most teasing of the petty annoyances which buzzed round Keats's ears on his return to town was the suggestion that he was indebted to Hunt in the writing of *Endymion*. Since Hunt had not seen a line of the poem, this implication was peculiarly galling. Keats's indignation bursts out in his first letter to Bailey. After quoting a long passage from a letter written to his brother George "in the Spring," part of which I have already given,[1] he goes on:

> "You see Bailey how independent my Writing has been. Hunt's dissuasion was of no avail — I refused to visit Shelley that I might have my own unfettered scope; — and after all, I shall have the Reputation of Hunt's élève. His corrections and amputations will by the knowing ones be traced in the Poem. This is, to be sure, the vexation of a day — nor would I say so many words about it to any but those whom I know to have my welfare and reputation at heart."

[1] See Vol. I, p. 306.

It was not long after this that Keats succumbed to overwork, worry, and, I very much fear, a sore throat. For, toward the end of the month, he writes to Bailey again, telling him that he has been shut up at Hampstead for two weeks, but is now out and about again. A week or more later, he says he has not "been well enough to stand the chance of a wet night," and so has not seen Haydon. Reynolds, he has seen, and doubtless Haslam, Severn, Dilke, and Brown kept his enforced house-keeping from being too dull. But the worries were not fanciful ones. Tom was really ill, and it was becoming evident that a Winter in London would be a dangerous thing for him to face. There was some talk of his going to Lisbon with John, but eventually it was decided that he should try Devonshire instead, and that George, not John, should be his companion.

A very much less important worry, but one which, nevertheless, deserves the name from the trouble it caused Keats, was the case of a young man named Cripps. Haydon had observed this young man at Oxford copying some pictures, and had asked Keats while there to hunt him up and communicate to him an offer from Haydon to take him as a pupil. Keats did so, but it soon appeared that Haydon required the usual apprenticeship fee. Keats, out of sheer kindness of heart, undertook to raise a subscription to meet it, and for some months his letters are full of Cripps, and Haydon's failure to keep his engagements in regard to him. Perhaps Cripps proved himself less talented than Haydon had at first thought, certainly his name has not come ringing down to us. The affair is only of moment as showing Keats's generous willingness to spend himself for other people, and Haydon's unreliability.

A third worry, of a much greater magnitude than the Cripps business, was the appearance in the October number of *Blackwood's Magazine* (the number which inaugurated the ruthless sway of Messrs. Wilson and

Lockhart) of the first of the series of articles on the *Cockney School.* This first article was an attack upon Hunt of the most abominable kind. Keats calls it "a flaming attack," and says of it:

> "I never read anything so virulent — accusing him of the greatest Crimes, depreciating his Wife, his Poetry, his Habits, his Company, his Conversation. These philippics are to come out in numbers called 'The Cockney School of Poetry.' There has been but one number published . . . to which they have prefixed a motto from one Cornelius Webb, Poetaster — who unfortunately was of our party occasionally at Hampstead, and took it into his head to write the following — something about, 'We'll talk on Wordsworth, Byron, a theme we never tire on;' and so forth till he comes to Hunt and Keats. In the motto they have put Hunt and Keats in large letters."

The motto to this outrageous sheaf of abuse reads in this wise:

> 'Our Talk shall be (a theme we never tire on)
> Of Chaucer, Spenser, Shakspeare, Milton, Byron,
> (Our England's Dante) — Wordsworth — HUNT, and KEATS,
> The Muses' Son of promise; and what feats
> He yet may do."
>
> CORNELIUS WEBB.

This naturally led Keats to fear that the next paper would be devoted to him, yet, not knowing the men with whom he had to deal, he seems to have believed that an advertisement in the *Examiner* for November Second, in which Hunt had challenged the writer of the anonymous article (it was signed simply "Z") to send his address to the printer "in order that Justice may be Executed on the proper person" would have the effect of putting a stop to the series. That it had quite the opposite effect, we shall very soon see. Keats could not help dreading the arrival of his turn, but, with admirable courage, he says:

> "I don't mind the thing much — but if he should go to such lengths with me as he has done with Hunt, I must infallibly call him to an Account if he be a human being, and appears in Squares and Theatres, where we might 'possibly meet' — I don't relish his abuse."

What else Keats may have said on the subject, we do not know, for these quotations are from a fragment of a letter to Bailey, postmarked November fifth, 1817, and the fragment ends with the above. Such a threat as that hinted in the *Examiner*, and practically uttered by Keats, was no mere rhodomontade in those days. Duelling, although against the law, was still not seldom resorted to as a means of wiping out an insult. In the sequel, these very *Blackwood* articles led to a duel in which poor John Scott was killed, but that was not until three years later. At the moment, nothing happened; for "Z" was not man enough to acknowledge his identity. It seems wiser to defer discussion of these *Cockney School* articles until a later chapter. It is enough to say, at this moment, that all mystery about them was dissipated years ago, and I shall give the whole history of them when, in the course of the narrative, we reach the time at which the one dealing with Keats was published.

We have now arrived at a point a few days later than the date on which Keats wrote the letter to Jane Reynolds, containing the *Ode to Sorrow*, transcribed in the last chapter. We have seen that Keats, after his long and unbroken concentration on *Endymion* was becoming impatient to try his hand at lyrics once more.[1] He wrote two, and managed to incorporate them in *Endymion*, but, shortly after, he was moved to write another, which no power could make a part of his great poem. It was, and is, a perfectly separate little piece, the only one we know of his permitting himself to write, with the exception of the Oxford parody, since beginning *Endymion*. The poem, which was first printed by

[1] See Vol. I, p. 440.

Lord Houghton, is entitled simply *To* ——. It is, naturally, far better known by its first two lines, which are:

> "Think not of it, sweet one, so;—
> Give it not a tear."

The date is given in the first Woodhouse Commonplace Book in this way: "Abt. 11 Novr. 1817. from K's ms," so there is room for a doubt as to the exact day. November eleventh was a Tuesday, which tells us nothing, of course. Another inconsiderable lyric of the same general character is given by Lord Houghton immediately after *Think not of it*. This second poem is called simply *Lines*, but is generally known, as in the previous case, by its first two:

> "Unfelt, unheard, unseen,
> I've left my little queen."

There is no merit in either of these poems. They read like exercises of lyric form rather than anything else. But, also, they seem an attempt to catch a gossamer beauty, a sort of beauty quite foreign to the type with which Keats had been busy for months. Needless to say, they fail, drooping weakly to the ground not undraggled by the sticky sweetness of Keats's early work. The last things they seem are records of any real occurrence. I am forced to the conclusion that they are simply and solely experiments on Keats's part to see if he had lost his versatility, and a sort of mental outlet to his brain, overworked with one point of view and, with the exception of the *Indian Maiden's Song*, one metre. There is also another possibility, and an extremely likely one, namely, that these two little songs represent new words to Charlotte Reynolds's music, for they are quite in keeping with the sentimental ditties of the period.

As November advanced, the Keats brothers' plans took shape. George and Tom were to go to Teignmouth in Devonshire, starting about the middle of December.

John was to stay in Hampstead, finish *Endymion* and get it ready for the press, and, when that was over, go down to Teignmouth and join his brothers. A pleasant arrangement, but *Endymion* would not allow itself to be finished. There were too many distractions, too many people to see, too many reasons for running hither and thither. The more Keats wanted to end the poem, the more he could not do so. The long and the short of it was that he could not stand things as they were in town; he must try his infallible remedy — change of scene. So off he went to Burford Bridge, to the little inn lying at the foot of Box Hill.

There is no more enchanting place in the home counties than Box Hill, and, if we can imagine ourselves back a hundred years, when trippers were unknown, and Dorking and Leatherhead country villages, with Box Hill itself a sylvan retreat, not a trodden highway — if we can imagine the thin sunshine of late November lightly spreading footpaths and lanes with a shadow-pattern of bare boughs and slender twigs on which sometimes a last dried leaf still clings and flutters, ditches choked with the debris of a season's blooming turned rustling highways to the skim of a passing wind, glimpses of hazy landscape with the little river Mole a blue streak dimming and brightening to the march of blowing clouds, and, from the top of the hill, the Autumn view of smoke-coloured woodlands fringing shorn meadows — we shall know it lovelier still, even on the days when mist hangs heavily about the heads of old oaks and the holly bushes glisten in the rain. Keats could not have chosen a more sympathetic, a more peaceful, or a more cheerful spot. Had he known or cared as much for recent history as he did for a remoter past, his delight in the place itself would have been augmented by the charm of reminiscence. Close to the hill stood Juniper Hall, the home of Madame de Staël, Talleyrand, Narbonne, and other *émigrés* for a time during the French Revolution. Norbury

Park, mentioned so often in Fanny Burney's Diary, was close by, and not far off was Camilla Cottage, which Madame d'Arblay had built with the proceeds of her novel of that name. A memory more likely to affect him lay in the fact that at the very inn where he was staying Nelson had spent a night on his way to Portsmouth to join the *Victory* just before Trafalgar. But, if Keats knew these things, he was not in the humour for them to count. At the moment, he was occupied with the moon and his poem, and the hill chiefly in so far as it brought the moon and his poem into fresh conjunction and gave his imagination a new fillip.

The actual day on which Keats went to Burford Bridge cannot be determined, but it was probably on either Thursday or Friday, November twentieth or twenty-first. He was certainly there on Saturday, the twenty-second, for on Friday or Saturday, he wrote to Bailey.[1] The world was still very much with him in this letter. There is not a word about the countryside, and only the fact that he has gone there to spur on *Endymion* as a reference to his poem. The letter begins with the Cripps worry. Haydon has written a disagreeable letter to Bailey on the subject, which gives Keats an opportunity to express what, from our point of view, is a most interesting opinion. This is what he says:

> [2] "What occasions the greater part of the world's quarrels? Simply this — two Minds meet, and do not understand each other time enough to prevent any shock or surprise at the conduct of either party. As soon as I had known Haydon three days, I had got enough of his Character not to have been surprised at such a Letter as he has hurt you with. Nor, when I knew it, was it a principle with me to drop his acquaintance; although with

[1] For dates of the letters from Burford Bridge to Bailey and Reynolds, see Vol. I, pp. 446–447.

[2] Quotations from this letter are corrected from the holograph. Author's Collection.

VIEW OF BOX HILL FROM NORBURY PARK

From an old engraving in the possession of the author

you it would have been an imperious feeling. I wish you knew all that I think about Genius and Heart — and yet I think that you are thoroughly acquainted with my innermost breast in that respect, or you could not have known me even thus long, and still hold me worthy to be your dear Friend. In passing, however, I must say one thing that has pressed upon me lately, and increased my Humility and capability of submission — and that is this truth — Men of Genius are great as certain ethereal Chemicals operating on the Mass of neutral intellect — but they have not any individuality, any determined Character — I would call the top and head of those who have a proper self, Men of Power.

But I am running my head into a subject which I am certain I could not do justice to under five Years' study, and 3 vols. octavo — and, moreover, long to be talking about the Imagination."

This theory of the impersonality of genius is a favourite speculation with Keats. He explains it more at length in a letter to Woodhouse written two years later. It does, indeed, throw considerable light on a condition of Keats's writing life — the power of reducing his own strong personality to a mere receiving medium, a sensitized plate on which impressions might record themselves untinged by his own ego. Keats's remarks here are not so much a truth as a haphazard shot at a bright speck which he feels may turn out to be a truth. He is a little troubled and perplexed at his shifting moods. Bailey does not shift, he is not two or three men within the hour as Keats is forced to realize that he himself is. Not seeing quite far enough into his own psychological processes, he is not a little shocked at this variability of attitude. Bailey being for the moment his ideal of purposeful endeavour, he wants to find himself more oriented in this respect, and is puzzled and annoyed to discover that he is, as he supposes, the very opposite. The answer is, of course, that Keats confused the necessarily diverse methods of endeavour of the artist and the mere man of brains, be he scholar, banker, what you will. Fumbling round amid the half-truths which his new experiences had scattered about his mind, he missed the reconciling fact of the total difference of the workings of the conscious and subconscious minds. The elementary facts of psychology had not become nursery proverbs to his generation as they have to ours. He knew himself for a man of brains, of far better brains than Bailey could boast, although that, of course, he would have denied. He also knew that he had the power to write poetry, but that the poetry turned him whither it would, and brushed his brains aside whenever it pleased; or rather, that his brains played him false and went rioting over to the side of poetry whenever poetry had a mind to call on them for assistance. This knowledge gave him a sense of bewilderment. Clearly, he was not the master of himself, and if he were not master, what was? He might rule for a day or two, but, whenever it liked, the poetry would come in and order him round like a slave. And the worst of it was that he was never so happy as when he was obeying. He wanted to be a sensitive recipient to his imagination, which to him represented the highest and most spiritual truth of which he was cognizant; but he also wanted, paradoxically, to guide this same imagination, and that he could by no means do. He felt this as a constant war when he felt it at all, which was, on the whole, far too often.

At the end of the letter, he returns again to his charge, fearful lest Bailey should be hurt at his seeming changes of heart. In this passage, he reveals what he seldom, in these early days, permitted anyone to see, the fundamental disbelief in happiness which dogged him all his life. But here it is only a shadow, a faint shadow, swiftly passing:

> "I scarcely remember counting upon any happiness — I look not for it if it be not in the present hour, — nothing startles me beyond the moment. The Setting Sun will always set me to rights, or if a Sparrow come before my

Window, I take part in its existence and pick about the gravel. The first thing that strikes me on hearing a misfortune having befallen another is this — 'Well, it cannot be helped: he will have the pleasure of trying the resources of his Spirit' — and I beg now, my dear Bailey, that hereafter should you observe anything cold in me not to put it to the account of heartlessness, but abstraction — for I assure you I sometimes feel not the influence of a passion or affection during a whole Week — and so long this sometimes continues, I begin to suspect myself, and the genuineness of my feelings at other times — thinking them a few barren Tragedy Tears."

The only comfort for an artist is to know himself for what he is, the possessor of an extremely exacting and disconcerting type of mind. Keats, not yet comprehending himself, is too harsh in his conclusions. Being a sentient, yet highly ethical, man, his quarrel with himself was unending. Since he could not analyze himself in the light of any guiding clue, we find him going at this same subject from different angles, again and again. His endeavours to probe himself are curiously persistent and pathetic, for sincerity was a dominating trait with him.

This letter contains the passage beginning "I am certain of nothing but the Holiness of the Heart's affections," which I quoted in the last chapter.[1] In connection with this, he refers to "the little Song I sent in my last," which, he says, is "a representation from the fancy" of what he has been saying. But no such song do we know. It was probably sent in the letter of November fifth, which has come down to us as a fragment merely, or in another letter that is lost. Certainly the description of it does not fit either of the love songs we have already considered.

Following immediately upon this passage, Keats returns to his and Bailey's long discussions on Milton by a reference to Adam's dream in the Eighth Book of *Paradise Lost*. He uses it to dot his argument:

[1] See Vol. I, p. 360.

[1] "The Imagination may be compared to Adam's dream, — he awoke and found it truth: — I am more zealous in this affair, because I have never yet been able to perceive how anything can be known for truth by consecutive reasoning — and yet it must be. Can it be that even the greatest Philosopher ever arrived at his Goal without putting aside numerous objections? However it may be, O for a life of Sensations rather than of Thoughts! It is 'a Vision in the form of Youth,' a shadow of reality to come — and this consideration has further convinced me, — for it has come as auxiliary to another favourite speculation of mine, — that we shall enjoy ourselves hereafter by having what we call happiness on Earth repeated in a finer tone and so repeated. And yet such a fate can only befall those who delight in Sensation, rather than hunger as you do after Truth. Adam's dream will do here, and seems to be a Conviction that Imagination and its empyreal reflection, is the same as human life and its spiritual repetition. But, as I was saying, the simple imaginative Mind may have its rewards in the repetition of its own silent Working coming continually on the Spirit with a fine Suddenness."

That is Keats, Keats as he saw himself to be in his moments of entranced rapture. Sensation was not to him a mere material thing, but the rift in the cloud through which he glimpsed the heavenly hosts. Yet, even as he describes his vision, even as he pulses with the power to evoke from sensation the dream of eternal loveliness and meaning, he is teased by the thought that the most completely developed type of man arrives at truth by another road:

"Sure this cannot be exactly the case with a complex mind — one that is imaginative, and at the same time careful of its fruits, — who would exist partly on Sensation, partly on thought — to whom it is necessary that 'years should bring the philosophic Mind'?[2] Such a one I consider yours."

Keats was shrewd enough to see a good way through

[1] Corrected from the original. Author's Collection.
[2] Wordsworth's *Ode to Immortality*.

Haydon, but he was greatly mistaken in Bailey. However, no matter for that just now. With his mind filled with these whys and wherefores, what room was there for *Endymion*, how could five hundred lines squeeze themselves in between so many fermenting ideas, doubts, and wonders? But Keats had an everlasting friend who never failed him, to whom the tide of his feelings always turned, the uniting symbol which welded his two combating halves into a quiet compromise and made him whole — Diana, the glorious, silent, distant, and comprehending moon. On Saturday night he went up to Box Hill, and saw and found his moon, and coming down "wrote some lines." Sensation conquered, he was stilled, succoured, turned once more upon his task; the last five hundred lines were begun.

Yet, even so, Keats, come down from the hill to his little room in the inn, cannot quite forget the world. His "some lines" written, his mind goes back to London and the life he has left behind. But this time he goes back in a somewhat altered frame of mind. It is Reynolds he writes to now, and Reynolds is a very different man from Bailey. The letter begins:

> "There are two things which teaze me here — one of them Cripps, and the other that I cannot go with Tom into Devonshire. However, I hope to do my duty to myself in a week or so; and then I'll try what I can do for my neighbour — now, is not this virtuous? On returning to Town I'll damn all Idleness — indeed, in superabundance of employment, I must not be content to run here and there on little two-penny errands."

It is just the "little two-penny errands" which have been sapping his vitality. Indeed, from his very mention of them, we can see that their ghosts haunt him still. But, after all, Tom seems better, he has just told Bailey so, and he is at liberty to plunge head over ears into poetry, if he can. He has only this minute taken a first dip, and the vigour he has gained from it tinges the very diction of his letter. He tells Reynolds that one of the three books he has brought with him is Shakespeare's *Poems*, and forthwith proceeds to quote passages and comment on them. One of these quotations is

> "... a poet's rage
> And stretched metre of an antique song." [1]

Having written that down, he is struck with its appositeness of description to his *Endymion* and exclaims promptly: "Which by the bye, will be a capital motto for my poem, won't it?" He treasured it up, and the last line was printed on the title-page of *Endymion*.

We have already noticed [2] that the "some lines" were, by ordinary counting, at least ninety-four. We can therefore see that his walk up Box Hill had put him into splendid cue. Indeed, the moment, whether through accident or design, was fortuitous, for the moon lacked but twenty-four hours of being at the full; and the weather was kind, providing one of those tumbled skies of jet and silver cloud-racks through which the moon breaks and beams from time to time. I believe, that night, he stopped in the middle of the song, just where he breaks off in the letter to Reynolds. Considering that the moon had set him going, it would be thoroughly in keeping for him to find that he had done enough for one bout at the lines:

> "The Star-Queen's Crescent on her marriage night:
> Haste, haste away!"

But he is all keyed up, we can feel his excitement in the manner in which he ushers in his quotation:

> "By the Whim-King! I'll give you a stanza, because it is not material in connexion, and when I wrote it I wanted you — to give your vote, pro or con. —"

[1] Shakespeare. Sonnet XVII. [2] See Vol. I, p. 446.

This stanza (as he calls it) begins with the line:

> "Crystalline brother of the belt of Heaven,"

and ends with those quoted above. A sort of quasi-evidence in favour of his having paused for the night at this point, is the fact that he follows his quotation with the sentence: "Now I hope I shall not fall off in the winding up."

Ninety-four lines is not a vast amount to do at a sitting. The ordinary double-spaced typewritten page of to-day contains about thirty-two lines, so we see that he need only have written three pages to fill his quota — by no means a large allowance. His stint of fifty lines a day at Oxford was, indeed, extremely small. There was plenty of time for his walk up Box Hill, his three pages of composition, and his letter to Reynolds, all accomplished in the same evening, for, on that short November day, the sun set at a quarter past four.

Wherever Keats stopped, his mood of joyous excitement continued and craved the imaginative relief of a comprehending response, so he shifted from *Endymion* to Reynolds and worked himself out in that way.

It is particularly interesting to watch how well Keats knew when he had worn his creating edge even a trifle dull, when he risked doing inferior work if he went on. It is most important to observe that he dropped his work then and there, even though the mood continued, and this bears out exactly what Woodhouse says of him: "The moment he feels any dearth he discontinues writing and waits for a happier moment." [1]

Apparently, from that Saturday evening, the world ceased to haunt him. At any rate, we know of no more letters from Burford Bridge, and I cannot help thinking that, if he had written, it would have been to Reynolds, for, when it was a question of poetry, there is no doubt that he found Reynolds more sympathetic than any one

[1] See Vol. I, p. 501.

else. No, it is evident that during all the next week Keats was fairly captured by his poem. On Saturday night he had got as far as line 590. There are one thousand and three lines in the Fourth Book, making four hundred and thirteen still to be written, as well as we can calculate, at the time he wrote to Reynolds. It took him just six days to do them, and on the following Friday, November twenty-eighth, he wrote the last line and dated his manuscript with the sense of a load lifted off his mind.

Endymion was finished, except for revision that is, and Keats could not, naturally, begin revising at once. But he could go home, and he did not. He wanted an empty space between the strenuous week he had just passed through and the taking up of his ordinary life. If solitude had ground upon him in the Spring, it was balm and healing to him now. He had completed it, his great task; the labour, the holding himself to a line, the long vista of days and days working to one end, was over. He was another man from the young fellow who had dreaded to begin his poem. This man who ended it and dated his release from a self-imposed tyranny, a tyranny the result of which was to make or mar all his poetical prospects, was a totally different person from the youth who had summoned his brother to keep him away from himself. He did not want to be kept away from himself now. On the contrary, he wanted an infinity of leisure to see into himself and weigh and appraise. He was in a mood for stock-taking, and under the plain necessity of dulling the sharp edge of his susceptibility a little before encountering the hustlings and well-meant impingements which his personality was sure to receive in town. He stayed on at Burford Bridge, then, for a week or more, perhaps. But we cannot be certain of the date of his return to town, as there is no letter extant from him until December twenty-eighth.

We can picture him walking about the country, enjoying to the full the sense of freedom and achievement. Looking at everything with that observant eye of his, and finding what he saw superlatively good and medicine to his soul. Did he realize that Shelley's father, Sir Timothy Shelley, lived at Field Place, some six miles beyond Dorking on the Brighton road? If he did, he probably gave its gates a wide berth. All that we actually know of these last days at Burford Bridge is that on one of them he wrote the little lyric, *In Drear-Nighted December*.

This poem has had rather a curious history, which it seems worth while to retail in full. In the first place, on Woodhouse's testimony, it was attributed to the year 1818; but the discovery of the second Woodhouse Commonplace Book (*Poems II*),[1] corrected what was all along an error on Woodhouse's part, for in that volume he carefully revises his former judgment by recording that Jane Reynolds had told him that it was written in December, 1817, while Keats was at Burford Bridge.

The poem was published in the *Gem*, a periodical edited by Thomas Hood, in 1829, and, in the same year, made one of the selections from Keats's work in the Galignani edition of the *Poems of Coleridge, Shelley, and Keats*. These practically contemporaneous printings have hitherto been supposed to be the first. I am, however, indebted to a correspondent in the London *Times Literary Supplement*,[2] for a still farther correction. It seems that some two or three weeks before its appearance in the *Gem*, the poem, in a slightly different version, was printed in the *Literary Gazette* for September nineteenth, 1829. There it was put in the selection *Original Poetry*, entitled merely *Stanzas* (*Unpublished*) and signed at the end "John Keats." Later, in the number for October twenty-fourth, 1829, at the end of a review of the *Gem*, the *Gazette* reviewer remarked: "There is a poem of the late J. Keats, which

[1] Crewe Collection.

[2] Letter to the *Times Literary Supplement* by George Dumas Stout. September 14, 1922.

appeared a few weeks since in the 'Literary Gazette': it is but justice to state that the proprietors had previously printed their version from another copy." There is a little confusion here as to whether "the proprietors" were those of the *Literary Gazette* or the *Gem*. But that is really immaterial. The point is that the poem was printed in perfectly good faith by two editors from different manuscripts, derived from different people. Hood undoubtedly got his version from his wife, he had married Jane Reynolds; the *Literary Gazette* probably received theirs from either Taylor or Woodhouse, since they also had copies. It is not my purpose here to enter into variant readings. But some obvious changes had crept into the printed versions which I agree entirely with Sir Sidney Colvin should now be suppressed, since Keats's holograph manuscript, as well as the copies made by Woodhouse and Brown, are without them. For the pleasure of having the original version here, I copy the poem as Sir Sidney gives it in his *Life of Keats*; also, sundry things have turned up which make a re-reading of it necessary.

"In drear-nighted December,
Too happy, happy tree,
Thy branches ne'er remember
Their green felicity:
The north cannot undo them,
With a sleety whistle through them;
Nor frozen thawings glue them
From budding at the prime.

In drear-nighted December,
Too happy, happy brook,
Thy bubblings ne'er remember
Apollo's summer look;
But with a sweet forgetting,
They stay their crystal fretting,
Never, never petting
About the frozen time.

Ah! would t'were so with many
  A gentle girl and boy!
But were there ever any
  Writh'd not at passed joy?
The feel of *not* to feel it,
When there is none to heal it,
Nor numbed sense to steel it,
  Was never said in rhyme."

In the *Literary Gazette*, the *Gem*, and the Galignani edition, and of course in all subsequent reprints, the first line reads "In a drear-nighted December," which is perhaps an improvement, but there is also a change from the holograph in the fifth line of the third stanza, which in the alteration reads: "To know the change and feel it." Sir Sidney has something so pertinent to say about this, that I shall quote his passage in part:

> "The new fifth line is to modern ears more elegant than the original, as getting rid of the vulgar substantive form 'feel' for feeling. But 'feel,' which after all had been good enough for Horace Walpole and Fanny Burney, was to Keats and the Leigh Hunt circle no vulgarism at all, it was a thing of every day usage both in verse and prose. And does not the correction somewhat blunt the point of Keats's meaning? To be poignantly aware of no longer feeling a joy once felt is a pain that may indeed call for steeling or healing, while to steel or heal a 'change' seems neither so easy nor so needful: at all events the phrase is more lax."

I am in entire accord with Sir Sidney in thinking that the alteration of the line seriously weakens its effect. But I fear Sir Sidney's suggestion that this alteration is due to the editing of, possibly, Hood, cannot stand, since the editor of the *Literary Gazette*, printing from a different manuscript, also has it. Sir Sidney goes on to state that a perfectly new version of the last stanza, copied in 1827 by one of Woodhouse's brothers, seems evidence that Keats did try variations of it. This stanza, quoted in his *Life of Keats*, is as follows:

"But in the Soul's December
The fancy backward strays,
And darkly doth remember
The hue of golden days,
In woe the thought appalling
Of bliss gone past recalling
Brings o'er the heart a falling
Not to be told in rhyme."

Of this stanza, Sir Sidney says: "This can hardly be other than an alternative version tried by Keats himself," and he goes on to show a precedent for "falling" in Wordsworth's *Ode to Immortality*, but adds, "and though 'the thought appalling' is a commonplace phrase little in Keats's manner, it is worth noticing that the word occurs in Bailey's report of his spoken comment on this very passage of Wordsworth." True, but that was *Bailey's report* of a spoken comment; what Keats really said, we have no idea, but the expression here is none of Keats's. He did not write that stanza; Woodhouse did. And I say this on no less an authority than Woodhouse himself. The information is contained in an unpublished letter to Taylor,[1] written on the twenty-third of November, 1820. Woodhouse is perfectly explicit:

"I have tried unsuccessfully to admire the 3d Stanza of 'Drear-nighted Dec.' as much as the 2 first — I plead guilty, even before I am accused, of an utter abhorrence of the word 'feel' for feeling (substantively). But Keats seems fond of it and will engraft it 'in æternam' on our language — Be it so — I will conquer my dislike — But the great objection to the 3rd stanza is that the 4 last lines are an excrescence — and ought to have had some connection with the 4 first which are an application of or rather an antithesis to the last stanza.

I wod not dream of entering into the lists with any poet that ever rhymed much less Keats. But as a specimen of the sort of Sentiment which shod terminate the song in my opinion 'see here.'"

[1] Woodhouse Book. Morgan Collection.

Some Greek words follow, and then, in the middle of the page, the very stanza of which I have been speaking, given, with the exception of the word "sadly" for "darkly," some unnecessary capitals, and a few differences in punctuation, exactly as Sir Sidney quotes it.

At the end of November, 1820, Keats was in Rome, and in no state to be consulted about alterations in his poems. Woodhouse seems to have got his knowledge of the poem from a book in which Reynolds copied his own poems and those of his friends, for, at the beginning of the letter, he says: "I return you . . . Reynolds's volume of poetry," and then mentions poems by Reynolds himself, Keats, and Hunt. The truth seems to be that the poem, as Keats wrote it and left it, is as given by Sir Sidney, and that none of the versions printed elsewhere have the slightest authority or value. Evidently it was thought a little too high-handed to change a whole stanza without Keats's consent, and very likely Keats's other friends saw how wretched Woodhouse's stanza was, but when it came to printing they did allow themselves to change the fifth line and so sent the poem out. I do believe, however, that only Woodhouse, Taylor, and Reynolds are responsible, since the *Gem* version certainly came from Reynolds, and, in view of this discussion, I think we may be sure that Woodhouse gave the editor of the *Literary Gazette* the one he used. That the two copies came originally from the same source seems proved, for in both the *Gem* and the *Literary Gazette* "steel" is spelt as here, while Galignani prints the obviously erroneous "steal."

It has often been pointed out that *In Drear-Nighted December* is written in something the same form as Dryden's *Spanish Friar*, but there is one marked difference. Keats does not rhyme his last line with the fourth as Dryden does. On the contrary, he experiments in a really unexpected way, rhyming his last lines with nothing in their own stanzas, but rhyming them all three together throughout.

The chief charm in this little lyric is its form; the chief interest, its reflection of Keats's state of mind. It is not happy in its use of words, and the thought it contains is not very clearly resolved. It is not worthy of the popularity it has gained, nor the space I have accorded it; but it does show that Keats realized the inevitable fact that, in opening some doors, he had involuntarily closed others and shut himself out from certain entrances; that he had turned away from his own boyhood and was set upon a track from which there was no going back. If he were strong with the sense of victory won in part, he was, at the same time, pensive in the knowledge that past days are not lived over, that feelings change before regret is numb. It was probably in some such mood as this that he returned to Hampstead to be with his brothers for a little while before they went to Devonshire.

CHAPTER VII

HORIZONS AND THUNDERHEADS

THE first salient event of Keats's return to Hampstead was his brothers' departure for Teignmouth; the second, his going to see Kean's return to the stage, after an illness, in Shakespeare's *Richard III*, on Monday, December fifteenth. The effect of this evening was to bring Keats out in print for the first time as the author of a prose article. A couple of weeks later, he tells his brothers that he is substituting for Reynolds as theatrical critic for the *Champion*, while Reynolds is in Exeter, but he does not speak as though this first paper were donc in the same official capacity. Perhaps it was, but I rather doubt it, and the difference in the way the two papers are written lends a very strong bias to my doubt. Keats seems to have produced this first paper in the height of enthusiasm. It is in no sense a criticism, being, in fact, an appreciation of the warmest kind. On the following Thursday, Keats again saw Kean as Luke in the tragedy of *Riches*, a modern bowdlerization of Massinger's *City Madam*. These two plays, and Kean's acting in them, were not to be resisted, and Keats dashed off his paper *con amore*. It was probably Reynolds's pleasure in what his friend had done which led to the article's appearance in the *Champion* for Sunday, December twenty-first, and to Reynolds's request that Keats take on his job while he went off for a Christmas holiday.

Keats dearly loved the theatre, particularly Shakespeare's plays in the theatre, acted and spoken as the great tradition of those days made inevitable. Later, one of his chief ambitions was to write poetical drama. What the theatre gave him when such a man as Kean played, can be seen by the opening paragraph of his paper:

"'In our unimaginative days' — Habeas Corpus'd as we are out of all wonder, curiosity, and fear; — in these fireside, delicate, gilded days, — in these days of sickly safety and comfort, we feel very grateful to Mr. Kean for giving us some excitement by his old passion in one of the old plays. He is a relict of romance; a posthumous ray of chivalry, and always seems just arrived from the camp of Charlemagne."

He goes on to analyze something of the peculiar qualities possessed by Kean, and the technical means which enabled him to achieve his extraordinary results. After a passage which I have already quoted,[1] Keats continues:

"The sensual life of verse springs warm from the lips of Kean, and to one learned in Shakesperean hieroglyphics — learned in the spiritual portion of those lines to which Kean adds a sensual grandeur; his tongue must seem to have robbed the Hybla bees and left them honeyless! There is an indescribable *gusto* in his voice, by which we feel that the utterer is thinking of the past and future while speaking of the instant."

Here follows a string of illustrations so vivid and pertinent that we who read do certainly seem to apprehend something of the reason of Kean's greatness, no mean thing for a writer to have accomplished, by the way. A shrewd observation is the following:

"Other actors are continually thinking of their sum-total effect throughout a play. Kean delivers himself up to the instant feeling, without a shadow of a thought about anything else."

There is little more to the paper, and it is marred by Keats's inveterate habit of quotation to point his meaning. The last sentence is pure rhapsody:

"Kean! Kean! have a carefulness of thy health, a nursing regard for thy own genius, a pity for us in these cold and

[1] See Vol. I, p. 382.

enfeebling times! Cheer us a little in the failure of our days! for romance lives but in books. The goblin is driven from the hearth, and the rainbow is robbed of its mystery."

Here is a queer and very youthful mixture of rhodomontade and intelligence. Keats was evidently writing to please himself, and not taking the pleasure too seriously.

A week later he went again to see Kean, on Monday, December twenty-second, in a telescoped adaptation of Shakespeare's three King Henry plays. This time he was the official reviewer of a paper, and he took the task very seriously indeed. His account of the play, which appeared on Sunday, December twenty-eighth, is written with seriousness and restraint and is full of knowledge of his subject and wise criticism of the feeble compilation he had witnessed. Few analyses of Shakespeare's poetry in his very different types of plays have been better than that led up to by a consideration of his English historical dramas, of which Keats says:

"They are written with infinite vigour, but their regularity tied the hand of Shakespeare. Particular facts kept him in the high road, and would not suffer him to turn down leafy and winding lanes, or to break wildly and at once into the breathing fields. The poetry is for the most part ironed and manacled with a chain of facts, and cannot get free; it cannot escape from the prison house of history, nor often move without our being disturbed with the clanking of its fetters. The poetry of Shakespeare is generally free as is the wind — a perfect thing of the elements, winged and sweetly coloured. Poetry must be free! It is of the air, not of the earth; and the higher it soars the nearer it gets to its home. The poetry of 'Romeo and Juliet,' of 'Hamlet,' of 'Macbeth,' is the poetry of Shakespeare's soul — full of love and divine romance. It knows no stop in its delight, but 'goeth where it listeth' — remaining, however, in all men's hearts a perpetual and golden dream. The poetry of 'Lear,' 'Othello,' 'Cymbeline,' &c., is the poetry of human passions and affections, made almost

> ethereal by the power of the poet. Again, the poetry of 'Richard,' 'John,' and the Henries is the blending of the imaginative with the historical: it is poetry! — but often times poetry wandering on the London Road."

This excellent criticism Keats half apologized for immediately, but wisely and rightly let it stand.

Where poetry was concerned, Keats was on his own ground, and that passage is both scholarly and full of imagination. In fact, the whole article shows thought and careful working up. His notes on Kean's acting are impressionistic, reminding one of the first article, but more coolly, appraisingly done, for instance:

> "His death was very great. But Kean always 'dies as erring men do die.' The bodily functions wither up, and the mental faculties hold out till they crack. It is an extinguishment, not a decay. The hand is agonized with death; the lip trembles with the last breath, as we see the autumn leaf thrill in the cold of evening. The very eye-lid dies."

There were moments during the evening which Keats's sense of humour could not let pass. How well we see the rather miscast actress of whom he writes:

> "Mrs. Glover chews the blank verse past endurance; her comedy is round and comfortable; her tragedy is worse than death."

In both these papers, but particularly in the last, the influence of Hazlitt is very noticeable.

Two more dramatic reviews did Keats do, and neither of them amounts to anything. They both appeared in the *Champion* for January fourth. One was on a modern tragedy, *The Chieftain's Daughter*, in which Macready appeared. Keats was evidently bored with the whole thing. He tells the story of the play at length, and mentions particular actors well or ill, but of these Macready is not one. The piece was bad and he says so, but in so youthful a tone and with so jejune a finality that we see how far he as yet was from being able to turn his critical faculty upon anything which did not interest him.

The other, and last, of these sallies in dramatic criticism has for subject the Christmas Drury Lane Pantomime, which that year, taking its cue from the success of Mozart's opera, was called *Don Giovanni.* Here Keats begs the whole question of play and observer, and contents himself with writing a nonsensical squib which is not even good nonsense at that. His real opinion of the pantomime, sent in a letter to his brothers, was wiser, merrier, wittier by far, and a better criticism. It is:

> "The Covent Garden pantomime is a very nice one, but they have a middling Harlequin, a bad Pantaloon, a worse Clown, and a shocking Columbine."

With the publication of his pantomime critique, Keats's connection with Grub Street ends, and leaves us wondering how far he could have learnt to overcome his distaste for the mere job work of letters if he had followed out his intention of two years later of applying himself to hack work for his daily bread.

Although Keats was alone in the Hampstead lodgings, he had enough work in correcting *Endymion* for the press, and enough society, to take up his time. We hear of him passing the night with Wells at his lodgings in Featherstone Buildings, dining "the Sunday after you left" (he is writing to his brothers) with Haydon, spending an evening with Dilke, and altogether moving pleasantly in a very pleasant circle.

An event which should have proved most agreeable, but which seems to have resulted in a good deal of a fizzle, was his meeting, or rather meetings, with Wordsworth. At the end of 1817, Wordsworth came up to London on a visit to his brother Christopher at the Rectory, Lambeth.

Crabbe Robinson mentions[1] his being in London on December fourth, so that he was already there when Keats returned from Burford Bridge. Naturally Keats was agog to see him, and the matter was characteristically arranged by Haydon, but not apparently as has hitherto been recorded. Haydon, in his *Autobiography*, says that the meeting took place at his house at dinner, the famous dinner of December twenty-eighth, and Hunt says[2] that it was at this dinner that Keats recited the *Ode to Pan* from *Endymion*, while Severn recollected the gathering in Haydon's studio at which the reading took place. Unfortunately none of these three gentlemen can be trusted in matters of date and detail. Perhaps equally untrustworthy, but at least new, is an account of this first meeting with Wordsworth which I have found in an unpublished letter of Haydon's[3] to an unknown correspondent, written in 1845. For the sake of comparison, and the possibility of its being the true version of the occasion, I will quote part of it:

> "When Wordsworth came to Town I brought Keats to him by his (Wordsworth's) desire — Keats expressed to me as we walked to Queen Anne St. East where Mr. Monkhouse Lodged, the greatest, the purest, the most unalloyed pleasure at the prospect. Wordsworth received him kindly, & after a few minutes, Wordsworth asked him what he had been lately doing, I said — he has just finished an exquisite Ode to Pan — and as he had not a copy I begged Keats to repeat it — which he did in his usual half chant, (most touching) walking up and down the room — when he had done I felt really, as if I had heard a young Apollo — Wordsworth dryly said
>
> 'A Very pretty piece of Paganism.'
>
> That was unfeeling, and unworthy of his high genius to a Young Worshipper like Keats — and Keats felt it *deeply* — so that if Keats has said anything severe about our Friend; it was because he was wounded and though he

[1] *Diary, Reminiscences, and Correspondence, of Henry Crabbe Robinson.*
[2] *Lord Byron and his Contemporaries*, by Leigh Hunt.
[3] Author's Collection.

dined with Wordsworth after at my table — he never forgave him . . .

I wish you would send this letter to Mr. Milnes . . .

All Hunt's assertions about this being said at my house is a mistake."

Monckton Milnes (Lord Houghton) can never have received the letter, for he followed Hunt and Severn in putting the recitation of the *Ode to Pan* as happening at Haydon's, although not at the dinner.

Keats may have been deeply wounded by Wordsworth's unenthusiastic comment, indeed his not mentioning it to his brothers (unless, which is not likely, it happened before they left Hampstead) would seem to point that way, but that he never forgave Wordsworth we must consider one of Haydon's exaggerations. What he seems to have found it much harder to forgive Wordsworth was the great poet's dining with one Kingston, a comptroller of stamps, whom Keats considered a fool and a philistine. He even went so far as to refuse an invitation of Kingston's to meet Wordsworth at dinner, because he would not go to the man's house. Certainly Wordsworth's treatment of Keats's poem was decidedly curt, but Wordsworth seems to have been in a disagreeable mood that Autumn. Crabbe Robinson speaks of his replying to a remark of Coleridge's "by dry unfeeling contradiction." He could not pardon Coleridge some of his remarks in the *Biographia Literaria*, in spite of the high praise which went with them. His general attitude at the time can be seen by this entry in Crabbe Robinson's diary describing an evening at Lamb's, two days after Hunt's dinner: "I heard a long time Coleridge quoting Wordsworth's verses; and W. quoting, not Coleridge's, but his own." [1]

The "immortal dinner," as Haydon calls it, took place in his painting-room on Sunday, December twenty-eighth,

[1] Quoted in the *Life of William Wordsworth*, by William Knight.

"with Jerusalem towering up behind us as a background." There were present Lamb, Wordsworth, Keats, and Monkhouse, with, of course, Haydon himself. After dinner, various other friends dropped in, among others, Ritchie, about to start for Africa, and the egregious Kingston, who had begged an invitation. It was a splendid evening, with Lamb in fine cue, uproarious cue, poking outrageous fun at Kingston, who was solemnly making an ass of himself. Finally Lamb was imprisoned in the painting-room, leaving the others stifling hopeless laughter. Ritchie, pleased, undoubtedly, at meeting the young poet of whom he had written so highly to his friend Garnett, was very polite to him, and promised to drop a copy of *Endymion* in the Desert of Sahara if Keats would give him one. Even Wordsworth seems to have forgotten to be pompous, if we can believe Haydon, who says: "It was delightful to see the good humour of Wordsworth in giving in to all our frolics without affectation and laughing as heartily as the best of us." "It was a night worthy of the Elizabethan age," continues its gratified originator, "and my solemn Jerusalem flashing up by the flame of the fire, with Christ hanging over us like a vision."

During Wordsworth's stay in town, Haydon painted him as one of the crowd in his picture, putting him just below Keats and beside Voltaire. This would have brought him to the painting-room several times, and he and Keats must have had at least one other meeting there, for both Severn and Hunt were present at one, and it was probably on this, or a similar, occasion, that Keats gave his *Poems* to Wordsworth.[1] How much interest Wordsworth took in them may be adduced by the fact that he cut only a fraction of the pages.[2]

These were not the only meetings between Keats and

[1] See Vol. I, pp. 126–127.

[2] From information supplied by F. Holland Day, Esq. who owns Wordsworth's copy of the *Poems*.

Wordsworth. Keats called on him, dined with him, and dined in his company. In fact, by January tenth he had, he tells Taylor, "seen Wordsworth pretty frequently." It speaks volumes for the esteem in which Keats was held by the group of literary men and artists whom Wordsworth knew, that he was asked so often to meet a man twenty-five years his senior. Considering the difference of age, it could hardly be expected that anything other than a formal acquaintance should have resulted, but there was more than mere disparity of years to make a barrier between the two men. Their natures could not accord. Keats loathed Wordsworth's adherence to the conservative party, and read in his tolerance of Kingston, and his dressing up to dine with him, a truckling to the existing order. This opinion came out mildly enough in Keats's writing to his brothers that, when he went to see Wordsworth on the afternoon of Kingston's dinner, he was "surprised to find him with a stiff collar"; but his verbal account of the incident had, according to Dilke, something of anger in it. Yet Keats's admiration for Wordsworth's poetry suffered no change. A week later he wrote to Haydon: "I am convinced that there are three things to rejoice at in this Age — The Excursion, Your Pictures, and Hazlitt's depth of Taste." Still he admitted that in everyday life his idol had feet of clay, and when the idol left London at the end of January, he not only did not know of his departure for some days, but when he did, he wrote, again to his brothers: "I am sorry that Wordsworth has left a bad impression wherever he visited in town by his egotism, Vanity, and bigotry." He adds, however, "Yet he is a great poet if not a philosopher."

Keats's justness of vision in regard to the poetical qualities of his contemporaries was seldom at fault, and never influenced by purely personal considerations, at least so far as adverse criticism was concerned. He had, it is true, an undue regard for Reynolds's work, biassed, of course, by his love for the man; but adversely this did not apply. He felt no particular congeniality toward Shelley, yet when in this December *Laon and Cythna* appeared, was recalled by its cowardly publishers, the Olliers, and a revision and expurgation of the book forced upon Shelley before its republication as the *Revolt of Islam*, Keats was all sympathy. He knew how unpleasantly the Olliers could make one of their authors feel. "Shelley's poem is out," he writes to his brothers on December twenty-eighth, "and there are words about its being objected to as much as 'Queen Mab' was. Poor Shelley, I think he has his Quota of good qualities, in sooth la!!"

From Keats's seeing Wordsworth so often, from his dining with Horace Smith, from his hobnobbing with "Bob" Harris on the steps of Covent Garden Theatre of which Harris was the manager, we can see that he is already an acknowledged member of what we should call to-day the young *intelligentsia*. He is no longer a mere neophyte, but distinctly one of those promising young fellows who count, who knows everybody in a certain *milieu*, and if that *milieu* be not yet the great world of art and letters, it is at least the quasi-bohemian vestibule to it which most youthful artists find its surest approach.

Keats had small patience with even the inspired dilettante. He did not enjoy the Smith dinner, possibly very largely on account of the presence of Kingston. His comment on the conversation of the party is highly significant:

> "These men say things which make one start, without making one feel; they are all alike; their manners are alike; they all know fashionables; they have all a mannerism in their very eating and drinking, in their mere handling a decanter. They talked of Kean and his low company. 'Would I were with that company instead of yours,' said I to myself! I know such like acquaintance will never do for me."

And no more it would. The affectations and cant shibboleths of the amateur of the arts made a stifling atmosphere to so perfectly sincere and natural a fellow as Keats. He felt no whit out of place with Wordsworth and Hazlitt, and perfectly in his element with various lively spirits of an entirely different sort, but in the presence of any kind of attitudinizing he was hopelessly out of place.

For the lively occasions, we are told of a supper and dance at the house of a Mr. Redhall, where the conversation certainly did not lack robustness and the dancing was of a prodigious fury. It is a comment on the manners of the day that Bailey, the budding clergyman, was there and "seemed to enjoy the evening."

Fanny Keats came up to town for the Christmas holidays, and she and John passed a good deal of time together to the complete satisfaction of both. He seems to have seen more of all his friends generally than ever before, and in an easier, more relaxed, sort of way. The fact of having published one book and being at the moment preparing another for the press, gave him a sense of security in his chosen career which was a spur to something I can find no better word for than jollity. Rice initiates him into "a little band," who talk a slang new to Keats and amuse him greatly; also he, and various other cronies, form a club to meet on Saturday evenings, and the joyous playing of concerts continues. Here is a specimen Sunday: "I saw Hunt and dined with Haydon, met Hazlitt and Bewick there, and took Haslam with me." A little note,[1] or announcement, in Keats's handwriting, very likely belongs to this time. We can imagine that Keats had dropped in at 93 Fleet Street in order to get Taylor to join some dinner or card party, and that Taylor, having alleged his inability to leave the shop in case of callers, Keats had dashed off this notice to show him how easily that obstacle could be disposed of. This seems to have been the way of it. At any rate, Taylor preserved the note, which is as follows:

[1] Author's Collection.

> "To any friend who may call.
> Mr. Taylor's Compt[s] to any Ladies or gentlemen his friends who may call, and begs they will pardon him for being led away by an unavoidable engagement, which will detain him till eleven o'clock to night."

Brown was away for the Christmas vacation, but Dilke remained and was a host in himself. "I and Dilke are getting capital friends," he writes his brothers. With Reynolds, he was as close as ever, but a severe quarrel between Reynolds and Haydon gave him pause and worried him not a little, calling forth a characteristic bit of probing delivered in one of his periodical letters to his brothers, that sort of probing into the bases of human relations and the life of man toward which his mind was forever straying:

> "I am quite perplexed in a world of doubts and fancies — there is nothing stable in the world; uproar's your only music — I don't mean to include Bailey in this and so I dismiss him from this with all the opprobrium he deserves — that is in so many words, he is one of the noblest men alive at the present day . . . So I do believe — not thus speaking with any poor vanity — that works of genius are the first things in this world. No! for that sort of probity and disinterestedness which such men as Bailey possess, does hold and grasp the tip-top of any spiritual honours that can be paid to anything in this world. And moreover having this feeling at this present come over me in its full force, I sat down to write to you with a grateful heart, in that I had not a Brother who did not feel and credit me for a deeper feeling and devotion for his uprightness, than for any marks of genius however splendid."

There is Keats, the ethical man that he, in his complete integrity, was, speaking out of his heart's core. It was hard to solve the why of the universe, and he no more than any other absolutely honest man of brains ever solved it; but, in spite of his perplexities as to the dual quality of his own nature, he never for a moment believed, or advocated, the atrophy of either side of it. Ethical he must be, that was how he saw himself in the face of life, in the face of his responsibility toward his poetry.

The Haydon-Reynolds quarrel brought out another expression of opinion from him which reveals all the tolerant sanity of his attitude toward the men with whom he was brought into intimate relations. It is to Bailey this time that he speaks his mind:

> "It is unfortunate — Men should bear with each other: there lives not the Man who may not be cut up, aye Lashed to pieces on his weakest side. The best of men have but a portion of good in them — a kind of spiritual yeast in their frames, which creates the ferment of existence — by which a Man is propelled to act, and strive, and buffet with Circumstance. The sure way, Bailey, is first to know a Man's faults, and then be passive — if after that he insensibly draws you towards him then you have no power to break the link. Before I felt interested in either Reynolds or Haydon, I was well read in their faults; yet, knowing them, I have been cementing gradually with both. I have an affection for them both, for reasons almost opposite — and to both must I of necessity cling, supported always by the hope that, when a little time, a few years, shall have tried me more fully in their esteem, I may be able to bring them together. The time must come, because they both have hearts: and they will recollect the best parts of each other, when this gust is overblown."

All this time, Keats had been revising the first book of *Endymion*. But, as usual with him, too much gadding was beginning to tell on his health. "I have been racketing too much, and do not feel over well," he tells Taylor on January tenth. Keeping in mind that he was, in all probability, already infected with tuberculosis, the wonder is that he felt as well as he did. But I think we must take his ill-health at this time as being also due to impatience with himself at having passed a month without having written anything new. He should have been satisfied with his revision of *Endymion*, but he was not. He should have minimized the parties, but he could not bring himself to do that either. The very next week after his note to Taylor, he apologizes to his brothers for a break in a letter to them in this wise:

> "I was called away, and have been about somewhere ever since. Where? What? . . . I cannot for the world recollect why I was called away, all I know is that there has been a dance at Dilke's, and another at the London Coffee House; to both of which I went."

On Tuesday, January sixteenth, his creative faculty woke up in him again, mildly, merrily, but still it was once more awake. He composed a sonnet to Mrs. Reynolds's cat. This is an amusing little piece, a parody of the Miltonian sonnet. We remember that Keats, at Oxford and after, had been poring much over Milton. Because of this Miltonian preoccupation, I do not hesitate to place another poem, *Welcome joy, and welcome sorrow*, as being written about this time, although no actual date, beyond that of the year 1818, can be assigned to it. It bears for motto a misquotation from *Paradise Lost*. The poem is an evocation of opposites, obviously started by the lilt of the opening lines. It is rather neatly done, but is, after all, only a fugitive piece of no real importance.

Well, he had written two poems, but they amounted to nothing. Things pressed, he felt no real desire to write, but he was irritated at feeling none, and the world, his world, went on. He took his First Book to Taylor, revised in a slovenly manner enough by scribblings and alterations made on the sheets of his first draft. Taylor read it and was flatteringly pleased. He even suggested printing the book as a quarto, if Haydon would make a drawing for the frontispiece. Keats was delighted and rushed at once to Haydon, who said he would do anything Keats liked, but that he should prefer to paint a finished picture from the poem. He also was struck with the First Book, which Keats showed him. The next day, however, he wrote that he thought a chalk sketch of Keats's head would be better, urging the lack of time necessary for a picture, but suggesting that the idea be held over until *Hyperion* was published, when he would paint something from that poem for the new volume. It is evident from this that Keats had not only decided that his next long poem should be on the subject of Hyperion, but that the fact was well known to his friends. On Friday, January twenty-third, he wrote to Haydon agreeing to this change of plan. I give his letter in full:

> [1]"MY DEAR HAYDON, —
>
> I have a complete fellow feeling with you in this business — so much so that it would be as well to wait for a choice out of 'Hyperion' — when that Poem is done there will be a wide range for you — in Endymion I think you may have many bits of the deep and sentimental cast — the nature of 'Hyperion' will lead me to treat it in a more naked and grecian Manner — and the march of passion and endeavour will be undeviating — and one great contrast between them will be — that the Hero of the written tale being mortal is led on, like Buonaparte, by circumstance; whereas the Apollo in Hyperion being a fore-seeing God will shape his actions like one. But I am counting, &c.
>
> Your proposal pleases me — and, believe me, I would not have my Head in the shop windows from any hand but yours — no by Appelles!
>
> I will write Taylor and you shall hear from me.
>
> Yours ever
>
> JOHN KEATS."

In the end, the whole scheme fell through, and *Endymion* was issued in octavo, minus a frontispiece. After Keats's death, Haydon blamed himself for the dilatoriness which

[1] Not given by Buxton Forman. Quoted by Sir Sidney Colvin in his *Life of John Keats*.

prevented him from carrying out Keats's request, but his prompt acceptance and subsequent non-performance were acutely characteristic.

On Wednesday, January twenty-first, Keats went to see Hunt, and Hunt, in great enthusiasm, showed him a lock of Milton's hair which had just been given him. "What a subject!" we can imagine Hunt saying. Hair which had actually grown on Milton's head! By all the gods they both revered, could anything be more moving, more proper to rouse the poetic impulse! Keats, who knew only too well that his poetic impulse needed rousing, listened and wrote. In a letter to Bailey, written two days later, he quotes the poem in full, but, as though the writing it out had revealed its paucity to him, he adds after it: "This I did at Hunt's, at his request — perhaps I should have done something better alone and at home." Very likely that is true, for the poem is not a success. I imagine that "alone and at home" Keats would probably have considered that, on the whole, there was no particular urge upon him to write a poem at all. The idea sprang from Hunt's sentimentality, but Keats evidently allowed himself to be persuaded that he must feel like writing a poem when he saw the hair. He was altogether too prone to think he must write on important occasions, as we shall have more than one opportunity to note when we come to his Scotch tour.

There is in existence a curious evidence of Hunt's anxiety to have Keats write at once. A note-book[1] in which Hunt was writing, or had written, his *Hero and Leander* contains two pages of the Milton poem in Keats's handwriting, which are the first seventeen lines. Why the poem was not continued in the note-book, was probably because Hunt's manuscript went on from there. We can suppose that Hunt, fumbling round for paper, took up his note-book, and running over the pages found two blank and

[1] Author's Collection.

handed the book to Keats. Keats certainly wrote the whole poem at Hunt's, so we can only think that the rest was jotted down on something else.

The poem is, as a poem written under such circumstances could hardly help being, inadequate enough. It is, indeed, worse than that, being full of most unhappy images. The first line, "Chief of organic numbers," is so good that we may be sure it was Keats's utterance of it which caused Hunt to give him the first blank paper at hand to go on with. But what can one say to the lines:

"Thy spirit never slumbers
But rolls about our ears."

Milton's wakeful spirit perpetually *rolling* about the ears of posterity is a sad picture, and Keats caps it in the next stanza by addressing Milton as "Live Temple of sweet noise." To be sure, his original expression was "O living fane of Sounds," which, although not too satisfactory, was much better. But the first line of this second stanza ended with "soundest," so the "sounds" had to come out; and then and there, with Hunt waiting for the finish of the poem, Keats changed it to the present reading. How little he cared for the poem can be seen by the fact that he never revised this line away, although he apparently thought enough of it to copy it into his folio Shakespeare.[1]

This Milton poem is one of those which are biographically of considerable importance. In this instance, we learn how very modest Keats still was; how well he understood his own immaturity. The last two stanzas tell the tale:

"When every childish fashion
Has vanished from my rhyme,
Will I, gray-gone in passion,
Leave to an after-time
Hymning and Harmony
Of thee, and of thy works, and of thy life;

[1] Dilke Collection.

But vain is now the burning and the strife,
Pangs are in vain, until I grow high-rife
With old Philosophy,
And mad with glimpses of futurity.

For many years my offering must be hush'd;
When I do speak, I'll think upon this hour,
Because I feel my forehead hot and flushed,
Even at the simplest vassal of thy power, —
A lock of thy bright hair, —
Sudden it came,
And I was startled when I caught thy name
Coupled so unaware;
Yet at the moment temperate was my blood.
I thought I had beheld it from the flood."

The last stanza contains a double revelation, for in it we see that, no matter how Keats thought he ought to feel at the sight of a lock of Milton's hair, in cold truth he felt nothing at all, which is the reason why I am convinced that "alone and at home" nothing would have been written.

Possibly Hunt praised the Milton poem, or it may have been that Haydon's and Taylor's enthusiasm over his First Book put Keats's perspicacity off its guard, or he may have felt that, considering how he had been wont to talk over his things with Hunt not so very long ago, a relation which that Wednesday visit put him in mind of, it would be almost an insult to keep *Endymion* from him any longer. At any rate, some time before the following Friday, Keats actually showed Hunt his First Book. Of course, he may have done this earlier, before taking his manuscript to Taylor, but in view of the Wednesday call on Hunt, I think that unlikely. How Hunt took this first reading of a poem from which he had been kept carefully away, Keats tells his brothers as follows:

"Leigh Hunt I showed my 1st Book to — he allows it not much merit as a whole; says it is unnatural and made ten objections to it in the mere skimming over. He says the conversation is unnatural and too high-flown for Brother and Sister — says it should be simple, forgetting do ye mind that they are both overshadowed by a supernatural Power, and of force could not speak like Francesca in the 'Rimini.' He must first prove that Caliban's poetry is unnatural. This with me completely overturns his objections. The fact is he and Shelley are hurt, and perhaps justly, at my not having showed them the affair officiously; and from several hints I have had they appear much disposed to dissect and anatomize any trip or slip I may have made. But who's afraid? Aye! Tom! Demme if I am."

Hunt's snappishness about *Endymion* naturally pushed him still farther out of the circle of Keats's more intimate friends. His poetry Keats had already outgrown. In the copy of Hunt's *Foliage*, published this year, which he gave to Keats,[1] there is not a single mark or annotation, and when we reflect how Keats scored and commented in the margins of the books that interested him, the lack of any such signs is highly significant.

The Milton poem was certainly a failure, but it seems to have loosed a bolt in Keats's brain, for suddenly poetry began to flood in upon him. The next day, Thursday, January twenty-second, as he was reading *King Lear*, he was seized with a desire to write upon it, and immediately composed the sonnet: *On sitting down to read "King Lear" once again*. Writing to Bailey on Friday, he tells him:

[2] "I sat down to read 'King Lear' yesterday, and felt the greatness of the thing up to the writing of a Sonnet thereto: in my next you shall have it."

Why he did not copy it then and there was because he had filled his sheet and had only half a "doubling" left to copy it upon. He did copy it in the letter I have just

[1] Author's Collection.
[2] Corrected from original letter. Author's Collection.

quoted from, to his brothers, written on this same Friday, and in this letter he describes certain changes which he perceives to be going on within him. His account of himself is particularly interesting in the light of his discussions with Bailey, and his questionings and probings into the workings of the universe and the highest peak of development possible to sentient man. This is the passage:

> "I think a little change has taken place in my intellect lately — I cannot bear to be uninterested or unemployed, I, who for so long a time have been addicted to passiveness. Nothing is finer for the purposes of great productions than a very gradual ripening of the intellectual powers. As an instance of this — observe — I sat down yesterday to read 'King Lear' once again: the thing appeared to demand the prologue of a sonnet, I wrote it, and began to read."

Here follows the sonnet, and after it he says:

> "So you see I am getting at it, with a sort of determination and strength, though verily I do not feel it at this moment — this is my fourth letter this morning, and I feel rather tired, and my head rather swimming."

What he was getting at was a sort of shadowy compromise between the life of sensation and the life of thought, that difficult paradox which overhangs all artists who are also thinking men. It is the same subject he had discussed at length in his letter to Bailey from Burford Bridge.

This sonnet, although not among Keats's best, is serious and full of underlying purpose. It contains the fine lines:

> ". . . for once again the fierce dispute
> Betwixt Hell torment and impassion'd Clay
> Must I burn through; once more assay
> The bitter-sweet of this Shakespearian fruit."

It should be stated that, in the later copies of the poem,

Keats corrected the short line by putting the word "humbly" before "assay."

Professor de Sélincourt thinks that the "golden-tongued Romance with serene Lute" from which he turned to read Shakespeare was the *Faerie Queene.* I think rather that he refers to all those mythological and symbolical conceptions which had held him enthralled for so long. At the moment, he was reaching out after a poetry of more depth and passion than can be found in even the most extraordinary and beautiful of imaginary evocations. Life, with its simple and huge pathos, tragedy, and mystery, was something which Keats never succeeded in rendering dramatically; but, even so early as this, he had begun to understand that the greatest poetry can be made of nothing else. The lines quoted above represent a new ideal for him, a "certain ripening of the intellectual powers."

Authentic as this mood was in Keats, and cropping up again and again as it does throughout his life, nevertheless we must not expect to find it static. Keats was a poet of many moods, of variously tinted shades of thought and feeling. What was true of him at one time was not necessarily true at another, and it is just this tissue of conflicting sensations which we must study and comprehend if we would know the man and his work as both really were, not pigeon-holed into a theoretical pocket, but free and variable as nature itself. Keats's was a personality rich in overtones, to catch which we must be forever on the watch. One of the tragedies of his life is that he died before he had given the sum total of them adequate utterance.

The poetry vein once tapped continued to flow. After the *King Lear* sonnet came another, written on either Thursday, Friday, or Saturday of that same week, for on Saturday Keats sat down to write to Reynolds. He was in a high flight of spirits, which we may guess to have been induced by the consciousness of having written two good sonnets. However that may be, he begins his letter by dashing off two little trifles in verse, and then suddenly says:

> "My dear Reynolds, you must forgive all this ranting — but the fact is, I cannot write sense this Morning — however you shall have some — I will copy out my last Sonnet."

This sonnet is *When I have fears that I may cease to be.*

The first two quatrains of the sonnet are nothing less than magnificent, and were it not for the change and drop in theme, tenor, and diction of the succeeding quatrain and couplet, *When I have fears* would rank among the best sonnets that Keats did. But this change is so lamentable that the sonnet, as a whole, fails to maintain itself. I say "as a whole," for, taken by themselves, nothing can mar the first eight lines. In order that the strange droop which follows them, a droop which ruined the poem, may be realized, I must give it entire:

> "When I have fears that I may cease to be
> Before my pen has glean'd my teeming brain,
> Before high-piled Books, in charactery,
> Hold like rich garners the full-ripen'd grain —
> When I behold, upon the night's starr'd face,
> Huge cloudy symbols of a high romance,
> And think that I may never live to trace
> Their shadows, with the magic hand of chance;
> And when I feel, fair creature of an hour,
> That I shall never look upon thee more,
> Never have relish in the faery power
> Of unreflecting Love; — then on the shore
> Of the wide world I stand alone, and think
> Till Love and Fame to nothingness do sink."

Reading this sonnet with the knowledge of Keats's abortive career in our minds, it seems the unconscious utterance of some terrible prophecy. To the young man who wrote it, it was merely the expression of a vague fear, one of his usual attacks of hypochondrianism venting itself in poetry; to us, it is the very tolling of the bell of doom. Because of its absolute faithfulness to his feeling at the moment, to what he knew in himself — his power, his abundant possibilities, his haunting perspective — it becomes a door through which we catch a sharp glimpse of his soul. Here is his ambition and his aim, and the lurking devil of his despondence; and here also is the best criticism of his work that has ever been made, for, in its entirety, what is it — all of it — measured and appraised, but "huge cloudy symbols of a high romance"? Is it not — *Hyperion* no less than *Endymion*, the odes, the sonnets, all of his serious poetry — as Dr. Bridges has said of *Endymion*,[1] "suggestive of meaning and full of shadowy outlines of mysterious truth," a characterization only a little less happy than Keats's own, but which amounts to the same thing.

Who the "fair creature of an hour" was, we can have no idea. References to such slight and fleeting preoccupations are frequent in the poems of this period, and they creep into the letters occasionally, but they all seem to refer to ladies encountered, or merely looked at, for the briefest of accidental intervals preceding their total eclipse. The "lady I met at Hastings," vague though she is, is the most solid of these momentary phantoms. The "fair creature of an hour," if she had any existence outside of Keats's fancy, which I am half inclined to doubt, serves only one purpose for us, which is to reveal the fact that Keats realized he could never experience the happiness of "unreflecting love." Alas! Was not the heart of the tragedy of his relations with Fanny Brawne just this, that he reflected upon them until his sick brain turned love itself into a monstrous torture?

When I have fears is noteworthy as being a sonnet in the Shakespearian form and almost the first which Keats wrote. I use the singular qualification "almost," because

[1] See Vol. I, p. 459.

his early sonnet, *On Peace*, written in either 1814 or 1815 was, as we have seen,[1] very nearly a Shakespearian sonnet, certainly it was not Petrarchan. Keats, it will be remembered, had taken Shakespeare's sonnets to Burford Bridge with him, and had re-read them there with infinite attention. In the letter to Reynolds written on the night after his arrival, he had said: "I never found so many beauties in the Sonnets — they seem to be full of fine things said unintentionally . . . He has left nothing to say about nothing or anything." Shakespeare's music ran in his head, and he longed to have a try at the same harmony. Why his first two sonnets of this Winter were in the Petrarchan form so familiar to him, it is not difficult to divine. The cat sonnet was a parody, and very likely an impromptu; the sonnet on King Lear was the first poem after his return which took a real hold on him, which insisted on being written, and he was too glad to find himself seized by the creative impulse once more, too much under an old influence, to write in any way to which he was not thoroughly accustomed. But the King Lear sonnet gave him confidence that he could both hold his inspiration and direct it toward those cadences he longed to essay. From this period on, he seems to have found the Shakespearian form more sympathetic, but his several departures from it suggest that it was death rather than decision which make him appear to have given it a permanent preference. As it is, he wrote thirty-eight Petrarchan sonnets as against sixteen Shakespearian.

The two light-hearted little pieces which precede *When I have fears* in the letter to Reynolds of Saturday, January thirty-first, are, first, an erotic trifle, *O Blush not so*, which we need not dwell upon beyond saying that it is not impossible that passages from Shakespeare's *Troilus and Cressida* are responsible for some of the concurrences in it. After jotting this down, Keats continues:

[1] See Vol. I, pp. 60–61.

> "Now I purposed to write you a serious poetical letter . . . Yet I cannot write in prose; it is a sunshiny day and I cannot, so here goes, —"

What goes is *Hence Burgundy, Claret, and Port.* This is a pretty bit of rhyming, which turns at the end into something like the expression of a real mood. The chief importance of the poem is the Blakeian ring of the last nineteen lines, but of Keats's indebtedness to Blake I shall speak in a moment. Both these "rantings," as he calls them, bear the hall-marks of being done on the instant. Keats was much in the habit of dashing off into verse when the rhyming mood came on him in the midst of a letter, but it is not difficult to tell which of such poems are copies of earlier drafts and which done on the spur of the moment. When no other indication is given, the quality of the poem is a sure guide.

The new year opened quite pleasantly, with what seemed good auguries. The news from Devonshire was on the whole encouraging. Tom was gaining strength, although the hæmorrhages continued. His London doctor, Mr. Sawrey, to whom Keats took the reports, expressed himself satisfied with Tom's progress. Brown had returned and Keats found dining with him, or with the Dilkes, very much to his taste. He got into the habit of taking his papers to Dilke's and copying them there, chatting at the same time — a dual occupation which did the revision of *Endymion* no service. One of his activities during January and February was going to hear Hazlitt's lectures on the English poets at the Surrey Institution. His comments on them in his letters are all too slight, but it is interesting to learn that he considered that Hazlitt "gave a very fine piece of Criticism on Swift, Voltaire, and Rabelais," and that he was "disappointed at his treatment of Chatterton." Hazlitt had had the temerity to declare that the chief interest in Chatterton's poems was the very youthful age of the author when he wrote them. Keats, who was probably more drawn to Chatterton on account of his youth than he was aware, naturally found such a statement most unsympathetic. Since he and Hazlitt were, as Mr. Howe happily expresses it, "rubbing elbows in the same society"[1] very frequently at this time, we may well believe that it was Keats's strenuous objections to his opinion which drew from Hazlitt the generous explanation of his point of view with which he began his last lecture of the series.

It is a curious commentary on Keats's state of mind that he did not go to Coleridge's lectures, delivered during the same weeks at a hall much nearer to Hampstead in Flower-de-Luce Court, Fetter Lane.[2]

However delightful the new friendship with Brown and Dilke may have been, it was evidently Reynolds who fitted in most closely with the mood of these early months of 1818. Reynolds was already engaged to Miss Drew and was considering, had indeed by this time decided, to give up his position in the insurance office and become an articled clerk to a Mr. Fladgate, a solicitor, the good James Rice paying the requisite fee. There would be less time for poetry as an embryo solicitor than as an insurance clerk with no studying to do, so Reynolds and Keats evidently reasoned, with the natural result that the two friends wrote and talked poetry as much as they could before Reynolds's incarceration took place, and whenever it so happened that they could not meet for a day or two, they exchanged letters. One of these letters from Keats to Reynolds, written on Tuesday, February third, contains two poems: *Lines on the Mermaid Tavern* and *Robin Hood*.

Although the Mermaid Tavern poem was copied last,

[1] Letter from P. P. Howe, author of the *Life of William Hazlitt*, to the London *Observer*. September 24, 1922.

[2] From a copy of the original prospectus for the lectures. Author's Collection.

it was clearly composed before the other, as Keats introduces it by saying: "Here are the Mermaid lines," as though he had already told Reynolds about them. The lines are not arresting, and we need not linger over them. Professor de Sélincourt suggests that Keats may have got his idea for the poem from *Master Francis Beaumont's Letter to Ben Jonson, written before he and Master Fletcher came to London with two of the precedent comedies, then not finished, which deferred their merry meetings*. But surely the legend of the Mermaid Tavern is part and parcel of the equipment of everyone in the least conversant with the history of English literature. A shrewder speculation is made by Mr. Finney,[1] who thinks that the poem derives from Drayton's *The Muse's Elysium*. Certainly Drayton's description of Elysium contains the germ of the Mermaid lines.

The *Mermaid Tavern* is only a sort of afterthought in this Tuesday letter, which was written to thank Reynolds for two sonnets on Robin Hood that he had sent to Keats, but the fact that Keats brings Robin Hood into the poem, which was written before he received them, implies that the sonnets were the outgrowth of some conversation which the friends had together. The letter begins very charmingly:

> "I thank you for your dish of Filberts — would I could get a basket of them by way of dessert every day for the sum of two-pence."

After some pleasant joking, Keats proceeds to comment on the sonnets:

> "About the nuts being worth cracking, all I can say is, that where there are a throng of delightful Images ready drawn, simplicity is the only thing. The first is the best on account of the first line, and the 'arrow, foil'd of its antler'd food,' and moreover (and this is the only word or two I find

[1] *Shakespeare and Keats*, by Claude L. Finney.

> fault with, the more because I have had so much reason to shun it as a quicksand) the last has 'tender and true.' We must cut this, and not be rattlesnaked into any more of the like."

Most excellent criticism truly, and how kindly put! Keats knew the secret of praising first where blame must follow. When Reynolds printed these poems three years later in his *Garden of Florence*, published after Keats's death, the offending "tender and true" had given place to "young as the dew," which, although none too good, is certainly better.

Keats prefaced the copying of his *Robin Hood* by remarking: "In return for your dish of filberts, I have gathered a few catkins. I hope they'll look pretty." They do, very pretty indeed; but the poem is little more than pretty. It is neatly rhymed and pleasantly imagined, and the trochaic metre is carefully and expertly kept throughout. *Robin Hood* is better handled than the *Lines on the Mermaid Tavern*. The picture is clear, simple, and sufficient, which cannot be said of the earlier poem, but both poems spring from one mood, only the mood itself had taken a firmer hold in *Robin Hood*, due, of course, to Reynolds's example.

How much the young men were together at this time can be seen by this sentence at the end of the letter: "I will call on you at 4 to-morrow and we will trudge together for it is not the thing to be a stranger in the Land of Harpsicols. I hope also to bring you my 2nd Book." There could not be enough talk about poetry with Reynolds, that is clear, and the Second Book was copied, this time decently, on new paper. Two days later, Keats writes to Taylor: "I have finished copying my Second Book — but I want it for one day to overlook it." [1] These two references have made possible the dating of an unpublished letter from

[1] Corrected from original letter. Author's Collection.

Keats to Haydon,[1] which I venture, for reasons to be given presently, to assign to February fifth.

"Thursday Morning.

My dear Haydon —

I was at Reynolds's when he received your Letter and am therefore up to Probabilities — The fact is Reynolds is very unwell — he has all Kinds of distressing Symptoms and I am on this account rather glad that he has not spare time for one of our right Sort meetings — he would go to[o] far for his health. I was right glad of your Letter from Devonshire whereby that is I hope one day to see it. Right sorry that you are back today. I hope 'tis not for long. I met a friend the other day who had seen Wordsworth's House the other Week. You will be glad to hear that I have finished my second Book that is if this catches you at your Street door. I have been gadding and did not see your Note time to answer it sooner. Let me hear from Devon again.

Yours like a Pyramid

John Keats.

My Brother George desires to be remembered to you."

At first glance, the reference to finishing the Second Book suggests that this letter was written in August, just before Keats went to Oxford. But this idea falls to the ground in the face of Haydon's distinct statement that his only outing during the Summer of 1817 was a short trip to Oxford and Blenheim, which we know to be true, because it was at Oxford that he encountered Cripps. The only other time when Keats could have said that he had finished his Second Book was when he had finished copying it, and the date of that occurrence is determined by the letters to Reynolds and Taylor. No other poem can come in question, as the only other of Keats's poems which contains a Second Book is *Hyperion*, and the Second Book of that was never finished. But here a difficulty presents itself, there is no record of Haydon's having been in

[1] Morgan Collection.

Devonshire during the Winter of 1818. The evidence on this point is purely negative and collateral, but, if carefully examined, extremely conclusive. There is a gap in Haydon's correspondence between January twenty-second and February sixth; on the latter date he was certainly in London, for he wrote to Miss Mitford from there on that day, the very next day to the one on which I suppose Keats's letter to have been written. There is no proof, but it is certainly not impossible for Haydon to have run down to Devonshire for a couple of weeks at the end of January. The collateral evidence is very strong. In the first place, the letter is dated Thursday morning, and February fifth was a Thursday. In the second, Keats has recently been at Reynolds's where we know he purposed going on Wednesday, February fourth. In the third place, Haydon has written inviting Reynolds to one of their usual evenings, and we know that Haydon tried very hard to patch up the quarrel; Reynolds has refused to go, and we have Keats's word for it that Reynolds rejected all Haydon's attempts at a reconciliation; and Keats is offering a mollifying reason for Reynolds's refusal, as, by his own showing, he was constantly doing. Again, Reynolds is far from well, which at this time was the case; by the end of February he was attacked with a rheumatic fever from which he suffered for months. In the fourth place, there is the evidence that Keats expects to go to Devonshire. In the fifth, we have the curious signature, which I feel sure was put into his head by the very gadding he mentions, for, having presumably "trudged" all the afternoon of Wednesday with Reynolds, he finished the day by passing the evening at Hunt's when he, Hunt, and Shelley wrote their competitive sonnets on the Nile. The connection between the Nile sonnets and this signature will appear in a moment. The message from George Keats is no hindrance to this train of reasoning; it was undoubtedly sent in a letter from Teignmouth. In view of all these interweaving strands of fact, I firmly believe that the letter is rightly placed here.

Keats was very busy on that Wednesday, for, according to Woodhouse, the sonnet *To a Lady seen for a few Moments at Vauxhall* was also written on that day. If Woodhouse be correct in his date, the sonnet was probably written in the morning, for in the afternoon Keats was off to Little Britain and Reynolds. The title I have used is that under which it is given in the Buxton Forman editions. Lord Houghton entitles it simply *To* ——. There is no real authority for Buxton Forman's title, he derived it from a statement by Woodhouse that the sonnet was addressed to "a lady whom he saw for some few moments at Vauxhall."

The sonnet is in the Shakespearian form which Keats was so determined to master. Here he certainly succeeded. Both Dr. Bridges and Professor de Sélincourt have pointed out its resemblance to Shakespeare's sonnets. This sonnet is a beautiful thing, but too reminiscent of Shakespeare to be as interesting as others which are more personal to Keats. The long pondering over Shakespeare's poems in the Autumn was bearing fruit in other matters than form. It is not, I think, the compliment which Dr. Bridges means it to be to say, as he does, that "it might almost have been written by Shakespeare." For the most important thing in a man's work is that it should be his own, without echo. This sonnet must be admitted to be a programme piece, written with infinite care to a pattern. The first line, "Time's sea hath been five years at its slow ebb," seems to have determined the poem, and the evocation of the lady seen so long before merely served as a sympathetic idea to go on with. Granted, then, that the poem owes its existence to Keats's recently conceived desire to write sonnets in the Shakespearian form, and the sudden starting into his mind of the first line, nevertheless Keats here produced a very fine sonnet. The first six lines are perfectly successful; with the seventh his inspiration lags and falls back upon such ancient *clichés* as "rose's dye," "my soul doth take its flight," and "fond ear." The twelfth line is weak, and fails to end the quatrain which is run on into the couplet. For all these reasons, readers at large, who know nothing of derivations or manners, will always repeat the first line, and be unable to recall a single other one in the poem. The sonnet is, in the final reckoning, a study, and a remarkably satisfactory study, but lacking the personal and peculiar touch which is the hall-mark of Keats's best work.

Sir Sidney Colvin's effort to identify the lady seen at Vauxhall with the "fair creature of an hour" of *When I have fears* and the much earlier nymph of *Fill for me a Brimming Bowl* does not seem to me to maintain itself. Apparently, in the Woodhouse Transcripts (*Poems II*),[1] Woodhouse suggests that *Fill for me a Brimming Bowl* was written to a lady seen at Vauxhall. I have not seen this volume, but in the Woodhouse Book in the Morgan Library, where the poem is copied twice, there is no mention of her. Woodhouse, as I have shown, is often lax in details, tacking data belonging to one poem on another, giving names wrong, and various things of the sort. An instance of this appears in his transcript in the Morgan Library Woodhouse Book of *Hadst thou liv'd in days of old*,[2] which we know to have been written to Georgiana Wylie, but which he states to have been sent "as a valentine . . . to Miss Mary F." Later he refers to the same poem as "To xxxx" with "Mary" in brackets, even though, in this last place, he says that the poem was written for George Keats to send to a lady as a valentine. Evidently Keats preserved the anonymity of his future sister-in-law by inventing a mythical Mary F. as a sop to Woodhouse's curiosity. Considering this, it seems not unlikely that "a lady seen for a few moments at Vauxhall" became a

[1] Crewe Collection. [2] See Vol. I, p. 62.

generic term for any lady about whom he was tempted to write, a convenient alias to put Woodhouse off with, for Woodhouse's questions as to the genesis of poems, however flattering in principle, must often have been a nuisance.

There is another objection to Sir Sidney's theory to be found in the poems themselves, which is that the tone of *Fill for me a Brimming Bowl* has no resemblance to that of the last two sonnets, so that, if all three poems refer to the same person, Keats's heart must have become marvellously fonder during the years when he had not seen her, and such a persisting and increasing admiration would have meant a far deeper feeling than could be assuaged by a couple of sonnets. No, in spite of the romantic charm of Sir Sidney's suggestion, I fear we shall be wiser to consider that such slight episodes, fit to be utilized as needed in poems, were a very usual part of Keats's daily life in his early years, and are to be taken for just what we see them to be worth and no more.

Having trudged with Reynolds, or merely stayed and paid a call on him if Reynolds's "distressing symptoms" prevented the proposed walk, Keats dropped in at Hunt's in Lisson Grove. Here he found Shelley up from Marlowe on a few days' visit to Hunt. This was an excellent opportunity for Hunt's favourite indoor sport — competitive sonnet writing. He proposed it, of course, and the subject chosen was the Nile. The sonnets were to be in the Petrarchan form and the time allowed for composition was a quarter of an hour. Shelley and Keats were up to time, but Hunt, it is said,[1] worked over his poem for half the night. This gave him an unfair advantage, obviously, but however that may be, his sonnet is far better than either of the other two.

For fruitful comparison, here are the three sonnets. Keats's shall come first:

[1] Colvin.

"Son of the old moon-mountains African!
Chief of the Pyramid and Crocodile!
We call thee fruitful and, that very while,
A desert fills our seeing's inward span;
Nurse of swart nations since the world began,
Art thou so fruitful? or dost thou beguile
Such men to honour thee, who, worn with toil,
Rest for a space 'twixt Cairo and Decan?
O may dark fancies err! they surely do;
'Tis ignorance that makes a barren waste
Of all beyond itself, thou dost bedew
Green rushes like our rivers, and dost taste
The pleasant sun-rise, green isles hast thou too,
And to the sea as happily dost haste."

Here is Shelley's:

"Month after month the gather'd rains descend,
Drenching yon secret Æthiopian dells,
And from the Desert's ice-girt pinnacles,
Where Frost and Heat in strange embraces blend
On Atlas, fields of moist snow half depend.
Girt there with blasts and meteors, Tempest dwells
By Nile's aërial urn, with rapid spells
Urging its waters to their mighty end.
O'er Egypt's land of memory floods are level,
And they are thine, O Nile! and well thou knowest
That soul-sustaining airs and blasts of evil,
And fruits and poisons spring where'er thou flowest.
Beware, O man! for knowledge must to thee,
Like the great flood to Egypt, ever be."

Hunt's sonnet is:

"It flows through old hush'd Ægypt and its sands,
Like some grave mighty thought threading a dream;
And times and things, as in that vision, seem
Keeping along it their eternal stands, —
Caves, pillars, pyramids, the shepherd bands
That roam'd through the young world, the glory extreme
Of high Sesostris, and that southern beam,

The laughing queen that caught the world's great hands.
Then comes a mightier silence, stern and strong,
As of a world left empty of its throng,
And the void weighs on us; and then we wake,
And hear the fruitful stream lapsing along
'Twixt villages, and think how we shall take
Our own calm journey on for human sake."

Hunt's sonnet is certainly the best he ever wrote, and he printed it in his volume, *Foliage*, published later in the year. Shelley's, one of the worst he ever wrote, was lost until it unexpectedly came to light in 1876; up to that time his *Ozymandias* was supposed to be his contribution. Keats's sonnet was first printed by Lord Houghton, but Keats wrote out a fair copy of it in a copy of *Endymion* [1] which contains many transcripts by Keats of his poems of this time.

Keats's sonnet is remarkable for his slight knowledge of Egypt and his abiding joy in English scenery. There are no "green rushes like our rivers" in the Nile, but Keats can conceive of no river without them. The Nile in his hands, through courtesy and compliment, turns into an English stream.

It seems very probable that Keats harked back to his recollections of Diodorus when he pictured the Nile. In Book I, Chapter Three, of that amazing and amusing history, there is a description of the Nile, where, among other things, is this:

> "It runs down from the mountains of Ethiopia, till it empties itself into the sea . . . In its course it makes many islands."

Later in the same chapter, speaking of the inundations of the Nile, Diodorus, quoting Democritus the Abderite, says:

> "These vapours . . . are driven about by the Etesian

[1] Dilke Collection.

> winds, till they fall upon the highest mountains, which are, (as he affirms, in Ethiopia.)"

In Chapter One of the same Book, we find the genesis for the Nile's fruitfulness. Here is the passage:

> "For this river being very fruitful, and apt to bring forth many animals, yields, of itself, likewise food and nourishment for the things produced. For it yields the roots of canes, the fruit of the lote-tree," etc.

To Keats's prejudiced affection "the roots of canes" become the green rushes of English waters. In the same chapter, it is again spoken of as "the most fruitful and richest river of any that is known in the world." There is a long and vivid account of the crocodile, and pyramids abound, naturally.

Diodorus declares that life was first produced in Egypt, from the action of the sun on the mud of the Nile, and states that

> "The Egyptians report, that, at the beginning of the world, the first men were created in Egypt,"

which statement gave Keats the line

> "Nurse of swart nations since the world began."

For men who

> ". . . worn with toil
> Rest for a space 'twixt Cairo and Decan"

we may imagine Keats beguiled into a remembrance of Ritchie's long journey, even though the route were different.

Pondering on this sonnet on Thursday morning, working over it very likely, Keats's thoughts were naturally full of Egypt when he sat down to answer Haydon's note, and his "Yours like a Pyramid" becomes lucidly clear in the light of another passage from Diodorus which was probably, in connection with the others, surging round in his head. This passage is so pertinent to the meaning of his expression that I give it here:

> "The three pyramids, which were accounted among the seven wonders of the world . . . The greatness of these works, and the excessive labour of the workmen seen in them, do even strike the beholders with admiration and astonishment. The greatest is built of solid marble throughout, or rough work, but of perpetual duration."

It is, of course, the last sentence which Keats had principally in mind. But may he not also have intended a little joke about the drudgery of copying, copying, copying his *Endymion?*

I do not suppose Keats to have remembered these passages otherwise than generally, unless, indeed, a copy of Diodorus was at Hunt's that night, and talk of it led to the choice of the Nile as the subject for the sonnets, which is quite possible.

On this same Thursday, Keats went to town on "very particular employ in the affair of Cripps" whatever that may have been, and drifted in to the Reynoldses' before coming home. There he found Reynolds's married sister, Mrs. Longmore, and at her request he then and there wrote a sonnet to Spenser and gave it to her.

As we should expect, from his preoccupation at the moment, the sonnet was Shakespearian. There is no doubt that, until the last year of his writing life, Keats found the sonnet, whether Petrarchan or Shakespearian, a particularly handy form in which to encase all sorts of fleeting interests and emotions. He wrote it, always easily, and sometimes surprisingly well. *To Spenser* is rather pleasing, and the idea that to write on Spenser needs the twin enticements of Summer and leisure, is nicely put. Keats, being both in the middle of Winter and in the middle of his long labour of revising *Endymion*, was in no mood to do justice to the subject. What he did was to beg the question by enlarging upon the idea I have just paraphrased. The "last eve" in the third line would seem to put the sonnet as having been written on the day subsequent to the request, but the date is written on the manuscript by Mrs. Longmore and she is responsible for the account I have given. A tenable explanation is that Mrs. Longmore proffered her request on Wednesday, and when, on Thursday, Keats appeared again empty-handed, teased him into writing what he could on the spot.

Reynolds seems to have been poetizing as much as possible during these weeks, anticipating his forthcoming total immersion in the law. Among other things, he composed a sonnet in praise of dark eyes, presumably Miss Drew's; this he showed to Keats, who immediately countered with his sonnet *Blue! 'Tis the life of Heaven.* In spite of the fact that Reynolds's sonnet followed the Petrarchan mode, Keats clung to his new love, the Shakespearian. Keats's sonnet was written on Sunday, February eighth. A week later, Reynolds wrote his *Farewell to the Muses*, so we can imagine that Monday, the sixteenth, saw him perched up at a desk in Fladgate's office, if, indeed this event were not postponed by his illness.

Blue! 'Tis the life of Heaven is neatly arranged as to its juxtapositions, and the detail is both happy and imaginative; but the couplet is a sad thing. With this scanty consideration we may leave it.

So time moved on until the middle of February; composing, revising, and gadding sharing Keats's days. No proofs of *Endymion* were as yet forthcoming, but by February sixteenth he had seen a trial sheet, and had hopes that the proofs would begin to arrive before long. In the meanwhile, he was well ahead of the printers, which was satisfactory; and he was beginning to taste the fruits of a modest notoriety, which seemed to his inexperience delightful, although he had too just a sense of proportion, and too lively a sense of humour, to be in the least overbalanced by them. Writing to his brothers on Monday, February sixteenth, he describes the situation:

> "I am in the high way of being introduced to a squad of people, Peter Pindar, Mrs. Opie, Mrs. Scott — Mr. Robinson,[1] a great friend of Coleridge's, called on me. Richards tells me that my Poems are known in the west country, and that he saw a very clever copy of verses, headed with a Motto from my Sonnet to George — Honours rush so thickly upon me that I shall not be able to bear up against them. What think you — am I to be crowned in the Capitol, am I to be made a Mandarin — No! I am to be invited, Mrs. Hunt tells me, to a party at Ollier's, to keep Shakespeare's birthday — Shakespeare would stare to see me there."

Shakespeare would stare because less than a year had elapsed since Keats and the Olliers had parted anything but friends. But he was near enough to being somebody now for them to think it worth while to bury the hatchet. Only posterity can know what an accolade Crabbe Robinson's call was. That the indefatigable busy-body and lion-hunter chose to seek him out, speaks eloquently to the fact that Robinson's set had its eye upon him. His social horizons were widening out in every direction, and he was young enough to enjoy the fact, an enjoyment which he was so soon to lose. Still more important was the increasing extent of his mental horizon. On Thursday, February nineteenth, he wrote a very wise and very beautiful letter to Reynolds, then already ill, and in the letter he copied his poem entitled by subsequent editors: *What the Thrush said.*

> "My dear Reynolds,
>
> I had an idea that a man might pass a very pleasant life in this manner — let him on a certain day read a certain

[1] Henry Crabbe Robinson, the diarist.

Page of full Poesy or distilled Prose, and let him wander with it, and muse upon it, and reflect upon it, and bring home to it, and prophesy upon it, and dream upon it, until it becomes stale — and when will it do so? Never. When Man has arrived at a certain ripeness in intellect any one grand and spiritual passage serves him as a starting-post towards all 'the two-and-thirty Palaces.' How happy is such a voyage of conception, what delicious diligent Indolence! . . . Nor will this sparing touch of noble Books be any irreverence to their Writers — for perhaps the honours paid by Man to Man are trifles in comparison to the Benefit done by great Works to the 'Spirit and pulse' of good by their mere passive existence. Memory should not be called Knowledge. Many have original minds who do not think it — they are led away by Custom. Now it appears to me that almost any Man may like the spider spin from his own inwards his own airy Citadel — the points of leaves and twigs on which the spider begins her work are few, and she fills the air with a beautiful circuiting. Man should be content with as few points to tip with the fine Web of his Soul, and weave a tapestry empyrean full of symbols for his spiritual eye, of softness for his spiritual touch, of space for his wandering, of distinctness for his luxury. But the Minds of Mortals are so different and bent on such diverse journeys that it may at first appear impossible for any common taste and fellowship to exist between two or three under these suppositions. It is however quite the contrary. Minds would leave each other in contrary directions, traverse each other in numberless points, and at last greet each other at the journey's end. An old Man and a child would talk together and the old Man be led on his path and the child left thinking. Man should not dispute or assert but whisper results to his neighbour and thus by every germ of spirit sucking the sap from mould ethereal every human might become great, and Humanity instead of being a wide heath of Furze and Briars with here and there a remote Oak or Pine, would become a grand democracy of Forest Trees! It has been an old comparison for our urging on — the Beehive; however, it seems to me that we should rather be the flower than the Bee — for it is a false notion that more is gained by receiving than giving — no, the receiver and the giver are equal in their benefits. The flower, I doubt not, receives a fair guerdon from the Bee — its leaves blush deeper in the next spring — and who shall say between Man and Woman which is the most delighted. Now it is more noble to sit like Jove than to fly like Mercury — let us not therefore go hurrying about and collecting honey, beelike buzzing here and there impatiently from a knowledge of what is to be aimed at; but let us open our leaves like a flower and be passive and receptive — budding patiently under the eye of Apollo and taking hints from every noble insect that favours us with a visit — sap will be given us for meat and dew for drink."

That passage shows so much reflection, and there is such a depth of truth in it, that I have given it practically in full. Possibly the most remarkable idea in it is that "Many have original minds who do not think it — they are led away by Custom." In Keats's day, this would have been a startling and subversive opinion had it ever passed beyond the bounds of private correspondence and risked itself in the great world. Only now, a century later, has some dim knowledge of the kind penetrated the minds of educators here and there. But Keats was no propagandist. What thoughts that came to him he "whispered" to his friends between his letter sheets. Shelley flung his immature half-thinkings forth on every wind that blew, and when the world would not listen corked them up in bottles and floated them out to sea, vaguely content that, like soap-bubbles, he had at least wafted them away. Not so Keats; he sat open to impressions, harking to the promptings of his own ripening intellect, willing to leave all these things to work their will on his mind and his poetry in their own good time. He believed, as all great poets have done, that there is a "Benefit done by great Works to the 'Spirit and pulse' of good by their mere passive existence"; and if his conception that a world of men following the truths that are in them would all be great is perhaps slightly idealistic, even this cannot be gainsaid if we take it as partial, not complete, fact.

Following this passage, Keats goes on:

"I was led into these thoughts, my dear Reynolds, by the beauty of the morning operating on a sense of Idleness — I have not read any Books — the Morning said I was right — I had no idea but of the morning, and the thrush said I was right — seeming to say,

O thou whose face hath felt the Winter's wind,
Whose eye has seen the snow-clouds hung in mist,
And the black elm-tops 'mong the freezing stars,
To thee the Spring will be a harvest-time.
O thou, whose only book has been the light
Of supreme darkness which thou feddest on
Night after night when Phœbus was away,
To thee the Spring shall be a triple morn.
O fret not after knowledge — I have none,
And yet my song comes native with the warmth.
O fret not after knowledge — I have none,
And yet the Evening listens. He who saddens
At thought of idleness cannot be idle,
And he's awake who thinks himself asleep."

That is a poem to stamp any day with gold and crimson. Idle, forsooth! Was any day ever better spent? The long hours occupied in soaking in the sunny day, with his "snail-horn perception of beauty" at its most sentient and eager; the comparatively short period of writing. Yet Keats, half in earnest, half a little overcome by his own philosophizing at the beginning of the letter, ends it with a quasi-deprecatory gesture in this wise:

"Now I am sensible this is a mere sophistication (however it may neighbour to any truths), to excuse my own indolence — so I will not deceive myself that Man should be equal with Jove — but think himself very well off as a sort of scullion-Mercury, or even a humble Bee. It is no

> matter whether I am right or wrong, either one way or another, if there is sufficient to lift a little time from your shoulders."

Now Keats was not apt to be deprecatory in regard to the poems he sent his friends. If they were frankly jokes, he laughed with them and at them; if they were serious, he left them to take their chance, often giving them a sort of appreciative pat as he turned them out for contemplation. Why, then, this attitude toward such an excellent thing as he ought to have known this was? The answer, I think, is that Keats was more completely possessed by this poem than by any he had written for a long while. Nothing that he had done since finishing *Endymion* is at all equal to it. No short poem written since the sonnet *On the Sea* can touch it for intensity and beauty sustained throughout. Keats had been writing a good deal since his return to Hampstead; some of the work had been fairly good, but most of it had been decidedly poor. All the poems written immediately after his return from Oxford read more like pieces that he had set himself to write than *con amore* flashes which would come out. I say this with due consideration for his best work of the Winter, since, as we have seen, even those poems which are the most successful fail in sustaining themselves to the end. In the *Thrush's Song*, he appears thoroughly under the influence of his subconscious mind. I do not know whether any holograph of the poem is known other than that in the letter. I have never heard of one. But I suspect that, if a first draft ever comes to light, it will be found to contain a minimum of corrections, possibly, even, none at all. Corrections are no fault in a poem, often a poem is practically made during correction, but on those infinitely rare occasions when one drops down upon its author in a beautiful ready-made precision, when, I say, such a thing does happen, there is a finality and rightness about it which cannot be mistaken.

I judge that this poem came to Keats in this way because of its form. It came in a hurry and unrhymed. This is more important than it may at first seem. Keats rhymed easily and well, but we shall see later that the recurring rhymes in both the sonnet forms were not completely satisfactory to him. The scheme of the poem has the appearance of a sonnet, but it is in blank verse. Why? Because the lines came into his mind so fast and so perfectly tuned that he would not stop to rhyme them. The significant fact is that they came unrhymed. Here let me make a digression which we shall find in a moment is a sort of explanation.

Buxton Forman makes a very interesting suggestion. He says:

> "Keats seems to have been really writing in a kind of spiritual parallelism with the thrush's song: it will be noted that line 5 repeats the form of line 1, line 8 of line 4, while lines 11 and 12 are a still closer repetition of lines 9 and 10 . . . Having regard to the varieties of sonnet metre used by Keats, his bold boyish attempt at emancipation in making five syllables without a rhyme serve as a full line, and his sonnet protest . . . against chaining our English 'by dull rhymes,' I think it hardly fantastic to suppose that he consciously translated the wild melody of the thrush into an unrhymed sonnet structure."

We may dismiss at once Buxton Forman's "boyish attempt," and his five syllables made to serve as a full line. The truncated line in the second sonnet to Haydon never purported to be a full line, but boldly pronounced itself a short one. This daring attempt at introducing a rest does, however, show how very musical Keats's ear naturally was, and how unboyishly he could flout conventions. Having scuffed aside these misconceptions, there is yet considerable to ponder over in this passage. Buxton Forman's contention is arresting, but it leaves the whole *raison d'être* of the form still to be accounted for from any but a superficial point of view. In the first place,

Keats's impatience with "dull rhymes" in the sonnet did not manifest itself until over a year later. I take issue with Buxton Forman exactly at the word "consciously," for, as I have said, this poem seems to me to be an almost perfectly subconscious one. Is then Buxton Forman wrong about the parallel with the thrush's song? Yes, and no. The thrush, like all birds, repeats his song over and over, and Keats had been more affected by the repetitive structure of the song than he was aware, undoubtedly. On the other hand, the kind of repetition in which Keats indulges here is very common in poetry. Certainly Keats made no effort to reproduce the cadences of the thrush's song. He was not in the least ripe for such an idea to occur to him, nor had any such stretching of the rhythmic possibilities of verse occurred to anybody at the period in which he lived. Let us suppose Keats *unconsciously* saturated with this bird-call repeated again and again, his subconsciousness seized upon the fact and projected it into the poem as an inherent atmospheric necessity. But lying in his mind also were the rhythms of the Shakespearian sonnet. During the two weeks preceding that Thursday, he had written four sonnets, three Shakespearian and one Petrarchan. What more natural, under the circumstances, than that the repetition here should drop into the form of quatrains. But the bird's cadences were not of equal length, and, after two quatrains, a certain monotony jarred across the subconscious free rhythm implanted in Keats's unconscious ears by the thrush and for that reason become symbolic of place, time, and idea. Immediately the repetition takes on, first, a new form, and second, a slightly uneven cadence, for the first figure consists of two lines, the second of one line and a half. But again the sonnet form obtrudes, and ends the poem at fourteen lines — since Keats has been in the habit of fitting such conceptions into just fourteen lines — and by this end the sonnet sense is satisfied in both its manifestations, as the Shakespearian sonnet always, and the Petrarchan not seldom, finishes with a couplet, which, from the connection of idea in them, we may consider the last two lines of *What the Thrush Said* to be. The form of the poem then, viewed from the psychological angle, becomes, not a conscious experiment at all, but a permeation of atmosphere infused through psychical and physical being alike, plus a well rooted complex in favour of the sonnet form.

Keats's peculiar excellence lies in a sort of selflessness. Which is odd, because few men have had a more vivid personality than he. It is just his personality which makes his letters one of the most satisfying and remarkable books in English literature. But when he writes poetry, he seems to become a clear glass through which beauty itself may shine. We do not read so much as see through his eyes and with his super-sensitive mind. As he grew and learnt, he acquired some of the architectonics of poetry, at least in certain *genres*. The type of short poem which he calls an "ode," for example, he came to manage triumphantly, and he was making strides in the direction of both pictorial narrative and symbolistic lyric when he died. The marvel is that all his effort and achievement toward the mere building of a poem should have left his delicate recording power intact. But it did. Because he could learn and not lose, is the reason for believing that he had not reached his poetic maturity at the time of his death. To point to the eclipse of his creative power during the last year of his life as a refutation of his farther advance, is unintelligent, for then he was a dying man; to all intents and purposes, indeed, he was already dead, and, as far as poetry is concerned, may, and should, be counted so. When *Endymion* was written, he knew practically nothing of poetic architectonics, therefore we cannot expect to find much sense of structure in that poem, but what we do find is the mirror quality I have spoken of, and that in superb abundance.

It is this mirror quality, but in this instance reflecting

melody rather than vision, which makes *What the Thrush Said* so immensely interesting at just this point in his life. For Keats clung to the sonnet form precisely because it gave him a defined structure and saved him the trouble of finding one. Yet here, at a moment when his desire for change bade him turn from one sonnet form to another, he is suddenly jerked out of himself by the force of an aural impression, and so violently that the result is this varied and repetitive blank verse lyric.

There was also another influence at work upon him, although he scarcely realized it, and his aptitudes were not yet sufficiently advanced for him to take all the advantage from it he might have done. That influence, vague and fitful though it were, was William Blake. There is no specific trace of this influence in *What the Thrush Said*, but there are well defined evidences of it in two of the little fragments usually printed under the heading, *Extracts from an Opera*.

What the opera was, we do not know, nor indeed whether there ever was any opera. Lord Houghton printed six poems under this caption, so it is presumable that some of Keats's friends told him of a projected opera of which these six poems were fragments. But, indeed, so fragmentary are they, and so disconnected one with another, that we cannot glean from them the remotest inkling of what the opera was to be about. Only two of these poems are worth mentioning in detail. These two are *Daisy's Song*, and the one beginning *The stranger lighted from his steed*, and in both of them there is a decidedly Blakeian influence. Dante Gabriel Rossetti long ago pointed out a resemblance between *The Stranger* and Blake's *The Will and the Way*, and Professor de Sélincourt has suggested another to Blake's *Love's Secret*. There is, however, a much stronger resemblance to Blake in *Daisy's Song*, which has to a nicety the tricks of Blake's style in the *Songs of Innocence* and the *Songs of Experience*; at least it has them in the first and last stanzas, the second is less in Blake's manner. For purposes of comparison, I give the poem.

"DAISY'S SONG

The sun, with his great eye,
Sees not so much as I;
And the moon, all silver-proud,
Might as well be in a cloud.

And O the spring — the spring!
I lead the life of a King!
Couch'd in the teeming grass,
I spy each pretty lass.

I look where no one dares,
And I stare where no one stares,
And when the night is nigh,
Lambs bleat my lullaby."

Minus the second stanza, that poem might have been written by Blake. The metre is exactly that of *I love the jocund dance* in the *Poetical Sketches*, and of *The Little Girl Lost*, *The Little Girl Found*, and *The Human Abstract* in the *Songs of Experience*; even the employment of a line beginning with an anapest in Keats's first and third stanzas has its counterpart in the first and the last of these poems of Blake's. Lambs are Blake's most common furniture in the *Songs of Innocence and Experience*, but it is the last stanza of *The Shepherd* which seems to echo most persistently in the last two lines of Keats's last stanza, for witness:

"For he hears the lamb's innocent call,
And he hears the ewe's tender reply;
He is watchful while they are in peace,
For they know when their Shepherd is nigh."

Keats may never have seen any of Blake's Prophetic Books, for although we know that Dilke was a Blake collector, he may not have begun his collection in Keats's lifetime. But whether Keats knew the Prophetic Books, with their superb and audacious rhythmical experimentation, or not, there were enough strange cadences and broken rhythms in the *Poetical Sketches*, in such poems as *To Spring* and *To the Evening Star*, to have opened his eyes to something new. The last of these two poems, by the way, may not inconceivably be more than a little responsible for *What the Thrush Said*, for, in spite of its syncopated cadences and over-long and over-short lines, it purports to be in blank verse and has just fourteen lines.

The only other noteworthy thing in these *Extracts from an Opera* is a little expression in one of them which is so charming that I cannot forbear mentioning it. This little chip from an otherwise inconsiderable trifle is "the May-fly's small fan-horns," which is perfectly Keatsean and perfectly delightful.

I should add that my putting the *Extracts from an Opera* here is a perfectly arbitrary act on my part. Lord Houghton assigns them to 1818, and the early Winter seems the only time during the year when they could have been written. The shadowy connection between Blake's *To the Evening Star* and *What the Thrush Said* is my sole reason for placing them immediately after that poem. But where no clues whatever as to their exact date exist, even so vague and hazardous a one as this gains a certain plausibility. *To the Evening Star* is of course "cadenced verse," or *vers libre*, as it is more commonly called, based upon an iambic rhythm; Keats's *What the Thrush Said* is strict blank verse, yet there is a kind of psychologic rhythmic parallel between the two which must not be overlooked.

By this time, George Keats was beginning to be a little restless at his enforced stay in Devonshire. On the twenty-eighth of February he would come of age, an event of unusual importance in the Keats family, for it meant escape from Abbey's jurisdiction. In George's case, this emancipation heralded the taking of a bold step; nothing less, in fact, than emigration to America, if such a scheme could be embarked upon with any likelihood of success. He was itching to come up to town and prospect for possible chances, but Tom seemed to be gaining in Devonshire and to bring him back to London while Winter was still in the air was not to be thought of. Besides this, George had the greatest regard for Keats's work, and on no account wished to hurry him in his revision of *Endymion*. So matters stood, and seemed likely to stand, for Tom could not be left alone. Keats had written on the sixteenth of February that he longed to be at Teignmouth, but thought he had better finish his Third Book first, an indefinite date for his impatient brothers to reckon upon. We can readily suppose that, without mentioning any particular reason, it was nevertheless some hint of desire to have him come on the part of George or Tom which induced him suddenly to give up some of the gadding and work more steadily. At any rate, on the same idle, and very fruitful, day on which he had written to Reynolds, he wrote to Horace Smith, throwing over an engagement to pass the day on the plea that his brothers were expecting him in Devonshire and that he had some days' work still to do before he could go thither.

Apparently he had no idea that his going down meant George's coming up. George probably did not tell him, realizing what disappointing news it would be. But Keats found out in an amusing manner and with a cleverness of induction worthy of a detective. Writing to his brothers on Saturday, February twenty-first, after admitting that he has been "abominably idle," he adduces, in proof of having "just turned over a new leaf," his breaking his engagement with Horace Smith, and adds:

> "The occasion of my writing to-day is the enclosed letter — by Postmark from Miss W[ylie]. Does she expect you in town George?"

So the cat was out of the bag, and there was all the more reason for him to hurry down to Teignmouth. Try as he would, there was still a lot to be done before he could start. The proofs were beginning to come in, and Taylor, after the manner of publishers, was pressing him for his last two Books, declaring that he should bring the poem out in a month. Things were beginning to look a little gloomy too, for Reynolds was really extremely ill:

> "Reynolds has been very ill for some time, confined to the house, and had leeches applied to his chest; when I saw him on Wednesday he was much the same, and he is in the worst place for amendment, among the strife of women's tongues, in a hot and parch'd room."

Clearly the Reynolds girls were losing favour in Keats's eyes; we suspect them of being too all-pervasive when he went to call on their brother. On the other hand, Dilke and Brown, and the double house in which they lived, Wentworth Place, were increasing in attraction, for Keats says:

> "I am a good deal with Dilke and Brown; we are very thick; they are very kind to me, they are well; I don't think I could stop in Hampstead but for their neighbourhood."

"They are well" is very illuminating. Reynolds's illness evidently preyed upon Keats, facing a long sojourn with the sick Tom. He was worn fine with work, and needed to be surrounded by vigour and health. Brown's robustness and Dilke's sensible interest in things intellectual braced him up like a full-bodied wine. In Brown's positively rude health, we have one of the cords which attached Keats so closely to him in the sequel. Keats was feeding his own intellect very sturdily, in spite of all his poetical work. Humorously observing his own changes of mood, he tells George and Tom:

> "I am reading Voltaire and Gibbon, although I wrote to Reynolds the other day to prove reading of no use."

But the thrushes and blackbirds are singing even though the wind is "boisterous," and he has not read Shelley's Poem[1] yet, and Lord Byron's Fourth Canto[2] is expected out, and he has heard somewhere that Walter Scott has a new poem in readiness, and so the letter gossips on to the end.

The "new leaf" was turned to some purpose, for six days later, on February twenty-seventh, he wrote to Taylor that he had finished the Third Book and begun the Fourth. There was no question of delaying his journey any longer, the time had come when he absolutely must go down and relieve George. But before we follow him to Devonshire, we must take note of a few more poems which we know to have been written this year, and undoubtedly, I think, while he was still at Hampstead, but the exact dates of which being lost, I could not deal with in the narrative proper.

Among these undated poems are two little songs of no particular interest, entitled *Fairy Songs.* The first is the better of the two, the opening four lines of it are very quotable and often quoted:

> "Shed no tear! O shed no tear!
> The flower will bloom another year.
> Weep no more! O weep no more!
> Young buds sleep in the root's white core."

The second song, which begins with the line, *Ah! woe is me! poor silver-wing!* is worthy of no more than a citation. Another, exceedingly poor, song is *Spirit here that Reignest.* This poem was written on a blank page of a volume of Beaumont and Fletcher, but, although the song may conceivably be addressed to the spirit of the plays, it is quite as probable that it has nothing to do with the book. In Lord Houghton's first edition it was printed as an independent poem, but in his Aldine edition it was included

[1] *Laon and Cythna.* [2] *Childe Harold.*

among the *Fairy Songs*, supposedly because of information supplied by some of Keats's friends.

A trifle of little significance, sarcastically inclined, and most likely a joke piece, called *Modern Love* need not be considered beyond its mention.

Two poems of this undated group are interesting, one very much so. These two are the sonnet *To Homer* and the *Fragment of "The Castle Builder."* The first is dated by Woodhouse "1818." My reasons for putting it here are threefold. The first is that there seems very little likelihood that Keats wrote this sonnet at any other time during the year. It does not in the least harmonize with his mood either in Teignmouth or Scotland, and I do not suppose it to have been written after his return from Scotland on account of my second and third reasons. Of these, the second may appear slight and fantastic, but it is not lacking in plausibility. Keats's twelfth line in this sonnet is:

> "There is a triple sight in blindness keen."

Now Keats had been set very hard upon Milton by Bailey, and we know from his letters after his return from Oxford that he was still much concerned with *Paradise Lost*, even, it appears, to the extent of giving a copy of it to Mrs. Dilke, a copy annotated by himself. There is no clue as to when the annotations were made, the inscription to Mrs. Dilke is undated, but the volume was probably one used by Keats and only subsequently given to Mrs. Dilke. In view of the circumstance of Keats's interest in Milton at this time, there seems little doubt that the notes and underscorings in Mrs. Dilke's copy were made during the Autumn and Winter of 1818. One of these notes contains this pregnant passage:

> "A Poet can seldom have justice done to his imagination — for men are as distinct in their conceptions of material shadowings as they are in matters of spiritual understanding: it can scarcely be conceived how Milton's Blindness

> might here aid the magnitude of his conceptions as a bat in a large gothic vault."

A bat in a gothic vault does not seem a very happy illustration of Keats's meaning. A much better one is the line I have just quoted from the Homer sonnet.

My third reason is, I believe, not the least cogent of the three. It is simply that while during January and February he wrote no less than eight sonnets, on his return from Scotland until the end of the year he wrote no sonnets at all, for his translation of a sonnet by Ronsard cannot be considered an original piece. At the end of the year, therefore, he was clearly not in a sonnet mood, nor did he write another, as far as our knowledge goes, until the Spring of 1819.

To Homer takes a middle place among Keats's sonnets. It is not one of the most successful, nor one of the least so. I think we shall do well to rank it among the set pieces, but it contains the excellent line:

> "There is a budding morrow in midnight,"

a line which Rossetti told Buxton Forman he considered one of the finest "in all poetry."

The *Fragment of "The Castle Builder"* has come down to us with no date at all, not even the year. I put it here on the strength of another annotated passage in the *Paradise Lost.*

The *Castle Builder* is an evocation of pure fancy. We may take it as a catalogue of indoor "luxuries," just as *I Stood Tip-toe* was a catalogue of outdoor "luxuries." It is Keats's imagination rampant among the richest conceptions he can conjure up. Here is a room "rich and sombre," flooded by the silver light of a full June moon. The moonlight, quivering through gold-fish bowls, makes a "glassy diamonding on Turkish floor." The wind blows softly across a terrace, rustling the leaves of orange-trees.

Within the room are various romantic objects: a guitar-ribbon, a lady's glove, a viol-bow lying across a folio of Anacreon, an hour-glass twined in passion-flowers slowly spilling its sand, a skull upon a mat of roses. A cloud crosses the moon, and the poet calls for lights, which being brought reveal the room still farther, showing, among other things "ebon sofas," black and white fleeces, and, most curious of all, a large mirror on which is written "in letters raven-sombre" the old warning: "Mene, Mene, Tekel Upharsin." But this is by no means the end; there are pictures, mostly Salvator Rosas with a few Titians, and

> "... one, though new,
> Of Haydon's in its fresh magnificence."

Only one picture of Haydon's! To be sure Haydon is the sole modern painter admitted to this remarkable assemblage of *objets de virtu*, but — only one! Here is the evidence of a little wind blowing up a change in Keats's mental atmosphere. And there is a still more significant witness to an alteration in Keats's habit of mind in these lines:

> "Greek busts and statuary have ever been
> Held, by the finest spirits, fitter far
> Than vase grotesque and Siamesian jar;
> Therefore 'tis sure a want of Attic taste
> That I should rather love a Gothic waste
> Of eyesight on cinque-coloured potter's clay,
> Than on the marble fairness of old Greece."

Where did Keats run across that "cinque-coloured potter's clay"? If we knew that, we could fix the date of the poem. Now we must rely upon two rather vague hints as to it, and they both come from the annotated copy of *Paradise Lost.* The first is an underscored passage and its attendant note, in which, I believe, we have the genesis of Keats's poem. The passage from Milton is from the First Book. I give it somewhat shortened:

"Anon out of the earth a fabric huge
Rose like an exhalation . . .

. . . .

Built like a temple, where pilasters round
Were set, and Doric pillars overlaid
With golden architrave; nor did there want
Cornice or frieze, with bossy sculptures graven:
The roof was fretted gold . . .

. .

. . . The ascending pile
Stood fixed her stately highth; and straight the doors,
Opening their brazen folds, discover, wide
Within, her ample spaces o'er the smooth
And level pavement: from the arched roof,
Pendent by subtle magic, many a row
Of starry lamps and blazing cressets, fed
With naphtha and asphaltus, yielded light
As from a sky."

Against this passage, Keats wrote:

> "What creates the intense pleasure of not knowing? A sense of independence, of power, from fancy's creating a world of its own by the sense of probabilities. We have read the Arabian Nights and hear there are thousands of those sort of Romances lost—we imagine after them . . ."

Keats's picture is, in tone, treatment, and detail, quite unlike Milton's, and yet there is the parallelism of opposites. Milton's temple is all gold and lamp-fire; Keats's room is silver and black. Yet the shining of the "starry lamps" is duplicated by the moonlight, the "level pavement" by the "Turkish floor," the "brazen doors" by the "four large windows." Still it is not such things on which I would lay great stress, it is on the picture as a whole, inducing Keats to try what he could do in the same kind. However, this is not all. Let us keep in mind Keats's colour scheme of black and silver. There is a note to a long underscored passage, the advance of Azazel's army, in the same volume of Milton. This note begins:

"The light and shade — the sort of black brightness — the ebon diamonding — the Ethiop Immortality — the sorrow, the pain, the sad-sweet Melody . . ."

Not only is "black brightness" the very hue of the *Castle Builder*, but here are both "ebon" and "diamonding," words carried over bodily, it would seem, and even the "sad-sweet Melody" is remembered by implication, for Keats tells us that his dream chamber is

"... a gorgeous room, but somewhat sad;
The draperies are so, as tho' they had
Been made from Cleopatra's winding-sheet."

Cleopatra connotes the Nile; the Nile, his sonnet upon it; the sonnet, his "Moon mountains African"; Africa is Ethiopia. Have we not our poem dated pretty conclusively? I think so.

It is rather amusing to observe that what Milton gave Keats in this instance, Keats passed on to Poe and the French poet, Albert Samain. Both these poets constructed imaginary rooms, and both of these rooms are more like Keats's than Keats's room is like Milton's temple.

Poe's room appears in his essay, *Philosophy of Furniture*. Let us look at it a moment and follow, just for fun, his indebtedness to Keats. In the first place, the time is night. Poe's room has only two windows, but they "open on an Italian *veranda*," which is, of course, Keats's orange-tree-embowered terrace. No moon is mentioned, but the windows have crimson tinted glass, a statement which was certainly intended to imply a moon, for, with no light to shine through them, the windows would be dark, and the hue of them of no importance to the description. Evidently Poe made the same mistake that Keats did in the *Eve of St. Agnes* and supposed that stained glass retains its colour by moonlight. The main tint of Poe's room is crimson and gold, but the windows have inner curtains of silver tissue and the crimson outer curtains are lined with the same. Keats's "Turkish floor," by which he presumably meant to imply Oriental rugs, is changed by Poe into a carpet of "Saxony material," while the "diamonding" effect of moonlight through the gold-fish bowls is imitated by the application of a gold cord "thrown upon" the carpet "in such a manner as to form a succession of short irregular curves — one occasionally overlaying the other." How many "ebon sofas" Keats had, he does not say; Poe very carefully designates two, but Poe's sofas are of rosewood. Keats's lute is duplicated by a piano, but Poe will have none of his "cinque-coloured potter's clay," instead he desires "four large and gorgeous Sèvres vases." He admits a mirror, not very large and "nearly circular," whatever shape that may be, yet, in spite of its very original contour, Poe's mirror is a poor thing compared with Keats's. Poe, too, will have pictures, and the list of his preferences in this line is not a little odd. There are to be "fairy grottoes" by Clarkson Stanfield, the *Lake of the Dismal Swamp* by Chapman, and "three or four female heads . . . in the manner of Sully." There is more, but farther detail is unnecessary. Poe is writing in prose, in a prose far less inspired than is his wont, but even without reflecting on his style, his heavy and decidedly garish conception leaves him far behind his original.

Samain also writes in prose; in his case, however, a certain poetical charm relieves the too great ornamentation of his ideal apartment. He also sees his room at night, for, in telling us that it has no window, he explains that it is only used by artificial light. Like Poe, he mentions no moon, and indeed it would be useless where there was no window. Samain forces the silver of metal to do duty for the silver of moonlight, since he, like Keats, would make his prevailing colour scheme black and silver. The walls are "hung with velvet of steel-coloured grey, with blue lights in it," at the corners of the ceiling are embossed designs of old silver, on the floor is "a carpet with a silver knap." There is considerably more of this silver, but we need not enumerate it all; where Keats has given his tone with a touch, Samain requires long and minute description. So much for the silver, and the ebony is not lacking. There is "an ebony table with silver lion's claws for feet," and "an Etruscan armchair, made entirely of ebony, with silver nails." Over this armchair is flung a grey bearskin; Keats's black and white fleeces are used as table covers apparently, and I must say that, in the disposition of his bearskin, I think Samain made an improvement. Instead of pictures, Samain has books: Corbière, Mallarmé, *Fleurs du Mal*. Nothing is more interesting about these rooms than the way in which Keats's and Poe's lists of pictures, and Samain's list of books, reveal the differing periods in which the three men lived. All three are not only true to themselves, but true to their times, and all are curiously local. For who, to-day, would, above all other paintings, choose those of Salvator Rosa or Haydon, Clarkson Stanfield or Chapman, or even, beyond everything else in literature, select the poems of Mallarmé and Baudelaire? Titian is the only choice which marks a universality transcending place and period, and Titian falls to the lot of Keats.

There has recently been discovered another fragment of the *Castle Builder*.[1] Professor de Sélincourt calls it the "opening," but I cannot see any reason to suppose that such is the case. In the first place, it begins in the middle of a sentence, for it is written in the form of a dialogue between a person designated as Castle Builder and some one, apparently a friar, named Bernadine. The scene is laid somewhere out of England, Sir Sidney Colvin thinks in Italy, but I think in France, partly because of the form of the friar's name, partly because Keats speaks of

> ". . . that imperial host
> Who came unmaimed from the Russian frost,"

[1] Woodhouse Commonplace Book (*Poems II*). Crewe Collection. Quoted in the notes to *The Poems of John Keats*, edited by E. de Sélincourt. Fourth Edition.

and certainly Napoleon's troopers who returned from Moscow were prevailingly French. This fragment of twenty-three lines is in a jocular vein full of slang and local allusions. It is broken three times, breaks indicated by asterisks, as though various fillings-in were to be added later. It very likely precedes the printed version, for toward the end occurs this passage:

> "In such like nonsense would I pass an hour
> With random Friar, or Rake upon his tour,"

but it clearly does not immediately run on into the printed text. That Keats intended to keep the vein of fooling throughout when he began, is shown by the first two lines of the published text:

> "To-night I'll have my friar — let me think
> About my room, — I'll have it in the pink."

"In the pink" gives his original intention away, even if the new fragment were not here to prove it. But, when it came to the room, Keats's imagination galloped off with him full tilt. The conceiving of a series of beautiful objects was too much, he could not keep to his key, but became seriously obsessed and eager, and the jocularity vanished forthwith, leaving in its place only a half-whimsical sort of comedy. Probably it was the difficulty of resolving his new fragment with his old that led him to abandon the poem.

A few stanzas of the *Pot of Basil* were written during this February, but as the larger part of the poem was done at Teignmouth, I will postpone all mention of it until we reach the time when Keats was really occupied with it.

How and when did Keats go to Devonshire? That I think we can tell quite easily, or at least within a couple of days. An unpublished letter from Hessey to Taylor,[1]

[1] Woodhouse Book. Morgan Collection.

dated "Mar. 6, 1818," gives the chief clue in this pregnant paragraph:

> "George Keats called here to day to say that his Brother the Poet is gone into Devonshire & has left the third Book with him — he will have it here either to morrow or on Monday — The Proofs he wishes to have sent to Mr. Charles Clarke, 6 Little Warner Street, Clerkenwell — Keats went off on the night of the Storm on the *outside* of the Coach."

March sixth was a Friday, and Keats did not go off "yesterday" or "day before yesterday," but "on the night of the storm," which must, it would seem, have been earlier in the week. Now, to go to Teignmouth, one took coach to Exeter, and from there changed into what *Cary's New Itinerary* calls a "provincial coach" for the fifteen miles to Teignmouth. This Teignmouth coach ran only on Monday, Wednesday and Friday afternoons. The last dated letter we have from Keats from Hampstead was written on Friday, February twenty-seventh, therefore the first coach he could get out of Exeter after that would have been on the following Monday, March second. As he would certainly not have wished to linger a day at Exeter, he would plan to reach that city on the morning of the afternoon that he was to leave it, which by this showing would be on either Monday or Wednesday. Of course, he might have hired a post-chaise to carry him to Teignmouth, but a man who booked a passage *outside* a coach in a storm cannot have been so flush of money as to contemplate travelling post. The fact that he went by night limits the possible coaches which he might have taken out of London. Bearing this in mind, I think we may be fairly sure that he left town by the Royal Mail, starting from The Swan with Two Necks Inn in Lad Lane at seven o'clock in the evening of Sunday, March first, or at half-past seven on Tuesday, March third, and reached the New

London Inn, Exeter, at nine o'clock in the morning of the next day, whichever it was, and from thence proceeded to Teignmouth, where he arrived somewhat less than twenty-four hours after his departure from London.

For a man with incipient tuberculosis to travel on a stormy night on the top of a coach was, of course, madness. Even granted that he did not know the state of his health, it was most imprudent. How horrified Hessey was at such a proceeding is evident by his underlining the word "outside."

The two brothers may have been together for a day or so at Hampstead before John left, but I think it more likely that they crossed each other on the road, for I imagine from George's not bringing the Third Book with him when he went to Taylor and Hessey's on Friday that he wanted a day or two to read it before turning it in. That Charles Cowden Clarke was entrusted with the proofs, shows how intimate Keats's relations with him still were. Keats himself would be at too great a distance from London to make proof-reading practicable, and he had enough to do with the Fourth Book to revise and the Preface to write, and all this with Taylor anxious to publish in a few weeks. It has hitherto been supposed that Keats did not reach Teignmouth until the middle of the month, because the first letter extant from there appears to have been written on March thirteenth. But I think his silence as far as letters are concerned is due to a feverish working at his revision of his final Book, which he finished copying on Saturday, the fourteenth.

George and Tom Keats, like their brother, possessed the happy faculty of making friends. They had been at Teignmouth three months and had already "dug themselves in" in the society of that little town. The family with whom they appear to have been most intimate were the Jeffreys, a mother and two daughters. Mrs. Jeffrey seems to have been a long time a widow when the Keats brothers knew her, for she is listed under her own name, Margaret Jeffrey, as one of the taxpayers of Teignmouth so early as 1800.[1] Of the daughters, Sarah never married, but Marianne eventually became the wife of a Mr. Prowse, and their son, W. Jeffrey Prowse, was one of the original contributors to *Punch*.[2] In 1830, as Mrs. I. S. Prowse, Marianne published a volume of contemplative and sentimental verse which contained more than one allusion to Keats, then dead. Local tradition in Teignmouth has it that she was in love with him; but, if so, her feelings were not reciprocated. Anything less like love-letters than Keats's few letters to her and her sister cannot well be imagined. But a habit of mild flirtatious fooling seems to have sprung up between these girls and George and Tom, which atmosphere Keats found awaiting him on his arrival. The Jeffreys — warm-hearted mother, blithe and intelligent daughters — must have been a godsend, first to George and then to John in their worry and anxiety over Tom. That John should make a good impression on these new friends was a matter of prime importance to George. A hitherto unpublished letter[3] written to "the steady, quiet Marianne and laughing thoughtless Sarah" shows his eagerness on the subject:

> "How do you like John? is he not very original? he does not look by any means so handsome as four months ago, but is he not handsome? I am sure you must like him very much, but don't forget *me*. I suppose Tom gets more lively as his health improves. Tell me what you think of John."

The first part of this letter gives a vivid picture of the innocent, intimate relations of which I have spoken. Locks of hair are mentioned — treasured from one girl, demanded of the other — and kisses remembered.

[1] From information supplied by Dr. Luke of Teignmouth to Mr. Louis A. Holman. [2] From a letter from Mr. Launcelot Archer to Mr. A. Forbes Sieveking. Bemis Collection. [3] Owned by Professor Edward S. Burgess of New York University.

There were other pleasant people in Teignmouth: Dr. Turton, who was taking care of Tom, a physician with a passion for conchology, whose *Conchological Dictionary of the British Islands* was published the following year; by an odd turn of fortune his collection of shells is now in the National Museum in Washington. We hear of a Mr. and Mrs. Atkins, of Mr. Bartlett, a surgeon, of a Captain Tonkin, a Miss Mitchell, and a Mr. Stanbury — just the sort of people we should expect to find in a little town, which is also something of a watering-place, in the early nineteenth century; the list of them reads like a page out of Jane Austen.

What Keats had expected of the Devonshire climate is not said, what he got was rain. It rained gently, steadily, persistently. He was none too husky just then, I fear, although no direct suggestion of ill-health has come down to us, if we except George's statement that he was not looking as handsome as four months earlier. The "gaddings" of the Winter, combined with the work he had managed to get through, had told, evidently.

Keats is very amusing about Devonshire. He calls it "a splashy, rainy, misty, snowy, foggy, haily, floody, muddy, slipshod county. The hills are very beautiful, when you get a sight of 'em — the primroses are out, but then you are in — the Cliffs are of a fine deep colour, but then the clouds are continually vieing with them —" Fresh from the kind of society he had been frequenting in London, he found that of Teignmouth an impossibly thin sort of gruel. He liked the women, but considered the men very poor stuff indeed, and the provincialism of the place got on his nerves. "Moore's Almanack is here a Curiosity" he exclaims in genuine, if humorous, impatience. With his Fourth Book finished and posted off to London, he had time to take stock of his surroundings and he did not find them exhilarating. To give himself the vicarious illusion of companionship, he fell back on letters. The first of which we have any knowledge was written to Bailey. In it, Keats reveals himself at work on his continual questioning. Toward the end of the letter, he breaks out into sharp expression of both his melancholy and his eternal endeavour to find some stable spiritual ground where he may rest in peace. For the first, we have this strange sentence, purporting to refer to his poor opinion of the Devonshire men, but in reality cloaking feelings far more personal: "O Devonshire, last night I thought the moon had dwindled in heaven —" The next sentence contains the following:

> [1] "You know my ideas about Religion. I do not think myself more in the right than other people, and that nothing in this world is proveable. I wish I could enter into all your feelings on the subject, merely for one short 10 minutes, and give you a page or two to your liking. I am sometimes so very sceptical as to think Poetry itself a mere Jack o' Lantern to amuse whoever may chance to be struck with its brilliance. As tradesmen say everything is worth what it will fetch, so probably every mental pursuit takes its reality and worth from the ardour of the pursuer — being in itself a Nothing. Ethereal things may at least be thus real, divided under three heads — Things real — things semi-real — and Nothings. Things real, such as the existances of Sun, moon, & Stars and passages of Shakespeare. — Things semi-real, such as love, the Clouds &c., which require a greeting of the Spirit to make them wholly exist — and Nothings, which are made great and dignified by an ardent pursuit . . . I have written a sonnet here of a somewhat collateral nature — so don't imagine it an 'apropos des bottes' —"

Here he copies his sonnet: *The Human Seasons*, published the following year in Leigh Hunt's *Literary Pocket-Book* with the signature "I." After a few more speculations, Keats remarks, with the charming humility he often evinces when he has been moved to philosophize:

[1] Corrected from the original letter. Author's Collection.

> "Now, my dear fellow, I have not one idea of the truth of any of my speculations — I shall never be a reasoner, because I care not to be in the right, when retired from bickering and in a proper philosophical temper."

The Human Seasons is, as we should expect, Shakespearian in form. The version here set down differs markedly from that published the next year, but in neither version is the sonnet anything but dull. It is chiefly interesting as another example of Keats's favourite figure of the four ages of man, which had already occupied him in *Sleep and Poetry* and was to bring from him a very interesting prose passage in a letter to Reynolds two months later.

The probings and questionings which Keats was constantly undergoing have occasioned the spilling of much ink on the part of a host of critics, who have misinterpreted their cause and found answers which I believe to be unwarranted. Keats was very human as a man, but he was a poet through and through. No teasing examination of his meaning can turn him into a philanthropist, or force him to play the rôle of one of those baleful persons who believe in doing good through the medium of art. He believed that art was an end in itself, and, so believing, felt that to produce it was good. He never got very far along the road of reasoning how the good was to come. Sometimes he felt that he was too far removed from the world, that the salvation of his art would come from getting nearer to it. But he never acted upon what was, after all, only a spasmodic impulse. What really troubled him was the dislocation between himself and his time. He is always, in his poetry, struggling to find a new way, a road down which his thought can run unhampered. For brief intervals, in certain poems, he found it. But in its entirety he never really achieved a conclusion. He questions — questions — studies — learns — but always he had outgrown the men he studied; or rather, they steadily led him toward goals which were none of his. So the search continued, and in the end he had found no solution. Such a havoc in the very centre where there should be calm, in that centre and core of being in which lies the root of one's direction, could not fail to produce restlessness, merging at times into discouragement. When he says: "I lay awake last night listening to the Rain, with a sense of being drowned and rotted like a grain of wheat," we know that all is not right with him. But it was never his power which he doubted, he believed always that his power was capable of enormous growth; it was his direction which puzzled him. His friends never understood this. In fact, he never told them in so many words, but I think they were too much a part of the whole in which they lived to have understood it, even if he had.

The first days in Devonshire were peaceful. Even if the downpour were continuous, his own particular sky was clear. Then suddenly, out of the open blue of this personal sky, the dim outline of a cloud swelled up — that cloud of recurring trouble which was to engulf him in the end. The first sign of its coming was that Tom had a relapse. But he pulled up from it, and things appeared to be going well, and then — then Keats wrote a Preface to *Endymion* and the other edge of the cloud poked above the horizon. To us who know the sequel, all this is like listening to the idle, premonitory clicking of the shears of Atropos. But before considering this Preface, let us stop a moment and take a look at him valiantly living down the days of his moist *villeggiatura.*

Writing to Reynolds on Saturday, March fourteenth, he gives a picture of his environment in a couple of sentences:

> "Being agog to see some Devonshire, I would have taken a walk the first day, but the rain would not let me; and the second, but the rain would not let me; and the third, but the rain forbade it. Ditto 4 — ditto 5 — ditto — so I made up my Mind to stop in-doors, and catch a sight flying between the showers: and, behold I saw a pretty valley —

> pretty cliffs, pretty Brooks, pretty Meadows, pretty trees, both standing as they were created, and blown down as they are uncreated. The green is beautiful, as they say, and pity it is that it is amphibious . . . I have copied my Fourth Book and shall write the Preface soon. I wish it was all done; for I want to forget it and make my mind free for something new. Atkins the coachman, Bartlett the surgeon, and the Girls over at the Bonnet-shop, say we shall now have a month of seasonable weather — warm, witty, and full of invention."

Tom's relapse, as nearly as I can calculate it with the available dates, occurred on Friday, March thirteenth. In the letter to Bailey, written on that day, Keats tells him that Tom "has just this moment had a spitting of blood."

The hæmorrhage was a terrible blow to all three brothers, who had believed that Tom was really much better. George, on hearing the unfortunate news, immediately wrote to John in what appears a somewhat severe strain, for he says:

> "I hope and trust that your *kind* superintendence will prevent any violent bleeding in future . . . Tom must never again presume on his strength, at all events until he has completely recovered."

What does George mean by underlining the word kind? With Keats's sensitiveness, it is hardly possible to conceive him as being anything but kind to the sick brother whom he adored. We have a clue to the word, however, when we remember George's remarks on John's habit of pouring out his feelings to his brothers, and that Tom understood him better than any one. John was homesick and bored to distraction, that is the long and the short of it. It may be that in the momentary lull between showers he wanted to go out for a stroll, but did not like to leave Tom. We can imagine Tom assuring him that he was quite well enough for a little walk, a very little one, and John let himself be persuaded that such was the case, with the result of the subsequent hæmorrhage. George is exhorting John to keep Tom quiet mentally as well as physically, hence the cryptic, but pregnant, "kind."

In this letter, George encloses a bill of twenty pounds, which he hopes will reach John "before you are quite aground." Woodhouse records that, at one time during the Teignmouth sojourn, Keats was so low in funds as to be obliged to borrow of his landlady.[1]

On Saturday, March twenty-first, Keats wrote to Haydon, a letter which Buxton Forman, quite erroneously I believe, attributes to the fourteenth. The various reasons for my belief would take longer to state than my space warrants. I shall therefore not detail them. The important thing is that, by this Saturday, the Devonshire climate had so far modified its lachrymatory energy as to permit the unexpected dawning of three fine days. When Keats wrote, it was raining again; but the three days had been, and they had done him a world of good. He had "enjoyed the most delightful walks," for these days had been of the superlative kind which Devonshire knows so well how to produce when it pleases. The result, sent promptly off to Haydon, was a set of stanzas, which posterity calls sometimes *Teignmouth* and sometimes *Here all the summer could I stay*; Keats calls them "some dogrel." Geographically and rhythmically the verses are pleasant, but they are chiefly remarkable for the number of real place names which Keats has crowded into them. The mention of white violets and primroses gives us a vivid picture of the kind of walks these were and what a solace they must have been — violets and primroses sparkling with recent rain.

Following the "dogrel," Keats wrote "Perhaps you would like a bit of B-hrell:" and immediately jots down *Where be ye going, you Devon maid?* This is an extremely

[1] Woodhouse Book. Morgan Collection.

charming little bit of nothing, a puff-ball of evanescent verse; its value lies in its gay simplicity. Haydon had the wit to find it good. He acknowledged it by saying: "Your br-ell as you call it is beautiful." Dante Gabriel Rossetti pointed out to Buxton Forman that the first stanza of the poem was undoubtedly a reminiscence of one of the songs in Chatterton's *Ælla.* The stanza of Chatterton's poem which Keats is supposed to have had in mind is:

> "Mie husbande, Lorde Thomas, a forrester boulde,
> As ever clove pynne, or the baskette,
> Does no cherysauncys from Elynour hould,
> I have ytte as soon as I ask ytte."

The chief resemblance between the two stanzas, so far as I can see, is the rhyme of "basket" and "ask it." But the real point here is that two days before, on Thursday, the nineteenth, Keats had written his first Preface to *Endymion* and his first dedication to Chatterton. Chatterton therefore was running in his head, and up popped "basket" and "ask it" just when they would be most apropos.

So here we are back at the Preface again, and why? Because Brown had written Keats that the printers had taken a sudden spurt and finished all the copy they had, and were clamouring for the Fourth Book and Preface. The Fourth Book was ready, but the Preface had to be written. Keats wrote it on Thursday, and on Saturday sent it off to Taylor. Here it is:

> "In a great nation, the work of an individual is of so little importance; his pleadings and excuses are so uninteresting; his 'way of life' such a nothing, that a Preface seems a sort of impertinent bow to strangers who care nothing about it.
>
> A Preface, however, should be down in so many words; and such a one that by an eye-glance over the type the Reader may catch an idea of an Author's modesty, and non-opinion of himself — which I sincerely hope may be seen in the few lines I have to write, notwithstanding many

proverbs of many ages old which men find a great pleasure in receiving as gospel.

About a twelvemonth since, I published a little book of verses; it was read by some dozen of my friends who lik'd it; and some dozen whom I was unacquainted with, who did not.

Now, when a dozen human beings are at words with another dozen, it becomes a matter of anxiety to side with one's friends — more especially when excited thereto by a great love of Poetry. I fought under disadvantages. Before I began I had no inward feel of being able to finish; and as I proceeded my steps were all uncertain. So this Poem must rather be considered as an endeavour than a thing accomplished; a poor prologue to what, if I live, I humbly hope to do. In duty to the Public I should have kept it back for a year or two, knowing it to be so faulty: but I really cannot do so, — by repetition my favourite passages sound vapid in my ears, and I would rather redeem myself with a new Poem should this one be found of any interest.

I have to apologize to the lovers of simplicity for touching the spell of loneliness that hung about Endymion; if any of my lines plead for me with such people I shall be proud.

It has been too much the fashion of late to consider men bigoted and addicted to every word that may chance to escape their lips; now I here declare that I have not any particular affection for any particular phrase, word, or letter in the whole affair. I have written to please myself, and in hopes to please others, and for a love of fame; if I neither please myself, nor others, nor get fame, of what consequence is Phraseology?

I would fain escape the bickerings that all Works not exactly in chime bring upon their begetters — but this is not fair to expect, there must be conversation of some sort and to object shows a man's consequence. In case of a London drizzle or a Scotch mist, the following quotation from Marston may perhaps 'stead me as an umbrella for an hour or so: 'let it be the curtesy of my peruser rather to pity my self-hindering labours than to malice me.'

One word more — for we cannot help seeing our own affairs in every point of view — should any one call my dedication of Chatterton affected I answer as followeth: 'Were I dead, sir, I should like a Book dedicated to me.'

TEIGNMOUTH,

March 19th, 1816."

Had Keats been writing in a diary, that would have been a most interesting entry; as a Preface, it was about as bad as it could be. No critic save posterity could be expected to treat a poem so heralded with lenience. It was too open to what Keats would have called "smoking." Fortunately for him, it was unanimously condemned by the friends to whom he sent it. On Thursday, April ninth, he answered to Reynolds:

"Since you all agree the thing is bad, it must be so — though I am not aware there is anything like Hunt in it (and if there is, it is my natural way, and I have something in common with Hunt.) Look it over again, and examine into the motives, the seeds, from which any one sentence sprung — I have not the slightest feel of humility towards the public — or to anything in existence, — but the eternal Being, the Principle of Beauty, and the Memory of Great Men . . . a Preface is written to the Public; a thing I cannot help looking upon as an Enemy, and which I cannot address without feelings of Hostility. If I write a Preface in a supple or subdued style, it will not be in character with me as a public speaker — I would be subdued before my friends, and thank them for subduing me — but among Multitudes of Men — I have no feel of stooping, I hate the idea of humility to them. I never wrote one single Line of Poetry with the least Shadow of public thought."

Then, with a last, final spurt of annoyance:

"I would jump down Ætna for any great Public good, but I hate a Mawkish Popularity."

Nevertheless he gave up the Preface (I fancy he knew that it was bad) and set to work immediately on another, which he sent off the next day to Reynolds who would, he hoped, find it "tolerable." His eagerness to have this new Preface pass muster, and his weariness of the whole thing, appear in a rather wistful sentence:

> "I had an idea of giving no Preface; however, don't you think this had better go? O, let it — one should not be too timid — of committing faults."

The second Preface is a beautiful piece of writing, but it was poor policy to print it. It was not wise to open one's heart to such gentry as Messrs. Lockhart, Wilson, and Croker.

Many as are the letters of Keats which we have, there must have been numberless others which we have not. Keats and Brown were certainly corresponding at this time, but not a single letter to Brown of this date has ever turned up. This is a pity, for the difference of Keats's letters to his various friends is of great psychological interest. While always holding fast to his own personality, a personality so strong that he could not have concealed it even if he had wanted to, yet to each one of his friends Keats turns a slightly different side. To Bailey, he philosophizes and opens up the heart of his spiritual puzzles; to Haydon, he chats about art, gossips of mutual friends, and falls in, as far as may be, with what he knows Haydon to be preoccupied with at the time; to Reynolds, he talks pure poetry, and often merely rambles on after the thread of his wandering fancies, certain that Reynolds will understand; to his brothers, he is everything by turns, but always in a taken-for-granted sort of way, quite unlike his attitude toward any one else. The richness of his capacity for human intercourse with many kinds of men is one of his most remarkable traits. Did we know the exact relations he had with his different friends, we should, I think, be amazed at the versatility of his sympathies. For instance, James Rice. We know very little of Rice, have no letters from him, and only three from Keats to him, and these at widely spaced intervals. Yet Rice's personality is very distinct. On two occasions during the Teignmouth weeks he appears to us, and both times with extraordinary clarity.

The first of these appearances is due to a letter which Keats wrote him on Tuesday, March twenty-fourth. This is a letter of rather muddled nonsense. A touch of raciness peeps in at the end, a touch which we gather to have been extremely agreeable to Rice. Rice was very fond of Devonshire. Keats begins his letter: "Being in the midst of your favourite Devon," and in the middle gives a genial little picture, by implication, of Rice in this manner: "Some of the little Bar-maids look'd at me as if I knew Jem Rice — but when I took [cherry? [1]] Brandy they were quite convinced." At the end of the letter, Keats says: "I went yesterday to Dawlish fair," and at once writes down a poem of which only the first stanza has hitherto been printed. Apparently the holograph of this letter was never seen by Buxton Forman. It is quoted by Lord Houghton with a good many inaccuracies, and with the whole of the Dawlish fair poem except the first stanza suppressed. Whether this squeamishness in regard to a very harmless bit of fooling is due to Lord Houghton, or to someone else who may have copied the letter for him, of course we do not know. At any rate, apropos of this suppression, Buxton Forman says: "Whether the rest is observation or (as is more probable) mere rhyme, I cannot say." What it is can easily be seen by reading it. It is Keats in one of the Rice moods, in one of his own moods, and as such does, I think, deserve to be given in full. I copy it from the original letter: [2]

"Over the Hill and over the dale.
And over the bourne to Dawlish.
Where Ginger-bread wives have a scanty sale,
And ginger-bread nuts are smallish.

[1] There is a hole in the letter just where this word came.
[2] Author's Collection.

Rantipole Betty she ran down a hill
And kick'd up her petticoats fairly
Says I I'll be Jack if you will be Gill.
So she lay on the Grass debonnairly.

Here's somebody coming, here's somebody coming!
  Says I 'tis the wind at a parley
So without any fuss any hawing or humming
  She lay on the grass debonnairly —

Here's somebody here and here's somebody there
  Says I hold your tongue you young Gipsey.
So she held her tongue and lay plump and fair
  And dead as a venus tipsy.

O who wouldn't hie to Dawlish fair
  O who wouldn't stop in a Meadow
O [who] wouldn't rumple the daisies there
  And make the wild fern for a bed do."

I think we can guess, without much difficulty, that this little piece of high spirits was an impromptu, composed on the instant of its writing. Let us be thankful for this mood of hilarity; it was but a moment's brightness in the midst of gloom. For Keats was in no jocular state of mind in the core of him, rather he was struggling like a buffeted swimmer in a tide of troubles. How anxiously he strove to hide his feelings from his friends, can be seen by the letters to Haydon and Rice, with their rollicking verses. The gaiety induced by his trip to Dawlish fair was of very short duration; already, by the next day, the momentary relief of his outing has passed. Very different in tone, touch, and intention is another poem sent to Reynolds on Wednesday. This poem known as *Epistle to John Hamilton Reynolds* is, in fact, practically the whole letter, with the slightest of prefaces to explain it. Keats writes:

"In hopes of cheering you through a Minute or two, I was determined will he nil to send you some lines, so you

> will excuse the unconnected subject and careless verse. You know, I am sure, Claude's Enchanted Castle, and I wish you may be pleased with my remembrance of it."

The poem itself is very strange. "Unconnected" it certainly is. We can only account for it at all by realizing that it was probably jotted down just as it came into Keats's head and sent off entirely without correction. It may even have been written directly into the letter. I can say nothing of this with certainty as I have not seen the holograph. What does seem certain, however, is that Keats set out to make a picture solely to amuse and give pleasure to his sick friend. He really did not know how to begin it. A recollection of Claude's *Enchanted Castle* was all he had to go upon, and he was writing plainly against his mood. He was evidently trying after something of the same sort as the *Castle Builder*. In that poem, he had begun with joking, but had presently found himself driven along on the swift tide of imaginative conception. The *Castle Builder*, although he had not been able to finish it, had "points," there was quite a little that was good in it. He hoped for the same sort of luck with the Enchanted Castle. He did not find it. It is no matter that his picture is not in the least like Claude's. Claude's painting, probably known to him solely through the black and white of an engraving, was merely to serve as a spring-board from which to leap (if he could) into the teeming immensity of his own fancy. But, try as he would, his take-off failed to project him into the desired atmosphere. Let me change the metaphor and say that his fancy would not budge an inch, but remained, a Pegasus with its wings obstinately folded, stuck to the ground; he was obliged to use both whip and spur to move it at all, and even then only got a little foot-high flutter out of the balky thing. Words — words — words — there are plenty of words, but, with a single exception, not a line or passage pierces the reader and startles him to admiring astonishment. Keats builds a castle surely, and out of his head (for he has evidently forgotten all but the fact and general impression of Claude's picture); but, however he tries, his castle stays a weird jumble of unrelated dream architectures until his mood flames in and obliterates his original intention, leaving only his sincere bitterness and revolt.

We have watched Keats's depression growing daily, a depression haunted by the vision of a universe of wanton cruelty. Tom is very ill; Tom, not yet nineteen! He himself is tortured by this, and by the constant drain on his time and vitality, not only because of Tom, but because of the thousand and one things that hedge and beset him, among others his growing intellect and his lack of the knowledge of how to satisfy it and gain a surer footing for his poetry. And "the rain it raineth every day," soaking his nerves to an aching pulp. For a man in his state of mind, the weather was annihilating. Just before copying the poem, he tells Reynolds that "The Rain is come on again — I think with me Devonshire stands a very poor chance, I shall damn it up hill and down dale, if it keep up to the average of six fine days in three weeks." He longs to get away from this reality of rain, illness, and tormenting thoughts. In the eighth stanza of the poem, he breaks out:

> "O that our dreamings all, of sleep or wake,
> Would all their colours from the sunset take:
> From something of material sublime
> Rather than shadow our own soul's day-time
> In the dark void of night . . ."

There is no farther question of the castle; from this point on to the end — which is no end, merely an abrupt ceasing to write — the picture vanishes in the cloud of Keats's own questionings:

> ". . . Oh, never will the prize,
> High reason, and the love of good and ill,

Be my award! Things cannot to the will
Be settled, but they tease us out of thought;
Or is it that imagination brought
Beyond its proper bound, yet still confin'd,
Lost in a sort of Purgatory blind,
Cannot refer to any standard law
Of either earth or heaven? It is a flaw
In happiness to see beyond our bourne, —
It forces us in summer skies to mourn,
It spoils the singing of the Nightingale.

Dear Reynolds! I have a mysterious tale,
And cannot speak it."

No, even *his* words could do no more than faintly shadow the horror in which he was engulfed. Yet it is strange that just here occurs the single memorable passage in the poem — memorable as poetry, that is — one which I have already quoted:[1]

". . . 'Twas a quiet eve,
The rocks were silent, the wide sea did weave
An untumultuous fringe of silver foam
Along the flat brown sand."

Here, and then, he says, he would have been happy, but he

". . . saw
Too far into the sea, where every maw
The greater on the less feeds evermore. —
But I saw too distinct into the core
Of an eternal fierce destruction."

That very day, he goes on, he has gathered periwinkles and wild strawberries; but, even while so engaged, the everlasting destruction of nature obsesses him, he thinks of a shark, a "Hawk at pounce," even of "the gentle robin . . . ravening a worm."

[1] See Vol. I, p. 99.

Poor fellow! Both his mind and his imagination are at work to flay him. And no one to give him a moment's ease. Strangers all about him; no one to whom he can speak but the sick Tom, who is himself despondent, and whom he must spare, if he can.

The first month at Teignmouth was productive of little but anxiety, misery, and spleen, hidden from prying eyes beneath a cloak of iridescent wit and fun. The weather was really insupportable, it weighed heavily on the spirits of both brothers. But Tom seemed to be getting better, and there was talk of returning to town in April. Keats was planning to go on a walking tour in Scotland with Brown during the Summer, and that was something to look forward to. Yet Tom's very gain appeared to put a spoke in the wheel of Keats's fortune, for the poor boy had grown to have such confidence in the conchological Dr. Turton that it seemed most unwise to move him. This meant an indefinite stay for John, who must have regarded such a change of plan a bit ruefully as it affected himself. Rain — rain — rain — and then suddenly a brief mitigation, which he commemorated in the sonnet *To J. R.*

It has long been surmised that "J. R." was James Rice, and not John Hamilton Reynolds, as Buxton Forman, following Lord Houghton, imagined. The sonnet has hitherto been supposed to date from the Winter of 1818, but a most unlooked-for discovery has led me to assign it, on what I think is the best of circumstantial evidence, to the end of April. I will go even farther and say that it was, in all probability, written on either April twentieth or twenty-first.

The discovery to which I owe my information is the existence of a copy of the third English edition of the old Spanish Romance, *Guzman d'Alfarache*, which belonged to Keats. It was known that Keats had owned such a book, for it is listed in the catalogue of his library,[1] but its

[1] Woodhouse Book. Morgan Library. Published by Sir Sidney Colvin.

whereabouts had long been lost sight of. The volume was among those bequeathed to the New York Authors Club by the late Richard Henry Stoddard. Stoddard bought the book in 1878. He paid fifty dollars for it, and sold a sonnet, which he promptly wrote upon it, for twenty-five dollars, so that the whole transaction was an eminently satisfactory one for him. But the result to the world was that the volume vanished out of memory. It was recently found in the Authors Club library by one of the members,[1] who very kindly communicated his discovery to me. The committee of the club at once gave me permission to examine the book, and copy its underscorings and annotations.[2] These have proved neither so interesting, nor so pertinent, as I had hoped, but two inscriptions in the volume are of high importance. The first, on the top margin of the first page in what I take to be Rice's handwriting, is: "John Keats. From his Friend J^s^ Rxxx 20th April 1818." The second, at the top of the page containing the dedication reads: "Purchased by me A.D. 1818 — and given to John Keats and upon his death 1821 — returned to me. Rice." At first I did not think of the sonnet *To J. R.*, I thought only of the time, and realized that Keats was in Devonshire. Could Rice have sent this enormously heavy book (it is a calf-bound folio weighing four pounds, two ounces, I weighed it) as a coach parcel? Considering the rates for packages at that period, and the fact that Keats was expected home within a few days (hc had written to Reynolds on April ninth that he should "be in Town in about Ten days"), this seemed preposterous. Suddenly there leapt into my mind the recollection that Rice had a great affection for Devonshire; and then, I do not know how, the sonnet *To J. R.* flashed upon me. In that sonnet, it was clear that Rice had come from somewhere for a couple of days only and then departed again. Does not the sonnet speak of "this morn" and "yester-evening"?

[1] Mr. Gardner Teall. [2] See Appendix C.

But I will quote it. To read it is to strengthen the impression.

"TO J. R.

O that a week could be an age, and we
Felt parting and warm meeting every week,
Then one poor year a thousand years would be,
The flush of welcome ever on the cheek:
So could we live long life in little space,
So time itself would be annihilate,
So a day's journey in oblivious haze
To serve our joys would lengthen and dilate.
O to arrive each Monday morn from Ind!
To land each Tuesday from the rich Levant!
In little time a host of joys to bind,
And keep our souls in one eternal pant!
This morn, my friend, and yester-evening taught
Me how to harbour such a happy thought."

There is nothing in the letters from Teignmouth to make either for or against the possibility of Rice's having gone down to Devonshire and stopped over a week-end with Keats. April nineteenth was a Sunday. Nothing is said in the letters, but there is a fairly eloquent silence, for, after the letter of the ninth of April to Reynolds, there is no letter until the twenty-fourth, and that letter is to Taylor to whom Keats would not be likely to speak of a visit from Rice, also the letter is a quasi-business one. On the twenty-seventh, Keats again writes to Reynolds and tells him he has heard from Rice that morning; he mentions no visit, probably because Rice had gone back to London and would already have told Reynolds all about it.

It is quite as foolish to suppose that Rice travelled with this mighty tome which is *Guzman* as to think that he posted it, and I suppose no such thing. I believe he bought it somewhere in Devonshire; Keats seems to have bought a black-letter Chaucer there.[1] I do suppose, however,

[1] Letter to Reynolds. May 3, 1818.

that the two friends chuckled over the volume that Sunday, and that Rice ended by giving it to Keats. It had been such a pleasant Sunday, refreshing to the soul of the despondent, friend-starved, literary-conversation-starved, homesick young fellow, shut up at Teignmouth and beginning to fear that his exile might continue for the whole Summer. Musing over the fun he had had with Rice, the pleasure it had been to see him, he sat down and wrote this sonnet. This may be supposititious reasoning, yet I believe it to point very clearly to a fact.

There is something curiously attractive about this sonnet, but I confess I am puzzled to say just why. Probably the answer lies in that penumbra which surrounds all enduring poetry and seems to give it the power of perpetuating itself beyond any reasoning or argument on theme or structure which we have the perspicuity to apply to it. *To J. R.* has no lines nor passages of a "fine excess"; there are no pictures, no sentiments marvellously flashed up by a single word. Yet here is that indescribable thing — charm; although, to account for it, the only clue we can find is that the sonnet is so undeniably *felt*.

I happen to possess an unknown holograph of this sonnet, the only one in existence apparently, and for the sake of the curious in such matters I may note that it contains a variant reading, which is, at the same time, happily cancelled. The last two lines were started thus:

> "This morn and yester eve my friend has taught
> Such Greediness of Pleasure"

but Keats discarded them even in the writing, and put the far better ending I have quoted above.

Rice gone, Keats set himself to contemplate the idea of a Summer in Devonshire. He mused on it in his walks, when he could take them, in lanes "banked on each side with store of Primroses." The result of his self-communing was the realization that, even in poetry, knowledge is valuable.

That, to write great poems, he must know more than his meagre education had permitted. Convinced of this, he writes to Taylor on Friday, April twenty-fourth:

"I was proposing to travel over the North this summer. There is but one thing to prevent me. — I know nothing — I have read nothing — and I mean to follow Solomon's directions, 'Get learning — get understanding.' I find earlier days are gone by — I find that I can have no enjoyment in the world but continual drinking of knowledge. I find there is no worthy pursuit but the idea of doing some good in the world. Some do it with their society — some with their wit — some with their benevolence — some with a sort of power of conferring pleasure on all they meet . . . there is but one way for me. The road lies through application, study, and thought. I will pursue it; and for that end purpose retiring for some years. I have been hovering for some time between an exquisite sense of the luxurious, and a love for philosophy, — were I calculated for the former I should be glad. But as I am not, I shall turn my soul to the latter."

This is strange speech from a man who has just received a first copy of his new book, a book which has occupied him for over a year, which has worn him, and torn him, and taught him. Holding *Endymion* printed and bound in his hands, turning its pages, what has Keats to say to the publisher who has believed in him? This — for the paragraph I have just quoted is the third of the letter — this, which is the first:

"I think I did wrong to leave to you all the trouble of Endymion — But I could not help it then — another time I shall be more bent to all sorts of troubles and disagreeables. Young men for some time have an idea that such a thing as happiness is to be had, and therefore are extremely impatient under any unpleasant restraining. In time, however, of such stuff is the world about them, they know better, and instead of striving from uneasiness, greet it as an habitual sensation, a pannier which is to weigh upon

> them through life. And in proportion to my disgust at the task is my sense of your kindness and anxiety. The book pleased me much. It is very free from faults; and, although there are one or two words I should wish replaced, I see in many places an improvement greatly to the purpose."

To trace the passage of Taylor's or Woodhouse's editing hand through the pages of *Endymion* is the task of a commentator not of a biographer. All I shall do here, then is to point out that the sight of the volume produced no elation in Keats's mind, no sense of pride; on the contrary, it induced in him a vast humility that he had done so ill, fallen so far short of his conception of great poetry. *Endymion*, at last issued and on sale, was to him merely an illustration of his prevailing dissatisfaction, and the contemplation of it led naturally to his remarks at the end of the letter. We hear no more of *Endymion* for a long time to come, and this silence in regard to it is full of meaning. He had learnt to think of it as a stage already outdistanced; it is the future which occupies him, not the past. He is not ashamed of his earlier self; he has merely outlived the boy he was, although he regards him with tolerance as a fellow who did his best with what equipment he had.

To increase his equipment, that is his present concern. Ten days after writing to Taylor, he tells Reynolds that were he to study medicine again he is sure it would make no difference to his poetry. He is glad that he did not give away his medical books and he intends to look them over again so as not to forget what he knows, and he hopes through Reynolds and Rice to learn something about the law, for

> "Every department of Knowledge we see excellent and calculated towards a great whole . . . An extensive knowledge is needful to thinking people — it takes away the heat and fever; and helps, by widening speculation, to ease the Burden of the Mystery, a thing which I begin to understand a little."

All very well, but Tom is ill. With a strange, pertinacious wisdom, he adds, "it is impossible to know how far knowledge will console us for the death of a friend, and the ill 'that flesh is heir to.'" Truly the two months at Teignmouth had been agitating and busy ones. However much he may have chafed at them, we can see the maturing effect they had had upon him. He should have blessed them, rain and all, as, beginning with the sonnet *To J. R.*, they brought him some of his best poetry.

I said, a little while ago, that Keats started his *Isabella, or The Pot of Basil* in February at Hampstead. It seems that some time during the Winter Keats and Reynolds agreed to write a book together. The volume was to consist of certain tales from Boccaccio's *Decameron*, freely adapted and made into poems. The book was not to be in any sense a collaboration. Each poet was to write his own poems, but they were to be printed together. Keats was before Reynolds in producing a poem for this scheme, for Reynolds was too ill to think of writing; but evidently, after the first few stanzas, Keats left his poem for the rest of the Winter, probably because he found that he could not concentrate upon anything at all sustained and revise *Endymion* at the same time. Exactly when he resumed work upon it, we do not know, but it is safe to assume that he took it up only after the final work upon *Endymion*, including the much debated Preface, was done.

Writing to Reynolds on April twenty-seventh, he says:

> "I have written for my folio Shakespeare, in which there are the first few stanzas of my 'Pot of Basil.' I have the rest here finished, and will copy the whole out fair shortly, and George will bring it to you."

On May third, Keats wrote again to Reynolds:

> "I have written to George for the first stanzas of my 'Isabel,' — I shall have them soon, and will copy the whole out for you."

Probably he tinkered at the poem for some couple of months more, until he set out for Scotland, in fact. Brown told Lord Houghton that the poem was only just finished when Keats and he started on their Scotch tour, on June twenty-second; but Keats, in a letter to Bailey on June tenth, remarks:

> "I want to read you my 'Pot of Basil' — if you go to Scotland, I should much like to read it there to you, among the snows of next winter."

In the Woodhouse Commonplace Book,[1] at the end of Woodhouse's transcript of the poem, is this inscription:

> "Written at Teignmouth in the Spring of 1818 at the suggestion of J. H. R."

Evidently the stanzas Keats sent for were laid into the Shakespeare, for the volume is in the Dilke Collection and nothing of the sort is written in it.

The *Pot of Basil* represents a transition period in Keats's life. If we take those poems of his which I may call sustained — by which word I mean poems of greater length and with a much more weighty volume of content than is proper to either sonnets or short lyrics, no matter how rich in thought and emotion these latter may be — we shall find that they marshal roughly into two distinct groups. An earlier group and a later one. *Endymion*, viewed from this angle, becomes not so much a new departure (although it is this, too, taken from another standpoint) as the culmination of the same youthful urge which produced *I Stood Tip-toe* and *Sleep and Poetry*. The later group forms itself inevitably of the *Eve of St. Agnes*, *Lamia*, *Hyperion* (both versions), and the five great *Odes*. In neither of these groups does the *Pot of Basil* belong. It stands by itself, in a sort of no man's land of time. It stretches forward into the future, but also harks back to the past. It

[1] Owned by Sir Sidney Colvin.

completely lacks the gush and gusto of the earlier group, and is without its most glaring immaturities; but, also, we do not find in it any suggestion of the firm modelling and checked luxuriance which mark the poems of the later group. Sentimentality has not yet mellowed into sentiment; statement still lords it over suggestion. What Keats said of *Endymion* in his published Preface to that poem, may serve us here as a perfect criticism of the *Pot of Basil*:

> "The imagination of a boy is healthy, and the mature imagination of a man is healthy; but there is a space of life between, in which the soul is in a ferment, the character undecided, the way of life uncertain, the ambition thick-sighted: thence proceeds mawkishness, and all the thousand bitters . . ."

That passage applies far better to the *Pot of Basil* than it does to *Endymion*. Keats's point of view in *Endymion* is so adolescent that we need strain no point in considering it as boyish. The sustained poems of the later group are clearly the work of a man; a young man, of course, but one whose boyhood is a thing of the past. What irks us in the *Pot of Basil* is the disjunction of its various parts. Prosodiacally, it records an advance; in theme and structure, it stands still; in emotion, it retrogrades. Keats's poetical voice, in this poem, is the breaking voice of a boy in his 'teens; now it is deep and full like a man's, then it cracks, shrills, and becomes once more the shallow pipe of a child. There is no question about the increased expertness in versification here. Keats manages his rhymes and lines far more deftly than he has ever done before; he has shed much of his blissful disregard of the dictionary, and there are no coined words. Even the word "leafits," which used to be considered as such, has its precedents. We find it in no less than two botanical works of the eighteenth century, and again in Keith's *Plant Botany*, published in 1816. The source from which Keats probably derived it was

Coleridge's *The Nightingale: A Conversational Poem*, published in the *Lyrical Ballads* in 1798.[1] The *Oxford Dictionary* characterizes "leafits" as obsolete, yet even so late as 1830 it appeared in a book entitled *Insect Architecture*, by J. Remick. But if awkwardness has disappeared, artifice is more in evidence than it had ever been before or was ever to be again. There is a self-consciousness about the poem, an effort at fine writing, which is regrettable. Inversions abound, and even at that time poets were beginning to look askance at the inversion. I possess a copy of *Sibylline Leaves* annotated by Coleridge, in which he carefully deletes an inversion in the text and writes beside it the straightforward order of the words. But there are worse things than inversions in the *Pot of Basil*. Keats descends to tortured similes and forced metaphors to an extent that sets one's teeth on edge. One of these occurs in the passage:

> "So the two brothers and their murder'd man
> Rode past fair Florence."

Hunt calls[2] the adjective "murder'd," applied to a man still very much alive, but about to be murdered, "a masterly anticipation of his end." But this is just the type of elegant artifice which Hunt admired. To a more carping taste, it is error and confusion. That Lamb should have shared Hunt's opinion, as he did, proves Lamb to have been a better judge of prose than of poetry, which, indeed, we knew before. The worst of these unsatisfactory attempts at picturesque epithet is to be found in Stanza XLVII, where Isabella is digging up Lorenzo's corpse, in which her breasts are presented as

> "Those dainties made to still an infant's cries."

[1] Professor de Sélincourt says that Coleridge altered the word to "leaflets" in his later editions. In *Sibylline Leaves*, however, published in 1817, "leafits" is still retained; the alteration does not appear until the Pickering edition of 1828.

[2] From Hunt's review of the *Lamia* volume, reprinted by Buxton Forman in his Library Edition.

The suggestion in the passage that Isabella is, by Lorenzo's death, deprived of both past and future, of the lover that was and the children that might have been, is a clever touch and would have been a moving one but for the execrable expression of the idea and the confusion of images involved in it. The word "dainties" cannot be too severely dealt with. It is totally inadequate for the emotion of the scene, a cloying word, and here, before the stark reality of death, not a little disgusting. It belongs to the same family as the "amorous nipping" in *O blush not so*, and brings me to the confusion I have spoken of, for "dainties" refers to the lover's attitude and has no place in the child's. The word here comes precariously near to being vulgar; it is, in fact, the only approach to real vulgarity I can find in Keats's work. That his idea, in this line, was far from vulgar, is quite evident; but it is equally evident that his expression could not reach the level of what he had in mind. This stanza is an evidence of the breaking voice effect I have spoken of. The first five lines, somewhat highly coloured though they are, nevertheless are full and strong; with the sixth line, the tone cracks to a weak falsetto, but resumes its sonority in the last two lines. Perhaps, for the benefit of readers who have not the poem by them, I had better give the stanza:

"Soon she turn'd up a soiled glove, whereon
Her silk had play'd in purple phantasies,
She kiss'd it with a lip more chill than stone,
And put it in her bosom, where it dries
And freezes utterly unto the bone
Those dainties made to still an infant's cries:
Then 'gan she work again; nor stay'd her care,
But to throw back at times her veiling hair."

The poem is really mawkish. The very thing Keats most feared and hated overtook him in it, and the sad part is that it is mawkish in exactly the same way that Hunt is mawkish in *Rimini*. In spite of his firmer grasp and vivid envisioning of his subject, there is not a little in the *Pot of Basil* which reminds one of *Rimini*. It is just this note which I had in mind when I said that as far as emotion was concerned the poem was a retrogression. The emotion is distinctly a harking back to the Huntian mood of the year before. Even Hunt's jaunty colloquialism is not absent, for witness Lorenzo's farewell to Isabella: "Good bye! I'll soon be back."

Yet, with all its infelicities, the poem has a dramatic quality which far outdistances anything Keats had previously done. The digging up of Lorenzo's body is a remarkably well-managed combination of horror and pathos. And here, and in the succeeding stanzas where the planting of Lorenzo's head in the basil pot is described, Keats for once overcomes his usual abhorrence of the grim and tells his tale in a manner that conveys, and often states without any attempt at evasion, the loathly details of the action. These are, indeed, as he says himself of something else, "accomplished horrors," yet around and infusing them there is the cleansing sobriety of grief. It is the presentation of grief that lifts the end of the poem far above the embroidered beginning. To Keats's set, to whom embroidery of this sort was by no means disagreeable, the poem stood as a beautiful example of love and woe. That it has aged beyond any of Keats's sustained poems is natural. Fine writing bears its doom within itself; only the simplicity and strength of plain speaking can carry down the years. Fashion changes, but the heart of man is a changeless thing and rules beyond the customs of ephemeral moments.

Curiously enough, Keats's realism stands out clearly in this poem. Two notable examples are to be found in Stanzas XLI and XLV. The first contains this passage:

"As when of healthful midnight sleep bereft,
Thinking on rugged hours and fruitless toil,

We put our eyes into a pillowy cleft,
And see the spangly gloom froth up and boil."

We have already noticed how well Keats can describe the on-coming of sleep.[1] Here he gives the very picture of a night when sleep will not come. Genius is behind such realism as this. Professor de Sélincourt has recorded a conversation between Browning and a friend[2] in which it is said that Browning "quoted these lines as an instance of Keats's supreme mastery of language, adding, 'They have for me an additional pathos because they record a personal experience. It is what Keats, poor fellow, must himself have seen many a night in the early stages of consumption!'" Keats was in the early stages of consumption undoubtedly, little as he suspected the fact, but even without having consumption one may have experienced just such a vision of bright and seething darkness as Keats describes. How many nights during the dreary sojourn at Teignmouth must he have undergone such an experience!

The other realistic passage is this:

"Who hath not loiter'd in a green church-yard,
And let his spirit, like a demon-mole,
Work through the clayey soil and gravel hard,
To see scull, coffin'd bones, and funeral stole;
Pitying each form that hungry Death hath marr'd,
And filling it once more with human soul?"

The value of that passage, apart from its excellence as poetry, lies in its morbidness, for this is a morbidness common to all human beings possessed of imagination. With most imaginative persons, however, morbidness of this kind takes one of two forms. Either they shun it, and conceal, as far as possible from themselves and invariably from others, the fact that they are the victims of it; or they go to the other extreme and flaunt the quality, tossing it above their heads like a plume. Poe, for instance,

[1] See Vol. I, pp. 350, 352. [2] Mr. F. S. Storr.

loves this sort of thing, as does Baudelaire and a host of other writers. Keats's originality and sincerity lie in the fact that he falls into neither category. He neither flees nor flaunts; he merely states what is to him a plain truth. It is admirable, and a touchstone by which to gauge both his courage and his innate sanity. He sees as a man of imagination sees, and records as a man of science records. For it cannot be too strongly insisted upon that both these aspects of mind were in Keats, and that gradually pushing itself through the crust of his period was a strangely modern man. Nothing shows this modernity in Keats better than the fact that he came to distrust the *Pot of Basil* profoundly. There is much of this a year later, which we shall notice all in good time. His friends continued to dote upon the poem, but he knew better; he was a most competent critic.

The decided change in literary taste which has marked the beginning of the twentieth century has displaced the *Pot of Basil* from the position it has hitherto held in Keats's work. The poem has not worn well. The very fact that it was so admired in its day shows how perfectly it fitted that day. But what Keats thought about it in 1819 is what the world thinks about it now. For one reader of the *Pot of Basil* to-day, there are probably hundreds of the *Eve of St. Agnes*, *Lamia*, and the *Odes*. Even *Endymion*, in the fragments which are all most people know of it, would count more readers than the *Pot of Basil*, I believe, if a tally could be made. If, *con amore*, the poem is not loved as it used to be, it is still interesting as a mental costume plate of a bygone era, and also, and more, because of its function as an analysis of the developing methods by which Keats approached the great creations of his last period.

I think it not fantastic to say that Keats definitely entered on his last period with a little fragment of a poem, fourteen lines long, written on Friday, May first, 1818. This fragment of an unfinished *Ode to Maia*, is, in its kind, as excellent a piece of work as Keats ever did, and would be a perfect thing but for the false rhyme of Maia and Baiæ; and the realization that Keats probably pronounced the two words Maya and Baya only makes the matter worse. Keats's knowledge of classical pronunciation was almost nil. There exists a copy of the proof-sheets of *Lamia*,[1] corrected by Woodhouse, with the classical names in the poem all carefully listed and the pronunciations indicated, undoubtedly for Keats's guidance.

Apart from this one infelicity, the fragment is utterly beautiful. Beauty of thought, beauty of phrase, beauty of movement — they are all here, joined to a music which eludes, baffles, and enchants, no matter how often the poem is read. Here is the clear, reticent line so entirely missing in the *Pot of Basil*. The quiet of the poem is rest and refreshment; the sober strength of it, abiding peace. It floats into our ears like a melody come from a wide distance; it is solace to questioning, an answer to many doubts. The "span of heaven" stretches above it, and we of the "few ears" listen and are content. Greek, is it — as critic after critic has said? No, scarcely Greek. The Greeks spoke in other accents than this. They, too, understood the combination of simplicity and strength, but theirs was neither this simplicity nor this strength. It is England speaking here, and the Englishman who speaks is John Keats. This is Keats at his rare best. To what sprouting of impulse the poem owes its inception, we do not know. It may have been an unconscious reaction from the vivid, restless style of the *Pot of Basil*. That the *Ode to Maia* is one of that small group of poems which flowered suddenly, inconceivably, in Keats's mind from no volition on his part, seems evident. Why it was not finished, the lines themselves declare. Nothing farther came, and Keats was too wise to attempt to finish by force of mere desire what the something in him which he could by no means guide

[1] White Collection.

had begun. On May third, he wrote to Reynolds that he intended to finish the *Ode* "all in good time." But apparently the "good time" was not vouchsafed him, for no more was ever written.

It is a curious commentary on Keats's changing moods that the letter in which he copied his *Fragment of an Ode to Maia*, contains not only the passage on the necessity for knowledge which I quoted some pages back, but a long thoughtful consideration of the different types of mind of Wordsworth and Milton. The passage is too long to give in full; but one part of it, where Keats again refers to the different ages of man, and this time under a new figure, cannot be omitted. We have only to remember his ages of man in *Sleep and Poetry* to see how far he has outdistanced the conceptions of a year and a half before:

> "I compare human life to a large Mansion of many apartments, two of which I can only describe, the doors of the rest being as yet shut upon me. The first we step into we call the Infant, or Thoughtless Chamber, in which we remain as long as we do not think. We remain there a long while, and notwithstanding the doors of the second Chamber remain wide open, showing a bright appearance, we care not to hasten to it; but are at length imperceptibly impelled by the awakening of the thinking principle within us — we no sooner get into the second Chamber, which I shall call the Chamber of Maiden-Thought, than we become intoxicated with the light and the atmosphere, we see nothing but pleasant wonders, and think of delaying there for ever in delight. However among the effects this breathing is father of is that tremendous one of sharpening one's vision into the heart and nature of Man — of convincing one's nerves that the world is full of Misery and Heartbreak, Pain, Sickness, and oppression — whereby this Chamber of Maiden Thought becomes gradually darkened, and at the same time, on all sides of it, many doors are set open — but all dark — all leading to dark passages. We see not the balance of good and evil; we are in a mist, *we* are now in that state, we feel the 'Burden of

the Mystery.' To this point was Wordsworth come, as far as I can conceive, when he wrote 'Tintern Abbey,' and it seems to me that his genius is explorative of those dark Passages. Now if we live, and go on thinking, we too shall explore them."

Beyond this, he does not go, but returns to Wordsworth and Milton. I fain would copy all, yet this is enough. For indeed the passage he wanders in is dark. "Tom has spit a *leetle* blood this afternoon, and that is rather a damper — but I know — the truth is, there is something real in the World." Something real in the world — the religion that is left him, to which he must perforce cling. And only six months before, at Burford Bridge, a sparrow hopping about the gravel could set him to rights! How inconceivably sad, the life of this man! Yet, "the leaves have been out here for many a day"— so his observation of beauty strives again to solace him.

Tom's second hæmorrhage may have shaken his faith in Dr. Turton, or else the evident uselessness of a longer exile operated with his own and John's desire to be in town to determine the brothers to go thither at once. A journey by coach was not to be thought of. No, they must post to London by way of Bridport and Dorchester as the shortest route. One day then (exactly which we do not know, but it was probably during this first week of May), a post-chaise jangled up to the door of the house opposite the bonnet-shop. At the window stood poor little Tom, hoping for one more glimpse of his friends, the Jeffreys; but the doctor had forbidden the agitation of good-byes, and they did not come. John brought him their farewells, and the two brothers got into the chaise and were driven away under the full-leaved trees to London and the brooding future.

END OF VOLUME I